D0808305

OXFORD ILLUSTRATED

Shakespeare Dictionary

DAVID & BEN CRYSTAL

ILLUSTRATED BY KATE BELLAMY

OXFORD
UNIVERSITY PRESS

CONTENTS

OXFORD
UNIVERSITY PRESS
Great Clarendon Street, Oxford OX2 6DP.
United Kingdom

Oxford University Press is a department of the University of Oxford. It furthers the University's objective of excellence in research, scholarship, and education by publishing worldwide. Oxford is a registered trade mark of Oxford University Press in the UK and in certain other countries

Data available

ISBN: 9780192737502

10 9 8 7 6 5 4 3 2 1

Paper used in the production of this book is a natural, recyclable product made from wood grown in sustainable forests. The manufacturing process conforms to the environmental regulations of the country of origin.
Printed in Italy

INTRODUCTION *by David and Ben Crystal*

Why do we need a Shakespeare dictionary?

Most of the time, when we watch or read Shakespeare, we don't need a dictionary. The majority of the words in a Shakespeare play have the same meaning as those we use today, and if a play is performed well, the speeches will make sense even if we don't understand every single word in them. But as soon as we want to explore the plays more deeply, a dictionary can help, especially to understand the words that have changed their meaning since Shakespeare's day.

'Words, words, words'—Hamlet Some of these words will of course be explained in the notes that accompany an edition of a play. However, these editions rarely explain all the difficult words; nor will they tell us about the way these words are used, or about how they are used in other plays. If we want to understand Shakespeare's remarkable inventiveness in using language, making up new words and using older words in new ways, we need a dictionary.

Not just a dictionary

The type of words we use tell other people about the world we live in, and about the thoughts, beliefs, and feelings that we have. Exploring Shakespeare's vocabulary gives us an insight into the ways Elizabethan people thought, which were often very different from those we have today.

Many still believed that the Sun orbited the Earth, and there was a widespread belief in witchcraft. People wondered whether it was possible to create matter by the power of the mind, or to turn lead into gold. And they would all know about the gods, personalities, and myths of ancient Greece and Rome, such as Mars, Venus, and the story of the Gorgon.

'Bless thy five wits'—King Lear The mind and the body were thought to work differently from how we understand them now. Humans were considered not only to have five senses – sound, vision, touch, smell, and taste – but also five mental faculties or wits: common sense, imagination, fantasy, estimation, and memory.

They also believed their emotions were subject to different amounts of liquids, or humours: an excess of blood, phlegm, choler, or melancholy would mean, respectively, a particularly sociable, peaceful, ambitious, or analytical person.

All of our panels and illustrations, and many of our entries, introduce you in a more encyclopedic way to the mindset of the Elizabethans. In the centre of the book we have illustrations of things you'd wear, things you'd do, things you'd see in the world, and ways you'd navigate that world.

'If thou thou'st him some thrice, it shall not be amiss'—Twelfth Night Another important difference was that in Shakespeare's time you could address someone by either 'thou' or 'you'. The choice (like *tu* vs *vous* in French, or *te* and *usted* in Spanish) tells us what type of relationship there might be between characters.

These words turn up on virtually every page in a play, so it's good to notice how characters refer to each other, and that when they switch from 'thou' or 'you', or vice versa, they are altering the temperature of the conversation (like switching from calling someone *Benjy...* to *Benjamin*!). They might even be insulting each other. You'll find more details on p.146.

Shakespeare's vocabulary

The entries in this dictionary also show us Shakespeare's readiness to use words in new ways. Many of the words appear in English for the first time in his plays, either because they were personal coinages—something that all dramatists did at the time—or because he was the first writer we know to put them into the mouths of characters. When the Chorus describes the fields of France as 'vasty' or Lady Macbeth calls on the spirits to 'unsex' her, we find these words new and intriguing—as would an Elizabethan audience.

'A man of fire-new words'—Love's Labour's Lost
It's the breadth of Shakespeare's vocabulary that is so impressive. The son of a glove-maker, his early years in Warwickshire gave him an understanding of nature and country life, and his Stratford-upon-Avon schooling gave him a great knowledge of Latin and classical literature.

Unlike many of his fellow playwrights, he didn't have a university education, but his life experience in London was wide-ranging, including at one extreme the taverns and 'low' life, and at the other the refined practices and behaviour of the court, where his theatre company presented plays for the entertainment of the monarch.

'Art thou base, common, and popular?'—Henry V A dictionary is a guide to the society of its time. In Shakespeare's day, there were four main levels:

AT THE TOP
- The monarch
- The nobility

THE GENTRY (or gentlemen)
- Younger sons of nobles (who were not classed with the nobility)
- Major land-owners
- Knights, with their squires and pages
- Magistrates
- Professional people, such as lawyers, physicians, and the clergy

THE TRADERS
- Merchants
- Yeomen farmers (owning land)
- Craftsmen (tailors, carpenters etc) and their apprentices
- Husbandmen (small farmers, usually renting land)

THE LOWER ORDERS
- Day labourers and cottagers
- Servants
- Beggars

All of these levels are present in the characters of Shakespeare's plays, and his inventive and broad vocabulary reflects the speech of everyone from kings to beggars.

Shakespeare's styles

The ability to speak or write effectively—rhetoric—was once a standard part of education, and was a highly regarded skill. Choosing the right word would be at the heart of this, along with the choices in grammar and pronunciation that make up what we call a writer's style. There are sections on Shakespeare's grammar and pronunciation, as well as an account of his use of French and Latin, at the back of this book.

It's important to be aware that these other factors sometimes influence the way a word is used. When Shakespeare writes, in the opening Chorus of *Henry V*: *Can this cockpit hold the vasty fields of France,* the extra syllable added to 'vast' is there to make the rhythm of the poetic line work well. If we try saying this line without the -y, we feel the line stumble awkwardly at 'vast fields'.

'Speak the speech, I pray you'—Hamlet
We encounter a number of different styles in the plays. They silently tell us what type of character is speaking, or what type of mood that character might be feeling.
Many characters speak in prose, the closest reflection of everyday speech. This is easy to see on the page, as the lines reach the right-hand margin and don't look particularly structured:

> *I will tell you why. So shall my anticipation prevent your discovery, and your secrecy to the King and Queen moult no feather. I have of late—but wherefore I know not—lost all my mirth, forgone all custom of exercises.*

But characters also speak in poetry, or verse—something that no-one would naturally do in life. As today, if someone starts to speak poetically, or begins to rhyme, it's because they're playing with language, or because what they're saying has special importance to them. We can tell if something is written in verse because each line begins with a capital letter; and there will be a distinctive rhythm, or metre, to the lines too.

Shakespeare used a metre that had become fashionable among writers at the end of the 16th century. It would typically have ten syllables in every line, with a strong beat on every second syllable. This kind of rhythm reflects the natural 'de-DUM de-DUM de-DUM de-DUM de-DUM' rhythm of spoken English: I **went** to **town** to **buy** a **coat** to**day**.

This rhythm is called 'iambic pentameter.' 'Iambic' is a word that describes the 'de-DUM' rhythm; *penta* is the Greek word for five. So, in a line of iambic pentameter there will be five such units. Shakespeare uses this rhythm to guide us towards the more important words or syllables in the line: *Once* **more** *un***to** *the* **breach** *dear* **friends** *once* **more**.

'By the pricking of my thumbs / Something wicked this way comes' – Macbeth

Very often, and especially in his later writing, we find Shakespeare departing from this regular rhythm. Sometimes there are eleven or more syllables in a line of verse, and sometimes fewer than ten, reflecting the natural breaks in human speech or the broken state of mind of a character. Sometimes two characters will share a line of metre, which means they're interrupting each other or speaking quickly. A short line often allows a character a pause–time to think.

Some types of character are associated with different types of metre. The Witches in Macbeth and the Fairies in *A Midsummer Night's Dream* usually talk in eight-syllable lines (so the different rhythm makes them sound less human). And they love to rhyme. If a character speaks in rhyme there's something extra-special in what they're saying, perhaps even magical. And if someone sings, then–much like in a modern musical–it's because there's no other way to express what they're feeling!

THE PLAYS IN PRINT

The dictionary also introduces us to the chief notions associated with Elizabethan publishing and printing. Books came in two main forms, and so two main prices.

- If you folded a piece of paper once, you would have four sides to print words on. Books made like this were called Folios.
- If you folded a piece of paper twice you would have eight sides to print on. Books made like this were called Quartos.

A Quarto would therefore be half the size of a Folio, and much cheaper (because the paper was being used more efficiently). We can think of the difference as similar to today's hardback and paperback editions. It was incredibly rare for playwrights to have their works printed in Folio, as this format was reserved for high art, and plays were very much considered to be low art forms.

'What is't you read, my Lord?' – Hamlet

Half of the plays Shakespeare wrote were printed unofficially in his lifetime in the cheaper Quarto format. The other half were printed for the first time seven years after he died in a collection of all the plays called the First Folio. (He didn't seem to be interested in making his plays available to be read: they were written to be seen.) It's described as the 'first' because new editions of this collection later appeared, called the Second Folio, the Third Folio, and so on. Similarly, further Quarto editions of a play are referred to as the First Quarto, the Second Quarto, etc.

So there were different versions of Shakespeare's plays circulating 400 years ago, and because we don't have any of his original manuscripts, modern editors often disagree over which version is the best one. In this dictionary, you'll see we make references to the Folio spellings or the First or Second Quarto spellings, whenever a word has been treated differently by modern editors.

HANDLING THE WORDS

The Where?

This dictionary brings together all the difficult words you're likely to meet in twelve of Shakespeare's most performed and studied plays: *Hamlet, Henry V, Julius Caesar, King Lear, Macbeth, A Midsummer Night's Dream, The Merchant of Venice, Much Ado About Nothing, Othello, Romeo and Juliet, The Tempest,* and *Twelfth Night.*

The What?

These are the types of difficult words we've included:

- words Shakespeare made up that aren't in everyday language
- words that have gone out of use since his time
- words that have changed their meaning since his time
- the names of antiquated or fictional people and places

If a word had the same meaning to Shakespeare as it does to us today, we didn't include it in this dictionary.

We've also done things that dictionaries don't normally do. In particular, we've grouped together words that, in meaning, belong together. It didn't make sense to us to have 'accommodate' at one end of the alphabet and 'unaccommodated' at the other. So in our book we've brought them together, which we hope will help you remember them more easily. Sometimes the 'family' of words has several members, such as 'cozen', 'cozenage', 'cozener', and 'cozening: you'll find them all together at 'cozen'.

The Who?

We show you the extract in which a word appears, and tell you who said it, and why: the context of the word. If it's in a difficult passage, we explain that bit too. Also, for every word, we give an example of its use in one of the plays. There wasn't room to include every instance of when a word is used, so be careful when you look up a word that has more than one meaning. You have to choose the meaning you think is right.

And The Why?

For example, if you see the word *utter,* and look it up, you'll find three meanings: 'exhale', 'offer for sale', or 'commemorate'. The game is to choose the meaning that works in the context.

- *The Apothecary tells Romeo about his drugs: 'Mantua's law / Is death to any he that utters them'.*

The law is unlikely to dictate that anyone who talks about drugs will be put to death, so that rules out the meaning of 'exhale'. It's also hard to imagine a death penalty being put in place if someone 'commemorates' drugs. So we can deduce the meaning is likely to be the second, 'offer for sale'. This makes sense, as Romeo is trying to buy poison from the Apothecary. (See p.8 for an explanation of the / sign.)

Ergo*: The Deduction

Follow this process of deduction when using this dictionary. If the example you're looking for isn't there, mentally remove the alternatives that don't fit, one by one, until you're left with one that fits better than the others: *'Mantua's law / Is death to any he that offers them for sale'.*

Don't be distracted by meanings that are the same as ones you probably know in modern English. That's why we often begin an entry by saying: 'as well as...':

> **companion**
>
> as well as meaning 'comrade', you'll find: rogue
>
> - *Brutus orders an irritating poet to leave: 'Companion, hence!'*

We're pointing out that, although *companion* does sometimes mean 'comrade' in Shakespeare, in this example from *Julius Caesar* it doesn't.

***see Latin, p.352**

HOW TO USE THIS DICTIONARY

Each entry consists of the following elements:

HEADWORD

–a word or phrase in **bold type**

–for some words, there is an alternative spelling:

clerestory also spelled **clearstory**

PART OF SPEECH

–if the heading is a single word, we tell you which word class (or 'part of speech') it belongs to:

NOUN, VERB, ADJECTIVE, ADVERB, CONJUNCTION, PREPOSITION, INTERJECTION

PRONUNCIATION GUIDE

–if the headword needs pronunciation guidance, we give a sound-alike re-spelling in square brackets, with a hyphen between syllables and the main stress in bold:

Aeneas NOUN [pronounced a-**nee**-as]

DEFINITION

–the definition uses only words included in the *Oxford English Dictionary for Schools*; if a word has more than one meaning, the different definitions are numbered in sequence:

fell ADJECTIVE

1 fierce

• *(MND 5.1.217) Snug the joiner describes his character as 'A lion fell'.*

2 terrible

• *(Mac 1.5.45) Lady Macbeth wants no natural feelings to 'Shake my fell purpose'.*

WARNING NOTE

–if you see this sign ⚠ it means 'take care', to avoid being misled by a modern meaning you may already be familiar with:

rehearse VERB

⚠*Don't read in the meaning of 'practise'.*

utter

• *(MND 5.1.380) Titania tells the Fairies: 'rehearse your song by rote'.*

USAGE NOTE

–this sign ✒ introduces a comment which tells you more about how a word is used

apothecary or **pothecary** NOUN

one who prepares and sells medicinal drugs

• *(RJ 5.1.37) Romeo remembers where he can get some poison: 'I do remember an apothecary'.*

✒*We include the alternative spelling because the word sometimes drops its first syllable to fit the rhythm of a line.*

–it also introduces a comment about the sources where the word may be found:

wonder NOUN

4 astonishing course of events

• *(Ham 4.5.88) Claudius says Laertes 'Feeds on this wonder'.*

✒*The Second Quarto text has 'this wonder'. The First Folio has 'his wonder' (which would mean 'his grief').*

–modern editions of Shakespeare will sometimes translate words into their modern equivalent; we provide the old version, but will point out if such a change is made:

shale NOUN

shell

• *(H5 4.2.18) The Constable says the French will suck away the souls of the English, 'Leaving them but the shales and husks of men'.*

✒*This is the spelling in the First Folio. Several editions replace it with 'shells'.*

THEATRE NOTE

– this sign 🎭 introduces a comment about the cultural background, Elizabethan ways of thinking, or the theatrical practices of the time

groundlings NOUN

audience standing in a theatre courtyard around the stage

• *(Ham 3.2.10) Hamlet criticizes actors who 'split the ears of the groundlings'.*

🎭*The groundlings would have paid the cheapest entrance fee, and would thus be considered poor and badly educated. Cheap entrance to the courtyard is also a feature of the reconstructed Shakespeare's Globe in London, where standing members of the audience are still called groundlings.*

CITATION

—a quotation, showing the use of the word in a play, and always saying who is speaking (see Abbreviations); all quotations are taken from the *Oxford School Shakespeare*:

brake NOUN
bush

- *(MND 2.1.227) Demetrius tells Helena he will 'run from thee and hide me in the brakes'.*

—when there is a / in the quotation it shows a break between lines of verse, as in the example from *Twelfth Night* on p.11 (at **abjure**).

—we often include an extra gloss to help you with the sense:

coverture NOUN
canopied bower

- *(MA 3.1.30) Ursula sees Beatrice hiding 'in the woodbine coverture'—a honeysuckle covered enclosure in the garden.*

RELATED WORDS

—this sign **›** introduces a word with a related meaning to the main headword

bolted ADJECTIVE
refined

- *(H5 2.2.134) Henry is dismayed at Scroop's treachery, 'so finely bolted didst thou seem'—so well-refined.*

  › unbolted ADJECTIVE
  unrefined

  - *(KL 2.2.62) Kent threatens Oswald: 'I will tread this unbolted villain into mortar'.*

CROSS REFERENCE

Sometimes we make a link between entries in the A to Z section:

auchient see **ancient**

demi-natured see **nature**

If a word you're looking up is treated in the *Panels* or *Thematic* pages, it is listed in the *A to Z section,* with a cross-reference:

adieu see GOODBYE, p.121
ergo see LATIN, p.352

ABBREVIATIONS AND VARIATIONS

Abbreviations

All quotations are from the *Oxford School Shakespeare* editions, using the following abbreviations to refer to a particular play:

ABBR.	PLAY
H5	Henry V
Ham	Hamlet
JC	Julius Caesar
KL	King Lear
MA	Much Ado About Nothing
Mac	Macbeth
MND	A Midsummer Night's Dream
MV	The Merchant of Venice
Oth	Othello
RJ	Romeo and Juliet
Tem	The Tempest
TN	Twelfth Night

Line references are to Act.Scene.Line:
(TN 3.1.55) = *Twelfth Night* Act 3. Scene 1. Line 55

Line number variations

If you are using another edition of a play, you may find that the line numbers are different, especially when the quotation is from a passage of prose. Usually, line numbers will differ only by a line or two, but where a scene is very long, the differences towards the end can be up to ten lines or so (as in *Hamlet* 3.2) – so you may have to look carefully to find the word you've just looked up.

Scene number variations

Editors sometimes have different opinions on where a scene ends and a new one begins, so the numbering in this book might not be the same as in yours. We follow the decisions used by the editor of the *Oxford Schools Shakespeare*. Here are the cases where *Oxford* scene divisions are different from the editions we use in our book and our website *Shakespeare's Words*:

OXFORD SCHOOLS SHAKESPEARE	SHAKESPEARE'S WORDS
Mac 5.6	*Mac 5.6, lines 1-10*
Mac 5.7	*Mac 5.6, lines 11-39*
Mac 5.8	*Mac 5.6, lines 40-73*
Mac 5.9	*Mac 5.6, lines 74-114*
H5 3.2	*H5 3.2.1-53*
H5 3.3	*H5 3.2.54-135*
H5 3.4	*H5 3.3*
H5 3.5	*H5 3.4*
H5 3.6	*H5 3.5*
H5 3.7	*H5 3.6*
H5 3.8	*H5 3.7*

Name variations

Editors also have differing opinions on the names of characters. There are some names and spellings in the *Oxford Schools Shakespeare* series which differ from other editions:

OXFORD SCHOOLS SHAKESPEARE	SHAKESPEARE'S WORDS
Ham Osric	Osrick
Ham Gravedigger	First Clown
Ham Other	Second Clown
H5 Bourbon	Britaine (and in 3.8, 4.2, and 4.5 speeches assigned to Bourbon are given to Dauphin)
H5 Llewellyn	Fluellen
H5 Orléans	Orleans
JC Calpurnia	Calphurnia
JC Murellus	Marullus
JC Claudio	Claudius
JC Popillius	Popilius
JC Varrus	Varro
MA Conrad	Conrade
Mac Donaldbain	Donalbain
Mac Caithness	Cathness
Mac Menteith	Menteth
Mac Siward	Seyward
MV Balthazar	Balthasar
MV Lancelot	Launcelot
MV Salarino	Salerio
RJ Friar Lawrence	Friar Laurence

abate VERB
make less
• *(MND 3.2.432) Helena pleads with the night to be over soon, so she can return to Athens all the sooner: 'Abate thy hours'.*

› **abatement** NOUN
lessening
• *(KL 1.4.56) A knight observes there is a 'great abatement of kindness' towards Lear in Goneril's household.*

abide VERB
await
• *(Mac 3.1.142) Macbeth tells the Murderers to wait for him in another room: 'abide within'.*

› **abode** NOUN
1 staying
• *(Oth 4.2.222) Iago says Othello is going to Mauritania, 'unless his abode be lingered here by some accident'—unless something happens to make him extend his stay.*
2 delay
• *(MV 2.6.22) Lorenzo apologizes for keeping everyone waiting: 'your patience for my long abode'.*

abjure VERB
swear to abandon, promise to quit
• *(TN 1.2.40) The Captain tells Viola that Olivia 'hath abjur'd the company / And sight of men'.*

above see STAGE DIRECTIONS, p.285

Abraham Cupid
an unusual description of the god of love, probably referring to beggars known as 'Abraham coves' who pretended to be mad to get money
• *(RJ 2.1.13) Mercutio describes the god of love as 'Young Abraham Cupid'.*
Mercutio has just called Romeo a 'madman', and goes on to talk of the king who loved a beggar-maid.

Abram NOUN
the original name of 'Abraham', portrayed in the Bible as the founder of the Jewish race
• *(MV 1.3.67) Shylock tells a story about Jacob, the grandson of 'our holy Abram'.*

abridgement NOUN
1 shortening
• *(H5 5.Chorus.44) The Chorus apologizes for not giving all the details of what happened to Henry: 'Then brook abridgement'—permit me to cut the story short.*
2 pastime, an enjoyable way to pass the time more quickly
• *(MND 5.1.39) Theseus asks Philostrate: 'what abridgement have you for this evening?'*

abroach ADVERB
in action
• *(RJ 1.1.98) Montague asks Benvolio, 'Who set this ancient quarrel new abroach?'*

absolute ADJECTIVE
1 perfect
• *(H5 3.8.24) The Constable describes the Duke of Bourbon's horse as 'a most absolute and excellent horse'.*
2 literal-minded
• *(Ham 5.1.125) Hamlet remarks on the way the First*

Aa b c d e f g h i j k l m n o p q r s t u v w x y z

Gravedigger replies to him: 'How absolute the knave is'.
3 curt
• *(Mac 3.6.41) A Lord reports a messenger speaking 'with an absolute "Sir, not I"'.*
4 without any conditions
• *(Tem 1.2.109) Prospero describes his brother Antonio as wanting to be 'Absolute Milan'—a ruler with no restrictions on his power.*

abstemious also spelled **abstenious** ADJECTIVE
stopping oneself from doing something
• *(Tem 4.1.53) Prospero tells Ferdinand to control his passions when he is with Miranda: 'Be more abstemious'.*

abstract NOUN
summary
• *(Ham 2.2.512) Hamlet describes the Players as 'the abstract and brief chronicles of the time'—they are like stories that sum up all that happens.*

abuser NOUN
deceiver
• *(Oth 1.2.78) Brabantio accuses Othello of being 'an abuser of the world'.*

› **self-abuse** NOUN
self-deception
• *(Mac 3.4.142) Macbeth thinks that Banquo's ghost was an image conjured up by his own mind, and that he is tormenting himself: 'My strange and self-abuse'.*

aby VERB [pronounced a-**by**]
suffer for
• *(MND 3.2.335) Demetrius threatens Lysander over Helena: 'If thou dost intend / Never so little show of love to her, / Thou shalt aby it'.*

abysm NOUN
abyss, a deep dark cavernous space
• *(Tem 1.2.50) Prospero asks Miranda what she can remember of when she was a little child, 'In the dark backward and abysm of time'.*
Some editions replace 'abysm' with 'abyss'.

accent NOUN
as well as meaning 'someone's regional pronunciation', you'll find:
1 way of talking
• *(RJ 2.4.29) Mercutio describes Tybalt as one of the 'new tuners of accent!'—using the latest turns of phrase.*
2 language
• *(JC 3.1.113) Cassius says their killing of Caesar will become a famous story, told 'In states unborn and accents yet unknown!'*

› **second accent**
echo
• *(H5 2.4.127) Exeter says the Dauphin will hear the sound of his mockery return as the sound of Henry's cannon-fire ('ordinance'): 'In second accent of his ordinance'.*

accident NOUN
⚠ *Don't read in the modern meaning of 'an event that causes injury or damage', such as a car crash.*
event
• *(MND 4.1.67) Oberon says Bottom will 'think no more of this night's accidents' other than that they were a dream.*

accommodate VERB
equip
• *(KL 4.6.81) Edgar sees Lear strangely dressed with wild flowers, and thinks 'The safer sense will ne'er accommodate / His master thus'—a sane mind would never let its body dress in this way.*

› **unaccommodated** ADJECTIVE
possessing nothing
• *(KL 3.4.103) Lear reflects on seeing naked Poor Tom: 'unaccommodated man is no more but such a poor, bare, forked animal as thou art'.*

accompt see **account**

accordant or **according** ADJECTIVE
ready to agree
• *(MA 1.2.13) Antonio has heard that the Prince plans to tell Hero that he loves her, and 'if he found her accordant' he will then inform her father.*
• *(RJ 1.2.19) Capulet gives his 'consent and fair according voice' to Paris, agreeing that he should marry Juliet.*

account or **accompt** NOUN
1 amount
• *(Oth 1.3.5) A senator reports that estimates of the size of the Turkish fleet do not agree about the exact ('just') number: 'they jump not on a just accompt'.*
2 judgement, especially one made by God about the life you have led
• *(Ham 1.5.78) The Ghost says he was given no chance to obtain forgiveness for his bad deeds: 'sent to my account / With all my imperfections on my head'.*
'Accompt' sometimes appears shortened as 'compt', and 'account' as 'count', often to fit the metre of the line.
• *(Oth 5.2.271) Othello tells the dead Desdemona they will meet again at the day of judgement: 'When we shall meet at compt'.*

› **accountant** ADJECTIVE
accountable
• *(Oth 2.1.282) Iago admits to having had lustful*

thoughts about Desdemona: 'peradventure / I stand accountant for as great a sin'.
Some editions replace 'accountant' by 'accomptant'.
Don't read in the modern meaning of 'account', 'money in the bank', or 'accountant', 'financial book-keeper'.

accouter also spelled **accoutre** VERB
dress
• *(MV 3.4.63) Portia plans her disguise with Nerissa: 'When we are both accoutred like young men'.*

ace NOUN
in card-games, an ace is a card with one spot, and in dice-games it ranks as the lowest score of one
• *(MND 5.1.294) Demetrius has just heard Bottom, playing Pyramus, kill himself, saying die several times, and he jokes: 'No die, but an ace for him; for he is but one'.*
A 'die' is a dice; but to get the joke Demetrius is making, you have to know that in Shakespeare's time 'ace' was pronounced like the word 'ass'. So Demetrius is saying that Bottom is as stupid as a donkey.

acerb also spelled **acerbe** ADJECTIVE
[pronounced a-**serb**]
bitter
• *(Oth 1.3.344) Iago says the nice-tasting food that Othello is now eating (meaning Desdemona) will soon be 'as acerb as the coloquintida'—a kind of fruit with a very bitter—or acerbic—taste.*

Acheron NOUN [pronounced **ak**-eron]
in classical mythology, a great abyss (pit) in the Underworld, where a river flowed that the souls of the dead had to cross
• *(Mac 3.5.15) Hecate tells the Witches to meet her 'at the pit of Acheron'—the implication is that they will be meeting Macbeth at the gates of hell.*

acknow on VERB
admit to
• *(Oth 3.3.320) Iago tells Emilia she must not let Desdemona know she has taken a handkerchief: 'Be not acknown on't'.*

acquit VERB
as well as meaning 'complete a piece of work well' or (in court) 'be found not guilty of a charge', you'll find:
1 release
• *(TN 3.4.195) Cesario says to Olivia 'I will acquit you'—he will not make Olivia stand by what she has said.*
2 forgive
• *(H5 2.2.141) King Henry sends the traitors to be executed and asks God to 'acquit them of their practices'—forgive them for their wicked deeds.*

› **acquittance** NOUN
1 excusing
• *(Ham 4.7.1) Claudius persuades Laertes that he had nothing to do with the death of Polonius: 'Now must your conscience my acquittance seal'—you must believe my excuses.*
2 satisfaction
• *(Oth 4.2.189) Roderigo has sent Desdemona jewels, and hopes for a favourable response: 'comforts of sudden respect and acquittance'.*
'Acquittance' appears in the First Quarto text of 'Othello'. In the First Folio it is printed as 'acquaintance', 'getting to know me better'.

action-taking ADJECTIVE
taking legal action
• *(KL 2.2.16) Kent describes Oswald as an 'action-taking' rogue—the kind of annoying person who always wants to take people to court for the slightest reason.*

adage NOUN
saying
• *(Mac 1.7.45) Lady Macbeth compares her husband's change of mind about killing King Duncan to 'the poor cat i'th'adage'—a cat who wanted to eat fish in a pool but would not wet its feet.*

Adam NOUN
in the Bible, the first human being, expelled from the Garden of Eden for breaking God's law
• *(H5 1.1.29) Canterbury recalls how Henry, on becoming king, lost 'th'offending Adam' that was in him—his sinful character.*

Adam NOUN
Adam Bell, a legendary archer—at the time as famous as Robin Hood is today
• *(MA 1.1.236) Benedick, imagining himself a target in archery practice, says that anyone hitting him should be 'clapped on the shoulder and called Adam'.*

adamant NOUN
legendary substance of great hardness, believed to have magnetic force
• *(MND 2.1.195) Helena tells Demetrius she can't stop following him: 'You draw me, you hard-hearted adamant!'*

addiction NOUN
Don't read in the modern meaning of 'being addicted to drugs'.
inclination
• *(H5 1.1.54) The Archbishop talks about Henry's former behaviour, when 'his addiction was to*

warning note *usage note* *theatre note*

Aa b c d e f g h i j k l m n o p q r s t u v w x y z

courses vain'—his inclination was for worthless activities.

addition NOUN

⚠*Don't read the modern maths meaning of 'adding up' into these senses.*

1 title

• *(Mac 1.3.104) Ross formally greets Macbeth with the title 'Thane of Cawdor': 'In which addition, hail'.*

2 mark of honour (such as would be shown by a new symbol on a coat of arms)

• *(KL 5.3.300) Albany tells Edgar and Kent that their rights will be restored, with 'such addition as your honours / Have more than merited'.*

3 credit

• *(Oth 3.4.188) Cassio asks Bianca to leave him, as it would be 'no addition, nor my wish'—no credit to him for Othello to see him in the company of a woman.*

4 exaggeration

• *(Ham 4.4.17) The Captain answers Hamlet's question by saying he is going to tell him the truth, 'with no addition'.*

addle ADJECTIVE

addled, rotten

• *(RJ 3.1.23) Mercutio says Benvolio's head 'hath been beaten as addle as an egg for quarrelling'—its inside must now be as rotten as a bad egg.*

address VERB

as well as meaning 'speak to someone in a formal way', you'll find:

1 get ready

• *(MND 5.1.106) Philostrate tells Theseus that the players are ready to perform: 'the Prologue is address'd'.*

2 direct

• *(TN 1.4.15) Orsino tells Viola to go to Olivia: 'address thy gait unto her'—move your steps in her direction.*

adhere VERB

suit

• *(Mac 1.7.52) Lady Macbeth tells her husband that, when he first confided his thoughts to her, 'Nor time nor place / Did then adhere'—the situation wasn't right for a murder to take place.*

adieu see **GOODBYE, p.121**

admire VERB

marvel at

• *(H5 3.7.117) The French Herald Montjoy tells Henry that the English will 'admire our sufferance'—be amazed at the patience of the French.*

› **admiration** NOUN

amazement

• *(Ham 1.2.192) Horatio tells Hamlet to keep his emotions under control until he has reported the whole story of the Ghost: 'Season your admiration for a while'.*

› **admirable** ADJECTIVE

wondrous

• *(MND 5.1.27) Hippolyta finds the events of the night to have been 'strange and admirable'.*

› **admired** ADJECTIVE

to be wondered at

• *(Tem 3.1.37) Ferdinand addresses Prospero's daughter: 'Admir'd Miranda, / Indeed the top of admiration'.*

➨*'Admiration' doesn't necessarily mean that the person likes what is the cause of the wonder:*

• *(Mac 3.4.110) Lady Macbeth is angry with her husband for having upset everyone at dinner 'With most admir'd disorder'.*

ado NOUN

fuss, bustle

• *(RJ 3.4.23) Capulet tells Paris he won't invite many people to Juliet's wedding: he will 'keep no great ado—a friend or two'.*

🎭*'Much Ado About Nothing' literally means a great fuss over nothing; but there are two puns hidden in the title: (1) 'nothing' used to be pronounced like 'noting', and indeed a lot of observing and reporting goes on; (2) the play tells two love stories (Claudio and Hero, Benedick and Beatrice), neither of which proceeds smoothly, and 'nothing' was an impolite way of talking about the shape of the female genitals (an O).*

adoption NOUN

⚠*Don't read in the modern meaning of 'taking a child into your family'.*

relationship

• *(Ham 1.3.62) Polonius advises Laertes: 'Those friends thou hast, and their adoption tried, / Grapple them unto thy soul'—stay really close to them once you've tested the relationship with them.*

adulterate ADJECTIVE

adulterous

• *(Ham 1.5.42) The Ghost of Hamlet's father calls Claudius 'that adulterate beast'.*

🎭*'Adultery' was often used to mean any kind of sexual relationship thought to be wrong, not just to do with a married person having sex with someone other than their spouse.*

advantage see **vantage**

adventure VERB

dare to go

• *(RJ 2.2.84) Romeo tells Juliet that even if she were*

at the other end of the earth he 'should adventure for such merchandise'.

› at all adventures

⚠*Don't read in the modern meaning of 'an exciting story'.*

regardless of the risks

• *(H5 4.1.112) Bates thinks Henry would rather be up to his neck in the cold River Thames than be waiting for a battle at Agincourt, 'and I by him, at all adventures'—anywhere else would be better, even if it were dangerous.*

› misadventure NOUN

misfortune, bad happenings

• *(RJ 5.1.29) Balthasar tells Romeo that his looks 'are pale and wild, and do import / Some misadventure'—signify some misfortune.*

› misadventured also spelled **misadventur'd** ADJECTIVE

disastrous

• *(RJ Prologue.7) The Prologue informs the audience that the lovers suffered 'misadventur'd piteous overthrows'—a disastrous, saddening destruction.*

advertisement NOUN

⚠*Don't read in the modern meaning of 'commercials to make you buy things'.*

advice

• *(MA 5.1.32) Leonato says he won't listen to Antonio because his griefs 'cry louder than advertisement'—the sound of his sorrow would drown out any advice.*

advocation NOUN

advocacy, counsel

• *(Oth 3.4.117) Desdemona tells Cassio that she can't put his case to Othello, as he is so angry with her: 'My advocation is not now in tune'.*

Aegles NOUN [pronounced **ee**-glayz]

in Greek mythology, one of the women loved (and deserted) by Theseus

• *(MND 2.1.79) Oberon reminds Titania of how she made Theseus 'with fair Aegles break his faith'—persuaded him to be unfaithful to her.*

Aeneas NOUN [pronounced a-**nee**-as]

in Greek mythology, a hero who escaped from the city of Troy after it was conquered by the Greeks; he is remembered as the founder of ancient Rome

• *(JC 1.2.112) Cassius remembers the way 'Aeneas, our great ancestor' saved his father from the burning city.*

aerial ADJECTIVE

airy

• *(Oth 2.1.39) Montano tells everyone to look for Othello's ship as far as the eye can see, until 'we make the main and th'aerial blue / An indistinct regard'—where it's difficult to tell where the sea ends and the sky begins.*

Aeson NOUN [pronounced **ee**-son]

in Greek mythology, the father of Jason, who went in search of the Golden Fleece, and who was magically restored to youth by Medea

• *(MV 5.1.14) Jessica imagines a night when 'Medea gather'd the enchanted herbs / That did renew old Aeson'.*

affect VERB

1 favour

• *(KL 1.1.1) Kent opens the play by asking Gloucester whether 'the king had more affected the Duke of Albany than Cornwall'—which of his two sons-in-law he likes more.*

2 love

• *(MA 1.1.270) Don Pedro asks Claudio if he has fallen in love with Hero: 'Dost thou affect her?'*

affect NOUN

desire

• *(Oth 1.3.260) Othello says he wants Desdemona to come with him to Cyprus if it is her wish to do so, and not to satisfy 'the young affects' in him—the kind of desires he had when he was younger.*

› affected ADJECTIVE

inclined, disposed

• *(KL 2.1.97) Regan believes Edgar's bad behaviour comes from mixing with the followers of Lear: it's no surprise that 'he were ill affected'.*

affection NOUN

as well as meaning 'a real liking for someone', you'll find:

1 feeling

• *(MV 3.1.53) Shylock says that a Jew also has 'senses, affections, passions'.*

2 desire

• *(RJ 2.5.12) Juliet thinks the Nurse would travel faster if she had 'affections and warm youthful blood'—joking that desire makes the blood run warmer.*

3 love

• *(Tem 1.2.449) Ferdinand hopes that Miranda's 'affection' has 'not gone forth'—that she is not in love with someone else.*

4 character

• *(Mac 4.3.77) Malcolm admits to enormous greed growing in his 'most ill-compos'd affection'—that his personality contains all sorts of wickedness.*

5 being biased

• *(RJ 3.1.173) Lady Capulet tells the Prince that Benvolio is lying because he is a friend of Romeo: 'Affection makes him false'.*

☞ *'Affection' was sometimes confused by*

printers with 'affectation', meaning 'artificiality' or 'posing'.

• *(Ham 2.2.431) Hamlet remembers a play in which there was 'no matter in the phrase that might indict the author of affection'—nothing in the language that would let you accuse the author of writing in an artificial way.*

'Affection' is the word that appears in the Second Quarto text of the play. In the First Folio it is printed as 'affectation'.

affectioned ADJECTIVE
putting on airs, pretending to be something you're not

• *(TN 2.3.132) Maria says Malvolio is 'an affectioned ass'—a posturing fool.*

affeered also spelled **affeer'd** ADJECTIVE
legally confirmed

• *(Mac 4.3.34) Macduff talks about Macbeth becoming king: 'The title is affeer'd'.*

affiance NOUN [pronounced a-**fie**-ance]
trust

• *(H5 2.2.124) Henry tells the traitors that they have 'with jealousy infected / The sweetness of affiance'—spoilt the solid principle of people trusting each other.*

affine VERB
bind by ties

• *(Oth 2.3.202) Montano advises Iago to tell the truth about Cassio's brawl, even if he is 'partially affin'd or leagued in office'—even if he wants to take Cassio's side because they're close friends or colleagues.*

› **affined** also spelled **affin'd** ADJECTIVE
obliged

• *(Oth 1.1.39) Iago asks Roderigo if there is any good reason to be 'affin'd / To love the Moor'.*

› **affinity** NOUN
kinship

• *(Oth 3.1.45) Montano is described as being a person 'of great fame in Cyprus / And great affinity'—he has high-ranking relations and friends.*

affray VERB
startle from sleep

• *(RJ 3.5.33) The singing of the morning lark tells Juliet it is time for her and Romeo to separate: 'arm from arm that voice doth us affray'—scares us into separating.*

affront VERB
⚠*Don't read in the modern meaning of 'insult, offend'.*

come face to face with

• *(Ham 3.1.31) Claudius says he has called Hamlet into the hall where Ophelia is, so that he 'may here / Affront Ophelia'.*

again ADVERB
as well as meaning 'once more', you'll find:
in reply

• *(MND 5.1.179) After Bottom has cursed Wall, Theseus interrupts: 'The wall, methinks, being sensible, should curse again'—because it has feelings, the wall should curse in reply.*

Agamemnon NOUN
[pronounced aga-**mem**-non]
in Greek mythology, the commander of the victorious Greek forces at the city of Troy

• *(H5 3.7.6) The Welsh Captain describes the Duke of Exeter as being 'as magnanimous as Agamemnon'—showing the same courage and bravery.*

agate NOUN
dwarf

• *(MA 3.1.65) Hero says that if Beatrice sees a short man, she compares him to 'an agate very vilely cut'—like a tiny figure or dwarf badly carved in a type of hard, ornamental stone.*

aggravate VERB
intended to mean 'moderate'—make quieter

• *(MND 1.2.70) Bottom tells Quince that if he is allowed to play the Lion, he will 'aggravate' his voice to avoid frightening the ladies.*

The joke could still work today because 'aggravate' still has the negative meaning of 'make worse' or 'be annoying'.

agitation NOUN
⚠*In these senses, the modern meaning of 'being upset in your mind' is not the dominant one.*

1 movement—especially backwards and forwards repeatedly

• *(Mac 5.1.10) The Doctor describes Lady Macbeth's sleepwalking as 'slumbery agitation'.*

2 consideration

• *(MV 3.5.4) Lancelot tells Jessica what he thinks about her situation: 'now I speak my agitation of the matter'.*

agnize VERB
acknowledge

• *(Oth 1.3.229) Othello tells the Duke: 'I do agnize / A natural and prompt alacrity / I find in hardness'—he recognizes in his own personality a quick willingness to seek out harsh or difficult situations in life.*

ague NOUN [pronounced **ay**-gyoo]
fever, especially one that causes the body to shake
• *(Mac 5.5.4) Macbeth says the besieging army can wait outside his castle 'Till famine and the ague eat them up'.*

> **ague-proof** ADJECTIVE
> resistant to fevers
> • *(KL 4.6.104) Lear tells everyone: 'I am not ague-proof'.*

a-hold ADVERB
a sailing term meaning 'close to the wind', to hold a boat steady
• *(Tem 1.1.46) The Boatswain shouts through the storm to the sailors: 'Lay her a-hold'.*

aidant ADJECTIVE
helpful
• *(KL 4.4.17) Cordelia asks the herbs of the earth to help her sick father: 'be aidant and remediate / In the good man's distress!'*

air-drawn ADJECTIVE
moving in the air; or drawn (unsheathed) out of the air; or created ('drawn') by air and light
• *(Mac 3.4.62) Lady Macbeth reminds her husband of 'the air-drawn dagger' which led him to Duncan.*

Ajax NOUN [pronounced **ay**-jaks]
in Greek mythology, a hero who fought against Troy, proverbial for his terrific size and strength
• *(KL 2.2.121) Kent is dismissive of Oswald and his fellows: 'None of these rogues and cowards / But Ajax is their fool'—they have such high opinions of themselves that they think even Ajax would look foolish alongside them.*

alablaster NOUN
an alternative spelling of 'alabaster'—a type of ornamental white stone with a very smooth surface, often used for carving
• *(MV 1.1.84) Gratiano tries to cheer up Antonio: 'Why should a man whose blood is warm within / Sit like his grandsire cut in alablaster?' —as still as a grandfather in a carving.*
'Alablaster' is the spelling in the First Folio. Some editions replace this with 'alabaster'.
People would talk about having skin 'as smooth as alablaster' or 'as white as alablaster'. Unlike today, the nobility in Shakespeare's time wanted to have smooth white skin, and used make-up (often lead-based, which would create terrible sores) to give such an effect; a suntan was the mark of the working classes.

alack see REGRETTING, p.250

alarum or **alarm** NOUN
1 call to arms
• *(H5 4.6.35) King Henry hears the sound of an alarm that tells him the French are attacking again: 'what new alarm is this same?'*
2 encouragement
• *(Oth 2.3.23) Iago suggests to Cassio that when Desdemona speaks 'is it not an alarum to love?'—a wake-up call.*

alarum VERB
urge on
• *(Mac 2.1.53) Macbeth describes a murderer as being 'Alarum'd by his sentinel, the wolf'.*
For 'alarum' in stage directions, see ALARUMS AND EXCURSIONS.

ALARUMS AND EXCURSIONS

The modern meanings of 'alarm'—'a feeling of worry or fear', and 'a warning that something bad is about to happen'—are found in Shakespeare, but 'alarum' usually has a much stronger meaning, announcing a battle or fight, or telling us that a noisy, dangerous, or exciting event is going to take place. The commonest use is in stage directions (see p.285).

An 'alarum' is often followed by an 'excursion'—a bout of fighting that takes place across the stage—as in the middle of the Battle of Philippi.
• *(JC 5.3.1) Stage direction: 'Alarum. Excursions. Enter Cassius and Titinius'.*

The intensity of the alarum is sometimes mentioned.
• *(JC 5.2.3) During the Battle of Philippi, the stage direction says 'Loud alarum'.*

Any noisy instrument can signal an alarum, usually a trumpet, bell, or drum.
• *(Mac 2.3.71) In Macbeth's castle, Macduff alerts people to the murder of Duncan: 'Ring the alarum bell!'*

alas see REGRETTING, p.250

Albion NOUN [pronounced **al**-bee-on]
an ancient legendary name for Britain, suggesting a realm of a different time
• *(H5 3.6.14) The Duke of Bourbon threatens to buy*

Aa b c d e f g h i j k l m n o p q r s t u v w x y z

a farm in the 'isle of Albion' if the French fail to stand up to the English—in other words, I'll eat my hat!

Alcides NOUN [pronounced al-**sigh**-deez]
in Greek mythology, the original name of Hercules (after his grandfather, Alceus)
• *(MV 3.2.55) Portia says Bassanio has more love even 'Than young Alcides' when he rescued a Trojan princess from being sacrificed to a sea-monster.*

alderman see **OCCUPATIONS, p.166**

Alexander NOUN
Alexander the Great, a 4th-century BC Macedonian king and soldier, known for his great empire
• *(H5 3.1.19) Henry describes the fathers of his soldiers as 'many Alexanders' who fought in France before them.*

alla stoccata see **RECREATION, p.170**

alliance NOUN
as well as meaning 'an agreement between countries or political parties' you'll find:
marriage
• *(RJ 2.3.91) The Friar hopes that the 'alliance' between Romeo and Juliet will help to bring the two families together.*

> **ally** NOUN
> kinsman, a family member or close friend
> • *(RJ 3.1.105) Romeo describes Mercutio as 'the prince's near ally'.*

all-licensed also spelled **-licens'd** ADJECTIVE
allowed to do anything
• *(KL 1.4.190) Goneril angrily tells Lear about the bad behaviour of his followers, including 'your all-licens'd fool'.*

all the world to nothing see **nothing**

all thing also spelled **all-thing** ADVERB
completely
• *(Mac 3.1.13) Lady Macbeth tells Macbeth that it would have been 'all thing unbecoming'—a terrible social blunder—if Banquo had not been invited to their feast.*

ally see **alliance**

Almain also spelled **Almaine** NOUN
[pronounced **al**-mayn]
German
• *(Oth 2.3.73) Iago boasts about the drinking abilities of an Englishman: 'he sweats not to overthrow your Almain'—drinking more than a German (considered at the time to be great drinkers of alcohol) doesn't even bring him out in a sweat.* see **MAP, p.176**

alms NOUN
good deed
• *(MA 2.3.155) Don Pedro and Claudio discuss what should happen to Benedick if he continues to tease Beatrice: 'it were an alms to hang him'.*

aloft see **STAGE DIRECTIONS, p.285**

aloof ADVERB
▲*Don't read in the modern meaning of 'being unfriendly'.*
a short distance away
• *(MV 3.2.42) Portia tells her attendants, 'stand all aloof'.*

amain ADVERB
at full speed
• *(Tem 4.1.74) Iris describes the arrival of the goddess Juno, and the birds that pull her chariot: 'Her peacocks fly amain'.*

ambassage see **embassage**

amble VERB
as well as meaning 'walk at a slow and easy pace', you'll find:
walk in an unnatural way
• *(Ham 3.1.144) The angry Hamlet says that women 'jig and amble'.*

> **ambling** NOUN
> false way of moving around
> • *(RJ 1.4.11) Romeo doesn't like the idea of performing a slow stately dance at the Capulets' party: 'I am not for this ambling'.*

ambuscado NOUN
[pronounced am-bus-**kah**-doh]
a playfully fake Spanish word for 'ambush'
• *(RJ 1.4.84) Mercutio describes how soldiers dream 'of cutting foreign throats, / Of breaches, ambuscadoes'.*

amerce VERB [pronounced a-**murse**]
penalize—from a French word (related to 'mercy') meaning 'to punish with a fine'
• *(RJ 3.1.186) The Prince says how he will punish those involved with the killing of Tybalt: 'I'll amerce you with so strong a fine'.*

amiable ADJECTIVE
▲*Don't read the modern meaning of 'friendly' into these senses; the emotion is always much stronger.*
1 lovable
• *(MND 4.1.2) Titania, in love with Bottom, wants to stroke his 'amiable cheeks'.*
2 amorous, passionate
• *(MA 3.3.140) Borachio describes his mock-wooing of Margaret as an 'amiable encounter'.*

Anchises NOUN [pronounced an-**kigh**-seez]
in Greek mythology, the father of the Trojan hero Aeneas, saved by his son from the burning city of Troy by being shoulder-carried out of the city
• *(JC 1.2.114) Cassius remembers how Aeneas 'Did from the flames of Troy upon his shoulder / The old Anchises bear'.*

anchor NOUN
recluse
• *(Ham 3.2.211) The Player Queen assures the Player King (during the 'play within a play') that, were he to die, 'An anchor's cheer in prison be my scope'—her new way of life would be as a hermit in a cave.*

ancient also spelled **aunchient** NOUN
⚠ *Don't read in the meaning of 'very old'; most uses of 'ancient' refer to events within living memory.*
most experienced person
• *(KL 5.1.32) Albany intends to discuss his plans with 'th'ancient of war on our proceeding'—with his senior officers.*
🎭 *When this word is used as a title, it has nothing to do with age: it simply means 'ensign' ('standard-bearer'), or 'right-hand man'—examples are 'Ancient Pistol' in 'Henry V' and Iago in 'Othello', who is described as 'Ancient to the General'. The old pronunciation of 'ensign' sounded very like the old pronunciation of 'ancient', so that the two words became confused.*

ancientry NOUN
old-fashioned dignity
• *(MA 2.1.69) Beatrice describes a wedding as being like a stately dance, 'full of state and ancientry'.*

Andrew NOUN
the name of a Spanish galleon (the *Saint Andrew*) captured at Cadiz in 1596
• *(MV 1.1.27) Salarino imagines one of his ships running aground—'my wealthy Andrew dock'd in sand'.*

angel see **MONEY, p.197**

Anne, Saint
the mother of the Virgin Mary
• *(TN 2.3.104) Feste swears 'by Saint Anne'—an oath that would offend a Puritan like Malvolio.*

annexment NOUN
attachment, something added on
• *(Ham 3.3.21) Rosencrantz says that if the monarchy were to fall, even tiny things that depend on it, 'Each small annexment', would come to ruin.*

anon ADVERB
soon
• *(Mac 2.3.18) The Porter shouts to whoever is knocking at the gate: 'Anon, anon'—I'll be with you shortly.*

Anthropophagi NOUN
[pronounced an-throw-**pof**-a-jie]
a mythical race of man-eaters
• *(Oth 1.3.143) Othello recounts his tales of 'the cannibals that each other eat, / The Anthropophagi'.*

antic also spelled **antick, anticke, antique**
ADJECTIVE
fantastic, playful
• *(Ham 1.5.180) Hamlet says he may put on 'an antic disposition'—bizarre, extrovert, comical, mad behaviour.*

antic NOUN
buffoon, fool
• *(H5 3.2.28) The Boy describes Pistol, Nym, and Bardolph: 'three such antics do not amount to a man'.*

› **anticly** ADVERB
like a buffoon or fool
• *(MA 5.1.96) Antonio condemns 'boys' like Claudio and Don Pedro who 'Go anticly'.*
➨ *The two words 'antic' and 'antique' (see below) have very different meanings and origins, but in Shakespeare's time they were spelled in the same way.*

Antiopa NOUN [pronounced an-**tie**-op-a]
in Greek mythology, an Amazon woman loved (and deserted) by Theseus
• *(MND 2.1.80) Oberon reminds Titania of how she made Theseus break up with other lovers—'break his faith / With Ariadne, and Antiopa'.*

antique also spelled **antick, anticke, antic**
ADJECTIVE
⚠ *Don't read the modern meaning of 'antiques' into these senses—'old precious objects'.*
1 ancient
• *(H5 5.Chorus.26) The Chorus compares English councillors to 'the senators of th'antique Rome'.*
2 old-fashioned, vintage
• *(TN 2.4.3) Orsino wants to hear again 'That old and antic song we heard last night'.*

› **antique Roman**
a man from the time of ancient Rome (when suicide was an honourable act)
• *(Ham 5.2.334) Horatio, after seeing Hamlet die, says: 'I am more an antique Roman than a Dane'—he is prepared to kill himself.*
🎭 *'Antique' is usually pronounced with the stress on the first syllable, ['an-tik'], so*

*that it sounds like 'antic' (unlike in modern English, where the stress is on the second syllable, ['an-**teek**']).*

antre NOUN [pronounced **an**-ter]
cave, cavern
• *(Oth 1.3.139) Othello explains how he told Desdemona and her father tales about 'antres vast and deserts idle'.*

apart see **STAGE DIRECTIONS, p.285**

Apollo NOUN
in Greek mythology, the sun god, who pulls the sun across the sky in a horse-drawn chariot
• *(MND 2.1.231) Helena says she will run after Demetrius, reversing the story of Daphne running away from Apollo: 'Apollo flies, and Daphne holds the chase'.*
See also SWEARING, p.298

apoplexed also spelled **apoplex'd** ADJECTIVE
paralysed
• *(Ham 3.4.73) Hamlet tells his mother that her ability to sense things clearly must have been lost when she chose Claudius: 'but sure that sense / Is apoplex'd'.*

apothecary or **pothecary** NOUN
one who prepares and sells medicinal drugs (but not usually poison)
• *(RJ 5.1.37) Romeo remembers where he can get some poison: 'I do remember an apothecary'.*
The word can drop its first syllable to fit the rhythm of a line.

apparel NOUN
clothes
• *(Ham 1.3.72) Polonius advises Laertes that 'the apparel oft proclaims the man'—you can tell a lot about someone from the clothes.*

apparel VERB
clothe
• *(MA 4.1.226) The Friar predicts that when Claudio realizes that Hero died because of what he said about her, she will seem to be 'apparell'd in more precious habit'—everything about her will appear more precious.*

› **well-apparelled** also spelled **-apparell'd** ADJECTIVE
well-dressed
• *(RJ 1.2.27) Capulet describes the month of April as being 'well-apparell'd' coming soon after winter, it's a time when you can shed your winter clothes and dress more finely.*

apparent ADJECTIVE
obvious
• *(MV 4.1.21) The Duke condemns Shylock for his 'strange apparent cruelty'.*

› **appear** VERB
⚠ *Don't read in the modern meaning of 'appearing to be true'. 'Appear' does not mean 'might be the case' but 'definitely is the case'.*
be obvious
• *(H5 1.2.88) Canterbury explains why being descended from a woman is no reason to deny Henry a claim to the throne of France, because the French kings 'all appear / To hold in right and title of the female'—it's obvious they all have a female ancestor.*

appertain VERB
be relevant
• *(KL 1.1.283) Goneril tells her sister that she has a lot to say 'of what most nearly appertains to us both'—something very relevant to both of them.*

› **appertaining** ADJECTIVE
relevant
• *(Tem 3.1.95) Prospero, having observed the meeting of Ferdinand and Miranda, says that he has to 'perform / Much business appertaining'—to stop them getting too close too quickly.*

› **appertinent** also spelled **appurtenant** NOUN
gift, object, or land that a person has a legal right to
• *(H5 2.2.84) Henry describes how he favoured the Duke of Cambridge by providing him 'with all appurtenants / Belonging to his honour'—everything that comes as a result of being granted such a title.*

› **appurtenance** NOUN
usual accompaniment
• *(Ham 2.2.361) Hamlet tells Rosencrantz and Guildenstern that 'Th'appurtenance of welcome is fashion and ceremony'—people usually dress smartly and formally to greet a guest.*

appetite NOUN
⚠ *Don't read in the modern meaning of 'desire for food'.*
desire
• *(TN 1.1.3) Orsino wants to hear so much music (which he calls 'the food of love') that 'The appetite may sicken, and so die'—his desire for Olivia will eventually cease.*

applause NOUN
⚠ *Don't read in the modern meaning of 'clapping after a performance'.*
shout of approval
• *(JC 1.2.133) Brutus hears loud shouting and thinks*

that 'these applauses are / For some new honours that are heap'd on Caesar'.

The word can be used in the plural, unlike today.

apple NOUN
as well as meaning 'fruit', you'll find:
the pupil of the eye
• *(MND 3.2.104) Oberon drops the love-juice into Demetrius' eyes: 'Sink in apple of his eye'.*

The phrase 'apple of the eye' arose because people felt that the round shape of the pupil was like an apple.

appoint VERB
as well as meaning 'choose for a job', you'll find:
1 give
• *(JC 4.1.30) Antonio says he treats Lepidus as he does his horse: 'I do appoint him store of provender'—plenty of 'provender' (dry animal food, such as hay) to eat.*
2 decide
• *(Mac 2.3.48) Lennox asks Macbeth if Duncan intends to leave, and Macbeth replies 'he did appoint so'.*

› **appointment** NOUN
equipment
• *(Ham 4.6.15) Hamlet tells Horatio of a pirate-ship 'of very warlike appointment'—bristling with weapons.*

› **disappointed** ADJECTIVE
⚠*Don't read in the modern meaning of 'not having your hopes met'.*
unprepared
• *(Ham 1.5.77) The Ghost tells Hamlet that he was killed: 'Cut off even in the blossoms of my sin, / Unhousel'd, disappointed'—he was spiritually unprepared to die.*

› **well-appointed** ADJECTIVE
well-equipped
• *(H5 3.Chorus.4) The Chorus describes King Henry as 'The well-appointed king'—a king who is well-armed and supplied for war.*

apprehensive ADJECTIVE
⚠*Don't read in the modern meaning of 'anxious, worried'.*
quick-learning, capable of understanding
• *(JC 3.1.67) Casear tells everyone that 'men are flesh and blood, and apprehensive'—just before he is killed.*

approbation NOUN
1 proof
• *(TN 3.4.162) Sir Toby says a good swear-word 'gives manhood more approbation than ever proof itself would have earned him'—swearing shows that you're a man more than proving yourself in an actual fight.*
2 proving true
• *(H5 1.2.19) Henry tells Canterbury that many men 'Shall drop their blood in approbation / Of what your reverence shall incite us to'—men will die for you, to endorse whatever it is you urge as a worthy cause.*

appropriation NOUN
special feature
• *(MV 1.2.39) Portia says the Neapolitan prince talks only about his horse, and 'makes it a great appropriation to his own good parts'—is very proud of his ability to shoe the horse himself.*

appurtenant see **appertain**

aqua-vitae NOUN [pronounced **ak**-wa-**vee**-tay]
strong alcoholic drink—a Latin word meaning 'water of life'
• *(RJ 3.2.88) The Nurse is so shocked at the killing of Tybalt that she needs a drink: 'Give me some aqua-vitae'.*

arbitrament also spelled **arbitrement** NOUN
settling of a dispute, fight
• *(KL 4.7.94) A Gentleman comments on the news that there will soon be a battle: 'The arbitrement is like to be bloody'.*

arch NOUN
chief, lord
• *(KL 2.1.58) Gloucester describes the Duke of Cornwall as 'My worthy arch and patron'.*

› **arch-mock** NOUN
chief mockery
• *(Oth 4.1.70) Iago says it is the Devil's chief source of fun—'the fiend's arch-mock'—to make you think that a lover who lets herself be kissed in a carefree way is actually virtuous.*

argal ADVERB
a version of the Latin word *ergo*—therefore
• *(Ham 5.1.17) The First Gravedigger reaches a conclusion to his argument: 'Argal, he that is not guilty of his own death shortens not his own life'.*

Argier NOUN [pronounced are-**jeer**]
Algiers
• *(Tem 1.2.261) Ariel tells Prospero where the witch Sycorax was born: 'Sir, in Argier'.*
see also MAP, p.176

This is the spelling used in the First Folio. Some editions of the play replace it with the modern name 'Algiers'.

argosy see SHIPS, p.168

Aa b c d e f g h i j k l m n o p q r s t u v w x y z

Argus NOUN
in Greek mythology, a giant with a hundred eyes, whose task was to guard the nymph and priestess Io
• *(MV 5.1.230) Portia warns Bassanio not to spend a single night away from home: 'Watch me like Argus'.*

Ariadne NOUN [pronounced a-ree-**ad**-nee]
in Greek mythology, one of the women loved (and deserted) by Theseus
• *(MND 2.1.80) Oberon reminds Titania of how she made Theseus break off his relationship 'With Ariadne'.*

Arion NOUN [pronounced a-**rie**-on]
in Greek mythology, a great musician, who was about to be killed by sailors, and was allowed to sing one last song; he leapt overboard and was carried by a dolphin to safety
• *(TN 1.2.15) The Captain tells Viola that he saw Sebastian tied to a mast 'like Arion on the dolphin's back'.*

arithmetician NOUN
⚠ *Don't read in the meaning of 'someone who is good at arithmetic'.*
someone who knows how do something in theory, but not in practice
• *(Oth 1.1.19) Iago is disgusted that Cassio has been promoted, calling him 'a great arithmetician'—someone who's never actually fought in a battle.*

› **arithmetic** NOUN
calculation
• *(RJ 3.1.98) Mercutio says contemptuously that Tybalt 'fights by the book of arithmetic'—he does it by numbers, planning so much that there's no room for improvisation.*

aroint VERB
a word used only as a command—be gone!
• *(Mac 1.3.5) The First Witch tells the others how a woman shouted at her: 'Aroint thee, witch'.*

arrant ADJECTIVE
absolute, utter
• *(Ham 3.1.129) Hamlet warns Ophelia to keep away from men: 'We are arrant knaves all'.*
'Arrant' is always used along with a noun that refers to a bad person, such as 'knave', 'whore', 'traitor', 'rascal', and 'villain'.

arras NOUN see **ILLUSTRATION, p.57**
wall tapestry hanging
• *(Ham 3.3.28) Polonius tells Claudius he will hide himself to hear the conversation between Hamlet and Ophelia: 'Behind the arras I'll convey myself'.*

arrivance NOUN
arrival
• *(Oth 2.1.42) The rulers of Cyprus are waiting on the quay for Othello and his associates: 'every minute is expectancy / Of more arrivance'.*

artere or **artire** NOUN [pronounced **are**-teer]
sinew, muscle
• *(Ham 1.4.82) Hamlet feels his decision to follow the Ghost has made every little muscle—'each petty artire in this body'—as strong as a lion.*
'Artere' is an early spelling of 'artery'; the word does not refer to blood vessels here.

Arthur's bosom
intended to be 'Abraham's bosom'—a way of describing heaven (from the Bible, where Abraham is seen as the father of the Israelites)
• *(H5 2.3.8) The Hostess, mourning the death of Falstaff, misuses the phrase, saying he is 'in Arthur's bosom'.*

artificial ADJECTIVE
⚠ *Don't read the modern meaning of 'not genuine' or 'phoney' into these senses.*
1 produced by the black arts
• *(Mac 3.5.27) Hecate says her magic will raise 'artificial sprites'.*
2 artistically skilful
• *(MND 3.2.203) Helena reminds Hermia of their childhood needlework, when they created sewing-pictures 'like two artificial gods'.*

artire see **artere**

Ash Wednesday
in the Christian calendar, the first day of Lent
• *(MV 2.5.26) Lancelot, talking nonsense to Shylock, says his nose bled 'on Ash Wednesday was four year in th'afternoon'.*

aside see **STAGE DIRECTIONS, p.285**

askant PREPOSITION
aslant, at an angle over
• *(Ham 4.7.166) Gertrude describes the place where Ophelia drowned: 'There is a willow grows askant the brook'.*

aspersion NOUN
⚠ *Don't read in the modern idiom of 'casting aspersions'—attacking someone's character.*
sprinkling
• *(Tem 4.1.18) Prospero warns Ferdinand to treat Miranda well, otherwise 'No sweet aspersion shall the heavens let fall / To make this contract grow'.*

aspicious ADJECTIVE
intended for 'suspicious'
• *(MA 3.5.44) Dogberry reports that his watchmen*

have arrested 'two aspicious persons'.
➳ *Some editions use the 'aspitious' spelling from the First Folio, which probably represents the word 'auspicious' (meaning 'prosperous').*

assailing ADJECTIVE
amorous
• *(RJ 1.1.207) Romeo says that Rosaline can't stand 'th'encounter of assailing eyes'—either she's shy (she doesn't like being looked at) or she's jealous (she doesn't like others looking at Romeo).*

assigns NOUN
accessories
• *(Ham 5.2.142) Osric describes 'six French rapiers and poniards, with their assigns, as girdle, hanger, and so on'.*

associate NOUN
companion
• *(Ham 4.3.43) Polonius tells Laertes that 'Th'associates tend'—his fellow-travellers are waiting for him.*

associate VERB
accompany
• *(RJ 5.2.6) Friar John tells of looking for another friar 'to associate me, / Here in this city visiting the sick'.*

Ate NOUN [pronounced **ah**-tay]
in Greek mythology, the goddess of discord and vengeance
• *(JC 3.1.271) Antony says Caesar's spirit wants revenge, 'With Ate by his side'.*

Athenian NOUN
a native of Athens in Greece, a city known for its philosophers
• *(KL 3.4.173) Lear, having previously called Poor Tom a 'Noble philosopher', goes on to call him a 'good Athenian'.*

ATTENTION SIGNALS

Here are some of the words people use to get others to look, listen, or pay attention.

Look!

behold
• *(Oth 5.2.257) Othello tells everyone: 'Behold, I have a weapon.'*

lo
• *(Tem 2.2.14) Caliban sees Trinculo approaching: 'Lo, now, lo, / Here comes a spirit.'*
➳ *'Lo' is a short form of the word for 'look' in Old English.*

Listen!

hark or **hark you**
• *(KL 2.1.78) Gloucester hears a trumpet call: 'Hark! the Duke's trumpets. I know not why he comes.'*
• *(H5 3.7.79) The Welsh Captain hears a drum: 'Hark you, the king is coming.'*
🎭 *Important people had their own trumpet call or drum beat to signify their approach.*

Be quiet!

hush
• *(Tem 4.1.126) Prospero tells Ferdinand: 'Hush, and be mute, / Or else our spell is marr'd.'*

peace
• *(JC 3.2.231) The citizens tell each other to keep quiet so they can hear what Mark Antony wants to say: 'Peace ho, hear Antony, most noble Antony!'*

mum
• *(Tem 3.2.49) Stephano tells Trinculo to shut up: 'Mum, then, and no more.'*
➳ *A word which reflects the way the lips come together when you're not talking.*

Wait a moment!

soft or **soft you**
• *(RJ 2.2.2) Romeo suddenly sees Juliet on her balcony: 'But soft, what light through yonder window breaks?'*
• *(Ham 3.1.88) Hamlet sees Ophelia approaching, and brings his soliloquy to an end: 'Soft you now, / The fair Ophelia!'*
🎭 *The actors could also be asking the rowdy Elizabethan audience to be quiet.*

Pay attention!

mark
⚠ *This is the verb meaning 'notice'. Duncan's first name is not Mark!*
• *(Mac 1.2.28) The Captain tells Duncan to note what's coming next in his tale: 'Mark, King of Scotland, mark.'*

🎭 *When speakers are really excited or upset, they can string these together.*
• *(Ham 1.1.129) Horatio sees the Ghost and tells Barnardo and Marcellus: 'But soft, behold. Lo, where it comes again.'*

Aa b c d e f g h i j k l m n o p q r s t u v w x y z

atomy plural **atomi, atomies** NOUN
tiny being
• *(RJ 1.4.57) Mercutio describes Queen Mab's chariot as being 'Drawn with a team of little atomi'.*

atone VERB
⚠ *Don't read in the modern meaning of 'make amends for doing something wrong'. In the following situation, Desdemona has done nothing wrong.*
unite—make 'at one'
• *(Oth 4.1.228) Desdemona, talking of the row between Othello and Cassio, says she would 'do much / T'atone them'.*

attach VERB
⚠ *Don't read the modern meanings of 'joining one thing to something else' or 'being very fond of someone' into these senses.*
1 seize
• *(Tem 3.3.5) Alonso says he suddenly feels tired, 'attach'd with weariness'.*
2 arrest
• *(Oth 1.2.77) Brabantio tells Othello: 'I ... attach thee / For an abuser of the world'.*

attaint NOUN
1 sign of fatigue
• *(H5 4.Chorus.39) The Chorus describes Henry as someone who 'overbears attaint / With cheerful semblance'—hiding his tiredness by appearing to look happy.*
2 condemnation, punishment
• *(KL 5.3.84) Albany arrests Edmund for treason, and also Goneril 'in thy attaint'—punished along with him.*

> **unattainted** ADJECTIVE
> not emotionally involved
> • *(RJ 1.2.87) Benvolio tells Romeo to look at Rosaline 'with unattainted eye' when comparing her to other women.*

attask also spelled **attax** VERB
blame
• *(KL 1.4.334) Goneril accuses her husband of being often 'attax'd for want of wisdom'—badly thought of because he shows a lack of good sense.*

attent ADJECTIVE
attentive
• *(Ham 1.2.193) Horatio tells Hamlet to listen carefully, 'With an attent ear'.*

attribute NOUN
reputation
• *(Ham 1.4.22) Hamlet says that the carousing in the Danish court takes away 'The pith and marrow of our attribute'.*

atwain also spelled **a-twain** ADVERB
in two parts
• *(KL 2.2.70) Kent describes Oswald as one of those rogues who 'Like rats, oft bite the holy cords a-twain'—the special bonds that join people together.*

auger hole also spelled **auger-hole** NOUN
tiny hole made by a carpenter's drill
• *(Mac 2.3.118) Donaldbain tells Malcolm he is worried that their fate, 'hid in an auger hole may rush / And seize us'—treachery could come from out of the smallest place.*

aught NOUN
anything
• *(Ham 3.1.96) Hamlet tells Ophelia: 'I never gave you aught'.*

augur also spelled **augure** NOUN
[pronounced **aw**-gur]
prophecy
• *(Mac 3.4.124) Macbeth tells his wife that 'augures' can help reveal even the most secret murderer.*

> **augurer** NOUN
> religious official in ancient Rome who could see into the future and foretell events
> • *(JC 2.2.37) Caesar asks his servant: 'What say the augurers?'*

> **augury** NOUN
> omens (good or bad)
> • *(Ham 5.2.204) Hamlet tells Horatio: 'We defy augury'.*

aunchient see **ancient**

aunt NOUN
old woman
• *(MND 2.1.51) Puck tells how he tricks 'The wisest aunt, telling the saddest tale'—telling a really serious story.*
🎭 *'Aunt' usually has the same meaning as today, but here it refers to a gossiping old woman.*

Aurora NOUN [pronounced aw-**roar**-a]
in Roman mythology, the goddess of the dawn
• *(RJ 1.1.130) Montague describes the sun drawing 'The shady curtains from Aurora's bed'.*

avaunt INTERJECTION [pronounced a-**vawnt**]
go away
• *(Mac 3.4.93) Macbeth tells the ghost of Banquo: 'Avaunt and quit my sight!'.*

avouch NOUN
assurance
• *(Ham 1.1.60) Horatio says he would never have believed stories about the Ghost 'Without the sensible and true avouch / Of mine own eyes'.*

avouch VERB
1 justify
• *(Mac 3.1.122) Macbeth tells the Murderers that he could easily get rid of Banquo 'And bid my will avouch it'—I have the power to do what I like.*
2 declare
• *(MND 1.1.106) Lysander tells Theseus that Demetrius once loved Helena, and will now remind him of it: 'I'll avouch it to his head'—tell it to his face.*

› **avouchment** NOUN
confirm (the word here is intended to be the verb 'avouch')
• *(H5 4.8.34) The Welsh captain hopes Henry 'will avouchment that this is the glove of Alençon'—will confirm that this is the glove of the French lord Alençon.*

aye ADVERB
always, ever
• *(Ham 3.2.192) The Player King tells his wife: 'This world is not for aye'—life on earth is not for ever.*

ay me see **REGRETTING, p.250**

Burbage

Richard Burbage was Shakespeare's lead tragedian and the first actor to play Richard III, Hamlet, Othello, and King Lear. Richard and Shakespeare may have first met when they were both children. Richard was in Stratford with the theatre company of his father James Burbage, who was also an actor, manager, and pioneering theatre maker.

Bacchanal NOUN [pronounced **bak**-a-nal]
a follower of the Roman god of wine, Bacchus
• *(MND 5.1.48) Theseus reads out the title of a play: 'The riot of the tipsy Bacchanals'—the rampage of the drunk followers of Bacchus.*

baffle VERB
⚠ *Don't read in the modern meaning of 'puzzle' or 'confuse'.*
treat shamefully
• *(TN 5.1.357) Olivia sympathizes with Malvolio about the way he has been tricked: 'how have they baffled thee!'*

balance NOUN
scales
• *(MV 4.1.253) Shylock asks: 'Are there balance here to weigh / The flesh?'*

baldric or **baldrick** see **SWORDS AND DAGGERS, p.156**

ball NOUN
1 golden globe, held in the hand, showing that someone is a monarch
• *(Mac 4.1.120) Macbeth sees apparitions holding 'two-fold balls and treble sceptres'—implying they are shades of future kings.*
The two balls (or 'orbs') represent the crowns of England and Scotland. 'Macbeth' was written soon after James VI of Scotland was crowned James I of England in 1603.
2 cannon-ball
• *(H5 5.2.17) Queen Isabel sees friendship in King Henry's eyes rather than 'The fatal balls of murdering basilisks'—balls fired from large cannons (with a nice pun on eyeballs).*

ballow NOUN
cudgel
• *(KL 4.6.236) Edgar dares Oswald to 'try whither your costard or my ballow be the harder'—see if your head is harder than my stick.*

a Bb c d e f g h i j k l m n o p q r s t u v w x y z

balm VERB
soothe
• *(KL 3.6.96) Kent hopes Lear will have the chance of a rest that 'might yet have balm'd thy broken sinews'—ease the pain of torn muscles.*

› **balm** NOUN
sweet-smelling oil used to anoint a king at his coronation
• *(H5 4.1.248) Henry reflects on some of the things that go with being a king: 'the balm, the sceptre, and the ball' (see sense 1 of ball).*

› **balmy** ADJECTIVE
⚠ *Don't read the modern meaning of 'warm and calm', as in 'balmy weather', into these senses.*
1 soothing
• *(Oth 2.3.241) Othello tells Desdemona that it is a 'soldier's life / To have their balmy slumbers wak'd with strife'.*
2 sweet-smelling
• *(Oth 5.2.16) Othello kisses sleeping Desdemona: 'O balmy breath'.*

ban NOUN
⚠ *Don't read in the modern meaning of 'an order that forbids something'.*
curse
• *(KL 2.3.19) Edgar says how he will behave when disguised as a beggar, travelling about 'Sometime with lunatic bans, sometime with prayers'.*

› **banning** ADJECTIVE
cursing
• *(Oth 2.1.11) A Gentleman tells Montano the weather is so bad that to 'stand upon the banning shore' would make you think the waves were cursing the land, smashing so hard against the rocks.*

bane VERB
kill
• *(MV 4.1.46) Shylock says, if he had a rat in his house, there would be nothing to stop him paying a huge amount of money 'To have it ban'd' – pronounced [baynd].*

› **bane** NOUN
destruction
• *(Mac 5.3.60) Macbeth says he will 'not be afraid of death and bane, / Till Birnam Forest come to Dunsinane'.*

bankrout also spelled **bankerout, bancrout** NOUN
bankrupt
• *(MV 4.1.122) Shylock says he is sharpening his knife 'To cut the forfeiture from that bankrout there'.*
✒ *'Bankrout' is the spelling in the First Folio. Some editions avoid the less familiar word and use the modern 'bankrupt' instead.*

banquet also spelled **banket** NOUN
⚠ *Don't read in the modern meaning of 'a large ceremonial feast'.*
light meal
• *(RJ 1.5.121) Capulet invites Romeo and Benvolio to his 'trifling foolish banquet' (though it would actually have been more sumptuous than a modern light meal).*

Barabbas NOUN
in the Bible, a robber released at the Feast of Passover instead of Christ, who was then crucified
• *(MV 4.1.294) Shylock would rather have his daughter married to 'any of the stock of Barabbas'—to any child of a wicked person, such as Barabbas—rather than a Christian.*

Barbary ADJECTIVE **see MAP, p.176**
the Barbary Coast of North Africa, famous for its swift horses
• *(Ham 5.2.140) Osric tells Hamlet that Claudius has wagered 'six Barbary horses' on the outcome of the fencing match.*

Barbason NOUN [pronounced **bar**-ba-son]
name of a demon from hell
• *(H5 2.1.48) Nym reacts to Pistol's high-flown way of talking, which sounds as if he is exorcising a demon: 'I am not Barbason, you cannot conjure me'.*

barber-monger NOUN
frequenter of the barber shop
• *(KL 2.2.30) Kent calls Oswald a 'whoreson cullionly barber-monger'—a despicable bastard who is always going to the barber's to make himself look nice.*

bare ADJECTIVE
1 simple
• *(Ham 3.1.76) Hamlet talks about how someone might kill himself 'With a bare bodkin'—an ordinary dagger.*
2 lean (of body)
• *(RJ 5.1.68) Romeo describes the Apothecary as 'bare and full of wretchedness'.*
3 unsheathed
• *(Oth 5.1.2) Iago advises Roderigo: 'Wear thy good rapier bare'—with your sword drawn, ready for a fight.*

› **bare-gnawn** ADJECTIVE
worn away to nothing
• *(KL 5.3.121) Edgar describes himself as 'By treason's tooth bare-gnawn'—his being has been totally eaten up through treason.*

barful ADJECTIVE
full of hindrances
• *(TN 1.4.41) Viola reflects that to woo Olivia for Orsino is 'a barful strife'—an endeavour full of difficulties—as she is in love with him herself.*

bark also spelled **barque** NOUN
ship
• *(Ham 4.3.42) Claudius tells Hamlet 'The bark is ready' for his journey to England.*

bark about VERB
form a crust (making a cover just as tree-bark covers the wood)
• *(Ham 1.5.71) The Ghost tells Hamlet how, after he was poisoned, 'a most instant tetter bark'd about ... / All my smooth body'—scaly skin eruptions immediately spread everywhere.*

barley broth also spelled **barley-broth** NOUN
ale
• *(H5 3.6.19) The French nobles can't understand how the watery ale drunk by the English (and even given to horses)—'their barley-broth'—can heat their blood to make them so brave.*

barm NOUN
froth on the top of beer while it is being made, or the yeast that causes this to happen
• *(MND 2.1.38) The Fairy asks Puck if he is the one who makes 'the drink to bear no barm'—who stops the chemical process of fermentation taking place and makes the beer taste awful.*

barn also spelled **barne** NOUN
farm building *or* child
• *(MA 3.4.44) Beatrice makes a joke by punning on the meaning of 'farm building': 'if your husband have stables enough, you'll see he shall lack no barns'.*
'Barn' is still used in some dialects today to mean 'child', usually spelled 'bairn'—a word also found in Shakespeare, pronounced [bearn].

barnacle NOUN
Don't read in the meaning of 'a small shellfish that attaches itself to the bottoms of ships'.
a species of wild goose
• *(Tem 4.1.246) Caliban is scared that, if Stephano and Trinculo don't hurry up, Prospero will use his magic, and they will 'all be turn'd to barnacles, or to apes'.*
The bird comes from the Arctic, but visits the British coast in winter. Because people didn't know where its breeding grounds were, they imagined it coming magically out of the trees or shells on the sea-shore—hence the connection with sea barnacles.

barren ADJECTIVE
dull
• *(Ham 3.2.39) Hamlet criticizes stage clowns who try to make 'some quantity of barren spectators to laugh', even when the subject-matter of the play doesn't warrant it.*

› **barren-spirited** ADJECTIVE
dull-minded
• *(JC 4.1.36) Antony describes Lepidus as 'A barren-spirited fellow'.*

barricado NOUN [pronounced bar-i-**kay**-doh]
barricade
• *(TN 4.2.35) Feste uses nonsensical contradictions to confuse Malvolio: 'bay-windows transparent as barricadoes'—you can't see through a barricade (and he adds 'south-north' in the next line, to make him even more confused).*

Bartholomew-tide NOUN
around the time of St Bartholomew's Day, 24 August
• *(H5 5.2.293) The Duke of Burgundy compares 'maids' who have been well looked after during summer-time, to 'flies at Bartholomew-tide' —when late summer warmth makes them sluggish, so that they can be caught more easily.*

base ADJECTIVE
base is always to do with a type of 'lowness'
1 of low character, unworthy
• *(JC 4.3.24) Brutus tells Cassius that they should not 'Contaminate our fingers with base bribes'.*
2 of low rank in society, low-born
• *(KL 1.2.20) Edmund boasts how he will succeed over Edgar: 'Edmund the base / Shall top th'legitimate'.*
3 of low quality, wretched
• *(KL 2.3.7) Edgar says he will adopt 'the basest and most poorest shape'.*
4 of low value, worthless
• *(MV 2.9.19) Arragon describes the three caskets: 'Gold, silver, and base lead'.*

› **baseness** NOUN
1 a quality considered to be lower-class
• *(Ham 5.2.34) Hamlet once thought it 'A baseness to write fair'—because good handwriting was something 'lower-class' people (such as secretaries) did.*
2 cowardly nature
• *(TN 5.1.141) Olivia explains to Cesario that it is only 'the baseness of thy fear', which has made him deny being her husband in front of Orsino.*
3 lowly activity
• *(Tem 3.1.2) Ferdinand reflects on his job as a*

log-carrier: 'some kinds of baseness / Are nobly undergone'.

› baseless ADJECTIVE

⚠ *Don't read in the modern meaning of 'unjustifiable'.*

without substance

• *(Tem 4.1.151) Prospero talks of life as a dream, like 'the baseless fabric of this vision' Ferdinand and Miranda have just seen.*

basilisk NOUN

a very large cannon that could fire a cannon-ball of around 200 lb / 90 kg

• *(H5 5.2.17) Queen Isabel remembers 'The fatal balls of murdering basilisks' used when the English army defeated the French.*

🎭 *There was a fashion in the Middle Ages to name a piece of artillery after a venomous reptile. A 'basilisk' was a mythical serpent that killed just by looking at someone. Other types of cannon, such as a 'culverin' and a 'serpentine', were also named after snakes.*

bass VERB

utter with a bass voice, very loudly

• *(Tem 3.3.99) Alonso imagines hearing the thunder speak the name of Prospero: 'it did bass my trespass'—proclaim his wrongdoing in conspiring against Prospero.*

bastardy NOUN

condition of being illegitimate

• *(JC 2.1.138) Brutus thinks that if any of the conspirators break any part of their promise to kill Caesar, every single drop of blood within them will be 'guilty of a several bastardy'—will prove each of them not to be true Romans.*

baste VERB

sew loosely

• *(MA 1.1.261) Benedick reacts to the mocking speech of Don Pedro and Claudio by describing it as nothing more than 'guarded with fragments, and the guards are but slightly basted on' —decorated with bits of rubbish, and these 'decorations' are only loosely sewn on.*

bate VERB

a shortened form of 'abate'

1 reduce

• *(Tem 1.2.250) Ariel tells Prospero that 'Thou did promise / To bate me a full year'—lessen my term of service by a year.*

2 lose

• *(Ham 5.2.23) Hamlet tells Horatio that Claudius' letter to the English king asks for Hamlet to be executed, 'no leisure bated'—with no delay.*

🎭 *Being executed without time to pray for forgiveness of one's sins was considered a terrible way to die.*

3 lose weight

• *(MV 3.3.32) Despite the terrible situation he is in, Antonio shows a sense of humour to Solanio: 'These griefs and losses have so bated me / That I shall hardly spare a pound of flesh'.*

4 flutter (as a falcon beats its wings)

• *(RJ 3.2.14) Juliet excitedly talks of the blood 'bating in my cheeks'.*

› unbated ADJECTIVE

1 undiminished

• *(MV 2.6.12) Gratiano says no horse can go back the way it came down a path 'with the unbated fire / That he did pace them first'—with the same energy it had when it first walked along it.*

2 not blunted

• *(Ham 4.7.138) Claudius tells Laertes he will have a chance to kill Hamlet in a fencing match by using 'A sword unbated'.*

🎭 *When fencing became a sport, the sharp point of a sword was blunted or had a 'button' put on its end; being a sport, the idea was to score points, not to draw blood.*

bat-fowling NOUN

the sport of catching birds at night while they are roosting

• *(Tem 2.1.181) Sebastian responds to Gonzalo's sarcasm by claiming he and Antonio would not only find it easy to move the moon, but that afterwards they would have energy left to go 'a-bat-fowling'.*

batten VERB

grow fat on

• *(Ham 3.4.67) Hamlet harangues his mother for no longer feeding on the 'fair mountain' of his father, but going to 'batten on this moor'—a piece of open waste ground covered with rough grass (not a Moor in the sense of a person of African descent, like Othello).*

battle NOUN

⚠ *Don't read the related meaning of 'major combat' into these senses.*

1 army

• *(JC 5.1.4) Octavius tells Antony that the enemy forces are near: 'their battles are at hand'.*

2 battle array

• *(H5 4.3.2) Bedford reports that Henry has gone to look at the French war formation: 'The king himself is rode to view their battle'.*

bauble NOUN
1 plaything
• *(Oth 4.1.133) Cassio describes his girlfriend Bianca as a 'bauble'.*
2 decorated rod carried by a Fool
• *(RJ 2.4.84) Mercutio is happy that lovesick Romeo is no longer acting like a half-wit 'lolling up and down to hide his bauble in a hole'.*
Mercutio is also making a rude joke about Romeo wanting to have sex.

› **baubling** ADJECTIVE
contemptible
• *(TN 5.1.49) Orsino describes Antonio's ship as 'A baubling vessel'.*

bawcock see TERMS OF ADDRESS, p.306

bawd NOUN
pimp
• *(KL 3.2.90) The Fool prophesies about a time to come in England when 'bawds and whores do churches build'.*

› **bawdry** NOUN
bawdiness
• *(Ham 2.2.488) Hamlet describes Polonius as someone who likes 'a jig or a tale of bawdry'—a dance or a story that talks about sex in a humorous way.*

› **bawdy house** NOUN
also spelled **bawdy-house**
brothel
• *(H5 2.1.32) The Hostess is horrified to think that, if she takes in female lodgers, 'it will be thought we keep a bawdy house'.*
Women in Shakespeare's time rarely lived alone, and if they did they were thought to be spinsters (single women unlikely to marry), prostitutes, nurses (meaning nannies), or low-born and destitute.

bay VERB
force a hunted animal to its last stand
• *(MND 4.1.112) Hippolyta tells of how Hercules and Cadmus once 'bay'd the bear / With hounds of Sparta'.*
Sparta was the city-state of Ancient Greece, home to the dominant military land power; the implication is that dogs from there would be ferocious.

› **bay about** VERB
surround
• *(JC 4.1.49) Octavius tells Antony that they 'are at the stake / And bay'd about with many enemies'—like a bear tied to a stake surrounded by hounds.*
see RECREATION, p.170

bay ADJECTIVE see COLOURS, p.164

beadle see OCCUPATIONS, p.166

beak see SHIPS, p.168

beam NOUN
the cross-bar on a set of scales
• *(Ham 4.5.156) Laertes tells Ophelia 'thy madness shall be paid with weight / Till our scale turn the beam'—he will tilt the balance so that his revenge will weigh heavier than Ophelia's madness.*

Bear see COSMOS, p.174

bear-baiting see RECREATION, p.170

beard VERB
defy
• *(Ham 2.2.412) Hamlet jokes with one of the actors who has grown a beard: 'Com'st thou to beard me in Denmark?'*

› **in one's beard**
to someone's face
• *(H5 3.3.16) The Welsh Captain tells Gower that he will call McMorris an ass when he sees him: 'I will verify as much in his beard'.*

bear hard
bear ill will towards
• *(JC 1.2.311) Cassius reflects about how 'Caesar doth bear me hard, but he loves Brutus'.*

bear in hand past form **borne in hand**
deceive
• *(Mac 3.1.82) Macbeth reminds the Murderers of what he had earlier told them: 'how you were borne in hand' by Banquo.*

bearward or **bearherd** NOUN
bear-keeper
• *(MA 2.1.35) Beatrice is certain she will never marry: 'I will even take sixpence in earnest of the bearherd and lead his apes into hell'—she will pay a bear-keeper sixpence in advance to buy his apes so that she can perform the role of the proverbial 'old maid'.*
Apes were sometimes baited as an additional spectacle in bear-baiting events. The proverb 'they that die maids must lead apes in hell' arose in the 16th century, probably as a Protestant reaction to Catholic celibacy.
The spelling in the First Folio is 'berrord', which some editors interpret as 'bearward 'and others as 'bearherd'.

beastly ADJECTIVE
'Beastly' has a much stronger force than is found in the modern colloquial use of the word to mean 'horrid'.
abominable
• *(KL 2.2.65) Cornwall rebukes Kent for insulting*

Oswald: 'You beastly knave, know you no reverence?'

beaten ADJECTIVE
well-tried
• *(Ham 2.2.265) Hamlet asks Rosencrantz and Guildenstern 'in the beaten way of friendship, what make you at Elsinore?'—as one old friend to another, what are you doing here?*

beaver see **ARMOUR, p.154**

bechanced also spelled **bechanc'd** ADJECTIVE
happening
• *(MV 1.1.38) Salarino thinks of what happens when a ship is lost at sea: 'such a thing bechanc'd would make me sad'—such an event would make me miserable.*

beckon VERB
⚠*Don't read in the modern meaning of 'bid a person approach you'.*
make a meaningful gesture
• *(Oth 4.1.130) Othello notes Iago's signal that he should now pay attention to the story Cassio is telling: 'Iago beckons me'.*
In this situation, Iago is not calling Othello over. On the contrary: he wants him to stay where he is and observe.

becomed ADJECTIVE
[pronounced in this line as be-**come**-id]
becoming, fitting
• *(RJ 4.2.26) Juliet tells her father that when she met Paris, she 'gave him what becomed love I might'—staying within the boundary of polite etiquette.*

› **misbecome** VERB
appear unbecoming to
• *(H5 2.4.119) Exeter tells the Dauphin how much Henry scorns him with words of contempt 'that may not misbecome / The mighty sender'—that are unsuitable coming from the mouth of a prince.*

Bedlam NOUN
madman
• *(KL 3.7.100) A servant suggests that mad Tom can help blind Gloucester: 'get the Bedlam / To lead him where he would'.*
The Hospital of St Mary of Bethlehem, situated in Bishopsgate, London, was an asylum for the mentally ill. 'Bethlehem' was pronounced [bedlem] in everyday speech at the time.

› **Tom o'Bedlam**
madman
• *(KL 1.2.129) Edmund adopts a false, sad manner, sighing as he sees Edgar approaching: 'my cue is villainous melancholy, with a sigh like Tom o' Bedlam'.*
It's an interesting coincidence that his brother Edgar later assumes this name when disguising himself as a beggar.

› **bedlam** ADJECTIVE
mad
• *(H5 5.1.17) Pistol asks the Welsh Captain, who has just insulted him: 'art thou bedlam?'*

bed-right NOUN
sexual intercourse
• *(Tem 4.1.96) Iris says that Ferdinand and Miranda will not be allowed to sleep together until the wedding ceremony is properly performed: 'no bed-right shall be paid / Till Hymen's torch be lighted'.*

Beelzebub NOUN [pronounced bee-**ell**-zi-bub]
one of the names for the Devil
• *(Mac 2.3.4) The Porter asks, with a curse, who's knocking at the gate 'i'th'name of Beelzebub'.*

beetle VERB
overhang—like threatening eyebrows
• *(Ham 1.4.71) Horatio describes a cliff 'That beetles o'er his base into the sea'.*

beetle ADJECTIVE
overhanging
• *(RJ 1.4.32) Mercutio shows Romeo his mask: 'Here are the beetle brows shall blush for me'.*

before ADVERB
1 ahead
• *(KL 1.5.1) Lear tells Kent: 'Go you before to Gloucester'—go on ahead of us to Gloucester's castle.*
2 in the front
• *(Mac 5.9.12) Siward asks about his dead son: 'Had he his hurts before?'—die fighting face-to-face, and not turning his back as a coward.*
3 in support
• *(H5 1.2.307) Henry affirms: 'God before, / We'll chide this Dauphin at his father's door'—with God on our side.*

before-breach see **breach**

beggar VERB
impoverish
• *(Ham 4.5.91) Claudius, worried that he will be implicated in Polonius' death, says 'necessity, of matter beggar'd, / Will nothing stick our person to arraign'—with no facts to go on, people won't hesitate to accuse the king.*

› **beggared** also spelled **beggar'd** ADJECTIVE
impoverished
• *(H5 4.2.43) Grandpré pours scorn on the English: 'Big Mars seems bankrupt in their*

beggar'd host'—the god of war can see no value in their poverty-stricken army.

› **beggarly** ADJECTIVE
impoverished
• *(RJ 5.1.45) Romeo describes the contents of the apothecary's shelves: 'A beggarly account of empty boxes'.*

beguile VERB
1 deceive
• *(Ham 1.3.131) Polonius tells Ophelia that Hamlet has made his vows of love to her sound holy, 'The better to beguile'.*
2 charm
• *(Oth 1.3.66) The Duke tells Brabantio that he can rely on the law to bring to justice whoever it is that 'Hath thus beguil'd your daughter of herself'—has made her act so out of character.*
3 while away
• *(Ham 3.2.218) The Player King says to his wife: 'I would beguile / The tedious day with sleep'.*
4 disguise
• *(Oth 2.1.121) Desdemona says to herself that, although she isn't feeling happy, 'I do beguile / The thing I am by seeming otherwise'.*

behold see ATTENTION SIGNALS, p.23

behove VERB
befit
• *(Ham 1.3.97) Polonius tells Ophelia that, if she has been giving freely and warmly letting Hamlet spend time with her, such behaviour is not 'As it behoves my daughter and your honour', because she isn't of royal blood.*

behove NOUN
benefit
• *(Ham 5.1.60) The First Gravedigger grunts as he digs, and sings about loving a woman when he was a young man: 'Methought it was very sweet: / To contract—O—the time for—a—my behove'—(I thought it was a great idea to shorten—O—the time for my benefit) – the sexual allusions in the speech suggest he means to have sex quickly.*

› **behoveful** ADJECTIVE
necessary
• *(RJ 4.3.8) Juliet tells her mother that she has 'cull'd such necessaries / As are behoveful for our state tomorrow'—chosen what she needs for the celebration of her marriage to Paris.*

behowl VERB
howl at
• *(MND 5.1.355) Puck describes the night-time, when 'the wolf behowls the moon'.*

Bel NOUN
in the Bible, a Babylonian god
• *(MA 3.3.125) Borachio talks of how quickly clothing fashions change—one minute like Pharaoh's soldiers, the next like those of 'god Bel's priests in the old church window'.*
Bel's priests were killed by the king of Persia when the prophet Daniel denounced them. The reference is to a stained-glass portrayal in a church window, but it's not known where this might have stood.

beldam also spelled **beldame** NOUN
old hag
• *(Mac 3.5.2) Hecate tells her witches why she is angry: 'Have I not reason, beldams, as you are, / Saucy and over-bold?'—because they've been acting without her permission.*

belie VERB
slander
• *(MA 4.1.145) Beatrice tells Benedick: 'My cousin is belied'.*

belike ADVERB
probably
• *(Ham 3.2.133) Ophelia asks Hamlet what the actors are doing: 'Belike this show imports the argument of the play'—perhaps the dumb show is explaining the plot.*

bellman see OCCUPATIONS, p.166

Bellona NOUN
the Roman goddess of war
• *(Mac 1.2.54) Macduff in battle is described as 'Bellona's bridegroom'—the god of war on a battlefield.*
When Ross says 'Bellona's bridegroom', who is he referring to? It's traditionally thought to be Macbeth, coming soon after the Captain has described Macbeth's bravery in fighting Macdonald. But Ross seems to have been at a different battlefield, far away from where Macbeth and Banquo were fighting—in Fife, Macduff's territory—so he might actually be describing Macduff.

belly-pinched ADJECTIVE
starving
• *(KL 3.1.13) A Gentleman says that Lear is out in a storm that even wild animals would shelter from: 'The lion and the belly-pinched wolf / Keep their fur dry'.*

below see STAGE DIRECTIONS, p.285

bemadding ADJECTIVE
making mad
• *(KL 3.1.38) Kent asks a Gentleman to go to Dover*

to report to Cordelia about the 'unnatural and bemadding sorrow' that Lear is having to suffer.

bemonster VERB
make monstrous
• *(KL 4.2.63) Albany rages at Goneril: 'Be-monster not thy feature'—don't deform your beauty.*

benefice NOUN
church appointment
• *(RJ 1.4.81) Mercutio says what happens when Queen Mab visits a clergyman: 'Then he dreams of another benefice'.*

benison NOUN
blessing
• *(Mac 2.4.40) An Old Man says goodbye to Ross: 'God's benison go with you'.*

bent NOUN
1 direction
• *(RJ 2.2.143) Juliet asks Romeo if 'thy bent of love be honourable'.*
2 temperament
• *(MA 4.1.185) Benedick describes the princes Pedro and Claudio as having 'the very bent of honour' —their nature is made out of honour.*
3 extent
• *(Ham 3.2.368) Hamlet talks to himself about the way people treat him: 'They fool me to the top of my bent'—to my utmost limit (as much as an archery bow can be bent).*

bent ADJECTIVE
decided
• *(Ham 4.3.43) Claudius tells Hamlet that the preparations for his voyage are complete: 'everything is bent / For England'.*

berattle VERB
fill with noise
• *(Ham 2.2.334) Rosencrantz describes how the child players 'berattle the common stages'.*

Bergomask ADJECTIVE
in the manner of the people of Bergamo, northern Italy
• *(MND 5.1.337) Bottom asks Theseus if he wants 'to hear a Bergomask dance between two of our company' (confusing 'hear' and 'see').*

Bermoothes NOUN
[pronounced ber-**moo**-thuz]
the Bermuda islands
• *(Tem 1.2.229) Ariel recalls how Prospero once sent him to 'the still-vex'd Bermoothes'—always beset with storms.*
This is the name that appears in the First Folio. Some editions replace this with 'Bermudas'.

bescreen VERB
hide from sight
• *(RJ 2.2.52) Juliet asks 'What man art thou that thus bescreen'd in night / So stumblest on my counsel?'—she can't see who has overheard her, because it's so dark.*

beseech see **POLITENESS, p.230**

beshrew VERB
1 blame
• *(RJ 5.2.26) Friar Lawrence worries that Juliet 'will beshrew me much that Romeo / Hath had no notice of these accidents'.*
2 curse
• *(MV 2.6.53) Lorenzo is in no doubt about Jessica: 'Beshrew me but I love her heartily'.*
'Beshrew' is often used as a mild form of swearing in such phrases as 'beshrew me' and 'beshrew your heart'. It is sometimes shortened to ''shrew'.

besmirch VERB
discolour
• *(H5 4.3.110) Henry tells Montjoy that 'Our gayness and our gilt are all besmirch'd / With rainy marching'—his joy and his golden armour are both dampened by marching in the rain.*
⚠ *Don't read in the modern meaning of 'gay' —same-sex attraction.*

besort NOUN
attendants
• *(Oth 1.3.236) Othello asks that Desdemona be well looked after while he is away, 'With such accommodation and besort / As levels with her breeding'.*

besort VERB
be suitable for
• *(KL 1.4.240) Goneril tells Lear to cut down the number of his followers, leaving just a few 'as may besort your age'.*

bespeak past forms **bespake, bespoke** VERB
1 order
• *(TN 3.3.40) Antonio tells Sebastian he will go ahead to the inn: 'I will bespeak our diet'—order our food.*
2 address
• *(TN 5.1.182) Cesario tells Sir Andrew, 'I bespake you fair'—I spoke to you politely.*
3 speak for
• *(KL 5.3.90) Albany tells Regan that 'My lady is bespoke'—his wife Goneril is already engaged (to Edmund).*

best NOUN

› at the best

1 at the highest point

• *(RJ 1.5.118) At Capulet's party, Benvolio tells Romeo, 'the sport is at the best'—it's a good time to leave.*

2 as well as you can

• *(Oth 1.3.171) The Duke tells Brabantio that he must make the best of a complicated situation: 'take up this mangled matter at the best'.*

› in all my best

to the best of my ability

• *(Ham 1.2.120) Hamlet tells his mother: 'I shall in all my best obey you'.*

› in the best

in the very best version

• *(Ham 1.5.27) The Ghost of Hamlet's father tells his son about the way he was killed: 'Murder most foul, as in the best it is, / But this most foul, strange and unnatural'.*

› you/thou were best

or **you/thou are best** you are best advised

• *(Oth 5.2.160) Othello tells Emilia to be quiet: 'Peace, you were best'.*

For the difference between 'thou' and 'you', see p.346.

best-conditioned see **condition**

bestrew VERB

cover all over

• *(Tem 4.1.20) Prospero tells Ferdinand and Miranda not to have sex before the holy ceremonies are performed, otherwise 'discord shall bestrew / The union of your bed'—disagreement will spread throughout your marriage.*

bestride VERB

stand over, as if with legs astride

• *(JC 1.2.135) Caesar 'doth bestride the narrow world / Like a Colossus'—like a gigantic figure from Greek mythology, looking down on all.*

betake VERB

commit oneself

• *(TN 3.4.200) Sir Toby tells Cesario: 'That defence thou hast, betake thee to't'—trust your life to whatever weapon you have.*

beteem VERB

allow

• *(Ham 1.2.141) Hamlet says his father loved his mother so much that he would not 'beteem the winds of heaven / Visit her face too roughly'.*

betimes ADVERB

1 early in the morning

• *(Oth 1.3.367) Roderigo tells Iago: 'I'll be with thee betimes'.*

2 early in life

• *(Ham 5.2.208) Hamlet asks Horatio: 'Since no man, of aught he leaves, knows aught, what is't to leave betimes?'—since nobody knows anything about what he leaves behind when he dies, what does an early death matter?*

3 early on

• *(MV 3.1.19) Salarino hopes that Antonio will lose no more ships, and Solanio is quick to agree: 'Let me say "amen" betimes'.*

› betime ADVERB

early

• *(Ham 4.5.49) Ophelia sings: 'All in the morning betime'.*

betray VERB

⚠ *Don't read in the meaning of 'treacherously put someone into the power of an enemy'.*

deceive

• *(Oth 5.2.6) Othello says Desdemona must die 'else she'll betray more men'.*

bettered also spelled **better'd** ADJECTIVE

more skilful

• *(Ham 5.2.248) Claudius tells Hamlet that while Laertes 'is better'd'—held to be the better fencer—he will nonetheless still bet on Hamlet to win.*

bewhore VERB

call a prostitute

• *(Oth 4.2.114) Emilia tells Iago that Othello has called Desdemona a whore: 'my lord hath so bewhor'd her'.*

bewray VERB

reveal

• *(KL 2.1.106) Gloucester says that Edmund exposed Edgar's treachery: 'He did bewray his practice'.*

bias NOUN

⚠ *Don't read the meaning of 'favouring one side rather than the other' into these senses.*

1 inclination

• *(KL 1.2.105) Gloucester tells Edmund that Lear has changed: 'the king falls from bias of nature'—has lost his natural affection.*

2 indirectness

• *(Ham 2.1.65) Polonius asks Reynaldo to find out what Laertes gets up to in France 'with assays of bias'—with indirect attempts.*

biddy see **TERMS OF ADDRESS, p.306**

bide VERB

1 endure

• *(TN 2.4.122) Orsino tells Cesario to express his*

a Bb c d e f g h i j k l m n o p q r s t u v w x y z

love to Olivia: 'bide no denay'—don't tolerate any denial.
2 await
• *(TN 1.5.58) Olivia tells Feste, 'for want of other idleness, I'll bide your proof'—as I've nothing better to do, I'll listen to you.*

› **biding** NOUN
place to stay
• *(KL 4.6.219) Edgar tells Gloucester: 'I'll lead you to some biding'.*

bilboes NOUN
shackles
• *(Ham 5.2.6) Hamlet tells Horatio he couldn't sleep on board ship: 'I lay / Worse than the mutines in the bilboes'—in worse discomfort than mutineers in chains.*

bill NOUN
a weapon with a long handle and a curved blade at the top
• *(MA 3.3.40) Dogberry tells the watchmen: 'have a care that your bills be not stolen'.*

bill NOUN
⚠ *Don't read the money meaning of 'a statement of charges' into these senses.*
1 list
• *(MND 1.2.91) Quince tells his companions: 'I will draw a bill of properties'—make a list of props needed for the play.*
2 written order
• *(JC 5.2.1) Brutus tells Messala: 'give these bills / Unto the legions on the other side'.*

bird-bolt NOUN
short blunt-headed arrow for shooting birds
• *(MA 1.1.38) Beatrice says what she thinks of Benedick's ability as a soldier: 'my uncle's fool ... challenged him at the bird-bolt'—Leonato's jester challenged him at a very elementary level of archery.*

birdlime NOUN
sticky substance spread on branches to snare birds
• *(Oth 2.1.125) Iago tells Desdemona that he finds it hard to think up something clever to say: 'my invention / Comes from my pate as birdlime does from frieze'—his inventiveness comes out of his head as something sticky comes from a rough woollen cloth—with great difficulty.*

Birnam Wood also spelled **Birnan**
a forested area in Birnam, Dunkeld, eastern Scotland
• *(Mac 4.1.92) The Third Apparition tells Macbeth that he will not be defeated 'until / Great Birnam Wood to high Dunsinane Hill / Shall come against him'.*

birthdom NOUN
native land
• *(Mac 4.3.4) Macduff tells Malcolm they need to 'Bestride our downfall birthdom'—protect their birthright (their country) from its descent into chaos.*

bisson ADJECTIVE
blinding
• *(Ham 2.2.494) The First Player describes the distraught Hecuba running up and down the city streets 'With bisson rheum'—her eyes filled with blinding tears.*

bite one's thumb
a gesture of insult or defiance, made by inserting the thumb nail into the mouth, and making it click againt the upper teeth upon release
• *(RJ 1.1.37) Sampson tells Gregory he is going to show contempt to Montague's men: ' I will bite my thumb at them'.*
🎭 *This was an old rude Italian gesture, similar to 'giving someone the finger' today. The significance of the old gesture is lost, but it probably suggested cowardice in the person towards whom it was directed.*

black ADJECTIVE
⚠ *Don't read in the modern racial meaning.*
of dark complexion or with black hair
• *(Oth 2.1.130) Desdemona asks Iago what he thinks of a woman who is 'black and witty'.*

black in the phrase **let the devil wear black**
see **let**

Black Monday
in the Christian calendar, the day after Easter—perhaps recalling an Easter Monday in 1360, during the Hundred Years War, when bad weather devastated the English army
• *(MV 2.5.24) Lancelot, talking to Shylock, says his nose 'fell a-bleeding on Black Monday last'.*
🎭 *Shylock has just told Lancelot he dreamed of money-bags last night. Lancelot mocks his master by reporting superstitions of his own.*

bladder NOUN
container (made from an animal's remains) for storing liquids
• *(RJ 5.1.46) Romeo describes the contents of the shelves in the apothecary's shop: 'empty boxes, / Green earthen pots, bladders'.*

blank NOUN
bullseye—the white spot in the centre of a target
• *(Ham 4.1.42) Claudius talks about the way slander*

goes straight to its target 'As level as the cannon to his blank'.

› blank VERB
make pale
- *(Ham 3.2.212) The Player Queen assures her husband that, if she were ever to marry again, 'Each opposite, that blanks the face of joy, / Meet what I would have well'—let every adversity that drains joy from the face fall on her.*

blaspheme VERB
⚠ *Don't read in the meaning of 'speak irreverently against God'.*
speak evil of
- *(Mac 4.3.108) Macduff condemns Malcolm as someone who 'does blaspheme his breed'—defame his ancestry.*

blast VERB
blight, disease
- *(Ham 3.1.160) Ophelia sadly reflects on the way Hamlet's youthful bloom has been 'Blasted with ecstasy'—destroyed by madness.*

blast NOUN
storm
- *(Mac 1.7.22) Macbeth imagines pity spreading with the news of Duncan's murder, 'like a naked newborn babe / Striding the blast'—riding on a rolling storm of upset and indignation.*

› blastment NOUN
blight
- *(Ham 1.3.42) Laertes advises Ophelia to be wary of the blights that can harm a young woman: 'in the morn and liquid dew of youth / Contagious blastments are most imminent'—when you're young and naive, you can be easily destroyed.*

› blasted ADJECTIVE
⚠ *Don't read in the modern meaning of 'blasted' as a swear-word.*
blighted
- *(Mac 1.3.75) Macbeth asks the Witches why they have met him 'Upon this blasted heath'—a place where nothing grows.*

blazon NOUN
1 banner showing a coat-of-arms
- *(TN 1.5.273) Olivia thinks Cesario has displayed 'five-fold blazon'—a way of saying (by using a term from heraldry) that he has shown five marks of gentility.*

2 description
- *(MA 2.1.274) Don Pedro agrees that Beatrice's representation of Claudio is correct: 'I think your blazon to be true'.*

› blazon VERB
display—as on a coat-of-arms
- *(RJ 2.6.26) Romeo asks Juliet if the amount of her joy is like to his, and if she has the skill 'To blazon it'—to proclaim it.*

› blazoning ADJECTIVE
praising
- *(Oth 2.1.63) Cassio describes Desdemona as someone 'that excels the quirks of blazoning pens'—who surpasses the verbal flourishes of any writer who tried to praise her.*

blent ADJECTIVE
blended
- *(TN 1.5.219) Cesario describes Olivia's face: ''Tis beauty truly blent'—like a great portrait, where the paints have been skilfully blended.*

bless VERB
protect
- *(MA 5.1.141) Claudio reacts to Benedick's approach: 'God bless me from a challenge'—I hope he's not going to ask me for a fight!*

see also HELLO, p.133

blind ADJECTIVE
⚠ *'Blind' normally has the same meaning as today, but not in the quotation below. Henry's soldiers can see perfectly well.*
reckless
- *(H5 3.4.34) Henry warns the citizens of Harfleur to surrender, to avoid being attacked by 'The blind and bloody soldier'—headstrong and blood-thirsty.*

blind-worm NOUN
slow-worm
- *(Mac 4.1.16) The Witches add more items to their cauldron: 'Adder's fork, and blind-worm's sting'.*

🎭 *In the 16th century, the slow-worm was thought to carry a poisonous sting.*

blister NOUN
burn-mark—as made by a branding-iron on the forehead of a woman punished for being a prostitute
- *(Ham 3.4.44) Hamlet accuses Gertrude of being like a person who 'takes off the rose / From the fair forehead of an innocent love / And sets a blister there'.*

block **see HATS, p.160**

a
Bb
c
d
e
f
g
h
i
j
k
l
m
n
o
p
q
r
s
t
u
v
w
x
y
z

blood NOUN
showing strong emotions
1 of a sexual kind
• *(Ham 3.4.69) Hamlet tells his mother that at her age 'The heyday in the blood is tame'.*
2 of an angry kind
• *(Oth 2.3.189) Othello is furious to find Cassio fighting: 'My blood begins my safer guides to rule'—my anger is overcoming my normal peaceful instincts.*
3 of a high-spirited kind
• *(JC 4.3.262) Brutus tells Lucius: 'I know young bloods look for a time of rest'—hot-blooded fellows need their sleep.*
see also **HUMOURS, p.137**

blood NOUN
showing character or ancestry
1 disposition
• *(MA 1.1.118) Beatrice tells Benedick 'I thank God and my cold blood' that she is like him in not wanting a lover.*
2 relative
• *(RJ 3.1.185) The Prince reproaches Montague for the death of Mercutio: 'My blood for your rude brawls doth lie a-bleeding'.*
3 good parentage
• *(KL 3.1.40) Disguised Kent says who he is: 'I am a gentleman of blood and breeding'.*

› **half-blooded** ADJECTIVE
having only one noble parent
• *(KL 5.3.81) Albany calls Edmund a 'Half-blooded fellow'—a 'bastard', with a mother belonging to a lower class than the wife of Gloucester.*

blood-boltered also spelled **-bolter'd** ADJECTIVE
with hair matted in blood
• *(Mac 4.1.122) Macbeth sees an apparition: 'the blood-bolter'd Banquo smiles upon me'.*

bloody ADJECTIVE
⚠*Don't think of 'bloody' as a swear-word.*
1 blood-thirsty
• *(MV 3.3.34) Antonio describes Shylock as 'my bloody creditor'.*
2 causing bloodshed
• *(Mac 2.3.136) Donaldbain tells Malcolm: 'the nea'er in blood, / The nearer bloody'—the closer relatives are, the more likely they are to kill each other.*
3 showing that blood is going to be shed
• *(H5 1.2.101) Canterbury advises Henry: 'unwind your bloody flag'.*

blossoms NOUN
prime
• *(Ham 1.5.76) The Ghost says he was 'Cut off even in the blossoms of my sin'—with his sins unforgiven, in full flower.*

blow VERB
1 bloom
• *(MND 2.1.249) Oberon tells Puck: 'I know a bank where the wild thyme blows'.*
2 contaminate
• *(Tem 3.1.63) Ferdinand says he would normally not tolerate wood-carrying work, any more than he would allow 'The flesh-fly blow my mouth'—to lay eggs in his flesh.*
3 puff up
• *(TN 2.5.40) Fabian describes Malvolio's imaginings: 'Look how imagination blows him'—makes him arrogant.*

› **blown** ADJECTIVE
1 in full bloom
• *(Ham 3.1.159) Ophelia describes Hamlet: 'That unmatch'd form and feature of blown youth'.*
2 swollen
• *(KL 4.4.27) Cordelia reflects that 'No blown ambition doth our arms incite'—she and the French army are not fighting because of a desire to become great.*
3 whispered—blown around like the wind
• *(Oth 3.3.184) Othello says he would never listen to 'exsufflicate and blown surmises'—exaggerated and whispered insinuations.*

board VERB
1 approach
• *(Ham 2.2.170) Polonius tells Claudius and Gertrude that he will tackle Hamlet soon: 'I'll board him presently'.*
2 get on board (by sailing close to an enemy ship, so that you can jump on to it)
• *(Tem 3.2.3) Stephano tells the others to drink up: 'bear up and board 'em'—be brave and reckless in your drinking.*

bob VERB
cheat
• *(Oth 5.1.16) Iago thinks about the way he swindled Roderigo: 'gold and jewels that I bobb'd from him'.*

bobtail ADJECTIVE
with a docked tail
• *(KL 3.6.68) Poor Tom shouts at all sorts of dogs, including a 'bobtail tike'—a mongrel with its tail cut short.*

bodement NOUN
omen
• *(Mac 4.1.95) Macbeth is pleased with the Third Apparition's warning: 'Sweet bodements'.*

› **boding** ADJECTIVE
ominous
• *(Oth 4.1.22) Othello describes the way a raven makes people feel superstitiously that something bad is going to happen: 'Boding to all!'*

› **bode** VERB
predict
• *(Ham 1.1.72) Horatio thinks that the appearance of the Ghost 'bodes some strange eruption to our state'—predicts an abnormal disturbance.*
People in Shakespeare's time were terribly supersitious, much more so than we are now, and took all kinds of positive and negative meanings from objects and happenings in nature.

bodkin see **SWEARING, p.298, SWORDS AND DAGGERS, p.156**

body forth
give a shape in the mind
• *(MND 5.1.14) Theseus reflects that 'imagination bodies forth / The forms of things unknown', which the poet can then write down.*

boisterous also spelled **boist'rous** ADJECTIVE
Don't read the modern meaning of 'good-natured, noisy, lively', as when children are playing, into these senses.
1 violent
• *(Oth 1.3.226) The Duke describes Othello's visit to Cyprus as a 'stubborn and boisterous expedition'—a demanding and fierce voyage.*
2 painful
• *(RJ 1.4.26) Romeo says love is not a tender thing: it is 'too boist'rous'.*

bolster VERB
share a pillow
• *(Oth 3.3.400) Iago curses Desdemona and Cassio if they ever go to bed together: 'If ever mortal eyes do see them bolster'.*

bolted ADJECTIVE
Don't read the modern meaning of '(un) fastened with a bolt' into these senses. The words come from 'bolt' meaning 'to sift flour'.
refined
• *(H5 2.2.134) Henry is dismayed at Scroop's treachery, 'so finely bolted didst thou seem'—so well-refined.*

› **unbolted** ADJECTIVE
unrefined
• *(KL 2.2.62) Kent threatens Oswald: 'I will tread this unbolted villain into mortar'.*

bombard NOUN
a large leather wine-jug
• *(Tem 2.2.21) Trinculo describes a black cloud overhead as 'a foul bombard that would shed his liquor'.*

bombast ADJECTIVE
bombastic
• *(Oth 1.1.13) Iago says Othello responded to requests 'with a bombast circumstance'—vague and wordy circumlocution.*

bondman or **bond-slave** NOUN
slave
• *(JC 3.2.29) Brutus asks the people: 'Who is here so base that would be a bondman?'—so lowly that they want to drop in social status to become a slave.*
• *(TN 2.5.177) Sir Toby asks Maria if he could 'become thy bond-slave'.*

bones NOUN
as well as meaning 'parts of a skeleton', you'll find:
bobbins (cylinders that hold thread) made of bone
• *(TN 2.4.44) Orsino says that Feste's song was sung by carefree weavers—'the free maids that weave their threads with bones'.*
see also **MUSIC, p.172**

bonnet see **HATS, p.160**

book VERB
record
• *(H5 4.7.67) Montjoy asks Henry for permission 'To book our dead'—make a list of those killed.*

› **bookish** ADJECTIVE
of mere book-learning
• *(Oth 1.1.24) Iago describes Cassio's military knowledge as nothing more than 'bookish theoric'—theory obtained from books.*

› **unbookish** ADJECTIVE
ignorant (because not educated from books)
• *(Oth 4.1.101) Iago describes Othello's temperament as 'unbookish jealousy'.*

› **by the book**
as if following instructions in a manual
• *(RJ 1.5.109) Juliet tells Romeo 'You kiss by*

a
Bb
c
d
e
f
g
h
i
j
k
l
m
n
o
p
q
r
s
t
u
v
w
x
y
z

th'book'—expertly (or possibly politely—having not used his tongue).

› in your books

favour

• *(MA 1.1.69) The Messenger sees that Beatrice does not like Benedick very much: 'the gentleman is not in your books'—not in your good books.*

Book of Numbers

in the Bible, the fourth book of the Old Testament, in which a census is taken of the Israelites

• *(H5 1.2.98) Canterbury refers to the Bible to justify Henry's claim to the French throne: 'For in the Book of Numbers is it writ'.*

boon NOUN

⚠ *Don't read in the modern meaning of 'something very useful', as in 'a real boon'.*

plea

• *(KL 4.7.10) Kent asks Cordelia not to reveal his true identity: 'My boon I make it that you know me not'.*

boot NOUN

advantage

• *(KL 5.3.300) Albany tells Edgar and Kent (who have been in disguise and lost their identity, land, and rights) that they shall regain their rights 'With boot'—they'll get back what they originally had, and more.*

› make boot

plunder

• *(H5 1.2.194) Canterbury describes honey-bees that 'Make boot upon the summer's velvet buds'.*

› to boot

in addition

• *(Mac 4.3.37) Macduff says he would not be the kind of villain Malcolm thinks he is even if he were given—not only Scotland—but 'the rich East to boot'.*

The Asian East was thought to be a place of much wealth—the source of spices, cloths, foods, and valuable minerals.

bootless ADJECTIVE

useless

• *(MV 3.3.20) Antonio decides there's no point in asking Shylock to change his mind: 'I'll follow him no more with bootless prayers'.*

bootless ADVERB

uselessly

• *(JC 3.1.75) Caesar tells Brutus his request is in vain: 'Doth not Brutus bootless kneel?'*

bo-peep see **RECREATION, p.170**

boresprit see **SHIPS, p.168**

borne in hand see **bear in hand**

borrowed also spelled **borrow'd** ADJECTIVE

pretended

• *(RJ 4.1.104) The Friar tells Juliet that the potion will give her the 'borrow'd likeness of shrunk death'—she will look as if she is dead.*

bosky ADJECTIVE

covered with bushes

• *(Tem 4.1.81) Ceres tells Iris how the two ends of the rainbow 'dost crown / My bosky acres'—she rules over the whole world of nature.*

bosomed also spelled **bosom'd** ADJECTIVE

intimate

• *(KL 5.1.13) Regan thinks that Edmund has been having an affair with Goneril: 'you have been conjunct / And bosom'd with her'—coupled and close.*

botcher see **OCCUPATIONS, p.166**

bottle NOUN

as well as meaning 'a container for liquids', you'll find:

1 bundle—when talking about hay or straw

• *(MND 4.1.32) Bottom tells Titania what he would like to eat: 'I have a great desire to a bottle of hay'.*

2 basket

• *(MA 1.1.234) Benedick tells Don Pedro that, if he ever falls in love, he should 'hang me in a bottle like a cat, and shoot at me'.*

In Shakespeare's time, cats were sometimes used in archery practice, put inside a bottle-shaped container made of willow twigs or leather.

bottle-ale ADJECTIVE

immoral

• *(TN 2.3.26) Feste talks jestingly to Sir Andrew, concluding: 'the Myrmidons are no bottle-ale houses'.*

No-one has been able to work out what Feste is talking about in this speech, which brings together apparently unrelated statements. The meaning of some of these 400-year-old jokes is often lost. The Myrmidons were the warlike followers of the Greek hero Achilles. The name may have been a slang term for a kind of tavern frequented by 'low life', as during the 17th century 'myrmidon' is found as a label for a hired ruffian.

bottom NOUN

as well as meaning 'lowest part', you'll find:

vessel—when talking about ships

• *(MV 1.1.42) Antonio says that his 'ventures are*

not in one bottom trusted'—he hasn't put all his goods into just one ship's hold.

bound NOUN
1 limit
• *(Tem 1.2.97) Prospero describes how his brother Antonio developed 'A confidence sans bound'—a boldness without limit.*
2 region
• *(KL 1.1.62) Lear makes Goneril lady 'Of all these bounds' shown on his map of the country.*

bourn NOUN
frontier
• *(Ham 3.1.79) Hamlet talks about death, 'from whose bourn / No traveller returns'.*

bout in the phrase **walk a bout**
make a circuit around the dance floor
• *(MA 2.1.77) Don Pedro asks Hero: 'will you walk a bout with your friend?'*

bower VERB
enclose
• *(RJ 3.2.81) Juliet talks of Romeo as someone who did 'bower the spirit of a fiend / In mortal paradise of such sweet flesh'—like a devil sent in the disguise of a beautiful human.*

box-tree NOUN
type of large ornamental thick shrub
• *(TN 2.5.13) Maria tells the others: 'Get ye all three into the box-tree'—hide behind the big bush.*

brabble NOUN
brawl
• *(TN 5.1.60) The Officer tells Orsino that he caught Antonio in the streets 'In private brabble'—in a noisy quarrel involving just two people.*

brace NOUN
state of readiness
• *(Oth 1.3.24) The First Senator tells the Duke that, unlike Rhodes, Cyprus 'stands not in such warlike brace'—is not so prepared for war.*

brach NOUN
bitch-hound
• *(KL 3.6.67) Poor Tom shouts at all sorts of dogs, including a 'Hound or spaniel, brach or lym'.*

brainish ADJECTIVE
deluded
• *(Ham 4.1.11) Gertrude tells Claudius that Hamlet has killed Polonius in a fit of 'brainish apprehension'—deranged (mis)understanding.*

brain-sickly ADVERB
foolishly
• *(Mac 2.2.49) Lady Macbeth tells her husband not 'to think / So brain-sickly of things'.*

brake NOUN
bush
• *(MND 2.1.227) Demetrius tells Helena he will 'run from thee and hide me in the brakes'.*

branched ADJECTIVE
embroidered
• *(TN 2.5.44) Malvolio sees himself 'in my branched velvet gown'.*

brass or **braze** VERB
harden—like brass
• *(Ham 3.4.37) Hamlet tells Gertrude he wants to wring her heart, 'If damned custom have not braz'd it so'—if the way she has been behaving hasn't made it so hard that it can no longer be affected.*

brassy ADJECTIVE
⚠ *Don't read in the modern informal meaning of 'loud and vulgar'.*
unfeeling—hard as brass
• *(MV 4.1.31) Antonio has lost so much that his situation would evoke sympathy even 'From brassy bosoms and rough hearts of flint'.*

brave ADJECTIVE
⚠ *Don't read in the modern meaning of 'having or showing courage'.*
splendid
• *(Tem 5.1.183) Miranda exclaims upon seeing everyone: 'O brave new world / That has such people in't!'*

› **bravely** ADVERB
splendidly
• *(Tem 5.1.241) Ariel asks Prospero if he has done well, and Prospero replies: 'Bravely, my diligence'.*

brave VERB
challenge
• *(Oth 5.2.322) Cassio discovers how Roderigo was made to 'Brave me upon the watch'—provoke him to a fight.*

› **bravery** NOUN
1 extravagant show
• *(Ham 5.2.79) Hamlet says his anger against Laertes was triggered by 'the bravery of his grief' over the death of Ophelia.*
2 show of daring
• *(Oth 1.1.101) Brabantio accuses Roderigo of coming to disturb him 'Upon malicious bravery'—with evil-minded bravado.*

breach NOUN
1 disregarding
• *(Ham 1.4.16) Hamlet regrets that Claudius' drinking and marriage celebration is 'a custom / More honour'd in the breach than the observance'—it would be more honourable*

a

Bb

c d e f g h i j k l m n o p q r s t u v w x y z

for Denmark if it were neglected rather than practised.

2 breaking of the waves

• *(TN 2.1.20) Sebastian tells Antonio that Viola drowned 'some hour before you took me from the breach of the sea'—within an hour of saving me.*

› before-breach NOUN

previous breaking

• *(H5 4.1.162) Henry thinks of war as a place where 'men are punished for before-breach of the king's laws'.*

break VERB

1 speak, raise a matter

• *(MA 1.1.283) Don Pedro tells Claudio that, if he loves Hero, he will 'break with her and with her father'.*

2 reveal

• *(H5 5.2.235) Henry asks Katherine: 'break thy mind to me in broken English'.*

3 default

• *(MV 3.1.102) Tubal says that Antonio 'cannot choose but break'—not keep his word to his creditors.*

4 graze

• *(RJ 1.3.39) The Nurse describes how baby Juliet 'broke her brow'—grazed her forehead.*

breast NOUN

as well as the modern sense, the word reflects what goes on within the breast

1 singing voice

• *(TN 2.3.17) Sir Andrew says, after Feste's song, 'the fool has an excellent breast'—a good pair of lungs.*

2 heart

• *(Mac 4.3.113) Macduff expresses his despair: 'O my breast, / Thy hope ends here'.*

breath NOUN

as well as the modern sense, the word expresses several notions related to breathing:

1 speech

• *(MA 5.1.256) Leonato confronts Borachio: 'Art thou the slave that with thy breath hast kill'd / Mine innocent child?'—because of your false accusation.*

2 sound (especially when singing)

• *(MND 2.1.151) Oberon describes a mermaid 'Uttering such dulcet and harmonious breath'.*

3 life

• *(RJ 5.3.229) The Friar reflects that his 'short date of breath / Is not so long as is a tedious tale'—the amount of time he has left to live isn't enough to tell the story at length.*

4 energy

• *(Ham 5.2.256) Claudius addresses the court: 'The king shall drink to Hamlet's better breath'.*

› breathing ADJECTIVE

1 word-of-mouth

• *(MV 5.1.141) Portia wants to welcome Antonio to her house with deeds not words, and so she will 'scant this breathing courtesy'—shorten her verbal welcome.*

2 exercising

• *(Ham 5.2.164) Hamlet tells Osric 'it is the breathing time of day with me'.*

› breathing NOUN

delay

• *(MA 2.1.334) Don Pedro sees Claudio is unhappy at the thought of having to wait a week for his wedding: 'you shake the head at so long a breathing'.*

› unbreathed also spelled **unbreath'd** ADJECTIVE

untrained

• *(MND 5.1.74) Philostrate describes the rustics as having prepared their play with 'unbreath'd memories'—not learned their parts properly.*

breech VERB

cover—as if with cloth (breeches being short trousers)

• *(Mac 2.3.112) Macbeth describes Duncan's attendants: 'their daggers / Unmannerly breech'd with gore'—covered improperly (because they are the king's guards) with blood.*

bridal NOUN

wedding

• *(Oth 3.4.144) Desdemona thinks that women should not look in men 'for such observancy / As fits the bridal'—have as tender attention as on the day they were married.*

bride NOUN

spouse—here referring to the bridegroom

• *(RJ 3.5.145) Capulet is pleased he has found in Paris a good husband for Juliet: 'So worthy a gentleman to be her bride'.*

briefness NOUN

speedy action

• *(KL 2.1.18) Edmund hopes his plan will succeed if he acts quickly (and has luck on his side): 'Briefness and Fortune, work!'*

brinded see COLOURS, p.164

broach VERB

pierce

• *(H5 5.Chorus.32) The Chorus describes a General 'Bringing rebellion broached on his sword'—*

alluding to the campaign in 1599 by the Earl of Essex to quell rebellion in Ireland.

broad ADJECTIVE
1 unrestrained
• *(Ham 3.4.2) Polonius advises Gertude to tell Hamlet that 'his pranks have been too broad to bear with'—people cannot cope with his outrageous behaviour.*
2 frank
• *(Mac 3.6.21) Lennox gives a Lord his private opinion about Macduff's location 'from broad words'—to speak candidly.*
3 obvious
• *(RJ 2.4.79) Romeo plays with the word 'broad' to prove that Mercutio is 'a broad goose'—a plain prostitute.*

brock NOUN
badger—here used to mean a stinker
• *(TN 2.5.97) Sir Toby says of Malvolio: 'hang thee, brock!'*

broil NOUN
1 turmoil
• *(Oth 1.3.87) Othello tells the senators he can only speak of what 'pertains to feats of broil and battle'.*
2 quarrel
• *(KL 5.1.30) Goneril advises everyone to focus on the French enemy and put aside 'these domestic and particular broils'—their private arguments.*

broken ADJECTIVE
1 left-over
• *(KL 2.2.13) Kent describes Oswald as 'an eater of broken meats'.*
2 arranged for different instruments
• *(H5 5.2.233) Henry, proposing marriage, plays with words in asking Kate to give him an 'answer in broken music, for thy voice is music, and thy English broken'—she's not a fluent English speaker.*

brood in the phrase **on brood**
brooding, moping
• *(Ham 3.1.165) Claudius tells Polonius that Hamlet's 'melancholy sits on brood'.*

brother NOUN
as well as meaning 'a sibling', you'll find:
equal
• *(KL 5.3.62) Albany tells Edmund: 'I hold you but a subject of this war, / Not as a brother'—as a subordinate, not as an equal.*
Albany is aware that Edmund has been having an affair with Regan, and may also be hinting at his role as a possible brother-in-law.
see also FAMILY, p.103

› sworn brother
companion-in-arms, comrade
• *(MA 1.1.64) Beatrice says that Benedick 'hath every month a new sworn brother'.*

brow NOUN
as well as referring to the eyebrows or the forehead, you'll also find:
1 appearance
• *(Ham 1.2.4) Claudius tells his court that King Hamlet's death has caused the whole kingdom 'To be contracted in one brow of woe'—drawn together in a single face of sadness.*
2 overlooking shore
• *(Oth 2.1.53) A Gentleman tells Montano that he can see people standing 'on the brow o' the sea'.*

Brownist NOUN
a follower of Robert Browne, the founder of a 16th-century Puritan religious sect (with strong views on self-indulgence and sex)
• *(TN 3.2.28) Sir Andrew says he would rather 'be a Brownist as a politician'.*

bruit VERB [pronounced broot]
announce
• *(Mac 5.7.23) Macduff hears a noise (a trumpet-call or battle-cry) which suggests 'one of greatest note / Seems bruited'—someone important has arrived.*

Brutus NOUN
Lucius Junius Brutus, founder of the Roman republic in 509 BC
• *(H5 2.4.37) The Constable compares Henry's youthful follies to 'the outside of the Roman Brutus'—a man who pretended to be slow-witted to save his life (just as Henry pretended to be idle and foolish in his younger days).*
Shakespeare wrote about Henry's youthful behaviour in the two plays 'Henry IV Part 1' and 'Part 2'.

Brutus NOUN
Marcus Junius Brutus, a leader of the conspiracy to assassinate Julius Caesar in 44 BC
• *(Ham 3.2.99) Polonius says he played the part of Julius Caesar once: 'Brutus killed me'.*

bubukle also spelled **bubuckle** NOUN
inflamed swelling—a blend of 'bubo' and 'carbunkle' (words for boils or skin inflammations)
• *(H5 3.7.95) The Welsh Captain describes Bardolph's face as 'all bubuckles'.*

buckler see ARMOUR, p.154

a
Bb
c d e f g h i j k l m n o p q r s t u v w x y z

budge VERB
flinch
• *(JC 4.3.44) Brutus asks Cassius: 'Must I budge?' —must I let your anger make me give way?*

bug NOUN
⚠ *Don't read in the modern meaning of 'insect'.*
bugbear, an imaginary terror
• *(Ham 5.2.22) Hamlet describes how Claudius' letter talks of the 'bugs and goblins'—the terrors and dangers—in his life.*

bulk NOUN
1 the part of a building that sticks out at the front
• *(Oth 5.1.1) Iago tells Roderigo to hide in order to surprise Cassio: 'stand behind this bulk'.*
2 body
• *(Ham 2.1.95) Ophelia says that Hamlet's sigh was so pitiful 'it did seem to shatter all his bulk'.*

bully see TERMS OF ADDRESS, p.306

bum-baily NOUN
sheriff's officer
• *(TN 3.4.158) Sir Toby tells Sir Andrew to look out for Cesario 'at the corner of the orchard, like a bum-baily'—in case he tries to sneak up behind them.*

burden also spelled **burthen** NOUN
as well as the usual meaning of 'heavy load' or 'something troublesome', you'll find musical senses:
1 refrain
• *(Tem 1.2.380) Ariel tells the other spirits to take up the chorus of his song: 'sweet sprites bear / The burden'.*
2 bass line accompanying a song
• *(MA 3.4.41) Margaret suggests that Beatrice sings a song 'that goes without a burden'—that doesn't need a bass line (but also making a pun: that doesn't bear the weight of a man).*

burgher NOUN
citizen
• *(MV 1.1.10) Salarino describes Antonio's ships as being so large and rich that they are like 'signors and rich burghers', looking down on smaller ships as they pass by.*

burning zone see COSMOS, p.174

buskined also spelled **buskin'd** ADJECTIVE
wearing high hunting boots (known as *buskins*)
• *(MND 2.1.71) Titania describes Hippolyta to Oberon as 'Your buskin'd mistress'.*

busy ADJECTIVE
interfering
• *(Ham 3.4.33) Hamlet tells the dead Polonius: 'Thou find'st to be too busy is some danger'—being an interfering busybody can get you into trouble.*

butt NOUN
⚠ *Don't read such modern meanings as 'cigarette butt' or 'buttocks' into these senses.*
1 target (as in archery)
• *(Oth 5.2.265) Othello, having learned the truth, reflects on the end of his life: 'Here is my journey's end, here is my butt / And very sea-mark of my utmost sail'—the final objective and last beacon guiding his ultimate voyage.*
2 barrel
• *(Tem 2.2.117) Stephano reports how he escaped from the sinking ship 'upon a butt of sack' —holding on to a floating barrel of wine.*
3 old hulk
• *(Tem 1.2.146) Prospero and Miranda were sent away from Milan on 'A rotten carcass of a butt'—a ramshackle boat.*

› **butt-shaft** NOUN
blunt-headed arrow
• *(RJ 2.4.16) Mercutio describes Cupid's arrow as 'the blind bow-boy's butt-shaft'—sent by the god of love.*

buttery bar NOUN
ledge by the hatch of a liquor store
• *(TN 1.3.64) Maria invites Sir Andrew: 'bring your hand to th' buttery bar and let it drink'—referring in a flirtatious way to her breasts.*

button NOUN
1 bud
• *(Ham 1.3.40) Laertes warns Ophelia that disease can infect young flowers 'Too oft before their buttons be disclos'd'—even before their buds show (suggesting she is the young flower and Hamlet the disease before she matures).*
2 knob at the top of a cap
• *(Ham 2.2.226) Guildenstern and Rosencrantz joke with Hamlet that 'on Fortune's cap we are not the very button'—their fortunes are not at the highest point.*

buxom NOUN
⚠ *Don't read in the meaning of 'a woman with large breasts'.*
cheerful
• *(H5 3.7.25) Pistol describes Bardolph as 'a soldier firm and sound of heart, and of buxom valour'.*

buzz NOUN
rumour
• *(KL 1.4.316) Goneril tells her husband that Lear's knights will threaten them by responding to 'every*

dream, / Each buzz, each fancy' that he might have.

› buzzer NOUN

⚠ *Don't read in the modern meaning of 'an electrical device that makes a buzzing noise'.*

rumour-monger

• *(Ham 4.5.89) Claudius knows that Laertes 'wants not buzzers to infect his ear'—doesn't lack people around him whispering rumours about his father's murderer.*

buzz buzz see EXCLAMATIONS, p.99

by ADVERB

nearby

• *(TN 4.3.24) Olivia invites Sebastian 'Into the chantry by'.*

› by and by

⚠ *'By and by' can also mean 'later on, in due course', as it does today; so look carefully at the context in order to judge the sense of intended urgency.*

straightaway

• *(RJ 3.1.165) 'Tybalt fled; / But by and by comes back to Romeo'.*

› by this

by this time

• *(JC 1.3.125) Cassius tells Casca of their fellow-conspirators: 'by this they stay for me / In Pompey's Porch'—they're waiting for me there.*

bye see GOODBYE, p.121

byle NOUN

boil

• *(KL 2.4.220) Lear calls Goneril 'a byle, / A plague-sore'.*

✒ *Shakespeare sometimes helps us work out what an unfamiliar word means by using another word with a similar meaning immediately afterwards—a plague-sore is similar to a byle. The First Folio spelling is 'byle', but some editions replace this with the more familiar word 'boil'.*

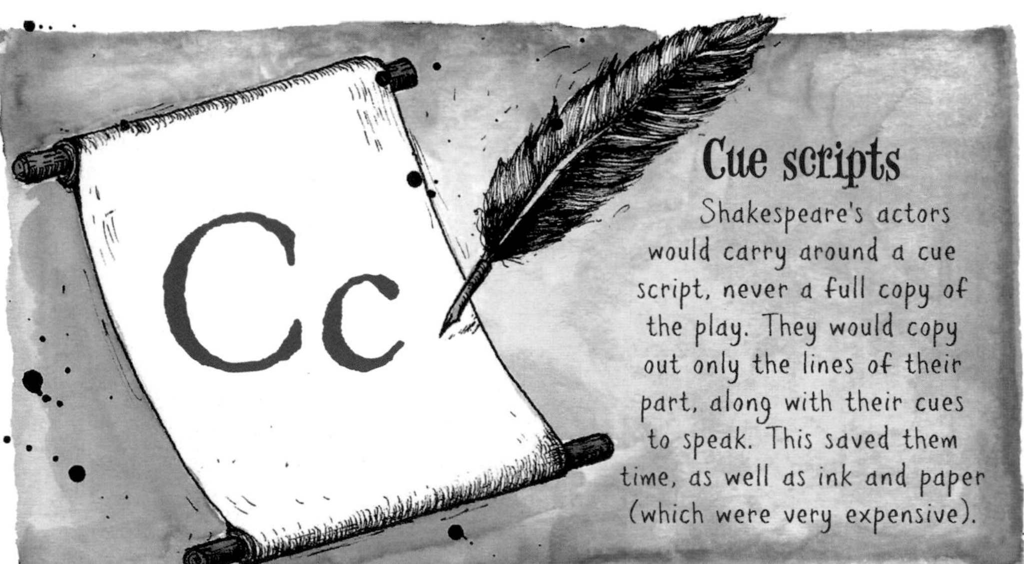

cable NOUN

scope

• *(Oth 1.2.17) Iago believes Brabantio will put whatever restraint upon Othello that the law 'Will give him cable'—will allow him to do.*

cadent ADJECTIVE

falling

• *(KL 1.4.275) Lear asks Nature to curse Goneril, so that her child will let 'cadent tears fret channels in her cheeks'—cause her immense grief.*

Cadmus NOUN

in Greek mythology, the founder of Thebes

• *(MND 4.1.111) Hippolyta recalls a time when she 'was with Hercules and Cadmus'.*

Cadwallader NOUN

[pronounced kad-**wa**-la-der]

in Welsh legend, a 7th-century warrior king

• *(H5 5.1.25) The Welsh Captain demands that Pistol eat his leek, to which Pistol replies: 'Not for Cadwallader and all his goats'—being scornful about the legendary Welsh king and his favourite animals.*

Caesar NOUN
Julius Caesar, 1st-century BC Roman general and ruler (whose assassination is central to the plot of Shakespeare's play, *Julius Caesar*)
• *(Ham 5.1.197) Hamlet, at a graveside, reflects on 'Imperious Caesar, dead and turn'd to clay'.*

'cagion see **'casion**

Cain NOUN
in the Bible, a son of Adam and Eve, who killed his brother Abel (and so became the first murderer)
• *(Ham 5.1.72) Hamlet sees the First Gravedigger throw a skull to the ground 'as if 'twere Cain's jawbone, that did the first murder'.*

caitiff NOUN [pronounced **kay**-tiff]
miserable wretch
• *(Oth 5.2.314) Othello calls Iago 'the pernicious caitiff!'—a villainous, miserable coward.*

caitiff ADJECTIVE
miserable
• *(RJ 5.1.52) Romeo describes the apothecary as 'a caitiff wretch'.*

calendar NOUN
as well as meaning 'a list of the dates in a year', you'll find:
standard
• *(Ham 5.2.107) Osric describes Laertes as 'the card or calendar of gentry'—the yardstick by which to judge good breeding.*

callet NOUN
a woman who is dirty or untidy
• *(Oth 4.2.120) Emilia is horrified that Othello called Desdemona a whore: 'A beggar in his drink / Could not have laid such terms upon his callet'—even a drunken beggar would not have used such a word to his female companion.*

calm VERB
⚠*Don't read in the meaning of 'become relaxed'.*
becalm, as when a sailing ship is cut off from the wind and brought to a halt
• *(Oth 1.1.30) Iago says the promotion of Cassio has made him 'lee'd and calm'd'.*

calumnious ADJECTIVE
slanderous
• *(Ham 1.3.38) Laertes warns Ophelia: 'Virtue itself scapes not calumnious strokes'—even the most virtuous person can't avoid being slandered.*

Camelot NOUN
the capital of King Arthur's legendary kingdom—here thought of as being on Salisbury Plain
• *(KL 2.2.80) Kent, calling Oswald a goose ('whore'), says that if he had him 'upon Sarum plain, / I'd drive ye cackling home to Camelot'.*

canakin see **cannikin**

canary NOUN
as well as meaning a kind of bird, you'll find:
sweet wine, from the Canary Islands
• *(TN 1.3.73) Sir Toby tries to cheer up Sir Andrew: 'thou lack'st a cup of canary'.*

candied ADJECTIVE
1 made of ice
• *(Tem 2.1.274) Antonio says that, even if he had twenty consciences, they would have to be frozen and melt before they would disturb him: 'candied be they, / And melt ere they molest'.*
2 flattering
• *(Ham 3.2.58) Hamlet tells Horatio: 'let the candied tongue lick absurd pomp'—leave it to flatterers to go in for tasteless splendour.*

candle-waster NOUN
someone who wastes candles by working late at night
• *(MA 5.1.18) Leonato asks Antonio if any such person exists who can forget about misfortune by burning the midnight oil: 'make misfortune drunk / With candle-wasters'.*
🎭*Scholars and bookworms who read by candlelight late into the night were often thought to be carrying out pointless activity, and thus wasting their time.*

Candy NOUN **see MAP, p.176**
Candia, a port in Crete, now known as Heraklion
• *(TN 5.1.56) An Officer identifies Antonio as the man 'That took the 'Phoenix' and her fraught from Candy'—captured the ship and her cargo.*

canker NOUN
1 a grub that destroys buds and leaves
• *(MND 2.2.3) Titania sends some of her fairies 'to kill cankers in the musk-rose buds'.*
2 disease, blight
• *(Tem 1.2.416) Prospero describes grief as 'beauty's canker'.*
3 wild rose
• *(MA 1.3.23) Don John says he would 'rather be a canker in a hedge' than a rose in his brother's favour—a plant that is wild and free rather than one pruned and cared for.*

canker VERB
decay
• *(Tem 4.1.192) Prospero describes Caliban as*

someone who, as he gets older, 'So his mind cankers'.

› **cankered** also spelled **canker'd** ADJECTIVE
rusted, malignant
• *(RJ 1.1.89) The Prince criticizes Capulet and Montague for fighting, which has caused people to take up weapons 'Canker'd with peace, to part your canker'd hate'—rusted and unused in peace time, but now taken up to separate deadly hatred.*

› **canker-bit** ADJECTIVE
worm-eaten
• *(KL 5.3.120) Edgar describes himself as 'By treason's tooth bare-gnawn, and canker-bit'—feeling totally eaten up as if by worms.*

› **canker-blossom** NOUN
grub that destroys the blossom (of love)
• *(MND 3.2.282) Hermia calls Helena 'you canker-blossom / You thief of love!'*

cannikin also spelled **canakin** NOUN
a little can—a small drinking vessel
• *(Oth 2.3.60) Iago sings a drinking song: 'And let me the cannikin clink'.*

canon NOUN
⚠ *Don't confuse this word with either the weapon ('cannon') or the clergyman ('canon').*
law
• *(Ham 1.2.132) Hamlet reflects on how God has 'fix'd / His canon 'gainst self-slaughter'—condemning suicide.*
Some editions have replaced 'canon' by 'cannon', giving a very different meaning.

canonized also spelled **canoniz'd** ADJECTIVE
buried with the rites of the Church
• *(Ham 1.4.47) Hamlet asks the Ghost why his 'canoniz'd bones' have come back from the dead.*

canton NOUN
song
• *(TN 1.5.250) Cesario tells Olivia he would write her 'loyal cantons of contemned love'—remain loyal to her, even though his songs would sing of despised and rejected love.*

cap see HATS, p.160

capable ADJECTIVE
1 willing to listen and respond
• *(Ham 3.4.127) Hamlet thinks the Ghost's physical appearance, along with its reasons for appearing, are so powerful that even if it preached to stones it 'Would make them capable'.*
2 comprehensive
• *(Oth 3.3.460) Othello wants 'a capable and wide revenge' in order to satisfy his bloody thoughts.*
3 able to inherit property
• *(KL 2.1.84) Gloucester tells Edmund that he will 'work the means / To make thee capable'.*
Edmund, being an illegitimate son of Gloucester, could by law receive no inheritance.
4 subject to
• *(Tem 1.2.352) Miranda tells Caliban he is a hateful slave, 'Being capable of all ill!'—with a nature that is open to every evil.*

capacity NOUN
⚠ *Don't read in the modern meanings of 'amount that can be held' or 'potential'.*
understanding
• *(MND 5.1.105) Theseus observes that simple but sincere people, even though they have difficulty expressing themselves, actually 'speak most, to my capacity'—if I am not mistaken.*

cap-a-pe also spelled **cap-à-pie** ADVERB
from head to foot
• *(Ham 1.2.200) Horatio describes the Ghost as being 'Armed at point exactly, cap-à-pie'—ready for battle, top to toe.*

capital ADJECTIVE
⚠ *Don't read the meaning of 'excellent' into these senses.*
1 main
• *(H5 5.2.96) Henry tells Queen Isabel that her daughter 'is our capital demand'.*
2 punishable by death
• *(Ham 4.7.7) Laertes asks Claudius why he did not act against Hamlet's actions, that were 'So crimeful and so capital in nature'.*

car NOUN
⚠ *Don't read in the modern meaning of 'motor car'. This is the sun god's chariot.*
chariot
• *(MND 1.2.29) Bottom declaims: 'Phibbus' car / Shall shine from far'.*

carbonado VERB
slash—as if preparing meat for a grill
• *(KL 2.2.35) Kent tells Oswald to fight or he will 'carbonado your shanks'—cut his legs to pieces.*

carbuncle NOUN
1 fiery, red precious stone
• *(Ham 2.2.451) Hamlet describes Pyrrhus: 'With eyes like carbuncles'.*
2 lump
• *(KL 2.4.221) Lear calls Goneril 'a boil, / A plague-sore, or embossed carbuncle'—a swollen tumour.*

a b Cc d e f g h i j k l m n o p q r s t u v w x y z

card NOUN
model
• *(Ham 5.2.107) Osric describes Laertes as 'the card or calendar of gentry'—the measure by which to judge good breeding.*

› **by the card**
with great precision
• *(Ham 5.1.125) Hamlet tells Horatio that, if they are going to talk to the First Gravedigger, 'We must speak by the card'.*
A compass-card showed the 32 points of the compass, providing sailors with an accurate guide to navigate by.

careful ADJECTIVE
as well as the modern meaning of 'avoiding damage' and 'serious-minded', you'll find:
1 anxious
• *(H5 4.1.218) Henry reflects on the way people make the king responsible for everything, including 'our debts, our careful wives'—wives who worry about us.*
2 caring
• *(RJ 3.5.107) Lady Capulet tells Juliet that she has 'a careful father'.*

› **carefully** ADVERB
considerately
• *(Ham 1.1.6) Francisco says to Barnardo: 'You come most carefully upon your hour'—it's considerate of you to relieve me on time.*

carnation see COLOURS, p.164

carol NOUN
⚠ *Don't read in the modern meaning of 'Christmas carol'.*
song of joy
• *(MND 2.1.102) Titania tells Oberon that, because of their arguing, 'No night is now with hymn or carol bless'd'.*

carpet consideration in the phrase **on carpet consideration**
for services given at court
• *(TN 3.4.215) Sir Toby describes Sir Andrew as a knight 'dubbed with unhatched rapier, and on carpet consideration'—he was made a knight for his duties at the royal court, and hasn't used his sword for service in the battlefield.*

carpet-monger NOUN
someone who pays frequent visits to a lady's bedroom chamber
• *(MA 5.2.30) Benedick reflects that he is in love more than 'a whole book full of these quondam carpet-mongers'—former ladies' men.*

carrack see SHIPS, p.168

carriage NOUN
as well as the meaning of 'vehicle' you'll find:
1 manner of behaviour
• *(MA 1.3.25) Don John says he will not 'fashion a carriage to rob love from any'—won't try to get people to like him by behaving differently.*
2 significance
• *(Ham 1.1.97) Horatio describes King Hamlet's deal with Norway: 'by the same cov'nant / And carriage of the article design'd'—according to the already agreed contract and the interpretation of its terms.*
3 burden
• *(Tem 5.1.3) Prospero tells Ariel that 'Time / Goes upright with his carriage'—there is so little left for Time to carry that he (Time) walks more easily.*
The personification of time, Father Time, was shown carrying an hourglass. As time passes, his burden lessens, and he moves faster.
see also SWORDS AND DAGGERS, p.156

carrion NOUN
1 rotting flesh of a dead animal
• *(Ham 2.2.182) Hamlet tells Polonius that a dead dog is 'a good kissing carrion'—good for breeding maggots.*
2 wretch, carcass
• *(MV 3.1.32) Solanio calls Shylock 'old carrion!'*

carrion ADJECTIVE
1 rotting
• *(JC 3.1.275) Antony says Caesar's murder is so foul it smells like 'carrion men groaning for burial'—as strong as the smell of dead flesh needing burial.*
2 loathsome
• *(MV 2.7.63) Morocco sees the contents of the gold casket: 'A carrion death'—a horrible death's-head (a skull), signalling the end of his attempt to woo Portia.*

› **carrion fly**
fly that preys on rotting flesh
• *(RJ 3.3.35) Romeo, reflecting on his banishment, says there is more value and honour 'In carrion flies than Romeo'—he feels he has lost all value in his being (because he can't be near Juliet).*

carry coals
1 submit to insult
• *(RJ 1.1.1) Sampson tells Gregory 'we'll not carry coals'.*
2 do degrading work
• *(H5 3.2.43) The Boy describes Pistol, Nym, and Bardolph as men who 'would carry coals'—a job for the lowest-born.*

carry it away
succeed
• *(Ham 2.2.351) Hamlet asks if the children's theatre*

companies have been successful: 'Do the boys carry it away?'

The expression comes from falconry, describing a bird that was successful in catching its prey.

cart NOUN

Don't read in the meaning we see in 'horse and cart'. This is the sun god's chariot.

chariot

• *(Ham 3.2.147) The First Player describes time passing as 'Phoebus' cart'—the sun—going around the earth.*

carve VERB

as well as the meaning of 'cut up', you'll find: choose—as when selecting a piece of meat

• *(Ham 1.3.20) Laertes tells Ophelia that Hamlet may not 'Carve for himself'—follow his own inclinations.*

case NOUN

as well as the meaning of 'container' (such as a suitcase), you'll find:

1 outer covering

• *(TN 5.1.160) Orsino asks Cesario how he will look 'When time hath sow'd a grizzle on thy case'—when he's grown a beard.*

2 mask

• *(RJ 1.4.29) Mercutio asks Romeo for 'a case to put my visage in'.*

› **casing** ADJECTIVE

surrounding

• *(Mac 3.4.23) Macbeth says the killing of Fleance along with Banquo would have made him 'As broad and general as the casing air'—far-reaching and all-embracing.*

› **in case to**

ready to

• *(Tem 3.2.25) Trinculo says he is 'in case to jostle a constable'—feels in such a fit state that he could deliberately elbow a constable.*

'casion or **'cagion** NOUN

cause—a short way of saying *occasion* in a West Country accent

• *(KL 4.6.230) Edgar, with a disguised voice, tells Oswald he will not let go of Gloucester's arm, 'without vurther 'casion'—unless you do something to make me.*

'Casion' is the spelling in the First Folio. The First Quarto text of the play has 'cagion'.

casque or **caske** see **ARMOUR, p.154**

casted ADJECTIVE

thrown aside

• *(H5 4.1.23) Henry comments on how, when a man's mind is lively, so the parts of his body 'newly move / With casted slough'—as if they had replaced an old skin by a new one.*

castiliano vulgo

[pronounced ka-stil-ee-**ah**-noh **vul**-goh]

an unclear expression, but the context suggests it means 'talk of the devil'

• *(TN 1.3.39) Sir Toby ends his conversation with Maria: 'Castiliano vulgo: for here comes Sir Andrew Agueface'.*

cast the water

inspect a sample of urine, in order to diagnose a disease

• *(Mac 5.3.51) Macbeth asks the Doctor to 'cast / The water of my land, find her disease'.*

casualty NOUN

Don't read 'a person injured or killed' into these senses.

1 chance occurrence

• *(KL 4.3.44) Kent tells how Lear's unkindness has turned Cordelia 'To foreign casualties'—to the uncertainties of living abroad.*

2 disaster

• *(MV 2.9.29) Arragon talks of the way a martlet bird builds a nest on an outside wall 'Even in the force and road of casualty'—despite the risks of being in the direct path of bad weather.*

cat NOUN

as well as its usual meaning, you'll find: civet cat—the source of a perfume

• *(KL 3.4.101) Lear tells Poor Tom that he owes 'the sheep no wool, the cat no perfume'—he has no beautiful fragrance about him.*

Cataian see **Cathayan**

catalogue NOUN

list

• *(Mac 3.1.94) Macbeth tells the Murderers that 'in the catalogue ye go for men'—in a roll-call of human beings, they would be registered as 'men', with nothing more to say about them (they're the same species, but the similarities end there).*

cataplasm NOUN

poultice—a soft, hot dressing

• *(Ham 4.7.143) Laertes knows a poison so powerful that 'no cataplasm so rare' can save an infected person from death—not even the finest poultice can help.*

catastrophe NOUN

Don't read in the modern meaning of 'sudden disaster'.

final event in a play

• *(KL 1.2.127) Edmund sees Edgar coming 'like the catastrophe of the old comedy'—he's calling his brother a clown.*

catch NOUN
musical round
• *(TN 2.3.16) Sir Toby suggests to Feste: 'Now let's have a catch'.*

catechize VERB
interrogate
• *(TN 1.5.56) Feste tells Olivia he must ask her a set of questions: 'I must catechize you'.*

cater-cousins NOUN [pronounced **kay**-tur]
good friends
• *(MV 2.2.121) Gobbo says that his son Lancelot and Shylock 'are scarce cater-cousins'—not really on the best of terms.*

Cathayan also spelled **Cataian** NOUN
[pronounced ka-**thay**-un or ka-**tay**-un]
person from Cathay (= China)
• *(TN 2.3.67) Sir Toby calls Olivia 'a Cataian'.*
It isn't clear what Sir Toby means. The name was often used to mean 'villain', so perhaps he is thinking of Olivia as a rogue if, as Maria suggests, she were to turn him out of the house.

Cato NOUN [pronounced **kay**-toe]
1st-century BC Roman politician, an opponent of Julius Caesar
• *(JC 2.1.295) Portia reminds Brutus that she is 'A woman well reputed, Cato's daughter'.*

cat o'mountain see ANIMALS, p.162

cause NOUN
as well as the meanings of 'reason' and 'subject-matter', you'll find:
1 business
• *(Mac 3.1.35) Macbeth tells Banquo that the next day 'we shall have cause of state / Craving us jointly'—state business that will require both of our attentions.*
2 court case
• *(KL 4.6.108) Lear imagines himself pardoning a condemned man and asks: 'What was thy cause?'—what have you been charged with?*
3 reason to engage in a duel—as set out in the fencing code of honour
• *(RJ 2.4.25) Mercutio describes Tybalt's fencing background: 'a gentleman of the very first house, of the first and second cause'—who learned all about the two main reasons for duelling (being accused of a major crime, and for personal or family honour) from the best training school.*

cautel NOUN [pronounced **kaw**-tul]
deceit
• *(Ham 1.3.15) Laertes talks to Ophelia about Hamlet: 'no soil nor cautel doth besmirch / The virtue of his will'—no blemish or deceit dirties his honourable intentions.*

cautelous ADJECTIVE [pronounced **kaw**-tul-us]
cautious
• *(JC 2.1.129) Brutus tells his fellow conspirators they have no need to swear, unlike 'priests and cowards and men cautelous'—because they are too honourable to need an oath to take their plan forward.*

Cavalery NOUN [pronounced ka-va-**leer**-ee]
Cavalier—a courtly gentleman
• *(MND 4.1.22) Bottom asks Mustardseed to 'help Cavalery Peaseblossom to scratch' his ears.*

caveto INTERJECTION [pronounced ka-**vee**-toh]
beware
• *(H5 2.3.45) Pistol advises his wife: 'caveto be thy counsellor'—take care, people say these days.*

caviary NOUN
caviare (the pickled eggs of certain types of fish)
• *(Ham 2.2.424) Hamlet describes a play as being 'caviary to the general'—only for those with an acquired taste.*
'Caviarie' is the spelling in the First Folio. Some editions avoid the less familiar word and use 'caviar' or 'caviare' instead.
In Shakespeare's England (where keeping fish cool was impossible) caviare was a new and incredibly expensive and rare delicacy, imported from Scandinavia; only someone of high birth and wealth would have been able to afford it. It's also a food that not everyone likes, and so is literally something of an acquired taste: you either like it or you don't.

'ce or **ise**
a dialect form of 'I shall'
• *(KL 4.6.235) Edgar tells Oswald to keep away from Gloucester, 'or ise try whither your costard or my ballow be the harder'—see if your head is harder than my stick.*

cell NOUN
⚠ *Don't read in the modern meaning of 'room where a prisoner is kept'.*
small humble dwelling
• *(Tem 1.2.20) Prospero describes himself as 'master of a full poor cell'.*

cellarage NOUN
cellars
• *(Ham 1.5.159) Hamlet hears the Ghost talking from beneath the ground, 'in the cellarage'.*
At Shakespeare's Globe, there was space underneath the stage, and trapdoors allowed ghosts, demons, and spirits to 'rise' from hell,

or—as in the above quotation—voices to be heard from below.

censure VERB
as well as meaning 'criticize' or 'condemn', you'll find:
give an opinion (not involving blame)
• *(JC 3.2.16) Brutus asks the people: 'Censure me in your wisdom'—judge wisely what I have done.*

censure NOUN
opinion
• *(Ham 1.3.69) Polonius tells Laertes to 'Take each man's censure, but reserve thy judgement'—listen to what people have to say, but don't judge them for it.*

Centaur NOUN
a mythical creature with the upper half of a man and the bottom half and legs of a horse, known for its lecherous behaviour
• *(KL 4.6.122) Lear reflects on promiscuous women: 'Down from the waist they are Centaurs'.*

centre NOUN
centre of the Earth
• *(Ham 2.2.159) Polonius says he will find out the truth about Hamlet 'though it were hid indeed / Within the centre'.*

century NOUN
company of a hundred men
• *(KL 4.4.6) Cordelia commands soldiers to go looking for Lear: 'A century send forth'.*

cerecloth NOUN [pronounced **sear**-kloth]
shroud
• *(MV 2.7.51) Morocco thinks it unlikely that the dull leaden casket contains Portia's image, as it would be too inferior even 'To rib her cerecloth in the obscure grave'—to enclose her shrouded dead body.*

cerements NOUN [pronounced **sear**-ments]
grave-clothes
• *(Ham 1.4.48) Hamlet asks the Ghost why his bones have 'burst their cerements'.*

Ceres NOUN [pronounced **sair**-eez or **si**-reez]
in Roman mythology, the goddess of crops and fruit
• *(Tem 4.1.75) Iris calls Ceres to meet Juno: 'Approach, rich Ceres, her to entertain'.*

certes ADVERB [pronounced **sir**-teez]
certainly
• *(Tem 3.3.30) Gonzalo reacts to the spirit-beings who have brought in a banquet: 'certes these are people of the island'.*

cess NOUN
cessation, halt
• *(Ham 3.3.15) Rosencrantz reflects on what would happen after 'The cess of majesty'—if a king were to be harmed.*

cestern see **cistern**

Cham NOUN [pronounced **kam**]
Kubla Khan, a 13th-century emperor of the Mongols
• *(MA 2.1.249) Benedick asks Don Pedro to send him on an errand to 'fetch you a hair off the Great Cham's beard'—an impossible task—rather than talk to Beatrice.*

chamber NOUN
bedroom
• *(Mac 5.4.2) Malcolm hopes 'the days are near at hand / That chambers will be safe'—when they can sleep safely in their beds.*

> **› chamberlain** NOUN
> bedroom attendant, who would stay outside the room in case he was needed during the night
> • *(Mac 1.7.63) Lady Macbeth says she will ply with drink Duncan's 'two chamberlains'.*
>
> **› chamberer** NOUN
> man who makes social visits to ladies' houses and engages in conversation
> • *(Oth 3.3.266) Othello says he doesn't have 'those soft parts of conversation / That chamberers have'.*

chambers NOUN
cannons
• *(H5 3.Chorus.34) Stage direction: 'Alarm, and chambers go off'.*

champain NOUN
expanse of open countryside
• *(KL 1.1.64) Lear offers Goneril a part of the country 'With shadowy forests and with champains rich'd'.*

changeable ADJECTIVE
showing different colours
• *(TN 2.4.72) Feste expresses the wish to Orsino that 'the tailor make thy doublet of changeable taffeta'—of shiny, lustrous, colourful silk.*

changeling NOUN
1 child taken by fairies
• *(MND 2.1.23) Puck says Titania 'never had so sweet a changeling'.*
2 changeover
• *(Ham 5.2.53) Hamlet substitutes his own letter for Claudius', 'The changeling never known'.*

a b Cc d e f g h i j k l m n o p q r s t u v w x y z

a b Cc d e f g h i j k l m n o p q r s t u v w x y z

chanson NOUN [pronounced **shon**-sun]
song
• *(Ham 2.2.407) Hamlet tells Polonius that 'The first row of the pious chanson will show you more'—the first verse of the holy song (from the Bible).*

Chanticleer NOUN
[pronounced **chahnt**-i-clear]
rooster—a traditional name for a cockerel
• *(Tem 1.2.385) Ariel sings 'I hear / The strain of strutting Chanticleer'.*
Chanticleer was the cockerel from Chaucer's 'The Nun's Priest's Tale', which Shakespeare's audience would have known well. He would walk around very proudly, as he had the most beautiful call of 'cock-a-doodle-do' in all the land.

chantry NOUN
small private chapel
• *(TN 4.3.24) Olivia asks Sebastian: 'go with me and with this holy man / Into the chantry by'—into the nearby chapel.*

chapless see **chaps**

chaplet NOUN
garland
• *(MND 2.1.110) Titania describes 'An odorous chaplet of sweet summer buds'—a sweet-smelling wreath of flowers.*

chaps also spelled **chops** NOUN
jaws
• *(Mac 1.2.22) The Captain reports how Macbeth killed Macdonald: 'he unseam'd him from the nave to th'chaps'—split him in two from the navel to the jaws.*

› **chapless** ADJECTIVE
jawless
• *(RJ 4.1.83) Juliet imagines a charnel house (a vault where human bones are stored) filled with 'yellow chapless skulls'.*

character NOUN
as well as meaning 'personal identity or appearance', you'll find:
handwriting
• *(Ham 4.7.50) Claudius tells Laertes that a letter from Hamlet is written in 'Hamlet's character'.*

character VERB
inscribe
• *(Ham 1.3.59) Polonius gives advice to Laertes: 'these few precepts in thy memory / Look thou character'.*

› **charactery** NOUN
expression
• *(JC 2.1.308) Brutus says he will tell Portia the meaning of 'All the charactery of my sad brows'.*

charge NOUN
as well as the modern meanings of 'responsibility', 'accusation', and 'cost', you'll find:
1 command
• *(Mac 4.3.20) Malcolm observes that 'A good and virtuous nature may recoil / In an imperial charge'—it may fall away, faced with a royal command.*
2 official duty
• *(MA 3.3.7) Verges tells Dogberry to give the Watch 'their charge'—tell them what they have to do.*
3 important matter
• *(RJ 5.2.18) Friar Lawrence says his letter to Romeo was 'full of charge'.*
4 expense
• *(KL 2.4.236) Regan asks Lear why he needs so many knights, because 'both charge and danger / Speak 'gainst so great a number'—they cost so much to maintain, and Lear is in no danger.*

charge VERB
1 command
• *(KL 4.5.18) Oswald tells Regan he must obey Goneril: 'My lady charg'd my duty in this business'.*
2 overburden
• *(JC 3.3.2) Cinna has dreamed of Caesar, and now finds 'things unluckily charge my fantasy'—ominously make me imagine things.*

› **charged** ADJECTIVE
overburdened
• *(Mac 5.1.46) The Doctor observes of Lady Macbeth: 'The heart is sorely charged'.*

› **o'ercharg'd** ADJECTIVE
overburdened
• *(MND 5.1.85) Hippolyta tells Theseus: 'I love not to see wretchedness o'ercharg'd'—I don't like to see unhappy people overburdened with more unhappiness.*

› **uncharge** VERB
acquit of blame
• *(Ham 4.7.67) Claudius says the plot to kill Hamlet will be so good that 'even his mother shall uncharge the practice / And call it accident'.*

charter NOUN
assurance
• *(Oth 1.3.243) Desdemona begs the Duke: 'let me find a charter in your voice'.*

chartered also spelled **charter'd** ADJECTIVE
licensed
• *(H5 1.1.48) Canterbury says that, when Henry speaks, 'The air, a charter'd libertine, is still'—*

normally able to go anywhere (like a man allowed to do whatever he wants).

Charybdis NOUN [pronounced ka-**rib**-diss]
in Greek mythology, a whirlpool in the narrow strait between Sicily and the Italian mainland that swallowed ships whole
• *(MV 3.5.15) Lancelot tells Jessica that (being Jewish) neither of her parents offers her the hope of Christian salvation: 'when I shun Scylla your father, I fall into Charybdis your mother'.*
Scylla was a female sea monster. There was a very narrow safe passage between her cave and the whirpool Charybdis. **see MAP, p.176**

chase NOUN
as well as its meaning of 'pursuit', you'll find: in tennis, a forfeited point
• *(H5 1.2.266) Henry, having had a gift of tennis balls from the French, says that 'all the courts of France will be disturb'd / With chases'—with a pun on the meaning of 'pursuit'.*

chaudron also spelled **chawdron** NOUN
[pronounced **chaw**-drun]
entrails
• *(Mac 4.1.33) The Witches add 'a tiger's chawdron' to their brew.*

chawed ADJECTIVE
chewed
• *(H5 4.2.50) The French say that in the mouths of the English horses the bridle-bit 'Lies foul with chawed grass'.*
'Chaw'd' is the spelling in the First Folio. Some editions avoid the less familiar word and use 'chewed' or 'chew'd' instead.

che PRONOUN
a dialect form of 'I'
• *(KL 4.6.235) Edgar tells Oswald to keep away from Gloucester: 'che vor' ye'—I warn you.*

cheapen VERB
Don't read in the modern meaning of 'make something less expensive'.
bid for
• *(MA 2.3.30) Benedick says that any woman he might love has to be 'Virtuous, or I'll never cheapen her'—try to win her attention (not literally 'bid with money at an auction').*

check NOUN
rebuke
• *(Oth 4.3.20) Desdemona says she loves Othello so much that she finds grace and favour even in 'his checks, his frowns'.*

› **check** VERB
rebuke
• *(JC 4.3.97) Cassius says he has been 'check'd like a bondman'—scolded like a slave.*

› **check at** VERB
1 turn aside from
• *(Ham 4.7.62) Claudius wonders if Hamlet has returned to Denmark, 'checking at his voyage' to England.*
2 in falconry: swerve to pounce on
• *(TN 3.1.61) Viola says Feste is someone who has to 'check at every feather / That comes before his eye'.*

› **unchecked** ADJECTIVE
uncontradicted
• *(MV 3.1.2) Salarino says there is a rumour 'unchecked that Antonio hath a ship of rich lading wrecked'.*

cheer NOUN
Don't read the modern meaning of 'shouting out' into these senses.
1 entertainment
• *(RJ 4.5.87) Capulet instructs his servants to change 'Our wedding cheer to sad burial feast'.*
2 welcome
• *(Mac 3.4.33) Lady Macbeth rebukes her husband: 'You do not give the cheer'.*
3 lifestyle
• *(Ham 3.2.211) The Player Queen tells her husband that, rather than marry again after his death, 'An anchor's cheer in prison be my scope'—she would rather live in a cell like a hermit.*
4 expression
• *(MV 3.2.310) Portia tells Bassanio to 'show a merry cheer'.*
5 cheerfulness
• *(Ham 1.2.116) Claudius asks Hamlet to stay in Elsinore, 'Here in the cheer and comfort of our eye'.*

› **cheerly** ADVERB
cheerfully
• *(H5 2.2.188) Henry commands everyone to set sail for France: 'Cheerly to sea'.*
'Cheerly' is often used as a general shout of encouragement.
• *(RJ 1.5.87) Capulet greets his guests: 'Cheerly, my hearts!'—have fun!*

› **all-cheering** ADJECTIVE
filling with life and energy
• *(RJ 1.1.128) Montague wonders why Romeo keeps himself away from everyone, even from*

a b Cc d e f g h i j k l m n o p q r s t u v w x y z

warning note *usage note* *theatre note*

'the all-cheering sun'—he never goes out any more (or perhaps only at night).

› how cheer'st thou?
how are you feeling?
• *(MV 3.5.61) Lorenzo asks: 'How cheer'st thou, Jessica?'*

cherry-pit see RECREATION, p.170

Cheshu NOUN
Shakespeare's way of showing a Welsh pronunciation of 'Jesus'
• *(H5 3.3.8) The Welsh Captain swears 'By Cheshu'.*
see also SWEARING, p.298

chev'ril also spelled **cheverel, cheveril** ADJECTIVE
flexible—a quality of kid goat leather
• *(TN 3.1.11) Feste tells Cesario that 'A sentence is but a chev'ril glove to a good wit'—the words can be easily turned around.*

chide past form **chid, chidden** VERB
as well as meaning 'scold', you'll find:
1 quarrel
• *(Oth 4.2.166) Iago persuades Desdemona it is state business that causes Othello's mood that makes him 'chide with you'.*
2 command harshly
• *(MND 3.2.312) Helena tells Hermia that Demetrius 'hath chid me hence'—angrily driven me from him.*

› chidden ADJECTIVE
driven along
• *(Oth 2.1.12) The Second Gentleman looks out at the rough sea: 'The chidden billow seems to pelt the clouds'—the waves appear to crash up to hit the clouds.*

› chiding NOUN
angry noise
• *(MND 4.1.114) Hippolyta remembers Spartan hounds: 'never did I hear / Such gallant chiding'—fearless growling and barking.*

childing ADJECTIVE
fertile
• *(MND 2.1.112) Titania describes what has happened to 'The childing autumn' as a result of their quarrel.*

Child Rowland also spelled **Childe Roland**
The most famous knight of Emperor Charlemagne (9th century), the subject of many ballads
• *(KL 3.4.175) As Lear approaches Gloucester's castle, Edgar as Poor Tom begins a rhyme: 'Child Rowland to the dark tower came'.*

chill or **'chill**
a dialect form of 'I will'
• *(KL 4.6.230) Edgar refuses to let go of Oswald's arm: 'Chill not let go'.*

chinks NOUN
money-bags
• *(RJ 1.5.116) The Nurse tells Romeo about Juliet: 'he that can lay hold of her / Shall have the chinks'.*
The Nurse is speaking both literally and metaphorically. Juliet's family is noble, and she will come with a dowry of money and possibly land when she is married. But the Nurse also means: 'whoever is lucky enough to marry Juliet will hit the jack-pot'.

chirurgeonly ADVERB
[pronounced kigh-**rur**-jun-lee]
like a surgeon
• *(Tem 2.1.136) Antonio says that Sebastian should bring a plaster 'most chirurgeonly'.*

chivalry NOUN
knights
• *(H5 1.2.157) Canterbury reminds everyone of what happened to England 'When all her chivalry hath been in France'.*

choice-drawn ADJECTIVE
chosen with great care
• *(H5 3.Chorus.24) The Chorus describes the 'cull'd and choice-drawn cavaliers' who are going to France.*

choir also spelled **quire** NOUN
as well as meaning 'group of singers', you'll find:
group of people
• *(MND 2.1.55) Puck recounts how, after a bout of his mischief, 'the whole choir hold their hips and loffe'—all the onlookers laugh.*

choir VERB
sing in a choir
• *(MV 5.1.62) Lorenzo describes the stars as angels 'choiring to the young-eyed cherubins'.*

choler NOUN
anger
• *(RJ 1.1.3) Sampson tells Gregory that if 'we be in choler, we'll draw'—if we find ourselves getting into a fight, we'll unsheathe our weapons.*

› choleric ADJECTIVE
hot-tempered
• *(JC 4.3.43) Brutus tells Cassius: 'Go show your slaves how choleric you are'.*

see also HUMOURS, p.137

chop-fallen ADJECTIVE
downcast
• *(Ham 5.1.177) Hamlet talks to Yorick's skull: 'Quite chop-fallen?'*
Hamlet is making a pun on 'chop' meaning 'jaw-bone'. The jaw-bone is separate from the skull, and so a skull will look jawless ('chop-fallen') when held up.
see also chaps

chopine **see CLOTHING, p.158**

chopped ADJECTIVE
chapped, chafed
• *(JC 1.2.243) Casca tells Brutus how the rabble 'clapped their chopped hands'.*

chopped logic also spelled **chopt-logic**
using arguments intended to deceive
• *(RJ 3.5.149) Capulet is furious with Juliet's intricately expressed answer: 'How how, how how, chopt-logic?'*

choppy ADJECTIVE
chapped
• *(Mac 1.3.42) Banquo sees each Witch with 'her choppy finger laying / Upon her skinny lips'.*

chorus also spelled **Chorus** NOUN
Don't read in a meaning to do with singing.
the character in a play who speaks the prologue and comments on the course of events
• *(Ham 3.2.235) Ophelia tells Hamlet: 'You are as good as a chorus'.*
The Chorus remains outside of the world of the play. He is an observer rather than a participator.

chough see **chuff**

'chould see **chud**

Chrish NOUN
Shakespeare's way of showing an Irish pronunciation of 'Christ'
• *(H5 3.3.31) The Irish Captain swears 'By Chrish law'.*
see also SWEARING, p.298

christom ADJECTIVE
intended to mean 'christened'—innocent
• *(H5 2.3.10) The Hostess describes Falstaff dying like 'any christom child'.*

chrysolite NOUN
a type of precious stone
• *(Oth 5.2.144) Othello imagines a world 'Of one entire and perfect chrysolite'.*

chud or **'chud** also spelled **'chould**
a dialect form of 'I should'
• *(KL 4.6.233) Edgar tells Oswald: 'And 'chud ha' bin zwagger'd out of my life'—denying that he would have been scared out of his life by Oswald's bullying manner.*

chuff also spelled **chough** NOUN
chatterer
• *(Ham 5.2.87) Hamlet describes Osric as 'a chuff'.*
see also ANIMALS, p.162

churl NOUN
wretch, villain—but here used as a term of endearment
• *(RJ 5.3.163) Juliet finds the poison by dead Romeo: 'O churl, drunk all'.*

› **churlish** ADJECTIVE
as well as meaning 'rude', 'bad-tempered', you'll find:
rough
• *(H5 4.1.15) Henry tells Erpingham a soft pillow for his head 'Were better than a churlish turf of France'.*

cicatrice NOUN [pronounced **sick**-uh-triss]
scar
• *(Ham 4.3.60) Claudius reminds England that 'yet thy cicatrice looks raw and red', after war with Denmark.*

cinquepace NOUN [pronounced **sink**-uh-pace]
five-step capering dance
• *(MA 2.1.66) Beatrice compares wooing, wedding, and repenting to 'a Scotch jig, a measure, and a cinquepace'—in turn, an energetic, leisurely, and highly exhausting series of dances, matching the various stages of a relationship.*

cipher NOUN
nonentity—the figure nought
• *(H5 Prologue.17) The Chorus describes the actors portraying the Battle of Agincourt as 'ciphers to this great account'.*
It was normal for the Chorus to show humility, and beg forgiveness for the 'lack of ability' that the theatre company were about to demonstrate.

circumscribe VERB
restrict
• *(Ham 1.3.22) Laertes tells Ophelia that, as a prince, Hamlet is not free to choose a wife 'And therefore must his choice be circumscrib'd'.*

› **circumscription** NOUN
restriction

• *(Oth 1.2.27) Othello says he would never want his freedom to be 'Put into circumscription and confine'.*

circumstance NOUN
1 situation
• *(Ham 1.3.102) Polonius says Ophelia speaks like someone 'Unsifted in such perilous circumstance'—lacking experience in handling an emotionally risky situation.*
2 detail
• *(RJ 2.5.36) Juliet asks the Nurse if the news is good or bad: 'Say either, and I'll stay the circumstance'—I can leave the specifics until later.*
3 circumlocution
• *(MV 1.1.154) Antonio asks Bassanio to not 'wind about my love with circumstance'—get to the point.*
4 ceremony
• *(Oth 3.3.355) Othello bids farewell to all 'Pride, pomp, and circumstance of glorious war!'*

› **circumstanced** also spelled **circumstanc'd** ADJECTIVE
subject to the situation
• *(Oth 3.4.195) Bianca accepts that Cassio has to leave her: 'I must be circumstanc'd'.*

circumvent VERB
get the better of
• *(Ham 5.1.75) Hamlet describes a schemer as someone who 'would circumvent God'.*

cistern also spelled **cestern, cesterne** NOUN
⚠ *Don't read in the meaning of 'large water-container above a lavatory'.*
pond
• *(Oth 4.2.60) Othello calls Desdemona's body 'a cistern for foul toads / To knot and gender in'—get together and have sex.*
✒ *'Cesterne' is the spelling in the First Folio. Some editions avoid the less familiar word and use 'cistern' instead.*

civet NOUN
type of musky perfume—obtained from the glands of the civet cat
• *(MA 3.2.44) Don Pedro says that Benedick now 'rubs himself with civet'.*

civil ADJECTIVE
⚠ *Don't read the meaning of 'minimally polite', 'not rude', into these senses.*
1 refined
• *(TN 1.4.21) Orsino advises Cesario to 'leap all civil bounds' in going to see Olivia—disregard all normal courtesies.*
2 seemly
• *(TN 3.4.5) Olivia describes Malvolio as 'sad and civil'—serious and well behaved.*
3 of civil law
• *(MV 5.1.210) Bassanio explains that no woman had his ring, 'but a civil doctor'.*
4 of civil war
• *(RJ Prologue.4) Verona is described as a place 'Where civil blood makes civil hands unclean'—civil strife between the families has bloodied the hands of normally well-behaved citizens.*

› **uncivil** ADJECTIVE
unrefined
• *(TN 5.1.107) Orsino calls Olivia an 'uncivil lady'.*
🎭 *This would have been an extremely impolite thing to say to a lady at the time.*

clause NOUN
⚠ *Don't read in the 'grammar' meaning of 'clause' here.*
assertion
• *(TN 3.1.149) Olivia, having just expressed her love for Cesario, asks him not to 'extort thy reasons from this clause'—don't force yourself to think that, just because I've said I love you, you therefore mustn't say you love me.*

claw VERB
flatter
• *(MA 1.3.15) Don John tells Conrad: I 'claw no man in his humour'—I don't butter up any man because of the type of person he is.*

clear ADJECTIVE
as well as meaning 'easy to see', you'll find:
1 spotless, pure
• *(KL 4.6.73) Edgar tells Gloucester that 'the clearest gods' have preserved him.*
2 blameless
• *(Mac 2.1.28) Banquo agrees to support Macbeth as long as this does not harm his 'allegiance clear'—his untarnished loyalty to Duncan.*
3 cheerful
• *(MND 3.2.60) Demetrius says that Helena looks 'as bright, as clear, / As yonder Venus in her glimmering sphere'.*

clear ADVERB
cheerfully
• *(Mac 1.5.70) Lady Macbeth tells Macbeth to 'look up clear'.*

› **clearness** NOUN
freedom from suspicion
• *(Mac 3.1.135) Macbeth tells the murderers: 'I require a clearness'.*

Cleitus NOUN [pronounced **kly**-tus]
an officer and friend of Alexander the Great, killed by him in a drunken quarrel

• *(H5 4.7.40) The Welsh Captain recalls how 'Alexander killed his friend Cleitus, being in his ales and his cups'.*

Cleopatra NOUN
Queen of Egypt in the 1st century BC, renowned for her beauty
• *(RJ 2.4.41) Mercutio mocks Romeo's romantic view of his lady as someone who makes 'Cleopatra a gipsy'—look dusky (tanned, and thus unfashionable).*
She is portrayed in Shakespeare's play 'Antony and Cleopatra'. Pale skin was considered attractive (tanned skin meant you were 'common', and worked outside), so noblewomen wore white, lead-based make-up (which slowly poisoned them).

clepe past form **clept** VERB
[pronounced kleep]
call
• *(Ham 1.4.19) Hamlet tells Horatio what outsiders think of the Danes: 'They clepe us drunkards'.*

clerestory also spelled **clearstory** NOUN
window high up on a wall
• *(TN 4.2.36) Feste tells Malvolio about his prison: 'the clerestories toward the south-north are as lustrous as ebony'—are as bright as black wood (so, not bright at all).*

clerk NOUN
Don't read the meaning of 'office subordinate' or 'shop assistant' into these senses.
1 scholar
• *(MND 5.1.93) Theseus recalls making visits to places where 'great clerks have purposed / To greet me'.*
2 parish clerk
• *(MA 2.1.100) Margaret instructs Balthasar, who has been saying 'Amen' to her: 'Answer, clerk'—treating him as if he were a parish clerk who has to reply to a priest.*

climate or **clime** NOUN
region—but without any reference to the weather
• *(JC 1.3.32) Casca describes strange happenings as ominous 'Unto the climate that they point upon'—for the part of the country that they are directed at.*

› **climature** NOUN
region
• *(Ham 1.1.128) Horatio is gloomy about the way the appearance of the Ghost is a bad omen for 'our climatures and countrymen'.*

clipper NOUN
someone who cuts gold or silver from the edges of coins
• *(H5 4.1.216) Henry says 'it is no English treason to cut French crowns, and tomorrow the king himself will be a clipper'—with a pun on 'crown' meaning 'coin/head'.*

clodpole also spelled **clotpoll** NOUN
blockhead
• *(TN 3.4.170) Sir Toby says Cesario will think Sir Andrew's challenge-letter 'comes from a clodpole'.*

clog NOUN
Don't read in the meaning of 'a type of wooden shoe'.
heavy wooden block
• *(Oth 1.3.196) Brabantio thinks, if he had other children, he would 'hang clogs on them' to keep them at home.*

cloistered also spelled **cloister'd** ADJECTIVE
confined—as if in the cloister of a monastery
• *(Mac 3.2.41) Macbeth tells his wife that a wicked deed will be done before 'the bat hath flown / His cloister'd flight'—before the bat returns home from its night-flight (often within monastery walls).*

cloistress NOUN
nun who is a member of an enclosed order
• *(TN 1.1.28) Valentine describes Olivia: 'like a cloistress she will veiled walk'.*

close ADJECTIVE
as well as meaning 'near', you'll find:
1 secret, hidden
• *(Mac 3.5.7) Hecate describes herself as 'The close contriver of all harms'.*
2 secretive
• *(MV 2.6.48) Lorenzo asks Jessica to hurry, for 'the close night doth play the runaway'—is fast disappearing.*
3 private
• *(MND 3.2.7) Puck tells Oberon of the players 'Near to her close and consecrated bower'.*
4 confined
• *(Oth 5.2.331) Lodovico commands that Iago be held 'close prisoner'.*

close ADVERB
out of sight
• *(Ham 4.7.129) Claudius advises Laertes to 'keep close within your chamber'.*

close VERB
1 agree
• *(JC 3.1.202) Antony thinks he would never 'close / In terms of friendship' with Caesar's enemies.*
2 join together again
• *(Mac 3.2.14) Macbeth fears that, although he has*

a b Cc d e f g h i j k l m n o p q r s t u v w x y z

slashed through a snake—done some of the work needed to keep him safe as king—'She'll close, and be herself'—she'll heal and be as strong as before (there's more danger to come).

› **closely** ADVERB
secretly
• *(RJ 5.3.255) The Friar tells the Prince he intended to keep Juliet 'closely at my cell'.*

› **closeness** NOUN
solitude
• *(Tem 1.2.90) Prospero says his former life was 'all dedicated / To closeness and the bettering of my mind'.*

closet NOUN **see ILLUSTRATION opposite**
1 small private chamber (where one would pray or dress)
• *(Ham 3.2.316) Rosencrantz tells Hamlet that his mother 'desires to speak with you in her closet'.*
2 small cabinet in which valuable things are kept
• *(KL 3.3.10) Gloucester tells Edmund where he has put a letter: 'I have lock'd the letter in my closet'.*

clothier's yard NOUN
a measure (a yard = 36 inches or about 90 centimeters) that clothiers used for lengths of cloth
• *(KL 4.6.88) Lear addresses an archer: 'draw me a clothier's yard'—pull the bowstring out to the extent of a full arrow.*

clotpoll see **clodpoll**

clouds in the phrase **in clouds**
filled with uncertainties
• *(Ham 4.5.88) Claudius says Laertes 'keeps himself in clouds' about his father's death.*

clout NOUN
1 piece of cloth, handkerchief
• *(RJ 2.4.188) The Nurse says that Juliet 'looks as pale as any clout'.*
2 cloth patch marking the centre of a target in archery
• *(KL 4.6.92) Lear calls out that an arrow has hit its target 'i'th'clout'—hit the bullseye!*

clown NOUN
⚠ *Don't read in the modern meaning of 'circus performer'.*
country bumpkin—in a play, a low comic character
• *(MND 3.1.1) Stage direction: 'enter the Clowns'.*

cloy VERB
gorge
• *(H5 2.2.9) Exeter describes how Henry has treated Scroop: 'Whom he hath dull'd and cloy'd with gracious favours'—favoured Scroop so much that he has become too lazy to do anything for himself.*

› **cloyment** NOUN
gorging
• *(TN 2.4.97) Orsino compares women's appetite for love to someone's taste that undergoes 'surfeit, cloyment, and revolt'—becomes weary from taking in too much food.*

clyster-pipe NOUN
tube for giving an enema (to clean out the bowels)
• *(Oth 2.1.172) Iago compares Cassio's fingers, sending kisses from his lips to Desdemona, to 'clyster-pipes'.*
🎭 *Kissing your own hand with three fingers was a common courteous gesture from a gentleman to a lady (actual physical contact was considered impolite, especially from strangers). Malvolio is seen doing the same gesture in 'Twelfth Night' (3.4.42). It seems to have been considered foppish behaviour—extravagant, over the top, and even foolish.*

coagulate ADJECTIVE
clotted
• *(Ham 2.2.450) Hamlet recites lines about Pyrrhus being 'o'ersized with coagulate gore'—smeared all over with clotted blood.*

coals see **carry coals**

coat NOUN
as well as meaning 'outer garment', you'll find:
coat-of-arms
• *(MND 3.2.213) Helena reminds Hermia of how they grew up together, like figures united on 'coats in heraldry'.*

cobbler NOUN
clumsy workman
• *(JC 1.1.11) The Cobbler puns on the name of his trade: 'I am but, as you would say, a cobbler'.*

cock NOUN
⚠ *Don't read the meaning of 'penis' into these senses without looking carefully at the context.*
as well as meaning 'cockerel' and 'weathercock', you'll find:
1 dinghy
• *(KL 4.6.19) Edgar describes to Gloucester a 'tall anchoring bark / Diminish'd to her cock'—so far away it looks the size of a small boat.*
2 cocking-piece of a gun
• *(H5 2.1.46) Pistol says that his 'cock is up'—his gun is ready for firing (here there is a sexual pun).*
see also SWEARING, p.298

see p56 and p22

a b Cc d e f g h i j k l m n o p q r s t u v w x y z

cock-a-hoop in the phrase
set cock-a-hoop
put everything into disorder
• *(RJ 1.5.80) Capulet tells off Tybalt: 'You will set cock-a-hoop!'*

cockatrice see ANIMALS, p.162

cockle hat see HATS, p.160

cockney NOUN
⚠*Don't read the modern meaning of 'Londoner' into these senses.*
1 squeamish woman
• *(KL 2.4.118) The Fool encourages Lear to tell his heart to stay calm 'as the cockney did to the eels' that she put into a pie without killing them first.*
2 an indecisive or foolish boy
• *(TN 4.1.12) Feste thinks Sebastian's way of talking is foppish, and fears the whole world 'will prove a cockney'—will end up in the same way.*

cockpit NOUN see ILLUSTRATION, p.113
theatre pit
• *(H5 Prologue.Chorus.11) The Chorus asks the audience: 'Can this cockpit hold / The vasty fields of France?'*

codling NOUN
half-grown apple
• *(TN 1.5.147) Malvolio compares Cesario's age to 'a codling when 'tis almost an apple'.*

codpiece see CLOTHING, p.158

cog VERB
deceive
• *(MA 5.1.95) Antonio describes Claudio and Don Pedro as boys 'That lie and cog and flout'—lie, deceive, and scoff at others.*

› **cogging** ADJECTIVE
deceiving
• *(Oth 4.2.131) Emilia thinks 'Some cogging, cozening slave' has slandered Desdemona.*

cognizance NOUN
token
• *(JC 2.2.89) Decius interprets Calpurnia's dream as great men rushing to get from Caesar's blood 'tinctures, stains, relics, and cognizance'—any kind of memorial of him.*

cohort NOUN
company of soldiers
• *(KL 1.2.141) Edmund is reading a book which talks about the 'dissipation of cohorts'—the scattering of an army.*

coign NOUN [pronounced coin]
projecting corner of a building
• *(Mac 1.6.7) Banquo describes Macbeth's castle as a place where martlets nest in every 'coign of vantage'—any opportune corner.*

coil NOUN
turmoil
• *(Ham 3.1.67) Hamlet reflects on death, 'When we have shuffled off this mortal coil'—when we have left the bustle of life behind.*

coining NOUN
the making of coins
• *(KL 4.6.83) Lear announces: 'they cannot touch me for coining'—tell me off for making coins (as this was something the king was entitled to do).*

coistrel NOUN
low fellow
• *(TN 1.3.37) Sir Toby calls anyone not drinking a toast to his niece 'a coward and a coistrel'.*

Colchos NOUN [pronounced **kol**-kos]
a spelling of Colchis, an ancient region at the eastern end of the Black Sea
• *(MV 1.1.171) Bassanio says Portia's house is similar to 'Colchos' strand'—a majestic stretch of shore.*
In Greek mythology, Colchos was the home of the Golden Fleece—a fabulous prize which was the quest of Jason and the Argonauts.
see MAP, p.176

Colin o custure me
[pronounced **ko**-lin oh ku-**stoo**-ray may]
an unclear expression, thought to be a refrain from a popular Irish Gaelic ballad meaning 'Maiden, my treasure'
• *(H5 4.4.3) Pistol has heard a French prisoner say he is 'bon qualité' (or 'of high rank'), but misunderstands: 'Quality? "Colin o custure me"'—an appropriate remark, because he anticipates a high ransom in return for a prisoner of 'quality'.*

collar NOUN
as well as meaning 'piece of clothing that goes around the neck', you'll find:
hangman's noose
• *(RJ 1.1.4) Gregory tells Sampson to 'draw your neck out of collar'—keep clear of the hangman (he would be hanged if he started a fight and killed someone).*

collected ADJECTIVE
calm
• *(Tem 1.2.13) Prospero tells distraught Miranda to 'Be collected'—don't be upset!*

collection NOUN
as well as meaning 'accumulation of things', you'll find:
deduction
• *(Ham 4.5.9) Ophelia's incoherent talk moves 'The*

hearers to collection'—listeners have to work out what she means for themselves.

collied ADJECTIVE
darkened
• *(MND 1.1.145) Lysander talks about what can make love as 'Brief as the lightning in the collied night'.*

Colm see **Saint Colm's Inch**

Colmkill also spelled **Colmekill** NOUN
Iona, an island off the west coast of Scotland, the traditional burial place for Scottish kings
• *(Mac 2.4.33) Macduff says that Duncan's body has been 'Carried to Colmkill'.*

coloquintida NOUN
[pronounced kol-uh-**kwin**-ti-da]
bitter-apple
• *(Oth 1.3.345) Iago tells Roderigo that the nice-tasting food that Othello is now eating (meaning Desdemona) will soon taste as sharp 'as the coloquintida'.*

Colossus NOUN
a huge bronze statue of the sun god Apollo that used to straddle the harbour entrance to the port of Rhodes
• *(JC 1.2.136) Cassius describes Caesar as someone who 'doth bestride the narrow world / Like a Colossus'.*

colour NOUN
as well as the everyday sense, you'll find:
1 convincing reason
• *(JC 2.1.29) Brutus thinks any complaint to Caesar 'Will bear no colour for the thing he is'—there's no good reason for complaining in Caesar's present state of mind.*
2 pretext
• *(H5 2.2.113) Henry is scornful about devils who clumsily disguise their temptations by covering them 'With patches, colours, and with forms' that give the appearance of holiness.*
3 appearance
• *(Ham 1.2.68) Gertrude asks Hamlet to 'cast thy nighted colour off'—his black mourning clothes (or sad looks).*

colour VERB
1 disguise
• *(Ham 2.2.276) Hamlet sees in Rosencrantz and Guildenstern's faces a confession that they 'have not craft enough to colour'—not clever enough to hide.*
2 explain
• *(Ham 3.1.45) Polonius asks Ophelia to read a book to explain why (having previously been kept away from any opportunity to meet Hamlet) she is on her own when she encounters him—'That show of such an exercise may colour / Your loneliness'.*

› **colours** NOUN
as well as meaning 'battle-flags', you'll find: standard-bearer (a soldier who carries his army's emblem or flag)
• *(Mac 5.2.1) Stage direction: 'Drum and colours'.*

› **fear no colours**
fear nothing
• *(TN 1.5.5) Feste says 'he that is well hanged in this world needs to fear no colours'—with a pun on 'collars', the hangman's noose (as well as a possible sexual pun on large male genitals).*

combustion NOUN
⚠ *Don't read in the meaning of 'burning'.*
tumult
• *(Mac 2.3.53) Lennox describes the unnatural things that have taken place which prophesy 'dire combustion and confus'd events'.*

comedian NOUN
⚠ *Don't read in the modern meaning of 'stand-up comic'.*
actor
• *(TN 1.5.170) Olivia asks Cesario, who is about to deliver a speech: 'Are you a comedian?'*

come thy ways see **ways**

comfit also spelled **comfect** NOUN
sweetmeat
• *(MA 4.1.313) Beatrice sarcastically calls Claudio 'Count Comfit, a sweet gallant, surely'.*

comfort NOUN
happiness
• *(RJ 3.3.165) Romeo is glad to receive Juliet's ring: 'How well my comfort is revived by this'.*
🎭 *A ring would often be used as proof that the message one is being given by a third party is truly from the right person.*

comfort VERB
help
• *(KL 3.5.18) Edmund hopes to find Gloucester 'comforting the King', to support the case that his father is a traitor.*

› **discomfort** NOUN
loss of heart
• *(Mac 1.2.28) The Captain reports how, after making apparent progress in the battle, 'Discomfort swells'.*

› **discomfort** VERB
1 dishearten
• *(JC 5.3.106) Brutus says Cassius' funeral 'shall not be in our camp / Lest it discomfort us'.*
2 worry
• *(Ham 3.2.158) The Player Queen tells her*

a b Cc d e f g h i j k l m n o p q r s t u v w x y z

husband that her fears for him should not 'Discomfort you'.

comfortable ADJECTIVE

⚠ *Don't read the modern meanings of 'being at ease' and 'not feeling discomfort' into these senses.*

comforting

- *(RJ 5.3.148) Juliet addresses Friar Lawrence: 'O comfortable Friar!'*

  › uncomfortable ADJECTIVE
  comfortless
  - *(RJ 4.5.60) Capulet describes Juliet's death as an 'Uncomfortable time'.*

coming-in NOUN

income

- *(H5 4.1.231) Henry asks an imagined personification of ceremony about its benefits: 'What are thy comings-in?'*

comma NOUN

the smallest punctuation mark, *or* in music, a tiny interval of pitch

- *(Ham 5.2.42) Claudius tells England that peace should 'stand a comma 'tween their amities'—bring them closely together (not even the smallest trouble should cause friction between their countries).*

commeddle VERB

mix together

- *(Ham 3.2.67) Hamlet considers people blessed whose passion and reasonable way of thinking are 'well commeddled'.*

commend VERB

as well as meaning 'praise' and 'entrust', you'll find:

1 present

- *(H5 4.6.23) Exeter reports York's dying words: 'Commend my service to my sovereign'—report my loyal work to the king.*

2 show well

- *(Ham 1.2.39) Claudius tells the ambassadors: 'let your haste commend your duty'—if you are quick in your work, it will show your loyalty to me.*

see also GOODBYE, p.121

  › discommend VERB
  find fault with
  - *(KL 2.2.105) Kent tells Cornwall he will switch out of the dialect 'which you discommend so much'.*

commissioner NOUN

official who acts for the king in his absence

- *(H5 2.2.60) Henry asks: 'Who are the late commissioners?'—the recently appointed officials.*

commodity NOUN

1 supply

- *(TN 3.1.42) Feste implores Jove to give Cesario a beard 'in his next commodity of hair'.*

2 benefit

- *(KL 4.1.21) Gloucester reflects that often our personal defects 'Prove our commodities'.*

commoner NOUN

prostitute

- *(Oth 4.2.72) Othello calls Desdemona a 'public commoner!'*

commons NOUN

citizens

- *(JC 3.2.129) Antony asks if the people want to hear Caesar's will: 'Let but the commons hear this testament'.*

compact ADJECTIVE

1 in league

- *(KL 2.2.114) Oswald reports how Kent 'compact, and flattering his displeasure, / Tripp'd me behind'—conspiring with the king, and adding to his dislike of me, tripped me from behind.*

2 made up

- *(KL 1.2.7) Edmund reflects that his bodily dimensions 'are as well compact' as Edgar's—as well formed as his brother's.*

companion NOUN

as well as meaning 'comrade', you'll find:

rogue

- *(JC 4.3.138) Brutus orders an irritating poet to leave: 'Companion, hence!'*

comparison NOUN

scoffing allusion

- *(MA 2.1.135) Beatrice says that Benedick will 'break a comparison or two on me'—speak in a scoffing way.*

compass VERB

1 achieve

- *(TN 1.2.44) The Captain tells Viola that becoming a servant to Olivia 'were hard to compass'—would be a difficult task to pull off (because she's in mourning after the death of her brother).*

2 surround

- *(Mac 5.9.23) Macduff sees Malcolm 'compass'd with thy kingdom's pearl'—surrounded by the best of the nobles (and also, wearing the crown).*

3 go around

- *(MND 4.1.96) Oberon says he and Titania 'the globe can compass soon'—quickly make an orbit of the earth.*

compass NOUN

⚠ *Don't read the meanings of devices for 'showing direction' and 'drawing circles' into these senses.*

1 range

• *(RJ 4.1.47) The Friar says that Juliet's grief 'strains me past the compass of my wits'—her upset is so great that it is pushing him to the limit of his ability to deal with her.*

2 revolution

• *(Oth 3.4.67) Othello tells Desdemona of a prophetess who had 'number'd in the world / The sun to course two hundred compasses'—had lived 200 years.*

COMPARISONS

Here are twelve of Shakespeare's vivid similes, all introduced by 'like' or 'as'.

• *(MND 2.2.100) Helena thinks she is 'as ugly as a bear'.*
• *(RJ 2.5.13) Juliet wants the Nurse to be 'as swift in motion as a ball'.*
• *(Ham 4.5.191) Ophelia sings that Polonius' beard was 'as white as snow'.*
• *(H5 3.1.31) King Henry sees that his soldiers are ready to fight, standing 'like greyhounds in the slips'.*
• *(JC 3.2.114) A citizen describes Antony's eyes as 'red as fire with weeping'.*
• *(KL 4.3.22) A gentleman describes Cordelia's tears leaving her eyes 'As pearls from diamonds dropp'd'.*
• *(Mac 5.2.21) Angus says that Macbeth's title hangs loose about him 'like a giant's robe / Upon a dwarfish thief'.*
• *(MA 5.1.4) Leonato says advice falls into his ears 'as profitless / As water in a sieve'.*
• *(MV 4.1.183) Portia says that mercy 'droppeth as the gentle rain from heaven / Upon the place beneath'.*
• *(Tem 5.1.16) Ariel describes Gonzalo's tears running down his beard 'like winter's drops / From eaves of reeds'.*
• *(TN 2.4.113) Viola's imaginary unloved sister sat 'like Patience on a monument, / Smiling at grief'.*
• *(Oth 2.1.286) Iago says the thought that Othello has made love to Emilia 'Doth like a poisonous mineral gnaw my inwards'.*

compeer VERB

equal

• *(KL 5.3.70) In Regan's opinion, Edmund 'compeers the best'—he's the match of anyone.*

competency NOUN

a moderate lifestyle

• *(MV 1.2.9) Nerissa thinks that, compared with a way of life given over to excess, 'competency lives longer'.*

competent also spelled **computent** ADJECTIVE

1 equivalent

• *(Ham 1.1.93) King Hamlet received an amount of land from King Fortinbras, after killing him in a duel. He had pledged to give Fortinbras 'a moiety competent'—the same amount of land, if the victory had gone the other way.*

2 to be reckoned with

• *(TN 3.4.225) Sir Andrew's anger is said to derive from 'a very computent injury'—a wrong done to him that needs to be settled.*

competitor NOUN

⚠ *Don't read in the meaning of 'rival'.*

partner

• *(TN 4.2.10) Feste sees Sir Toby and Maria arrive: 'The competitors enter'.*

complain VERB

⚠ *Don't read in the meaning of 'make a complaint'.*

lament

• *(RJ 1.5.150) The Chorus says of Romeo: 'to his foe suppos'd he must complain'—he must pour out his grief to Juliet, whom people expect to be his enemy.*

comply VERB

1 observe the formalities

• *(Ham 2.2.362) Hamlet tells Rosencrantz and Guildenstern: 'Let me comply with you in this garb'—follow the formal fashion in welcoming someone.*

2 satisfy

• *(Oth 1.3.260) Othello wants Desdemona to go with him not simply 'to comply with heat'—to satisfy the hot passion he has for her.*

composition NOUN

⚠ *Don't read the meaning of 'school essay' into these senses.*

as well as meaning 'the make-up of' and 'something composed', you'll find:

1 truce

• *(Mac 1.2.59) Ross tells King Duncan that 'Sweno, the Norways' king, / Craves composition'.*

2 consistency

• *(Oth 1.3.1) The Duke has received differing*

a b Cc d e f g h i j k l m n o p q r s t u v w x y z

accounts about the size of the Turkish fleet: 'There is no composition in these news'.

compound VERB
as well as meaning 'combine', you'll find:
reach an agreement
• *(H5 4.3.80) Montjoy asks Henry 'If for thy ransom thou wilt now compound'—agree to surrender.*
make
• *(H5 5.2.200) Henry suggests that he and Katherine 'compound a boy, half French half English'.*

compound ADJECTIVE
composed of the elements
• *(Ham 3.4.49) Hamlet describes the Earth as 'this solidity and compound mass'.*

comprehend VERB
intended to mean 'apprehend'
• *(MA 3.3.23) Dogberry tells his Watch: 'you shall comprehend all vagrom men'—arrest all vagrants.*

compromise VERB
⚠*Don't read in the modern meaning of 'expose to danger' (as in 'our position was compromised').*
reach an agreement
• *(MV 1.3.73) Shylock tells the biblical story of how Jacob and Laban 'were compromis'd' to share their sheep.*

compt or **count** NOUN
the day of judgement
• *(Oth 5.2.271) Othello thinks about when he and Desdemona 'shall meet at compt'.*

› **in compt** or **count**
held in trust
• *(Mac 1.6.27) Lady Macbeth says everything they possess is 'in count' to King Duncan.*

comptible ADJECTIVE
sensitive
• *(TN 1.5.163) Cesario asks Olivia not to scorn him: 'I am very comptible, even to the least sinister usage'.*

compunctious ADJECTIVE
remorseful
• *(Mac 1.5.44) Lady Macbeth wants 'no compunctious visitings of nature' to make her change her mind.*

con VERB
⚠*Don't read in the modern slang meaning of 'swindle'.*
learn by heart
• *(MND 1.2.87) Quince gives his actors their parts for their play and says: 'con them by tomorrow night'.*

conceit NOUN
⚠*Don't read the meaning of 'vanity' or 'being vain' into these senses.*
1 imagination
• *(Ham 3.4.114) The Ghost is concerned about Gertrude's state of mind: 'Conceit in weakest bodies strongest works'.*
2 opinion
• *(MA 2.1.275) Don Pedro says of Claudio: 'his conceit is false'—he has got things wrong.*
3 design
• *(Ham 5.2.145) Osric describes the rapier accessories as being 'of very liberal conceit'—very fancy design.*
4 trinket
• *(MND 1.1.33) Egeus accuses Lysander of stealing his daughter's heart by giving her 'rings, gauds, conceits'.*

conceit VERB
1 imagine
• *(JC 3.1.192) Antony tells the conspirators: 'you must conceit me, / Either a coward or a flatterer'.*
2 speculate
• *(Oth 3.3.150) Iago describes himself as someone who 'imperfectly conjects'—doesn't predict well how things will turn out.*
✒ *'Conceits' is used in the First Folio text of the play. The First Quarto has 'conjects'.*

› **conceited** ADJECTIVE
of the same opinion
• *(TN 3.4.269) We hear that Cesario has as frightening an idea of Sir Andrew as Andrew has of Cesario: 'He is as horribly conceited of him'—they are both terrified of each other.*

concernancy NOUN
relevance
• *(Ham 5.2.119) Hamlet asks Osric to get to the point: 'The concernancy, sir?'*

conclusions see **try conclusions**

condition NOUN
as well as meaning 'situation' and 'terms', you'll find:
quality
• *(Oth 2.1.242) Roderigo describes Desdemona as being 'full of most blest condition'.*

› **best-conditioned** also spelled **-condition'd, best conditioned** ADJECTIVE
best-natured
• *(MV 3.2.291) Bassanio says Antonio has a 'best-condition'd and unwearied spirit' / In doing courtesies'—he's at his best when he's helping someone.*

condoling ADJECTIVE
moving
• *(MND 1.2.34) Bottom reflects on a character in their play: 'a lover is more condoling'.*

conduct NOUN
as well as meaning 'behaviour' and 'guide', you'll find:
1 leader
• *(RJ 5.3.116) Romeo addresses the poison: 'Come, bitter conduct, come, unsavoury guide!'*
2 protection
• *(TN 3.4.221) Cesario, fearful of an attack, wants 'some conduct of the lady'—bodyguard protection arranged by Olivia as he leaves.*

› **conductor** NOUN
⚠ *Don't read in the modern meanings to do with orchestras or buses.*
leader
• *(KL 4.7.88) A Gentleman asks about Cornwall: 'Who is conductor of his people?'*

confederate ADJECTIVE
allied
• *(Ham 3.2.245) The character of Lucianus (in the 'play within a play') finds it a 'Confederate season' to commit murder—a helpful time (as King Hamlet sleeps alone, outside in his orchard, during the daytime).*

confession NOUN
⚠ *Don't read in the meaning of 'admitting wrongdoing'.*
acknowledgement
• *(Ham 4.7.95) Claudius tells Laertes that Lamord 'made confession of you'—gave Claudius a report of Laertes' achievements during his time abroad.*

confidence NOUN
as well as meanings to do with 'trust', 'certainty' and 'secrecy', you'll find:
1 over-confidence
• *(JC 2.2.49) Calpurnia tells Caesar: 'Your wisdom is consum'd in confidence'—destroying your good judgement.*
2 intended to mean 'conference'
• *(MA 3.5.2) Dogberry addresses Leonato: 'I would have some confidence with you'.*

confine NOUN
1 place of confinement
• *(Tem 4.1.121) Prospero is able to call spirits 'from their confines'.*
2 domain
• *(RJ 3.1.6) Mercutio describes what happens when Benvolio 'enters the confines of a tavern'.*

› **confined** ADJECTIVE
bounded
• *(KL 4.1.73) Gloucester knows of a cliff near Dover whose top 'Looks fearfully in the confined deep'—a sea that has boundaries (the Channel between England and France).*

› **confineless** ADJECTIVE
boundless
• *(Mac 4.3.55) Malcolm claims he can cause 'confineless harms'—unlimited hurts.*

confound VERB
as well as meaning 'amaze', you'll find:
destroy
• *(H5 4.5.3) Bourbon laments: 'all is confounded, all!'—all is lost!*

› **confounded** ADJECTIVE
destroyed
• *(H5 3.1.13) Henry describes a cliff, battered by storms, overhanging 'his confounded base'.*

confusions in the phrase **try confusions**
intended to mean 'try conclusions'
see **try conclusions**
• *(MV 2.2.34) Lancelot decides to talk to his father, Gobbo: 'I will try confusions with him'.*

congree VERB
come together in agreement
• *(H5 1.2.182) Exeter says that, even though government is split between home and abroad, it 'doth keep in one consent, / Congreeing'—everyone agrees that England should go to war with France.*

congreet VERB
exchange greetings
• *(H5 5.2.31) The English and French kings 'have congreeted'.*

congrue VERB
agree
• *(Ham 4.3.64) Claudius asks the English king to kill Hamlet, in 'letters congruing to that effect'.*

conjecture NOUN
as well as meaning 'guess', you'll find:
1 suspicion
• *(Ham 4.5.15) Horatio fears Ophelia 'may strew / Dangerous conjectures in ill-breeding minds'.*
2 imaginary case
• *(H5 4.Chorus.1) The Chorus asks the theatre audience to 'entertain conjecture of a time'—use their imaginations to see the situation of the armies ready to do battle.*

› **conject** VERB see **conceit**

conjunct ADJECTIVE
united
• *(KL 5.1.12) Regan thinks that Edmund has been having an affair with Goneril: 'you have been conjunct / And bosom'd with her'—close and coupled (had sex with her).*

a b Cc d e f g h i j k l m n o p q r s t u v w x y z

conjunction NOUN
uniting
• *(H5 5.2.332) The French king describes the treaty with England as a 'dear conjunction'.*

> **conjunctive** ADJECTIVE
> closely united
> • *(Oth 1.3.360) Iago tells Roderigo: 'Let us be conjunctive in our revenge'—let's plan our revenge together.*

conjure VERB
as well as meaning 'cast magic spells' or 'bring about by magic', you'll find:
1 ask solemnly
• *(Mac 4.1.49) Macbeth addresses the Witches: 'I conjure you ... answer me'.*
2 exorcise
• *(MA 2.1.238) Benedick hopes that 'some scholar would conjure' Beatrice—thinking of her as someone possessed by a demon.*

> **conjuration** NOUN
> 1 entreaty
> • *(RJ 5.3.68) Paris rebuffs Romeo: 'I do defy thy conjuration'.*
> 2 incantation
> • *(Oth 1.3.92) Othello says he will reveal with 'What conjuration and what mighty magic' he won Desdemona's love.*

consanguineous ADJECTIVE
[pronounced kon-san-**gwin**-ee-us]
related in blood
• *(TN 2.3.69) Sir Toby asks of Olivia: 'Am I not consanguineous? Am I not of her blood?'*

conscience NOUN
as well as meaning 'knowledge of right and wrong', you'll find:
1 inmost thoughts
• *(H5 4.1.113) The disguised King Henry tells Bates: 'I will speak my conscience of the king'.*
2 feeling of obligation
• *(TN 3.3.17) Sebastian tells Antonio he would give him better reward, 'were my worth, as is my conscience, firm'—if his wealth were as secure as is his state of mind.*

conscionable ADJECTIVE
right-thinking
• *(Oth 2.1.230) Iago says Cassio gives only a superficial appearance of being scrupulous: 'no further conscionable than in putting on the mere form of civil and humane seeming'.*

consequence NOUN
course of events
• *(Oth 2.3.55) Iago hopes the 'consequence do but approve my dream'—confirm my expectations.*

> **in this consequence**
> in the following way
> • *(Ham 2.1.46) Polonius suggests to Reynaldo how an acquaintance of Laertes might speak to him: 'He closes with you in this consequence'—speaks confidentially to you in this way.*

> **consequently** ADVERB
> subsequently
> • *(TN 3.4.66) Malvolio next reads in Olivia's letter how he is to behave in front of everyone: she 'consequently sets down the manner how'.*

consideration NOUN
as well as meaning 'careful thought', you'll find:
spiritual self-examination
• *(H5 1.1.28) Canterbury describes how 'Consideration like an angel came' and changed Henry's youthful behaviour.*

consign VERB
agree
• *(H5 5.2.90) Henry tells his Council members to alter the treaty with France as they see fit 'And we'll consign thereto'.*

consonancy NOUN
1 accord
• *(Ham 2.2.280) Hamlet solemnly asks his friends to be frank with him 'by the consonancy of our youth'—swearing by their youthful companionship.*
2 consistency
• *(TN 2.5.120) Malvolio tries to interpret Olivia's letter: 'there is no consonancy in the sequel'—what comes next doesn't make sense.*

constable also spelled **Constable** see **OCCUPATIONS, p.166**

constellation NOUN
as well as meaning 'an arrangement of stars in the sky', you'll find:
disposition
• *(TN 1.4.35) Orsino tells Cesario that 'thy constellation is right apt' for approaching Olivia.*
Similarly to today's horoscopes, the stars were once thought to influence a person's character and mood.

conster VERB
1 explain
• *(TN 3.1.54) Feste says he will report Cesario's*

arrival to Olivia's household staff: 'I will conster to them whence you come'.

2 interpret

• *(Oth 4.1.101) Iago knows that Othello 'must conster / Poor Cassio's smiles, gestures, and light behaviours / Quite in the wrong'.*

'Conster' is used in the Quarto editions of 'Othello'. The First Folio has 'conserve', which some editors have taken to be an error for 'construe'.

› **misconster** VERB

misinterpret

• *(MV 2.2.175) Bassanio is worried in case Gratiano's wild behaviour makes him 'misconster'd in the place I go to'—give an unintentionally bad impression.*

construction NOUN

1 judgement

• *(TN 3.1.111) Olivia tells Cesario she regrets what she has done: 'Under your hard construction must I sit'—your painful judgement.*

2 interpretation

• *(TN 2.3.158) Maria tells the others to note how Malvolio responds to Olivia's letter: 'Observe his construction of it'.*

› **misconstruction** NOUN

misinterpretation

• *(KL 2.2.113) Oswald explains how Lear did 'strike at me, upon his misconstruction'—because of a misunderstanding.*

contagion NOUN

Don't read meanings to do with disease into these senses.

1 infectious influence

• *(TN 2.3.51) Sir Toby drunkenly reflects on Feste's song: 'To hear by the nose, it is dulcet in contagion'—sweet in its infection.*

2 poison

• *(Ham 4.7.147) Laertes says he will put poison on the end of the sword: 'I'll touch my point / With this contagion'.*

› **contagious** ADJECTIVE

1 harmful

• *(MND 2.1.90) Titania complains to Oberon that, because of their arguing, the winds 'have suck'd up from the sea / Contagious fogs'.*

2 catchy

• *(TN 2.3.49) Sir Toby says of Feste, after his song, that he has 'A contagious breath'.*

contemn VERB

despise

• *(KL 4.2.32) Albany criticizes Goneril for having a 'nature, which contemns its origin'.*

› **contemned** also spelled **contemn'd**

ADJECTIVE

despised

• *(KL 4.1.2) Edgar reflects that he would rather be in his despised state than 'still contemn'd and flatter'd'—always being praised by people who really despise you.*

contemplative ADJECTIVE

mindless

• *(TN 2.5.17) Maria says Olivia's letter to Malvolio 'will make a contemplative idiot of him'.*

contemptible ADJECTIVE

scornful

• *(MA 2.3.176) Don Pedro describes Benedick as having 'a contemptible spirit'.*

Note that the meaning of 'contemptible' is not directed at Benedick himself. Pedro is saying that Benedick readily scorns other people.

content ADJECTIVE

as well as meanings to do with being 'happy' and 'satisfied', you'll find:

1 agreeable—the usual way of saying that you agree with something

• *(MV 4.1.392) Shylock agrees to the conditions: 'I am content'.*

2 patient

• *(TN 5.1.339) Olivia asks the upset Malvolio to 'be content'.*

content VERB

1 calm down

• *(MA 5.1.87) Antonio tells angry Leonato: 'Content yourself'.*

2 reward

• *(Oth 3.1.1) Cassio tells the musicians: 'I will content your pains'.*

› **contented** ADJECTIVE

1 agreeable

• *(Mac 2.3.130) Everyone agrees with Macbeth's suggestion: 'Well contented'.*

2 calm

• *(KL 3.4.105) The Fool tries to calm Lear (who is tearing off his clothes): 'Prithee, nuncle, be contented'.*

a b **Cc** d e f g h i j k l m n o p q r s t u v w x y z

continent NOUN
⚠*Don't read the meaning of a 'major land mass on the Earth' into these senses.*
1 precis, outline
• *(MV 3.2.130) Bassanio reads the scroll which is 'The continent and summary of my fortune'.*
2 container
• *(Ham 4.4.64) Hamlet reflects on the small size of the contested land 'Which is not tomb enough and continent / To hide the slain'.*
3 globe
• *(TN 5.1.262) Viola describes the sun as 'that orbed continent the fire / That severs day from night'.*
4 bank
• *(MND 2.1.92) Titania describes how rivers 'have overborne their continents'.*

continent ADJECTIVE
self-controlled
• *(KL 1.2.157) Edmund begs Edgar to avoid his father and have 'a continent forbearance till the speed of his rage goes slower'—keep out of his way until he calms down.*

continuate ADJECTIVE
uninterrupted
• *(Oth 3.4.172) Cassio assures Bianca he will be with her 'in a more continuate time'.*

continuer NOUN
someone who can keep going
• *(MA 1.1.129) Benedick wishes his horse was as fast as Beatrice's tongue, 'and so good a continuer'.*

contraction NOUN
marriage contract
• *(Ham 3.4.46) Hamlet condemns Gertrude for an act that 'from the body of contraction plucks / The very soul'—it removes the essence of the marriage sacrament.*

> **sub-contracted** ADJECTIVE
> already betrothed
> • *(KL 5.3.87) Albany tells Regan that Goneril 'is sub-contracted to this lord'—Goneril has been engaged to Edmund at the same time as Regan (there is an analogy in a modern sub-let, where a tenant, having made an agreement with a landlord, makes a secondary agreement with a new tenant).*

contribution NOUN
supplies
• *(JC 4.3.206) Brutus tells Cassius, on their way to battle, that local people 'have grudg'd us contribution'.*

controversy NOUN
as well as meaning 'disagreement', you'll find:
struggle
• *(JC 1.2.109) Cassius recalls how he and Caesar swam in a raging river, 'stemming it with hearts of controversy'—getting to the other side with struggling spirits.*

contumely NOUN [pronounced **con**-tyoom-lee]
scorn
• *(Ham 3.1.71) Hamlet reflects on 'the proud man's contumely'—the scorn of men filled with pride.*

conveniency NOUN
opportunity
• *(Oth 4.2.176) Roderigo complains that every day Iago keeps from him 'all conveniency' to woo Desdemona.*

convent VERB
summon
• *(TN 5.1.369) Orsino says that he will marry Viola when 'golden time convents'—when a favourable time calls us together.*

converse NOUN
conversation
• *(Ham 2.1.43) Polonius tells Reynaldo to sound out 'Your party in converse'—try to engage Laertes' friends in conversation.*

conveyance NOUN
as well as meaning a legal document for land transfer, you'll find:
1 escort
• *(Oth 1.3.282) Othello has Iago accompany Desdemona on her voyage: 'To his conveyance I assign my wife'.*
2 skill
• *(MA 2.1.227) Benedick complains of Beatrice 'huddling jest upon jest with such impossible conveyance upon me'—piling mocking jokes on me with incredible skill.*

convince VERB
overpower
• *(Mac 4.3.142) The Doctor describes sick people whose 'malady convinces / The great assay of art'—defeats the best efforts of medical science.*

convocation NOUN
assembly
• *(Ham 4.3.20) Hamlet tells Claudius that Polonius is being eaten by 'A certain convocation of politic worms'—a group of crafty worms.*

cope VERB
⚠*Don't read the meaning of 'deal with a problem' into these senses.*
1 encounter (in a fight)
• *(KL 5.3.123) Edgar says he is as 'noble as the adversary / I come to cope'.*
2 give in recompense for
• *(MV 4.1.410) Bassanio offers Balthazar three*

thousand ducats in payment for his trouble: 'We freely cope your courteous pains withal'.

Cophetua NOUN [pronounced ko-**fet**-you-a]
an African king, whose love for a beggar-girl is told in a romantic ballad
• *(RJ 2.1.14) Mercutio describes Cupid shooting the arrow 'When King Cophetua lov'd the beggar-maid'.*

copy NOUN
as well as meaning 'duplicate', you'll find:
an example
• *(H5 3.1.24) Henry strongly encourages the nobles in his army: 'Be copy now to men of grosser blood'—of lower breeding.*

coraggio also spelled **coragio** INTERJECTION [pronounced ko-**ra**-gee-oh]
an Italian word for courage
• *(Tem 5.1.257) Stephano encourages Caliban: 'Coraggio, bully-monster, coraggio!'*

coranto NOUN [pronounced ko-**ran**-toh]
a lively dance with quick running steps
• *(H5 3.6.33) The French ladies have advised their nobles to go to English dancing-schools, where they would learn 'swift corantos'.*

cordial NOUN
⚠ *Don't read in the modern meaning of a 'fruit-flavoured drink'.*
restorative
• *(RJ 5.1.85) Romeo addresses the poison: 'Come, cordial and not poison, go with me'—it will 'restore' him to Juliet (in death).*

Corin NOUN
a traditional name given to a love-sick shepherd
• *(MND 2.1.66) Titania reminds Oberon of when he 'in the shape of Corin sat all day' singing to Phillida (a traditional name for a shepherd's beloved).*

corky ADJECTIVE
withered
• *(KL 3.7.28) Cornwall tells his servants to tie Gloucester up: 'Bind fast his corky arms'.*

cornet see MUSIC, p.172

corollary NOUN
extra one
• *(Tem 4.1.57) Prospero tells Ariel to 'Bring a corollary, / Rather than want a spirit'—bring too many spirits rather than too few.*

correspondent ADJECTIVE
responsive
• *(Tem 1.2.297) Ariel assures Prospero he will be 'correspondent to command'.*

corrigible ADJECTIVE
controlling
• *(Oth 1.3.321) Iago tells Roderigo that people have it in themselves to make their own decisions: 'the power and corrigible authority of this lies in our wills'.*

corroborate ADJECTIVE
made strong
• *(H5 2.1.108) Pistol says that Falstaff's heart 'is fracted and corroborate'—both broken and strengthened by what the king has said of him.*
Why he says 'corroborate' is unclear. It may be that Pistol is using a fine-sounding word he doesn't understand.

corse NOUN
corpse
• *(RJ 3.2.54) The Nurse describes Tybalt: 'A piteous corse, a bloody piteous corse'.*

costard NOUN
large kind of apple—used to describe a head
• *(KL 4.6.236) Edgar dares Oswald to 'try whither your costard or my ballow be the harder'—see if your head is harder than my stick.*

costly ADJECTIVE
as well as meaning 'expensive', you'll find:
bountiful
• *(MV 2.9.93) A Messenger describes a young Venetian announcing Bassanio's approach: 'A day in April never came so sweet / To show how costly summer was at hand'.*

cote VERB
pass by
• *(Ham 2.2.312) Rosencrantz tells Hamlet that he and Guildenstern saw the players on their way to Elsinore: 'We coted them on the way'.*
Hamlet's friends were very likely on horseback or in a carriage, whereas the Players were probably walking or in a slow-moving horse and cart (with all their luggage of costumes and props).

cot-quean NOUN
a man acting like a housewife
• *(RJ 4.4.6) The Nurse scolds Capulet: 'Go, you cot-quean, go'.*
It would have been highly unusual to find the head of a household taking a practical interest in the affairs of the kitchen.

a b Cc d e f g h i j k l m n o p q r s t u v w x y z

couch VERB
as well as meaning 'lie down' (on a couch or bed), you'll find:
1 hide
• *(Ham 5.1.206) Hamlet sees the funeral procession and tells Horatio: 'Couch we awhile'.*
2 find shelter
• *(KL 3.1.12) A Gentleman describes the storm as being one 'wherein the cub-drawn bear would couch'—even a starving bear (drained of milk by its cubs) wouldn't go out to hunt.*

› **couch down** VERB
crouch
• *(H5 4.2.37) The French Constable boasts that 'England shall couch down in fear, and yield'.*

› **couching** NOUN
bowing
• *(JC 3.1.36) Caesar rejects Metellus Cimber's kneeling before him to present his request—'These couchings, and these lowly courtesies'.*

counsel NOUN
as well as meaning 'advice', you'll find:
1 private thoughts
• *(RJ 2.2.53) Juliet asks who it is that 'stumblest on my counsel'—has overheard her.*
2 self-reflection
• *(MA 2.3.194) Claudio suggests that Beatrice will get over her love for Benedick 'with good counsel'—once she thinks seriously about it.*

› **keep counsel**
keep a secret
• *(Ham 3.2.135) Hamlet tells Ophelia: 'The players cannot keep counsel'.*

count NOUN
as well as meaning 'numerical count', you'll find:
trial
• *(Ham 4.7.17) Claudius explains to Laertes why he could not go 'to a public count' to prove how dangerous Hamlet is.*

countenance NOUN
as well as meaning 'face' or 'expression', you'll find:
1 favourable appearance
• *(Ham 1.3.113) Ophelia tells Polonius that Hamlet 'hath given countenance to his speech' with holy vows.*
2 authority
• *(KL 5.1.63) Edmund says he will use Albany's 'countenance for the battle'—he will assume the same power as Albany while the battle is ongoing.*
3 approval
• *(Ham 4.2.14) Hamlet calls Rosencrantz a sponge 'that soaks up the king's countenance'.*

› **countenance** VERB
confront
• *(Mac 2.3.77) Macduff calls others to come and 'countenance this horror'—of Duncan's murder.*

counter NOUN
1 taking an opposite path—a term from hunting
• *(Ham 4.5.109) Gertrude condemns the people who have risen against them: 'this is counter, you false Danish dogs'.*
2 a contemptuous way of referring to a coin
• *(JC 4.3.80) Brutus tells Cassius he would never 'lock such rascal counters from his friends'—withhold the money they need.*

› **counter-caster** NOUN
someone who works things out with the help of counters (as on an abacus)
• *(Oth 1.1.31) Iago describes Cassio as 'this counter-caster'—not a real soldier.*

counterfeit NOUN
as well as meaning 'false imitation', you'll find:
1 impostor
• *(MND 3.2.288) Helena calls Hermia 'you counterfeit'.*
2 likeness
• *(MV 3.2.115) Bassanio discovers in the casket 'Fair Portia's counterfeit!'—her picture.*

counterfeit VERB
1 pretend
• *(TN 4.2.19) Sir Toby praises Feste, who is playing the role of a priest called Sir Topas: 'The knave counterfeits well'.*
2 imitate
• *(RJ 3.5.131) Capulet compares Juliet's crying to a ship: 'Thou counterfeits a bark, a sea, a wind'—she creaks, cries watery tears, and howls.*

counterfeit ADJECTIVE
1 sham
• *(H5 5.1.64) Gower calls Pistol 'a counterfeit cowardly knave'.*
2 close portrayal
• *(Ham 3.4.54) Hamlet shows Gertrude images of Hamlet and Claudius—'The counterfeit presentment of two brothers'.*

countermine NOUN
tunnel made by the defenders of a fortress to intercept an enemy mine
• *(H5 3.3.8) The Welsh Captain says the enemy has dug 'four yard under, the countermines'.*

counterpoise VERB
match
• *(MA 4.1.27) Claudio asks Leonato what he can give in return for Hero 'whose worth / May counterpoise this rich and precious gift'—something as valuable as the gift he's receiving (Hero's hand in marriage).*

countervail VERB
counterbalance
• *(RJ 2.6.4) Romeo says of Juliet that no amount of sorrow could 'countervail the exchange of joy / That one short minute gives me in her sight'.*

country matters
sexual intercourse—with a rude pun on the first syllable
• *(Ham 3.2.112) Hamlet asks Ophelia: 'Do you think I meant country matters?'*
The previous line (where Hamlet asks to put his head in Ophelia's lap) seems to suggest the pun is to do with oral sex.

County NOUN
Count—a title
• *(RJ 1.3.105) Lady Capulet tells Juliet that Count Paris is waiting for her: 'the County stays'.*

couplet NOUN
pair of young
• *(Ham 5.1.273) Gertrude says Hamlet will be calm as a female dove when 'her golden couplets are disclos'd'—her two chicks are born.*

courage NOUN
man of spirit
• *(Ham 1.3.65) Polonius advises Laertes to keep away from 'each new-hatch'd, unfledg'd courage'—from immature young bloods.*

course NOUN
as well as meaning 'way of proceeding', you'll find:
1 sail attached to the lower parts of a sailing ship
• *(Tem 1.1.46) The Boatswain tries to save his ship: 'Set her two courses'—set two sails in place.*
2 attack by dogs in bear-baiting
• *(Mac 5.7.2) Macbeth concludes: 'bear-like I must fight the course'.*
3 Roman festive chase
• *(JC 1.2.25) Cassius asks Brutus: 'Will you go see the order of the course?'*

course VERB
hunt
• *(KL 3.4.56) Poor Tom says the Devil has made him 'course his own shadow'.*

› **courser** NOUN
swift horse
• *(H5 3.8.41) Bourbon has composed a sonnet addressed 'to my courser'.*

› **coursing** ADJECTIVE
swift-riding
• *(H5 1.2.143) Henry describes the Scots as 'coursing snatchers'—thieves who make quick raids into England.*

court-cupboard NOUN
sideboard
• *(RJ 1.5.5) A Servingman tells his fellow: 'remove the court-cupboard'.*

courtesan also spelled **courtezan** NOUN
prostitute
• *(KL 3.2.79) In the storm, the Fool says: 'This is a brave night to cool a courtezan'—so cold it would cool down the hot desire even of a prostitute.*

court holy-water
courtly flattery
• *(KL 3.2.10) In the storm, the Fool wishes Lear would accept his daughters' empty promises of hospitality: 'court holy-water in a dry house is better than this rain-water out o'door'.*

court of guard
place where there is a guard-room
• *(Oth 2.1.210) Iago says that Cassio 'tonight watches on the court of guard'—he's on duty at the guard-house.*

cousin see FAMILY, p.103

cout see **scout**

cover VERB
as well as meaning 'place over', you'll find:
1 lay the table
• *(MV 3.5.46) Lorenzo asks Lancelot: 'Will you cover then, sir?'*
2 put on a hat
• *(MV 2.9.43) Arragon reflects: 'How many then should cover that stand bare!'*
see also HATS, p.160

› **self-covered** ADJECTIVE
self-concealing
• *(KL 4.2.62) Albany calls Goneril a 'changed and self-cover'd thing'—hiding the devil within her.*

› **uncovered** ADJECTIVE
barefaced
• *(MA 4.1.303) Beatrice attacks the 'public accusation, uncovered slander' of Hero.*

a b **Cc** d e f g h i j k l m n o p q r s t u v w x y z

a b **Cc** d e f g h i j k l m n o p q r s t u v w x y z

coverture NOUN
canopied bower
• *(MA 3.1.30) Ursula sees Beatrice hiding 'in the woodbine coverture'—a honeysuckle-covered enclosure in the garden.*

cowish ADJECTIVE
cowardly
• *(KL 4.2.12) Goneril criticizes her husband Albany: 'It is the cowish terror of his spirit / That dares not undertake'—he is scared to commit himself.*

coxcomb see HATS, p.160

coy ADJECTIVE
⚠ *Don't read in the meaning of 'pretending to be shy'.*
distant
• *(MA 3.1.35) Hero describes Beatrice as 'coy and wild / As haggards of the rock'—as a wild hawk.*

coy VERB
stroke
• *(MND 4.1.2) Titania has Bottom sit down 'While I thy amiable cheeks do coy'.*

coz see FAMILY, p.103

cozen VERB
deceive
• *(KL 5.3.153) Goneril tells Edmund that he has been 'cozen'd and beguil'd'—deceived and tricked.*

› **cozenage** also spelled **coz'nage** NOUN
deception
• *(Ham 5.2.67) Hamlet describes how Claudius has dealt with him 'with such coz'nage'.*

› **cozener** NOUN
deceiver
• *(KL 4.6.159) Lear says: 'The usurer hangs the cozener'—the money-lender is the gallowsman to the trickster (the big cheat condemns the little cheat).*

› **cozening** ADJECTIVE
deceiving
• *(Oth 4.2.131) Emilia thinks 'Some cogging, cozening slave' has thought up the slander on Desdemona.*

cozier see OCCUPATIONS, p.166

crab NOUN
⚠ *Don't read in the meaning of 'shellfish'.*
crab-apple (a small, sour apple)
• *(MND 2.1.48) Puck lurks in an old woman's bowl 'In very likeness of a roasted crab'.*

crabbed ADJECTIVE
bad-tempered
• *(Tem 3.1.8) Ferdinand finds Miranda 'Ten times more gentle than her father's crabb'd'—than her father is irritable.*

crack VERB
as well as meaning 'break' or 'split', you'll find:
1 fall to pieces
• *(Tem 5.1.2) Prospero observes: 'My charms crack not'.*
2 clip—of gold taken illegally from a coin
• *(Ham 2.2.416) Hamlet hopes a young player's voice 'be not cracked within the ring'—with a pun on a voice breaking.*
see also **clipper**
On coins there was a circle (or ring) that went around the sovereign's head. There's also a possible pun on the way a voice can ring (when loud) and can break.

crack NOUN
explosive charge
• *(Mac 1.2.37) The Captain describes Macbeth and Banquo fighting 'As cannons over-charg'd with double cracks'.*

› **crack the wind**
over-use
• *(Ham 1.3.108) Polonius hopes his punning on the word 'tender' will not 'crack the wind of the poor phrase'—make the phrase lose its effect, as when an animal loses energy by being made to go too fast.*

crafty ADJECTIVE
as well as meaning 'cunning', you'll find:
skilfully made
• *(MA 3.1.22) Hero talks about 'little Cupid's crafty arrow'—so well crafted it nearly always hits its target.*

crant NOUN
garland
• *(Ham 5.1.216) Ophelia has been allowed burial dressed in 'her virgin crants' (despite any rumours of her relationship with Hamlet).*

crasing or **crased** see **crazing**

craven ADJECTIVE
cowardly
• *(Ham 4.4.40) Hamlet reflects on whether his inaction is because of 'some craven scruple'—a weak-hearted doubt.*

craven NOUN
coward
• *(H5 4.7.125) The Welsh Captain insists that a soldier should keep his oath: 'He is a craven and a villain else'.*

crazed also spelled **crased** ADJECTIVE
⚠ *Don't read in the meaning of 'insane'.*
flawed
• *(MND 1.1.92) Demetrius tells Lysander to give up 'Thy crazed title to my certain right'.*

crazing also spelled **crasing** NOUN
ricochet
• *(H5 4.3.105) Henry tells Montjoy that the English army will have a second impact 'like to the bullet's crazing'.*

cream VERB
⚠ *Don't read in a meaning to do with 'milk'.*
form a frothy layer on the surface
• *(MV 1.1.89) Gratiano describes men whose faces 'Do cream and mantle like a standing pond'—show no movement (like a pond covered with growth).*

Crécy NOUN
a battle fought in France in 1346 in which Edward III inflicted a major defeat on the French
• *(H5 2.4.54) The French King recalls the time 'When Crécy battle fatally was struck'.*

credent ADJECTIVE
trustful
• *(Ham 1.3.30) Laertes advises Ophelia not to listen to what Hamlet has to say 'with too credent ear'.*

credit NOUN
as well as meanings to do with 'credibility' and 'trust', you'll find:
report
• *(TN 4.3.6) Sebastian, looking for Antonio, says he found a 'credit / That he did range the town to seek me out'.*

crescent ADJECTIVE
as well as meaning 'in a curved shape' (like the moon), you'll find:
developing
• *(Ham 1.3.11) Laertes tells Ophelia that 'nature crescent does not grow' only in a physical way —the mind grows as well.*

crescive ADJECTIVE
growing
• *(H5 1.1.66) Ely describes King Henry's development from being a wild young prince as 'Unseen, yet crescive in his faculty'—with growing capability.*

Cressid or **Cressida** NOUN
in the Trojan Wars, a Trojan woman, beloved by Troilus, who deserted him for Diomed after being taken to the Greek camp
• *(MV 5.1.6) Lorenzo imagines a night when Troilus visited 'the Grecian tents, / Where Cressid lay that night'.*

crest see **ARMOUR, p.154**

Crete NOUN
Mediterranean island, known for its shaggy dogs
• *(H5 2.1.64) Pistol calls Nym a 'hound of Crete'.*
see **MAP, p.176**

crewel ADJECTIVE
made of a thin, coloured smooth yarn
• *(KL 2.4.7) The Fool describes Kent in the stocks: 'he wears crewel garters!'—with a pun on 'cruel'.*
✒ *'Crewell' is the spelling in the First Quarto text of the play. The First Folio has 'cruell'.*

crib NOUN
⚠ *Don't read in the meaning of 'cot for a baby'.*
manger—a long trough from which farm animals feed
• *(Ham 5.2.86) Hamlet says Osric is a beast whose 'crib shall stand at the king's mess'—he'll get his food at the king's table.*

crib VERB
shut in (as in a tiny dwelling)
• *(Mac 3.4.24) Macbeth complains that he is 'cabin'd, cribb'd, confin'd'.*

crime NOUN
⚠ *Don't read in the meaning of 'criminal offence' here.*
offence
• *(KL 1.3.5) Goneril says that Lear 'flashes into one gross crime or other'—moves abruptly to commit vile offences.*

› **crimeful** ADJECTIVE
criminal
• *(Ham 4.7.7) Laertes describes Hamlet's deeds as 'So crimeful and so capital in nature'—criminal and worthy of death (as judged by the natural order of things).*

crisp ADJECTIVE
⚠ *Don't read the modern meaning of 'dry' or 'brittle', as in 'potato crisps', into these senses.*
rippling
• *(Tem 4.1.130) Iris tells her water-nymphs to leave their 'crisp channels'.*

› **crisped** ADJECTIVE
stiffly curled
• *(MV 3.2.92) Bassanio reflects on the nature of 'crisped snaky golden locks' of hair.*

Crispian and **Crispin** NOUN
Crispianus and Crispinus, martyrs under Roman emperor Diocletian in AD 287, whose joint feast day is 25 October
• *(H5 4.3.57) Henry encourages his troops, reminding them that the day of their battle will be remembered as the feast of 'Crispin Crispian'.*

crooked ADJECTIVE
as well as meaning 'illegal', you'll find:
rounded
• *(H5 Prologue.15) The Chorus points out that 'a crooked figure may / Attest in little place a million'—a zero numeral can turn a small number into a large one.*

a b Cc d e f g h i j k l m n o p q r s t u v w x y z

cross VERB
1 prevent
• *(RJ 5.3.20) Paris hears someone approaching in the graveyard 'To cross my obsequies'—who he thinks will interrupt the funeral rites he is preparing for Juliet.*
2 contradict
• *(JC 5.1.19) Antony asks Octavius: 'Why do you cross me?'*
3 thwart, frustrate
• *(MA 1.3.58) Don John admits to hating Claudio: 'If I can cross him any way, I bless myself every way'.*
4 intercept
• *(Ham 1.1.130) Horatio, on seeing the Ghost, says: 'I'll cross it though it blast me'—I'll cross its path even if it destroys me.*

› **cross** ADJECTIVE
as well as meaning 'bad-tempered', you'll find:
1 perverse
• *(RJ 4.3.5) Juliet describes her state of mind as 'cross and full of sin'.*
2 forked
• *(JC 1.3.50) Cassius describes 'the cross blue lightning'.*

cross NOUN
1 obstacle
• *(MA 2.2.4) Don John wants to find 'Any bar, any cross, any impediment' to cause trouble to Claudio.*
2 trial
• *(KL 5.3.277) Lear says he would have dealt with enemies better as a youth: 'I am old now, / And these same crosses spoil me'—these trials devastate me.*

cross-gartering see CLOTHING, p.158

crossway NOUN
crossroad
• *(MND 3.2.383) Puck talks of damned spirits 'That in crossways and floods have burial'—were buried there because they had committed suicide and so (following Christian belief) could not be buried in a churchyard.*

crotchet NOUN
whimsical notion
• *(MA 2.3.56) Don Pedro jokes about the singer Balthasar that 'these are very crotchets that he speaks'—with an obvious pun on musical notes.*

crow NOUN
crowbar
• *(RJ 5.2.21) Friar Lawrence asks Friar John: 'Get me an iron crow'.*

crow-keeper NOUN
scarecrow
• *(KL 4.6.88) Lear comments on an archer: 'That fellow handles his bow like a crow-keeper'.*

crown NOUN
as well as meaning 'royal crown' and an old type of coin, you'll find:
head
• *(Tem 4.1.231) Caliban says of Prospero: 'From toe to crown he'll fill our skins with pinches'.*
see also MONEY, p.197

crowner NOUN
coroner
• *(Ham 5.1.4) The Second Gravedigger tells his colleague about the inquest on Ophelia: 'The crowner hath sat on her'—reached a decision about her death.*

crownet ADJECTIVE
entwined
• *(Ham 4.7.172) Ophelia climbs a willow to hang 'crownet weeds' from the boughs.*

cruels NOUN
cruel creatures or forms of cruelty
• *(KL 3.7.62) Gloucester imagines wolves howling at the gate of Regan's castle, and her telling the porter to open the door, 'All cruels else subscribe'—all other cruel creatures would be kind and so should you be too.*

crusado also spelled **cruzado** NOUN
Portuguese gold coin (which bore the figure of a cross)
• *(Oth 3.4.22) Desdemona would rather have lost her 'purse / Full of crusadoes' than lose her handkerchief.*

crush VERB
as well as meaning 'squeeze and break', you'll find:
1 drink down
• *(RJ 1.2.82) A Servant invites Romeo to 'come and crush a cup of wine'.*
2 force a meaning out of
• *(TN 2.5.129) Malvolio studies the initials written in his letter and tries 'to crush this a little'.*

› **crushed** ADJECTIVE
forced
• *(H5 1.2.175) Exeter says that keeping the army in England would be 'a crush'd necessity'—a need forced on us.*

cry NOUN
as well as meanings to do with 'shouting' and 'weeping', you'll find:
1 company—like a pack of hounds
• *(Ham 3.2.266) Hamlet imagines getting 'a*

fellowship in a cry of players'—becoming a partner in an acting company
2 rumour
• *(Oth 4.1.123) Iago asks Cassio about Bianca: 'the cry goes that you shall marry her'.*

cry VERB
demand
• *(Oth 1.3.273) The Duke tells Othello he must move quickly: 'Th'affair cries haste'.*

crystals NOUN
⚠ *Don't read in the meaning of anything to do with the authors of this book.*
eyes
• *(H5 2.3.46) Pistol tells his wife to wipe her eyes: 'Go, clear thy crystals'.*

cub-drawn ADJECTIVE
drained of milk by cubs
• *(KL 3.1.12) The night is so stormy that it would make 'the cub-drawn bear' stay in her lair, even if she were weak and ravenously hungry.*

cubiculo NOUN [pronounced kyoo-**bik**-you-loh]
bedroom
• *(TN 3.2.47) Sir Toby tells Sir Andrew they will meet 'at thy cubiculo'.*

cubit NOUN [pronounced **kyoo**-bit]
a measure of length or distance (from the length of an adult forearm: about 20 in / 50 cm)
• *(Tem 2.1.252) Antonio describes the distance between Tunis (where Sebastian's sister lives as queen) and Naples (where she is heir to the throne) as one where 'every cubit' sends him the same message—that Sebastian should seize the chance to advance himself as heir.*

cuckold NOUN
a man with an unfaithful wife—a mocking name (from an Old French word for 'cuckoo', a bird that lays its eggs in other birds' nests)
• *(Oth 4.3.74) Emilia asks: 'who would not make her husband a cuckold, to make him a monarch?'*

cuckold VERB
dishonour a man by making his wife unfaithful
• *(Oth 1.3.361) Iago prompts Roderigo to dishonour Othello: 'If thou canst cuckold him, thou dost thyself a pleasure'.*

cucullus see HATS, p.160

cullion NOUN
rascal
• *(H5 3.2.19) The Welsh Captain shouts at his men: 'Avaunt, you cullions!'*

› **cullionly** ADJECTIVE
rascally
• *(KL 2.2.30) Kent calls Oswald a 'whoreson cullionly barber-monger'.*

cullison NOUN
badge
• *(Ham 3.2.49) Hamlet quotes a playgoer saying: 'My coat wants a cullison'—needs a badge.*
This line appears only in the First Quarto text of the play. It is sometimes omitted from modern editions.

cumber VERB
distress
• *(JC 3.1.264) Antony predicts that 'fierce civil strife / Shall cumber all the parts of Italy'.*

cunning ADJECTIVE
as well as meanings to do with 'ingenuity' and 'craftiness', you'll find:
clever, highly skilled
• *(RJ 4.2.2) Capulet tells his Servingman: 'go hire me twenty cunning cooks'.*

cunning NOUN
ruse, deception
• *(KL 2.1.29) Edmund tells Edgar that 'In cunning I must draw my sword upon you'—to fool their father.*

Cupid NOUN
the Roman god of love, depicted as a winged boy with curved bow and arrows, and blindfolded
• *(RJ 1.1.203) Romeo regrets that Rosaline will 'not be hit / With Cupid's arrow'—she won't fall in love with him, no matter what he does or doesn't do.*

curb VERB
bend
• *(Ham 3.4.157) Hamlet tells Gertrude that Virtue must beg pardon of Vice—'curb and woo for leave to do him good'.*
These qualities were personified as female (Virtue) and male (Vice).

› **uncurbed** ADJECTIVE
unrestrained
• *(H5 1.2.244) Henry tells the French Ambassador to give his message 'with uncurbed plainness'.*

curd VERB
curdle
• *(Ham 1.5.69) The Ghost tells how the poison made his blood 'posset / And curd'—clot and curdle.*

cure NOUN
state of health
• *(Oth 2.1.51) Cassio says his hopes of Othello's safe arrival 'Stand in bold cure'—a confident state.*

› **cureless** ADJECTIVE
without remedy
• *(MV 4.1.142) Shylock tells Gratiano to be more intelligent: 'Repair thy wit, good youth, or it will fall / To cureless ruin'.*

a b Cc d e f g h i j k l m n o p q r s t u v w x y z

curious ADJECTIVE

⚠*Don't read the modern meanings to do with 'inquisitiveness' or 'strangeness' into these senses.*

1 attentive to detail

• *(RJ 1.4.31) Mercutio, putting on a mask, doesn't care if a 'curious eye doth cote deformities'—note the way his face is altered (or notice that he isn't a member of the Capulets).*

2 finely made

• *(KL 1.4.30) Kent says one of his skills is to 'mar a curious tale in telling it'—ruin a very well-written story in retelling it.*

› **curiosity** NOUN

attention to detail

• *(KL 1.4.65) Lear says he had noticed the servants' neglect but had put this down to his 'jealous curiosity'—suspicious fussiness.*

› **curiously** ADVERB

1 minutely

• *(Ham 5.1.190) Horatio tells Hamlet not to 'consider too curiously'—not to think about things in such detail.*

2 skilfully

• *(MA 5.1.152) Claudio says he will fight Benedick 'most curiously'.*

currance NOUN

torrent

• *(H5 1.1.34) Canterbury describes the way Prince Hal's reformation came 'With such a heady currance scouring faults'—his faults were cleared away like fast-flowing water.*

currier NOUN

messenger, courier

• *(Mac 1.7.23) Macbeth imagines cherubim (winged angels) riding 'Upon the sightless curriers of the air'—the winds.*

✒*'Curriors' is the spelling in the First Folio. Some editions use the more familiar spelling of 'couriers'.*

currish ADJECTIVE

snarling—like a dog

• *(MV 4.1.133) Gratiano says Shylock has a 'currish spirit'.*

cursitory ADJECTIVE

hurried

• *(H5 5.2.77) The French King says he has looked at the treaty with England 'but with a cursitory eye'—he only glanced at it.*

curst ADJECTIVE

1 bad-tempered

• *(MND 3.2.300) Helena tells Demetrius and Lysander: 'I was never curst'.*

2 angry

• *(KL 2.1.64) Edmund tells his father that he spoke to Edgar 'with curst speech'.*

curtain NOUN

as well as meaning 'covering for a window', you'll find:

banner

• *(H5 4.2.41) The French describe the English army: 'Their ragged curtains poorly are let loose'.*

curtle-axe see **SWORDS AND DAGGERS, p.156**

cushing NOUN

cushion

• *(KL 3.6.34) Kent invites Lear to 'lie down and rest upon the cushings'.*

✒*'Cushings' is the spelling in the First Quarto text of the play. The Second Quarto text has 'cushions'.*

customer NOUN

prostitute

• *(Oth 4.1.119) Cassio is appalled at the thought of marrying Bianca: 'A customer!'*

cut NOUN

as well as its meanings to do with 'separation' and 'wound', you'll find:

work-horse (used to pull ploughs or heavy carts)

• *(TN 2.3.169) Sir Toby tells Sir Andrew that if he does not obtain Olivia in the end, 'call me cut'—you can call me an old nag (old and tired before my time).*

cutpurse NOUN

thief

• *(H5 5.1.78) Pistol says he will become a 'cutpurse of quick hand'.*

cuz see **FAMILY, p.103**

Cyclops NOUN

one-eyed giants who aided Vulcan in forging armour for the gods

• *(Ham 2.2.477) The First Player compares the force of Pyrrhus' sword to 'the Cyclops' hammers' making the armour of Mars.*

cynne also spelled **cynna, cyme** NOUN

[pronounced **sin**-uh or sighm]

a drug that induces vomiting

• *(Mac 5.3.56) Macbeth asks the Doctor 'What rhubarb, cynne, or what purgative drug / Would scour these English hence?'*

'Cyme' may be a typesetter's error for 'cynna'—spelled today as 'senna'—a shrub with medicinal properties as a laxative.

cypress NOUN

Don't read in the meaning of a type of tree.

a type of lightweight fabric (originally from Cyprus), worn as a sign of mourning

• *(TN 3.1.117) Olivia tells Cesario: 'a cypress, not a bosom, / Hides my heart'.*

daff also spelled **doff** VERB

put off

• *(MA 5.1.78) Leonato confronts Claudio: 'Canst thou so doff me?'—brush me off like that?*

dainty ADJECTIVE

as well as meaning 'delicately pretty', you'll find:

1 splendid

• *(Tem 5.1.95) Prospero praises Ariel: 'Why, that's my dainty Ariel!'*

2 fastidious

• *(Mac 2.3.140) Malcolm suggests to Donaldbain: 'let us not be dainty of leave-taking'—let's not waste time being polite and saying goodbye to everyone.*

› **dainty** NOUN

prim response

• *(RJ 1.5.18) Capulet is critical of any lady who 'makes dainty' when invited to dance—who doesn't eagerly accept the offer.*

dalliance NOUN

1 frivolity

• *(H5 2.Chorus.2) The Chorus describes how young men are leaving idleness and their fancy clothes behind as they get ready to fight: 'silken dalliance in the wardrobe lies'.*

2 flirting

• *(Tem 4.1.51) Prospero warns Ferdinand: 'do not give dalliance / Too much the rein'.*

› **dally** VERB

as well as meaning 'act slowly' or 'treat in a casual way', you'll find:

flirt

• *(Ham 3.2.237) Hamlet tells Ophelia he could provide a commentary on her and a lover, imagining them as 'puppets dallying' (or: I could understand you and your love for me if only I could see the puppeteers pulling the strings).*

dam see FAMILY, p.103

damask see COLOURS, p.164

dame see TERMS OF ADDRESS, p.306

Damon NOUN

a man from Syracuse remembered as a model of faithful friendship (for offering his life to save his friend Pythias)

• *(Ham 3.2.270) Hamlet, in a mock ballad, calls Horatio 'O Damon dear'.*

a b c Dd e f g h i j k l m n o p q r s t u v w x y z

Dan see **Don**

Daniel NOUN
in the Bible, a Babylonian administrator and prophet, known for his wise judgements
• *(MV 4.1.221) Shylock calls Balthazar 'A Daniel come to judgement'.*

Dansker NOUN
Dane
• *(Ham 2.1.7) Polonius asks Reynaldo to check 'what Danskers are in Paris'.*

Daphne NOUN
in Greek mythology, a nymph, chased by the sun god Apollo, who was 'saved' by being turned into a laurel tree
• *(MND 2.1.231) Helena says she will run after Demetrius, reversing the story of Daphne fleeing from Apollo: 'Apollo flies, and Daphne holds the chase'—the pursuer becomes the pursued.*

Dardanian ADJECTIVE
a poetic name for a Trojan (in Greek mythology, Troy was founded by Dardanus)
• *(MV 3.2.58) Portia, awaiting Bassanio's choice, compares her followers to 'the Dardanian wives' waiting to hear the outcome of Hercules' exploits.*

dare VERB
as well as meaning 'challenge', you'll find:
1 deliver
• *(Ham 4.4.52) Hamlet reflects on Fortinbras confronting 'all that fortune, death, and danger dare'.*
2 terrify
• *(H5 4.2.36) The Constable boasts that the French approach 'shall so much dare the field' that England will yield.*

> **dareful** ADJECTIVE
> full of defiance
> • *(Mac 5.5.6) Macbeth reflects that, if his situation had been different, he would not have tolerated an English siege of his castle: 'We might have met them dareful'—we might have gone out earlier to fight with them.*

darkling ADVERB
in the dark
• *(MND 2.2.92) Helena asks Demetrius: 'O wilt thou darkling leave me?'*

darnel NOUN
a type of weed
• *(KL 4.4.5) Cordelia describes Lear crowned with 'Darnel, and all the idle weeds that grow / In our sustaining corn'.*

date NOUN
as well as meaning a particular day, you'll find:
period of existence, time
• *(MND 3.2.373) Oberon promises that the lovers will return to Athens with a union 'whose date till death shall never end'—it will last as long as they live.*

> **dateless** ADJECTIVE
> everlasting
> • *(RJ 5.3.115) Romeo gives his last kiss to Juliet as 'A dateless bargain to engrossing Death!'*

daub VERB
as well as meaning 'smear', you'll find:
fake
• *(KL 4.1.51) Edgar finds it difficult to keep up his pretence as Poor Tom: 'I cannot daub it further'.*

Dauphin also spelled **Dolphin** NOUN
the title of the eldest son of the King of France (comparable to Britain's Prince of Wales)
• *(H5 1.2.259) Henry says he is glad 'the Dauphin is so pleasant with us'.*

daw NOUN
jackdaw—thought of as a stupid bird
• *(TN 3.4.33) Malvolio sarcastically rejects Maria's enquiry about his health, making himself out to be a beautiful songbird of the night: 'Yes, nightingales answer daws!'*

dead ADJECTIVE
as well as meaning 'lifeless', you'll find:
1 deadly
• *(MND 3.2.57) Hermia says Demetrius looks like a murderer, 'so dead, so grim'.*
2 death-like
• *(Tem 5.1.230) The Boatswain says he and his men were 'dead of sleep'—sleeping like the dead.*

> **deadly** ADJECTIVE
> death-like
> • *(KL 5.3.289) Kent recounts what has happened: 'All's cheerless, dark, and deadly'.*

dear ADJECTIVE
as well as meaning 'expensive' and 'loved', you'll find:
1 grievous
• *(H5 2.2.177) Henry asks God to forgive the traitors' 'dear offences'.*
2 important
• *(KL 3.1.19) Kent tells a Gentleman 'a dear thing'.*
3 precious
• *(MV 1.1.62) Antonio tells his friends: 'Your worth is very dear in my regard'.*

dear ADVERB
keenly
• *(JC 3.1.196) Antony asks dead Caesar if making*

peace with his murderers will 'grieve thee dearer than thy death'.

› dearly ADVERB
keenly
• *(Ham 4.3.39) Claudius tells Hamlet: 'we dearly grieve / For that which thou hast done'.*

dearn also spelled **dern** ADJECTIVE
dreadful
• *(KL 3.7.60) Gloucester describes 'that dearn time' when Lear was out in the storm.*

death-practised also spelled **-practis'd** ADJECTIVE
whose death has been plotted
• *(KL 4.6.272) Edgar says he will show a paper to Albany, 'the death-practis'd Duke'.*

death's head also spelled **death's-head** NOUN
skull, used as a *memento mori*—a reminder of death
• *(MV 1.2.48) Portia says she would 'rather be married to a death's head' than to the suitors she describes.*

deathsman NOUN
executioner
• *(KL 4.6.253) Edgar regrets that Oswald 'had no other deathsman'.*

debate NOUN
as well as meaning 'formal discussion', you'll find:
quarrel
• *(MND 2.1.116) Titania tells Oberon that 'this same progeny of evils comes / From our debate'—all the bad things that have taken place come from their arguing.*

› debatement NOUN
discussion
• *(Ham 5.2.45) Hamlet's letter asks the English king to execute Rosencrantz and Guildenstern immediately, 'Without debatement further'.*

deboshed also spelled **debauched, deboysed** ADJECTIVE
depraved
• *(Tem 3.2.25) Trinculo calls Caliban 'thou deboshed fish'.*

decern VERB
a mistake for 'concern'
• *(MA 3.5.3) Dogberry tells Leonato that he wants to talk to him about something 'that decerns you nearly'—especially to do with you.*

declension NOUN
decline
• *(Ham 2.2.149) Polonius explains the stages through which Hamlet gradually became mad: he fell 'by this declension, / Into the madness wherein now he raves'.*

decoct VERB
warm up
• *(H5 3.6.20) The Constable asks how the English can 'Decoct their cold blood to such valiant heat'.*

decree NOUN
⚠ *Don't read the meaning of 'official order' into these senses.*
decision
• *(RJ 3.5.138) Capulet asks his wife about Juliet: 'Have you deliver'd to her our decree?'—told her of our plans.*

decree VERB
decide
• *(MA 1.3.29) Don John tells Conrad: 'I have decreed not to sing in my cage'.*

deer NOUN
animals
• *(KL 3.4.131) Poor Tom talks of his food as 'mice and rats and such small deer'.*

deface VERB
⚠ *Don't read in the meaning of 'damage'.*
cancel
• *(MV 3.2.297) Portia tells Bassanio to pay Shylock 'six thousand, and deface the bond'.*

defeat VERB
as well as meaning 'win a victory' and 'bring to nothing', you'll find:
1 spoil
• *(Oth 1.3.336) Iago tells Roderigo to 'defeat thy favour with an usurped beard'—alter your looks by wearing a false beard.*
2 destroy
• *(Oth 4.2.159) Desdemona fears that Othello's 'unkindness may defeat my life'.*

defeat NOUN
act of destruction
• *(Ham 2.2.557) Hamlet reflects on his father, 'Upon whose property and most dear life / A damn'd defeat was made'.*

defect NOUN
as well as meaning 'deficiency', you'll find:
intended to mean 'effect'
• *(MV 2.2.132) Gobbo tells Bassanio: 'That is the very defect of the matter'.*

defence NOUN
as well as meaning 'protection against attack', you'll find:
skill in fencing
• *(TN 3.4.200) Sir Toby advises Cesario: 'That defence thou hast, betake thee to't'.*

a b c **Dd** e f g h i j k l m n o p q r s t u v w x y z

defend in the phrase **God/heaven defend**
forbid
• *(MA 2.1.85) Hero hopes Don Pedro's face will be better than his mask: 'God defend the lute should be like the case'.*

definement NOUN
description
• *(Ham 5.2.110) Hamlet tells Osric he has described Laertes well: 'his definement suffers no perdition in you'—he loses nothing from the way you have described him.*

defunction NOUN
decease
• *(H5 1.2.58) Canterbury talks about the period 'After defunction of King Pharamond'—a 4th-century king of the French.*

defuse see **diffuse**

degree NOUN
⚠*Don't read meanings to do with 'temperature' or 'university qualification' into these senses.*
as well as meaning 'extent', you'll find:
1 social rank
• *(Mac 3.4.1) Macbeth tells his guests: 'You know your own degrees, sit down'—you know where you should sit in relation to me.*
2 stage
• *(TN 1.5.126) Olivia says Sir Toby is 'in the third degree of drink'—well on the way to being drunk.*

delated see **dilated**

deliberate ADJECTIVE
calculating
• *(MV 2.9.79) Portia describes her suitors as 'deliberate fools'.*

delicate ADJECTIVE
as well as meanings to do with 'fine quality', 'skilfulness', and 'fragility', you'll find:
1 delightful
• *(Mac 1.6.10) Banquo observes that, where martlet birds nest, 'The air is delicate'.*
2 pleasure-seeking
• *(MA 1.1.277) Claudio says that thoughts of war have been replaced by 'soft and delicate desires'.*

deliver VERB
as well as meaning 'hand over' and 'be born' you'll find:
tell
• *(Tem 5.1.313) Prospero informs Alonso: 'I'll deliver all'.*

› **redeliver** VERB
report (someone's words)
• *(Ham 5.2.168) Osric asks Hamlet if he should tell Claudius what has been said: 'Shall I redeliver you so?'*
➨*'Redeliver' is used in the First Folio. In the Quarto texts of the play, the verb is 'deliver'.*

delver see **OCCUPATIONS, p.166**

demand VERB
as well as meaning 'ask firmly or forcibly' you'll find:
ask (without any particular force)
• *(Tem 1.2.139) Prospero responds to Miranda's question: 'Well demanded, wench'.*

demand NOUN
question
• *(KL 1.5.3) Lear says that Kent shouldn't tell Regan anything more 'than comes from her demand out of the letter'—only answer questions that directly relate to the letter.*

demerits NOUN
⚠*Don't read in the modern meaning of 'fault'.*
merits
• *(Oth 1.2.22) Othello says 'my demerits / May speak unbonneted'—speak for themselves.*

demesnes NOUN [pronounced de-**meenz**]
lands (from an Old French word meaning 'belonging to a lord')
• *(RJ 3.5.180) Capulet describes Paris as 'A gentleman of noble parentage, / Of fair demesnes'.*

demi-natured see **nature**

demi-puppet NOUN
dwarf-like creature
• *(Tem 5.1.36) Prospero addresses the 'demi-puppets that / By moonshine do the green sour ringlets make'—their footsteps make circles in the grass.*

demi-wolf NOUN
a dog/wolf cross-breed
• *(Mac 3.1.96) Macbeth lists a number of animals including 'demi-wolves', which he says are all called dogs.*

demure ADJECTIVE
⚠*Don't read the modern meaning of 'shy and modest' into these senses.*
serious
• *(TN 2.5.50) Malvolio imagines giving the other members of Olivia's staff 'a demure travel of regard'—a serious look, moving from one to the next.*

› **demurely** ADVERB
in a serious way
• *(MV 2.2.179) Gratiano promises to change his ways and 'look demurely'.*

denay NOUN
refusal
• *(TN 2.4.123) Orsino tells Cesario to express his love to Olivia: 'bide no denay'—don't tolerate any denial.*

Denis, Saint
the first apostle of France, living in the 3rd century
• *(H5 5.2.177) Henry tries to speak French to Katherine and asks for supernatural help: 'Saint Denis be my speed!'*

denote VERB
⚠ *Don't read in the modern meaning of 'be a sign of'.*
reveal
• *(Oth 4.1.277) Iago says of Othello: 'his own courses will denote him'—his actions will reveal his state of mind.*

› **denotement** NOUN
description
• *(Oth 3.3.124) Iago says that Othello has devoted himself to admiring Desdemona and the 'denotement of her parts and graces'.*
✎ *This is the word that appears in the First Folio. The Second Quarto has 'devotement', meaning 'worship'.*

see also **dilation**

deny VERB
as well as meanings to do with 'refusal', you'll find:
disown
• *(RJ 2.2.34) Juliet talks in her mind to Romeo: 'Deny thy father and refuse thy name'.*

deplore VERB
⚠ *Don't read in the modern meaning of 'express strong disapproval'.*
tell with grief
• *(TN 3.1.158) Cesario tells Olivia that he will never again 'my master's tears to you deplore'.*

depositary NOUN
manager of affairs
• *(KL 2.4.248) Lear tells Goneril and Regan he made them 'my guardians, my depositaries'.*

deprave VERB
⚠ *Don't read in the modern meaning of 'pervert'.*
defame
• *(MA 5.1.95) Antonio describes Claudio and Don Pedro as boys who 'deprave and slander'.*

deracinate VERB
uproot
• *(H5 5.2.47) Burgundy bemoans the way the countryside has been ravaged by war in France, with weeds growing wild: 'the coulter rusts / That should deracinate such savagery'—the plough has rusted from lack of use.*

dern see **dearn**

derogate ADJECTIVE
degenerate
• *(KL 1.4.270) Lear curses Goneril's 'derogate body'.*

descry VERB
1 catch sight of
• *(Oth 2.1.4) Because of the storm, the people on shore cannot 'Descry a sail'.*
2 find out
• *(RJ 5.3.181) The First Watchman sees the bodies of Paris and Juliet: 'the true ground of all these piteous woes / We cannot without circumstance descry'—we need further information.*

descry NOUN
sighting
• *(KL 4.6.208) Edgar asks where the British army is, and is told: 'the main descry / Stands on the hourly thought'—we expect to see it at any hour.*

desert also spelled **desart** ADJECTIVE
⚠ *Don't read in the meaning of 'a large area of sand'.*
desolate
• *(Tem 2.1.35) Adrian is puzzled that 'this island seem to be desert'.*

desert NOUN
1 deserving
• *(MV 2.9.50) Arragon says: 'I will assume desert'—acquire what I deserve.*
2 worthy deed
• *(TN 3.4.322) Antonio asks Cesario if it is possible that 'my deserts to you / Can lack persuasion'.*

› **desertless** also spelled **desartless** ADJECTIVE
undeserving—intended to mean 'deserving'
• *(MA 3.3.8) Dogberry asks the Watch: 'who think you the most desertless man to be constable?'*

deserve VERB
as well as meaning 'be worthy', you'll find:
pay back
• *(Oth 1.1.183) Brabantio assures Roderigo: 'I'll deserve your pains'—I'll reward you for your trouble.*

design NOUN
as well as meaning 'scheme', you'll find:
undertaking, task
• *(Mac 2.1.55) Macbeth describes how murder moves stealthily 'towards his design'.*

› **designment** NOUN
undertaking, task
• *(Oth 2.1.22) A Gentleman reports that the storm has so badly affected the Turkish fleet that 'their designment halts'.*

a b c Dd e f g h i j k l m n o p q r s t u v w x y z

desire NOUN
as well as meanings to do with 'wanting something very much', you'll find:
1 good wishes
• *(Ham 2.2.60) Voltemand reports that the Norwegian king sends 'Most fair return of greetings and desires'.*
2 charm
• *(Oth 4.1.94) Iago describes Bianca as someone who lives by 'selling her desires'.*

> **desired** ADJECTIVE
> liked
> • *(Oth 2.1.197) Othello assures Desdemona: 'you shall be well desir'd in Cyprus'.*

despatch see **dispatch**

desperate ADJECTIVE
as well as meaning 'hopeless' and 'hazardous', you'll find:
reckless
• *(KL 2.4.303) Regan says that Lear 'is attended with a desperate train'—a wild band of followers.*

> **desperately** ADJECTIVE
> in a state of despair
> • *(KL 5.3.291) Kent tells Lear that his eldest daughters 'desperately are dead' (one has been poisoned, the other has killed herself).*

> **desperation** NOUN
> reckless despair
> • *(Ham 1.4.75) Horatio describes the Elsinore cliff as a place which 'puts toys of desperation' into the minds of anyone who looks down—foolish thoughts of suicide.*

despite NOUN
1 contempt
• *(Oth 4.2.115) Emilia says Othello has thrown 'such despite and heavy terms' on Desdemona.*
Note that 'despite' is not an adjective here.
2 hatred
• *(TN 3.4.202) Sir Toby describes Sir Andrew to Cesario as 'full of despite'.*

despite VERB
spite
• *(MA 2.2.29) Don John says of Claudio and Hero: 'to despite them I will endeavour anything'.*

determinate ADJECTIVE
1 intended
• *(TN 2.1.9) Sebastian says that his 'determinate voyage is mere extravagancy'—just wandering about.*
2 decisive
• *(Oth 4.2.223) Iago gives a good reason for keeping Othello in Cyprus: 'none can be so determinate as the removing of Cassio'—the only way he'll stay is if Cassio dies and thus cannot deputize for him.*

detraction NOUN
defamation
• *(TN 2.5.127) Fabian (unheard by Malvolio, who is about to read Olivia's letter) says: if 'you had any eye behind you, you might see more detraction at your heels than fortunes before you'—because he and his companions are insulting Malvolio while hiding behind him.*

device NOUN
1 plan
• *(MV 3.4.81) Portia promises to tell Nerissa 'all my whole device / When I am in my coach'—when they are on the road, travelling.*
2 planning
• *(Ham 4.7.64) Claudius tells Laertes of 'an exploit, now ripe in my device'—ready for action.*
3 apparatus
• *(Tem 3.3.53) Stage direction: 'with a quaint device, the banquet vanishes'—using an ingenious mechanism.*
4 excuse
• *(Oth 4.2.174) Roderigo complains that every day Iago puts him off 'with some device'.*
5 production
• *(MND 5.1.50) Theseus says one of the proposed court entertainments is 'an old device'.*

devise VERB
as well as meaning 'invent' or 'imagine', you'll find:
enlighten
• *(Ham 4.7.53) Claudius, baffled by Hamlet's letter, asks Laertes: 'Can you devise me?'*

devotement see **denote**

dewberry NOUN
a type of blackberry
• *(MND 3.1.152) Titania tells her fairies to feed Bottom 'apricocks and dewberries'.*

dewlap NOUN
the folds of loose skin that hang about an old person's neck
• *(MND 2.1.50) Puck makes an old woman spill her beer 'on her wither'd dewlap'.*

> **dewlapped** also spelled **dewlapp'd** ADJECTIVE
> with folds of loose skin hanging from the throat
> • *(Tem 3.3.45) Gonzalo talks of fabled mountain-dwellers 'Dewlapp'd like bulls'.*

dexteriously ADVERB
with easy skill
• *(TN 1.5.54) Feste tells Olivia he can prove her a fool 'Dexteriously'.*

› **dexterity** NOUN
agility
• *(Ham 1.2.157) Hamlet condemns his mother for getting into bed with Claudius so quickly: 'To post / With such dexterity to incestuous sheets'.*

diabolo NOUN [pronounced dee-**ab**-o-loh]
Spanish for 'the devil'
• *(Oth 2.3.145) Iago shouts out at the ringing of the alarm bell: 'Diabolo, ho!'*

dial NOUN
sundial
• *(H5 1.2.210) Canterbury observes that 'many lines close in the dial's centre'—all points come to the same place.*

Dian or **Diana** NOUN
the Roman goddess associated with the moon, chastity, and hunting
• *(RJ 1.1.203) Romeo describes Rosaline as having 'Dian's wit'—the cleverness to avoid lovers.*

Dido NOUN [pronounced **die**-doe]
Queen of Carthage, famous for her faithfulness, who fell in love with Aeneas when he was shipwrecked on her shores
• *(RJ 2.4.41) Mercutio mocks Romeo's romantic view of his lady as someone who makes 'Dido a dowdy'—look slovenly.*

diet NOUN
as well as meaning 'food' (in general), you'll find: board and lodging
• *(Ham 1.1.102) Horatio says Fortinbras has got together a gang of desperadoes who will take on any dangerous enterprise 'For food and diet'.*

diet VERB
feed to a satisfactory level
• *(Oth 2.1.283) Iago reflects on what he will do 'to diet' his revenge.*

difference NOUN
as well as meanings to do with 'not being the same' and 'quarrel', you'll find:
1 change
• *(KL 5.3.287) Kent tells Lear he has followed him since 'your first of difference and decay'.*
2 fine quality
• *(Ham 5.2.105) Osric describes Laertes as 'full of most excellent differences'.*
3 class difference
• *(KL 1.4.84) Kent threatens Oswald: 'I'll teach you differences'.*
4 distinguishing mark—showing a junior branch of a family on a coat-of-arms
• *(MA 1.1.61) Beatrice describes Benedick's wit: 'let him bear it for a difference between himself and his horse'—as a heraldic mark that will show the horse to be superior.*

diffuse also spelled **defuse** VERB
disguise
• *(KL 1.4.2) Kent says he will adopt a false accent 'That can my speech defuse'.*

› **diffused** also spelled **diffus'd** ADJECTIVE
disorderly
• *(H5 5.2.61) Burgundy describes France, where war has made even scholars adopt 'swearing and stern looks, diffus'd attire'—untidy clothes.*

digest also spelled **disgest** VERB
as well as meaning 'take in' and 'swallow', you'll find:
1 organize
• *(Ham 2.2.427) Hamlet describes a play, 'well digested in the scenes'.*
2 endure
• *(H5 2.Chorus.31) The Chorus, describing how the action will move from England to France, says the actors will 'digest / Th'abuse of distance'—swallow up the space between the countries to make the play happen.*

dilate VERB
relate in full
• *(Oth 1.3.152) Othello says how he talked to Desdemona: 'I would all my pilgrimage dilate'—tell her all about my travels.*

dilated also spelled **delated** ADJECTIVE
detailed
• *(Ham 1.2.38) Claudius tells the ambassadors their power is limited to 'the scope / Of these dilated articles'.*

dilation NOUN
indication
• *(Oth 3.3.124) Othello says that pauses in a just man are 'close dilations, working from the heart'—secret expressions of thought.*

'Dilations' is found in the First Folio text of the play. In the First Quarto, the word is 'denotements' (with the same meaning).

dild see POLITENESS, p.230

diluculo surgere see LATIN, p.352

dint NOUN
force
• *(JC 3.2.191) Antony addresses the people: 'I perceive you feel / The dint of pity'.*

a b c **Dd** e f g h i j k l m n o p q r s t u v w x y z

warning note · usage note · theatre note

a b c **Dd** e f g h i j k l m n o p q r s t u v w x y z

direct session
immediate trial
• *(Oth 1.2.86) Brabantio says Othello should go to jail until 'fit time / Of law and course of direct session' calls him to defend himself.*

dirt NOUN
⚠*Don't read in modern meanings to do with 'being rude'.*
a contemptuous way of talking about 'land'
• *(Ham 5.2.87) Hamlet says Osric is 'spacious in the possession of dirt'—he has a lot of land.*

Dis NOUN
Roman god of the underworld (also called Pluto), associated with wealth
• *(Tem 4.1.89) Ceres (the goddess of grain and agriculture) recalls the time that 'dusky Dis my daughter got'—Dis abducted Prosperina (no relation to Prospero) for six months of the year, thus causing the arrival of winter.*

dis-
You will find these words and their definitions in this dictionary without dis-:
disappointed, discommend, dishonest, dishonesty, dislike, dismantle, disnatured, disproportioned, disprove, disquantity, dis-seat.

disaster NOUN
as well as meaning 'very bad misfortune', you'll find:
unlucky sight
• *(Ham 1.1.121) Horatio lists different kinds of ominous events, such as 'Disasters in the sun'—unfavourable aspects of the heavenly bodies.*

discase VERB
take off outer garments
• *(Tem 5.1.85) Prospero tells Ariel: 'I will discase me'.*

discharge VERB
as well as meaning 'carry out' and 'pay', you'll find:
perform in a play
• *(MND 1.2.80) Bottom tells Quince he will play Pyramus: 'I will discharge it'.*

› discharge NOUN
performance
• *(Tem 2.1.249) Antonio plots with Sebastian, saying that what is to happen is 'In yours and my discharge'.*

disclaim VERB
disown
• *(KL 1.1.112) Lear tells Cordelia: 'I disclaim all my paternal care'.*

› disclaiming NOUN
disowning
• *(Ham 5.2.225) Hamlet hopes Laertes will accept his 'disclaiming from a purpos'd evil'—denying that he had any intention of harming Polonius.*

discomfort NOUN
discouragement
• *(Mac 1.2.28) The Captain reports: 'from that spring whence comfort seem'd to come, / Discomfort swells'.*

discomfort VERB
⚠*Don't read the modern meaning of 'feeling uncomfortable' into these senses.*
1 discourage
• *(JC 5.3.106) Brutus says that Cassius' funeral should not be in their camp 'Lest it discomfort us'.*
2 worry
• *(Ham 3.2.158) The Player Queen tells her husband that, though she fears for his health, 'Discomfort you, my lord, it nothing must'.*

discourse NOUN
as well as meaning 'talk', you'll find:
1 faculty of understanding
• *(TN 4.3.12) Sebastian reflects that the events happening to him 'exceed all instance, all discourse'.*
2 course
• *(Oth 4.2.152) Desdemona says she would never have offended Othello, 'Either in discourse of thought or actual deed'.*

discourse VERB
sound out
• *(Ham 3.2.344) Hamlet says the recorder 'will discourse most eloquent music'.*

discover VERB
as well as meaning 'find' or 'expose', you'll find:
1 reveal
• *(Tem 5.1.171) Stage direction: 'Prospero discovers Ferdinand and Miranda'.*
2 recognize
• *(JC 2.1.75) Lucius tells Brutus that he cannot tell who the masked visitors are: 'by no means I may discover them'.*

› discovery NOUN
1 disclosure
• *(MV 2.6.44) Jessica says being a torchbearer is 'an office of discovery'—a role that would reveal who she is, as the torch would light her face.*
2 reconnaissance
• *(Mac 5.4.6) Malcolm says that using branches as camouflage will 'make discovery / Err in*

report of us'—make it difficult for Macbeth's men to report the correct number of his soldiers.

3 exploration

• *(Tem 2.1.238) Antonio suggests that if Sebastian became King of Naples 'even / Ambition cannot pierce a wink beyond, / But doubt discovery there'—an ambitious person looking to explore beyond the goal of kingship wouldn't find anything greater.*

discreet ADJECTIVE

⚠ *Don't read in the meaning of 'not giving away secret information'.*

discerning

• *(RJ 1.1.187) Romeo describes love as 'a madness most discreet'.*

discuss VERB

⚠ *Don't read in the meaning of 'debate'.*

make known

• *(H5 3.3.6) The Welsh Captain says Gower should tell the Duke about the enemy activity: 'you may discuss unto the duke'*

disfigure VERB

⚠ *Don't read in the meaning of 'spoil the appearance'.*

intended to mean 'figure' ('represent')

• *(MND 3.1.51) Quince says one of the company has to 'disfigure, or to present the person of Moonshine'.*

disgest see **digest**

dishclout NOUN

dishcloth

• *(RJ 3.5.219) The Nurse says Romeo is 'a dishclout' compared to Paris.*

disjoint VERB

fall to pieces

• *(Mac 3.2.16) Macbeth says he would rather 'let the frame of things disjoint' than eat a meal in fear and have bad dreams.*

disjoint ADJECTIVE

falling to pieces

• *(Ham 1.2.20) Claudius recalls how young Fortinbras thinks the Danish state 'to be disjoint and out of frame'.*

› **disjoin** VERB

separate

• *(JC 2.1.18) Brutus reflects that 'Th'abuse of greatness is when it disjoins / Remorse from power'.*

disloyal ADJECTIVE

⚠ *Don't read in the meaning of 'being a traitor'.*

unfaithful

• *(MA 3.2.90) Don John accuses Hero: 'the lady is disloyal'.*

dismal ADJECTIVE

⚠ *Don't read in the modern meanings of 'gloomy' or 'feeble'.*

disastrous

• *(RJ 4.3.19) Juliet reflects: 'My dismal scene I needs must act alone'.*

dismissed ADJECTIVE

⚠ *Don't read in the modern meaning of 'permission to leave' or 'being sacked from a job'.*

rejected

• *(Tem 4.1.67) Iris describes the groves 'Whose shadow the dismissed bachelor loves'.*

dismount VERB

⚠ *Don't read in the meaning of 'getting off a horse or bicycle'.*

remove from its sheath

• *(TN 3.4.203) Sir Toby advises Cesario: 'Dismount thy tuck'—draw your sword.*

dispatch also spelled **despatch** VERB

as well as meaning 'send away' and 'kill', you'll find:

1 deal with promptly

• *(MV 3.2.320) Portia urges Bassanio: 'Dispatch all business and be gone'.*

2 hurry up

• *(Oth 4.2.29) Othello tells Emilia to get outside the door: 'Nay, dispatch!'*

3 deprive

• *(Ham 1.5.75) The Ghost recounts how he was 'Of life, of crown, of queen at once dispatch'd'.*

displant VERB

transplant

• *(RJ 3.3.59) Romeo, having been proclaimed an exile, asks the Friar if philosophy can 'Displant a town, reverse a prince's doom'.*

disport NOUN

diversion

• *(Oth 1.3.268) Othello assures the Duke that he will never allow his 'disports corrupt and taint my business'—pleasure to get in the way of work.*

dispose NOUN

as well as meanings to do with 'management',

'arrangement', and 'control', you'll find: manner
• *(Oth 1.3.388) Iago describes Cassio as someone with 'a smooth dispose'.*

› ill-disposed also spelled **ill dispos'd** ADJECTIVE
poorly presented
• *(H5 4.Chorus.51) The Chorus apologizes for the way the actors will present the battle with 'ragged foils / Right ill-dispos'd in brawl ridiculous'.*

› strange-disposed also spelled **strange disposed** ADJECTIVE
with strange happenings taking place
• *(JC 1.3.33) Cicero concurs with Casca's description of events: 'it is a strange-disposed time'.*

› disposition NOUN
1 state of mind
• *(TN 3.1.131) Cesario addresses Olivia: 'Grace and good disposition attend your ladyship'.*
2 affectation, emotional inclination
• *(Ham 1.5.180) Hamlet says he will 'put an antic disposition on'—he will behave in an extrovert way.*

disprized also spelled **dispriz'd** ADJECTIVE
unvalued, unrequited
• *(Ham 3.1.72) Hamlet reflects on 'The pangs of dispriz'd love'.*

dispute VERB
⚠ *Don't read meanings to do with 'arguing' or 'quarrelling' into these senses.*
1 discuss
• *(RJ 3.3.63) The Friar presses Romeo: 'Let me dispute with thee of thy estate'—discuss your situation.*
2 deal with
• *(Mac 4.3.222) Malcolm advises Macduff, who has just heard news of his murdered family: 'Dispute it like a man'.*

› disputation NOUN
words of conversation
• *(H5 3.3.38) The Welsh Captain asks McMorris for 'a few disputations with you'.*

disquietly ADVERB
uneasily
• *(KL 1.2.108) Gloucester tells Edmund: 'all ruinous disorders follow us disquietly to our graves'—terrible troubles stay with us until we die.*

dissemble VERB
1 disguise
• *(TN 4.2.4) Feste receives his Sir Topas disguise: 'I will dissemble myself in't'.*
2 pretend
• *(Oth 3.4.30) Othello finds it difficult to pretend politeness to Desdemona: 'O hardness to dissemble!'*

› dissembler NOUN
deceiver
• *(MA 5.1.53) Leonato calls Claudio 'thou dissembler, thou'.*

› dissembling ADJECTIVE
deceitful
• *(TN 5.1.159) Orsino calls Cesario 'thou dissembling cub!'*

› dissembly NOUN
intended to mean 'assembly'
• *(MA 4.2.1) Dogberry asks: 'Is our whole dissembly appeared?'*

dissipation NOUN
⚠ *Don't read in the meanings of 'wastefulness' or 'immoral way of living'.*
dispersal
• *(KL 1.2.141) Edmund is reading a book which talks about the 'dissipation of cohorts'—the scattering of an army.*

distemper NOUN
1 illness or strange behaviour
• *(Ham 2.2.55) Claudius tells Gertrude that Polonius has found 'The head and source of all your son's distemper'.*
2 state of drunkenness
• *(H5 2.2.53) Henry asks whether mercy should be shown to 'little faults, proceeding on distemper'.*

distemper VERB
disorder
• *(TN 2.1.4) Sebastian warns Antonio: 'the malignancy of my fate might perhaps distemper yours'—the evil influence of my destiny might perhaps put your own into disorder.*

› distempered ADJECTIVE
1 vexed
• *(Tem 4.1.145) Miranda says she has never seen Prospero 'touch'd with anger, so distemper'd'.*
2 disturbed
• *(RJ 2.3.33) The Friar tells Romeo he must have 'a distemper'd head / So soon to bid good morrow to thy bed'—to have got up so early.*
3 insane
• *(Mac 5.2.15) Caithness says that Macbeth cannot 'buckle his distemper'd cause / Within*

the belt of rule'—control his mad course of action by force.

› distempering ADJECTIVE
intoxicating
• *(Oth 1.1.100) Brabantio thinks Roderigo is 'full of supper and distempering draughts'.*

› distemperature also spelled **distemp'rature** NOUN
1 ailment
• *(RJ 2.3.40) The Friar thinks Romeo must be ill to be up so early: 'Thou art uprous'd with some distemp'rature'.*
2 disordered state
• *(MND 2.1.106) Titania describes the effects of her quarrel with Oberon: 'thorough this distemperature we see / The seasons alter'—they are so at one with Nature that their arguments are altering the seasons.*

distil VERB
1 melt
• *(Ham 1.2.204) Horatio describes the sentinels 'distill'd / Almost to jelly with the act of fear'.*
2 fall in tiny drops
• *(RJ 5.3.15) Paris describes his 'tears distill'd by moans'.*

› distilling ADJECTIVE
infusing
• *(RJ 4.1.94) The Friar tells Juliet to drink 'this distilling liquor'.*

› distilment NOUN
extract
• *(Ham 1.5.64) The Ghost describes how a 'leperous distilment' was poured into his ears.*

distinctly ADVERB
as well as meaning 'clearly', you'll find:
separately
• *(Tem 1.2.200) Ariel describes how he moved quickly all over the ship: 'on the topmast, / The yards and bowsprit would I flame distinctly'.*
see SHIPS, p.168

distract ADJECTIVE
mad
• *(JC 4.3.155) Brutus describes Portia's death: 'she fell distract / And, her attendants absent, swallow'd fire'.*

› distract VERB
⚠ *Don't read the meaning of 'taking attention away' into these senses.*
1 divide
• *(Oth 1.3.319) Iago describes the human body as a kind of garden where one could decide to 'supply it with one gender of herbs or distract it with many'.*
2 throw into confusion
• *(Oth 2.3.239) Othello instructs Iago to 'silence those whom this vile brawl distracted'.*

› distracted ADJECTIVE
1 confused
• *(Tem 5.1.12) Ariel tells Prospero how 'The king, / His brother, and yours, abide all three distracted'.*
2 foolish
• *(Ham 4.3.4) Claudius says Hamlet is 'lov'd of the distracted multitude'.*

› distractedly ADVERB
disjointedly
• *(TN 2.2.20) Viola reflects that Olivia 'did speak in starts, distractedly'.*

distressful ADJECTIVE
earned through great hardship
• *(H5 4.1.258) Henry reflects on the wretched slave who 'Gets him to rest, cramm'd with distressful bread'.*

distrust VERB
⚠ *Don't read in the meaning of 'be suspicious of'.*
be anxious about
• *(Ham 3.2.157) The Player Queen says to her husband: 'you are so sick of late ... / That I distrust you'.*

ditch-dog NOUN
a dead dog thrown in a ditch
• *(KL 3.4.125) Edgar says Poor Tom 'swallows the old rat and the ditch-dog'.*

ditcher NOUN
ditch-maker
• *(Ham 5.1.28) The First Gravedigger says there are 'no ancient gentlemen but gardeners, ditchers, and gravemakers'—the oldest trades.*

divers ADJECTIVE
several
• *(TN 1.5.224) Olivia tells Cesario: 'I will give out divers schedules of my beauty'.*

divide VERB
as well as meaning 'separate into parts', you'll find:
identify the qualities of
• *(Ham 5.2.111) Hamlet wonders how to describe Laertes: 'to divide him inventorially'—make a list of his qualities.*

a b c **Dd** e f g h i j k l m n o p q r s t u v w x y z

a b c Dd e f g h i j k l m n o p q r s t u v w x y z

divine NOUN
clergyman
• *(MV 1.2.14) Portia observes: 'It is a good divine that follows his own instructions'.*

› **divinity** NOUN
as well as meaning 'divine power', you'll find: theology
• *(Oth 2.3.328) Iago reflects on his apparent show of good advice to Cassio: 'Divinity of hell!'—his reasoning is like that of a theologian, but based on evil rather than good.*

division NOUN
1 disagreement
• *(KL 1.2.130) Edmund comments on what he has been reading: 'these eclipses do portend these divisions'—give warning of future discords.*
2 variation—as in music
• *(RJ 3.5.29) Juliet tells Romeo: 'Some say the lark makes sweet division'.*

divulge VERB
1 proclaim
• *(TN 1.5.240) Olivia says that Orsino is 'In voices well divulg'd'—he is well spoken of.*
2 become public
• *(Ham 4.1.22) Claudius regrets the way he has dealt with Hamlet's madness 'To keep it from divulging'.*

do VERB
as well as its meanings to do with 'performance', you'll find:
do harm
• *(Mac 1.3.9) The First Witch tells the others: 'I'll do, I'll do, and I'll do'—she says it three times to increase its harmful effect (three was considered to be a magic number).*

doctor NOUN
as well as its medical meaning, you'll find: scholar
• *(MA 5.1.197) Claudio says a man who dresses well but who has stopped using his wit will look better than an ape, 'But then is an ape a doctor to such a man'—the ape will behave more intelligently.*

doff see **daff**

dog at
good at
• *(TN 2.3.55) Sir Andrew claims: 'I am dog at a catch'.*

doit NOUN
tiny amount—a small Dutch coin that was worth about an eighth of an English penny
• *(Tem 2.2.31) Trinculo says English people would not 'give a doit to relieve a lame beggar'—wouldn't even give a beggar a penny.*

dole NOUN
grief
• *(MND 5.1.265) Bottom as Pyramus asks: 'What dreadful dole is here?'*

dolour NOUN
grief
• *(Mac 4.3.8) Macduff talks of heaven yelling, in sympathy with Scotland, a 'Like syllable of dolour'—a similar shout of grief.*

Dolphin see **Dauphin**

Don or **Dan** NOUN
⚠ *Don't think of this as the short form of 'Donald'.*
Sir—a short form of the Latin word for 'master', *dominus*, meaning the person so named is the equivalent of a knight
• *(MA 5.2.77) Benedick describes the conscience of a wise man as 'Don Worm'.*
The worm was a traditional image for the way the conscience works in the brain.

donation NOUN
⚠ *Don't read in the meaning of 'giving money'.*
gift
• *(Tem 4.1.85) Iris asks Ceres to make 'some donation freely to estate / On the bless'd lovers'—bestow a special favour on them.*

doom NOUN
1 judgement
• *(RJ 3.3.4) Romeo asks the Friar: 'What is the prince's doom?'*
2 doomsday—the last day of mankind, when the dead will be raised and judged
• *(Mac 2.3.75) Macduff describes Duncan's corpse as 'The great doom's image'—an image of the end of everything.*

doom VERB
decree
• *(RJ 3.1.130) Benvolio tells Romeo: 'the prince will doom thee death / If thou art taken'—you'll be sentenced to death if you're caught.*

dotage NOUN
as well as meaning 'feebleness of mind in old age' ('dotage' is used of King Lear), you'll find: doting
• *(MND 4.1.46) Oberon decides to do something about Titania's infatuation with Bottom (who has been turned into a half-donkey): 'Her dotage now I do begin to pity'.*

doublet and hose see p.225

doubt VERB
⚠*Don't read the meaning of 'a feeling of uncertainty' into these senses.*
1 fear
• *(Mac 4.2.64) A Messenger warns Macduff's wife: 'I doubt some danger does approach you nearly'.*
2 suspect
• *(RJ 5.3.44) Balthasar says of Romeo: 'His intents I doubt'.*

doubt NOUN
suspicion
• *(Oth 3.3.190) Othello insists he will not harbour 'The smallest fear or doubt' about Desdemona.*
› **in doubt**
without clear meaning
• *(Ham 4.5.6) A Gentleman says Ophelia 'speaks things in doubt'.*
› **doubtful** ADJECTIVE
fearful
• *(TN 4.3.27) Olivia hopes her 'most jealous and too doubtful soul / May live at peace'.*
› **redoubted** ADJECTIVE
feared
• *(MV 3.2.88) Bassanio says cowards put on the surface appearance of valour 'To render them redoubted'.*

dout VERB
extinguish
• *(H5 4.2.11) Bourbon wants the French nobles to spur their horses so that their hot blood will 'spin in English eyes / And dout them'—make them unable to see.*

dower NOUN
dowry (a gift of money or land given at a marriage)
• *(KL 1.1.107) Lear tells Cordelia 'thy truth then be thy dower'.*

dower VERB
endow
• *(KL 1.1.203) Lear says Cordelia has been 'Dower'd with our curse'.*
› **dowerless** ADJECTIVE
lacking a dowry
• *(KL 1.1.255) France tells Lear he will take 'Thy dowerless daughter'.*

dowl also spelled **dowle** NOUN
small feather
• *(Tem 3.3.65) Ariel says swords cannot 'diminish / One dowl that's in my plume'.*

down-gyved see **gyves**

downright ADJECTIVE
as well as meaning 'outright', you'll find:
1 plain, straightforward
• *(H5 5.2.142) Henry tells Katherine he has 'no cunning in protestation, only downright oaths'—he doesn't have any clever ways of declaring love, but has to speak in a straightforward way.*
2 directed straight down
• *(RJ 3.5.128) Capulet describes Juliet's tears: 'It rains downright'.*

down-roping see **roping**

downy ADJECTIVE
comfort-giving—soft as down
• *(Mac 2.3.73) Macduff calls to everyone: 'Shake off this downy sleep'.*

drab NOUN
prostitute
• *(Mac 4.1.31) The Third Witch tells of a baby 'Ditch-deliver'd by a drab'.*
› **drabbing** NOUN
visiting prostitutes
• *(Ham 2.1.26) Polonius imagines Laertes' behaviour: 'swearing, / Quarrelling, drabbing'.*

Dragon's tail see **COSMOS, p.174**

draw VERB
as well as meaning 'pull something' and 'draw a sword', you'll find:
1 draft
• *(MND 1.2.91) Quince says he will 'draw a bill of properties'—a list of props.*
2 drink down
• *(Tem 2.2.141) Trinculo compliments Caliban: 'Well drawn, monster'.*
3 carry a burden
• *(Oth 4.1.67) Iago tells Othello to reflect that 'every bearded fellow that's but yok'd / May draw with you'—every married man has the same problem.*

drawer see **OCCUPATIONS, p.166**

dread ADJECTIVE
as well as meaning 'feared', you'll find:
revered
• *(H5 1.2.97) The Archbishop of Canterbury addresses King Henry as 'dread sovereign'.*

dread-bolted ADJECTIVE
with frightening thunderbolts
• *(KL 4.7.33) Cordelia says her father should not have had to 'stand against the deep dread-bolted thunder'.*

a b c Dd e f g h i j k l m n o p q r s t u v w x y z

dreadful ADJECTIVE
⚠ *Don't read the modern meaning of 'very bad, awful' into these senses.*
1 causing fear—inspiring dread
• *(Oth 2.3.159) Othello shouts: 'Silence that dreadful bell'.*
2 fearful—full of dread
• *(Ham 1.2.207) Horatio describes how the sentinels told him of the ghost 'In dreadful secrecy'.*

drench NOUN
drink
• *(H5 3.6.19) The Constable describes English ale as 'sodden water, / A drench for sur-reined jades'—a drink only for over-worked old horses.*
› **drenched** ADJECTIVE
full of drink
• *(Mac 1.7.68) Lady Macbeth describes the state of Duncan's attendants: 'Their drenched natures lie as in a death'.*

dress VERB
as well as meaning 'put on clothes', you'll find:
1 prepare
• *(H5 4.1.10) Henry says the French presence teaches them to 'dress us fairly for our end'—prepare ourselves well for what is to come.*
2 provide
• *(Oth 1.3.26) The First Senator says that Cyprus hasn't the defences 'That Rhodes is dress'd in'.*
3 treat
• *(TN 5.1.196) Sir Andrew tells Sir Toby, both injured, 'we'll be dressed together'—have our wounds looked to at the same time.*

drive VERB
⚠ *Don't read the modern meaning of 'making a vehicle go' into these senses.*
1 hasten
• *(KL 3.6.89) Gloucester tells Kent: 'drive toward Dover'.*
2 rush
• *(Ham 2.2.460) The First Player describes how 'Pyrrhus at Priam drives'.*
› **driving** ADJECTIVE
drifting
• *(TN 1.2.11) The Captain describes what happened when Viola 'Hung on our driving boat'.*

drollery NOUN
show of entertainment
• *(Tem 3.3.21) Sebastian describes the spirits as 'A living drollery!'*

dropping ADJECTIVE
tearful—tear-dropping
• *(Ham 1.2.11) Claudius describes his mixed feelings about marrying Gertrude: 'With an auspicious and a dropping eye'—as if one eye were happy, the other sad.*

dropsy NOUN
a type of disease in which the body swells up with watery fluids
• *(Tem 4.1.228) Caliban curses Trinculo: 'The dropsy drown this fool!'*

drover or **drovier** NOUN
cattle-dealer
• *(MA 2.1.181) Benedick reacts to Claudio's reluctant expression of good wishes to the Prince: 'that's spoken like an honest drover'—like a friendly dairy-farmer who wishes a customer (who has bought a cow) good luck with it.*
✒ *'Drovier' is the spelling in the First Folio.*

drowning-mark also spelled **drowning mark** NOUN
indication of death by drowning
• *(Tem 1.1.27) Gonzalo says the Boatswain 'hath no drowning-mark upon him'.*
🎭 *Gonzalo is recalling the proverb: 'He that is born to be hanged shall never be drowned'.*

dry ADJECTIVE
as well as meaning 'not wet' and 'thirsty', you'll find:
1 barren—coming up with no results
• *(TN 1.5.35) Olivia calls Feste 'a dry fool'.*
2 withered
• *(MA 2.1.108) Ursula says the masked person she is dancing with must be Antonio: 'Here's his dry hand up and down'—she can feel it is withered all over.*

dry-beat VERB
thrash
• *(RJ 4.5.118) Peter says to a musician: 'I will dry-beat you with an iron wit'.*

dudgeon see **SWORDS AND DAGGERS, p.156**

duello NOUN
established code of practice for duelling
• *(TN 3.4.281) Sir Toby tells Cesario that Sir Andrew must fight with him: 'He cannot by the duello avoid it'.*
🎭 *The duello states that there must be witnesses to the proceedings of a challenge.*

dug NOUN
nipple
• *(RJ 1.3.27) The Nurse talks of when she was weaning Juliet: 'I had then laid wormwood to my dug'—put a bitter-tasting plant on her nipple to make it taste bitter, and so give the baby a bad association with breast-feeding.*

dull ADJECTIVE
as well as meaning 'stupid' and 'not sharp', you'll find:
1 sluggish
• *(Ham 2.2.553) Hamlet describes himself as 'A dull and muddy-mettled rascal' for not actively doing anything.*
2 gloomy
• *(RJ 1.4.21) Romeo describes his feelings as 'dull woe'.*

dull VERB
1 stupefy
• *(H5 2.2.9) Exeter says that Henry gave his friend Scroop so many favours that Scroop became 'dull'd'—incapable of doing anything for himself.*
2 make insensitive
• *(Ham 1.3.64) Polonius advises Laertes: 'do not dull thy palm with entertainment'—don't shake too many hands.*

› **dull-eyed** ADJECTIVE
easily deceived
• *(MV 3.3.14) Shylock says he will 'not be made a soft and dull-eyed fool'.*

› **dullness** also spelled **dulness** NOUN
sleepiness
• *(Tem 1.2.185) Prospero is making Miranda fall asleep: ''Tis a good dulness, / And give it way'—give in to it.*

dump NOUN
tune
• *(RJ 4.5.122) Peter quotes a line from a song 'And doleful dumps the mind oppress'—sad songs cause the mind distress.*

dun ADJECTIVE
dark, murky
• *(Mac 1.5.50) Lady Macbeth asks the night to cover everything with 'the dunnest smoke of hell'.*
see also COLOURS, p.164

› **dun's the mouse**
keep quiet, hush!
• *(RJ 1.4.40) Mercutio plays on the word 'done' with a proverb: 'dun's the mouse, the constable's own word'—as a policeman might say after seeing something suspicious.*

› **Dun** NOUN
a folk name for a horse—like 'Dobbin' today—used in a Christmas game in which players tug at a log 'horse' that has to be pulled out of mud—'drawing Dun out of the mire'
• *(RJ 1.4.41) Mercutio continues his wordplay to Romeo: 'If thou art Dun, we'll draw thee from the mire'.*

Dunsinane Hill [pronounced **dun**-si-nayn]
a hill in the middle of Dunsinnan estate, near Collace, Perthshire, eastern Scotland
• *(Mac 4.1.92) The Third Apparition tells Macbeth that he will not be defeated 'until / Great Birnam Wood to high Dunsinane Hill / Shall come against him'.*
Dunsinane is about 12 miles (20 km) from Birnam.

dup VERB
open—a short way of saying 'do up' (in the sense of 'open up' not 'decorate')
• *(Ham 4.5.53) Ophelia sings of a lover who 'dupp'd the chamber door'.*

durance NOUN
confinement
• *(TN 5.1.267) Viola says the Captain 'Is now in durance at Malvolio's suit'—Malvolio has taken out a lawsuit against him (though we're not told why).*

duty NOUN
as well as meaning 'a task that must be done', you'll find:
proper respect
• *(TN 3.1.91) Cesario greets Olivia, offering her 'My duty, madam, and most humble service'.*

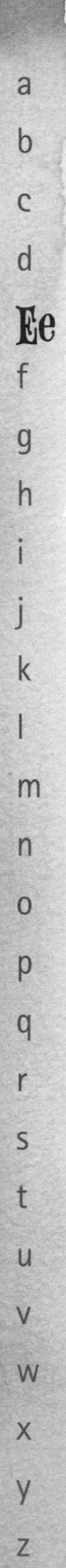

eager ADJECTIVE
1 biting
• *(Ham 1.4.2) Horatio feels the cold on the battlements: 'It is a nipping and an eager air'.*
2 sour
• *(Ham 1.5.69) The Ghost describes the working of the poison—'like eager droppings into milk'.*

eaning ADJECTIVE
lambing
• *(MV 1.3.82) Shylock tells a story about ewes at 'eaning time'—the time of year when lambs are born.*

› **eanling** NOUN
new-born lamb
• *(MV 1.3.74) In Shylock's story, Jacob would get 'all the eanlings which were streak'd and pied'—born with coats streaked with different colours.*

ear NOUN
as well as its usual meaning as a part of the body, you'll find:
listening
• *(KL 3.4.88) Poor Tom says he is 'light of ear'—always listening, and ready to believe anything.*

› **in the ear**
within earshot
• *(Ham 3.1.184) Polonius says he will listen in to the conversation between Hamlet and Gertrude—'in the ear / Of all their conference'.*

ear-bussing ADJECTIVE
reaching the ear only as rumours ('buss' means 'kiss')
• *(KL 2.1.7) Curan tells Edmund of the news that people are whispering—'ear-bussing arguments'.*

earn VERB
mourn
• *(H5 2.3.3) Pistol, leaving for the wars, admits to his wife: 'My manly heart doth earn'.*
'Erne' is the spelling in the First Folio. Some editions replace it with 'yearn'.

earnest NOUN
payment in advance
• *(KL 1.4.88) Lear gives Kent some money: 'there's earnest of thy service'.*

easiness NOUN
indifference
• *(Ham 5.1.64) Hamlet comments on the way the First Gravedigger deals with death: 'Custom hath made it in him a property of easiness'.*

Easter NOUN
the feast of Christ's resurrection
• *(RJ 3.1.27) Mercutio accuses Benvolio of falling out with a tailor 'for wearing his new doublet before Easter'—during Lent, a time for penitence, not fashion.*

eche also spelled **eke** VERB
stretch
• *(MV 3.2.23) Portia apologizes to Bassanio for speaking too long, saying it was to prolong the time, 'To eche it', before he makes his choice.*

ecstasy NOUN
⚠ *Don't read the modern meanings of 'rapturous delight' or anything to do with drugs into these senses.*
1 madness
• *(Ham 3.1.160) Ophelia describes Hamlet as 'Blasted with ecstasy'.*
2 frenzied behaviour
• *(MA 2.3.148) Leonato says, of Beatrice's supposed*

infatuation for Benedick, that 'the ecstasy hath so much overborne her'—almost overwhelmed her.
3 state of mind
• *(Mac 4.3.172) Ross describes Scotland as a place where 'violent sorrow seems / A modern ecstasy'—the normal state of affairs these days.*

edge NOUN
1 ardour
• *(Ham 3.2.239) Hamlet tells Ophelia: 'It would cost you a groaning to take off my edge'—satisfying my desire would make you groan (either with pleasure during sexual intercourse, or with pain when having a baby).*
2 keen delight
• *(Tem 4.1.29) Ferdinand assures Prospero he will do nothing 'to take away / The edge of that day's celebration'—his wedding-day.*
3 stimulus
• *(Ham 3.1.26) Claudius asks Rosencrantz and Guildenstern to find more things for Hamlet to enjoy: 'give him a further edge'.*

› **edged** ADJECTIVE
sharpened
• *(H5 3.6.38) The French King urges his nobles to fight 'with spirit of honour edg'd'.*

e'en see **even**

effect NOUN
as well as meaning 'result', you'll find:
1 purpose
• *(Ham 3.4.129) Hamlet begs the Ghost not to look directly at him in case this would 'convert / My stern effects'—make him alter his firm intentions.*
2 sign
• *(MA 2.3.110) Leonato asks about Beatrice's infatuation with Benedick: 'what effects of passion shows she?'*
3 benefit
• *(Ham 3.3.54) Claudius reflects: 'I am still possess'd / Of those effects for which I did the murder'.*

effusion NOUN
spilling
• *(H5 3.7.123) The French King tells Henry that the entire English army wouldn't be enough to make up for 'th'effusion of our blood'.*

eftest ADJECTIVE
quickest—perhaps intended to mean 'deftest'
• *(MA 4.2.34) Dogberry finds 'the eftest way' to proceed.*

egal also spelled **egall** ADJECTIVE
equal
• *(MV 3.4.13) Portia talks of companions 'Whose souls do bear an egall yoke of love'.*
'Egal' is the spelling in the First Folio. Some editions replace it with 'equal'.

egregious ADJECTIVE [pronounced e-**gree**-jus]
1 significant
• *(H5 4.4.9) Pistol demands 'egregious ransom' from his prisoner.*
2 outrageous
• *(H5 2.1.42) Pistol calls Nym an 'egregious dog'.*

eisel also spelled **eysell** NOUN
[pronounced **iy**-sul]
vinegar
• *(Ham 5.1.262) Hamlet challenges Laertes: 'Woo't drink up eisel?'—would you drink a bottle of vinegar?*

eke ADVERB
also
• *(MND 3.1.81) Thisbe addresses Pyramus: 'Most brisky juvenal, and eke most lovely Jew'—a lively youth as well as a lovely Jew.*

eke VERB see **eche**

elder gun also spelled **elder-gun** NOUN
pop-gun (whose shot wouldn't hurt anyone)
• *(H5 4.1.186) Williams dismisses the disguised Henry's remark: 'That's a perilous shot out of an elder gun'.*

election NOUN
as well as its political meaning, you'll find:
choice
• *(MV 2.9.3) Nerissa says that Arragon 'comes to his election presently'—he's coming right now to make his choice.*

element NOUN
1 substance
• *(MA 2.1.317) Leonata describes Beatrice: 'There's little of the melancholy element in her'.*
2 heavens
• *(JC 1.3.128) Cassius describes 'the complexion of the element' as being as fiery as the conspirators' intentions.*
3 social station
• *(TN 3.4.113) Malvolio addresses Sir Toby and the others: 'I am not of your element'.*

› **the elements**
1 the substances from which all material things

a b c d Ee f g h i j k l m n o p q r s t u v w x y z

are made—thought to be earth, water, air, and fire
• *(TN 2.3.9) Sir Toby asks Sir Andrew: 'Does not our life consist of the four elements?'*
2 the forces of nature
• *(KL 3.1.4) A Gentleman talks of Lear 'Contending with the fretful elements'.*

elf VERB
tangle
• *(KL 2.3.10) Edgar says he will 'elf all my hairs in knots'.*
› **elf-locks** NOUN
tangled hair (thought to be the work of elves)
• *(RJ 1.4.90) Mercutio describes the way Queen Mab tangles and hardens horses' manes—'bakes the elf-locks in foul sluttish hairs'—like the hair of untidy women.*

ell NOUN
a measure of length—in England, 45 in /about 114 cm (based on the length from the elbow to the tip of the middle finger)
• *(RJ 2.4.77) Mercutio describes Romeo's wit as something 'that stretches from an inch narrow to an ell broad!'*

Elysium NOUN [pronounced el-**iz**-ee-um]
in Greek mythology, the location of heaven
• *(TN 1.2.4) Viola thinks her brother has drowned and 'is in Elysium'.*

embar also spelled **imbar, imbare** VERB
reveal or prevent discovery of
• *(H5 1.2.94) Canterbury says the French would rather hide themselves in a net 'Than amply to embar their crooked titles'—honestly admit to the weaknesses in their claims.*

embassage also spelled **ambassage** NOUN
errand
• *(MA 1.1.256) Benedick tells Don Pedro that he has just about enough capacity to deliver his message to Leonato: 'I have almost matter enough in me for such an embassage'.*
› **embassy** NOUN
⚠ *Don't read in the modern meaning of 'the residence of a country's ambassador'.*
message
• *(TN 1.5.155) Olivia tells Maria: "We'll once more hear Orsino's embassy'.*

embay VERB
go within a bay
• *(Oth 2.1.18) Montano wonders if the Turkish fleet are 'enshelter'd and embay'd'.*

embossed ADJECTIVE
swollen, bulging
• *(KL 2.4.221) Lear calls Goneril 'a boil, / A plague-sore, or embossed carbuncle'—a swollen tumour.*

embrue see **imbrue**

emperious see **imperious**

empery NOUN
sovereignty
• *(H5 1.2.227) Henry predicts England will rule 'in large and ample empery / O'er France'.*

employment NOUN
⚠ *Don't read in the meaning of 'having a job'.*
matter, pursuit
• *(TN 2.5.76) Malvolio sees Olivia's letter: 'What employment have we here?'*

empty ADJECTIVE
unburdened
• *(JC 4.1.26) Antony proposes to remove responsibilities from Lepidus so that he is 'Like to the empty ass'.*

emulate ADJECTIVE
ambitious
• *(Ham 1.1.86) Horatio describes Fortinbras being 'prick'd on by a most emulate pride'.*
› **emulation** NOUN
ambitious rivalry
• *(JC 2.3.13) Artemidorus tries to warn Julius Caesar about his enemies, lamenting that 'virtue cannot live / Out of the teeth of emulation'—good cannot come from such competitive ill-will.*

enacture NOUN
performance
• *(Ham 3.2.189) The Player King says 'The violence of either grief or joy / Their own enactures with themselves destroy'.*

enamelled also spelled **enamell'd** ADJECTIVE
⚠ *Don't read in the meaning of 'coated with enamel'.*
with a hard, polished, brightly coloured surface
• *(MND 2.1.255) Oberon describes a bank where 'the snake throws her enamell'd skin'.*

encave VERB
conceal
• *(Oth 4.1.81) Iago tells Othello to 'encave yourself'.*

enchafed ADJECTIVE
angry
• *(Oth 2.1.17) The Second Gentleman says he 'never did like molestation view / On the enchafed flood'—such disturbance on the angry sea.*

enclog VERB
hinder
• *(Oth 2.1.70) Cassio describes the coastal rocks as ready 'to enclog the guiltless keel'—to bring down the approaching ship.*
✒ *This is the word used in the First Folio. Some editions replace it with the First and Second Quarto version, 'clog'.*

encompassment NOUN
roundabout means
• *(Ham 2.1.10) Polonius advises Reynaldo to find out about Laertes by 'encompassment and drift of question'.*

encounter VERB
as well as meaning 'meet', you'll find:
1 approach
• *(TN 3.1.71) Sir Toby asks Cesario to 'encounter the house'.*
2 stand opposite
• *(Tem 4.1.137) Iris calls to a group of men reaping the corn: 'these fresh nymphs encounter every one / In country footing'—each should take a partner for a dance.*

encumbered also spelled **encumber'd** VERB
folded
• *(Ham 1.5.182) Hamlet imagines Horatio and Marcellus standing 'With arms encumber'd thus'.*

endart VERB
send in—as an arrow
• *(RJ 1.3.99) Juliet promises her mother 'no more deep will I endart mine eye / Than your consent gives strength to make it fly'—she will encourage Paris only with her mother's approval.*

endite see **indite**

endue see **indue**

Endymion NOUN [pronounced en-**dim**-ee-on]
in Greek mythology, a young shepherd loved by the moon; Zeus granted his wish of eternal sleep, and thus he remained forever young.
• *(MV 5.1.109) Portia, returning home, calls to Lorenzo and Jessica, as if they were mythological lovers: 'The moon sleeps with Endymion / And would not be awak'd!'*

enforce VERB
as well as meaning 'force', you'll find:
emphasize
• *(JC 3.2.38) Brutus tells the people that Caesar's death has been officially recorded, without 'his offences enforced'—without stressing his faults.*

› **enforced** ADJECTIVE
violated
• *(MND 3.1.185) Titania describes the moon—thought of as the cause of dew—making flowers weep, 'Lamenting some enforced chastity'—feeling sorrow for times when a rape takes place.*

enfranchise VERB
set free
• *(MA 1.3.28) Don John complains that he has been 'enfranchised with a clog'—given the freedom of a beast with its legs hobbled.*
🎭 *Owners who were worried their animals might escape would 'hobble' them—tie something to their legs (or even break their legs) to ensure they didn't stray.*

› **enfranchisement** NOUN
giving the status of citizen
• *(JC 3.1.57) Cassius falls on his knees before Caesar 'To beg enfranchisement for Publius Cimber'—someone Caesar had banished.*

engaged also spelled **engag'd** ADJECTIVE
⚠ *Don't read in the meanings of 'promised to marry' or 'unavailable'.*
entangled
• *(Ham 3.3.69) Claudius addresses his soul 'that struggling to be free / Art more engag'd!'*

engendered also spelled **engender'd** ADJECTIVE
devised
• *(Oth 1.3.394) Iago thinks up his plan: 'I have't. It is engender'd'.*

› **high-engendered** ADJECTIVE
brought into being by the heavens
• *(KL 3.2.23) Lear calls down on his head the storm's 'high-engender'd battles'.*

engild VERB
brighten
• *(MND 3.2.187) Lysander says Helena has a face that 'engilds the night'.*

engine NOUN
⚠ *Don't read the modern meanings of 'steam engine' or 'search engine' into these senses.*
1 plot
• *(Oth 4.2.214) Iago promises Roderigo that he will get Desdemona for him, or else Roderigo can 'devise engines for my life'—plan ways to kill me.*
2 weapon
• *(Tem 2.1.157) Gonzalo says that in his imaginary world he would not have 'need of any engine'.*
3 lever
• *(KL 1.4.258) Lear says Cordelia's fault 'like an engine, wrench'd my frame of nature / From the*

fix'd place'—her behaviour led to a disruption in his normal state of being.

› **enginer** also spelled **engineer** NOUN
a builder of military works
• *(Ham 3.4.208) Hamlet finds it amusing 'to have the enginer / Hoist with his own petard'—see the plotter's plots blow up in his face.*
This line is not in all editions of Hamlet, as it appears in the Second Quarto text of the play, but not the First Folio.

englut VERB
swallow up
• *(H5 4.3.83) Montjoy tells Henry: 'thou art so near the gulf / Thou needs must be englutted'—you are bound to die because defeat is very near.*

engraffed, engrafted see **ingraft**

engrossing ADJECTIVE
Don't read in the modern meaning of 'fascinating'.
all-absorbing
• *(RJ 5.3.115) Romeo gives his last kiss to Juliet as 'A dateless bargain to engrossing Death!'*

enguard VERB
protect
• *(KL 1.4.317) Goneril fears the way Lear's knights would 'enguard his dotage'—protect his feebleness of mind.*

enjoy VERB
as well as meaning 'take pleasure in', you'll find:
have sex with
• *(KL 5.3.79) Goneril asks Regan about Edmund: 'Mean you to enjoy him?'*

enlarge VERB
1 release
• *(H5 2.2.40) Henry instructs: 'Enlarge the man committed yesterday'.*
2 extend
• *(Ham 5.1.210) The Priest says Ophelia's funeral rites 'have been as far enlarg'd / As we have warranty'—as she is presumed to be a suicide, he has done as much as Catholic law allows.*

enormous ADJECTIVE
Don't read in the modern meaning of 'huge'.
disordered or shocking
• *(KL 2.2.164) Kent hopes Cordelia will help find a remedy 'From this enormous state'—from this terrible situation.*

enow ADVERB
enough
• *(Mac 2.3.6) The Porter tells visitors to 'have napkins enow about you'—handkerchieves to mop up their sweat.*
'Enow' is the word used in the First Folio. Some editions replace it with 'enough'.

enraged also spelled **enrag'd** ADJECTIVE
Don't read in the modern meaning of 'very angry'.
passionate
• *(MA 2.3.103) Leonato says that Beatrice loves Benedick 'with an enraged affection'.*

enridged also spelled **enridg'd** ADJECTIVE
rippling
• *(KL 4.6.71) Edgar describes the beggar he saw as having horns twisted and curled 'like the enridged sea'.*

enrobe VERB
dress in a robe
• *(MV 1.1.34) Salarino imagines his merchant ship being wrecked by rocks which would 'Enrobe the roaring waters with my silks'.*

enrol VERB
Don't read in the meaning of 'become a member of something'.
record officially
• *(JC 3.2.37) Brutus says the manner of Caesar's death 'is enrolled in the Capitol'.*

enscarped also spelled **enscarp'd** ADJECTIVE
with sharp ridges
• *(Oth 2.1.70) Cassio describes dangerous rocks as being 'Traitors enscarp'd'.*
'Enscarped' is the spelling used in the First Quarto text of the play. The First Folio has 'ensteeped'.

enseamed ADJECTIVE
slimy
• *(Ham 3.4.92) Hamlet condemns Gertrude for living 'In the rank sweat of an enseamed bed'.*

ensteeped also spelled **ensteep'd** ADJECTIVE
submerged
• *(Oth 2.1.70) Cassio describes dangerous rocks as being 'Traitors ensteeped'.*
'Ensteeped' is the word that appears in the First Folio. Some editions use the First Quarto version, 'enscarped'.

entertain VERB
Don't read meanings to do with 'keeping someone amused' into these senses.

as well as meaning 'receive as a guest' and 'consider', you'll find:

1 welcome

• *(Tem 4.1.75) Iris tells Ceres to welcome Juno: 'Approach, rich Ceres, her to entertain'.*

2 hire

• *(JC 5.5.60) Octavius announces: 'All that serv'd Brutus, I will entertain them'.*

3 accept as true

• *(H5 4.Chorus.1) The Chorus asks the audience to imagine the next scene to be true: 'Now entertain conjecture of a time'—believe in the imaginary setting we are going to portray.*

4 maintain

• *(MV 1.1.90) Gratiano describes men whose faces 'do a wilful stillness entertain' in order to appear wise.*

› **entertainer** NOUN

receiver

• *(Tem 2.1.18) Gonzalo suggests that taking in every grief only causes more sorrow 'to th' entertainer'.*

› **entertainment** NOUN

1 reception

• *(TN 1.5.199) Cesario tells Olivia that his apparent rudeness 'have I learned from my entertainment'—from the way he has been treated.*

2 hospitality

• *(KL 2.4.203) Regan tells Lear that she hasn't enough in her house 'needful for your entertainment'.*

entreatment NOUN

interaction

• *(Ham 1.3.122) Polonius advises Ophelia to 'Set your entreatments at a higher rate / Than a command to parley'—don't talk to him just because he asks you to.*

enure see **inure**

envious ADJECTIVE

⚠ *Don't read the meaning of 'wanting something that someone else has' into these senses.*

malicious

• *(RJ 3.1.164) Benvolio reports that Tybalt killed Mercutio with 'An envious thrust'—an unfair fencing move.*

› **enviously** ADVERB

maliciously

• *(Ham 4.5.6) A Gentleman says that Ophelia 'Spurns enviously at straws'—treats little matters with spiteful contempt.*

› **envy** NOUN

malice

• *(MV 4.1.10) Antonio says of Shylock: 'no lawful means can carry me / Out of his envy's reach'.*

environ VERB

surround

• *(RJ 4.3.50) Juliet imagines herself distraught in the tomb, 'Environed with all these hideous fears'.*

envy see **envious**

Epicurus NOUN [pronounced e-pee-**cure**-us]

Greek philosopher of the 4th century BC, who viewed omens as mere superstitions and advocated a way of life based on pleasure and friendship

• *(JC 5.1.76) Cassius recalls how he formerly 'held Epicurus strong / And his opinion'—was convinced by Epicurus' views on omens.*

› **epicure** NOUN

pleasure-seeker

• *(Mac 5.3.8) Macbeth says the thanes 'mingle with the English epicures'.*

› **epicurism** NOUN

gluttony, pleasure-seeking

• *(KL 1.4.233) Goneril describes how Lear's knights have turned her house into a place of 'epicurism and lust'.*

epithet NOUN

turn of phrase

• *(MA 5.2.61) Benedick considers the phrase 'Suffer love' to be 'a good epithet'.*

equal ADJECTIVE

as well as meaning 'same in amount', you'll find:

exact

• *(MV 1.3.145) Shylock tells Antonio his forfeit will be 'an equal pound / Of your fair flesh'.*

› **equally** ADVERB

justly

• *(KL 5.3.46) Albany says he will treat his prisoners 'As we shall find their merits and our safety / May equally determine'.*

equinoctial see **COSMOS, p.174**

equinox NOUN

counterbalance

• *(Oth 2.3.110) Iago says that Cassio's vice is 'to his virtue a just equinox'—one is equal to the other.*

equity NOUN

justice

• *(KL 3.6.37) Lear describes the Fool as Poor Tom's 'yoke-fellow of equity'—fellow-judge.*

a b c d **Ee** f g h i j k l m n o p q r s t u v w x y z

a b c d Ee f g h i j k l m n o p q r s t u v w x y z

equivocation NOUN
double meaning
• *(Mac 5.5.42) Macbeth begins to doubt 'th'equivocation of the fiend'.*

› equivocator NOUN
someone who deals in double meanings
• *(Mac 2.3.8) The Porter imagines who is knocking at Macbeth's castle gate: 'Here's an equivocator that could swear in both the scales against either scale'—swear his support equally for either side of an argument (the figure of Justice is traditionally represented holding a pair of scales).*

Ercles see **Hercules**

ere CONJUNCTION
before
• *(Ham 3.2.316) Rosencrantz tells Hamlet that Gertrude wants to speak with him 'ere you go to bed'.*

Erebus NOUN [pronounced **e**-re-bus]
in Greek mythology, a place of darkness on the way from earth to the Underworld
• *(MV 5.1.87) Lorenzo says a man who has no music in him (who doesn't like music) has 'affections dark as Erebus'.*

erewhile ADVERB
a while before
• *(MND 3.2.274) Hermia says to Lysander: 'I am as fair now as I was erewhile'.*

ergo see **LATIN, p.352**

erring ADJECTIVE
⚠ *Don't read the modern meaning of 'making a mistake' into these senses.*
wandering
• *(Ham 1.1.159) Horatio talks of the way the 'erring spirit hies / To his confine'—rushes back to his prison.*

› error NOUN
wandering
• *(Oth 5.2.110) Othello claims that men are made mad by 'the very error of the moon'.*

erst ADVERB
formerly
• *(H5 5.2.48) Burgundy describes the French meadows 'that erst brought sweetly forth / The freckled cowslip'—that used to bloom with flowers.*

eruption NOUN
⚠ *Don't read in the meaning of a volcano exploding.*
disturbance
• *(JC 1.3.78) Cassius describes as fearful 'these strange eruptions' taking place in the city.*

escape see **scape**

escote past form spelled **escoted** or **escotted** VERB
pay for
• *(Ham 2.2.339) Hamlet asks how the child players are paid their wages: 'How are they escotted?'*

esperance NOUN
hope
• *(KL 4.1.4) Edgar reflects that even the lowest being 'Stands still in esperance'—still has hope.*

espial NOUN
watcher
• *(Ham 3.1.32) Polonius describes Claudius and himself as 'lawful espials' of Ophelia.*

espouse VERB
marry
• *(H5 2.1.67) Pistol suggests to Nym that he find Doll Tearsheet 'and her espouse'.*

essay NOUN
⚠ *Don't read in the meaning of a school essay.*
trial
• *(KL 1.2.44) Edmund tells Gloucester that Edgar's letter must have been written as 'an essay or taste of my virtue'.*

estate NOUN
⚠ *Don't read the modern meaning of an area of land with houses on it into these senses.*
1 situation
• *(MV 3.2.314) Antonio tells Bassanio in a letter: 'my estate is very low'.*
2 standing
• *(TN 1.5.239) Olivia describes Orsino as 'noble, / Of great estate'.*
3 kingdom
• *(Mac 1.4.37) Duncan says he will 'establish our estate upon / Our eldest, Malcolm'—making him next in line to be king.*

estate VERB
endow, give
• *(MND 1.1.98) Egeus says of Hermia: 'all my right of her / I do estate unto Demetrius'.*

estimation NOUN
as well as meanings to do with 'guessing' and 'calculating', you'll find:
reputation
• *(Oth 1.3.271) Othello insists that matters of*

the heart will never 'Make head against my estimation'—harm his reputation as a soldier.

eterne ADJECTIVE
eternal
• *(Ham 2.2.478) The First Player describes Mars' armour as 'forg'd for proof eterne'—it will last for ever.*

Ethiop also spelled **Ethiope** NOUN
1 dark-skinned person
• *(MND 3.2.257) Lysander shouts at Hermia: 'Away, you Ethiop!'*
2 someone from Africa (not necessarily from Ethiopia)
• *(RJ 1.5.45) Romeo compares Juliet's brightness in the dark to 'a rich jewel in an Ethiop's ear'.*

et tu, Brute **see LATIN, p.352**

Europa NOUN
1 in Greek mythology, a princess who was abducted by Zeus (the Greek name of Jove) who had disguised himself in the shape of a bull
• *(MA 5.4.46) Claudio jests with Benedick that, if he carries off a lover, 'As once Europa did at lusty Jove', everyone will rejoice.*
2 Europe
• *(MA 5.4.45) Claudio jests with Benedick, that 'all Europa shall rejoice at thee' if he manages to win his lady.*
see MAP, p.176

even also spelled **e'en** NOUN
1 evening
• *(H5 3.1.20) Henry remembers his soldiers' forefathers who 'Have in these parts from morn till even fought'.*
see also HELLO, p.133
2 plain truth
• *(H5 2.1.106) Nym reflects on how Henry treated Falstaff: 'The king hath run bad humours on the knight; that's the even of it'—caused harmful fluids to flow through him.*
see also HUMOURS, p.137

even ADJECTIVE
as well as meaning 'equal' and 'level', you'll find:
1 straightforward
• *(MA 4.1.262) Beatrice says to Benedick that there is 'A very even way' of showing friendship.*
2 steadfast
• *(JC 2.1.133) Brutus asks the conspirators not to make an oath, as this would 'stain / The even virtue of our enterprise'—because their plot is so honourable, they don't need a vow to make it happen.*

even ADVERB
1 exactly
• *(Ham 5.1.65) Hamlet agrees with Horatio: ' 'Tis e'en so'.*
2 right now
• *(Ham 4.3.20) Hamlet tells Claudius about Polonius—that worms 'are e'en at him'.*

› **evenly** ADVERB
1 directly
• *(H5 2.4.92) Exeter tells the French King that Henry is 'evenly deriv'd' from Edward III.*
2 along the same lines
• *(MA 2.2.7) Don John talks of Claudio: 'whatsoever comes athwart his affection ranges evenly with mine'—whatever goes against his wishes goes along with mine.*

› **even over** VERB
try to make sense of
• *(KL 4.7.80) The Doctor advises Cordelia that Lear should not 'even o'er the time he has lost'.*

› **even to't**
just go for it
• *(Ham 2.2.417) Hamlet tells the players about performing something: 'We'll e'en to it like French falconers, fly at anything we see'.*

even-Christen also spelled **-Christian** NOUN
fellow-Christian
• *(Ham 5.1.26) The First Gravedigger regrets that great people are allowed to kill themselves 'more than their even-Christen'—nobles are treated differently from common folk.*

even-pleached also spelled **-pleach'd** ADJECTIVE
with branches evenly layered
• *(H5 5.2.42) Burgundy describes France as a place where 'Her hedges, even-pleach'd', are now overgrown.*

event NOUN
⚠ *Don't read in the meaning of 'something that happens'. 'Event' usually means 'the result of something happening'.*
outcome
• *(TN 3.4.367) Fabian suggests he and Sir Toby follow Sir Andrew to see what happens: 'Come, let's see the event'.*

exaction NOUN
enforcing
• *(MV 1.3.160) Shylock asks: 'what should I gain / By the exaction of the forfeiture?'*

exactly ADVERB
completely
• *(Ham 1.2.200) Horatio describes the Ghost as 'Armed at point exactly'—correct in every detail.*

a b c d **Ee** f g h i j k l m n o p q r s t u v w x y z

excellent ADJECTIVE
⚠ *Don't read in the meaning of 'extremely good'.*
supreme
• *(KL 1.2.112) Edmund reflects on 'the excellent foppery of the world'—the greatest stupidity.*

except VERB
object to
• *(TN 1.3.6) Sir Toby says he will continue to take no notice of Olivia: 'let her except, before excepted'—object to something she's objected to before.*

excess NOUN
interest
• *(MV 1.3.57) Antonio tells Shylock that he doesn't lend or borrow 'By taking nor by giving of excess'.*

exclaim on VERB
denounce (loudly)
• *(MV 3.2.174) Portia tells Bassanio that if he gives her ring away, she will 'exclaim on' him.*

exclamation NOUN
intended to mean 'acclamation'
• *(MA 3.5.24) Dogberry tells Leonato that he hears 'as good exclamation on your worship as of any man in the city'.*

excrement NOUN
⚠ *Don't read in the meaning of 'waste matter from the bowels'.*
outgrowth of hair
• *(Ham 3.4.121) Gertrude describes Hamlet's hair: 'like life in excrements / Start up and stand an end'.*

excursions see **ALARUMS AND EXCURSIONS, p.17**

excuse see **scuse**

executor NOUN
1 performer
• *(Tem 3.1.13) Miranda says that Ferdinand's lowly work 'Had never like executor'—someone of his position in society has never had to work in this way.*
2 executioner
• *(H5 1.2.203) Canterbury describes a magistrate, like a honey-bee, 'Delivering o'er to executors pale / The lazy yawning drone'.*
3 disposer of remains
• *(H5 4.2.51) The French noble Grandpré describes the crows flying over the English army as 'their executors'—they will eat their dead bodies.*

exeunt see **STAGE DIRECTIONS, p.285**

exhalation NOUN
⚠ *Don't read the meaning of 'breathing out' into these senses.*
shooting star
• *(JC 2.1.44) Brutus describes 'The exhalations whizzing in the air'.*

› **exhale** VERB
as well as meaning 'cause to flow', you'll find:
draw forth (a sword)
• *(H5 2.1.55) Pistol tells Nym: 'Therefore exhale!'*

exhibit VERB
show
• *(MV 2.3.10) Lancelot bids farewell to Jessica: 'tears exhibit my tongue'—my tears express what my tongue would say.*
✒ *Lancelot might here be intending 'exhibit' to mean 'inhibit'.*

› **exhibiter** also spelled **exhibitor** NOUN
proposer
• *(H5 1.1.74) Canterbury tells Ely he thinks Henry supports their cause rather 'Than cherishing th'exhibiters against us'.*

› **exhibition** NOUN
⚠ *Don't read the modern meaning of 'a public display' into these senses.*
1 maintenance
• *(Oth 1.3.235) Othello asks the Duke to give Desdemona 'Due reference of place and exhibition'—appropriate lodging and support.*
2 gift
• *(Oth 4.3.72) Emilia says she would never be unfaithful to her husband for 'any petty exhibition'.*
3 intended to mean 'permission'
• *(MA 4.2.5) Verges tells the Sexton they 'have the exhibition to examine' the prisoners.*

exigent NOUN
critical time
• *(JC 5.1.19) Antony asks Octavius: 'Why do you cross me in this exigent?'—why are you arguing with me right now?*

exit see **STAGE DIRECTIONS, p.285**

exorcist NOUN
⚠ *Don't read in the modern meaning of 'one who drives out spirits'.*
one who summons spirits
• *(JC 2.1.323) Ligarius tells Brutus he will throw off his sickness: 'Thou, like an exorcist, hast conjur'd up / My mortified spirit'.*

EXCLAMATIONS

Shakespeare's characters have several ways of expressing their feelings of impatience, contempt, or disgust.

buzz
impatience when you are told something you already know
• *(Ham 2.2.383) Polonius tells Hamlet that a company of actors is coming to Elsinore, but Hamlet has already heard the news: 'Buzz, buzz'.*
Actors have found many different ways to say this line—pretending he's distracted by an imaginary fly, joking to his friends that Polonius' words are boring, pretending to hear a vibrating mobile phone: the possibilities with this line are fairly endless.

fie
disgust and contempt
• *(Ham 1.2.135) Hamlet thinks the world is an awful place: 'Fie on't, ah fie, 'tis an unweeded garden / That grows to seed'.*

a fig
said of anything that is small and has no value
• *(Oth 1.3.315) Iago is contemptuous when Roderigo says that his 'virtue' keeps him doting on Desdemona: 'Virtue? A fig!'*

fig's end
even smaller than a fig!
• *(Oth 2.1.243) Roderigo says that Desdemona is 'full of most blest condition', but Iago shows his contempt for that idea: 'Blest fig's end!'*

go to
impatience, similar to modern English 'come, come!'
• *(TN 4.1.2) Sebastian tries to stop Feste bothering him: 'Go to, go to, thou art a foolish fellow'.*

how
surprise and irritation, as when today we say 'What?!'
• *(KL 1.1.93) Lear is very surprised at Cordelia's expression of love for him: 'How, how, Cordelia! Mend your speech a little'.*

out on thee/you
angry reproach, as when today we say 'Away with you!'
• *(MA 4.1.55) Hero protests her innocence, but Claudio doesn't believe her: 'Out on thee! Seeming!'*
Some editions present this line differently, and have 'Out on thy seeming', in which case 'Out on' means 'That's enough of'.

pish
strong anger and disgust
• *(Oth 4.1.41) Othello trembles in fury to hear of Desdemona's supposed infidelity: 'It is not words that shakes me thus. Pish!'*

tilly-vally
impatient denial, similar to modern 'fiddlesticks' or 'nonsense'
• *(TN 2.3.69) Sir Toby dismisses Maria's worry that Olivia will turn him out of doors because of all the noise he's been making: 'Am I not of her blood? Tilly-vally!'*
The expression allows various interpretations, such as a serenading persuasion to Maria.

tush
impatient disregard for what has just been said
• *(RJ 4.2.39) Capulet dismisses his wife's worries that there isn't enough time to get things ready for Juliet's wedding: 'Tush, I will stir about, / And all things shall be well'.*

expectancy NOUN
hope for the future
• *(Ham 3.1.152) Ophelia describes Hamlet as 'Th'expectancy and rose of the fair state'.*

› **expectation** NOUN
hopefulness
• *(H5 3.4.44) The Governor tells Henry: 'Our expectation hath this day an end'.*

expedience NOUN
speed
• *(H5 4.3.70) Salisbury says the French 'will with all expedience charge on us'.*

expedition NOUN
1 speedy action
• *(Mac 2.3.106) Macbeth claims he killed Duncan's*

attendants because *'Th'expedition of my violent love / Outran the pauser, reason'.*
2 warlike enterprise
• *(JC 4.3.170) Brutus says the enemy powers are 'Bending their expedition toward Philippi'.*
3 ready awareness
• *(H5 3.3.22) The Welsh Captain describes Captain Jamy as someone 'of great expedition and knowledge in th'anchient wars'.*

expense NOUN
⚠*Don't read in the modern meaning of 'how much something costs'.*
spending
• *(KL 2.1.99) Regan thinks Lear's knights have persuaded Edgar to kill Gloucester to get his money—'To have th'expense and waste of his revenues'.*

experimental ADJECTIVE
⚠*Don't read in the modern meaning of 'scientific testing'.*
on the basis of experience
• *(MA 4.1.165) The Friar says his observation of Hero's innocence is confirmed by his 'experimental seal'.*

exposition NOUN
intended to mean 'disposition'- inclination
• *(MND 4.1.38) Bottom tells Titania: 'I have an exposition of sleep come upon me'.*

expostulate VERB
⚠*Don't read the modern meaning of 'protest strongly' into these senses.*
1 expound
• *(Ham 2.2.86) Polonius tells Claudius he is not going to 'expostulate / What majesty should be'.*
2 argue at length
• *(Oth 4.1.200) Othello says he will not 'expostulate with' Desdemona.*

express ADJECTIVE
⚠*Don't read in the modern meaning of 'fast'.*
well formed
• *(Ham 2.2.300) Hamlet describes the nature of man—'in form and moving how express and admirable'.*

expressure NOUN
expression
• *(TN 2.3.141) Maria says she will depict Malvolio in Olivia's letter by 'the expressure of his eye, forehead, and complexion'.*

exquisite ADJECTIVE
ingenious
• *(TN 2.3.127) Sir Toby asks Sir Andrew why he will beat Malvolio: 'Thy exquisite reason, dear knight?'*

exsufflicate ADJECTIVE
blown up out of all proportion
• *(Oth 3.3.184) Othello says he would never listen to 'exsufflicate and blown surmises'—exaggerations and insinuations.*

extempore ADVERB
spontaneously
• *(MND 1.2.60) Quince tells Snug, of the lion's part: 'You may do it extempore'—improvise it!*

extent NOUN
1 show (of politeness)
• *(Ham 2.2.363) Hamlet hopes his show of welcome—his 'extent to the players'—won't be more than that given to Rosencrantz and Guildenstern.*
2 assault
• *(TN 4.1.47) Olivia apologizes to Sebastian for 'this uncivil and unjust extent / Against thy peace'.*

extenuate VERB
lessen
• *(MND 1.1.120) Theseus tells Hermia about the force of the Athenian law 'Which by no means we may extentuate'.*

extinct ADJECTIVE
extinguished
• *(Ham 1.3.118) Polonius describes Hamlet's advances to Ophelia as 'Giving more light than heat, extinct in both / Even in their promise'—disappearing as soon as he makes them.*

› **extincted** ADJECTIVE
extinguished
• *(Oth 2.1.81) Cassio hopes Othello will 'Give renew'd fire to our extincted spirits'.*

extirpate VERB
drive away, exile
• *(Tem 1.2.125) Prospero tells Miranda how Antonio wanted to 'extirpate me and mine / Out of the dukedom'.*

extracting ADJECTIVE
preoccupying
• *(TN 5.1.272) Olivia explains that she forgot about Malvolio because of 'A most extracting frenzy of mine own'—her infatuation with Cesario.*

extravagancy NOUN
drifting around
• *(TN 2.1.10) Sebastian says that his 'determinate voyage is mere extravagancy'—the reason for his travelling is just to wander about.*

› **extravagant** ADJECTIVE
wandering
• *(Ham 1.1.159) Horatio has heard that the crowing of the morning cock makes*

'Th'extravagant and erring spirit' return to his prison.

extremes NOUN
desperate straits
• *(RJ 4.1.62) Juliet threatens to use a knife to mediate ' 'Twixt my extremes and me'.*

eyas NOUN
young hawk (taken from the nest to be trained)
• *(Ham 2.2.332) Rosencrantz describes the child players as 'an eyrie of children, little eyases'—like noisy young hawks.*

eye NOUN
as well as meaning the part of the body and 'sight', you'll find:
1 appearance
• *(Mac 4.3.188) Ross tells Malcolm: 'Your eye in Scotland / Would create soldiers'.*
2 tinge
• *(Tem 2.1.54) Sebastian says the ground has 'an eye of green in't'.*

› in his eye
in front of him
• *(Ham 4.4.6) Fortinbras says if Claudius wants to see him, 'We shall express our duty in his eye'—pay our respects in person.*

› eyne NOUN
an old-fashioned word for 'eyes'
• *(MND 1.1.242) Helena reflects that 'ere Demetrius looked on Hermia's eyne, / He hail'd down oaths that he was only mine'.*
'Eyne' is a useful alternative to 'eyes' if you want to make a rhyme. In this play, Shakespeare rhymes it four times—with 'mine' (three times) and 'divine'.

eysell see **eisel**

face VERB
as well as meaning 'confront', you'll find:
1 bully
• *(TN 4.2.89) Malvolio tells Feste that his enemies 'do all they can to face me out of my wits'.*
2 exclude
• *(TN 5.1.83) Antonio says Cesario's cunning 'Taught him to face me out of his acquaintance'—he was so devious he pretended that we weren't friends.*

› face out VERB
act shamelessly
• *(H5 3.2.30) The Boy says Bardolph 'faces it out but fights not'—is all talk (all bark but no bite).*

› outface VERB
overcome by confronting
• *(KL 2.3.11) Edgar says he will 'outface / The winds and persecutions of the sky'.*

fact NOUN
as well as meaning 'something true', you'll find:
deed, especially of a wicked kind
• *(Mac 3.6.10) Lennox describes Duncan's death as a 'Damned fact'.*

warning note *usage note* *theatre note*

factious ADJECTIVE
ready to form a faction or group
• *(JC 1.3.118) Casca suggests a course of action to Cassius: 'Be factious for redress of all these griefs'—let us gather together a group of like-minded people to find a remedy for our grievances.*

fade VERB
decay
• *(Tem 1.2.400) Ariel sings of Ferdinand's drowned father's body turning into beautiful underwater objects: 'Nothing of him that doth fade / But doth suffer a sea-change / Into something rich and strange'.*

fadge VERB
turn out
• *(TN 2.2.32) Viola reflects on her situation: 'How will this fadge?'*

fain ADVERB
gladly
• *(MA 3.5.28) Leonato tells Dogberry and Verges: 'I would fain know what you have to say'.*

fain ADJECTIVE
glad
• *(KL 4.7.38) Cordelia asks Lear: 'wast thou fain, poor father, / To hovel thee with swine'—to sleep with pigs, for lack of any better shelter.*

faint ADJECTIVE
1 half-hearted
• *(KL 1.4.64) Lear says he has 'perceived a most faint neglect of late'.*
2 faint-hearted
• *(RJ 4.3.15) Juliet reflects: 'I have a faint cold fear thrills through my veins'.*
3 weak
• *(H5 1.1.16) Canterbury lists the Church's losses, such as almshouses for 'indigent faint souls, past corporal toil'—needy people not able to work any more.*
4 pale-coloured
• *(MND 1.1.215) Hermia reminds Helena how they often 'Upon faint primrose beds were wont to lie'.*

› **faintly** ADVERB
half-heartedly
• *(Oth 4.1.112) Othello reflects on Cassio's supposed seduction of Desdemona: 'Now he denies it faintly'.*

fair ADJECTIVE
1 good-looking
• *(Tem 4.1.24) Ferdinand hopes for 'fair issue'—beautiful children.*
2 plausible
• *(Mac 1.7.81) Macbeth tells his wife to 'mock the time with fairest show'—to pass the time by behaving in an innocent way.*
3 proper
• *(RJ 2.3.19) The Friar reflects on the way all natural things are good unless 'strain'd from that fair use'—unless they're used in a way they shouldn't be.*

fair ADVERB
1 kindly
• *(TN 5.1.182) Cesario tells Sir Andrew that he answered him courteously: 'I bespake you fair, and hurt you not'.*
2 elegantly
• *(Ham 5.2.32) Hamlet tells Horatio how he 'Devis'd a new commission, wrote it fair'—created a new set of orders, and wrote them as elegantly as a clerk would do.*

fair NOUN
beauty
• *(MND 1.1.182) Helena complains to Hermia: 'Demetrius loves your fair'.*

› **fair hour**
time of youth
• *(Ham 1.2.62) Claudius wishes Laertes well: 'Take thy fair hour'—enjoy yourself while you're young.*

› **fairly** ADVERB
1 cordially
• *(Ham 2.2.364) Hamlet says his welcome to the players 'must show fairly outwards'—show every sign of warmth.*
2 completely
• *(RJ 2.4.45) Mercutio tells Romeo: 'You gave us the counterfeit fairly last night'—you gave us the slip really well.*

faith NOUN
fidelity
• *(MA 1.1.66) Beatrice says Benedick 'wears his faith but as the fashion of his hat'—he is unfaithful as often as he changes his hat.*
see also SWEARING, p.298

› **faith** VERB
believe
• *(KL 2.1.69) Edmund tells Gloucester that if he were to expose Edgar's villainy he would never be 'faith'd', because he is illegitimate (a bastard), and thus automatically considered less trustworthy.*

falchion **see SWORDS AND DAGGERS, p.156**

fallow ADJECTIVE
uncultivated
• *(H5 5.2.44) Burgundy describes what has happened to the 'fallow leas' of France—the open countryside.*

fallow NOUN
area of arable land
• *(H5 5.2.54) Burgundy describes how the French 'vineyards, fallows, meads and hedges' have become wild.*

false ADJECTIVE
as well as meaning 'untrue' and 'fake', you'll find:
1 treacherous
• *(Tem 1.2.77) Prospero tells Miranda of his brother, calling him 'Thy false uncle'.*
2 unfaithful
• *(Oth 4.2.38) Othello shouts at Desdemona: 'thou art false as hell'.*
3 not good enough
• *(JC 4.3.291) Lucius tells Brutus that the strings on his instrument 'are false'—out of tune.*

false ADVERB
in a wrong way
• *(Tem 5.1.172) Miranda, playing chess with Ferdinand, complains: 'you play me false'—you're cheating!*

false NOUN
a deceiving person
• *(TN 2.2.28) Viola talks about how 'the proper false'—a handsome deceiver, such as herself in a male disguise—can attract a woman.*

› **false fire**
the discharge of blank cartridges
• *(Ham 3.2.255) Hamlet observes Claudius' reaction to the play: 'What, frighted with false fire?'*

› **falsehood** NOUN
treachery
• *(Tem 1.2.95) Prospero tells Miranda how his trust in his brother Antonio 'did beget of him / A falsehood' gave Antonio an opportunity to betray him.*

FAMILY

The names for the members of your family have not changed very much since Shakespeare's time; but there are a few differences.

grandam
your grandmother
• *(MV 2.2.184) Gratiano says he will stop being wild, and will behave like someone who puts on a serious show 'To please his grandam'.*

grandsire
your grandfather
• *(Ham 2.2.452) Hamlet recites a speech about the Trojan Wars when the Greek warrior Pyrrhus seeks out the king of Troy, 'Old grandsire Priam'.*

stepdame also spelled **step-dame**
your stepmother
• *(MND 1.1.5) Theseus complains about waiting for his wedding-day, comparing it to the time a young man has to wait to get his inheritance if 'a step-dame' stands in the way.*

brother
could also be your brother-in-law
• *(KL 4.2.15) Goneril tells Edmund to take a message back 'to my brother'; she means Cornwall, who is married to her sister Regan.*

son
could also be your son-in-law
• *(KL 1.1.40) Lear calls the husbands of his two daughters 'Our son of Cornwall, / And you, our no less loving son of Albany'.*

dam
the mother of an animal, or someone who is said to be like an animal
• *(Mac 4.3.220) Macduff describes his murdered family as 'all my pretty chickens and their dam'.*

WHO CAN BE YOUR COUSIN?

In Shakespeare's day, you could call almost any relative your cousin, as well as people who did not belong to your family at all, but who were your social equals (as long as you were on good terms with them, or wanted to be).

• *(Ham 1.2.64) Claudius calls Hamlet 'my cousin Hamlet'—though he is actually his stepfather.*
• *(TN 1.5.109) Olivia asks Sir Toby 'What is he at the gate, cousin?'—though he is actually her uncle.*
• *(H5 1.2.235) King Henry refers to 'our fair cousin Dauphin'—though he is not actually related to him.*

When people know each other very well, they often shorten 'cousin' to 'coz' or 'cuz':
• *(MA 3.4.36) Hero greets Beatrice: 'Good morrow, coz'.*

a b c d e **Ff** g h i j k l m n o p q r s t u v w x y z

fancy NOUN
as well as meaning 'whim' and 'showiness', you'll find:
1 love
• *(MV 3.2.63) Words from a song while Bassanio chooses a casket: 'Tell me where is fancy bred'.*
2 lover
• *(Oth 3.4.59) Othello's mother was told that, if she lost her special handkerchief, his father 'should hunt / After new fancies'.*
3 imagination
• *(Ham 5.1.170) Hamlet describes Yorick as a man 'of most excellent fancy'.*
4 mind
• *(MA 3.1.95) Ursula asks Hero not to be angry with her for 'Speaking my fancy'.*
5 imagining
• *(Mac 5.3.39) The Doctor says Lady Macbeth is 'troubled with thick-coming fancies'.*

fancy VERB
⚠ *Don't read in the modern meaning of 'have a sudden liking' for someone or something.*
fall in love
• *(TN 2.5.23) Malvolio reflects about Olivia: 'should she fancy, it should be one of my complexion'.*

› **fancy-sick** ADJECTIVE
love-sick
• *(MND 3.2.96) Oberon describes Helena as being 'All fancy-sick'.*

fanned ADJECTIVE
well-sifted
• *(Ham 5.2.180) Hamlet comments on the way Osric copes with 'the most fanned and winnowed opinons'—the most tried and tested views.*

fantastico NOUN
absurd fop
• *(RJ 2.4.28) Mercutio describes Tybalt as one of the 'antic, lisping, affecting fantasticoes'—grotesque, mannered, and affected.*
'Fantasticoes' is the word used in the First Quarto text of the play. In the First Folio the word is printed as 'phantacies'. Some editions emend this to 'phantasimes'.

fantasy NOUN
1 imagining
• *(MND 2.1.258) Oberon threatens to make Titania 'full of hateful fantasies'.*
2 imagination
• *(JC 3.3.2) Cinna the poet reflects on his dream: 'things unluckily charge my fantasy'—ominously weigh down his mind.*
3 whim
• *(Oth 3.3.301) Emilia decides to give Desdemona's handkerchief to Iago 'to please his fantasy'.*

› **fantastic** ADJECTIVE
⚠ *Don't read in the modern colloquial meaning of 'really good'.*
fanciful, grotesque
• *(Ham 4.7.168) Gertrude describes the scene of Ophelia's death: 'fantastic garlands did she make'.*

› **fantastical** ADJECTIVE
1 fanciful, highly creative
• *(MA 2.3.20) Benedick finds Claudio's words to be 'a very fantastical banquet, just so many strange dishes'.*
2 imaginary
• *(Mac 1.3.51) Banquo asks the Witches: 'Are ye fantastical?'*

› **fantastically** ADVERB
fancifully
• *(KL 4.6.80) Stage direction: 'Enter Lear, fantastically dressed with wild flowers'.*
This is one of the most famous stage directions in Shakespeare. Most productions understand 'fantastically' in its modern meaning, and cover Lear in colourful flowers. But there were many meanings of the word in Shakespeare's time, and choosing which of these fits best will depend on what kind of entrance you want Lear to make: grotesque? bizarre? ridiculous...?

farce VERB
cram
• *(Mac 5.5.5) Macbeth says the besieging troops are 'farced with those that should be ours'—Scottish soldiers who have changed sides to fight against him.*
Some editions replace 'farced' with 'forced' or 'forc'd' (meaning 'reinforced'), which is the word that appears in the First Folio.

› **farced** ADJECTIVE
stuffed with flattery
• *(H5 4.1.251) Henry reflects on the long-winded way in which people address a king: 'The farced title running 'fore the king'.*

fardel NOUN
burden
• *(Ham 3.1.76) Hamlet reflects: 'Who would fardels bear, / To grunt and sweat'.*

fare VERB
turn out
• *(MA 4.1.221) The Friar predicts that Claudio will

come to prize what he has lost: 'So will it fare with Claudio'.

› how fares?

an enquiry as to how someone is coping with a situation

• *(Tem 5.1.253) Prospero asks Alonso: 'How fares my gracious sir?'*

farewell, fare thee/you well see GOODBYE, p.121

fashion-monging ADJECTIVE

dandified

• *(MA 5.1.94) Antonio describes Claudio and Don Pedro as 'fashion-monging boys'.*

fast ADJECTIVE

1 firm

• *(Oth 1.3.356) Roderigo asks Iago if he will be loyal: 'Wilt thou be fast to my hopes?'*

2 fast asleep

• *(RJ 4.5.1) The Nurse tries to wake Juliet: 'Fast, I warrant her'.*

fast VERB

do penance (suffer to obtain forgiveness for one's sins)

• *(Ham 1.5.11) The Ghost tells Hamlet how during the day he is 'confin'd to fast in fires'—because he was killed before his sins could be absolved.*

fasten VERB

as well as meaning 'attach one thing to another', you'll find:

establish

• *(JC 5.1.11) Antony considers what the enemy will do 'To fasten in our thoughts that they have courage'.*

› fastened ADJECTIVE

steadfast

• *(KL 2.1.76) Gloucester calls Edgar a 'strange and fast'ned villain!'*

fat ADJECTIVE

as well as meaning 'plump', you'll find:

heavy

• *(TN 5.1.104) Olivia says Orsino's love-suit is 'as fat and fulsome to mine ear / As howling after music'—gross and repulsive.*

fatal ADJECTIVE

as well as meaning 'causing death', you'll find:

ominous

• *(Mac 2.1.36) Macbeth describes his imaginary dagger as a 'fatal vision'.*

Fates NOUN

in Greek mythology, three goddesses who control human destiny, one of whom cuts the thread of life spun by the others

• *(MND 5.1.194) Thisbe says she will be faithful 'till the Fates me kill'.*

father NOUN

as well as its usual meaning of 'male parent', you'll find:

1 old man—as a term of address

• *(KL 4.6.72) The disguised Edgar tells Gloucester the gods have saved him: 'thou happy father'.*

This is often interpreted as Edgar calling Gloucester 'father' (male parent). Some productions choose this interpretation, portraying Edgar as forgetting he is in disguise.

2 stepfather

• *(Ham 3.4.8) Gertrude tells Hamlet: 'thou hast thy father much offended'.*

father VERB

1 resemble one's father

• *(MA 1.1.99) Don Pedro says, of Beatrice: 'the lady fathers herself'.*

2 be dealt with by a father

• *(KL 3.6.108) Edgar reflects on Lear: 'He childed as I father'd'—he was treated by his children as I was treated by my father.*

fathom NOUN

ability

• *(Oth 1.1.152) Iago reflects on the state's view of Othello: 'Another of his fathom they have none / To lead their business'—there's no-one else with skills like his to take command in the war.*

fault NOUN

Don't read the meaning of 'blame' into these senses.

as well as meaning 'offence', you'll find:

1 weakness

• *(H5 2.Chorus.20) The Chorus addresses England: 'thy fault France hath in thee found out'.*

2 loss of scent

• *(TN 2.5.119) Fabian says of Malvolio: 'the cur is excellent at faults'—good at picking up a scent that has gone cold.*

› for fault of

in the absence of

• *(RJ 2.4.111) Romeo replies to the Nurse's enquiry: 'I am the youngest of that name, for fault of a worse'—I'm the youngest in my family, in the absence of a younger sibling.*

a b c d e **Ff** g h i j k l m n o p q r s t u v w x y z

favour NOUN
1 appearance
- *(TN 3.4.302) The First Officer says to Antonio: 'I know your favour well'.*

2 charm
- *(Oth 4.3.21) Desdemona says that even Othello's frowns 'have grace and favour in them'.*

3 good will
- *(Ham 5.2.78) Hamlet says of Laertes: 'I'll court his favours'.*

4 gift
- *(MND 2.1.12) A Fairy describes the spots in cowslips as 'rubies, fairy favours'.*

5 token worn as a mark of identity or friendship
- *(H5 4.7.144) Henry asks the Welsh Captain: 'wear thou this favour for me'.*

6 pardon
- *(Mac 1.3.148) Macbeth begs the nobles' pardon for delaying: 'Give me your favour'.*

› **hard-favoured** also spelled **hard-favour'd** ADJECTIVE
ugly
- *(H5 3.1.8) Henry tells his soldiers: 'Disguise fair nature with hard-favour'd rage'.*

› **ill-favouredly** ADVERB
offensively
- *(H5 4.2.40) The French describe the English army as carcasses that 'Ill-favouredly become the morning field'—dead bodies that make the battlefield look ugly.*

› **well-favoured** ADJECTIVE
good-looking
- *(TN 1.5.149) Malvolio tells Olivia that Cesario 'is very well-favoured'.*

fay see **SWEARING, p.298**

fear VERB
1 as well as meaning 'feel fearful', you'll find: frighten
- *(MV 2.1.9) Morocco tells Portia: 'this aspect of mine / Hath fear'd the valiant'—my face has terrified even the most courageous men.*

2 fear for
- *(Ham 4.5.121) Claudius tells Gertrude: 'Do not fear our person'.*

3 doubt
- *(TN 5.1.212) Sebastian responds to Antonio's uncertainty over who he is: 'Fear'st thou that, Antonio?'*

fear NOUN
duty
- *(Ham 3.3.8) Guildenstern says that keeping people safe who depend on the king is a 'Most holy and religious fear'.*

feat ADJECTIVE
well fitting
- *(Tem 2.1.268) Antonio comments on 'how well my garments sit upon me, / Much feater than before'.*

› **featly** ADVERB
gracefully
- *(Tem 1.2.378) Ariel sings: 'Foot it featly here and there'.*

feat NOUN
⚠ *Don't read in the positive meaning of 'an action displaying skill or strength'.*
wicked deed
- *(H5 3.4.17) Henry describes the cruel acts of war: 'all fell feats / Enlink'd to waste and desolation'.*

fee in the phrase **in fee**
with complete possession, as a freehold
- *(Ham 4.4.22) The Captain says the land being fought over is worthless, even if it were 'sold in fee'.*

› **fee-simple** also spelled **fee simple** NOUN
complete possession
- *(RJ 3.1.31) Benvolio says, if he quarrelled as much as Mercutio, 'any man should buy the fee-simple of my life for an hour and a quarter'—because he would be dead by the end of that hour or so.*

fee-grief NOUN
individual sorrow
- *(Mac 4.3.198) Macduff asks if Ross's news is of general interest 'or is it a fee-grief / Due to some single breast?'*

felicitate ADJECTIVE
made happy
- *(KL 1.1.74) Regan tells Lear: 'I am alone felicitate / In your dear highness' love'—made happy only by the love I have for you.*

fell ADJECTIVE
1 fierce
- *(MND 5.1.217) Snug the joiner describes his character as 'A lion fell'.*

2 terrible
- *(Mac 1.5.45) Lady Macbeth wants no natural feelings to 'Shake my fell purpose'.*

fell ADVERB
fiercely
- *(Ham 5.2.61) Hamlet warns against coming between the 'fell incensed points / Of mighty opposites'—the fiercely inflamed swords of great opponents.*

fell NOUN
skin
- *(KL 5.3.24) Lear tells Cordelia their enemies shall be devoured, 'flesh and fell'—completely.*

fellow NOUN
as well as meaning 'companion', you'll find:
1 equal
• *(TN 3.4.72) Malvolio is impressed that Olivia has called him 'Not Malvolio, nor after my degree, but "fellow"'.*
2 spouse
• *(Tem 3.1.84) Miranda tells Ferdinand: 'To be your fellow / You may deny me'.*

› **fellowly** ADVERB
as companions
• *(Tem 5.1.64) Prospero says his tears are falling like Gonzalo's, with 'fellowly drops'.*

› **unfellowed** ADJECTIVE
unequalled
• *(Ham 5.2.136) Osric says of Laertes' fencing skill: 'he's unfellowed'.*

felly NOUN
a piece of curved wood forming part of a wheel rim
• *(Ham 2.2.483) The First Player asks the gods to take away power from Fortune: 'Break all the spokes and fellies from her wheel'.*

fence NOUN
fencing ability
• *(MA 5.1.75) Leonato talks of Claudio's 'nice fence and his active practice'.*

fenny ADJECTIVE
marsh-dwelling
• *(Mac 4.1.12) The Second Witch puts into the cauldron 'Fillet of a fenny snake'.*

fen-sucked ADJECTIVE
rising from marshes
• *(KL 2.4.163) Lear curses Goneril: 'Infect her beauty, / You fen-suck'd fogs'—thick mists.*
Fogs were supersititously thought to be harmful to humans, carrying infections and causing skin blisters.

festinate ADJECTIVE
speedy
• *(KL 3.7.10) Edmund is sent to tell Albany to make 'a most festinate preparation' for war.*

fet VERB
derive
• *(H5 3.1.18) Henry addresses his soldiers as men 'Whose blood is fet from fathers of war-proof'—whose fathers were soldiers experienced in battle.*

fetch VERB
as well as meaning 'bring', you'll find:
1 perform
• *(MV 5.1.73) Lorenzo describes a herd of male horses (colts) 'Fetching mad bounds'—making wild leaps.*
2 derive
• *(H5 2.2.113) Henry describes devils working with pretences 'fetch'd / From glistering semblances of piety'—derived from apparent instances of beautiful holiness.*

› **fetch in** VERB
trick into making a confession
• *(MA 1.1.203) Claudio accuses Don Pedro: 'You speak this to fetch me in'.*

› **fetch off** VERB
get back
• *(Tem 4.1.212) Stephano tells Trinculo: 'I will fetch off my bottle'.*

fettle VERB
make ready
• *(RJ 3.5.153) Capulet tells Juliet to be ready for her wedding: 'fettle your fine joints 'gainst Thursday next'.*

few in the phrase **in few**
in short
• *(Ham 1.3.126) Polonius sums up his advice about Hamlet: 'In few, Ophelia, / Do not believe his vows'.*

fico also spelled **figo** NOUN
[pronounced **fick**-oh or **fig**-oh]
a word used along with a rude gesture—putting the thumb between the first two fingers of a fist (like giving someone the finger today)
• *(H5 4.1.59) Pistol tells disguised King Henry: 'The 'fico' for thee, then!'*

fie away VERB
be off
• *(TN 2.4.52) Feste sings: 'Fie away, fie away breath'.*
see also EXCLAMATIONS, p.99

field NOUN
as well as its usual meaning of 'an enclosed piece of land', you'll find:
1 battlefield
• *(JC 5.3.107) Brutus tells young Cato: 'let us to the field'.*
2 duelling place
• *(RJ 3.1.55) Mercutio tells Tybalt: 'go before to field'.*

fig see **EXCLAMATIONS, p.99**

figo see **fico**

a b c d e **Ff** g h i j k l m n o p q r s t u v w x y z

figure NOUN
as well as meaning 'shape' and 'portrayal', you'll find:
1 figure of speech
• *(Ham 2.2.98) Polonius describes his use of language as 'A foolish figure'.*
2 comparison
• *(H5 4.7.29) The Welsh Captain compares Henry and Alexander the Great: 'there is figures in all things'.*
3 imagining
• *(JC 2.1.231) Brutus addresses sleeping Lucius: 'Thou hast no figures nor no fantasies'.*

filbert NOUN
hazel-nut
• *(Tem 2.2.166) Caliban promises to bring Stephano 'To clust'ring filberts'.*

file NOUN
register
• *(Mac 3.1.94) Macbeth tells the Murderers that a 'valu'd file' (an official register) of dogs gives details about different breeds, unlike a mere list of names.*

file VERB
defile
• *(Mac 3.1.66) Macbeth reflects: 'For Banquo's issue have I fil'd my mind'—I've corrupted myself for the benefit of Banquo's children.*

fill-horse NOUN
horse that goes between shafts to pull a cart
• *(MV 2.2.89) Gobbo compares Lancelot to 'Dobbin my fill-horse'.*

filthy-mantled see **mantle**

find VERB
as well as meaning 'discover', you'll find:
1 see through
• *(H5 4.1.247) Henry reflects on flattery: 'I am a king that find thee'.*
2 find the truth about
• *(Ham 3.1.185) Polonius says that, if Gertrude doesn't discover what is wrong with Hamlet, he should be sent away from Denmark: 'If she find him not, / To England send him'.*
3 provide
• *(H5 1.2.72) Canterbury tells how Hugh Capet proceeded 'To find his title with some shows of truth'.*
In the 'Henry V' quotation, 'find' is the word used in the First Folio. The Quarto text of the play has 'fine', meaning 'refine', and this is used in some editions.

› **finder** NOUN
a member of a jury whose role is to decide if someone is insane
• *(TN 3.4.127) Sir Toby tells Maria that the success of her scheme will 'crown thee for a finder of madmen'.*

fine ADJECTIVE
as well as meaning 'excellent' and 'full of tiny particles', you'll find:
1 graceful
• *(Tem 1.2.317) Prospero addresses Ariel: 'Fine apparition!'*
2 finely clothed
• *(Tem 5.1.262) Caliban looks at Prospero: 'How fine my master is!'*
3 artificially beautiful
• *(Ham 2.2.433) Hamlet describes a play he once saw as being 'very much more handsome than fine'—its beauty was much more natural than artificial.*
4 sensitive
• *(Ham 4.5.160) Laertes reflects on Ophelia: 'Nature is fine in love'—by its nature, love is sensitive.*

fine NOUN
⚠ *Don't read the meaning of 'financial punishment' into these senses.*
1 final result
• *(MA 1.1.223) Benedick concludes: 'the fine is ... I will live a bachelor'.*
2 agreement to transfer possession of land
• *(Ham 5.1.98) Hamlet reflects on a lawyer who might have been 'a great buyer of land, with his statutes, his recognizances, his fines'.*
Hamlet then plays with the word, imagining a skull he finds to be that of a lawyer: 'Is this the fine of his fines?'—the final result of his legal procedures.

› **in fine**
finally
• *(KL 2.1.47) Edmund tells Gloucester what Edgar said, concluding: 'in fine ... he charges home / My unprovided body'.*

fine VERB
pledge
• *(H5 4.7.63) Henry informs Montjoy: 'I have fin'd these bones of mine for ransom'.*
see also the note at **find** 3

› **fineless** ADJECTIVE
infinite
• *(Oth 3.3.175) Iago says that 'riches fineless is as poor as winter / To him that ever fears he shall be poor'—if someone is afraid of becoming poor, they always will be poor, no matter how much money they have.*

finical ADJECTIVE
nit-picking
• *(KL 2.2.17) Kent describes Oswald as a 'finical rogue'.*

firago NOUN [pronounced vi-**rah**-go]
a war-like person, a virago—usually said of a woman
• *(TN 3.4.252) Sir Toby describes Cesario's fighting skills: 'I have not seen such a firago'.*

firebrand NOUN
⚠ *Don't read in the meaning of 'a person who stirs up trouble'.*
will-o'-the-wisp
• *(Tem 2.2.6) Caliban fears that Prospero's invisible spirits will lead him in the dark 'like a firebrand'—a magical being, made of light, like the flickering sparks from burning wood.*

firk VERB
beat
• *(H5 4.4.23) Pistol says what he will do to the French soldier named Fer: 'I'll fer him, and firk him'.*

first NOUN
1 beginning
• *(Mac 5.2.11) Lennox describes English soldiers who 'Protest their first of manhood'—acting like men for the first time.*
2 first colour named in describing a coat-of-arms
• *(MND 3.2.213) Helena describes herself and Hermia as 'Two of the first, like coats in heraldry'.*

› **at first and last**
to one and all
• *(Mac 3.4.1) Macbeth greets his guests: 'at first and last, the hearty welcome'.*

› **upon our first**
on our first raising the matter
• *(Ham 2.2.61) Voltemand reports that Fortinbras 'Upon our first, he sent out to suppress / His nephew's levies'.*

firstling NOUN
first fruits
• *(Mac 4.1.146) Macbeth says: 'The very firstlings of my heart shall be / The firstlings of my hand'—he will turn his first thoughts immediately into actions.*

fitchew see ANIMALS, p.162

fitly ADVERB
1 fittingly
• *(KL 1.1.199) Lear offers Cordelia's hand in marriage to Burgundy if it 'may fitly like your grace'—if you feel it is fitting.*
2 at the right time
• *(KL 1.2.160) Edmund tells Edgar: 'I will fitly bring you to hear my lord speak'.*

fitness NOUN
⚠ *Don't read the meaning of 'being in good shape' into these senses.*
1 proper behaviour
• *(KL 4.2.63) Albany says he would hit Goneril 'Were't my fitness / To let these hands obey my blood'.*
2 inclination
• *(Ham 5.2.187) Hamlet 'If his fitness speaks, mine is ready'—I'm ready if Laertes is.*

flat ADJECTIVE
1 plain
• *(MA 2.1.205) Benedick describes 'The flat transgression of a schoolboy'.*
2 feeble
• *(H5 Prologue.9) The Chorus describes the players as 'flat unraised spirits'—dull and uninspired.*

flat-long ADJECTIVE
with the flat side of a sword
• *(Tem 2.1.177) Sebastian describes Gonzalo's reaction as being a blow 'fall'n flat-long'—ineffective.*

flattery NOUN
⚠ *Don't read the meaning of 'praising someone more than is deserved' into these senses.*
self-delusion
• *(Oth 4.1.128) Cassio says Bianca thinks he will marry her 'out of her own love and flattery'—she flatters herself to think he would do so.*

› **flattering-sweet** ADJECTIVE
delightfully appealing
• *(RJ 2.2.141) Romeo thinks seeing Juliet is a dream 'Too flattering-sweet to be substantial'.*

› **flatter with** VERB
encourage
• *(TN 1.5.283) Olivia wants Cesario 'not to flatter with his lord'.*

flaw NOUN
⚠ *Don't read the meaning of 'something imperfect' into these senses.*
1 gust
• *(Mac 3.4.63) Lady Macbeth criticizes her husband for his 'flaws and starts'—his sudden gusts of emotion.*
2 fragment
• *(KL 2.4.282) Lear says his heart 'Shall break into a hundred thousand flaws' before he'll weep.*

› **flawed** also spelled **flaw'd** ADJECTIVE
broken
• *(KL 5.3.195) Edgar reflects on Gloucester's 'flaw'd heart'.*

fleer VERB
sneer
• *(RJ 1.5.56) Tybalt is angry, thinking that Romeo

a
b
c
d
e
Ff
g
h
i
j
k
l
m
n
o
p
q
r
s
t
u
v
w
x
y
z

has come to the party *'To fleer and scorn at our solemnity'.*

fleer NOUN
sneer
• *(Oth 4.1.82) Iago tells Othello to watch Cassio carefully: 'mark the fleers, the gibes'.*

› **fleering** ADJECTIVE
sneering
• *(JC 1.3.117) Casca describes himself as someone 'That is no fleering tell-tale'.*

fleet VERB
1 turn
• *(MV 3.2.108) Portia reflects: 'How all the other passions fleet to air'.*
2 pass away (of a soul)
• *(MV 4.1.135) Gratiano tells Shylock he is like a hanged wolf that 'from the gallows did his fell soul fleet'.*

fleet NOUN
⚠ *Don't read in the meaning of 'a group of ships'.*
assembly (here, of people)
• *(MA 2.1.131) Beatrice says she is sure that Benedick 'is in the fleet'.*

flesh VERB
1 use a sword for the first time in battle
• *(H5 2.4.50) The French King says, of Henry, 'The kindred of him hath been flesh'd upon us'—he has shown his character by the way he has fought for the first time.*
2 initiate (in shedding blood)
• *(KL 2.2.43) Kent threatens to fight: 'I'll flesh ye'.*

› **fleshed** ADJECTIVE
1 well used to bloodshed
• *(H5 3.4.11) Henry describes 'the flesh'd soldier' in his army.*
2 ready for a fight
• *(TN 4.1.34) Sir Toby tells Sebastian 'you are well fleshed'.*

› **fleshment** NOUN
first achievement
• *(KL 2.2.119) Oswald describes how Kent followed up his first attack: 'in the fleshment of this dread exploit, / Drew on me here again'.*

flesh-fly NOUN
fly that lays its eggs in dead flesh
• *(Tem 3.1.63) Ferdinand says he would normally not do menial work any more than he would tolerate 'The flesh-fly blow my mouth'—lay eggs in his mouth.*

fleur-de-lis see **flower-de-luce**

flewed also spelled **flew'd** ADJECTIVE
with large cheek folds
• *(MND 4.1.119) Theseus describes his hounds as 'bred out of the Spartan kind, / So flew'd, so sanded'.*

flexure NOUN
bending (of the knee or head)
• *(H5 4.1.243) Henry asks, of greatness, 'Will it give place to flexure and low bending?'—will it yield before the kneeling and bowing of flattering courtiers?*

Flibbertigibbet NOUN
[pronounced flib-er-tee-**jib**-et]
one of the fiends of hell
• *(KL 4.1.60) Poor Tom says five fiends have possessed him, including 'Flibbertigibbet, of mopping and mowing'—a fiend who grimaces.*

flight NOUN
as well as meanings to do with flying or fleeing, you'll find:
1 archery contest
• *(MA 1.1.36) Beatrice says that Benedick 'challenged Cupid at the flight'.*
2 size and weight
• *(MV 1.1.141) Bassanio says that, when he had lost one arrow, 'I shot his fellow of the selfsame flight'.*

flighty ADJECTIVE
⚠ *Don't read in the modern meaning of 'silly and frivolous'.*
swiftly conceived
• *(Mac 4.1.144) Macbeth reflects: 'The flighty purpose never is o'ertook / Unless the deed go with it'—the idea that comes to you quickly is never achieved unless you immediately act on it.*

flirt-gill NOUN
loose woman
• *(RJ 2.4.140) The Nurse dismisses Mercutio: 'I am none of his flirt-gills'.*

float also spelled **flote** NOUN
sea
• *(Tem 1.2.234) Ariel tells Prospero that the rest of Antonio's fleet is returning to Naples 'upon the Mediterranean float'.*

'Flote' is the form that appears in the First Folio.

flood NOUN

Don't read the meaning of 'large amount of unexpected water' into these senses.

1 sea

• *(MND 2.1.127) Titania describes watching 'th'embarked traders on the flood'.*

2 river

• *(JC 1.2.103) Caesar challenges Cassius: 'Leap in with me into this angry flood'.*

3 time of flowing in

• *(JC 4.3.219) Brutus reflects: 'There is a tide in the affairs of men / Which, taken at the flood, leads on to fortune'.*

Florentine NOUN

someone from Florence in northern Italy

• *(Oth 3.1.39) Cassio, a native of Florence, is surprised at the apparent kindness of Iago, a Venetian: 'I never knew a Florentine more kind and honest'.*

flote see **float**

flourish NOUN

as well as meaning 'extravagant gesture' or 'showy ornamentation', you'll find:

musical fanfare (of trumpets) announcing someone's arrival—frequently in stage directions

• *(MV 2.1.1) Stage direction: 'A flourish of cornets. Enter the Prince of Morocco.'*

flout VERB

mock

• *(Mac 1.2.49) Ross describes the region of Fife 'Where the Norwegian banners flout the sky'—the foreign flags insult the Scottish skies.*

> **flouting** ADJECTIVE
>
> mocking
>
> • *(MA 1.1.167) Benedick asks Claudio: 'do you play the flouting Jack'?—be a scornful fellow.*

flower-de-luce also spelled **flower de luce** NOUN [pronounced flower-duh-**loos**]

heraldic lily that is the royal symbol of France

• *(H5 5.2.202) Henry addresses Kate as 'my fair flower de luce'.*

'Flower-de-Luce' is the form that appears in the First Folio. Some editions replace this with the modern 'fleur-de-lis'.

fly-blowing NOUN

having flies lay their eggs

• *(Tem 5.1.283) Trinculo says 'I shall not fear fly-blowing'—flies won't come near him because he is so full of liquor.*

foil NOUN

as well as meaning 'a light blunted sword used in fencing', you'll find:

1 defeat

• *(Tem 3.1.46) Ferdinand compares Miranda to other women, each of whom had a defect that 'Did quarrel with the noblest grace she ow'd, / And put it to the foil'—it caused their best feature to be ignored.*

2 setting

• *(Ham 5.2.240) Hamlet says to Laertes, punning on 'foil' meaning 'sword': 'I'll be your foil'—a background that will set him off to advantage (I'll make you look good).*

see also SWORDS AND DAGGERS, p.156

foin NOUN

sword-thrust

• *(KL 4.6.240) Edgar tells Oswald: 'no matter vor your foins'—your sword-thrusts don't bother me.*

> **foining** ADJECTIVE
>
> thrusting (in swordplay)
>
> • *(MA 5.1.84) Antonio threatens Claudio: 'I'll whip you from your foining fence'.*

foison also spelled **foizon** NOUN

[pronounced **foy**-zun]

abundance

• *(Mac 4.3.88) Macduff tells Malcolm that 'Scotland hath foisons to fill up your will'—an abundance of things to satisfy his greed.*

folly NOUN

as well as meaning 'foolishness', you'll find:

lewdness

• *(Oth 5.2.133) Othello says that Desdemona 'turned to folly'—she was unfaithful to him.*

fond ADJECTIVE

as well as meaning 'loving', you'll find:

foolish

• *(RJ 3.3.52) The Friar calls Romeo: 'Thou fond mad man'.*

fond VERB

dote

• *(TN 2.2.33) Viola reflects that she loves Orsino as much as he, in turn, loves Olivia: 'I, poor monster, fond as much on him'.*

a b c d e **Ff** g h i j k l m n o p q r s t u v w x y z

fool NOUN
as well as meaning 'simpleton', you'll find:
1 darling
• *(KL 5.3.304) Lear says of Cordelia: 'And my poor fool is hang'd'.*
There has been debate over whether this line could refer to Lear's Fool.
2 jester
• *(MND 4.1.207) Bottom reflects: 'man is but a patched fool'.*
Clowns, fools, and jesters would normally wear clothes of colourful patchwork.
3 plaything
• *(Ham 1.4.54) Hamlet describes people as 'fools of nature'.*

foot VERB
1 walk about
• *(KL 3.4.113) Poor Tom recites: 'Swithold footed thrice the wold'—St Withold walked around the South Downs three times.*
2 gain a foothold
• *(H5 2.4.144) Exeter tells the Dauphin that Henry is in France: 'He is footed in this land already'.*
3 kick
• *(MV 1.3.113) Shylock tells Antonio that he did 'foot me as you spurn a stranger cur'.*

› foot it
dance in a lively way
• *(RJ 1.5.25) Capulet tells the ladies: 'foot it, girls'.*

› at foot
close behind
• *(Ham 4.3.54) Claudius tells attendants to follow Hamlet: 'Follow him at foot'.*

› footing NOUN
1 landing—setting foot on shore
• *(Oth 2.1.76) Cassio anticipates the arrival of Iago, 'Whose footing here anticipates our thoughts'.*
2 footsteps
• *(MV 5.1.24) Jessica says: 'I hear the footing of a man'.*
3 dance
• *(Tem 4.1.138) Iris invites the harvest reapers to join the nymphs 'In country footing'.*

fop NOUN
fool
• *(KL 1.2.14) Edmund reflects that his state (of being illegitimate—a bastard) is preferable to someone who creates 'a whole tribe of fops'.*

› fopped ADJECTIVE
fooled
• *(Oth 4.2.193) Roderigo criticizes Iago's attitude towards him: 'I say 'tis very scurvy and begin to find myself fopped in it'.*

› foppery NOUN
foolishness
• *(MV 2.5.34) Shylock says he doesn't want 'the sound of shallow foppery' to come into his house.*

› foppish ADJECTIVE
foolish
• *(KL 1.4.158) The Fool tells Lear that 'wise men are grown foppish'.*

force VERB
as well as meaning 'make happen using power', you'll find:
bring about
• *(H5 2.Chorus.32) 'we'll digest / Th'abuse of distance, force perforce a play'—through necessity, we'll manage to put on a play.*
see also the note at **farce**

force NOUN
violence
• *(MV 2.9.29) Arragon reflects on the way the martlet bird builds its nest 'on the outward wall, / Even in the force and road of casualty'—despite this being in the path of violence and disaster.*

› of force
necessarily
• *(JC 4.3.203) Brutus tells Cassius: 'Good reasons must of force give place to better'.*

fordo also spelled **foredo** past forms **fordid, fordone** VERB
1 ruin
• *(Oth 5.1.129) Iago reflects: 'This is the night / That either makes me, or fordoes me quite'.*
2 kill
• *(KL 5.3.290) Kent tells Lear: 'Your eldest daughters have fordone themselves'.*
3 exhaust
• *(MND 5.1.357) Puck describes the sleeping ploughman 'All with weary task foredone'—completely tired out.*

forehand also spelled **fore-hand** NOUN
Don't read in any meaning to do with tennis.
superiority
• *(H5 4.1.268) Henry reflects on an ordinary worker having 'the forehand and vantage of a king'.*

forerank also spelled **fore-rank** NOUN
main section
• *(H5 5.2.97) Henry says his marriage to Katherine is named 'Within the forerank of our articles'.*

forerun also spelled **fore-run** VERB
foreshadow
• *(RJ 5.1.53) Romeo recalls earlier thinking about*

Cockpit see p58

a b c d e Ff g h i j k l m n o p q r s t u v w x y z

poison: *'this same thought did but forerun my need'.*

forespent also spelled **forspent** ADJECTIVE
now exhausted or previously displayed
• *(H5 2.4.36) The Constable talks of Henry's 'vanities, forespent'.*

forespurrer see **spur**

fore-vouched see **vouch**

forfend VERB
forbid
• *(Oth 5.2.185) All react to the news of Desdemona's murder: 'O, heavens forfend!'*

› **forfended** ADJECTIVE
forbidden
• *(KL 5.1.11) Regan asks Edmund if he has ever found Albany's way 'To the forfended place'—made love to his wife Goneril.*

forged ADJECTIVE
fictitious
• *(Ham 1.5.37) The Ghost tells Hamlet how the people of Denmark have been told 'a forged process of my death'—a fabricated account.*

› **forgery** NOUN
as well as meaning 'fraudulent imitation', you'll find:
fictitious account
• *(Ham 2.1.20) Polonius says Reynaldo can make up things to say about Laertes—'What forgeries you please'.*

forget VERB
as well as meaning 'fail to remember', you'll find:
behave inappropriately
• *(Oth 2.3.172) Othello asks Cassio: 'How comes it, Michael, you are thus forgot?'—you've forgotten yourself.*

fork NOUN
⚠ *Don't read the meaning of 'a device with prongs' into these senses.*
1 forked tongue
• *(Mac 4.1.16) The Second Witch adds to the cauldron an 'Adder's fork'.*
2 barbed arrow-head
• *(KL 1.1.143) Kent defies Lear's threat of an arrow: 'though the fork invade / The region of my heart'.*

› **forks** NOUN
legs
• *(KL 4.6.117) Lear describes a woman 'Whose face between her forks presages snow'—warns of sexual coldness (she does not welcome sex).*

› **forked** ADJECTIVE
1 two-legged
• *(KL 3.4.103) Lear describes Poor Tom as 'a poor, bare, forked animal'.*
2 two-horned
• *(Oth 3.3.278) Othello describes unfaithfulness in marriage as a 'forked plague'.*
A cuckold (a man whose wife has been unfaithful) was imagined as having two horns growing from his forehead. A horned animal cannot see its horns, just as a betrayed husband cannot see his wife's unfaithfulness.

formal ADJECTIVE
1 rational
• *(TN 2.5.110) Malvolio thinks the meaning of Olivia's letter is obvious 'to any formal capacity'—reasonable mind.*
2 external
• *(JC 2.1.227) Brutus advises the conspirators to appear to others 'With untir'd spirits and formal constancy'—behave with their usual outward self.*

former ADJECTIVE
foremost
• *(JC 5.1.79) Cassius reports two eagles perching 'on our former ensign'—their leading flag of war.*

forsooth see **SWEARING, p.298**

forspent see **forespent**

forswear past form **forsworn** VERB
1 swear falsely
• *(Mac 4.3.126) Malcolm tells Macduff that he 'never was forsworn'—he has never intentionally lied or perjured himself until now.*
2 give up
• *(MND 2.1.62) Titania says of Oberon: 'I have forsworn his bed and company'.*
3 deny
• *(RJ 1.5.51) Romeo sees Juliet and asks himself: 'Did my heart love till now? forswear it, sight!'*

forthright also spelled **forth-right** NOUN
straight path
• *(Tem 3.3.3) Gonzalo describes the way he and his companions have come: 'Here's a maze trod indeed / Through forth-rights and meanders!'*

Fortune NOUN
in Roman mythology, a goddess, often represented as a blind woman turning a wheel controlling the rise and fall of destinies
• *(H5 3.7.25) Pistol describes 'giddy Fortune's furious fickle wheel'.*

forward ADJECTIVE
1 ready
• *(Ham 3.1.7) Guildenstern tells Claudius of Hamlet: 'Nor do we find him forward to be sounded'—he doesn't want to be questioned.*
2 presumptuous
• *(MA 1.3.49) Don John describes Claudio as 'A very forward March chick!'—a very self-confident young man (chicks were normally born in March).*
It's possible that Don John is here referring to Hero, in which case 'forward' would mean 'precocious'.
3 early
• *(Ham 1.3.8) Laertes describes Hamlet's love for Ophelia as 'Forward, not permanent'.*

foul ADJECTIVE
as well as meaning 'dirty' and 'disgusting', you'll find:
plain-looking
• *(Oth 2.1.138) Desdemona asks Iago to describe a woman who is 'foul and foolish'.*
› **foulness** NOUN
immorality
• *(KL 1.1.226) Cordelia asks Lear to make it clear that her situation is not due to any 'vicious blot, murther, or foulness'.*

foundation NOUN
charitable institution
• *(MA 5.1.311) Dogberry thanks Leonato for his recompense: 'God save the foundation!'—as if he had received it, as beggars did, from a charity.*

founder VERB
make lame
• *(MA 4.1.30) Ferdinand thinks his wedding-night will not come quickly because 'Phoebus' steeds are foundered'—the horses drawing the chariot of the sun have collapsed, so that the sun is taking a long time to set.*

fox NOUN
as well as meaning the animal, you'll find:
a type of sword (with a fox-like engraving on it)
• *(H5 4.4.8) Pistol threatens a French soldier: 'thou diest on point of fox'.*

fracted ADJECTIVE
broken
• *(H5 2.1.107) Pistol describes Falstaff's heart as 'fracted'.*

frailty NOUN
Don't read the meaning of 'physical weakness' into these senses.
1 moral weakness
• *(Ham 1.2.146) Hamlet reflects: 'Frailty, thy name is woman'.*
2 body
• *(Mac 2.3.122) Banquo suggests a meeting 'when we have our naked frailties hid'—when we have got dressed.*

frame NOUN
1 structure
• *(TN 1.1.33) Orsino describes Olivia as having a loving heart of 'fine frame'.*
2 plan
• *(MA 4.1.127) Leonato wonders why he once criticized 'frugal nature's frame'—for having just one child.*
3 order
• *(Ham 3.2.294) Guildenstern asks Hamlet to 'put your discourse into some frame'.*
4 plotting
• *(MA 4.1.188) Benedick describes Don John, 'Whose spirits toil in frame of villainies'.*

frame VERB
1 make
• *(MA 5.1.242) Don Pedro says Don John 'is compos'd and fram'd of treachery'.*
2 plan
• *(KL 1.2.93) Gloucester tells Edmund to find Edgar: 'frame the business after your own wisdom'.*

franchised also spelled **franchis'd** ADJECTIVE
free from evil
• *(Mac 2.1.28) Banquo wishes to keep 'My bosom franchis'd and allegiance clear'.*

Francis, Saint
Francis of Assisi, a 13th-century Italian saint
• *(RJ 2.3.65) Friar Lawrence swears by 'Holy Saint Francis'—the founder of the Franciscan order to which he belongs.*

frank ADJECTIVE
Don't read in the meaning of 'candid'.
generous
• *(RJ 2.2.131) Juliet tells Romeo she would withdraw her love 'But to be frank and give it thee again'.*
› **frankly** ADVERB
with no ill-will
• *(Ham 5.2.237) Hamlet says to Laertes he 'will this brothers' wager frankly play'.*

Frateretto NOUN [pronounced fra-tuh-**ret**-oh]
the name of a devil
• *(KL 3.6.6) Edgar says a demon is talking to him: 'Frateretto calls me'.*

a b c d e Ff g h i j k l m n o p q r s t u v w x y z

fraught NOUN
1 freight
• *(TN 5.1.56) The First Officer identifies Antonio as the man who 'took the 'Phoenix' and her fraught from Candy'.*
2 burden
• *(Oth 3.3.450) Othello tells his heart: 'Swell, bosom, with thy fraught'.*

fraught ADJECTIVE
laden
• *(MV 2.8.31) Salarino has heard about the wreck of 'A vessel of our country richly fraught'.*

› **fraughting** ADJECTIVE
making up the freight
• *(Tem 1.2.13) Miranda describes the doomed ship and 'The fraughting souls within her'.*

› **o'erfraught** ADJECTIVE
too heavily laden
• *(Mac 4.3.212) Malcolm tells Macduff that 'the grief that does not speak, / Whispers the o'erfraught heart and bids it break'—grief should be expressed and not bottled up, for fear of breaking one's heart.*

free ADJECTIVE
1 generous
• *(Ham 1.3.93) Polonius says Ophelia has 'been most free and bounteous' to meet Hamlet in her spare time.*
2 noble
• *(TN 1.5.240) Olivia says Orsino is 'free, learn'd, and valiant'.*
3 untroubled
• *(Oth 3.3 341) Othello remembers when he was 'free and merry'.*
4 innocent
• *(Ham 2.2.549) Hamlet imagines a passion that would 'Make mad the guilty and appal the free'.*
5 on the loose
• *(JC 2.1.79) Brutus talks of conspiracy showing itself at night 'When evils are most free'.*
6 frank
• *(Mac 1.3.154) Macbeth invites Banquo to 'speak / Our free hearts each to other'.*
7 freely given
• *(Ham 4.3.61) Claudius anticipates the attitude of the king of England: 'thy free awe / Pays homage to us'.*

French-crown-colour see **COLOURS, p.164**

fresh NOUN
freshwater stream
• *(Tem 3.2.65) Caliban says he will not show Trinculo 'Where the quick freshes are'.*

fret past forms **fretted, fretten** VERB
as well as meaning 'worry', you'll find:
1 eat away
• *(KL 1.4.275) Lear hopes that any child of Goneril's will 'With cadent tears fret channels in her cheeks'—make her as miserable as she's made him.*
2 chafe
• *(MV 4.1.77) Antonio describes the tops of mountain pines waving 'When they are fretten with the gusts of heaven'.*
3 adorn elaborately
• *(JC 2.1.104) Cinna the poet points out the coming dawn: 'yon grey lines / That fret the clouds are messengers of day'.*

friend NOUN
as well as meaning 'a person you like', you'll find:
1 sweetheart
• *(MA 2.1.77) Don Pedro asks Hero: 'will you walk a bout with your friend?'*
2 relative
• *(RJ 3.5.75) Lady Capulet sympathizes with Juliet for feeling the loss of 'the friend / Which you weep for'—she means Tybalt.*

frieze NOUN
a type of rough woollen cloth
• *(Oth 2.1.125) Iago says creativity comes from his brain 'as birdlime does from frieze'—as the sticky material used in catching birds comes away from cloth (with great difficulty).*

frippery NOUN
second-hand clothes shop
• *(Tem 4.1.223) Trinculo tells Caliban: 'We know what belongs to a frippery'.*

frock see **CLOTHING, p.158**

front NOUN
1 forehead
• *(Ham 3.4.56) Hamlet says his father had 'the front of Jove himself'.*
2 forelock
• *(Oth 3.1.48) Emilia tells Cassio that Othello will 'take the safest occasion by the front'—the first opportunity to restore Cassio's position.*

› **frontlet** NOUN
headband—here, of frowns
• *(KL 1.4.179) Lear asks Goneril: 'What makes that frontlet on?'*

fruit NOUN
as well as its everyday meaning, you'll find:
dessert
• *(Ham 2.2.52) Polonius says his news can follow*

what the ambassadors have to say: 'My news shall be the fruit to that great feast'.

› **fruitful** ADJECTIVE
1 overflowing
• *(Ham 1.2.80) Hamlet says 'the fruitful river in the eye' does not truly show his grief.*
2 bountiful
• *(Oth 2.3.319) Iago describes Desdemona 'as fruitful / As the free elements'—she acts with the spontaneity of natural forces.*

› **fruitfulness** NOUN
generosity
• *(Oth 3.4.34) Othello thinks Desdemona's moist hand 'argues fruitfulness and liberal heart'.*

frutify VERB
intended to mean 'certify' or 'notify'
• *(MV 2.2.124) Lancelot tells Bassanio that Gobbo 'shall frutify unto you'—inform you of what Lancelot wants.*

fry NOUN
offspring
• *(Mac 4.2.81) A Murderer calls Macduff's son 'Young fry of treachery!'*

full-fraught also spelled **full fraught** ADJECTIVE
filled to the brim
• *(H5 2.2.136) Henry tells Scroop his fall 'hath left a kind of blot / To mark the full fraught man'—his betrayal will damage the reputation even of a man jam-packed full of fine qualities.*

fulsome ADJECTIVE
1 repulsive
• *(TN 5.1.104) Olivia says Orsino's love-suit is 'as fat and fulsome to mine ear / As howling after music'.*
2 randy
• *(MV 1.3.81) Shylock tells how Jacob placed sticks 'before the fulsome ewes', so that they would produce distinctive lambs.*

fumiter or **fumitory** NOUN
a type of weed
• *(KL 4.4.3) Cordelia describes Lear as 'Crown'd with rank fumiter and furrow-weeds'.*

Furies NOUN
in Greek mythology, three goddesses of vengeance, carrying torches and covered with snakes
• *(MND 5.1.271) Bottom calls on the gods: 'Approach, ye Furies fell!'—fierce avengers.*

furnish VERB
as well as meaning 'provide' or 'prepare', you'll find:
clothe
• *(RJ 4.2.35) Juliet asks the Nurse to find ornaments 'As you think fit to furnish me tomorrow'.*

› **furnishing** NOUN
outward sign
• *(KL 3.1.29) Kent describes Albany and Cornwall's actions as 'furnishings' of deeper motives.*

› **unfurnished** ADJECTIVE
1 unprepared
• *(RJ 4.2.10) Capulet is worried that they will not be ready for the wedding: 'We shall be much unfurnish'd for this time'.*
2 unfinished
• *(MV 3.2.126) Bassanio talks about leaving a portrait of Portia 'unfurnish'd'.*

fury NOUN
as well as meaning 'rage', you'll find:
zeal
• *(Oth 3.4.68) Othello tells Desdemona that a wise woman sewed her special handkerchief 'In her prophetic fury'—with frenzied inspiration.*

fust VERB
become musty
• *(Ham 4.4.39) Hamlet reflects that God did not give mankind the faculty of reason 'To fust in us unus'd'—to go mouldy through disuse.*

fustian NOUN
nonsense
• *(Oth 2.3.262) Cassio criticizes himself for getting drunk and talking 'fustian with one's own shadow!'*

fustian ADJECTIVE
full of lofty language
• *(TN 2.5.102) Fabian describes the riddle in Olivia's letter as 'A fustian riddle!'*

Globe's groundlings

Shakespeare's Globe Theatre was a roundish building with no roof, built on the south bank of the River Thames, outside the city walls. Much of the audience stood around the stage, and were known as the groundlings. This was the cheapest way to see a play, and a groundling ticket cost a penny.

gaberdine see CLOTHING, p.158

gad in the phrase **upon the gad**
suddenly—as if pricked with a goad (a spike)
• *(KL 1.2.26) Gloucester looks back on Lear's actions: 'All this done / Upon the gad!'*

gage NOUN
pledge (to fight a duel)
• *(H5 4.1.197) Henry asks Williams for 'any gage of thine and I will wear it in my bonnet'.*

gage VERB
pledge
• *(Ham 1.1.94) Horatio describes how the legal agreement between King Hamlet and Fortinbras 'Was gaged by our king'.*

gaingiving also spelled **gain-giving** NOUN
misgiving
• *(Ham 5.2.200) Hamlet describes his feelings—'a kind of gaingiving as would perhaps trouble a woman'.*

gait NOUN
as well as meaning 'manner of walking', you'll find:
course
• *(MND 5.1.399) Oberon tells 'Every fairy take his gait'—go on his way.*

gale NOUN
⚠ *Don't read in the meaning of 'very strong wind'.*
breeze
• *(Tem 5.1.314) Prospero promises Alonso 'calm seas, auspicious gales'.*

gall NOUN
1 bile—noted for its bitterness
• *(Mac 4.1.27) The Third witch adds 'Gall of goat' to the cauldron.*
2 bitterness
• *(RJ 1.1.188) Romeo describes love as 'A choking gall, and a preserving sweet'.*
3 angry spirit
• *(TN 3.2.43) Sir Toby advises Sir Andrew about writing a challenge: 'Let there be gall enough in thy ink'.*
4 irritation
• *(KL 1.4.107) Lear calls the Fool 'A pestilent gall to me!'*

gall VERB
1 irritate
• *(Oth 2.1.97) Cassio welcomes Emilia with a kiss, telling Iago: 'Let it not gall your patience'.*
2 chafe
• *(Ham 5.1.129) Hamlet reflects on how the behaviour of a peasant comes so close to that of a courtier that 'he galls his kibe'—rubs his toe against the courtier's inflamed heel.*
3 injure
• *(H5 1.2.151) Henry describes the Scots 'Galling the gleaned land with hot assays'—harming the bare land with fierce attacks.*
4 graze
• *(Ham 4.7.147) Laertes tells Claudius of how his poisoned sword would immediately kill Hamlet: 'if I gall him slightly, / It may be death'.*
5 scoff
• *(H5 5.1.68) Gower condemns Pistol's 'gleeking and*

galling' at the Welsh Captain—making jibes and scoffing.

› **galled** ADJECTIVE
1 swollen
• *(Ham 1.2.155) Hamlet reflects on his mother's 'galled eyes' at his father's funeral.*
2 chafed
• *(H5 3.1.12) Henry describes a 'galled rock'—battered by the sea.*

› **ungalled** ADJECTIVE
uninjured
• *(Ham 3.2.261) Hamlet recites lines from an old ballad: 'The hart ungalled play'.*

gallants see TERMS OF ADDRESS, p.306

Gallia NOUN
an old name for France (in Latin)
• *(H5 1.2.216) Canterbury tells Henry that even with just a quarter of an army he 'shall make all Gallia shake'.*
see MAP, p.176

galliard NOUN
a type of lively, high-spirited dance
• *(TN 1.3.106) Sir Toby asks Sir Andrew: 'What is thy excellence in a galliard, knight?'*

galloglass also spelled **gallowglass** NOUN
axe-wielding Irish soldier, hired to fight for foreign causes
• *(Mac 1.2.13) The Captain reports how Macdonald 'Of kerns and galloglasses is supplied'.*

gallow VERB
frighten
• *(KL 3.2.44) Kent sees 'the wrathful skies / Gallow the very wanderers of the dark'.*

game NOUN
as well as meaning 'amusement', you'll find:
1 amorous play
• *(Oth 2.3.18) Iago thinks Desdemona would be 'full of game'.*
2 gambling
• *(Ham 3.3.91) Hamlet thinks of occasions when he might kill Claudius, such as when he is 'At game'.*

› **gamesome** ADJECTIVE
full of sportive spirit
• *(JC 1.2.28) Brutus refuses to go to see a ceremonial procession, saying he is 'not gamesome'.*

garb NOUN
⚠ *Don't read in the meaning of 'distinctive clothing'.*
manner
• *(H5 5.1.70) Pistol thought the Welsh Captain 'could not speak English in the native garb'.*

garbage NOUN
⚠ *Don't read in the meaning of 'household rubbish'.*
entrails, intestines
• *(Ham 1.5.57) The Ghost tells Hamlet that lust will 'prey on garbage'—sexual desire will feed on the lowest things (thinking of Claudius).*

garner NOUN
granary
• *(Tem 4.1.111) Ceres sings: 'Barns and garners never empty'.*

garner VERB
store up
• *(Oth 4.2.56) Othello describes Desdemona as a place 'where I have garner'd up my heart'.*

gaskins see CLOTHING, p.158

gast VERB
frighten
• *(KL 2.1.54) Edmund says that Edgar probably fled, 'gasted by the noise I made'.*

› **gastness** NOUN
terror
• *(Oth 5.1.106) Iago asks of Bianca: 'Do you perceive the gastness of her eye?'*

gaud NOUN
trinket
• *(MND 1.1.33) Egeus says Lysander won Hermia by giving her 'rings, gauds, conceits'.*

gauntlet see ARMOUR, p.154

gayness NOUN
⚠ *Don't read in the modern meaning of 'attraction to people of one's own sex'.*
happiness
• *(H5 4.3.110) Henry tells Montjoy that 'Our gayness and our gilt are all besmirch'd / With rainy marching'—his happiness and his golden armour are dampened by marching in the rain.*

gear NOUN
⚠ *Don't read in the modern meaning to do with drugs.*
as well as meaning 'clothes', you'll find:
1 business
• *(MV 1.1.110) Antonio says he will join in the conversation: 'I'll grow a talker for this gear'.*
2 foul substance
• *(RJ 5.1.60) Romeo describes a poison as 'soon-speeding gear / As will disperse itself through all the veins'.*

geck NOUN
dupe
• *(TN 5.1.331) Malvolio complains to Olivia that*

a b c d e f Gg h i j k l m n o p q r s t u v w x y z

he has been made 'the most notorious geck and gull'—dupe and fool.

geld past form **gelt** VERB
castrate
• *(MV 5.1.144) Gratiano curses the clerk who took Nerissa's ring: 'Would he were gelt that had it'.*

gemelled, gemell'd see **gimmaled**

gender NOUN
kind
• *(Oth 1.3.319) Iago describes a body as a garden which can be supplied 'with one gender of herbs or distract it with many'—divided with many kinds.*

> **general gender**
> the general public
> • *(Ham 4.7.18) Claudius talks of 'the great love the general gender bear' towards Hamlet.*

gender VERB
beget
• *(Oth 4.2.61) Othello talks of Desdemona's body as a place where foul toads 'knot and gender in!'—get together and have sex.*

general NOUN
public
• *(JC 2.1.12) Brutus reflects that his opposition to Caesar is 'for the general'—for the common good.*

generous ADJECTIVE
⚠ *Don't read in the meaning of 'willing to share things'.*
noble-minded
• *(KL 1.2.8) Edmund reflects that he is 'as generous' as his brother.*

genius NOUN
⚠ *Don't read in the meaning of 'unusually clever person'.*
soul
• *(TN 3.4.117) Sir Toby says of Malvolio: 'His very genius hath taken the infection of the device'—his whole being has been taken in by the plot (just as a disease can take over a body).*

gentle ADJECTIVE
as well as meaning 'soft' and 'tender', you'll find:
1 noble
• *(RJ 1.4.13) Mercutio addresses his friend as 'gentle Romeo'.*
2 kind
• *(MV 4.1.34) The Duke tells Shylock: 'We all expect a gentle answer'.*
3 refined (person)
• *(TN 4.2.31) Sir Topas describes himself as 'one of those gentle ones that will use the devil himself with courtesy'—who would be courteous even to the devil.*
4 peaceful
• *(MA 5.3.25) Don Pedro describes the dawning of a 'gentle day'.*

gentle NOUN
dear one
• *(MV 2.6.52) Gratiano describes Jessica as 'a gentle and no Jew!'—with a pun on 'Gentile' ('non-Jew').*
see also TERMS OF ADDRESS, p.306

gentle VERB
make noble
• *(H5 4.3.63) Henry promises that, even if a soldier is of lowly birth, the forthcoming battle 'shall gentle his condition'.*

> **gentleness** NOUN
> nobility
> • *(MND 2.2.138) Helena tells Lysander she thought him 'lord of more true gentleness'.*
>
> **gently** ADVERB
> 1 with dignity
> • *(JC 4.2.31) Lucilius tells his army to 'March gently on'.*
> 2 quietly
> • *(Tem 1.2.298) Ariel tells Prospero he will be obedient and 'do my spriting gently'—without arguing.*
>
> **ungently** ADVERB
> unkindly
> • *(Tem 1.2.445) Miranda wonders why Prospero speaks 'so ungently'.*

gentleman, gentlewoman see **TERMS OF ADDRESS, p.306**

gentleman of a company
army volunteer with a status higher than a private, but not an officer
• *(H5 4.1.39) The disguised King Henry tells Pistol that he is 'a gentleman of a company'.*

George, Saint
the patron saint of England, who lived in the 3rd century AD
• *(H5 3.1.34) Henry encourages his troops with the call: 'God for Harry, England, and Saint George!'*

german also spelled **germane** NOUN
near relative
• *(Oth 1.1.114) Iago tells Brabantio his daughter will be mated with a horse (Othello): 'you'll have coursers for cousins, and jennets for germans'.*
🎭 *The word for a male horse (jennet) was slang for 'a prostitute'.*

german ADJECTIVE
connected
• *(Ham 5.2.150) Hamlet criticizes Osric's phrasing as not being particularly 'german to the matter'.*

GOODBYE

A simple goodbye

farewell or **fare thee/you well**
• *(JC 1.2.292) Casca says goodbye to Brutus and Cassius: 'Farewell both'.*
• *(MA 3.5.50) Leonato offers Dogberry a drink before he leaves: 'Drink some wine ere you go. Fare you well'.*

God buy, bu'y, or **bye**
the 'buy' or 'bye' is short for 'be with'
• *(TN 4.2.96) Feste takes his leave of the imaginary Sir Topas: 'God buy you, good Sir Topas!'*

A goodbye with time of day

good morrow
also used as a greeting (see HELLO, p.133)
• *(KL 2.2.153) Kent says goodbye as Gloucester leaves: 'Give you good morrow!'*

A goodbye with kind regards

commend me
• *(Oth 5.2.126) The dying Desdemona tells Emilia: 'Commend me to my kind lord'.*

A goodbye with a concern for well-being

rest you merry
• *(RJ 1.2.82) A servant takes his leave of Romeo: 'Rest you merry'.*

A goodbye which dismisses you

go thy ways
'be off with you'
• *(Ham 3.1.129) Hamlet ends a harangue of Ophelia with 'Go thy ways to a nunnery'.*

An emotional goodbye

adieu pronounced [a-jew]
a word from French (and still used today)
This expresses fondness, kind wishes, or sorrow at parting, and usually suggests the parting is going to be for a long time, or even that the people may never meet again.
• *(H5 2.3.54) The Hostess says it to Pistol, her husband, as he goes to the wars: 'Farewell, adieu'.*
• *(KL 1.1.185) The banished Kent says it to everyone as he leaves the court for the last time: 'Thus Kent, O princes, bids you all adieu!'*
• *(Ham 1.5.91) The Ghost says it repeatedly to Hamlet as he leaves: 'Adieu, adieu, adieu. Remember me'.*

germen NOUN
life-forming element
• *(KL 3.2.8) Lear addresses the storm: 'all germens spill at once'.*

get past form **got** VERB
beget
• *(Mac 1.3.65) The Third Witch tells Banquo: 'Thou shalt get kings'.*
• *(KL 2.1.77) Gloucester says of Edgar: 'I never got him'—he's no child of mine.*

› **getting** NOUN
begetting
• *(MA 2.1.299) Beatrice tells Don Pedro that for a husband she 'would rather have one of your father's getting'—someone like Don Pedro himself.*

ghastly ADJECTIVE
▲ *Don't read in the modern colloquial meaning of 'very bad'.*
full of fear
• *(Tem 2.1.304) Alonso asks the others: 'Wherefore this ghastly looking?'*

ghost NOUN
▲ *Don't read the meaning of 'apparition' into these senses.*
spirit
• *(KL 5.3.312) Kent tells Edgar to let Lear pass away in peace: 'Vex not his ghost'—don't trouble his spirit.*

› **ghostly** ADJECTIVE
spiritual
• *(RJ 2.6.21) Juliet greets the Friar: 'Good even to my ghostly confessor'.*

gib see ANIMALS, p.162

giddy ADJECTIVE
▲ *Don't read the meaning of 'dizzy' into these senses.*
1 frivolous
• *(H5 2.4.28) The Dauphin describes Henry as 'a vain, giddy, shallow, humorous youth'.*
2 wildly elated
• *(MV 3.2.144) Bassanio describes himself as 'Giddy in spirit'.*

› **giddily** ADVERB
1 lightly
• *(TN 2.4.82) Orsino says he rates Olivia's wealth*

'as giddily as fortune'—he won't depend on her wealth, any more than he would upon the fickle goddess, Fortune.
2 madly
• *(MA 3.3.122) Borachio talks about fashion: 'how giddily a turns about all the hot-bloods'—how it influences the behaviour of all the young men about town.*
› giddy-paced ADJECTIVE
whirling
• *(TN 2.4.6) Orsino asks for a song to relax him in 'these most brisk and giddy-paced times'.*

gild VERB
as well as meaning 'cover with a thin layer of gold', you'll find:
1 smear
• *(Mac 2.2.59) Lady Macbeth says she will 'gild the faces of the grooms' with blood.*
2 bring colour to
• *(Tem 5.1.280) Alonso asks how Stephano and Trinculo got the 'grand liquor that hath gilded 'em'—made them red-faced (from being drunk).*
3 enrich
• *(MV 2.6.50) Jessica tells Lorenzo: 'I will ... gild myself / With some moe ducats'.*
› gilded ADJECTIVE
1 glittering
• *(KL 5.3.13) Lear tells Cordelia that they will 'laugh / At gilded butterflies'.*
2 gold-bearing
• *(Ham 3.3.58) Claudius reflects that 'Offence's gilded hand may shove by justice'—judges can be bribed.*
› gilt NOUN
gold
• *(H5 2.Chorus.26) The Chorus records how the traitors have accepted 'the gilt of France'.*

gimmaled also spelled **gimmal'd, gemelled, gemell'd** ADJECTIVE
[pronounced **jim**-uld]
jointed (to make it move more easily)
• *(H5 4.2.49) The French describe how 'the gemell'd bit / Lies foul with chew'd-grass' in the mouths of the English horses.*
The reason there are so many spellings is that editors aren't sure how best to deal with the form printed in the First Folio: 'jymold'.

gin NOUN
⚠ *Don't read in the meaning of an alcoholic drink.*
snare
• *(TN 2.5.77) Fabian observes Malvolio: 'Now is the woodcock near the gin'—the stupid bird is near the trap.*

gipe see **gype**

gird VERB
surround
• *(H5 1.2.152) Henry describes the Scottish attacks: 'Girding with grievous siege castles and towns'.*
› girded ADJECTIVE
besieged
• *(H5 3.Chorus.27) The Chorus describes the cannons 'With fatal mouths gaping on girded Harfleur'.*
› ungird VERB
take off
• *(TN 4.1.13) Feste asks Sebastian to 'ungird thy strangeness'—don't behave as if you don't know me.*

girdle NOUN
waist
• *(KL 4.6.124) Lear reflects on the chastity of the gods: 'to the girdle do the gods inherit'—only as far down as the waist.*
see also **SWORDS AND DAGGERS, p.156**
› turn one's girdle
find an outlet for anger
• *(MA 5.1.139) Claudio says that Benedick 'knows how to turn his girdle'.*

Gis see **SWEARING, p.298**

given ADJECTIVE
disposed
• *(JC 1.2.197) Antony describes Cassius as 'a noble Roman and well given'—with a great temperament.*

glass NOUN
1 mirror
• *(Ham 3.1.153) Ophelia describes Hamlet as 'The glass of fashion'.*
2 crystal ball
• *(Mac 4.1.110) Stage direction: 'Enter a show of eight kings, and the last with a glass in his hand'.*
3 hourglass
• *(Tem 1.2.240) Prospero tells Ariel the time after noon: 'At least two glasses'—two hours.*
› glass eyes
spectacles
• *(KL 4.6.166) Lear tells blind Gloucester: 'Get thee glass eyes'.*
› glass-gazing ADJECTIVE
admiring oneself in a mirror
• *(KL 2.2.16) Kent describes Oswald as a 'glass-gazing ... rogue'.*

glaze VERB
gaze
• *(JC 1.3.21) Casca says: 'I met a lion / Who glaz'd upon me'.*

gleaned ADJECTIVE
stripped
• *(H5 1.2.151) Henry describes the Scots harming 'the gleaned land with hot assays'—fierce attacks.*

gleek NOUN
taunt
• *(RJ 4.5.110) Peter says he will give the musicians 'the gleek'—a contemptuous gesture.*

gleek VERB
jest
• *(MND 3.1.130) Bottom tells Titania: 'I can gleek upon occasion'.*

globe NOUN
head
• *(Ham 1.5.97) Hamlet promises to remember the Ghost 'whiles memory holds a seat / In this distracted globe'—in his bewildered brain (but with a pun on the rapt attention of the audience in the Globe Theatre).*

glose also spelled **gloze** VERB
interpret
• *(H5 1.2.40) Canterbury says 'the French unjustly glose' Salic land as belonging to France.*

glut VERB
swallow up
• *(Tem 1.1.56) Gonzalo says the Boatswain won't drown, though the waters 'gape at wid'st to glut him'—even though there's water everywhere waiting to engulf him.*

God-a-mercy see POLITENESS, p.230

golden fleece
in Greek mythology, a fabulous winged ram's fleece made of gold, eventually found by Jason
• *(MV 1.1.170) Bassanio describes Portia's hair hanging on her temples 'like a golden fleece'.*

Golgotha NOUN [pronounced **gol**-go-tha]
the place in Jerusalem where Christ was crucified
• *(Mac 1.2.40) A Captain says Macbeth and Banquo fought as if to 'memorize another Golgotha'—make the battle as memorable as the crucifixion of Christ.*

good NOUN
good fellow
• *(Tem 1.1.14) Gonzalo tells the Boatswain: 'Nay, good, be patient'.*

goodman see TERMS OF ADDRESS, p.306

good morrow see HELLO, p.133

Goodwins NOUN
Goodwin Sands—sands which are treacherous for ships, found off the Kent coast in the English Channel (the 'Narrow Seas')
• *(MV 3.1.4) Salarino thinks one of Antonio's ships has been wrecked on 'the Narrow Seas; the Goodwins'.*

goodyear in the phrase **what the goodyear** also spelled **good-year**
a mild exclamation (equivalent to 'what the dickens!' and such phrases)
• *(MA 1.3.1) Conrad addresses Don John: 'What the goodyear, my lord.'*

goose NOUN
1 prostitute
• *(RJ 2.4.69) Mercutio jokes with Romeo: 'Was I with you there for the goose?'*
2 a long-handled smoothing iron (for clothes)
• *(Mac 2.3.14) The Porter welcomes a tailor to the castle: 'here you may roast your goose'—heat up your iron.*

goose-pen NOUN
quill-pen
• *(TN 3.2.44) Sir Toby advises Sir Andrew about writing his letter: 'though thou write with a goose-pen, no matter'.*
Quill pens were often made from goose feathers, but the goose was traditionally thought of as a foolish bird—and Sir Toby is expecting Sir Andrew's letter to be foolish (as it turns out).

Gorboduc NOUN [pronounced **gaw**-buh-duk]
a legendary King of Britain
• *(TN 4.2.14) Feste talks nonsense in his character of Sir Topas: 'as the old hermit of Prague ... very wittily said to a niece of King Gorboduc'.*

gordian knot also spelled **Gordian**
apparently unsolvable problem
• *(H5 1.1.46) Canterbury says that Henry, faced with a matter of state business, 'The gordian knot of it he will unloose'.*

gorge NOUN
stomach contents
• *(Ham 5.1.172) Hamlet reflects on Yorick's skull: 'My gorge rises at it'.*

Gorgon NOUN
in Greek mythology, a monster whose staring eyes could turn people to stone
• *(Mac 2.3.69) Macduff tells everyone that looking into Duncan's chamber will 'destroy your sight / With a new Gorgon'.*

goss NOUN
gorse
• *(Tem 4.1.180) Ariel tells Prospero how the others*

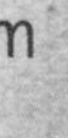

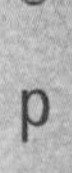

a b c d e f Gg h i j k l m n o p q r s t u v w x y z

are following him through 'pricking goss, and thorns'.

The word is printed in the First Folio as 'gosse'. Some editions replace this with 'gorse'.

gossip NOUN
as well as meaning 'idle talker', you'll find:
1 friend
• *(RJ 2.1.11) Mercutio calls to Romeo: 'Speak to my gossip Venus one fair word'.*
2 old woman
• *(MND 2.1.47) Puck says he sometimes lurks 'in a gossip's bowl'.*

gossip VERB
talk together
• *(MND 2.1.125) Titania says the mother of her changeling attendant often 'gossip'd by my side'.*

got see **get**

go thy/your ways see **ways**

gout NOUN
drop
• *(Mac 2.1.46) Macbeth sees on the imaginary dagger 'gouts of blood'.*

government NOUN
as well as meaning 'ruling a country', you'll find:
1 control
• *(RJ 4.1.102) The Friar tells Juliet the parts of her body will be 'depriv'd of supple government', after taking his potion.*
2 self-control
• *(Oth 3.3.258) Othello tells Iago: 'Fear not my government'.*

› **ungoverned** ADJECTIVE
uncontrolled
• *(KL 4.4.19) Cordelia asks people to look for Lear, to prevent him from harming himself through 'his ungovern'd rage'—uncontrolled madness.*

grace NOUN
as well as meaning 'gracefulness', you'll find:
1 honour
• *(JC 3.2.56) Brutus tells everyone to 'Do grace to Caesar's corpse'.*
2 good quality
• *(RJ 2.3.15) The Friar reflects that great 'is the powerful grace that lies / In plants'.*
3 favour
• *(Tem 5.1.295) Caliban tells Prospero he will 'seek for grace'—work hard to get back into Prospero's good books.*

grace VERB
do honour to
• *(JC 3.2.56) Brutus tells everyone to respect what Antony is about to say: 'grace his speech'.*

› **graced** ADJECTIVE
gracious
• *(Mac 3.4.40) Macbeth notes the absence from the feast of 'the grac'd person of our Banquo'.*

gracious ADJECTIVE
Don't read the meaning of 'generously kind' into these senses.
1 filled with divine grace
• *(Mac 3.1.67) Macbeth describes the murdered king as 'gracious Duncan'.*
2 holy
• *(Ham 1.1.169) Marcellus talks of Christmas night: 'So hallow'd and so gracious is that time'.*
3 blessed
• *(Ham 5.2.84) Hamlet tells Horatio that not knowing who Osric is makes Horatio's state 'the more gracious'.*
4 pleasing
• *(TN 2.3.20) Sir Andrew tells Feste that he was 'in very gracious fooling last night'—Feste sang, clowned, and fooled very well.*
5 elegant
• *(TN 1.5.242) Olivia describes Orsino as 'A gracious person'.*

› **ungracious** ADJECTIVE
1 wicked
• *(KL 4.6.271) Edgar says he will show Goneril's 'ungracious paper' to the Duke.*
2 unmannerly
• *(TN 4.1.41) Olivia calls Sir Toby an 'Ungracious wretch'.*

gramercy see **POLITENESS, p.230**

grandam, grandsire see **FAMILY, p.103**

grandsire NOUN
as well as meaning 'grandfather', you'll find:
old man
• *(Ham 2.2.452) The First Player recites a speech about 'Old grandsire Priam'.*

grandsire ADJECTIVE
long-established
• *(RJ 1.4.37) Romeo says he knows a proverb explaining why he will not dance: 'I am proverb'd with a grandsire phrase'—the onlooker (the 'candle-holder') sees the best of the game.*

grange NOUN
country house
• *(Oth 1.1.107) Brabantio tells Roderigo to stop shouting outside his house: 'My house is not a grange'—an isolated place where noisy behaviour wouldn't be noticed.*

grant NOUN
1 gift
• *(MA 1.1.291) Don Pedro tells Claudio that 'The fairest grant is the necessity'—the best gift is the one you really need.*
2 conveyance of land
• *(H5 5.2.318) Exeter points out that the French King has not yet agreed to the way Henry should be titled when requesting 'matter of grant'.*

gratify VERB
reward
• *(MV 4.1.404) The Duke suggests to Antonio that he should express his gratitude to Balthazar: 'gratify this gentleman'.*

gratillity NOUN
a humorous version of 'gratuity'
• *(TN 2.3.24) Feste tells Sir Andrew, making up his own words: 'I did impeticos thy gratillity'—I put your tip in my pocket.*

gratis ADVERB
free of charge
• *(MV 1.3.39) Shylock reflects on the way Antonio 'lends out money gratis'—without charging interest.*

grave ADJECTIVE
⚠ *Don't read in the meaning of 'serious' or 'solemn'.*
respected
• *(Mac 3.1.22) Macbeth says he will miss Banquo's advice, 'Which still hath been both grave and prosperous'—wise and beneficial.*

grave-beseeming also spelled **grave beseeming** ADJECTIVE
suitably dignified
• *(RJ 1.1.87) The Prince says the quarrel has made Verona's citizens 'Cast by their grave beseeming ornaments'—throw aside their dignified garments.*

gravity NOUN
1 respectability
• *(JC 2.1.149) Metellus says that Cicero's 'gravity' would help colour the actions of the conspirators.*
2 wisdom
• *(RJ 3.5.174) Capulet tells off the Nurse: 'Utter your gravity o'er a gossip's bowl'.*

grece see **grize**

Greek NOUN
1 buffoon—someone who talks nonsense
• *(TN 4.1.16) Sebastian tells Feste to go away: 'I prithee, foolish Greek, depart from me'.*
2 gibberish
• *(JC 1.2.282) Casca tells Brutus that what Cicero said 'was Greek to me'—I couldn't understand a word of it.*

green ADJECTIVE
as well as meaning the colour, you'll find:
1 recent
• *(H5 5.1.38) The Welsh Captain tells Pistol that a leek 'is good for your green wound'—its properties will help you fight off any infection.*
2 immature
• *(Oth 2.1.238) Iago describes Cassio as having all the attributes of people with 'green minds'.*
🎭 *Green was considered the colour of jealousy, as in Iago's warning to Othello about the 'green-eyed monster' (Oth 3.3.168).*

› **greenly** ADVERB
1 sheepishly, like a young lover
• *(H5 5.2.140) Henry tells Katherine he 'cannot look greenly'.*
2 unskilfully
• *(Ham 4.5.82) Claudius tells Gertrude that they have 'done but greenly' to bury Polonius in secret.*

green-sickness ADJECTIVE
affected by a kind of illness found in young women after puberty, where the skin has a greenish pallor
• *(RJ 3.5.156) Capulet calls Juliet a 'green-sickness carrion'—an anaemic carcass (like a corpse with the blood drained out of it).*

greet VERB
as well as meanings to do with 'addressing' and 'welcoming', you'll find:
lament
• *(TN 2.4.60) Feste sings sadly: 'not a friend greet / My poor corpse'.*

grief NOUN
as well as meaning 'great sorrow', you'll find:
grievance
• *(JC 1.3.118) Casca tells Cassius to be ready to form a faction 'for redress of all these griefs'.*

› **grieved** ADJECTIVE
wronged
• *(MA 4.1.88) Don Pedro describes Claudio as 'this grieved count'.*

grize also spelled **grece, grise** NOUN
step
• *(TN 3.1.120) Cesario denies that pity is a step on the way to love: 'No, not a grize'—not a bit.*

grizzle, grizzled see **COLOURS, p.164**

groat see **MONEY, p.197**

⚠ *warning note* ✒ *usage note* 🎭 *theatre note*

a b c d e f Gg h i j k l m n o p q r s t u v w x y z

groom NOUN
⚠ *Don't read in the meanings of 'bridegroom' or 'person who looks after horses'.*
attendant
• *(Mac 2.2.53) Lady Macbeth tells Macbeth to 'smear / The sleepy grooms with blood'.*

gross ADJECTIVE
as well as meanings to do with being 'bad', 'ugly', or 'disgusting', you'll find:
1 obvious
• *(Oth 1.2.72) Brabantio tells Othello, about Desdemona, that it is 'gross in sense / That thou hast practis'd on her with foul charms'.*
2 large
• *(KL 4.6.14) Edgar tells Gloucester that the birds flying around the cliff 'Show scarce so gross as beetles'—they look only as big as beetles.*
3 excessively luxuriant
• *(Ham 1.2.136) Hamlet, comparing the world to a garden, reflects that 'things rank and gross in nature / Possess it merely'—abundant foul weeds have entirely taken it over.*
4 weighty
• *(Ham 4.4.46) Hamlet reflects on why he hasn't yet acted against Claudius when 'Examples gross as earth exhort me'—he has plenty of evidence that pushes him to do something.*
5 ignorant
• *(TN 2.5.150) Malvolio promises to 'wash off gross acquaintance'—rid himself of stupid associates.*

gross NOUN
whole amount
• *(MV 3.2.158) Portia sums up her qualities: 'which to term in gross / Is an unlesson'd girl'—she hasn't had a formal education.*

› **grossly** ADVERB
1 openly
• *(KL 1.1.289) Goneril observes that Lear's poor judgement now 'appears too grossly'.*
2 with substance
• *(TN 5.1.228) Sebastian describes himself to Viola as a spirit 'grossly clad'—in earthly form.*
3 in a state of excess
• *(Ham 3.3.80) Hamlet reflects that Claudius 'took my father grossly, full of bread'—a state that would require God's forgiveness.*
4 coarsely
• *(MV 5.1.266) Portia tells Gratiano, who has just used the word 'cuckold': 'Speak not so grossly'.*

› **grossness** NOUN
1 obviousness
• *(MV 3.2.80) Bassanio reflects that even a great religious error can be covered over, 'Hiding the grossness with fair ornament'—polished words can hide even the most obvious sins.*
2 bodily form
• *(MND 3.1.142) Titania promises Bottom: 'I will purge thy mortal grossness', to make him more like a spirit.*

groundlings NOUN
audience standing in a theatre courtyard around the stage
• *(Ham 3.2.10) Hamlet criticizes actors who 'split the ears of the groundlings'.*
🎭 *Cheap entrance to the courtyard is also a feature of the reconstructed Shakespeare's Globe in London, where standing members of the audience are still called 'groundlings' (and beer is still sold).*

guardage NOUN
protection
• *(Oth 1.2.70) Brabantio tells Othello he can't believe that Desdemona would want to 'Run from her guardage to the sooty bosom / Of such a thing as thou'.*

guarded ADJECTIVE
ornamented
• *(MA 1.1.260) Benedick likens the way Don Pedro and Claudio have been talking to a garment 'guarded with fragments', where 'the guards are but slightly basted on'—the trimmings are sewn on very loosely.*

guards see THE COSMOS, p.174

gudgeon NOUN
a type of fish used as a bait
• *(MV 1.1.102) Gratiano tells Antonio: 'fish not with this melancholy bait / For this fool gudgeon, this opinion'—don't use melancholy as a way of gaining a reputation.*
✒ *Anyone who was particularly gullible would be called a 'gudgeon'.*

guerdon NOUN [pronounced **gur**-don]
recompense
• *(MA 5.3.5) Claudio reads about Hero: 'Death, in guerdon of her wrongs, / Gives her fame'.*

guidon NOUN [pronounced **guide**-on]
pennant, flag
• *(H5 4.2.60) The Constable says he is ready for battle: 'I stay but for my guidon'.*

guiled ADJECTIVE
[pronounced in this line as two syllables: **gy**-lid]
treacherous
• *(MV 3.2.97) Bassanio reflects that 'ornament is but the guiled shore / To a most dangerous sea'—the love of bling can lead people into danger.*

guinea-hen NOUN
an informal name for a prostitute
• *(Oth 1.3.311) Iago says he would rather turn into a baboon than drown himself 'for the love of a guinea-hen'.*

gules see COLOURS, p.164

gulf NOUN
1 whirlpool
• *(Ham 3.3.16) Rosencrantz describes the loss of monarchy as something that 'like a gulf doth draw / What's near it with it'.*
2 huge stomach
• *(Mac 4.1.23) The Third Witch adds to the cauldron: 'maw and gulf / Of the ravin'd salt-sea shark'—the throat and guts of a shark stuffed with prey.*

gull NOUN
1 fool
• *(TN 5.1.198) Sir Toby calls Sir Andrew 'a thin-faced knave, a gull!'*
2 hoax
• *(MA 2.3.120) Benedick wonders whether what the others are saying is 'a gull'.*

gull VERB
trick
• *(TN 2.3.121) Maria promises to trick Malvolio so much that his name will become proverbial for 'fool': 'gull him into a nayword'.*

› **gull-catcher** NOUN
fool-trapper
• *(TN 2.5.173) Fabian sees Maria: 'Here comes my noble gull-catcher'.*

gum NOUN
⚠ *Don't read in the meaning of 'chewing gum'.*
mucus
• *(H5 4.2.48) The French describe the English horses as having 'gum down-roping from their pale dead eyes'—trickling down.*

gype NOUN [pronounced jipe]
Shakespeare's way of showing a Welsh pronunciation of the word 'jibe'
• *(H5 4.7.43) The Welsh Captain says that Falstaff was 'full of jests and gypes'.*

gyves NOUN [pronounced jives]
1 shackles
• *(RJ 2.2.179) Juliet describes a captive bird 'Like a poor prisoner in his twisted gyves'.*
2 handicaps, faults
• *(Ham 4.7.21) Claudius says, of Hamlet, that the general public 'Convert his gyves to graces'.*

› **gyve** VERB
shackle
• *(Oth 2.1.165) Iago considers how he will snare Cassio: 'I will gyve thee in thine own courtship'.*

› **down-gyved** ADJECTIVE
hanging down like shackles
• *(Ham 2.1.80) Ophelia describes Hamlet with 'his stockings foul'd, / Ungarter'd and down-gyved to his ankle'.*

Holinshed's Chronicles

Raphael Holinshed's book, The Chronicles of England, Scotland and Ireland, was the chief source for the plot of Macbeth and many of Shakespeare's history plays, including Henry V. First published in 1577, it was the first comprehensive work on British history and a common plot-source for Elizabethan writers.

habit NOUN

⚠*Don't read the modern meaning of 'addiction' into these senses.*

as well as meaning 'regular behaviour', you'll find:

1 clothing

• *(H5 3.7.107) The herald Montjoy tells Henry: 'You know me by my habit'.*

2 covering

• *(Oth 1.3.108) The Duke describes Brabantio's arguments against Othello as 'thin habits'—flimsy guises.*

3 demeanour

• *(MV 2.2.177) Gratiano promises Bassanio he will 'put on a sober habit'.*

› **habited** ADJECTIVE

clothed

• *(Tem 4.1.138) Stage direction: 'Enter certain reapers, properly habited'—clothed in a way that suits their occupation as harvesters of grain.*

hag NOUN

as well as meaning 'ugly old woman', you'll find: wicked fairy

• *(RJ 1.4.92) Mercutio describes Queen Mab as a 'hag'.*

› **hag-born** ADJECTIVE

born of a witch

• *(Tem 1.2.283) Prospero describes Caliban as 'A freckled whelp, hag-born'.*

› **hag-seed** NOUN

witch-child

• *(Tem 1.2.364) Prospero tells Caliban: 'Hag-seed, hence!'*

Hagar NOUN [pronounced **hay**-gar]

in the Bible, a handmaid of Abraham's wife, who bore him a child that he then rejected

• *(MV 2.5.42) Shylock calls Lancelot 'that fool of Hagar's offspring'—a descendant of servants.*

haggard NOUN

wild hawk

• *(MA 3.1.36) Hero describes Beatrice's spirits as 'coy and wild / As haggards of the rock'.*

haggard ADJECTIVE

wild

• *(Oth 3.3.262) Othello reflects on how he would cast Desdemona off, 'If I do prove her haggard'—if he can prove she's been disloyal.*

haggle VERB

hack

• *(H5 4.6.11) Exeter describes York, after the battle, as 'all haggled over'—hacked to pieces.*

hail see HELLO, p.133

hair in the phrase **against the hair**

contrary to inclination (like stroking a cat the wrong way)

• *(RJ 2.4.86) Mercutio jokes with Benvolio: 'Thou desirest me to stop in my tale against the hair'—with a sexual pun.*

halcyon ADJECTIVE [pronounced **hal**-see-un]

like a kingfisher

• *(KL 2.2.74) Kent describes Oswald as a flatterer following every whim of his master, just as dead kingfishers, hung up to dry, 'turn their halcyon beaks'—have their heads moved about by the wind.*

hale VERB
pull
• *(MA 2.3.59) Benedick thinks it strange that the sound of a stringed instrument 'should hale souls out of men's bodies'—that listening to the music of stringed instruments can make people so emotional.*

half-blooded see **blood 2**

halfpence see **MONEY, p.197**

halloo also spelled
halloa, hallow, holla, hollow VERB
shout
• *(TN 1.5.252) Cesario tells Olivia that, if he loved her, he would 'Halloo your name to the reverberate hills'—make her name echo around the hills.*

halt VERB
⚠*Don't read in the modern meaning of 'stop'.*
limp
• *(TN 5.1.185) Sir Andrew sees 'Sir Toby halting'.*
› **halting** ADJECTIVE
limping
• *(MA 5.4.87) Claudio describes 'A halting sonnet' written by Benedick—with a faltering stop-start rhythm to the metre.*

halter NOUN
⚠*Don't read in the meaning of 'a strap around a horse's head'.*
hangman's noose
• *(KL 1.4.311) The Fool sings: 'If my cap would buy a halter'.*

Hampton NOUN
a short form of Southampton, one of the main port cities in the south of England
• *(H5 2.2.88) Henry describes how the Duke of Cambridge had plotted 'To kill us here in Hampton'.*

hams NOUN
thighs
• *(Ham 2.2.199) Hamlet tells Polonius that old men have 'most weak hams'.*

handsaw NOUN
⚠*Don't read in the meaning of 'a carpenter's tool'.*
heron
• *(Ham 2.2.369) Hamlet says he can tell 'a hawk from a handsaw'.*

handsome ADJECTIVE
⚠*Don't read the meaning of 'good-looking' into these senses.*
1 naturally graceful
• *(Ham 2.2.433) Hamlet describes a play he once saw as being 'very much more handsome than fine'—more natural than artificial.*
2 proper
• *(MA 4.2.83) Dogberry describes himself as someone who 'hath two gowns, and everything handsome about him'—he has two outfits kept only for special occasions, and everything else he owns is nice too.*
› **handsomely** ADVERB
beautifully
• *(Tem 5.1.293) Prospero tells Caliban to decorate their dwelling 'handsomely'.*
› **unhandsome** ADJECTIVE
inadequate
• *(Oth 3.4.145) Desdemona describes herself as an 'unhandsome warrior'.*

handy-dandy see **RECREATION, p.170**

hanger see **SWORDS AND DAGGERS, p.156**

hangman NOUN
as well as meaning 'executioner', you'll find:
rascal
• *(MA 3.2.10) Don Pedro describes Cupid as a 'little hangman'.*

hap NOUN
1 fortune
• *(RJ 2.2.189) Romeo says he will seek out the Friar, 'His help to crave, and my dear hap to tell'.*
2 accident
• *(MA 3.1.105) Hero tells Ursula that 'loving goes by haps'—love is caused by chance events.*
3 happening
• *(RJ 3.3.171) The Friar tells Romeo that Romeo's servant will communicate 'Every good hap to you that chances here' (in Verona, while Romeo is exiled).*

hap VERB
happen
• *(TN 1.2.60) Viola tells the Captain: 'What else may hap, to time I will commit'—time will tell.*
› **haply** ADVERB
perhaps
• *(H5 5.2.93) Queen Isabel tells Henry that 'Haply a woman's voice may do some good'.*

happily ADVERB
as well as meaning 'fortunately' and 'aptly', you'll find:
perhaps (an alternative to 'haply' above)
• *(Ham 2.2.374) Rosencrantz agrees that Polonius is like a new-born baby in swaddling clothes: 'Happily he is the second time come to them, for they say an old man is twice a child'—in his second childhood.*

a b c d e f g Hh i j k l m n o p q r s t u v w x y z

a b c d e f g Hh i j k l m n o p q r s t u v w x y z

happy ADJECTIVE
as well as meaning 'contented', you'll find:
1 fortunate
• *(RJ 3.3.137) The Friar reminds Romeo that Juliet is alive: 'There art thou happy'.*
2 opportune
• *(JC 2.2.60) Caesar tells Decius that he has arrived 'in very happy time'.*
The phrase 'in happy time' was often used as a greeting, meaning 'well met!' or 'you've come at just the right time'.

› **unhappy** ADJECTIVE
as well as meaning 'sad', you'll find:
miserable (used as an insult)
• *(KL 4.6.223) Oswald calls Gloucester 'Thou old unhappy traitor'.*

› **unhappily** ADVERB
1 disastrously
• *(KL 1.2.136) Edmund tells Edgar about an author he has been reading: 'the effects he writes of succeed unhappily'—the events he writes about will have disastrous consequences.*
2 in a way that isn't comfortable to hear
• *(Ham 4.5.13) A Gentleman describes Ophelia's speech as being 'nothing sure, yet much unhappily'—saying things that, while not entirely clear, are uncomfortably near the truth.*

harbinger NOUN
forerunner
• *(MND 3.2.380) Puck points out the morning star (the planet Venus, often visible in the east before sunrise): 'yonder shines Aurora's harbinger'.*

hard-favoured see **favour**

hardness NOUN
hardship
• *(Oth 1.3.231) Othello acknowledges 'A natural and prompt alacrity / I find in hardness'—an eager readiness to get into harsh situations.*

hardy ADJECTIVE
bold
• *(TN 2.2.8) Olivia tells Cesario, of Orsino: 'be never so hardy to come again in his affairs'—don't ever dare to come to me with business to do with him.*

hark see **ATTENTION SIGNALS, p.23**

harlot NOUN
prostitute
• *(RJ 2.4.42) Mercutio jokes that Queen Helen of Troy and Hero (in Greek mythology, a priestess in love with Leander) were 'hildings and harlots'—good-for-nothings and prostitutes compared to Romeo's Rosaline (even though Helen was renowned for her beauty and Hero for her loyalty).*

› **harlotry** NOUN
1 prostitute
• *(Oth 4.2.230) Iago tells Roderigo that Cassio 'sups tonight with a harlotry'—he means Bianca (but perhaps implicating Desdemona).*
2 little wretch
• *(RJ 4.2.14) Capulet describes Juliet as 'A peevish self-will'd harlotry'.*

harness NOUN
as well as meaning 'straps for a horse', you'll find:
armour
• *(Mac 5.5.51) Macbeth, referring to himself using the 'royal we', anticipates dying 'with harness on our back'.*

harp VERB
give voice to
• *(Mac 4.1.73) Macbeth reflects on what the First Apparition has said: 'Thou hast harp'd my fear aright'.*

harpy NOUN
a mythical bird, half woman and half vulture
• *(Tem 3.3.52) Stage direction: 'Enter Ariel, like a harpy'.*

haste-post-haste ADJECTIVE
with all possible speed
• *(Oth 1.2.37) Cassio tells Othello that the Duke 'requires your haste-post-haste appearance'.*

hatchment NOUN
a tablet displaying a coat-of-arms
• *(Ham 4.5.210) Laertes asks why Polonius has been buried with 'No trophy, sword, nor hatchment o'er his bones'.*

hautboy see **MUSIC, p.172**

have after
let's follow
• *(Ham 1.4.89) Horatio agrees with Marcellus that they must follow Hamlet and the Ghost: 'Have after'.*

having NOUN
wealth
• *(TN 3.4.318) Cesario tells Antonio: 'My having is not much'.*

hawk at VERB
pursue
• *(Mac 2.4.13) An Old Man recounts that a falcon 'Was by a mousing owl hawk'd at and kill'd'.*
This would have been a highly unusual event, as a falcon is much bigger and more

powerful than an owl, which usually hunts mice.

hay see **RECREATION, p.170**

hazard NOUN
as well as meaning 'danger', you'll find:
1 chance
• *(MV 2.1.45) Portia tells Morocco he can choose from the three boxes later: 'after dinner / Your hazard shall be made'.*
2 in the game of royal tennis, an opening in the wall of the court from which one couldn't return the ball (and so would lose the point)
• *(H5 1.2.263) Henry sends a message to the Dauphin that he will 'strike his father's crown into the hazard'—so that the French King will lose.*
Royal tennis (these days usually called real tennis) is the game from which modern lawn tennis is descended. It was played in a large indoor court with hiqh walls and slopinq roofs, against which a servicc ball had to bouncc before entering the receiver's end (containing the hazard).

hazard VERB
take a chance
• *(MV 3.2.2) Portia, using the same phrasing as she did with the Prince of Morocco, asks Bassanio to 'pause a day or two / Before you hazard'.*
› **come / go to hazard**
make a bet
• *(H5 3.8.79) Rambures asks the French nobles 'Who will go to hazard with me for twenty prisoners?'*

head NOUN
as well as its usual meanings of 'part of the body' and 'leader', you'll find:
1 army
• *(JC 4.1.42) Antony tells Octavius that 'we must straight make head'—we must immediately form an army.*
2 uprising
• *(Ham 4.5.100) A messenger brings news of Laertes leading 'a riotous head'.*
3 headway
• *(Oth 1.3.271) Othello affirms that if love-making should ever stop him doing his job, he would permit all kinds of unworthy attacks to 'Make head against my estimation'—his reputation.*
› **head and front**
greatest extent
• *(Oth 1.3.80) Othello explains that 'The very head and front of my offending' was in marrying Desdemona.*

headborough NOUN
parish officer
• *(MA 3.5.1) Stage direction: 'Enter Leonato, Dogberry the constable, and Verges the Headborough'.*
A headborough was a law-enforcement officer in a small parish community. This was quite a senior position, but subordinate to the local constable.

head-lugged also spelled **-lugg'd** ADJECTIVE
dragged along by the head, and thus enraged
• *(KL 4.2.42) Albany describes Lear, 'Whose reverence even the head-lugg'd bear would lick'.*

heady ADJECTIVE
1 violent
• *(H5 3.4.32) Henry warns the citizens of Harfleur of 'heady murder, spoil, and villainy'.*
2 impulsive
• *(KL 2.4.106) Lear says he has 'fall'n out with my more headier will'—he will try to control his impulsive temper.*

hcarkcn VERB
pay attention to
• *(Tem 3.2.36) Caliban asks Stephano 'to hearken once again to the suit I made to thee'.*
› **hearken after** VERB
inquire into
• *(MA 5.1.206) Claudio tells Don Pedro, of Borachio and Conrad: 'Hearken after their offence'.*

hearse VERB
put in a coffin
• *(MV 3.1.80) Shylock wishes Jessica 'were hearsed at my foot, and the ducats in her coffin'.*

hearted ADJECTIVE
1 heartfelt
• *(Oth 1.3.359) Iago tells Roderigo: 'My cause is hearted'.*
2 heart-centred
• *(Oth 3.3.449) Othello asks love to yield 'thy crown and hearted throne / To tyrannous hate!'*

heartless ADJECTIVE
Don't read in the meaning of 'cruel'.
cowardly
• *(RJ 1.1.60) Tybalt asks Benvolio: 'art thou drawn among these heartless hinds?'—have you drawn your sword along with these cowardly animals?*

hearts see **TERMS OF ADDRESS, p.306**

heat NOUN
as well as meaning 'state of being hot' and 'strong emotion', you'll find:
1 urgency
• *(Oth 1.2.40) Cassio brings Othello a message from the Duke: 'It is a business of some heat'.*
2 normal body temperature
• *(TN 1.5.123) Feste says, of a drunken man, 'one*

draught above heat makes him a fool'—alcohol raises the body temperature, making a man foolish.

› in the heat
while feeling heated—soon!
• *(KL 1.1.304) Goneril tells Regan that they have to do something, 'and i'th'heat'—they need to strike while the iron is hot.*

heavy ADJECTIVE
as well as meaning 'weighty', you'll find:
1 sad
• *(JC 2.1.275) Portia asks Brutus to tell her 'Why you are heavy'.*
2 weary
• *(Tem 2.1.184) Gonzalo tells Antonio: 'I am very heavy'.*
3 dark
• *(Oth 5.1.42) Lodovico is cautious about venturing into the streets: 'It is a heavy night'.*
The action is taking place in Cyprus, so there's a suggestion that the air is hot and oppressive.

› heavy hand
oppressive behaviour
• *(Mac 3.1.91) Macbeth reminds the Murderers how Banquo's 'heavy hand hath bowed you to the grave'—made you old before your time.*

› heavily ADVERB
sadly
• *(Tem 4.1.138) Stage direction, of the spirit dancers: 'they heavily vanish'.*

› heaviness NOUN
1 sadness
• *(RJ 3.4.11) Lady Capulet describes Juliet as 'mew'd up to her heaviness'—confined (keeping to herself) in her grief.*
2 sleepiness
• *(Tem 1.2.307) Miranda tells Prospero that 'The strangeness of your story put / Heaviness in me'.*

hebona or **hebenon** NOUN
[pronounced **heh**-bo-na]
a kind of poisonous plant (of uncertain identity)
• *(Ham 1.5.62) The Ghost says he was killed 'With juice of cursed hebona'.*

Hecate NOUN [pronounced **heh**-cut]
in Greek mythology, the goddess of the underworld, associated with magic and witchcraft
• *(Mac 2.1.52) Macbeth reflects on how 'Witchcraft celebrates / Pale Hecate's off'rings'.*

hectic NOUN
persistent fever
• *(Ham 4.3.66) Claudius says Hamlet rages like 'the hectic in my blood'.*

Hecuba NOUN [pronounced **heh**-cue-ba]
the wife of Trojan king Priam, and mother of 18 children, all killed after the Greeks took Troy following a long siege
• *(Ham 2.2.489) Hamlet asks the First Player to 'come to Hecuba' in his recitation—get to the point in the siege where Hecuba arrives.*

hedge VERB
protect
• *(Ham 4.5.122) Claudius claims there is a divinity that 'doth hedge a king'.*
A monarch was thought to be God's representative on earth.

› hedge in VERB
restrict
• *(JC 4.3.30) Cassius tells Brutus: 'You forget yourself / To hedge me in'—you forget who you're talking to when you try to limit my authority.*

hedge-pig NOUN
hedgehog
• *(Mac 4.1.2) The Second Witch tells the others: 'Thrice and once the hedge-pig whin'd'.*

heir general NOUN
an heir from either the male or the female line
• *(H5 1.2.66) Canterbury describes King Pepin (king of the Franks in the 8th century) as 'heir general, being descended / Of Blithild'.*
Heirs to a royal throne were usually from the male line. In some other Shakespeare plays you will find the expression 'heir apparent', meaning the next in line to the throne.

Helen NOUN
a Greek woman renowned for her beauty, whose abduction by Paris of Troy caused the Trojan War
• *(RJ 2.4.41) Mercutio mocks Romeo's romantic view of his lady as someone who makes the famed 'Helen and Hero hildings and harlots'—look like good-for-nothings and prostitutes.*

Hellespont NOUN [pronounced **hell**-uh-spont]
a narrow strait in north-west Turkey, today called the Dardanelles, that connects the Aegean Sea and the Sea of Marmara
• *(Oth 3.3.457) Othello says his bloody thoughts race on like the fast current that flows from the Pontic Sea (now called the Black Sea) 'To the Propontic and the Hellespont'.*
see MAP, p.176

helm NOUN
1 helmet
see **ARMOUR, p.154**
2 covering of hair
• *(KL 4.7.36) Cordelia imagines Lear on the heath 'With this thin helm'.*

hempen ADJECTIVE
in clothing made of hemp
• *(MND 3.1.65) Puck sees the rustics: 'What hempen homespuns have we swaggering here'.*

hent NOUN
opportunity or grasp
• *(Ham 3.3.88) Hamlet decides to kill Claudius later: 'Up, sword, and know thou a more horrid hent'.*

Hercules NOUN [pronounced **her**-cue-leez]
in Greek mythology, a demi-divine hero famous for his amazing strength, who had to perform twelve great tasks, or 'labours'
• *(MV 3.2.85) Bassanio describes cowards who grow beards like the gods to make them appear brave: 'The beards of Hercules and frowning Mars'.*
Several characters are described with reference to Hercules, especially in comedy.
• *(MND 1.2.23) Bottom fancies himself playing the part of Hercules: 'I could play Ercles rarely'.*

here-remain see **remain**

Hermes NOUN [pronounced **her**-meez]
in Greek mythology, the winged messenger of the gods, the inventor of the lyre and flute
• *(H5 3.8.17) Bourbon boasts that the sound of his horse's hoof 'is more musical than the pipe of Hermes'.*

hermit NOUN
Don't read in the meaning of 'a person who lives alone'.
one who prays for another
• *(Mac 1.6.21) Lady Macbeth thanks Duncan for the honours he has bestowed: 'We rest your hermits'—we continue to pray for you.*

Hero NOUN
a priestess of Aphrodite, loved by Leander—who each night swam across the Hellespont to be with her, guided by her lamp, until one night the lamp blew out, he drowned, and Hero committed suicide by throwing herself into the river
• *(RJ 2.4.41) Mercutio mocks Romeo's romantic view of his lady as someone who makes the famed 'Helen and Hero hildings and harlots'—look like good-for-nothings and prostitutes.*

HELLO

A SIMPLE GREETING
how now
• *(MV 3.1.21) Solanio greets Shylock: 'How now, Shylock, what news among the merchants?'*
well met
• *(H5 2.1.1) Bardolph meets Nym along the way: 'Well met, Corporal Nym'.*
hail
used to kings, emperors, and princes, or to people who are being treated as if they were royal
• *(MND 3.1.161) Peaseblossom greets Bottom: 'Hail, mortal!'*

A GREETING WITH TIME OF DAY
good morrow
also used as a goodbye (see Goodbye, p.121)
• *(JC 2.2.109) Publius greets Julius Caesar: 'Good morrow, Caesar'.*
good even
• *(RJ 2.6.21) Juliet greets Friar Lawrence: 'Good even to my ghostly confessor'.*

A GREETING WITH A CONCERN FOR WELL-BEING
well be with you
• *(Ham 2.2.370) Polonius greets Hamlet and his friends: 'Well be with you, gentlemen'.*

A GREETING WITH A DIVINE WISH
God bless you
• *(Ham 3.2.357) Hamlet greets Polonius: 'God bless you, sir'.*
God save you
• *(Oth 4.1.212) Lodovico greets Othello: 'God save you, worthy general!'*
God speed
• *(MND 1.1.180) Hermia meets Helena as she is leaving: 'God speed, fair Helena! Whither away?'*

Herod NOUN
in the Bible, the Judean king who tried to eliminate Jesus by having all the male newborn children of Bethlehem killed
• *(Ham 3.2.14) Hamlet condemns players who shout so much on stage that 'It out-Herods Herod'—they surpass his angry raging.*

a b c d e f g Hh i j k l m n o p q r s t u v w x y z

hest NOUN
command
• *(Tem 3.1.37) Miranda tells Ferdinand her name, then remembers Prospero's command, and speaks as if to her father: 'I have broke your hest to say so'.*

hic et ubique see **LATIN, p.352**

hie VERB
hurry
• *(RJ 3.5.26) Juliet tells Romeo: 'hie hence, be gone, away!'*

Hiems NOUN [pronounced **hie**-emz]
winter personified—thought of as an old man
• *(MND 2.1.109) Titania describes how the seasons have changed, with summer buds settling on 'old Hiems' thin and icy crown'.*
'Hiems' is the Latin word for 'winter'.

high ADJECTIVE
as well as meanings to do with 'height', you'll find:
1 very great
• *(Oth 5.2.94) Othello says: 'The noise was high'.*
2 important
• *(KL 3.6.109) Edgar advises himself to 'Mark the high noises'—note what the important people are talking about.*
3 sophisticated
• *(Tem 3.3.88) Prospero observes: 'My high charms work'.*

› **highly** ADVERB
ambitiously
• *(Mac 1.5.19) Lady Macbeth reflects about her husband: 'What thou wouldst highly, / That wouldst thou holily'—you want to become great, but in a righteous way.*

high-day also spelled **highday** NOUN
day of celebration
• *(Tem 2.2.181) Caliban celebrates: 'Freedom, high-day!'*

› **high-day** also spelled **highday** ADJECTIVE
befitting a holiday
• *(MV 2.9.97) Portia is taken with the Messenger's description of her visitor: 'Thou spend'st such highday wit in praising him'.*

high-engendered see **engendered**

high-lone ADJECTIVE
without support
• *(RJ 1.3.37) The Nurse remembers Juliet as a baby, when 'she could stand high-lone'.*

high-proof ADJECTIVE
tested to the highest level
• *(MA 5.1.122) Claudio says he and Don Pedro are in a state of 'high-proof melancholy'.*

hight VERB [pronounced hiet]
is called
• *(MND 5.1.138) Quince describes Snug in the play: 'This grisly beast, which Lion hight by name'.*
'Hight' was already an old-fashioned usage in Shakespeare's day.

high-wrought ADJECTIVE
extremely rough
• *(Oth 2.1.2) A Gentleman describes the sea: 'it is a high-wrought flood'.*

hilding NOUN
good-for-nothing
• *(RJ 3.5.168) Capulet shouts about Juliet: 'Out on her, hilding!'—be gone with her, the baggage!*

hilding ADJECTIVE
worthless
• *(H5 4.2.29) The Constable describes the English army as 'a hilding foe'.*

hint NOUN
1 occasion
• *(Tem 2.1.3) Gonzalo tells Alonso: 'Our hint of woe / Is common'—many people suffer in this way.*
2 opportunity
• *(Oth 1.3.141) Othello recounts his moment of story-telling: 'It was my hint to speak'.*

hip in the phrase **on/upon the hip**
at a disadvantage (the expression comes from wrestling)
• *(MV 1.3.41) Shylock thinks about how he can catch Antonio 'once upon the hip'.*

hoar ADJECTIVE
1 see **COLOURS, p.164**
2 mouldy
• *(RJ 2.4.120) Mercutio jokes about a pie that is 'something stale and hoar'—making a pun on 'whore'.*

hob, nob
have it or have it not
• *(TN 3.4.219) Sir Toby describes Sir Andrew's attitude in a fight: 'Hob, nob, is his word'—he will fight regardless of what the other person does.*

hobby-horse NOUN
1 prostitute
• *(Oth 4.1.152) Bianca tells Cassio to give the handkerchief to 'your hobby-horse'.*
2 buffoon
• *(MA 3.2.63) Benedick tells Leonato he wants to say something to him away from Don Pedro and*

Claudio—'which these hobby-horses must not hear?'

Hoberdidance NOUN
[pronounced hob-er-**did**-ance]
one of the fiends of hell
• *(KL 4.1.59) Poor Tom says five fiends have possessed him, including 'Hoberdidance, prince of dumbness'.*

hogshead NOUN
barrel
• *(Tem 4.1.249) Stephano wants Caliban to accompany him to 'where my hogshead of wine is'.*

Hold-fast also spelled **Holdfast** NOUN
a name which appears in an old proverb: 'Brag is a good dog, but Hold-fast is a better'—silent steadfastness is better than boasting
• *(H5 2.3.44) Pistol advises his wife to stay quiet and steady in what she does: 'Hold-fast is the only dog'.*

holidam see SWEARING, p.298

holla, hollow see **halloo**

hollow ADJECTIVE
insincere
• *(JC 4.2.23) Brutus reflects on the nature of 'hollow men'.*

> **hollowly** ADVERB
insincerely
• *(Tem 3.1.70) Ferdinand affirms to Miranda that he does not speak 'hollowly'.*

> **hollowness** NOUN
insincerity
• *(KL 1.1.153) Kent tells Lear that people 'whose low sounds / Reverb no hollowness' are not empty-hearted—they send out no echoes of insincerity.*

holp past form of **help** VERB
helped
• *(Mac 1.6.23) Duncan says that Macbeth's great love 'hath holp him / To his home before us'—Macbeth's love for his wife has helped him ride fast and arrive ahead of them.*

home ADVERB
1 fully
• *(Tem 5.1.71) Prospero tells Gonzalo: 'I will pay thy graces / Home'.*
2 deeply
• *(Oth 5.1.2) Iago advises Roderigo to 'Wear thy good rapier bare, and put it home'—keep it drawn, and thrust it into the heart.*
3 bluntly
• *(Oth 2.1.161) Cassio says that Iago 'speaks home'.*

homespun NOUN
peasant
• *(MND 3.1.65) Puck sees the rustics: 'What hempen homespuns have we swaggering here?'*

honest ADJECTIVE
⚠ *Don't read the meaning of 'being truthful' into these senses.*
1 chaste
• *(Oth 3.3.385) Othello tells Iago: 'I think my wife be honest, and think she is not'—there's a silent 'yet' implied after 'and'.*
2 honourable
• *(JC 3.1.126) Antony says that 'Brutus is noble, wise, valiant, and honest'.*
3 genuine
• *(Ham 1.5.144) Hamlet tells Horatio and Marcellus: 'It is an honest ghost'.*
4 innocent
• *(MA 3.1.84) Hero says she will 'devise some honest slanders / To stain my cousin with'.*

> **honesty** NOUN
1 chastity
• *(Ham 3.1.107) Hamlet tells Ophelia: 'your honesty should admit no discourse to your beauty'—you're obviously lying (about why you're giving me back my love-letters), because otherwise why would your pureness interact with your beauty (why would you blush)?*
2 honour
• *(MA 2.1.350) Don Pedro says that Benedick is a man of 'confirmed honesty'.*
3 decency
• *(TN 2.3.78) Malvolio harangues Sir Toby and the others for their late-night noise-making: 'Have you no wit, manners, nor honesty?'*

> **dishonest** ADJECTIVE
⚠ *Don't read meanings of 'being untruthful' or 'being a thief' into these senses.*
1 unchaste
• *(H5 1.2.49) Canterbury recounts the 'dishonest manners' of German women.*
2 dishonourable
• *(TN 3.4.359) Sir Toby calls Cesario 'A very dishonest paltry boy'.*
3 unreliable
• *(TN 1.5.36) Olivia tells the newly returned Feste: 'you grow dishonest'.*

> **dishonesty** NOUN
dishonour
• *(TN 3.4.360) Sir Toby describes Cesario's behaviour: 'His dishonesty appears in leaving his friend here in necessity'.*

a b c d e f g Hh i j k l m n o p q r s t u v w x y z

honour NOUN
as well as meaning 'fame' and 'good name', you'll find:
noble rank
• *(KL 5.3.128) Edgar says he has the right to draw his sword: 'it is the privilege of mine honours'.*

hood see **HATS, p.160**

hoodman-blind see **RECREATION, p.170**

hoodwink VERB
as well as meaning 'deceive', you'll find:
1 blindfold
• *(RJ 1.4.4) Benvolio says they will gatecrash the Capulets' party without an introductory speech: 'We'll have no Cupid hoodwink'd with a scarf'—just as Cupid (who is blind) doesn't need to be blindfolded, so they don't need a speech to excuse their arrival.*
2 cover up
• *(Tem 4.1.205) Caliban tells Stephano that 'the prize I'll bring thee to / Shall hoodwink this mischance'—make him forget the mishap he has just experienced.*

hoop NOUN
⚠ *Don't read in the meaning of 'a large ring used as a toy'.*
a posture that takes on the shape of a circle
• *(Tem 1.2.259) Prospero describes Sycorax 'who with age and envy / Was grown into a hoop'.*

Hoppedance NOUN [pronounced **hop**-a-dance]
the name of a devil
• *(KL 3.6.30) Poor Tom imagines his hunger as a fiend yelling inside him: 'Hoppedance cries in Tom's belly for two white herring'.*

horn NOUN
1 drinking-horn (an animal's horn, sealed with leather, used to carry water)
• *(KL 3.6.73) Poor Tom says that his 'horn is dry'.*
2 hunting-horn or bugle
• *(MA 2.3.60) Benedick rates the music of sport and war more highly than romantic music: 'a horn for my money'.*

horn-mad ADJECTIVE
enraged (like a mad bull)
• *(MA 1.1.245) Claudio says a married Benedick would 'be horn-mad'—with a pun on horns as the sign of a man with an unfaithful wife.*

horologe NOUN [pronounced **ho**-ruh-lodge]
clock
• *(Oth 2.3.116) Iago says that Cassio will 'watch the horologe a double set'—stay awake to drink while the clock goes round twice.*

hose see **CLOTHING p.158**

host NOUN
army
• *(H5 3.6.50) The French King tells his nobles to attack Henry: 'Rush on his host'.*

hot ADJECTIVE
as well as meanings to do with 'high temperature', you'll find:
1 angry
• *(RJ 3.5.175) Lady Capulet tells her husband: 'You are too hot'.*
2 enthusiastic
• *(KL 5.3.67) Goneril warns Regan: 'Not so hot'—don't get too excited.*
3 lecherous
• *(Oth 3.3.404) Iago imagines Cassio and Desdemona 'as hot as monkeys'.*
4 vigorous
• *(H5 3.2.2) Nym finds the fighting too tough: 'The knocks are too hot'.*

› **hotly** ADVERB
1 ardently
• *(KL 4.6.158) Lear imagines a beadle who 'hotly lusts' after a whore.*
2 urgently
• *(Oth 1.2.44) Cassio tells Othello: 'You have been hotly call'd for'.*

house NOUN
as well as meanings to do with 'buildings' and 'households', you'll find:
1 school of fencing
• *(RJ 2.4.24) Mercutio describes Tybalt as 'a gentleman of the very first house'—trained at the best fighting school.*
2 heavenly domain
see **THE COSMOS, p.174**

housekeeper also spelled **house-keeper** NOUN
1 householder
• *(TN 4.2.8) Feste reflects on the nature of 'an honest man and a good housekeeper'.*
2 house-dog
• *(Mac 3.1.99) Macbeth distinguishes types of dog, such as 'the swift, the slow, the subtle, / The housekeeper'.*

housewife also spelled **huswife** NOUN [pronounced **huz**-if]
as well as meaning 'a woman who looks after a home', you'll find:
prostitute
• *(Oth 4.1.94) Iago goes to 'question Cassio of Bianca, / A housewife'.*

howbeit CONJUNCTION [pronounced how-**be**-it]
however
• *(H5 1.2.91) Canterbury tells Henry the French*

position with regard to the English king's right to rule France: 'Howbeit, they would hold up this Salic law / To bar your highness'.

› howbeit that

although

• *(Oth 2.1.277) Iago talks about Othello: 'The Moor, howbeit that I endure him not, / Is of a constant, loving, noble nature'.*

howlet see ANIMALS, p.162

how now see HELLO, p.133

howsomever CONJUNCTION

in whatever way

• *(Ham 1.5.84) The Ghost begins a warning to Hamlet: 'But howsomever thou pursuest this act...'*

This word often appears split in two:

• *(Ham 1.5.178) Hamlet tells Horatio and Marcellus of the way he is thinking: 'How strange or odd some'er I bear myself'.*

how's the day?

what's the time?

• *(Tem 5.1.3) Prospero asks Ariel 'How's the day?' and Ariel replies 'On the sixth hour'.*

hugger-mugger NOUN

secrecy

• *(Ham 4.5.82) Claudius tells Gertrude that they have failed 'In hugger-mugger' to bury Polonius—to keep Hamlet's role in Polonius' death out of the public eye.*

hull VERB

lie (as if at port, with sails furled)

• *(TN 1.5.189) Cesario tells Maria, who has asked him to 'hoist sail', that he is not leaving: 'I am to hull here a little longer'.*

humane ADJECTIVE

1 polite

• *(Oth 2.1.231) Iago says that Cassio puts on the 'form of civil and humane seeming'.*

2 civil

• *(Mac 3.4.76) Macbeth talks about former bloodshed 'Ere humane statute purg'd the gentle weal'—before law and order cleansed society and made it more benevolent.*

humour also spelled **humor** NOUN

⚠ *Don't read the modern meaning of 'funny' into these senses.*

1 mood

• *(JC 4.3.46) Brutus asks Cassius: 'Must I stand and crouch / Under your testy humour?'*

2 fancy

• *(H5 2.1.49) Nym threatens Pistol: 'I have an humour to knock you indifferently well'—to give you a thorough beating.*

3 way

• *(H5 2.3.52) Nym says farewell: 'I cannot kiss, that is the humour of it'.*

4 fluid

• *(RJ 4.1.96) The Friar tells Juliet that, after taking his potion, through her veins 'shall run / A cold and drowsy humour'.*

5 vapour

• *(JC 2.1.262) Portia asks Brutus if it is healthy 'To walk unbraced and suck up the humours / Of the dank morning'—to walk around with your chest bare.*

HUMOURS

In Shakespeare's time, people thought that four different fluids—or 'humours'—inside your body controlled the way you behaved. If these humours were in a state of balance, you would be in good health. But if one of the humours became more powerful than the others, this would affect your mood.

blood

if your most important humour was blood, you would be passionate, optimistic, and courageous (which is how Mercutio thinks of Romeo here)

• *(RJ 2.1.7) Mercutio calls on Romeo to show himself: 'Romeo! humours! madman! passion! lover!'*

phlegm

if your most important humour was phlegm, you would be full of water rather than blood, and this would make you dull, lazy, and cowardly

• *(H5 3.2.29) The Boy describes Bardolph as 'white-livered and red-faced'.*

choler

if your most important humour was choler, you would be angry, irritable, and bad-tempered

• *(JC 4.3.43) Brutus tells Cassius to 'Go show your slaves how choleric you are'.*

melancholy

if your most important humour was melancholy, you would be sad, gloomy, and depressed

• *(MA 2.1.5) Hero describes Count John: 'He is of a very melancholy disposition'.*

› humorous ADJECTIVE
1 moody
• *(H5 2.4.28) The Dauphin calls Henry 'a vain, giddy, shallow, humorous youth'.*
2 damp
• *(RJ 2.1.31) Benvolio says Romeo has hid himself 'To be consorted with the humorous night'.*

hunt's-up NOUN
a daybreak song to wake huntsmen (or a newly married wife)
• *(RJ 3.5.34) Juliet tells Romeo that the lark is 'Hunting thee hence with hunt's-up to the day' —telling him to leave with its daybreak song.*

hurdle NOUN
cart
• *(RJ 3.5.155) Capulet threatens to drag Juliet to church 'on a hurdle'.*

hurricano NOUN [pronounced hu-ri-**kay**-no]
water-spout—a whirling column of water formed when a whirlwind draws up a mass of water from the sea
• *(KL 3.2.2) Lear addresses the storm: 'You cataracts and hurricanoes, spout'.*

hush see **ATTENTION SIGNALS, p.23**

huswife see **housewife**

Hybla NOUN [pronounced **high**-bla]
a town in Sicily, famed for its honey
• *(JC 5.1.34) Cassius says Antony's words (of friendship after the assassination of Caesar) were so sweet that they 'rob the Hybla bees / And leave them honeyless'.*

Hydra-headed ADJECTIVE
[pronounced **high**-dra]
many-headed
• *(H5 1.1.35) Canterbury describes the way Henry cast off his 'Hydra-headed wilfulness'.*
The Hydra in Greek mythology was a snake with many heads that grew again if they were cut off.

Hymen NOUN [pronounced **high**-men]
in Greek mythology, a goddess who led a wedding procession, carrying a torch
• *(Tem 4.1.23) Prospero warns Ferdinand to respect Miranda's virginity, 'As Hymen's lamps shall light you'—if you want Hymen's torch to shine brightly at your wedding (foretelling a happy marriage).*

hyperbolical ADJECTIVE
outrageous
• *(TN 4.2.24) Feste shouts at the devil in Malvolio: 'Out, hyperbolical fiend!'*

Hyperion NOUN [pronounced high-**peer**-ee-on]
in Greek mythology, the sun god, who travels in a horse-drawn chariot
• *(H5 4.1.263) Henry reflects on the wretched slave who each day 'after dawn / Doth rise and help Hyperion to his horse'—he is up before sunrise.*

Hyrcan or **Hyrcanian** ADJECTIVE
[pronounced **her**-kan, her-**kay**-nee-an]
from Hyrcania, an ancient Persian region by the Caspian Sea, known for its ferocious wild animals
• *(Mac 3.4.101) Macbeth says even 'th'Hyrcan tiger' does not scare him.*
see **MAP, p.176**

hysterica passio see **LATIN, p.352**

Iceland NOUN
a country once known for its dogs with long hair, pointed ears, and a bad temper
• *(H5 2.1.38) Pistol calls Nym a 'prick-eared cur of Iceland'.*

ides also spelled **Ides** NOUN
the halfway point in a month (in the Roman calendar)
• *(JC 1.2.18) A Soothsayer calls to Caesar: 'Beware the Ides of March'—the fifteenth day.*

idle ADJECTIVE
⚠ *Don't read the meaning of 'lazy' into these senses.*
1 useless
• *(KL 4.4.5) Cordelia describes the way Lear is crowned with 'idle weeds'.*
2 mad
• *(Ham 3.2.88) Hamlet sees people coming and tells Horatio: 'I must be idle'—I must pretend to be mad again.*
3 foolish
• *(RJ 1.4.97) Mercutio says that dreams are 'the children of an idle brain'.*
4 unimportant
• *(Oth 1.2.95) Brabantio tells an Officer: 'Mine's not an idle cause'.*
5 frivolous
• *(Tem 2.1.162) Antonio mocks the subjects in Gonzalo's commonwealth: 'all idle—whores and knaves'.*
6 careless
• *(Ham 2.2.138) Polonius tells Claudius he would not have looked on Hamlet's love of Ophelia 'with idle sight'.*
7 unmoving
• *(KL 4.6.21) Edgar describes the sea 'That on th'unnumber'd idle pebble chafes'—a gentle sea-shore.*
8 empty or barren
• *(Oth 1.3.139) Othello recounts stories of 'deserts idle'.*

› **idleness** NOUN
foolishness
• *(TN 1.5.58) Olivia says she will listen to Feste 'for want of other idleness'—as she has nothing better to do.*

ignorance NOUN
⚠ *Don't read meanings to do with 'being stupid' into these senses.*
negligence
• *(KL 4.5.9) Regan says of Gloucester that letting him live 'was great ignorance'.*

› **ignorant** NOUN
unaware people
• *(Ham 2.2.550) Hamlet thinks that someone with his motivation would 'Confound the ignorant' —amaze those with no knowledge of the crime.*

'ild see POLITENESS, p.230

Ilium NOUN [pronounced **ill**-ee-um]
the city of Troy
• *(Ham 2.2.462) The First Player tells how Pyrrhus' sword falls on Priam so forcefully that even 'senseless Ilium'—a city that lacks human sensation—seems to feel the blow.*
see MAP, p.176

a b c d e f g h Ii j k l m n o p q r s t u v w x y z

ill ADJECTIVE
as well as meaning 'sick', you'll find:
1 bad
• *(TN 1.5.144) Malvolio says Cesario is 'Of very ill manner'—incredibly impolite.*
2 evil
• *(Tem 1.2.458) Miranda says of Ferdinand: 'There's nothing ill can dwell in such a temple'.*
3 poor
• *(MA 2.3.79) Balthasar describes himself as 'an ill singer'.*
4 unskilful
• *(Ham 2.2.119) Hamlet thinks he is no good at writing verses: 'I am ill at these numbers'.*

ill ADVERB
badly
• *(JC 4.3.275) Brutus complains: 'How ill this taper burns!'*

ill NOUN
evil
• *(MV 2.5.17) Shylock thinks 'There is some ill a-brewing towards my rest'—something bad is coming that will keep me awake.*

ill-beseeming ADJECTIVE
unseemly
• *(RJ 1.5.73) Capulet tells Tybalt that his frowns are 'An ill-beseeming semblance for a feast'.*

ill-breeding ADJECTIVE
mischief-making
• *(Ham 4.5.15) Horatio thinks Ophelia's behaviour 'may strew / Dangerous conjectures in ill-breeding minds'—arouse suspicions about how her father died.*

ill-composed also spelled **-compos'd** ADJECTIVE
made up of wicked elements
• *(Mac 4.3.77) Malcolm claims he has a 'most ill-compos'd affection'—a character emotionally disturbed by evil.*

ill-disposed see **dispose**

ill-divining ADJECTIVE
giving premonitions of harm
• *(RJ 3.5.54) Juliet says she has 'an ill-divining soul'.*

ill-favouredly see **favour**

illness NOUN
▲ *Don't read in the modern meaning of 'sickness'.*
wickedness
• *(Mac 1.5.19) Lady Macbeth thinks Macbeth wants to be great 'but without / The illness should attend it'.*

ill-tempered see **temper**

ill-well ADVERB
cruelly accurately
• *(MA 2.1.107) Ursula says the masked Antonio could never simulate the real Antonio 'so ill-well unless you were the very man'.*

Illyria NOUN [pronounced ill-**li**-ree-a]
the eastern shore of the Adriatic Sea and its hinterland (present-day Croatia), which Shakespeare created as the setting for 'Twelfth Night'
• *(TN 1.2.2) The Captain tells Viola where they have come to shore: 'This is Illyria, lady'.*
see MAP, p.176

imbar, imbare see **embar**

imbrue also spelled **embrue** VERB
pierce
• *(MND 5.1.329) Flute, as Thisbe, addresses a sword: 'Come blade, my breast imbrue!'*

immediacy NOUN
being next in status
• *(KL 5.3.67) Regan tells Albany that Edmund has been acting for her, 'The which immediacy may well stand up / And call itself your brother'.*

> **immediate** ADJECTIVE
1 close in succession
• *(Ham 1.2.109) Claudius tells Hamlet: 'You are the most immediate to our throne'.*
2 nearest to the heart
• *(Oth 3.3.157) Iago says a good name in men and women 'Is the immediate jewel of their souls'.*

immured also spelled **immur'd** ADJECTIVE
enclosed
• *(MV 2.7.52) Morocco wonders, of Portia, if 'in silver she's immur'd'—if her portrait is within the silver casket.*

imp NOUN
▲ *Don't read in a meaning of 'mischievous creature'.*
child
• *(H5 4.1.45) Pistol describes Henry as 'a lad of life, an imp of fame'.*

impasted ADJECTIVE
made into a paste
• *(Ham 2.2.447) The First Player describes blood 'Bak'd and impasted with the parching streets'—which has become solid and sludgy under the sun.*

impawn VERB
1 pledge as security
• *(H5 1.2.21) Henry warns Canterbury: 'take heed*

how you impawn our person'—be careful about how you use my name when promising things.

2 wager

• *(Ham 5.2.141) Osric describes what Laertes has 'impawned' for the fencing match.*

impeach VERB

⚠ *Don't read the meaning of 'bringing an important political figure to trial' into these senses.*

discredit

• *(MND 2.1.214) Demetrius tells Helena: 'You do impeach your modesty too much' to follow someone who doesn't love you.*

> **impeachment** NOUN
>
> hindrance
>
> • *(H5 3.7.135) Henry tells Montjoy he would like to 'march on to Calais / Without impeachment'.*

imperfect ADJECTIVE

1 unfinished

• *(KL 4.3.3) A Gentleman explains that the French King returned home because of 'Something he left imperfect in the state'.*

2 ambiguous

• *(Mac 1.3.68) Macbeth calls the Witches 'imperfect creatures'—he can't tell exactly what they are.*

imperious also spelled **emperious** ADJECTIVE

imperial

⚠ *Don't read in the meaning of 'arrogant and bossy'.*

• *(Ham 5.1.197) Hamlet reflects on 'Imperious Caesar'.*

impertinent ADJECTIVE

⚠ *Don't read the meaning of 'being insolent' into these senses.*

1 irrelevant

• *(Tem 1.2.138) Prospero says he must tell Miranda about what is happening, 'without the which this story / Were most impertinent'.*

2 intended to mean 'pertinent'

• *(MV 2.2.127) Lancelot tells Bassanio that his request 'is impertinent to myself'.*

> **impertinency** NOUN
>
> nonsense
>
> • *(KL 4.6.170) Edgar describes Lear's speech as 'matter and impertinency mix'd'—sense and nonsense all mixed up.*

impeticos or **impetticoat** VERB

a humorous version of 'put in my inside pocket', derived from 'petticoat'

• *(TN 2.3.24) Feste tells Sir Andrew, making up his own words: 'I did impeticos thy gratillity'—pocketed your tip.*

impiteous ADJECTIVE

impetuous

• *(Ham 4.5.99) A Messenger describes the arrival of Laertes with 'impiteous haste'.*

✒ *'Impitious' is the spelling in the First Folio. Some editions replace this with 'impetuous'.*

implorator NOUN

solicitor

• *(Ham 1.3.129) Polonius tells Ophelia not to believe Hamlet's vows as they are 'mere implorators of unholy suits'—only attempts at sinful courtship.*

import VERB

⚠ *Don't read the meaning of 'bring goods into a country' into these senses.*

1 mean

• *(Oth 4.2.30) Desdemona asks Othello: 'what doth your speech import?'*

2 concern

• *(Ham 5.2.21) Hamlet describes the content of Claudius' letter 'Importing Denmark's health, and England's too'.*

import NOUN

importance

• *(RJ 5.2.19) Friar Lawrence says his letter to Romeo was 'full of charge, / Of dear import'.*

> **importing** PREPOSITION
>
> concerning
>
> • *(Ham 1.2.23) Claudius tells his court of messages from Fortinbras 'Importing the surrender' of land.*

importance NOUN

as well as meaning 'significance' or 'great authority', you'll find:

urging

• *(TN 5.1.351) Fabian recounts that Maria wrote the letter to Malvolio 'at Sir Toby's great importance'.*

> **important** ADJECTIVE
>
> demanding
>
> • *(MA 2.1.62) Beatrice advises Hero: 'If the Prince be too important, tell him there is measure in everything'—there's nothing that can't wait a while.*

importune VERB

1 urge

• *(KL 3.4.154) Kent tells Gloucester to ask Lear to enter the castle: 'Importune him once more to go'.*

2 beg

• *(Oth 2.3.298) Iago advises Cassio to ask Desdemona for help: 'Importune her help to put you in your place again'.*

> **importunate** ADJECTIVE
>
> persistent
>
> • *(Ham 4.5.1) A Gentleman tells Gertrude that*

a b c d e f g h Ii j k l m n o p q r s t u v w x y z

Ophelia insists on speaking to her: 'She is importunate'.

› **importuned** also spelled **importun'd** ADJECTIVE
beseeching
• *(KL 4.4.26) Cordelia says the French king has taken pity on her 'mourning and importun'd tears'.*

› **importunity** NOUN
persistent urging
• *(MV 4.1.159) Bellario says that he has formed a legal opinion which Balthazar will deliver 'at my importunity'.*

impossible ADJECTIVE
as well as meaning 'not possible', you'll find:
preposterous
• *(MA 2.1.127) Beatrice says Benedick has a gift 'in devising impossible slanders'.*

imposthume NOUN
[pronounced im-**posst**-youm]
abscess
• *(Ham 4.4.27) Hamlet describes the Polish conflict as 'th'impostume of much wealth and peace'—resulting from a period of peacetime affluence.*

impotent ADJECTIVE
⚠ *Don't read the meaning of 'unable to engage in sex' into these senses.*
powerless
• *(Ham 1.2.29) Claudius describes old Fortinbras as 'impotent and bedrid'.*

› **impotence** NOUN
powerlessness
• *(Ham 2.2.66) Voltemand describes old Fortinbras' 'sickness, age, and impotence'.*

impress VERB
⚠ *Don't read a meaning to do with 'admiring' into these senses.*
conscript
• *(Mac 4.1.94) Macbeth reflects on the Third Apparition's warning: 'Who can impress the forest?'*

impress NOUN
conscription
• *(Ham 1.1.78) Marcellus asks Horatio: 'Why such impress of shipwrights?'—why are there so many ship-makers?*

› **impressed** also spelled **impress'd** ADJECTIVE
conscripted
• *(KL 5.3.51) Edmund is aware that popular support for Lear could 'turn our impress'd lances in our eyes'—make the conscripted soldiers rise against them.*

impressure NOUN
mark made by a seal
• *(TN 2.5.87) Malvolio examines Olivia's letter, seeing the picture of Lucrece on her seal: 'the impressure her Lucrece'.*
Nobles had their own distinct mark, which they would press into the melted wax that sealed a letter up. The seal would tell the receiver who the letter was from, and—if the wax wasn't broken—that the letter hadn't yet been read.

improve VERB
as well as meaning 'make better', you'll find:
make good use of
• *(JC 2.1.159) Cassius thinks Antony has means that could harm the conspirators' cause, 'If he improve them'.*

› **unimproved** ADJECTIVE
untried or undisciplined
• *(Ham 1.1.99) Horatio describes young Fortinbras as a man 'Of unimproved mettle'—he hasn't yet had an opportunity to prove his worth.*

imputation NOUN
reputation
• *(Ham 5.2.135) Osric praises 'the imputation laid on' Laertes' fencing skill by those who are expert in swordplay.*

incapable ADJECTIVE
not aware
• *(Ham 4.7.178) Gertrude describes Ophelia as 'one incapable of her own distress'.*

incardinate ADJECTIVE
intended to mean 'incarnate'—embodied in flesh
• *(TN 5.1.175) Sir Andrew describes Sebastian as 'the very devil incardinate'.*

incarnadine VERB
turn into the colour of blood
• *(Mac 2.2.65) Macbeth thinks the blood on his hand will 'The multitudinous seas incarnadine, / Making the green one red'.*
Shakespeare seems to realize that his audience might not understand this word, and explains it himself in the next line.

incarnation ADJECTIVE
intended to mean 'incarnate'—embodied in flesh
• *(MV 2.2.24) Lancelot describes Shylock as 'the very devil incarnation'.*

incensement NOUN
anger
• *(TN 3.4.217) Sir Toby says Sir Andrew's 'incensement at this moment' cannot be calmed.*

Inch see **Saint Colm's Inch**

inchmeal in the phrase **by inchmeal** also spelled **inch-meal**
inch by inch
• *(Tem 2.2.3) Caliban curses Prospero, asking infections to fall on him and 'make him / By inchmeal a disease!'*

inclining ADJECTIVE
compliant
• *(Oth 2.3.318) Iago thinks it is easy 'Th'inclining Desdemona to subdue / In any honest suit'—to persuade her to agree to any honourable request.*

inclining NOUN
faction
• *(Oth 1.2.82) Othello tells everyone to calm down, 'Both you of my inclining and the rest'—his followers and everyone else.*

incontinency NOUN
⚠ *Don't read the modern meaning of 'inability to control bladder or bowels' into these senses.*
lack of sexual restraint
• *(Ham 2.1.30) Polonius says that Reynaldo must not go around saying that Laertes 'is open to incontinency'—that he is promiscuous.*

› **incontinent** ADVERB
immediately
• *(Oth 4.3.12) Desdemona says Othello 'will return incontinent'.*

› **incontinently** ADVERB
immediately
• *(Oth 1.3.302) Roderigo tells Iago: 'I will incontinently drown myself'.*

inconvenience NOUN
⚠ *Don't read in the meaning of 'slight difficulty'.*
harm
• *(H5 5.2.66) Burgundy hopes peace will 'expel these inconveniences' that have affected France during the war.*

incorporal ADJECTIVE
lacking substance
• *(Ham 3.4.118) Gertrude asks Hamlet why he is talking to 'th'incorporal air'.*

incorporate ADJECTIVE
united in one body
• *(MND 3.2.208) Helena reminds Hermia of a time when they were so close as friends it seemed that 'our hands, our sides, voices, and minds / Had been incorporate'.*

incorporate VERB
unite
• *(RJ 2.6.37) The Friar tells Romeo and Juliet that they may not 'stay alone / Till Holy Church incorporate two in one'.*

incorpsed also spelled **incorps'd** ADJECTIVE
made into one body
• *(Ham 4.7.87) Claudius describes Lamord's horse-riding skill as if he had 'been incorps'd and demi-natur'd / With the brave beast'.*

increase NOUN
produce
• *(MND 2.1.114) Titania says autumn and winter have got so mixed up that people 'By their increase now knows not which is which'—it's no longer possible to tell the seasons by which fruits and vegetables are growing.*

Ind NOUN
the Indies
• *(Tem 2.2.57) Stephano asks Caliban if he is playing tricks 'with savages and men of Ind'.*
🎭 *Stephano is probably thinking of the West Indies, given the earlier reference in the play to the 'Bermoothes' (the Bermuda Islands), but the name was also used for the East Indies and for India.*

index NOUN
prologue
• *(Ham 3.4.52) Gertrude asks Hamlet what is the act that 'thunders in the index'—the noisy prelude to what you are about to say (what are you shouting about?).*

indifferent ADJECTIVE
⚠ *Don't read meanings to do with 'not caring' or 'not very good' into these senses.*
1 impartial
• *(H5 1.1.72) Canterbury says that Henry, in relation to a contentious bill, 'seems indifferent'.*
2 typical
• *(Ham 2.2.224) Rosencrantz tells Hamlet that he and Guildenstern are getting on 'As the indifferent children of the earth'—not too badly, fairly well.*

› **indifferent** ADVERB
moderately
• *(TN 1.5.227) Olivia describes her lips, 'indifferent red'.*

› **indifferently** ADVERB
1 impartially
• *(JC 1.2.87) Brutus tells Cassius, of honour and death, 'I will look on both indifferently'.*
2 fairly well
• *(Ham 3.2.35) The First Player tells Hamlet, of their performing style, 'I hope we have reformed that indifferently'.*

indign ADJECTIVE
unworthy
• *(Oth 1.3.270) Othello would welcome 'all indign*

⚠ *warning note* ✒ *usage note* 🎭 *theatre note*

and base adversities' if he allowed his love-making to get in the way of his profession.

indirection NOUN
1 roundabout means
• *(Ham 2.1.66) Polonius advises Reynaldo: 'By indirections find directions out'—find out information by being indirect.*
2 devious means
• *(JC 4.3.75) Brutus says he would never extract money from peasants 'By any indirection'.*

indirectly ADVERB
as well as meaning 'not directly', you'll find:
wrongfully
• *(H5 2.4.95) Exeter says the French King must resign his 'crown and kingdom, indirectly held'.*

indistinguished also spelled **indistinguish'd** ADJECTIVE
limitless
• *(KL 4.6.266) Edgar reflects on Goneril's plot: 'O indistinguish'd space of woman's will'.*

indite or **endite** VERB
a deliberate mistake for 'invite'
• *(RJ 2.4.116) Benvolio suggests that the Nurse is planning to ask Romeo to dinner: 'She will indite him to some supper'.*
Benvolio seems to be mocking the way the Nurse talks, as she has just asked Romeo for 'some confidence'—meaning 'conference'.

indue or **endue** VERB
1 endow
• *(TN 1.5.89) Feste compliments Olivia for speaking well of fools: 'Now Mercury endue thee with leasing'—grant you the art of lying.*
2 bring
• *(Oth 3.4.140) Desdemona reflects that an aching finger 'endues / Our other healthful members even to a sense / Of pain'.*

› **indued** or **endued** ADJECTIVE
endowed
• *(Ham 4.7.180) Gertrude describes the drowning Ophelia as if she were like 'a creature native and indued / Unto that element'—supplied with the qualities needed to live in water.*

inevitable ADJECTIVE
impossible to avoid
• *(TN 3.4.254) Sir Toby describes Sir Andrew's fencing thrusts as having 'such a mortal motion that it is inevitable'—he is bound to kill someone.*

inexecrable ADJECTIVE
relentless or damnable
• *(MV 4.1.128) Gratiano calls Shylock an 'inexecrable dog'.*

infection NOUN
⚠ *Don't read the meaning of 'disease' into these senses.*
1 rottenness
• *(Tem 2.2.1) Caliban curses Prospero with 'All the infections that the sun sucks up / From bogs, fens, flats'—the sun's heat drawing up bacteria from low-lying lands and waters.*
2 intended to mean 'affection'
• *(MV 2.2.116) Gobbo tells Bassanio that Lancelot 'hath a great infection' to serve him.*

inform VERB
⚠ *Don't read the meaning of 'give information' into these senses.*
1 provide evidence
• *(Ham 4.4.32) Hamlet reflects: 'How all occasions do inform against me'—accuse him of not doing anything.*
2 appear in a shape
• *(Mac 2.1.48) Macbeth ponders the dagger he sees: 'It is the bloody business which informs / Thus to mine eyes'.*

ingener NOUN [pronounced in-**gen**-er]
inventor
• *(Oth 2.1.65) Cassio says Desdemona's beauty 'Does tire the ingener'—goes well beyond what a creative artist can express.*

ingenious ADJECTIVE
⚠ *Don't read in the meaning of 'cleverly inventive'.*
fully conscious
• *(KL 4.6.275) Gloucester says he has 'ingenious feeling / Of my huge sorrows!'*

ingraft also spelled **engraffed** ADJECTIVE
deep-rooted
• *(Oth 2.3.126) Montano says Cassio is 'one of an ingraft infirmity'—he has a fundamental weakness.*

› **ingrafted** or **engrafted** ADJECTIVE
deep-rooted
• *(JC 2.1.184) Cassius describes 'the engrafted love' Antony has for Caesar.*

› **long-ingraffed** or **-engraffed** ADJECTIVE
habitual
• *(KL 1.1.294) Goneril discusses with Regan their father's 'imperfections of long-engraffed condition'.*

ingrate ADJECTIVE
ungrateful
• *(TN 5.1.108) Orsino describes himself as making offerings at Olivia's 'ingrate and unauspicious altars'—thinking of her as an ungrateful and unfavourable goddess.*

inherit VERB
as well as meaning 'receive something after the death of its previous owner', you'll find:
1 possess
• *(KL 4.6.124) Lear reflects on the chastity of the gods: 'to the girdle do the gods inherit'—they have power only down to the waist.*
2 inhabit
• *(Tem 4.1.154) Prospero sees everything dissolving, including 'the great globe itself', and 'all which it inherit'.*

› **inheritor** NOUN
owner
• *(Ham 5.1.104) Hamlet says a great landowner will have documents that would hardly fit in a coffin big enough for 'th'inheritor himself'.*

inhibition NOUN
⚠ *Don't read the meaning of 'not expressing your emotions' into these senses.*
official ban
• *(Ham 2.2.325) Rosencrantz says the players have been given an 'inhibition'—they have been prohibited to play in the city.*

› **inhibited** ADJECTIVE
forbidden
• *(Oth 1.2.79) Brabantio claims Othello is 'a practiser / Of arts inhibited'.*

initiate ADJECTIVE
beginner's
• *(Mac 3.4.143) Macbeth explains his feelings as 'the initiate fear that wants hard use'—a fear that comes from not being experienced enough.*

injoint VERB
join up
• *(Oth 1.3.35) A Messenger reports that the Turkish ships have 'injointed with an after fleet'—a secondary fleet.*

injury NOUN
as well as meaning 'damage to a body', you'll find:
1 insult
• *(MND 2.1.147) Oberon promises to torment Titania 'for this injury' done to him.*
2 abscess
• *(H5 3.7.115) Montjoy tells Henry that the French have decided not to 'bruise an injury till it were full ripe'—squeeze a boil until it is ready to burst.*

innocent ADJECTIVE
silly
• *(MA 5.2.35) Benedick says he can find 'no rhyme to "lady" but "baby"—an innocent rhyme'.*

innovation NOUN
1 disturbance
• *(Oth 2.3.34) Cassio says he is affected by even a single drink: 'behold what innovation it makes here'.*
2 new fashion or insurrection
• *(Ham 2.2.326) Rosencrantz says the players have been banned because of 'the late innovation' —the new fashion of using child actors.*
🎭 *This could equally be a reference by Shakespeare to the insurrection of the Earl of Essex in 1601 against Queen Elizabeth, as his followers requested a performance of Shakespeare's 'Richard II', including a famous scene where the monarch is deposed.*

inoculate VERB
graft
• *(Ham 3.1.118) Hamlet says 'virtue cannot so inoculate our old stock' it isn't possible to graft virtue into human nature or into his family (like a bud can be grafted onto a tree).*

insinuation NOUN
⚠ *Don't read in the meaning of 'making an unpleasant suggestion'.*
fawning
• *(Ham 5.2.59) Hamlet says the downfall of Rosencrantz and Guildenstern 'Does by their own insinuation grow'—he thinks it's their own fault for being loyal to Claudius instead of to him.*

› **insinuating** ADJECTIVE
fawning
• *(Oth 4.2.130) Emilia says: 'Some busy and insinuating rogue' has slandered Desdemona.*

instance NOUN
as well as meaning 'example', you'll find:
1 proof
• *(MA 2.2.38) Borachio tells Don John to inform Claudio and Don Pedro of Hero's infidelity: 'Offer them instances'.*
2 reason
• *(H5 2.2.116) Henry tells Scroop that the devil 'Gave thee no instance why thou shouldst do treason'.*

instrument NOUN
as well as meaning 'musical instrument', you'll find:
1 means
• *(Tem 3.3.54) Ariel talks of destiny 'That hath to instrument this lower world'—uses the lower world (hell) as its means of action.*
2 faculty
• *(JC 2.1.66) Brutus reflects on the time between planning a dreadful deed and carrying it out, when 'The genius and the mortal instruments /*

a b c d e f g h Ii j k l m n o p q r s t u v w x y z

Are then in council'—the spirit and human faculties confer.
3 weapon
• *(Mac 4.3.242) Malcolm says: 'the powers above / Put on their instruments'—take up their weapons—to shake Macbeth.*

insubstantial ADJECTIVE
lacking real substance
• *(Tem 4.1.155) Prospero describes his 'insubstantial pageant'.*

INSULTS

Some of Shakespeare's most vivid vocabulary appears in the way characters insult each other.

• *(MND 3.2.296) Hermia calls Helena a 'painted maypole'—presumably because she is tall and thin, and wears a lot of make-up.*
• *(TN 2.3.132) Maria calls Malvolio 'a time-pleaser, an affectioned ass'—a follower of fashion and a pretentious idiot.*
• *(H5 5.1.5) The Welsh Captain describes Pistol as a 'rascally, scald [scabby], beggarly, lousy, pragging [show-off] knave'.*
• *(Tem 1.1.38) Sebastian calls the Boatswain a 'bawling, blasphemous, incharitable dog'.*
• *(KL 2.2.19) Kent says Oswald is a 'knave, beggar, coward, pandar [pimp], and the son and heir of a mongrel bitch'.*
• *(MA 5.1.94) Antonio describes Claudio and Don Pedro as 'Scambling, outfacing, fashion-monging boys'—quarrelsome, bluffing, and dandified.*
• *(TN 5.1.197) Sir Toby calls Sir Andrew 'An ass-head, and a coxcomb, and a knave, a thin-faced knave, a gull!'—a simpleton.*
• *(KL 1.4.82) Kent describes Oswald as a 'base foot-ball player'—a game of the gutter that nobles would never dream of playing.*

insuppressive ADJECTIVE
indomitable, can't be defeated
• *(JC 2.1.134) Brutus reminds the conspirators of 'th'insuppressive mettle of our spirits'.*

intelligent ADJECTIVE
⚠ *Don't read in the meaning of 'great mental ability'.*
giving inside information
• *(KL 3.5.9) Edmund says Gloucester's letter proves him to be 'an intelligent party to the advantages of France'.*

intend VERB
pretend
• *(MA 2.2.32) Borachio advises Don John to 'Intend a kind of zeal both to the prince and Claudio'.*

› **intendment** NOUN
intention
• *(H5 1.2.144) Henry says he fears 'the main intendment of the Scot'.*

intentively ADVERB
paying continuous attention
• *(Oth 1.3.154) Othello describes how Desdemona would listen to his stories 'Whereof by parcels she had something heard, / But not intentively'—she'd heard bits of stories before, but never a single one all the way through.*

intercession NOUN
plea
• *(RJ 2.3.54) Romeo asks the Friar for help: 'My intercession likewise steads my foe'—what I'm asking for is not selfish, as it will also benefit my enemy (the Capulets).*

interdiction NOUN
prohibition
• *(Mac 4.3.107) Macduff condemns Malcolm, who 'By his own interdiction stands accurs'd'—has accused himself of being guilty.*

interess VERB
admit
• *(KL 1.1.84) Lear tells Cordelia that both France and Burgundy 'Strive to be interess'd' to her love.*

interest NOUN
⚠ *Don't read the meaning of 'mild curiosity' into these senses.*
1 rights of possession
• *(KL 1.1.49) Lear tells his daughters he will give up his 'Interest of territory'.*
2 personal involvement
• *(RJ 3.1.184) The Prince tells Montague he has 'an interest in your hearts' proceeding'—he feels involved in their quarrel in a personal way (possibly because he is related to Mercutio, who is a close friend of Romeo).*
✒ *'Hearts' is the reading in the First Folio. The First Quarto text of the play has 'hates'.*

interlude NOUN
⚠ *Don't read in the meaning of 'interval'.*
short play
• *(MND 1.2.5) Quince gives out the parts to those who are 'to play in our interlude'.*

intermission NOUN

⚠ *Don't read the meaning of 'interval between parts of a film or a show' into these senses.*

1 delay

• *(Mac 4.3.235) Macduff asks the heavens to 'Cut short all intermission'.*

2 pause

• *(KL 2.4.32) Kent reports how a messenger delivered letters 'spite of intermission'—without pausing to draw breath.*

intermit VERB

withhold

• *(JC 1.1.56) Murellus asks the gods 'to intermit the plague' that will fall on the people for their behaviour.*

interrogatory NOUN

questioning

• *(MV 5.1.298) Portia asks everyone to enter her house to 'charge us there upon inter'gatories' —make me answer all your questions.*

✒ *The shortened spelling is to fit the metre of the line.*

intrenchant ADJECTIVE

uncuttable

• *(Mac 5.8.9) Macbeth boasts that it would be easier for Macduff to cut 'the intrenchant air' than to make him bleed.*

intrince also spelled **intrinse** ADJECTIVE

intricate or secret

• *(KL 2.2.71) Kent attacks Oswald as a rogue who bites apart the bonds of natural affection 'Which are too intrince t'unloose'.*

inure also spelled **enure** VERB

accustom

• *(TN 2.5.136) Olivia's letter advises Malvolio 'to inure thyself to what thou art like to be'—get used to the idea of what could lie in store for you.*

inurn VERB

bury

• *(Ham 1.4.49) Hamlet recalls the Ghost's tomb 'Wherein we saw thee quietly inurn'd'.*

invention NOUN

⚠ *Don't read a meaning to do with 'making something for the first time' into these senses.*

as well as meaning 'innovation', you'll find:

1 imagination

• *(H5 Prologue.2) The Chorus asks for 'a muse of fire, that would ascend / The brightest heaven of invention'.*

2 composition

• *(TN 5.1.321) Malvolio asks Olivia if the letter is 'not your invention'.*

3 trickery

• *(TN 5.1.332) Malvolio says he's been made the greatest fool 'That e'er invention play'd on'.*

4 fiction

• *(Mac 3.1.34) Macbeth reports that Malcolm and Donaldbain are 'filling their hearers / With strange invention'—spreading rumours about their father's death.*

inventorially ADVERB

in detail (as in an inventory)

• *(Ham 5.2.111) Hamlet says to Osric how difficult it would be to list all of Laertes' attributes—'to divide him inventorially'.*

invest VERB

⚠ *Don't read meanings to do with 'money' or 'honours' into these senses.*

1 clothe

• *(Tem 2.1.221) Antonio compares Sebastian's ambition to a desirable garment: 'how in stripping it / You more invest it'—the more you take it off, the more you want to wear it.*

2 permeate

• *(H5 4.Chorus.26) The Chorus describes the sadness of the English army, 'Investing lank-lean cheeks'.*

3 urge

• *(Ham 1.3.83) Polonius tells Laertes: 'The time invests you'—hurry up!*

› **investments** NOUN

clothes

• *(Ham 1.3.128) Polonius says Hamlet's vows of love are 'Not of that dye which their investments show'—they are not what they appear to be, but cover a hidden meaning.*

invisible ADJECTIVE

unforeseeable

• *(Ham 4.4.50) Hamlet is impressed by Fortinbras, who 'Makes mouths at the invisible event'—is scornful of what the future may hold.*

inwardness NOUN

attachment

• *(MA 4.1.244) Benedick says his 'inwardness and love / Is very much unto the prince and Claudio'.*

iron NOUN

sword

• *(TN 4.1.34) Sir Toby tells Sebastian: 'put up your iron'.*

irreconciled ADJECTIVE

unabsolved

• *(H5 4.1.145) Henry describes someone who dies 'in*

many irreconciled iniquities'—who dies without having had his sins forgiven.

ise see **'ce**

issue NOUN
1 child (or children)
• *(MV 2.4.37) Lorenzo says Jessica is 'issue to a faithless Jew'.*
2 outcome
• *(MA 2.2.28) Borachio asks Don John: 'Look you for any other issue?'*
3 action
• *(JC 3.1.294) Antony says he will tell the people about 'The cruel issue of these bloody men'.*

issue VERB
descend from
• *(Tem 1.2.59) Prospero describes Miranda as 'his only heir / And princess no worse issued'—his only child, and a princess, and the daughter of a princess too.*

itching palm
desire for personal gain
• *(JC 4.3.10) Brutus accuses Cassius of having 'an itching palm'.*

iterance NOUN
repetition
• *(Oth 5.2.149) Othello asks Emilia why she has repeated the words 'My husband': 'What needs this iterance, woman?'*

iwis ADVERB [pronounced i-**wiss**]
certainly
• *(MV 2.9.67) Arragon reads about the portrait: 'There be fools alive iwis'.*
✑ *This was an old-fashioned word in Shakespeare's time.*

James I

King James VI of Scotland succeeded Queen Elizabeth I in 1603 as James I of England, and wrote a book about witches called Daemonologie. He also survived an assassination attempt by Guy Fawkes on November 5th. The plot of Macbeth – written the following year and featuring the killing of a Scottish king, and witches – may well have had some personal significance to him.

Jack also spelled **jack** NOUN
1 ill-mannered fellow
• *(MA 5.1.91) Antonio calls Claudio and Don Pedro 'Boys, apes, braggarts, jacks, milksops!'*
2 practical joker
• *(Tem 4.1.197) Stephano tells Caliban that the fairy who has been leading them astray (Ariel) 'has done little better than played the jack with us'.*

jackanapes NOUN
monkey
• *(H5 5.2.139) Henry tells Katherine he could sit firmly on a horse 'like a jackanapes, never off'.*

Jack-sauce also spelled **Jack Sauce** NOUN
impudent fellow
• *(H5 4.7.133) The Welsh Captain calls anyone who does not keep his oath 'a villain and a Jack Sauce'.*

Jacob NOUN
in the Bible, the younger son of Isaac, and a grandson of Abraham (and so technically an ancestor of Shylock, who proudly tells a story of Jacob's ingenuity)
• *(MV 1.3.66) Shylock talks of Jacob, who 'graz'd his uncle Laban's sheep'.*

jade NOUN
worn-out horse
• *(MA 1.1.131) Beatrice accuses Benedick of always ending a conversation 'with a jade's trick'—like a nag that refuses to go further.*

jade VERB
deceive
• *(TN 2.5.152) Malvolio is sure he isn't fooling himself, 'to let imagination jade me'.*

jakes NOUN
lavatory
• *(KL 2.2.63) Kent threatens to turn Oswald into mortar and 'daub the wall of a jakes with him' —beat him up so much it'll be like plastering him all over a lavatory wall.*

Janus see SWEARING, p.298

Jason NOUN
in Greek mythology, the leader of a band of heroes who went in search of a fabulous golden fleece
• *(MV 1.1.172) Bassanio talks of the 'many Jasons' who come to Belmont to win Portia.*

jaunce NOUN
fatiguing journey
• *(RJ 2.5.26) The Nurse complains to Juliet: 'What a jaunce have I!'*

jaunce VERB
run around
• *(RJ 2.5.52) The Nurse complains she will catch her death 'with jauncing up and down!'*

jealous ADJECTIVE
⚠ *Don't read meanings to do with 'envy' or 'resentfulness' into these senses.*
1 suspicious
• *(KL 1.4.65) Lear has noticed the servants' neglect, 'which I have rather blamed as mine own jealous curiosity'.*
2 doubtful
• *(JC 1.2.162) Brutus affirms to Cassius: 'That you do love me, I am nothing jealous'.*
3 worried
• *(H5 4.1.273) Erpingham tells Henry that his nobles are 'jealous of your absence'.*

› **jealousy** NOUN
1 suspicion
• *(Ham 2.1.113) Polonius curses his mistrust: 'But beshrew my jealousy!'*
2 worry
• *(TN 3.3.8) Antonio followed Sebastian because of 'jealousy what might befall your travel'.*

jealous-hood also spelled **jealous hood** NOUN
example of female jealousy
• *(RJ 4.4.13) Capulet calls his wife 'A jealous hood'.*
see also CLOTHING, p.158

jennet also spelled **gennet** NOUN
a small Spanish horse
• *(Oth 1.1.114) Iago tells Brabantio if his daughter goes out with a horse (that is, Othello) he'll have 'jennets for germans'—horses as blood relations.*

Jephthah NOUN
in the Bible, a leader who promised God to sacrifice the first living thing he met if he returned home victorious—this proved to be his daughter
• *(Ham 2.2.392) Hamlet, talking to Polonius, calls out: 'O Jephthah, judge of Israel, what a treasure hadst thou!'*

jerkin see CLOTHING, p.158

jess NOUN
a short strap fastened to the legs of a hawk to keep it from flying away
• *(Oth 3.3.263) Othello says he would cast Desdemona off, 'Though that her jesses were my dear heart-strings'.*

jest VERB
make believe
• *(Ham 3.2.225) Hamlet assures Claudius that the players 'do but jest'.*

Jesu see SWEARING, p.298

jet VERB
strut
• *(TN 2.5.29) Fabian says of Malvolio: 'How he jets under his advanced plumes!'*
🎭 *Some productions dress Malvolio in a heavily plumed hat, to make the point.*

jewel NOUN
as well as meaning 'precious stone', you'll find:
miniature picture in a jewelled setting
• *(TN 3.4.188) Olivia gives Cesario a gift: 'wear this jewel for me, 'tis my picture'.*

Jezebel NOUN
in the Bible, the wife of King Ahab, known for her pride (and her painted face)
• *(TN 2.5.38) Sir Andrew reacts in disgust to Malvolio's self-importance: 'Fie on him, Jezebel!'*

jig-maker NOUN
comic performer
• *(Ham 3.2.120) Hamlet describes himself: 'O God, your only jig-maker'—God's champion jester.*

a b c d e f g h i Jj k l m n o p q r s t u v w x y z

jocund ADJECTIVE
merry
• *(Mac 3.2.40) Macbeth tells his wife: 'be thou jocund'.*

John-a-dreams NOUN
an idle dreamer
• *(Ham 2.2.554) Hamlet reflects that he mopes around 'Like John-a-dreams'—not actually doing anything.*

joint in the phrase **out of joint**
out of order
• *(Ham 1.5.196) Hamlet reflects: 'The time is out of joint'—everything in this current period of his life is in chaos.*

jointress NOUN
woman who has a right to property from her deceased husband
• *(Ham 1.2.9) Claudius describes Gertrude as 'Th'imperial jointress to this warlike state'.*

joint-ring also spelled **joint ring** NOUN
finger-ring made in two parts
• *(Oth 4.3.70) Emilia says she would not be unfaithful just 'for a joint-ring'.*

joint-stool NOUN
well-made stool
• *(KL 3.6.51) The Fool says to a stool, that Lear sees as Goneril: 'Cry you mercy, I took you for a joint-stool'—excuse me for not seeing you.*
The expression was used proverbially as a mocking apology for overlooking someone.

jointure NOUN
marriage settlement
• *(RJ 5.3.297) Capulet gives Montague his hand: 'This is my daughter's jointure'—a sign that they finally end their quarrel.*

journeyman NOUN
hired workman
• *(Ham 3.2.33) Hamlet describes some of the players he has seen as 'Nature's journeymen'—their performance is good, but not great.*

Jove or **Jupiter** NOUN
in Roman mythology, the king of the gods, associated with thunder and lightning
• *(H5 2.4.101) Exeter tells the French that Henry is coming to France 'like a Jove'.*
see also SWEARING, p.298

jovial ADJECTIVE
as well as meaning 'merry', you'll find:
majestic—like Jove
• *(KL 4.6.194) Lear says 'I will be jovial!'*

judicious ADJECTIVE
fitting
• *(KL 3.4.71) Lear comments on the state of discarded fathers: 'Judicious punishment!'*

Jug NOUN
a pet name for 'Joan'
• *(KL 1.4.214) The Fool comes out with: 'Whoop, Jug, I love thee!'—the meaning is unclear, but it's perhaps a line from a song, or just a cheeky reply to Goneril.*

Julius see **Caesar**

jump ADVERB
exactly
• *(Oth 2.3.363) Iago plans to bring Othello 'jump when he may Cassio find / Soliciting his wife'—the exact moment when he will see Cassio and Desdemona together.*

jump VERB
1 agree
• *(MV 2.9.31) Arragon says he 'will not jump with common spirits', and choose what many men desire (gold).*
2 risk
• *(Mac 1.7.7) Macbeth thinks that achieving success is worth risking the future he sees himself having: 'We'd jump the life to come'.*

Juno NOUN
in Roman mythology, the queen of the gods (the wife of Jupiter), associated with marriage
• *(Tem 4.1.125) Prospero sees that 'Juno and Ceres whisper seriously'.*
see also SWEARING, p.298

Jupiter see **Jove** **see also SWEARING, p.298**

just ADJECTIVE
as well as meaning 'fair' and 'right', you'll find:
1 exact
• *(MV 4.1.325) Balthazar tells Shylock he must take 'a just pound'.*
2 loyal
• *(JC 3.2.84) Antony says Caesar was his friend, 'faithful and just to me'.*

just ADVERB
1 exactly
• *(RJ 3.3.85) The Nurse describes Romeo's distress to be exactly like Juliet's: 'Just in her case'.*
2 quite so
• *(MA 2.1.23) Beatrice responds to Leonato's 'God will send you no horns' (comparing her to a*

bad-tempered cow) with 'Just, if he send me no husband'—that's fine, as long as he doesn't send me a husband.

› **justly** ADVERB
exactly
• *(RJ 3.2.78) Juliet harangues Romeo: 'Just opposite to what thou justly seem'st'—the exact opposite of what you truly seemed to be.*

justify VERB
prove
• *(Tem 5.1.128) Prospero tells Sebastian and Antonio that he could 'justify you traitors'.*

jutty NOUN
part of a building that sticks out from the rest
• *(Mac 1.6.6) Banquo talks of the martlet making its home in any 'jutty' it can find.*

jutty VERB
jut out over
• *(H5 3.1.13) Henry describes a sea-battered cliff that does 'O'erhang and jutty his confounded base'.*

juvenal NOUN
young man
• *(MND 3.1.81) Flute (as Thisbe) calls Pyramus 'Most brisky juvenal'—lively youth.*

kecksie NOUN
a kind of hollow-stalked plant
• *(H5 5.2.52) Burgundy describes France as a country where nothing grows 'But hateful docks, rough thistles, kecksies, burrs'.*

keen ADJECTIVE
cutting
• *(MND 3.2.323) Helena describes Hermia, when she's angry, as 'keen and shrewd'.*

keep below stairs
remain a servant
• *(MA 5.2.9) Margaret asks Benedick: 'shall I always keep below stairs?'*

keep time
be restrained
• *(Oth 4.1.92) Iago advises Othello to control himself: 'But yet keep time in all'.*

kerchief see HATS, p.160

kern NOUN
lightly armed Irish foot-soldier
• *(Mac 1.2.13) The Captain reports how Macdonald 'Of kerns and galloglasses is supplied'—he has hired mercenaries armed in different ways (some with battle-axes).*

kettle NOUN
⚠ *Don't read in the meaning of 'a vessel for boiling water'.*
kettle-drum
• *(Ham 5.2.260) Claudius commands: 'let the kettle to the trumpet speak'.*

kibe NOUN
chilblain, especially on the heel
• *(Ham 5.1.129) Hamlet reflects on how a peasant is now so close to a courtier (in terms of their wit)*

that 'he galls his kibe'—his toe rubs against the courtier's inflamed heel.

kickshaw NOUN
trivial distraction
• *(TN 1.3.102) Sir Toby asks Sir Andrew if he is 'good at these kickshawses'—masques and revels.*

kid-fox NOUN
crafty young cub
• *(MA 2.3.42) Claudio tells Don Pedro about Benedick: 'We'll fit the kid-fox with a pennyworth'—pay him well for hiding so craftily.*
Both the First Folio and Quarto texts have 'kid-fox'; but some editions replace it by 'hid fox'.

kind NOUN
as well as meaning 'manner' and 'type', you'll find:
1 nature
• *(Ham 1.2.65) Hamlet reacts to Claudius, who has just called him 'cousin' and 'son': 'A little more than kin, and less than kind'—more than a cousin, but certainly not a natural son.*
2 role
• *(Tem 3.3.88) Prospero praises the way his 'meaner ministers / Their several kinds have done'.*

kind ADJECTIVE
as well as meaning 'friendly' and 'type', you'll find:
1 showing natural feeling
• *(MA 1.1.25) Leonato describes the tears shed by Claudio's uncle (after hearing of Claudio's achievements) as 'A kind overflow of kindness' —an understandable reaction from a close relative.*
2 happy
• *(Tem 3.1.69) Ferdinand asks heaven to bless what he has to say 'with kind event'—a happy outcome.*

› **kindless** ADJECTIVE
unnatural
• *(Ham 2.2.568) Hamlet describes Claudius as a 'lecherous, kindless villain!'*

› **kindly** ADJECTIVE
natural
• *(MA 4.1.73) Claudio tells Leonato to use his 'fatherly and kindly power' to make Hero speak the truth.*

› **kindly** ADVERB
1 with natural affection
• *(Tem 5.1.24) Prospero says he must be 'kindlier moved' than Ariel in dealing with his enemies —he feels he must treat them better.*
2 convincingly
• *(RJ 2.4.54) Mercutio says that Romeo 'hast most kindly hit it'—responded perfectly to his wordplay.*

› **unkind** ADJECTIVE
with unnatural feeling
• *(KL 3.4.68) Lear thinks Poor Tom's low state is due to his 'unkind daughters'—behaving against nature (not as daughters should treat their father).*

› **unkindly** ADVERB
cruelly or unnaturally
• *(JC 3.2.178) Antony imagines Caesar's shed blood rushing out, whether 'Brutus so unkindly knock'd or no'—whether Brutus asked it to or not.*

› **unkindness** NOUN
1 ingratitude
• *(Mac 3.4.42) Macbeth says Banquo's absence from the banquet is something he will 'challenge for unkindness'.*
2 ill-will
• *(JC 4.3.159) Brutus toasts Cassius with wine: 'In this I bury all unkindness'.*

kite NOUN
⚠ *Don't read in the modern meaning of a kind of toy.*
a bird of prey, thought to be of ill omen
• *(KL 1.4.252) Lear calls Goneril a 'Detested kite'.*

knack NOUN
knick-knack
• *(MND 1.1.34) Egeus says Lysander has stolen Hermia's heart with 'Knacks, trifles, nosegays, sweetmeats'.*

knap VERB
1 knock
• *(KL 2.4.119) The Fool tells a story of a woman and the eels she was cooking: 'She knapp'd 'em o'th' coxcombs with a stick'—hit them over the head.*
2 bite into
• *(MV 3.1.9) Solanio talks of an old woman who 'ever knapped ginger'—who always nibbled ginger-snaps.*

knave VERB
as well as meaning 'rogue', you'll find:
1 servant
• *(KL 1.4.40) Lear asks: 'Where's my knave? my fool?'*
2 boy
• *(JC 4.3.269) Brutus addresses the sleeping Lucius: 'Gentle knave, good night'.*

› **knavery** NOUN
1 trickery
• *(MND 3.1.99) Bottom thinks his friends have*

tricked him: 'This is a knavery of them to make me afeard'.
2 treachery
• *(Ham 3.4.207) Hamlet tells his mother that Rosencrantz and Guildenstern will 'marshal me to knavery'—lead him into a trap.*

› knavish ADJECTIVE
mischievous
• *(Ham 3.2.231) Hamlet describes the play as 'a knavish piece of work'.*

knight NOUN

as well as its usual military meaning, you'll find:
servant (male or female)
• *(MA 5.3.13) Balthasar sings to Diana, the goddess of the night, describing Hero as her 'virgin knight'.*

knot VERB

gather together
• *(Oth 4.2.61) Othello talks of Desdemona's body as a place where foul toads 'knot and gender in!' —get together and have sex.*

knot NOUN

company
• *(JC 3.1.117) Cassius believes that often 'shall the knot of us be call'd / The men that gave their country liberty'.*

knot-grass NOUN

a type of creeping weed
• *(MND 3.2.329) Lysander tells Hermia (presumably as she clings to him) that she is made 'of hindering knot-grass'.*

know VERB

as well as meanings to do with 'gaining knowledge' and 'understanding', you'll find:
1 remember
• *(MND 1.1.68) Theseus tells Hermia: 'Know of your youth'.*
2 recognize
• *(JC 2.1.255) Portia imagines her husband so changed that 'I should not know you, Brutus'.*
3 have sexual intercourse with
• *(MA 4.1.47) Claudio denies Leonato's suggestion that he has slept with Hero: 'If I have known her, / You will say she did embrace me as a husband'.*

› unknown to
not having had sexual intercourse with
• *(Mac 4.3.126) Malcolm says he is 'yet / Unknown to woman'.*

knowledge NOUN

as well as meanings to do with 'information', you'll find:
familiar territory
• *(H5 3.8.120) Orléans criticizes Henry for wandering about 'with his fat-brained followers so far out of his knowledge'.*

Armour

Battles take place in many of Shakespeare's plays, and characters might wear protective armour (made from metal or tough leather) over their clothes every day of the year. Some of the words may look familiar to you, but don't let yourself be fooled by 'beaver' or 'target' —they meant something quite different.

EXAMPLES OF CASQUES AND HELMS

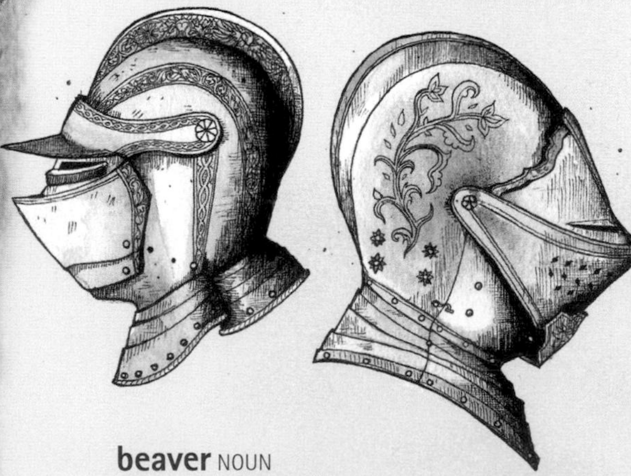

beaver NOUN

⚠ *Don't read in the modern meaning of an 'aquatic rodent'.*

the visor of a helmet, which acts as a face-guard

• *(Ham 1.2.229) Horatio tells Hamlet that he could see the Ghost's face because 'He wore his beaver up'.*

casque also spelled **caske** NOUN

a helmet

• *(H5 Prologue.14) The Chorus wonders if it's possible to fit into a small theatre 'the very casques / That did affright the air at Agincourt'—all the helmet-wearing soldiers that fought in the battle.*

crest NOUN

head-piece, helmet (often with a plume of feathers)

• *(Mac 5.6.50) Macbeth taunts Macduff, believing he cannot be harmed: 'Let fall thy blade on vulnerable crests'—attack someone who is able to be hurt.*

helm NOUN

a helmet

• *(KL 4.2.57) Goneril tells Albany that the French army is coming: 'With plumed helm thy state begins to threat'—to threaten his rule.*

✒ *Helm is a useful alternative to helmet when the metre requires only one syllable (as in the King Lear quote here).*

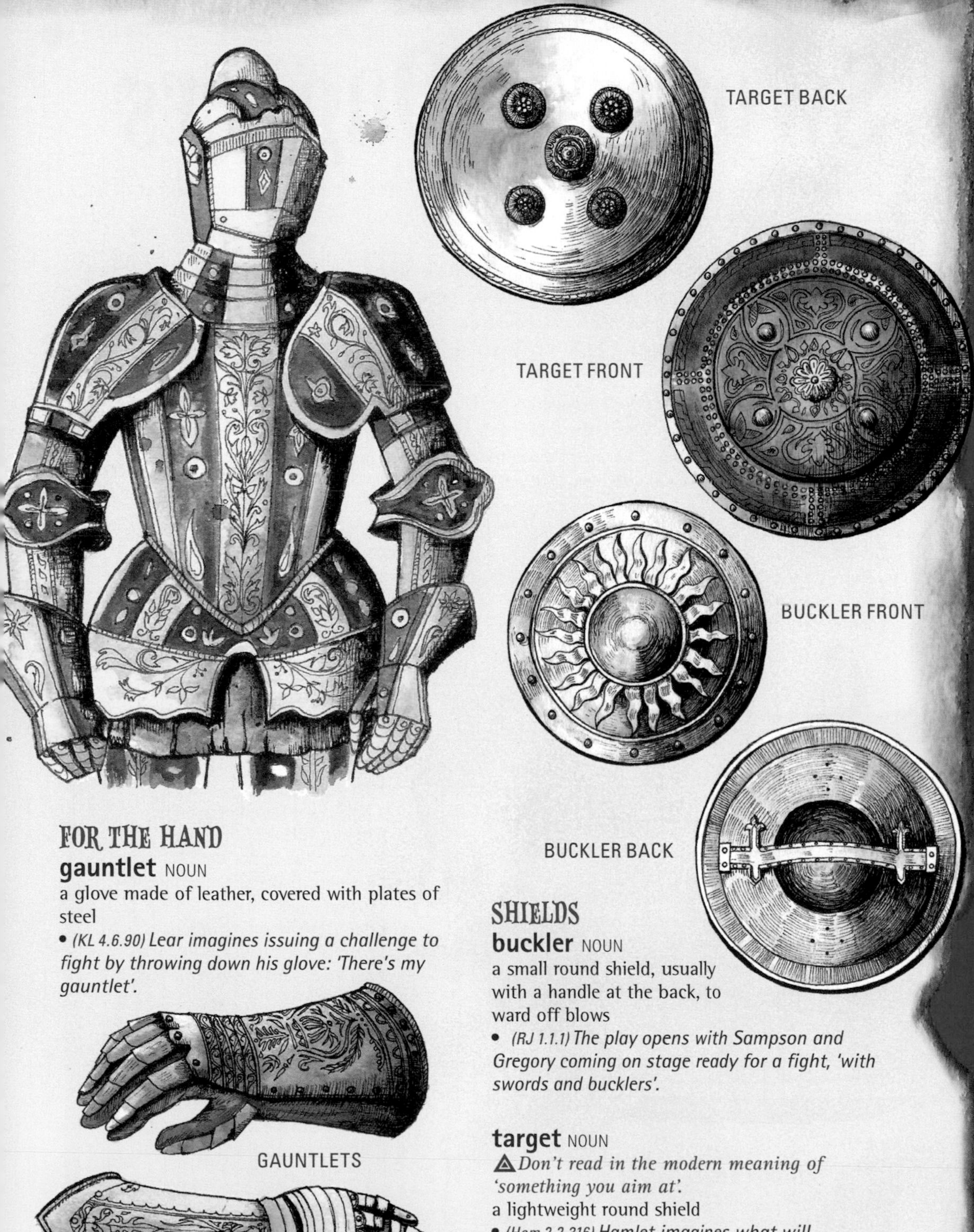

FOR THE HAND

gauntlet NOUN

a glove made of leather, covered with plates of steel

• *(KL 4.6.90) Lear imagines issuing a challenge to fight by throwing down his glove: 'There's my gauntlet'.*

SHIELDS

buckler NOUN

a small round shield, usually with a handle at the back, to ward off blows

• *(RJ 1.1.1) The play opens with Sampson and Gregory coming on stage ready for a fight, 'with swords and bucklers'.*

target NOUN

⚠ *Don't read in the modern meaning of 'something you aim at'.*

a lightweight round shield

• *(Ham 2.2.316) Hamlet imagines what will happen when the players arrive to perform: 'the adventurous knight shall use his foil and target'—his sword and shield.*

Swords and Daggers

Shakespeare often liked to end his plays with a big fight! The fights use different weaponry, depending on whether they're set in a palace or on the battle-field.

In day-to-day life men would normally carry a thin sword (a rapier), and sword fighting—or duelling—was a common way of finishing an argument. The slightest scratch would mean you won, as your opponent could die from a simple skin cut—there were no antibiotics in Shakespeare's time to treat an infection.

Practising your sword-play was a popular pastime, and several styles of fighting came to England from Europe, with different types of weapons used in different ways. Do you want to run someone through with a sharp point? Use a rapier. Do you want to chop someone's arm off with a long blade? Use a curtal-axe.

bodkin NOUN
a short pointed weapon, such as a dagger
• *(Ham 3.1.76) Hamlet reflects on someone committing suicide 'With a bare bodkin'.*

BODKIN

curtle-axe also spelled **curtal-axe** NOUN
a short, broad cutting sword that delivers slashing blows
• *(H5 4.2.21) The Constable thinks there is not enough blood in the veins of the English soldiers 'To give each naked curtal-axe a stain'.*
The word comes from 'cutlass', which people heard as 'cutting axe'. The weapon is not an axe at all.

CURTLE-AXE

dudgeon NOUN
hilt, handle
• *(Mac 2.1.46) Macbeth talks to his imaginary dagger: 'on thy blade and dudgeon gouts of blood'.*

DUDGEON

falchion NOUN
[pronounced **fall**-shun]
a curved broad sword, with the edge on the outer side, like a scimitar
• *(KL 5.3.275) Lear remembers the days when he would fight with 'my good biting falchion'.*

FALCHION

foil NOUN
a light sword used in fencing, with a blunt edge and a dulled tip, or button, at the point, making it a harmless weapon
• *(MA 5.2.12) Margaret describes Benedick's wit being 'as blunt as the fencer's foils, which hit but hurt not'.*

FOIL

partisan NOUN
a type of spear, with a long handle, a broad triangular double-edged head, and two upturned backward-facing points at its base (making it harder to remove from the flesh)
• *(Ham 1.1.143) Marcellus asks Horatio what he should do to the Ghost: 'Shall I strike at it with my partisan?'*

PARTISAN

pike NOUN
a type of spear, with a long wooden shaft and a pointed steel head
• *(H5 4.1.40) Pistol asks the disguised Henry if he is in the infantry: 'Trail'st thou the puissant pike?'—pull the powerful pike behind you.*
Soldiers on the march would ease the labour of carrying a pike by holding them by the head and allowing the handle to trail behind them along the ground.

poniard NOUN
a small, slim dagger
• *(MA 2.1.229) Benedick describes Beatrice's wit: 'She speaks poniards, and every word stabs'.*

PONIARD

rapier NOUN see **ILLUSTRATION p283**
a long thin sharp-pointed sword designed chiefly for thrusting, often used in fencing
• *(RJ 1.5.54) Tybalt is furious to see Romeo at the Capulets' party, and calls his servant: 'Fetch me my rapier, boy'.*

RAPIER

scimitar NOUN
a short curved single-edged sword, used especially in Turkey and the Middle East
• *(MV 2.1.24) Morocco swears by his sword that he would do anything to win Portia: 'By this scimitar'.*

tuck NOUN
a long slender thrusting sword, shorter than a rapier, and with a simpler design to the knuckle guard
• *(TN 3.4.203) Sir Toby tells Cesario to be ready to fight: 'Dismount thy tuck'—remove your sword from its sheath.*

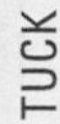
TUCK

SCIMITAR

PIKE

ACCESSORIES

baldric also spelled **baldrick** NOUN
a leather strap worn over a shoulder, across the breast, and under the opposite arm, holding a horn, sword, or other piece of equipment
• *(MA 1.1.220) Benedick, having just referred to a horn-call, insists he will not let any woman 'hang my bugle in an invisible baldric'—doubtless intending a bawdy pun.*

carriages NOUN
a loop attached to a sword-belt, for holding a sword

girdle NOUN
belt

hanger NOUN
a short sword that hangs from the belt
• *(Ham 5.2.143) Osric says the fencing prizes include several sword-fighting accessories, 'as girdle, hanger, and so. Three of the carriages, in faith, are very dear to fancy'.*

pilcher NOUN
a contemptuous way of describing a scabbard—from 'pilchard', thought of as a small and contemptible fish
• *(RJ 3.1.77) Mercutio taunts Tybalt: 'Will you pluck your sword out of his pilcher by the ears?'*

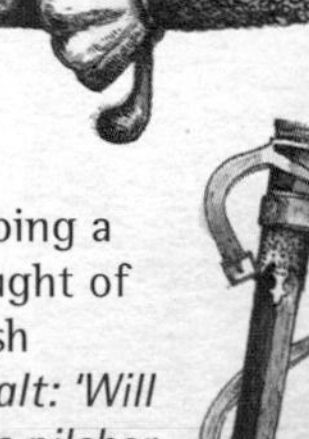

Clothing

People in Shakespeare's time dressed very differently from today, and while the clothes themselves are quite simple variations on things we wear now, several of them—and more importantly their names—have changed or simply gone out of fashion.

CODPIECE

STOCK

NETHER-STOCK

CROSS-GARTER

FOR THE LEGS

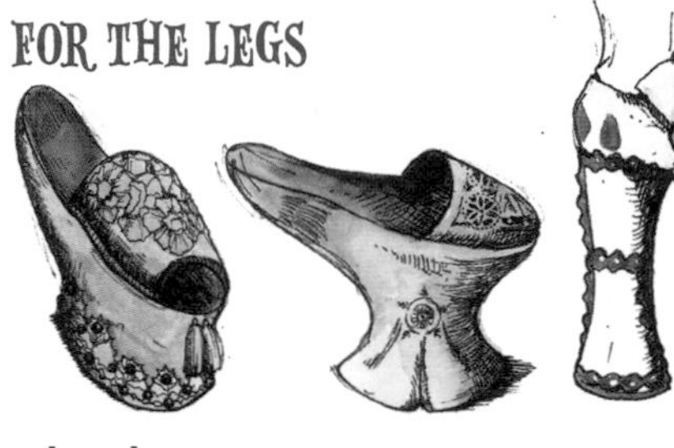

chopine NOUN (pronounced cho-**peen**)
a shoe with a high base made from cork, often worn by actors playing women on stage
• *(Ham 2.2.415) Hamlet tells a boy-actor that he 'is nearer to heaven than when I saw you last by the altitude of a chopine'—the shoes have made him look tall.*

gaskins NOUN
wide, loose-fitting trousers (coming from Gascony in south-west France)
• *(TN 1.5.22) Maria tells Feste that if the ribbons keeping his trousers up break, 'your gaskins fall'.*

SLOPS

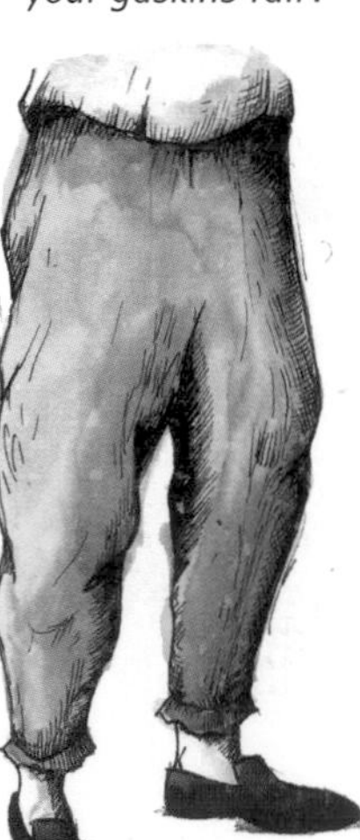
GASKINS

slop or **slops** NOUN
wide, loose-fitting trousers
• *(RJ 2.4.44) Mercutio greets Romeo with bon jour ('good morning'): 'There's a French salutation to your French slop' —one that suits the style of trousers you're wearing.*

cross-gartering NOUN
wearing bands of fabric (garters) crossed along the legs and tied tightly to stop stockings from falling down.
• *(TN 3.4.19) Malvolio finds that 'this does make some obstruction in the blood, this cross-gartering'.*

stock NOUN
a stocking, either for the whole leg or just for the lower leg
• *(TN 1.3.120) Sir Andrew thinks his leg looks very nice 'in a dun-coloured stock'.*

› **nether-stock** NOUN
a stocking for the lower leg
• *(KL 2.4.10) The Fool describes the stocks (a wooden structure used for punishment) holding down Kent's legs as if they were items of clothing: 'wooden nether-stocks'.*

round hose NOUN
very full short trousers that give the hips a rounded look
• *(MV 1.2.69) Portia tells Nerissa that her suitor Baron Falconbridge bought 'his round hose in France'.*

codpiece NOUN
a triangular flap at the front of male breeches, often decorated and padded
• *(MA 3.3.128) Borachio describes a tapestry showing Hercules, 'where his codpiece seems as massy as his club'.*

FOR THE BODY

doublet and **hose** NOUN see **ILLUSTRATION p225**
usual clothing for noblemen and gentlemen in Shakespeare's time
doublet: a close-fitting waist-length jacket
hose: close-fitting stockings for the legs and lower body
• *(MA 5.1.195) Don Pedro reflects on Benedick's unexpected challenge to fight Claudio: 'What a pretty thing man is when he goes in his doublet and hose and leaves off his wit!'*

frock NOUN
today, frocks are worn only by women and girls, but in Shakespeare's time it was also a long tunic worn by men, sometimes part of a uniform, such as a monk's habit
• *(Ham 3.4.166) Hamlet tells his mother that repeated actions can create good habits that are as easy to acquire as putting on 'a frock or livery'.*

mantle NOUN
a loose sleeveless coat
• *(JC 3.2.168) Antony shows everyone what Caesar was wearing: 'You all do know this mantle'.*

gaberdine NOUN
a loose upper garment, like a cloak or cape, made of some coarse material
• *(MV 1.3.107) Shylock reminds Antonio: 'You ... spit upon my Jewish gaberdine'.*

rebato NOUN (pronounced ri-**bah**-toe)
a stiff ornamental collar, or ruff
• *(MA 3.4.6) Margaret tells Hero, who is deciding on what to wear for her wedding, that she thinks 'your other rebato were better'.*

jerkin NOUN
a waistcoat, or sleeveless jacket, worn by men as an outer garment
• *(Tem 4.1.234) Stephano sees an array of clothes hanging from a line and asks: 'is not this my jerkin?'*

sea-gown NOUN
a robe with a high collar, short sleeves, and mid-leg length, worn when travelling by sea
• *(Ham 5.2.13) Hamlet tells Horatio how, on his sea voyage to England, he left his cabin 'My sea-gown scarf'd about me'.*

SEA-GOWN

Hats

Hats weren't only used to keep your head warm, or to protect you from the heat of the sun. The type of hat you wore often told people what job you did (a sailor, a fool, a soldier) and what type of life you lived—if you were rich your hat might be made of fine, expensive cloth.If you were not wearing a hat, you would be 'going bare-headed'. People usually wore hats, so to go without one would show that something unusual was happening.

• *(KL 3.2.60) Kent is shocked that the King should be outside without a hat: 'Alack, bare-headed?'*

No matter who you were, there was one 'hat' that would force you to remove yours—the crown. Everyone would have to uncover their head before their King or Queen.

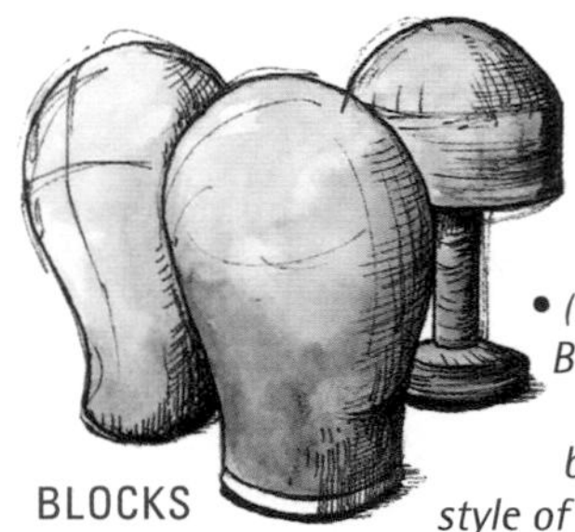

BLOCKS

block NOUN
a piece of wood used to make a mould for a hat
• *(MA 1.1.68) Beatrice describes Benedick as someone whose loyalty to friends 'changes with the next block'—that is, as often as a new style of hat is made, which was very often.*
(KL 4.6.179) King Lear enters—'crowned with wild flowers', as some editions say—and interrupts what he is saying with the words 'This's a good block'. Some productions have him take off his flower-crown at this point; others have him pointing to someone's hat.

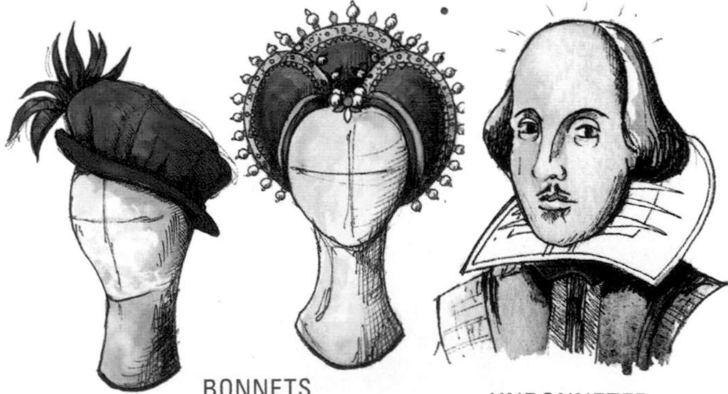

BONNETS

UNBONNETED

bonnet NOUN
an outdoor soft-cloth head-dress, not covering the forehead, different from a hat because it had no brim
• *(Ham 5.2.91) Hamlet tells Osric to put his hat on: 'Your bonnet to his right use: 'tis for the head'.*
Bonnets without a brim were later worn only by women, girls, and babies, but in Shakespeare's time they were also worn by men and boys.

› **unbonneted** ADJECTIVE
bare-headed
• *(KL 3.1.14) When a gentleman describes Lear as running around 'unbonneted', he means the king is going about so wildly that he has lost the hat he would normally wear.*

tire NOUN
a head-dress—a shortened form of attire
• *(MA 3.4.12) Margaret tells Hero she likes 'the new tire'.*

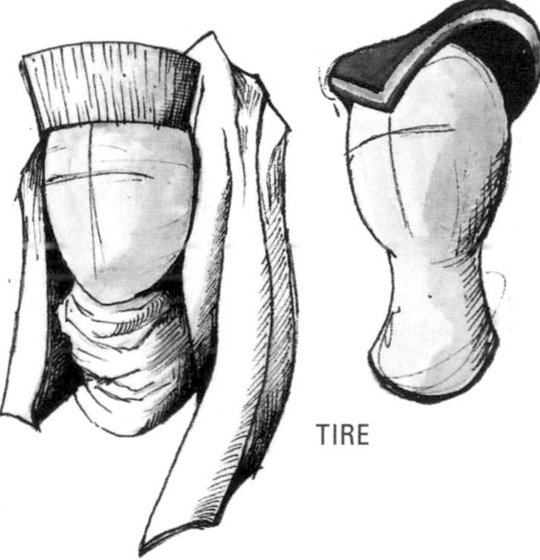

TIRE

cucullus NOUN (pronounced koo-**kull**-us)
the Latin word for a hood, heard in the expression *cucullus non facit monachum*, 'the hood does not make the monk'
• *(TN 1.5.50) Feste uses the expression to tell Olivia that he has a brain, despite his foolish appearance.*
Today we would say 'You can't tell a book by its cover' or 'Appearances are deceptive'.

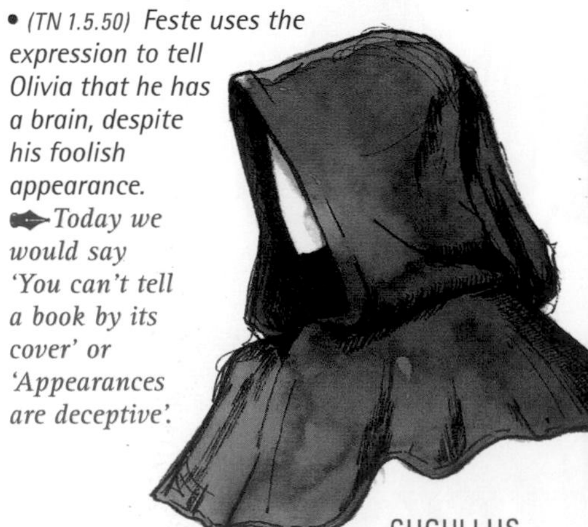

CUCULLUS

hood NOUN
a covering made of soft material for the head and neck, also used to describe a whole person
• *(RJ 4.4.13) Capulet calls his wife 'a jealous hood'.*

hood VERB
to cover up, or hide, as with a hood
• *(MV 2.2.180) Gratiano says he will 'hood' his eyes with his hat to show he will behave himself.*
Hood is sometimes used in swearing.
• *(MV 2.6.52) Gratiano swears 'by my hood'.*
see SWEARING, p.298

cockle hat
a hat with a cockle shell stuck in it
• *(Ham 4.5.25) Ophelia in her madness sings about a man wearing 'his cockle hat and staff'.*
Pilgrims wore cockle hats when they were travelling to the shrine of St James of Compostela in Spain. A legend says that St James once rescued a knight from drowning, and when he came out of the water he was covered with these shells.

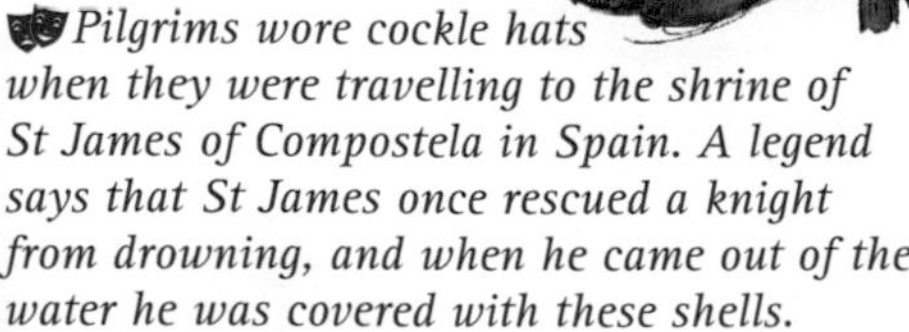

COCKLE HAT

coxcomb NOUN (pronounced **coks**-kum)
1 a special cap worn by the fool, or jester, who was part of the household of a monarch or nobleman; the top had the shape and colour of a cockerel's crest
• *(KL 1.4.96) The Fool in King Lear wears one, and offers it to Kent for being so foolish as to follow Lear: 'take my coxcomb'.*
2 a comical way of describing a head
• *(TN 5.1.184) Sir Andrew describes Sir Toby as having 'a bloody coxcomb'.*
3 an insult, used for any fool or simpleton, sometimes quite mild and friendly, but usually much stronger in force
• *(Oth 5.2.231) The strongest use of all is when Emilia calls Othello, after he has killed Desdemona, a 'murderous coxcomb'.*

COXCOMB

cap NOUN
a head-covering worn by both men and women (unlike today, when caps are usually worn by men and boys): for a man, a hat made of soft cloth without a brim, as today; for a woman, a loose-fitting decorative head-dress
• *(MA 3.4.66) Beatrice has a cold and isn't feeling very well, so when her maid makes a joke she responds crossly: 'you should wear it in your cap'—like a fool.*
Caps came in many different styles and fashions, and could also identify particular groups of people, or perhaps what beliefs they had, like a badge or a ribbon today.

FEMALE NIGHT-CAP

› night-cap NOUN
Don't read in the meaning of 'an alcoholic drink taken at the end of an evening before going to bed'.
a piece of headwear worn at night to keep the head warm
• *(JC 1.2.244) Casca tells Brutus how the crowd cheered and threw up their 'sweaty nightcaps' in praise of Julius Caesar.*

MALE NIGHT-CAP

› sea-cap NOUN
a sailor's cap
• *(TN 3.4.303) Officers recognize the sailor Antonio even though 'you have no sea-cap on your head'.*

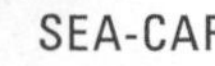

SEA-CAP

› off-cap VERB
to take off one's cap
• *(Oth 1.1.10) Iago talks about people who 'off-capped' to Othello—took off their hats in respect.*

OFF-CAP

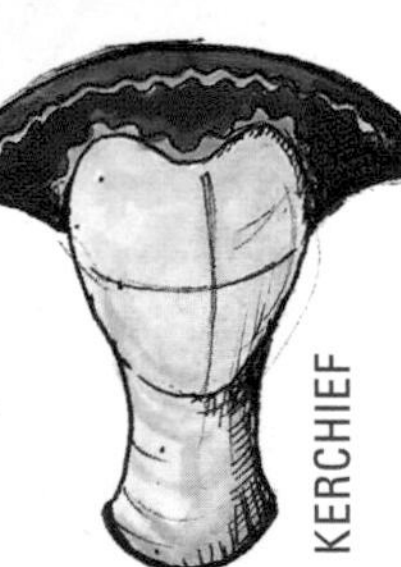

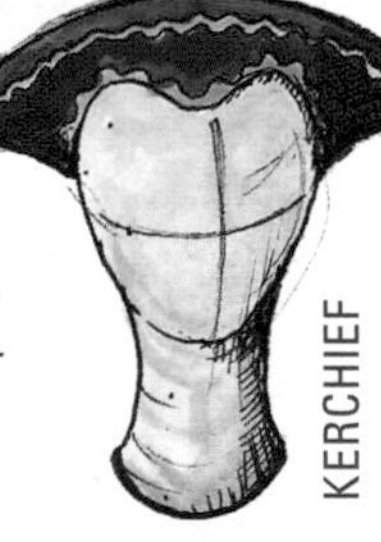

KERCHIEF

kerchief NOUN (pronounced '**ker**-cheef')
a cloth head-covering or scarf
• *(JC 2.1.321) When sick Ligarius meets Brutus, he is wearing one to keep his head warm, but 'He pulls off his kerchief' to become part of the plot to kill Caesar.*
The word comes from 'coverchief', originally a French word meaning 'cover for the head'.

KERCHIEF

Animals

Most animal names from Shakespeare's time are familiar to us today, but a few need explanation. Many animals, such as the kangaroo or the panda, aren't mentioned in the plays because they hadn't yet been discovered by the western world.

BIRDS

MARTLET

CHOUGH

chough NOUN (pronounced **chuff**)
jackdaw
• *(MND 3.2.21) Puck describes 'russet-pated choughs ... Rising and cawing'—with dull-reddish-brown heads.*

martlet NOUN
house martin
• *(MV 2.9.27) Arragon compares the superficial attraction of gold to the way 'the martlet / Builds in the weather on the outward wall'.*

howlet or **owlet** NOUN
small or young owl
• *(Mac 4.1.17) The Second Witch puts into the cauldron 'Lizard's leg and howlet's wing.'*

HOWLET

LEGENDARY ANIMAL

cockatrice NOUN (pronounced cock-a-**triss**)
a mythical murderous serpent that kills with its eye
• *(TN 3.4.192) Sir Toby says Cesario and Sir Andrew 'will kill one another by the look, like cockatrices'.*

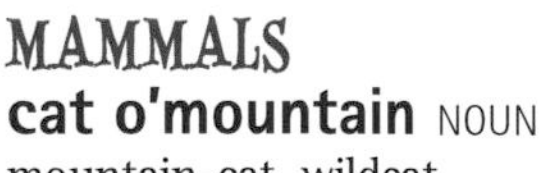

MAMMALS

cat o'mountain NOUN
mountain-cat, wildcat
see **pard**

gib NOUN
(pronounced **gib**, not **jib**)
tom-cat
• *(Ham 3.4.192) Hamlet tells Gertrude that she must hide her knowledge of Hamlet's true behaviour from Claudius, just as she would hide it 'from a paddock, from a bat, a gib'.*
These animals were all thought to act as a witch's familiar—an attendant spirit, usually in the form of an animal, that was a powerful source of magic and capable of reading minds.

GIB

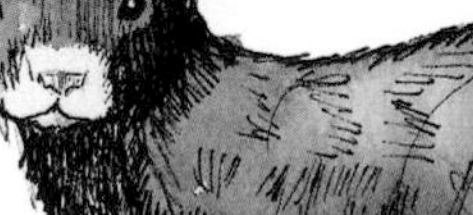

fitchew NOUN
polecat, skunk
• *(Oth 4.1.144) Cassio greets the arrival of Bianca: ''Tis such another fitchew! Marry, a perfumed one!'*
The name was also applied to prostitutes.

paddock NOUN
as well as meaning 'horse enclosure', you'll find: toad
• *(Mac 1.1.10) The Second Witch hears her personal demon calling her: 'Paddock calls!'*
Some editions give the name as Padock, which is the spelling used in the First Folio.

pard NOUN
leopard, panther
• *(Tem 4.1.259) Prospero tells Ariel to pinch Caliban, Stephano, and Trinculo so much that they will be 'more pinch-spotted ... / Than pard or cat o'mountain'.*

OUNCE

PARD

ounce NOUN
as well as meaning a unit of measurement, you'll find: lynx
• *(MND 2.2.36) Oberon tells sleeping Titania she will fall in love with the first thing she sees when she wakes up, 'Be it ounce or cat or bear'.*

shough NOUN (pronounced **shok**)
shaggy-haired Icelandic dog
• *(Mac 3.1.96) Macbeth tells the murderers they can be called 'men' only in the same way as 'Shoughs, water-rugs, and demi-wolves are clept / All by the name of dogs'.*

SHOUGH

water-rug NOUN
rough-haired water-dog
see **shough**

Colours

As well as everyday words such as red, yellow, and green, Shakespeare sometimes used more unusual words and phrases to describe the colour of things. The colours are all the same as today; it's just the words that are unfamiliar.

bay ADJECTIVE
reddish-brown—a colour used only when describing horses
• *(KL 3.4.55) Edgar, disguised as Poor Tom, rambles on about how the devil made him 'ride on a bay trotting-horse'.*

brinded ADJECTIVE
brownish with streaks of another colour
• *(Mac 4.1.1) The First Witch tells the others: 'Thrice the brinded cat hath mewed'.*

dun ADJECTIVE
dull greyish-brown
• *(TN 1.3.119) Sir Andrew thinks his leg looks very nice 'in a dun-coloured stock'.*
Dun most often describes the colour of asses, cows, and other bovine animals (none of them famed for their intelligence).

carnation ADJECTIVE
flesh-coloured, pink (like the flower)
• *(H5 2.3.30) The Hostess says that Falstaff 'could never abide carnation, 'twas a colour he never liked'.*

damask ADJECTIVE
light red, blush-coloured—the colour of the damask rose
• *(TN 2.4.110) Cesario describes a woman who never expressed her love, letting 'concealment, like a worm i'the bud, / Feed on her damask cheek' - eat away the colour in her face, like a worm eats a rosebud.*
Shakespeare often uses 'damask' to describe the colouring in a woman's face, especially her lips and cheeks.

rubious ADJECTIVE
ruby-coloured, deep red
• *(TN 1.4.32) Orsino is fascinated by Cesario's face, comparing it to the Roman goddess of chastity: 'Diana's lip / Is not more smooth and rubious'.*

French-crown-colour ADJECTIVE
the light yellow colour of a French crown coin
• *(MND 1.2.82) Bottom lists the beard-colours he would use to play the part of Pyramus, including a 'French-crown-colour beard, your perfect yellow'.*

gules ADJECTIVE (pronounced **gyoolz**)
red—a term used in heraldry for one of the colours in a coat-of-arms

• *(Ham 2.2.445) The First Player describes Pyrrhus as 'Head to foot, / Now is he total gules'—completely covered with the blood of those he has killed.*

sable ADJECTIVE
black—a term used in heraldry for one of the colours in a coat-of-arms
• *(Ham 2.2.440) Hamlet quotes lines about Pyrrhus, whose 'sable arms, / Black as his purpose, did the night resemble'.*

› **sable** NOUN
black colour
• *(Ham 1.2.242) Horatio describes the Ghost's beard: 'A sable silvered'.*

russet ADJECTIVE
dull reddish-brown
• *(Ham 1.1.171) Horatio describes the colour of the early-morning sky 'in russet mantle clad'—as if it was wearing a cloak of that colour.*
It was a familiar sight to see country people dressed in a russet cloak made of a coarse woollen cloth. And choughs were sometimes described as russet-pated.
(see ANIMALS, p162)

grizzled ADJECTIVE
grey
• *(Ham 1.2.240) Hamlet asks Horatio if the Ghost's beard had any grey hairs: 'His beard was grizzled, no?'*

› **grizzle** NOUN
sprinkling of grey hairs
• *(TN 5.1.163) Orsino asks Cesario how he will behave 'When time hath sowed a grizzle on his face'.*

hoar ADJECTIVE
grey-white
• *(Ham 4.7.167) Gertrude describes the way the willow 'shows his hoar leaves in the glassy stream'.*

parti-coloured ADJECTIVE
multi-coloured
• *(MV 1.3.85) Shylock tells a biblical story about the birth of 'parti-coloured lambs'.*

saffron ADJECTIVE
orange-red
• *(Tem 4.1.78) Ceres describes Iris as having 'saffron wings'.*

pied ADJECTIVE
multi-coloured
• *(Tem 3.2.61) Caliban scolds Trinculo for his behaviour: 'What a pied ninny's this!'*
Court jesters such as Trinculo would wear brightly coloured clothes.

Occupations

Living in Shakespeare's England, you would have encountered many people being paid to do jobs that just don't exist any more—or if they do exist, we know them by different names. Several are to do with the early police force, or to do with people who made things with their hands (craftsmen), or the men who worked to help run towns and cities. One in particular, the town crier, was the only way the public could hear the day's news, as the daily newspaper hadn't been invented yet! He would walk through the town, and shout out all that had happened.

IN TOWNS AND CITIES

❶ alderman NOUN

a senior officer of a town or city council, next in dignity to a mayor

• *(RJ 1.4.56) Mercutio describes Queen Mab as being as tiny as 'an agate-stone / On the forefinger of an alderman'.*

A seal-ring on the forefinger would show that the wearer was in a position of authority.

❷ beadle NOUN

a parish constable whose job included punishing minor offences

• *(KL 4.6.156) Lear imagines himself talking to a constable whipping a prostitute: 'Thou rascal beadle, hold thy bloody hand'.*

❸ bellman NOUN

a bell-ringer who went around a town to announce a death, or a death that was about to happen (as to a condemned prisoner)

• *(Mac 2.2.3) Lady Macbeth hears an owl, and it reminds her of 'the fatal bellman / Which gives the stern'st good-night'—as it would seem to someone condemned to die.*

❹ constable NOUN

the chief officer of the body of watchmen tasked with keeping the peace

• *(MA 3.3.9) Dogberry asks his men: 'who think you the most desertless man to be constable?'—he means 'deserving'.*

> **Constable** NOUN

⚠ *Don't read in the modern meaning of 'police officer'.*

the chief officer of a royal household, as in England and France

• *(H5 3.7.1) The scene begins: 'Enter the Constable of France'.*

sheriff NOUN

⚠ *Don't read in the meaning of a modern American law-enforcement officer.*

the chief officer who administered the law in a county

• *(TN 1.5.139) Malvolio tells Olivia that Cesario intends to 'stand at your door like a sheriff's post' until she agrees to see him.*

A tall decorated door-post stood outside the house of a sheriff, to show that a person of authority lived there. No-one would ever dare move it!

❺ town-crier NOUN

an officer who makes public announcements in the streets of a town

• *(Ham 3.2.3) Hamlet advises the players to speak their lines naturally, and not to sound like 'the town-crier'.*

❻ whiffler NOUN

an armed attendant whose job was to keep the way clear when a procession was taking place

• *(H5 5.Chorus.12) The Chorus describes the sea 'Which like a mighty whiffler fore the King / Seems to prepare his way'.*

A wifle was an old word for a javelin or spear.

❼ yeoman NOUN

1 a man who owns a small amount of property but who does not have the rank of a gentleman

• *(KL 3.6.10) The Fool asks Lear: 'tell me whether a madman be a gentleman or a yeoman'.*

2 a middle-ranking attendant in a royal or noble household

• *(TN 2.5.37) Malvolio recalls that 'The lady of the Strachy married the yeoman of the wardrobe'—an upper-class lady (no-one has yet been able to identify what Strachy refers to) married her attendant.*

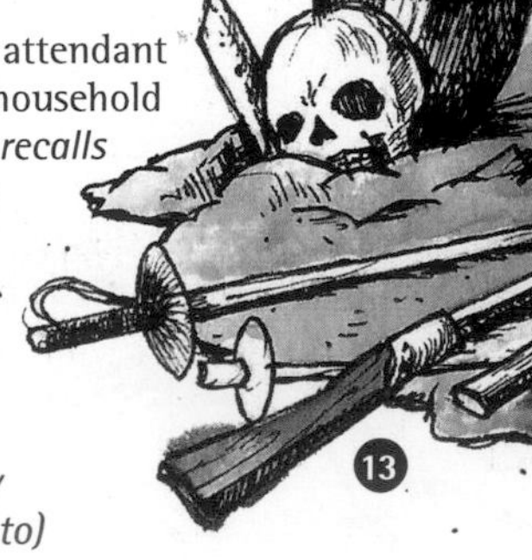

› yeoman's service

good and faithful service, such as would come from a loyal servant

• *(Ham 5.2.36) Hamlet tells Horatio that he was glad he was good at handwriting: 'It did me yeoman's service'—as it enabled him to copy the writing in Claudius' letter.*

IN THE SHOPS

8 botcher NOUN

a mender of old clothes

• *(TN 1.5.40) Feste tells Olivia that a dishonest man should mend his ways by himself, but if he can't, 'let the botcher mend him'.*

9 cozier NOUN

cobbler

• *(TN 2.3.80) Malvolio is furious with Sir Toby and the others for their loud singing: 'ye squeak out your coziers' catches'.*

Cobblers were well-known for singing while they worked.

10 delver NOUN

a digger—such as a gravedigger or (in farming) a tiller of the ground

• *(Ham 5.1.12) The Second Gravedigger asks the First to listen to him: 'Nay, but hear you, Goodman Delver'.*

The First Gravedigger is called Clown in the First Folio.

11 drawer NOUN

a barman—someone who draws drink from a barrel

• *(RJ 3.1.9) Mercutio describes a person in a bar who is always ready for a fight 'and draws him on the drawer, when indeed there is no need'—takes out his sword to attack the bartender for no reason at all.*

12 mechanical NOUN

craftsman

• *(MND 3.2.9) Puck describes the rustics who have come into the forest: 'A crew of patches, rude mechanicals'—fools, uncultivated manual workers.*

13 sutler NOUN

seller of provisions to the army

• *(H5 2.1.96) Pistol tells Nym: 'I shall sutler be unto the camp'.*

1.ALDERMAN 2.BEADLE 3.BELLMAN 4.CONSTABLE 5.TOWN-CRIER 6.WHIFFLER 7.YEOMAN 8.BOTCHER 9.COZIER 10. DELVER 11. DRAWER 12. MECHANICAL 13.SUTLER

Ships

Ships were the most important method of transportation in Shakespeare's time. You could travel by foot, horse, carriage, cart, canal, or boat—but if you had goods to trade or information to pass from country to country, or indeed if you wanted to protect your land from invaders, then the seas were the highways, freeways, and fibre-optic cables. Shakespeare's audience would have had a broad understanding of the various parts of a ship, in the same way as most of us know the various parts of a car.

Passage on the huge, ocean-faring ships was terribly dangerous. Pirates and foreign invaders aside, many waters were uncharted, weather was unpredictable, and cargo holds were often overladen. A journey by sea could easily end in shipwreck, with frequent loss of life and goods, and whilst it was certainly quicker than transporting freight by land, a relatively simple journey across the North Sea from Denmark to England could take over a week.

beak NOUN
the front end of a ship, prow
• *(Tem 1.2.196) Ariel tells Prospero how he moved about the sinking ship: 'Now on the beak'.*

carrack also spelled **carack** NOUN
a large merchant ship, also fitted out for warfare
• *(Oth 1.2.50) Iago reports that Othello has 'boarded a land carrack'.*

topmast NOUN
on a ship, a section of mast fitted to the top of a lower mast
• *(Tem 1.1.32) The Boatswain tells his men: 'Down with the topmast!'*

top-gallant NOUN
on a ship, the platform at the top of the highest part of a mast
• *(RJ 2.4.173) Romeo says he has a rope-ladder which will let him climb 'to the high top-gallant of my joy' —the very highest point.*

yard NOUN
the crossbar on a mast that supports a sail
• *(Tem 1.2.200) Ariel reports to Prospero that he appeared like flame all over the ship, including 'the topmast,/ The yards'.*

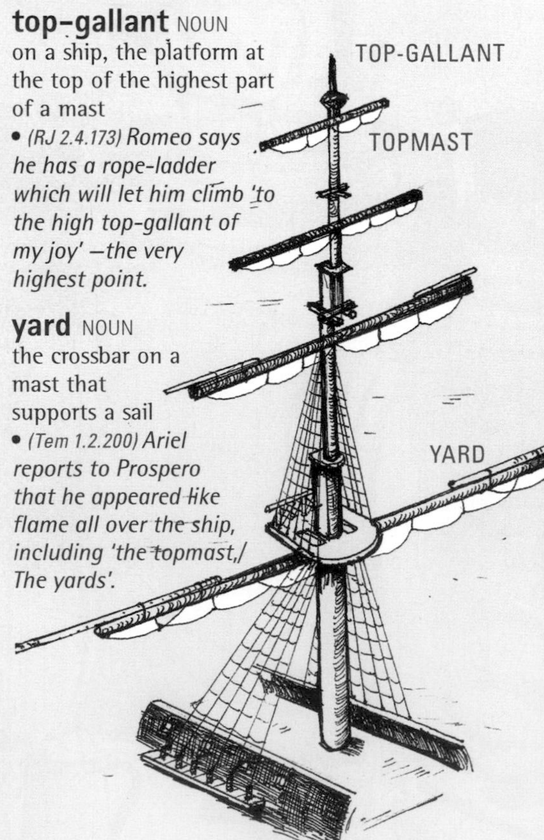

argosy NOUN
the largest merchant-vessel known in Shakespeare's time
• *(MV 1.3.15) Shylock considers the whereabouts of Antonio's ships: 'he hath an argosy bound to Tripolis, another to the Indies'.*

boresprit NOUN
bowsprit—on a sailing-boat, the boom at the front to which the front sail is fastened
• *(Tem 1.2.200) Ariel reports to Prospero that he appeared like flame all over the ship, including 'The yards, and boresprit'.*

main-course NOUN
the principal sail of a ship
• *(Tem 1.1.33) The Boatswain tells his men: 'Bring her to try with main-course' - so that the bow is into the wind.*

topsail NOUN
on a ship, a sail placed above the lower set of sails
• *(Tem 1.1.6) The Boatswain tells his men: 'Take in the topsail!'*

waist NOUN
the middle of the upper deck of a ship
• *(Tem 1.2.197) Ariel tells Prospero how he moved about the sinking ship: 'Now in the waist, the deck'.*

Recreation

Apart from going to the theatre, there were many ways to keep yourself entertained in Shakespeare's time, and plenty of sports and games for children and adults to watch or play. Football existed, but was considered a game only for the poor and rowdy.

bear-baiting NOUN
the sport of setting dogs to attack a bear chained to a stake
• *(TN 1.3.85) Sir Andrew wishes he had spent more time studying languages than 'in fencing, dancing, and bear-baiting'.*

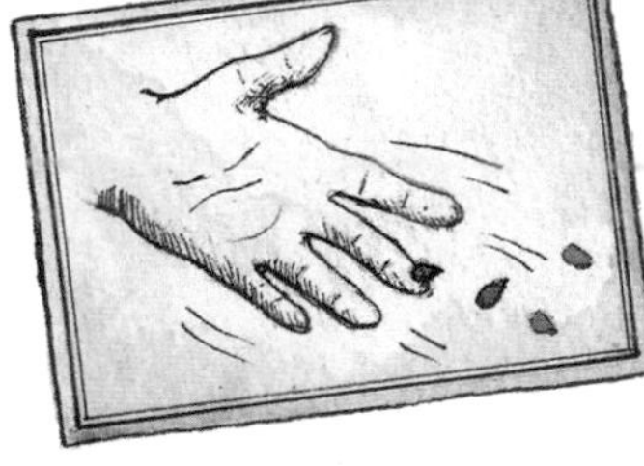

cherry-pit NOUN
a game in which children compete to throw cherry-stones into a small hole
• *(TN 3.4.107) Sir Toby taunts Malvolio that it is 'not for gravity to play at cherry-pit with Satan'—a respectable person shouldn't play children's games with the devil.*

hoodman-blind NOUN
blind-man's buff
• *(Ham 3.4.78) Hamlet says his mother must have been blind to go from his father to Claudius, as if a devil 'hath cozened you at hoodman-blind'—had fooled her to go in the wrong direction.*

loggets NOUN
a game in which sticks are thrown at a stake, with the one closest to the stake the winner—the same principle as in modern bowls
• *(Ham 5.1.91) Hamlet sees the gravedigger throwing human bones around and asks Horatio: 'Did these bones cost no more the breeding but to play at loggets with 'em?—is that all they were brought up to be?*

nine-men's-morris NOUN
a two-person game using nine playing pieces on each side, played on a board or (as here) in the open air, with squares marked out on the ground
• *(MND 2.1.98) Titania describes the things that have gone wrong as a result of her quarrel with Oberon: 'The nine-men's-morris is filled up with mud'.*

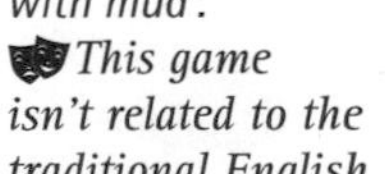

This game isn't related to the traditional English 'morris' dance. It's more like a game of noughts-and-crosses, in which the players move their pieces along the lines to get three in a row.

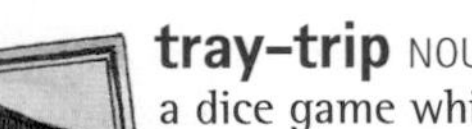

tray-trip NOUN
a dice game which depends on the throw of a three to win
• *(TN 2.5.176) Sir Toby is so pleased with the success of Maria's scheme that he asks her: 'Shall I play my freedom at tray-trip and become thy bond-slave?'—someone who will serve you for ever.*

handy-dandy NOUN
a children's game in which you choose which hand holds a hidden object
• *(KL 4.6.149) Lear says there is often no difference between the behaviour of a judge and that of a thief: 'change places and, handy-dandy, which is the justice, which is the thief?'—make your choice.*

bo-peep NOUN
peep-bo, peek-a-boo—a game played with babies
• *(KL 1.4.167) The Fool sings to Lear: 'That such a king should play bo-peep'—behave like a child.*

whirligig NOUN
spinning top, roundabout
• *(TN 5.1.363) Feste explains that his part in the fooling of Malvolio was to get his own back for the way Malvolio insulted him: 'And thus the whirligig of time brings in his revenges'—'what goes around, comes around', as people say these days.*

FENCING

When you had a sword fight, you hoped to fight someone who had learned the same fighting style as you had, so you would know how they were going to attack you or defend themselves. The more flamboyant French and Italian sword-fighting styles were becoming popular while Shakespeare was writing, and the ways of describing some of the moves came from those languages too.

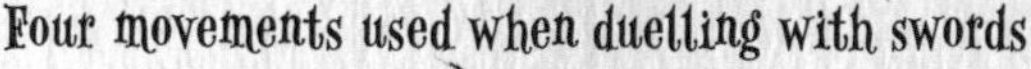

alla stoccata
thrust—the Italian phrase means 'to *the swordpoint*'
• *(RJ 3.1.71) Mercutio tells Romeo someone should fight Tybalt: 'Alla stoccata carries it away'—a sudden thrust will win the day.*

hay INTERJECTION
the home thrust, when you hit an opponent—the Italian word means 'you have it'
• *(RJ 2.4.25) Mercutio describes the way Tybalt fights: 'the immortal passado! the punto reverso! the hay!'*

punto reverso
a lunge forward and to the side of your opponent, combined with a back-handed thrust with a foil, with the palm of the hand upwards—the Italian phrase means 'reverse point'
see **hay**

passado NOUN
a forward thrust with the foil, with the rear foot moving forward at the same time—the Italian word means 'passing'
see **hay**

Music

Much like in a modern film, if you went to see a Shakespeare play 400 years ago, you would be entertained by music playing before and after the show. The musicians would usually play on the balcony above the stage, where the audience could clearly see them.

Women from rich families were taught to play an instrument, but their performance was restricted to the home. It was illegal for them to play (or act) at the theatre.

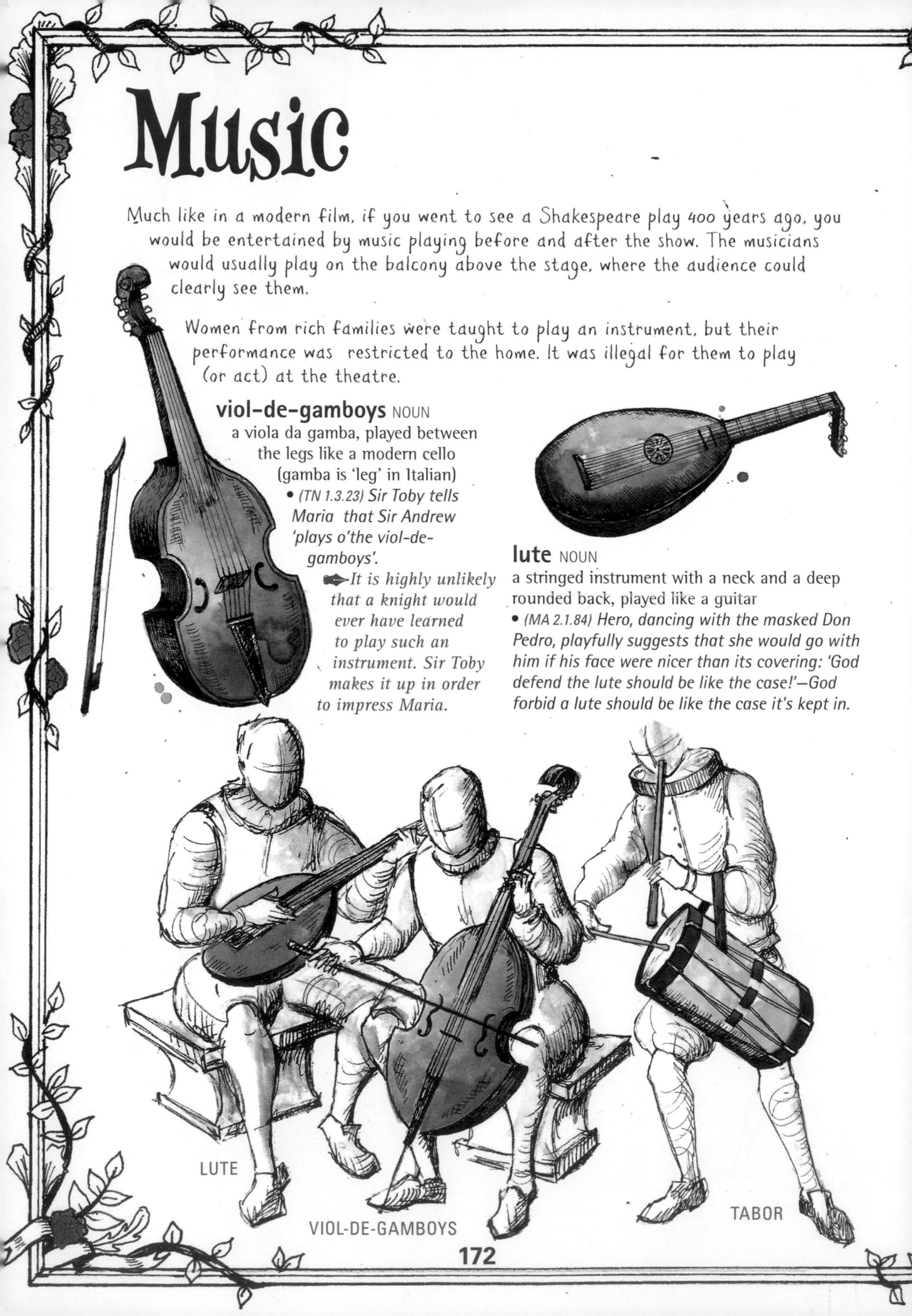

viol-de-gamboys NOUN
a viola da gamba, played between the legs like a modern cello (gamba is 'leg' in Italian)
• *(TN 1.3.23) Sir Toby tells Maria that Sir Andrew 'plays o'the viol-de-gamboys'.*

✒ *It is highly unlikely that a knight would ever have learned to play such an instrument. Sir Toby makes it up in order to impress Maria.*

lute NOUN
a stringed instrument with a neck and a deep rounded back, played like a guitar
• *(MA 2.1.84) Hero, dancing with the masked Don Pedro, playfully suggests that she would go with him if his face were nicer than its covering: 'God defend the lute should be like the case!'—God forbid a lute should be like the case it's kept in.*

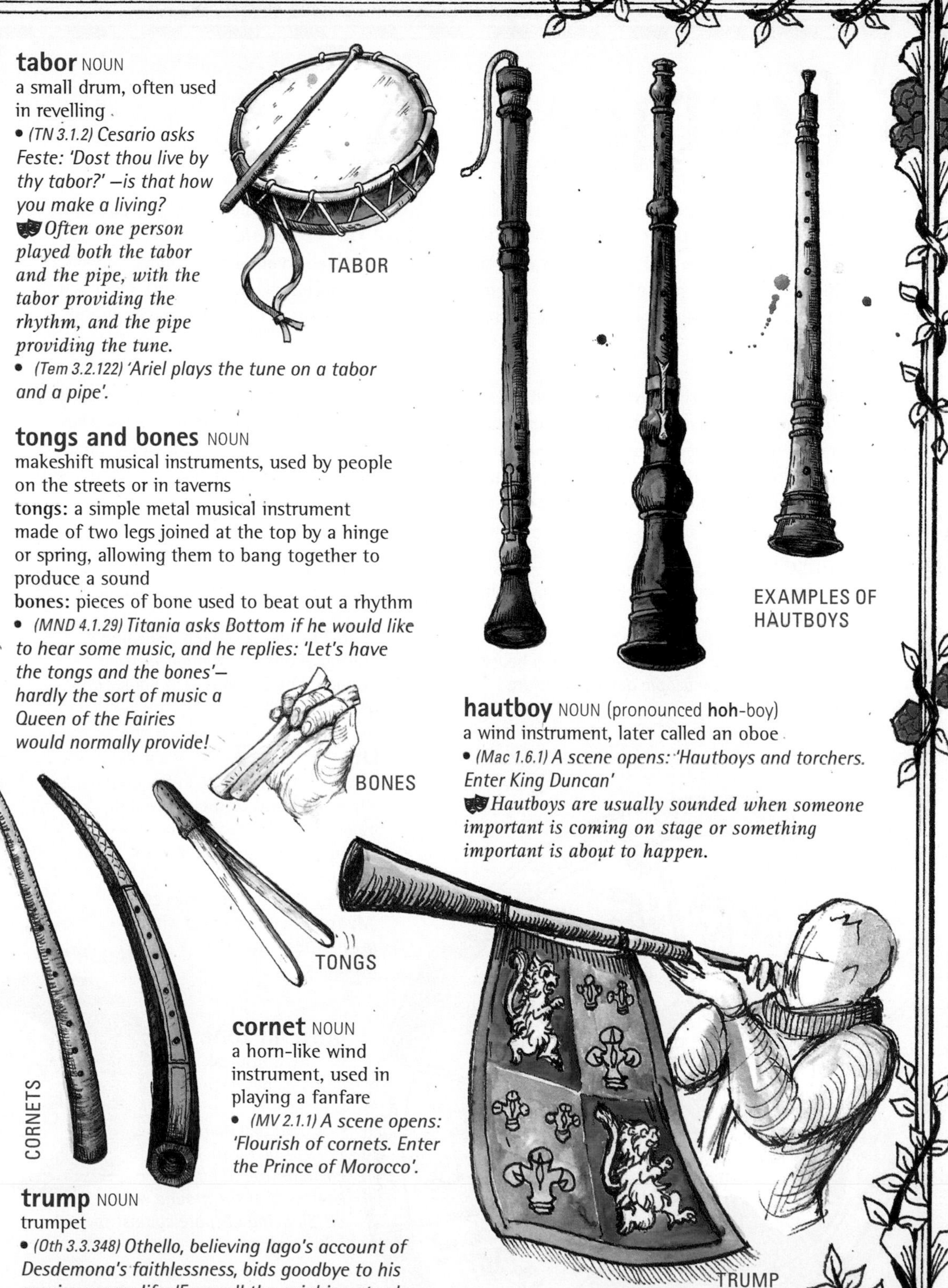

tabor NOUN
a small drum, often used in revelling
• *(TN 3.1.2) Cesario asks Feste: 'Dost thou live by thy tabor?' —is that how you make a living?*
Often one person played both the tabor and the pipe, with the tabor providing the rhythm, and the pipe providing the tune.
• *(Tem 3.2.122) 'Ariel plays the tune on a tabor and a pipe'.*

tongs and bones NOUN
makeshift musical instruments, used by people on the streets or in taverns
tongs: a simple metal musical instrument made of two legs joined at the top by a hinge or spring, allowing them to bang together to produce a sound
bones: pieces of bone used to beat out a rhythm
• *(MND 4.1.29) Titania asks Bottom if he would like to hear some music, and he replies: 'Let's have the tongs and the bones'—hardly the sort of music a Queen of the Fairies would normally provide!*

hautboy NOUN (pronounced **hoh**-boy)
a wind instrument, later called an oboe
• *(Mac 1.6.1) A scene opens: 'Hautboys and torchers. Enter King Duncan'*
Hautboys are usually sounded when someone important is coming on stage or something important is about to happen.

cornet NOUN
a horn-like wind instrument, used in playing a fanfare
• *(MV 2.1.1) A scene opens: 'Flourish of cornets. Enter the Prince of Morocco'.*

trump NOUN
trumpet
• *(Oth 3.3.348) Othello, believing Iago's account of Desdemona's faithlessness, bids goodbye to his previous army life: 'Farewell the neighing steed, and the shrill trump'.*

Cosmos

Shakespeare's audience was very superstitious and had a strong belief in the power of the stars and planets above them. They believed the Ptolemaic model of the solar system to be true – that the sun and the planets revolved around the Earth. Indeed, they thought the planets' spheres—their orbits—were so close together that they would scrape as they passed each other, creating a sound that was called 'the music of the spheres'.

While not quite thinking of the planets as gods (as the Greeks and Romans used to do), Elizabethans strongly believed that the position of the planets and stars in the sky when you were born would influence your personality. For example, if you were born when the orbit of the descending moon intersected with the orbit of the sun, you would be more inclined to excessive or offensive sexual desire.

house NOUN
in astrology, one of the twelve divisions of the heavens
• *(RJ 4.1.8) Paris says he hasn't talked of love to Juliet, because 'Venus smiles not in a house of tears'—unhappy people don't appreciate receiving tenders of love.*

equinoctial NOUN
the celestial equator—with nights and days of equal length
• *(TN 2.3.21) Sir Andrew vaguely remembers Feste talking about 'the Vapians passing the equinoctial of Queubus'. The names are invented nonsense.*

Dragon's tail
in astrology, the place in the cosmos where the orbit of the descending moon intersects that of the sun—thought to be associated with lechery
• *(KL 1.2.123) Edmund believes 'My father compounded with my mother under the Dragon's tail'.*

burning zone
the inter-tropical domain that encircles the Earth
• *(Ham 5.1.268) Hamlet talks of piling so much earth on top of him and Laertes that the ground would be 'Singeing his pate against the burning zone'.*

HOUSE

DRAGON'S TAIL

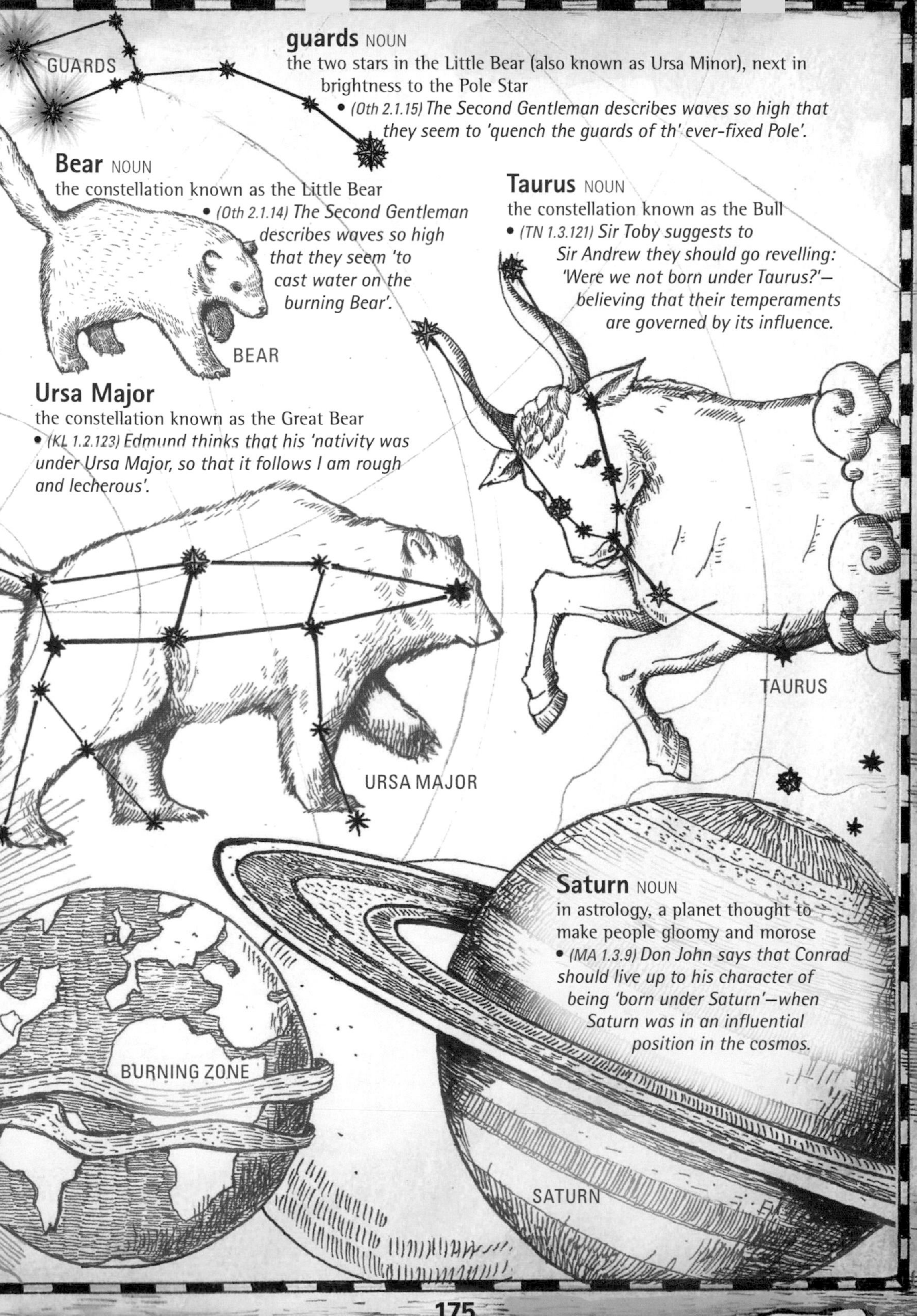

guards NOUN
the two stars in the Little Bear (also known as Ursa Minor), next in brightness to the Pole Star
• *(Oth 2.1.15) The Second Gentleman describes waves so high that they seem to 'quench the guards of th' ever-fixed Pole'.*

Bear NOUN
the constellation known as the Little Bear
• *(Oth 2.1.14) The Second Gentleman describes waves so high that they seem 'to cast water on the burning Bear'.*

Taurus NOUN
the constellation known as the Bull
• *(TN 1.3.121) Sir Toby suggests to Sir Andrew they should go revelling: 'Were we not born under Taurus?'—believing that their temperaments are governed by its influence.*

Ursa Major
the constellation known as the Great Bear
• *(KL 1.2.123) Edmund thinks that his 'nativity was under Ursa Major, so that it follows I am rough and lecherous'.*

Saturn NOUN
in astrology, a planet thought to make people gloomy and morose
• *(MA 1.3.9) Don John says that Conrad should live up to his character of being 'born under Saturn'—when Saturn was in an influential position in the cosmos.*

SHAKESPEARE'S EUROPE
AND THE MEDITERRANEAN
ICELAND
ALMAIN
EUROPA
Calais
Harfleur
GALLIA
BERMOOTHES
Mount
Olympus
Mount
Ossa
ILLYRIA
Venice
Messaline
Florence
THESSALY
Scylla and
Charybdis
Thebes
Messina
Sparta
Argier
BARBARY
TUNIS
Tripolis
AFRIC

Afric (Tem 2.1.67)–Africa
Almain (Oth 2.3.73) - Germany
Arabia (Tem 3.3.22)
Argier (Tem 1.2.260) - Algiers
Barbary (Ham 5.2.140) - N Africa
Bermoothes (Tem 1.2.229)–Bermuda
Calais (H5 3.4.56)
Candy (Tn 5.1.56) - Heraklion, Crete
Colchos (MV 1.1.171)–Colchis, e of Black Sea
Crete (H5 2.1.64)
Europa (MA 5.4.45)–Europe
Gallia (H5 1.2.216)–France
Harfleur (H5 3.4.1)–France
Hellespont (Oth 3.3.457)–Dardanelles
Hyrcania (Ham 2.2.438)–Iran, on Caspian Sea
Iceland (H5 2.1.38)
Ilium (Ham 2.2.462)–Troy, W Turkey
Illyria (TN 1.2.2)–Dalmatian Coast
Ind (Tem 2.2.57), Indies (MV 1.3.16)–East Indies
Mediterranean (tem 1.2.234)
Messaline (TN 2.1.15)–Marseilles
Messina (MA 1.1.1)–Sicily
Olympus (JC 4.3.92)–N Greece
Ossa (Ham 5.1.269)–N Greece
Paphos (Tem 4.1.93)–Cyprus
Parthia (JC 5.3.37)–PERsia (iran)
Philippi (JC 4.3.170)–Thrace, Asia Minor
Phrygia (TN 3.1.49)–Asia Minor
Pontic Sea (Oth 3.3.454)–Black Sea
Propontic Sea (Oth 3.3.457)–Sea of Marmara, Turkey
Sardis (JC 4.2.28)–Lydia, Asia Minor
Scylla and Charybdis (MV 3.5.14)–Straits of Messina
Sparta (MND 4.1.113)–Peloponnesia, S Greece
Tartary (TN 2.5.191)–Tartar, C Asia
Taurus (MND 3.2.141)–Turkey
Thasos (JC 5.3.104)–Thassos, N Greece
Thebes (KL 3.4.150)–Boeotia, SE Greece
Thessaly (MND 4.1.121)–NE Greece
Tripolis (MV 1.3.16)–Tripoli, Libya
Troy (JC 1.2.113)–W Turkey
Tunis (tem 2.1.71)–Tunisia
Venice (MV)

Lord Chamberlain's Men

Every theatre company needed a patron. Shakespeare's actors quickly gained Queen Elizabeth I as theirs, under the careful watch of her most senior royal official, the Lord Chamberlain, which gave them their name. Under James I, they became The King's Men.

Laban NOUN [pronounced **lay**-ban]
in the Bible, the father-in-law and uncle of Jacob (the ancestor of the tribes of Israel)
• *(MV 1.3.66) Shylock tells a story about Jacob grazing 'his uncle Laban's sheep'.*

label NOUN
additional clause (in a contract)
• *(RJ 4.1.57) Juliet threatens to use her hand to kill herself rather than as 'the label to another deed'—to sign a new (marriage) contract that would cancel the one she has with Romeo.*

label VERB
attach as an additional note
• *(TN 1.5.226) Olivia says every part of her beauty will be listed and 'labelled to my will'—in a series of clauses attached to her will.*

lack in the phrase **it lacks of**
a little before
• *(Ham 1.4.3) Horatio tells Hamlet the time: 'I think it lacks of twelve'.*

lackey NOUN
as well as meaning 'servant', you'll find:
non-fighting follower in an army camp
• *(H5 4.4.65) The Boy says: 'I must stay with the lackeys with the luggage of our camp'.*

lading NOUN
cargo
• *(MV 3.1.3) Salarino reports that 'Antonio hath a ship of rich lading wrecked'.*

lady see **SWEARING, p.298, TERMS OF ADDRESS, p.306**

lag of
lagging behind
• *(KL 1.2.6) Edmund says he is 'some twelve or fourteen moonshines / Lag of a brother'—12 or 14 months younger than Edgar.*

laid see **lay**

Lammas-eve NOUN
the day before the harvest festival, 31 July
• *(RJ 1.3.18) The Nurse works out Juliet's age: 'Come Lammas-eve at night shall she be fourteen'.*

If we count how many lines Juliet speaks from when she wakes up in the crypt to when she kills herself, we find one line for every year of her life. Ben thinks this is very significant.

Lammas-tide NOUN
the harvest festival, 1 August
• *(RJ 1.3.16) The Nurse asks Lady Capulet: 'How long is it now / To Lammas-tide?'*

lanch'd see **latch**

lanthorn NOUN [pronounced **lan**-torn]
lantern
• *(MND 5.1.229) Starveling as Moonshine presents his props: 'This lanthorn doth the horned moon present'—the crescent moon (with horns at each end).*

lap VERB
wrap
• *(Mac 1.2.54) Macbeth is described in battle as 'lapp'd in proof'—clad in battle-tested armour.*

lapse VERB
seize
• *(TN 3.3.36) Antonio tells Sebastian of his worry about being in Illyria: 'if I be lapsed in this place, / I shall pay dear'.*

lard VERB
1 strew
• *(Ham 4.5.38) Ophelia sings of her father's shroud: 'Larded with sweet flowers'.*
2 enrich (with blood)
• *(H5 4.6.8) Exeter describes dead York, 'Larding the plain'—the battlefield.*

large ADJECTIVE
as well as meaning 'big' and 'great', you'll find:
1 lavish
• *(Mac 3.4.11) Macbeth tells everyone at the banquet: 'Be large in mirth'.*
2 coarse
• *(MA 2.3.190) Don Pedro says Benedick has a way of making 'large jests'.*
3 grandiose
• *(KL 1.1.183) Kent hopes Goneril and Regan's actions will fulfil the promise of their 'large speeches'.*

› **largely** ADVERB
in full
• *(MA 5.4.69) The Friar speaks to Don Pedro and Claudio: 'I'll tell you largely of fair Hero's death'.*

› **at large**
in full
• *(H5 1.1.78) Canterbury says he has approached Henry about matters to do with France, 'Which I have open'd to his grace at large'.*

lass-lorn ADJECTIVE
forsaken by a sweetheart
• *(Tem 4.1.68) Iris describes the shadowy groves that 'the dismissed bachelor loves, / Being lass-lorn'.*

latch VERB
1 receive
• *(Mac 4.3.197) Ross says the words of his message should be 'howl'd out in the desert air / Where hearing should not latch them'.*
2 nick
• *(KL 2.1.51) Edmund tells Gloucester that Edgar's sword 'latched mine arm'.*
'Latched' is the word used in the First Folio. The First Quarto text has 'lancht', and this is used in some editions as it is the source for the word 'lanch'd', meaning 'pierced'.
3 secure or moisten
• *(MND 3.2.36) Oberon asks Puck if he has 'yet latch'd the Athenian's eyes / With the love juice'.*

late ADJECTIVE
Don't read in the meaning of 'recently died'.
as well as meaning 'after the expected time', you'll find:
1 recent
• *(KL 1.2.98) Gloucester ponders the significance of the 'late eclipses in the sun and moon'.*
2 recently appointed
• *(H5 2.2.60) Henry asks: 'Who are the late commissioners?'*

› **lated** ADJECTIVE
overtaken by the night
• *(Mac 3.3.6) The First Murderer reflects: 'Now spurs the lated traveller apace / To gain the timely inn'—the traveller spurs his horse to make it to his lodging in time.*

› **latest** ADJECTIVE
as well as meaning 'most recent', you'll find:
final
• *(H5 3.4.2) Henry tells the citizens of Harfleur: 'This is the latest parle we will admit'—the final negotiation.*

lath NOUN
thin wood
• *(RJ 1.4.5) Benvolio rejects the idea of going to the Capulets' party by dressing up as Cupid and carrying a 'painted bow of lath'.*

laud NOUN
hymn
• *(Ham 4.7.177) Gertrude says Ophelia 'chanted snatches of old lauds'—sang bits of old hymns.*

laughter NOUN
as well as finding 'the act or sound of laughing', you'll find:
laughing-stock
• *(JC 1.2.72) Cassius denies he is 'a common laughter'.*

Laura NOUN
the beautiful lady addressed in much of the love poetry written by Petrarch (the 14th-century Italian poet whose works were a principal source for Shakespeare)
• *(RJ 2.4.39) Mercutio mocks Romeo's romantic view of his lady: 'Laura to his lady was a kitchen wench'—in comparison to Rosaline, Laura was nothing but a lowly servant.*

lave VERB [pronounced layv]
bathe
• *(Mac 3.2.33) Macbeth, fearful of Banquo, tells his wife that they are 'unsafe the while, that we / Must lave our honours in these flattering streams'—keep our honourable titles safe by bathing them in flattery.*

a b c d e f g h i j k Ll m n o p q r s t u v w x y z

lavish ADJECTIVE
⚠*Don't read in the modern meanings of 'generous' or 'plentiful'.*
wild
• *(Mac 1.2.57) Ross reports that Macbeth has defeated the Norwegian king, 'Curbing his lavish spirit'.*

lavolta NOUN [pronounced la-**vol**-ta]
lively high-leaping dance
• *(H5 3.6.33) The French ladies have advised their nobles to go to English dancing-schools, where they would learn 'lavoltas high'.*

lawn NOUN
⚠*Don't read in the meaning of 'area of mown grass'.*
fine linen
• *(Oth 4.3.71) Emilia says she would not be unfaithful for 'measures of lawn'.*

lay NOUN
song
• *(Ham 4.7.182) Gertrude recounts how Ophelia sang 'her melodious lay' before drowning.*

lay past form **laid** VERB
as well as meaning 'put', you'll find:
1 bet
• *(H5 4.1.212) Henry says the French 'may lay twenty French crowns to one they will beat us'.*
2 appease
• *(RJ 2.1.26) Mercutio makes a joke about Romeo raising a spirit 'in his mistress' circle ... letting it there stand / Till she had laid it'.*
Demons and spirits were thought to be summoned and contained within a magic circle. Mercutio is also making a sexual pun on 'circle' (vagina), 'stand' (erection), and 'laid' (had sex).
3 ascribe, attribute
• *(Ham 4.1.17) Claudius fears that the responsibility for Polonius' death 'will be laid to us'—he'll get the blame.*

lay NOUN
bet
• *(Oth 2.3.303) Iago promises Cassio that his situation will improve: 'My fortunes against any lay worth naming'.*

› **lay down** VERB
work out
• *(H5 1.2.137) Henry says the English 'must lay down our proportions to defend / Against the Scot'—decide how much of their army to send north.*

› **lay home** VERB
talk severely
• *(Ham 3.4.1) Polonius advises Gertrude about Hamlet: 'Look you lay home to him'.*

› **lay knife aboard**
make a claim
• *(RJ 2.4.184) The Nurse tells Romeo that Paris 'would fain lay knife aboard'—would like to assert his claim to Juliet.*
The expression was proverbial. It may have originated in the practice of diners in taverns to use their own knives to mark their place at a table ('board') or to get hold of a piece of food.

› **lay on** VERB
perform vigorously
• *(Tem 3.2.147) Stephano admires the drummer he can hear: 'he lays it on'.*

› **lay to** VERB
bring into action
• *(Tem 4.1.248) Stephano tells Caliban to help carry the barrel of wine: 'lay to your fingers'.*

layer-up NOUN
preserver
• *(H5 5.2.221) Henry describes old age as 'that ill layer-up of beauty'—age is a bad preserver of good looks.*

lazar NOUN
leper
• *(H5 1.1.15) Canterbury discusses what is needed for the 'relief of lazars'.*

lazar ADJECTIVE
leprous
• *(H5 2.1.66) Pistol tells Nym to go and find 'the lazar kite of Cressid's kind'—the leprous bird of prey with the (unfaithful) nature of Cressida (he means Doll Tearsheet).*
In Greek legend, the lady Cressida is punished with leprosy by the god of love for being unfaithful to the Trojan hero Troilus. Shakespeare tells the story of their love in his play 'Troilus and Cressida'.

› **lazar-like** ADJECTIVE
leprous
• *(Ham 1.5.72) The Ghost says the poison made his body 'Most lazar-like'.*

leasing NOUN
skill in lying
• *(TN 1.5.89) Feste compliments Olivia for speaking well of fools: 'Now Mercury endue thee with leasing'.*

lee VERB
make helpless
• *(Oth 1.1.30) Iago says the promotion of Cassio has left him 'lee'd and calm'd'—like a sailing ship that has been cut off from the wind and becalmed.*

lees NOUN
dregs
• *(Mac 2.3.91) Macbeth reacts to Duncan's death: 'The wine of life is drawn, and the mere lees / Is left this vault to brag of'—figuratively, there are only dregs left on earth to boast about; literally, Duncan's body is almost drained of blood.*

leet NOUN
a local court of justice
• *(Oth 3.3.141) Iago says nobody can stop filthy ideas keeping 'leets and law-days'—holding court in the brain.*

legerity NOUN
nimbleness
• *(H5 4.1.23) Henry says a lively spirit makes the limbs move with 'fresh legerity'.*

Legion NOUN
in the Bible, the name of a devil possessing a madman
• *(TN 3.4.79) Sir Toby says he will speak to Malvolio, even if 'Legion himself possessed him'.*

leman NOUN [pronounced **leh**-man or **lee**-man]
sweetheart
• *(TN 2.3.23) Sir Andrew tells Feste that he gave him a tip: 'I sent thee sixpence for thy leman'—not a terrific amount of money to give someone to spend on their love!*

lendings NOUN
borrowings
• *(KL 3.4.104) Lear removes his clothes: 'Off, off, you lendings!'—thinking of clothes as being lent to humans by the animals providing the material.*

lenity NOUN
gentleness
• *(H5 3.2.22) Pistol begs the Welsh Captain to 'Use lenity'.*

lenten ADJECTIVE
1 meagre
• *(TN 1.5.8) Maria tells Feste that his reply was 'A good lenten answer'—lacking any substance (Lent being the season for fasting).*
2 made in the penitential season of Lent
• *(RJ 2.4.119) Mercutio jokes about 'a lenten pie'—a pie which would normally contain no meat.*

leperous ADJECTIVE
infected
• *(Ham 1.5.64) The Ghost describes how his murderer poured a 'leperous distilment' into his ears.*

let VERB
as well as meaning 'allow', you'll find the opposite meaning:
hinder
• *(Ham 1.4.85) Hamlet threatens to 'make a ghost of him that lets me'—he'll kill anyone that tries to prevent him from following the Ghost.*

let NOUN
hindrance
• *(H5 5.2.65) Burgundy asks the two kings if he 'may know the let why gentle peace / Should not ... bless us'.*

› **let-alone** NOUN
ability to hinder
• *(KL 5.3.80) Albany tells Goneril: 'The let-alone lies not in your good will'.*

› **let blood**
kill
• *(JC 3.1.152) Antony asks the conspirators: 'Who else must be let blood'.*

› **let the devil wear black**
a way of saying 'to hell with mourning!'
• *(Ham 3.2.124) Hamlet ironically remarks that, as so much time has passed since his father's death, 'let the devil wear black, for I'll have a suit of sables'—I'll wear something posh.*

lethargy NOUN
as well as meaning 'lack of vitality', you'll find:
coma
• *(Oth 4.1.53) Iago says that Othello's 'lethargy must have his quiet course'—he suffers from fits that Iago describes as epilepsy.*

lethargy VERB
subdue
• *(KL 1.4.218) Lear thinks 'his discernings / Are lethargied'—his abilities to understand are dulled.*

Lethe NOUN [pronounced **lee**-thee]
1 in Greek mythology, a river whose waters make people forget everything
• *(TN 4.1.56) Sebastian wonders what is happening to him: 'Let fancy still my sense in Lethe steep'—let my imagination drown my reason in the river of forgetfulness.*

› **Lethe** also spelled **lethe** NOUN
life-blood
• *(JC 3.1.206) Antony tells the dead Caesar his murderers were 'crimson'd in thy Lethe'.*

a b c d e f g h i j k Ll m n o p q r s t u v w x y z

letter NOUN
personal recommendation (as expressed in a letter)
• *(Oth 1.1.36) Iago complains that 'Preferment goes by letter and affection'.*

› letters NOUN
great learning
• *(Tem 2.1.146) Gonzalo says that in his commonwealth 'Letters should not be known'.*

level VERB
aim
• *(MA 4.1.236) The Friar outlines his proposal, adding that it provides an alternative 'If all aim but this be levell'd false'—if we miss our goal in all other respects.*

› level at VERB
as well as meaning 'aim at', you'll find:
guess correctly
• *(MV 1.2.36) Portia tells Nerissa to describe her suitors and then 'level at my affection'—guess how much I like them.*

› level with VERB
be in keeping with
• *(Oth 1.3.237) Othello asks that his wife be looked after in a manner 'As levels with her breeding'—befits someone of her social position.*

Leviathan NOUN [pronounced leh-**vie**-ath-an]
whale (a name that comes from the Bible)
• *(H5 3.4.26) Henry says it is as impossible to stop the onslaught of violent soldiers 'As send precepts to the Leviathan / To come ashore'.*

levy NOUN
⚠ *Don't read a meaning to do with 'collecting taxes' into these senses.*
recruitment of soldiers
• *(Ham 2.2.62) Voltemand says old Fortinbras has suppressed 'His nephew's levies'.*

levy VERB
muster
• *(Tem 1.2.128) Prospero describes how he was exiled by 'A treacherous army levied'.*

lewd ADJECTIVE
As well as meaning 'indecent', you'll find:
wicked
• *(MA 5.1.325) Leonato describes Borachio as 'this lewd fellow'.*

› lewdness NOUN
obscenity
• *(Ham 1.5.54) The Ghost says true virtue 'never will be mov'd / Though lewdness court it in a shape of heaven'.*

liberal ADJECTIVE
1 overgenerous
• *(Oth 3.4.42) Othello says Desdemona has 'A liberal hand!'—she is too touchy-feely.*
2 coarse
• *(MA 4.1.91) Don Pedro describes Hero's supposed lover as 'a liberal villain'.*
3 fanciful
• *(Ham 5.2.145) Osric describes the swordbelt loops as being 'of very liberal conceit'—lavishly designed.*

liberal ADVERB
freely
• *(Oth 5.2.218) Emilia says she 'will speak as liberal as the north'—the north wind.*

liberal arts
subjects of study considered essential to a gentleman's education (grammar, logic, rhetoric, arithmetic, geometry, music, astronomy)
• *(Tem 1.2.73) Prospero says he was renowned 'for the liberal arts'—for his wide learning.*

libertine NOUN
1 debaucher, someone who indulges excessively in sex, alcohol, or drugs
• *(MA 2.1.128) Beatrice says of Benedick: 'None but libertines delight in him'—only such people like his company.*
2 free spirit
• *(H5 1.1.48) Canterbury says that, when Henry speaks, 'The air, a chartered libertine, is still'—normally allowed to wander wherever it wants, the air stops as if to listen.*

liberty NOUN
innovative plays which break the traditional laws of drama
• *(Ham 2.2.391) Polonius describes the players as the best men 'For the law of writ, and the liberty'—to present plays that follow the established rules of play-writing as well as those that don't.*

licensed see **all-licensed**

Lichas NOUN [pronounced **lie**-cas]
in Greek mythology, the servant of Hercules
• *(MV 2.1.32) Morocco reflects that a lesser person than he might win Portia, just as the servant might 'If Hercules and Lichas play at dice'.*

lie in the phrase **give the lie**
an expression with several meanings: deceive; throw down (as in wrestling); lose the ability to perform sexually; cause the need to urinate
• *(Mac 2.3.32) The Porter says too much drink leaves a man in a sorry state after 'giving him the lie'.*

lief in the phrase **had as lief** also spelled **lieve** [pronounced leaf or leev]
had rather
• *(MA 2.3.85) Benedick says he 'had as lief have heard the night-raven'—he would rather have listened to an unpleasant bird-song—than hear Balthasar sing.*

liege see **TERMS OF ADDRESS, p.306**

liegeman NOUN
subject (of a monarch)
• *(Ham 1.1.16) Marcellus identifies himself and Horatio as being 'liegemen to the Dane'.*

lifelings see **SWEARING, p.298**

light ADJECTIVE
1 joyful
• *(RJ 4.2.46) Capulet says his heart 'is wondrous light'.*
2 easy
• *(Tem 1.2.452) Prospero decides to make it harder for Ferdinand and Miranda to come together as a couple, 'lest too light winning / Make the prize light' (for this second use of 'light', see sense 3 below).*
3 of little value
• *(H5 2.2.86) Henry says Cambridge became a traitor 'for a few light crowns'.*
4 frivolous
• *(RJ 2.2.105) Juliet hopes Romeo will 'not impute this yielding to light love'.*
› **light o'love**
promiscuous
• *(MA 3.4.42) Beatrice tells Margaret that if she danced to the tune of 'Light o' love' she would be 'Light o' love with your heels!'—she would dance energetically in a sexy way.*
'Light o' love' was a lively popular song, written probably in the 1570s. It's mentioned three times in Shakespeare's plays.

light NOUN
signal
• *(TN 5.1.324) Malvolio asks Olivia why she gave him 'such clear lights of favour'—clear signs that he should try to woo her.*

light VERB
1 alight
• *(Ham 5.2.348) Hamlet affirms that 'th'election lights on Fortinbras'—that the next king would be Fortinbras.*
Denmark had an elective system of monarchy. In a circumstance where there was no obvious heir, the people would vote and the monarch would be chosen by election.
2 give light to
• *(Mac 5.5.21) Macbeth reflects that 'all our yesterdays have lighted fools / The way to dusty death'.*
› **lightly** ADVERB
readily
• *(H5 2.2.86) Henry says Cambridge 'lightly conspir'd' with France for money.*
› **lightness** NOUN
lightheadedness
• *(Ham 2.2.149) Polonius suggests that Hamlet fell 'into a weakness, / Thence to a lightness'.*

like ADVERB
as well as meanings to do with 'being similar', you'll find:
likely
• *(Ham 1.2.235) Hamlet agrees with what Horatio has just said: 'Very like'.*
› **the like**
the same
• *(Tem 2.1.290) Antonio tells Sebastian: 'when I rear my hand, do you the like'.*

like VERB
as well as meanings to do with 'someone enjoying something', you'll find:
please
• *(H5 3.Chorus.32) Henry rejects the proposals from the French King: 'The offer likes not'.*
› **dislike** VERB
displease
• *(Oth 2.3.40) Cassio is reluctant to invite the revellers in: 'I'll do't, but it dislikes me'.*

Limander NOUN
intended to mean 'Leander', the lover of Hero
• *(MND 5.1.193) Pyramus tells Thisbe: 'like Limander am I trusty still'.* see also **Hero**

limbeck NOUN
apparatus for distilling
• *(Mac 1.7.67) Lady Macbeth says the grooms will be so drunk that the thinking part of their brain will be 'A limbeck only'—clouded with fumes.*

lime NOUN
birdlime—a sticky substance spread on branches to catch birds
• *(Tem 4.1.243) Trinculo tells Caliban to 'put some lime on your fingers'—so that he can steal things more easily.*

lime VERB
catch (as if with birdlime)
• *(TN 3.4.68) Malvolio says of Olivia: 'I have limed her'.*
› **limed** ADJECTIVE
trapped (as if with birdlime)
• *(Ham 3.3.68) Claudius addresses his 'limed soul, that struggling to be free / Art more engag'd!'—in trying to free itself, it becomes more ensnared.*

a b c d e f g h i j k Ll m n o p q r s t u v w x y z

limitation NOUN
allotted time
• *(JC 2.1.283) Portia complains to Brutus: 'Am I your self / But, as it were, in sort or limitation?'—am I your other half only in certain ways and at certain times?*

limited ADJECTIVE
appointed
• *(Mac 2.3.46) Macduff says he will wake the king, 'for 'tis my limited service'.*

line NOUN
line of descent
• *(H5 2.4.89) Exeter tells the French king that Henry sends him 'this most memorable line'—presumably a family tree to show the French King how Henry has a right to the French throne.*

› **by line and level**
very methodically
• *(Tem 4.1.237) Trinculo takes clothing that is hanging from a line, telling Stephano that 'we steal by line and level'—as if with a plumb line (used to determine the depth of water) and a carpenter's level (used to determine an exact horizontal plane), and thus making a joke about stealing in a scientific way.*

line VERB
strengthen
• *(H5 2.4.7) The French King tells the Dauphin 'To line and new repair our towns of war'.*

line NOUN
⚠ *Don't read in the modern meaning of 'washing line'.*
lime tree
• *(Tem 4.1.193) Prospero tells Ariel, of the clothes: 'hang them on this line'.*

line NOUN
grove of lime trees
• *(Tem 5.1.10) Ariel tells Prospero he has put the king and his followers 'In the line-grove which weather-fends your cell'—the grove that protects your dwelling from the wind.*

lineal ADJECTIVE
lineally descended
• *(H5 1.2.82) Canterbury describes how Queen Isabel 'Was lineal of the Lady Ermengard'.*

› **unlineal** ADJECTIVE
of different descent
• *(Mac 3.1.64) Macbeth reflects on how his sceptre will be taken away from him 'with an unlineal hand, / No son of mine succeeding'.*

lineament NOUN
features
• *(RJ 1.3.84) Lady Capulet tells Juliet to look carefully at Paris: 'Examine every married lineament'—his well-proportioned features.*

linstock NOUN
stick that holds a flame for firing a cannon
• *(H5 3.Chorus.33) The Chorus describes how 'the nimble gunner / With linstock now the devilish cannon touches'.*

Lipsbury NOUN
space between the lips
• *(KL 2.2.8) Kent threatens to have Oswald 'in Lipsbury pinfold'—in 'lip-town', trapped between his teeth.*
There isn't a real town called Lipsbury in Britain. Some think this is a name for an old wrestling move.

lisp VERB
⚠ *Don't read in the meaning of a speech defect.*
talk in an affected way (carefully and unnaturally)
• *(Ham 3.1.144) Hamlet finds fault with women: 'You jig and amble, and you lisp'.*

list NOUN
1 combat arena at a tournament
• *(Mac 3.1.72) Macbeth wants Fate to come 'into the list, / And champion me'.*
2 band
• *(Ham 1.1.101) Horatio describes Fortinbras' army as 'a list of lawless resolutes'—desperadoes.*
3 limit
• *(TN 3.1.73) Cesario tells Sir Toby that Olivia 'is the list of my voyage'—my destination.*
4 wish
• *(Oth 2.1.104) Iago says his wife is always talking 'when I have list to sleep'.*

list VERB
1 wish, like
• *(MA 3.4.76) Margaret tells Beatrice: 'I am not such a fool to think what I list'—I don't think whatever I please, like a fool.*
2 listen or listen to
• *(Ham 1.5.22) The Ghost appeals to Hamlet: 'List, list, O list!'*

liver NOUN
the part of the body thought to be the seat of the passions, especially sexual desire
• *(TN 2.4.96) Orsino says women's love 'may be call'd appetite, / No motion of the liver'—their love shows no impulse of sexual desire.*

living NOUN
means of support
• *(MV 5.1.286) Antonio tells Portia: 'you have given me life and living'.*

lo see ATTENTION SIGNALS, p.23

lob NOUN
clown
• *(MND 2.1.16) The Fairy calls Puck 'thou lob of spirits'.*

locust NOUN
locust-bean—the fruit of the carob tree
• *(Oth 1.3.344) Iago talks of food 'as luscious as locusts'.*

lodestar NOUN
guiding star
• *(MND 1.1.183) Helena tells Hermia: 'Your eyes are lodestars'.*

lodge VERB
flatten
• *(Mac 4.1.54) Macbeth demands an answer from the Witches, 'Though bladed corn be lodg'd and trees blown down'.*

> **lodged** also spelled **lodg'd** ADJECTIVE
> deep-rooted
> • *(MV 4.1.60) Shylock describes the 'lodg'd hate' he has for Antonio.*

loggerhead NOUN
blockhead
• *(RJ 4.4.21) Capulet tells his servant 'thou shalt be loggerhead'—you shall be an idiot—with a pun on fetching logs for the fire.*

loggets see **RECREATION, p.170**

long-engraffed also spelled **-ingraffed** see **ingraft**

loon see **lown**

looped also spelled **loop'd** ADJECTIVE
full of holes
• *(KL 3.4.31) Lear describes wretches as being clothed in a 'loop'd and window'd raggedness'.*

loose VERB
cancel
• *(MV 4.1.24) The Duke hopes Shylock will 'loose the forfeiture'.*

lost ADJECTIVE
1 ruined
• *(Tem 4.1.202) Trinculo warns Caliban that if Stephano takes a dislike to him, 'Thou wert but a lost monster'.*
2 groundless
• *(Oth 5.2.267) Othello assures Gratiano there's nothing to be afraid of: ''Tis a lost fear'.*

lot in the phrase **by lot**
by chance
• *(Ham 2.2.404) Hamlet quotes a line from a ballad: 'As by lot God wot'—God knows.*

lottery NOUN
chance
• *(JC 2.1.119) Brutus talks of how tyranny could continue 'Till each man drop by lottery'.*

louse VERB
become infected with lice
• *(KL 3.2.29) The Fool sings that, if a man has no home for his head, 'The head and he shall louse'.*

Louvre NOUN [pronounced **loo**-vruh]
the palace of the French kings in Paris
• *(H5 2.4.133) Exeter tells the Dauphin that Henry will 'make your Paris Louvre shake' for the insult he received.*

love NOUN
⚠ *Don't read the meaning of 'sexual love' or 'sexual partner' into these senses.*
as well as meaning 'lover', you'll find:
dear friend
• *(MV 4.1.275) Antonio asks Portia to judge 'Whether Bassanio had not once a love'.*

> **lover** NOUN
> dear friend
> • *(JC 3.2.13) Brutus addresses the crowds: 'Romans, countrymen, and lovers, hear me for my cause'.*

low ADJECTIVE
as well as meaning 'not high', you'll find:
1 humble
• *(KL 2.3.17) Edgar reflects on beggars asking for charity 'from low farms'.*
2 short (in stature)
• *(MA 1.1.156) Benedick says Hero is 'too low for a high praise'.*

> **lowly** ADJECTIVE
> humble
> • *(TN 3.1.95) Olivia says the world hasn't been a happy place 'Since lowly feigning was call'd compliment'—since pretended humility was thought a good thing.*

lown also spelled **loon** NOUN
rogue
• *(Oth 2.3.81) Iago sings of King Stephen: 'he call'd the tailor lown'.*
🎭 *Iago is getting Cassio drunk, and reminding him of England. He sings a stanza from a popular Scottish song about an argument between a man and his wife. The man says he needs a new cloak to keep out the winter cold; his wife says his old cloak will do, and in this version of the song she recalls an English king who made do with cheap clothes rather than use an expensive tailor. She wins the argument.*

⚠ *warning note* ➡ *usage note* 🎭 *theatre note*

a b c d e f g h i j k Ll m n o p q r s t u v w x y z

lubber NOUN
blundering fool
• *(TN 4.1.12) Feste describes the world as a 'great lubber'.*

Lucifer NOUN
the chief devil in hell—sometimes called a 'prince' of devils
• *(H5 4.7.130) The Welsh Captain says a man must keep his oath, even though he is 'as good a gentleman as the devil is, as Lucifer'.*

lucky ADJECTIVE
⚠ *Don't read in the meaning of 'resulting from happy chance'.*
successful
• *(H5 2.2.180) Henry hopes for 'a fair and lucky war'.*

› **unlucky** ADJECTIVE
⚠ *Don't read in the meaning of 'resulting from unhappy chance'.*
disastrous
• *(Oth 5.2.337) Othello describes what has happened as 'these unlucky deeds'.*

› **unluckily** ADVERB
ominously
• *(JC 3.3.2) Cinna the poet reflects on how 'things unluckily charge my fantasy'—his mind is filled with ominous thoughts.*

Lucrece NOUN [pronounced loo-**krees**]
a legendary Roman heroine of the 6th century BC, who killed herself after being raped by Tarquin
• *(TN 2.5.87) Malvolio examines the seal on Olivia's letter: 'the impressure her Lucrece'—the image of Lucrece is on the stamp that she uses.*

Lupercal NOUN [pronounced **loo**-per-cal]
in ancient Rome, a feast in honour of Lupercus, the god of shepherds, held on 15 February
• *(JC 3.2.94) Antony reminds the people how he offered Caesar a kingly crown 'on the Lupercal'.*

lurk VERB
⚠ *Don't read in the meaning of 'hiding with the intention of doing something wicked'.*
stay out of sight
• *(KL 3.6.113) Edgar decides he will have to 'Lurk, lurk'.*

lustihood NOUN
youthful vigour
• *(MA 5.1.76) Leonato describes Claudio as a man in 'His May of youth and bloom of lustihood'.*

lusty ADJECTIVE
as well as meaning 'strong' and 'vigorous', you'll find:
1 merry
• *(RJ 1.4.113) Romeo cheers on his friends: 'On, lusty gentlemen'.*
2 sensual
• *(RJ 1.2.26) Capulet describes the feelings of 'lusty young men'.*

› **over-lusty** ADJECTIVE
1 excessively merry
• *(H5 4.Chorus.18) The Chorus describes 'The confident and over-lusty French'.*
2 too vigorous
• *(KL 2.4.9) The Fool comments on what happens when 'a man's over-lusty at legs, then he wears wooden nether-stocks'—when he's been too active with his legs (after fighting), he's put in the wooden stocks (which keep your legs from moving).*

lute see MUSIC, p.172

luxury NOUN
⚠ *Don't read the meaning of 'something expensive and comfortable' into these senses.*
lust
• *(Ham 1.5.83) The Ghost appeals to Hamlet to not let the Danish royal bed be 'A couch for luxury and damned incest'.*

› **luxurious** ADJECTIVE
lustful
• *(MA 4.1.40) Claudio says Hero 'knows the heat of a luxurious bed'.*

lym NOUN
bloodhound on a leash
• *(KL 3.6.67) Poor Tom says he shouts at all sorts of dogs, including a 'brach or lym'.*

machine NOUN
⚠*Don't read in the modern meaning of 'something mechanical'.*
human body
• *(Ham 2.2.123) Hamlet ends his letter to Ophelia with the salutation 'Thine ... whilst this machine is to him'—for the rest of his life.*

mad ADJECTIVE
as well as meaning 'angry' and 'insane', you'll find:
faithless
• *(Oth 4.3.27) Desdemona tells the story of her mother's maid, whose lover 'prov'd mad / And did forsake her'—gave her up.*

mad VERB
madden
• *(KL 4.2.43) Albany accuses Goneril: 'A father ... have you madded'.*

made men NOUN
men with fortunes made
• *(MND 4.2.15) Snug says that if they had been able to perform their play, 'we had all been made men'.*

madonna NOUN
⚠*Don't read in the title of the Virgin Mary (or the stage name of a famous pop singer).*
my lady—used as an affectionate, jocular term of endearment
• *(TN 1.5.54) Feste calls Olivia 'good madonna'.*

maggot-pie NOUN
magpie
• *(Mac 3.4.125) Macbeth says murderers have been revealed by talking birds—'maggot-pies, and choughs, and rooks'.*

magnanimous ADJECTIVE
⚠*Don't read in the meaning of 'generously forgiving'.*
valiant
• *(H5 3.7.6) The Welsh Captain says the Duke of Exeter 'is as magnanimous as Agamemnon'.*

magnifico NOUN
Venetian leader
• *(MV 3.2.278) Salarino says, of Shylock, that 'the magnificoes / Of greatest port have all persuaded with him'—the most eminent nobles have argued with him.*

Mahu NOUN [pronounced **mah**-hoo]
one of the fiends of hell
• *(KL 4.1.59) Poor Tom says five fiends have possessed him, including 'Mahu, of stealing'.*

maid NOUN
as well as meaning 'maidservant', you'll find:
1 mortal woman (and not a spirit)
• *(Tem 1.2.428) Ferdinand asks Miranda 'If you be maid or no?'*
2 virgin (male)
• *(TN 5.1.254) Sebastian tells Olivia she is 'betroth'd both to a maid and man'—to a virgin youth—but also suggesting she has married both Viola (in mind) and Sebastian (in body).*

maidenhead NOUN
virginity
• *(RJ 1.3.2) The Nurse swears 'by my maidenhead'.*

a b c d e f g h i j k l **Mm** n o p q r s t u v w x y z

maidhood NOUN
maidenhood
• *(Oth 1.1.172) Brabantio believes love-potions have abused 'the property of youth and maidhood' in Desdemona.*

maimed ADJECTIVE
incomplete
• *(Ham 5.1.203) Hamlet wonders who the funeral is for, 'with such maimed rites'—the minimum of ceremony.*

main NOUN
1 open sea
• *(Oth 2.1.3) The First Gentleman says he can't see any ship between 'the heaven and the main'.*
2 mainland
• *(KL 3.1.6) A Gentleman says Lear is commanding the wind to 'swell the curled waters 'bove the main'.*
3 central part
• *(Ham 4.4.15) Hamlet asks whether Fortinbras' army goes 'against the main of Poland'.*
4 chief concern
• *(Ham 2.2.56) Gertrude thinks the cause of Hamlet's madness 'is no other but the main'—his father's death.*
5 strength
• *(Oth 2.1.13) The Second Gentleman describes the waves, 'with high and monstrous main'.*
'Maine' is the spelling in the First Folio for sense 5, and 'mayne' in the First and Second Quarto text. Some editions emend to 'mane' (as on a lion).

› **main flood** NOUN
high tide
• *(MV 4.1.72) Antonio says trying to persuade Shylock is like commanding 'the main flood bate his usual height'—like trying to hold back the sea.*

main-course see SHIPS, p.168

make VERB
as well as its usual meaning of 'bring into existence', you'll find:
1 have to do
• *(RJ 5.3.280) The Prince asks Paris' page why they were in the cemetery: 'what made your master in this place?'*
2 make a case
• *(RJ 5.3.225) The Friar realizes that he is under suspicion because 'the time and place / Doth make against me'.*
3 prosper
• *(Tem 2.2.30) Trinculo imagines bringing Caliban to England: 'There would this monster make a man'*
see also **made men**
4 raise
• *(Oth 1.3.349) Iago tells Roderigo: 'Make all the money thou canst'.*

› **make forth** VERB
come forward
• *(JC 5.1.25) Antony tells Octavius to 'Make forth' to talk to Brutus and Cassius.*

› **make from** VERB
avoid or release
• *(KL 1.1.142) Lear threatens Kent: 'The bow is bent and drawn; make from the shaft'.*

› **make good** VERB
justify
• *(TN 1.5.6) Maria tells Feste to 'Make that good'—prove your point.*

› **make to** VERB
go towards
• *(JC 3.1.18) Brutus notes of Popillius: 'Look how he makes to Caesar'.*

› **make up** VERB
arrange
• *(KL 1.1.205) Burgundy reacts to Lear's offer of Cordelia's hand in marriage: 'Election makes not up in such conditions'—it isn't possible to choose, based on these terms.*

make in the phrase **mate and make** see **mate and make**

malady of France
venereal disease
• *(H5 5.1.75) Pistol has heard that Doll died in hospital 'of a malady of France'.*

malapert ADJECTIVE
impudent
• *(TN 4.1.38) Sir Toby tells Sebastian: 'I must have an ounce or two of this malapert blood from you'.*

malediction NOUN
cursing
• *(KL 1.2.139) Edmund describes someone writing about 'menaces and maledictions against king and nobles'.*

malicho see **miching mallecho**

malicious ADJECTIVE
⚠ *Don't read in the meaning of 'spiteful'.*
violent
• *(Ham 1.1.151) Marcellus says striking out against the Ghost is 'malicious mockery'—because they'll never hit it.*

malignancy NOUN
evil influence
• *(TN 2.1.4) Sebastian tells Antonio he will go on alone: 'the malignancy of my fate might perhaps distemper yours'—my bad luck might transfer to you.*

Mall, Mistress
Mistress Mary—possibly the name of a lady-in-waiting involved in a scandal
• *(TN 1.3.113) Sir Toby asks if Sir Andrew's gifts are 'like to take dust, like Mistress Mall's picture' —hidden by a curtain to protect them from dust and sunlight.*

mallecho see **miching mallecho**

mallow NOUN
a type of wild plant
• *(Tem 2.1.140) Sebastian suggests Gonzalo might plant 'docks, or mallows' in the island as remedies for nettle-stings.*

mammer VERB
hesitate
• *(Oth 3.3.70) Desdemona says she would not deny a request of Othello's, 'Or stand so mammering on' as he is doing with her request about Cassio.*

mammet NOUN
puppet
• *(RJ 3.5.184) Capulet calls Juliet 'A whining mammet'.*

mandragora NOUN
[pronounced man-**drag**-or-a]
a mandrake plant (which provides a sedative drug)
• *(Oth 3.3.331) Iago reflects that neither 'poppy nor mandragora' will help Othello sleep from now on.*

mandrake NOUN
a type of poisonous plant (believed to emit a lethal shriek when its forked, human-shaped roots are pulled from the earth)
• *(RJ 4.3.47) Juliet imagines the tomb as a place with 'shrieks like mandrakes torn out of the earth'.*

manikin NOUN
little man
• *(TN 3.2.48) Fabian comments to Sir Toby about Sir Andrew: 'This is a dear manikin to you'.*

mannerly ADJECTIVE
seemly
• *(RJ 1.5.97) Juliet describes Romeo as displaying 'mannerly devotion'.*

› **unmannerly** ADVERB
improperly
• *(Mac 2.3.112) Macbeth describes the grooms' daggers 'Unmannerly breech'd with gore'.*

man of wax NOUN
faultless (as a wax model would be)
• *(RJ 1.3.77) The Nurse describes Paris as 'a man of wax'.*

mansionry NOUN
place of habitation
• *(Mac 1.6.5) Banquo says the martlet bird's 'lov'd mansionry' shows the pleasant character of Macbeth's castle.*

mantle NOUN
1 covering (of vegetable matter)
• *(KL 3.4.126) Poor Tom says he 'drinks the green mantle of the standing pool'—the stagnant water.*
2 a loose sleeveless cloak
see **CLOTHING, p.158**

mantle VERB
1 form a scum
• *(MV 1.1.89) Gratiano talks of men 'whose visages / Do cream and mantle like a standing pond'.*
2 cover
• *(Tem 5.1.67) Prospero describes how he is lifting from his enemies 'the ignorant fumes that mantle / Their clearer reason'.*

› **mantled** ADJECTIVE
slime-covered
• *(Tem 4.1.182) Ariel says he left Stephano and the others 'I' th' filthy-mantled pool beyond your cell'.*

› **dismantle** VERB
1 take away
• *(KL 1.1.216) France wonders what monstrous thing Cordelia could have done 'to dismantle / So many folds of favour'.*
2 deprive
• *(Ham 3.2.271) Hamlet makes up a verse of a ballad: 'This realm dismantled was / Of Jove himself'—this state that has been stripped apart was made by a god (Hamlet thinking of his dead father as god-like).*

many a day in the phrase
for this many a day
during these past few days
• *(Ham 3.1.91) Ophelia asks Hamlet: 'How does your honour for this many a day?'—how have you been since we saw each other last?*

a b c d e f g h i j k l Mm n o p q r s t u v w x y z

The phrase 'for this many a day' usually means 'these past few days', but it may have been weeks or months since Hamlet and Ophelia last saw each other.

March chick also spelled **-chick**
precocious youth
• *(MA 1.3.49) Don John describes Claudio as 'A very forward March chick!'—like a newborn bird (as chicks usually hatch in March).*

marchpane NOUN
marzipan
• *(RJ 1.5.7) A Servingman preparing Capulet's feast asks: 'save me a piece of marchpane'.*

margent NOUN
margin
• *(RJ 1.3.87) Lady Capulet tells Juliet that she will find out more about Paris 'written in the margent of his eyes'—in the way that he looks at her.*

mark VERB
see **ATTENTION SIGNALS, p.23**

mark NOUN
1 target
• *(MA 2.1.228) Benedick says what it was like to be verbally attacked by Beatrice: 'I stood like a man at a mark, with a whole army shooting at me'.*
2 birthmark
• *(MND 5.1.395) Oberon promises that no 'mark prodigious' shall be on the children of the lovers.*
see also **POLITENESS, p.230**

Mark Antony
Roman leader in the 1st century BC, a friend of Julius Caesar
• *(H5 3.7.13) The Welsh Captain thinks Pistol 'is as valiant a man as Mark Antony'.*

marl NOUN
clay
• *(MA 2.1.55) Beatrice says she will not have a husband and have to 'make an account of her life to a clod of wayward marl'.*

married ADJECTIVE
as well as its meaning of 'wedded', you'll find:
well proportioned
• *(RJ 1.3.84) Lady Capulet tells Juliet to look carefully at Paris: 'Examine every married lineament'—joined in harmony, as in a marriage.*

marry see **SWEARING, p.298**

Mars NOUN
the Roman god of war
• *(H5 Prologue.6) The Chorus imagines King Henry on a stage where he would 'Assume the port of Mars'—take on a warlike, godly bearing in his stance.*

mart NOUN
1 market
• *(MV 3.1.41) Shylock describes Antonio as 'a beggar that was used to come so smug upon the mart'.*
2 trading
• *(Ham 1.1.77) Marcellus asks why Denmark is engaged in such 'foreign mart for implements of war'.*

mart VERB
market
• *(JC 4.3.11) Brutus accuses Cassius of being one who is ready 'To sell and mart your offices for gold'.*

martlet see **ANIMALS, p.162**

mask VERB
take part in a masque (a formal dance where the participants wore stylized masks)
• *(RJ 1.5.36) Capulet reminisces with his cousin: 'Some five and twenty years, and then we mask'd'.*

Mass see **SWEARING, p.298**

massy ADJECTIVE
massive
• *(Tem 3.3.67) Ariel tells the nobles: 'Your swords are now too massy for your strengths'.*

masterdom NOUN
supremacy
• *(Mac 1.5.69) Lady Macbeth tells Macbeth their plan will give them 'solely sovereign sway and masterdom'.*

masterless ADJECTIVE
abandoned
• *(RJ 5.3.142) The Friar asks why there are 'masterless and gory swords' in the cemetery.*

masterly ADJECTIVE
of one's mastery
• *(Ham 4.7.96) Claudius tells Laertes that Lamord 'gave you such a masterly report'—of Laertes' fencing skill.*

masterly ADVERB
from experience
• *(TN 2.4.21) Orsino tells Cesario: 'Thou dost speak masterly'.*

masters see **TERMS OF ADDRESS, p.306**

match NOUN
as well as meanings to do with 'equality' and 'competing', you'll find:

1 bargain
• *(MV 3.1.39) Shylock complains of Antonio: 'There I have another bad match'.*
2 victory
• *(RJ 2.4.65) Romeo wants Benvolio to come between him and Mercutio as fast as he can 'or I'll cry a match'—claim the victory in their jesting.*

match VERB
marry
• *(MA 2.1.57) Beatrice says 'Adam's sons are my brethren, and truly I hold it a sin to match in my kindred'—so she won't marry any man, as they are all her relatives.*

mate VERB
astound
• *(Mac 5.1.70) The Doctor says of Lady Macbeth: 'My mind she has mated'.*

mate and make
husband and wife
• *(KL 4.3.34) Kent says the stars must govern our characters, otherwise, 'one self mate and make could not beget' daughters so different as Lear's.*

material ADJECTIVE
full of substance
• *(KL 4.2.35) Albany, addressing Goneril, says she who cuts herself off 'From her material sap' must wither.*

matin NOUN
morning
• *(Ham 1.5.89) The Ghost says: 'The glow-worm shows the matin to be near'.*

matter NOUN
1 substance
• *(MA 2.1.306) Beatrice says she was 'born to speak all mirth and no matter'.*
2 significance
• *(Ham 4.1.1) Claudius says to Gertrude: 'There's matter in these sighs'.*
3 issue
• *(Oth 1.2.38) Othello asks Cassio why the Duke wants to see him: 'What is the matter, think you?'*
⚠ *Don't read in the meaning of 'What's wrong?'*
4 means—here, energetic means
• *(MA 1.1.255) Benedick assures Don Pedro he can deliver a message: 'I have almost matter enough in me for such an embassage'.*

mattock NOUN
a tool for loosening hard ground
• *(RJ 5.3.22) Romeo tells Balthasar: 'Give me that mattock'.*

mature ADJECTIVE
ripe
• *(KL 4.6.270) Edgar says he will show Goneril's letter to Albany 'in the mature time'—when the time is ripe.*

maugre PREPOSITION [pronounced **maw**-guh]
in spite of
• *(TN 3.1.147) Olivia tells Cesario that she loves him 'maugre all thy pride'.*

maw NOUN
belly or throat
• *(RJ 5.3.45) Romeo calls Juliet's tomb 'Thou detestable maw, thou womb of death'.*

maze NOUN
⚠ *Don't read in the meaning of 'an artificial labyrinth designed as a puzzle'.*
bewildering arrangement of naturally formed paths
• *(Tem 5.1.242) Alonso says: 'This is as strange a maze as e'er men trod'.*

› **mazed** ADJECTIVE
bewildered
• *(MND 2.1.113) Titania recounts how 'the mazed world' can no longer tell the difference between autumn and winter.*

mazzard NOUN
skull
• *(Oth 2.3.138) Cassio threatens Montano: 'I'll knock you o'er the mazzard'.*

mead NOUN
meadow
• *(KL 1.1.64) Lear gives Goneril land 'With plenteous rivers and wide-skirted meads'.*

mean ADJECTIVE
1 of low rank
• *(H5 4.Chorus.45) The Chorus describes Henry visiting everyone in the camp, 'mean and gentle all'—of low and high rank.*
2 lowly
• *(Tem 3.1.4) Ferdinand describes his log-carrying as a 'mean task'.*
3 middling
• *(MV 1.2.6) Nerissa tells Portia that 'It is no mean happiness ... to be seated in the mean'—not a low level of happiness to be in the middle between poverty and riches.*

mean NOUN
means
• *(Oth 3.1.36) Iago says he will 'devise a mean to draw the Moor / Out of the way'.*

mean VERB
as well as meaning 'explain' and 'intend', you'll

a b c d e f g h i j k l Mm n o p q r s t u v w x y z

find:
mourn
• *(MND 5.1.308) Demetrius comments on Thisbe: 'And thus she means'.*

measure NOUN
as well as meanings to do with 'extent' and 'course of action', you'll find:
1 limit
• *(MA 1.3.2) Conrad asks Don John: 'Why are you thus out of measure sad?'—so excessively gloomy.*
2 due proportion
• *(Mac 5.9.40) Malcolm promises future deeds 'in measure, time, and place'.*
3 slow stately dance
• *(RJ 1.5.49) Romeo looks for Juliet: 'The measure done, I'll watch her place of stand'.*
4 metre
• *(H5 5.2.132) Henry says he has 'neither words nor measure'—not enough poetic skill—to woo Katherine.*

measure VERB
1 travel
• *(MV 3.4.84) Portia tells Nerissa they 'must measure twenty miles today'.*
2 give out
• *(RJ 1.4.10) Benvolio plans the visit to the Capulets' party: 'We'll measure them a measure and be gone'—give them just one dance.*

meat NOUN
as well as meaning 'flesh of animals', you'll find:
1 food (in general)
• *(JC 1.2.149) Cassius wonders 'Upon what meat doth this our Caesar feed / That he is grown so great?'*
2 edible part
• *(KL 1.4.151) The Fool talks about cutting an egg in the middle 'and eat up the meat'.*
3 scraps
• *(KL 2.2.13) Kent calls Oswald 'an eater of broken meats'.*

mechanic ADJECTIVE
worker
• *(H5 1.2.200) Canterbury describes the 'poor mechanic porters' among the honey-bees.*

mechanicals see OCCUPATIONS, p.166

meddle VERB
⚠ *Don't read the meaning of 'tinkering with something' into these senses.*
1 fight
• *(TN 3.4.229) Sir Toby tells Cesario: 'meddle you must'.*
2 busy oneself
• *(RJ 1.2.39) The Servant (mixing up the professions) reflects that 'the shoemaker should meddle with his yard' (a measuring stick used by tailors).*

› **meddle or make**
interfere
• *(MA 3.3.50) Dogberry advises his men not to 'meddle or make' with a thief.*

› **meddle with** VERB
enter into
• *(Tem 1.2.22) Miranda tells Prospero that knowing more about his history 'Did never meddle with my thoughts'.*

Medea NOUN [pronounced mi-**dee**-a]
in Greek mythology, the daughter of the king of Colchis, who helped Jason to obtain the Golden Fleece and then married him
• *(MV 5.1.13) Jessica imagines a night when 'Medea gather'd the enchanted herbs' that made Jason's father young again.*

medicine NOUN
as well as meaning 'remedy', you'll find:
1 drug (used for purposes other than healing)
• *(Oth 1.3.61) Brabantio says Desdemona is 'corrupted / By spells and medicines bought of mountebanks'.*
2 poison
• *(KL 5.3.97) Goneril responds to Regan saying she is sick: 'If not, I'll ne'er trust medicine'.*

medlar NOUN
a variety of fruit (with a shape thought to resemble female genitals)
• *(RJ 2.1.36) Mercutio jokes about 'that kind of fruit / As maids call medlars, when they laugh alone'.*

meed NOUN
merit
• *(Ham 5.2.136) Osric says of Laertes' fencing skill that 'in his meed, he's unfellowed'—can't be matched.*

meet ADJECTIVE
1 fit
• *(JC 4.3.125) The Poet says there is a quarrel between Brutus and Cassius, so that it is 'not meet / They be alone'.*
2 even
• *(MA 1.1.42) Leonato tells Beatrice that Benedick will 'be meet with you'.*

› **unmeet** ADJECTIVE
improper
• *(MA 4.1.181) Hero asks Leonato to prove that she talked to a man 'At hours unmeet'.*

meiny NOUN [pronounced **may**-nee]
household retinue
• *(KL 2.4.34) Kent reports how Regan and Cornwall 'summon'd up their meiny'.*

melancholy (a type of humour)
see **HUMOURS, p.137**

memorize VERB
⚠ *Don't read in the meaning of 'learn off by heart'.*
make memorable
• *(Mac 1.2.40) The Captain says Macbeth and Banquo were so fierce it was as if they wanted to 'memorize another Golgotha'—create a scene as memorable as the crucifixion of Christ.*

merchant NOUN
as well as meaning 'trader' and 'fellow', you'll find:
merchant-ship
• *(Tem 2.1.5) Gonzalo tells Alonso that 'The masters of some merchant' have suffered shipwreck just like they have.*

› **merchant-marring** ADJECTIVE
capable of damaging a merchant-ship
• *(MV 3.2.269) Bassanio asks if any of Antonio's ships escaped 'the dreadful touch / Of merchant-marring rocks?'*

Mercury NOUN
in Roman mythology, the winged messenger of the gods, and the god of eloquence and deception
• *(H5 2.Chorus.7) The Chorus describes how young men are following Henry to battle 'With winged heels, as English Mercuries'.*

mere ADJECTIVE
as well as meaning 'not more than', you'll find:
1 complete
• *(Oth 2.2.3) A Herald announces 'the mere perdition of the Turkish fleet'—its total destruction.*
2 personal
• *(KL 4.1.20) Gloucester reflects that often 'our mere defects / Prove our commodities'—our own flaws turn out to be advantages.*

› **merely** ADVERB
completely
• *(Ham 1.2.137) Hamlet reflects on the world as an unweeded garden: 'things rank and gross in nature / Possess it merely'.*
⚠ *Look carefully at the context to decide whether 'mere' and 'merely' mean 'a little' or 'a lot'.*

merit NOUN
as well as meaning 'what one deserves', you'll find:
a deserving person
• *(Ham 3.1.74) Hamlet reflects on 'the spurns / That patient merit of th'unworthy takes'—the insults that a deserving person has to put up with from someone less deserving.*

› **unmeritable** ADJECTIVE
unworthy
• *(JC 4.1.12) Antony describes Lepidus as 'a slight, unmeritable man'.*

Merlin NOUN
a good wizard whose magic helped King Arthur
• *(KL 3.2.95) The Fool makes a series of prophecies, imagining he lived before the time of Merlin, and anticipating that 'This prophecy Merlin shall make' one day.*

merry ADJECTIVE
as well as meaning 'cheerful and lively', you'll find:
1 facetious
• *(Ham 3.2.117) Ophelia responds to Hamlet's punning: 'You are merry, my lord'.*
2 well
• *(JC 2.4.45) Portia tells Lucius: 'commend me to my lord, / Say I am merry'.*

mervailous ADJECTIVE
[pronounced **mer**-vay-us]
marvellous
• *(H5 2.1.43) Pistol and Nym exchange insults, and Pistol throws the word 'solus' ('alone') back at Nym: 'in thy most mervailous face!'*

mess NOUN
1 banqueting table
• *(Ham 5.2.86) Hamlet describes Osric as a beast whose manger 'shall stand at the king's mess'.*
2 serving of food
• *(Oth 4.1.195) Othello thinks of what he will do to Desdemona: 'I will chop her into messes'—little bits of meat.*

Messaline NOUN [pronounced **meh**-sa-leen]
an invented name, but probably related to the Latin name for Marseilles, France
• *(TN 2.1.15) Sebastian names his father as 'Sebastian of Messaline'.* **see MAP, p.176**

Messina NOUN [pronounced meh-**see**-na]
a port in Sicily, Italy
• *(MA 1.1.1) Leonato announces that 'Don Pedro of Aragon comes this night to Messina'.*
see MAP, p.176

metal of India
pure gold
• *(TN 2.5.11) Sir Toby greets Maria: 'How now, my metal of India?'*

metaphysical ADJECTIVE
supernatural
• *(Mac 1.5.28) Lady Macbeth reflects on the way*

a b c d e f g h i j k l **Mm** n o p q r s t u v w x y z

a b c d e f g h i j k l Mm n o p q r s t u v w x y z

'fate and metaphysical aid' seem to be predicting that Macbeth will be king.

meteor NOUN
⚠ *Don't read in the meaning of 'shooting star' here.*
aurora
• *(RJ 3.5.13) Juliet tells Romeo that the light is not daylight but 'some meteor that the sun exhal'd'.*

methinks past form **methought** VERB
it seems to me
• *(MND 1.1.3) Theseus sighs: 'O, methinks, how slow / This old moon wanes!'*
• *(Tem 3.3.96) Alonso thinks he has heard the name of Prospero: 'Methought the billows spoke'.*

method NOUN
table of contents
• *(TN 1.5.209) Cesario answers Olivia's question 'by the method'—imagining what he has to say as the text of a book.*

mew VERB
confine
• *(MND 1.1.71) Theseus tells Hermia what it would be like to be a nun 'in shady cloister mew'd'.*

› **mew up** VERB
confine
• *(RJ 3.4.11) Lady Capulet tells Paris that Juliet is 'mew'd up to her heaviness'—enclosed in sorrow.*

miching mallecho also spelled **malicho**
[pronounced **mitch**-ing ma-**lik**-oh]
sneaking mischief
• *(Ham 3.2.132) Hamlet describes the poisoning dumb show as 'miching malicho. It means mischief'.*

mickle ADJECTIVE
great
• *(RJ 2.3.15) The Friar reflects that 'mickle is the powerful grace that lies / In plants'.*

Midas NOUN [pronounced **my**-das]
in Greek mythology, a king who was granted his wish that everything he touched would turn to gold (thus including his food)
• *(MV 3.2.102) Bassanio calls gold 'Hard food for Midas'.*

mid-season NOUN
noon
• *(Tem 1.2.239) Ariel tells Prospero the time: 'Past the mid-season'.*

milch ADJECTIVE
moist
• *(Ham 2.2.505) The First Player recites how Hecuba's passion 'Would have made milch the burning eyes of heaven'—brought down tears like milk.*

mimic NOUN
burlesque actor
• *(MND 3.2.19) Puck tells Oberon about Bottom meeting his companions: 'forth my mimic comes'.*

mince VERB
as well as meaning 'chop into pieces', you'll find:
1 play down
• *(Oth 2.3.231) Othello tells Iago that his 'honesty and love doth mince this matter'—make little of Cassio brawling.*
2 give an affected appearance of
• *(KL 4.6.118) Lear imagines a woman's face 'That minces virtue'.*

mine NOUN
⚠ *Don't read meanings to do with 'explosives', or with 'places where valuable things are dug from the ground', in these senses.*
an excavated passage under a fortress wall
• *(H5 3.3.2) Gower tells the Welsh Captain: 'you must come presently to the mines'.*

mine VERB
undermine
• *(Ham 3.4.150) Hamlet tells his mother that 'rank corruption, mining all within, / Infects unseen'.*

mineral NOUN
1 mine
• *(Ham 4.1.26) Gertrude compares Hamlet's madness to gold which, 'Among a mineral of metals base, / Shows itself pure'.*
2 substance
• *(Oth 1.2.74) Brabantio accuses Othello of abusing Desdemona's 'delicate youth with drugs or minerals'.*

minikin ADJECTIVE
dainty
• *(KL 3.6.43) Poor Tom sings about a shepherd piping some music: 'one blast of thy minikin mouth'.*

minimus NOUN
tiniest of creatures
• *(MND 3.2.329) Lysander insults Hermia's size, calling her a 'minimus'.*

minion NOUN
⚠ *Don't read the meaning of 'humble servant' into these senses.*
1 darling
• *(TN 5.1.120) Orsino tells Olivia that Cesario is 'your minion, whom I know you love'.*
2 hussy
• *(RJ 3.5.151) Capulet harangues Juliet: 'mistress minion you'.*

minutely ADJECTIVE [pronounced **min**-it-lee]
⚠ *Don't read in the meaning of 'in a very small way'.*
taking place minute by minute
• *(Mac 5.2.18) Angus says people are rebelling against Macbeth's treachery: 'Now minutely revolts upbraid his faith-breach'—every minute a rebellion shows that they condemn the way he broke his promises.*

mirror NOUN
supreme example
• *(H5 2.Chorus.6) The Chorus says that young people in England are keen to follow Henry, 'the mirror of all Christian kings'.*

misadventure, misadventured see **adventure**

misbecome see **becomed**

miscarry VERB
⚠ *Don't read in the meaning of 'lose a baby before it is born'.*
1 come to harm
• *(TN 3.4.58) Olivia says, of Malvolio, that she 'would not have him miscarry'.*
2 go wrong
• *(Oth 5.1.6) Roderigo wonders about killing Cassio: 'I may miscarry in't'.*

mischief NOUN
⚠ *Don't read the meaning of 'naughty behaviour' into these senses.*
1 calamity
• *(Mac 1.5.49) Lady Macbeth calls on agents of evil who 'wait on nature's mischief '.*
2 evil deed
• *(JC 4.1.51) Octavius tells Antony: 'some that smile have in their hearts, I fear, / Millions of mischiefs'.*
3 harm
• *(KL 1.2.155) Edmund warns Edgar that even 'the mischief of your person' wouldn't calm their father's anger.*
4 disease
• *(MA 1.3.10) Don John criticizes Conrad for trying to apply 'a moral medicine to a mortifying mischief'—a medicine of philosophy to a deadly disease.*

› **mischievous** ADJECTIVE
harmful
• *(JC 2.1.33) Brutus imagines Caesar as a serpent's egg 'Which, hatch'd, would as his kind grow mischievous'.*

misconster see **conster**

misconstruction see **construction**

miscreate ADJECTIVE
wrongly created
• *(H5 1.2.16) Henry warns Canterbury to avoid 'opening titles miscreate'—bringing up illegitimate claims.*

misgive VERB
have misgivings
• *(Oth 3.4.85) Othello tells Desdemona to fetch her handkerchief: 'my mind misgives'—I have a bad feeling about this.*

misgovernment NOUN
wicked behaviour
• *(MA 4.1.97) Don John tells Hero: 'I am sorry for thy much misgovernment'.*

misgraffed ADJECTIVE
badly matched
• *(MND 1.1.137) Lysander tells Hermia that true love is often hindered by being 'misgraffed in respect of years'—one is too old or the other too young.*

mishaved ADJECTIVE
badly behaved
• *(RJ 3.3.143) The Friar criticizes Romeo for behaving like 'a mishaved and sullen wench'.*

misprision NOUN [pronounced miss-**priz**-ee-un]
mistake
• *(TN 1.5.49) Feste says Olivia has got things wrong: 'Misprision in the highest degree!'—of the worst kind.*

› **misprised** ADJECTIVE
mistaken
• *(MND 3.2.74) Demetrius denies to Hermia that he has done anything to Lysander: 'You spend your passion on a mispris'd mood'.*

misprize also spelled **misprise** VERB
despise
• *(MA 3.1.52) Hero describes Beatrice's eyes as 'Misprising what they look on'.*

miss VERB
1 do without
• *(Tem 1.2.311) Prospero tells Miranda they need Caliban as a servant: 'We cannot miss him'.*
2 be inadequate
• *(RJ Prologue.14) The Prologue apologizes for any inadequacies in the players' performance: 'What here shall miss, our toil shall strive to mend'.*

misshapen ADJECTIVE
gone awry
• *(RJ 3.3.131) The Friar criticizes Romeo's intelligence for allowing his manly form and love to be 'Misshapen in the conduct of them both'—badly directed.*

mistempered see **temper**

a b c d e f g h i j k l **Mm** n o p q r s t u v w x y z

misuse VERB
1 disgrace
• *(MA 2.1.221) Benedick complains to Don Pedro that Beatrice 'misused me past the endurance of a block'—even a hard-hearted person wouldn't stand for it.*
2 deceive
• *(MA 2.2.26) Borachio assures Don John that he will provide 'Proof enough to misuse the Prince'.*

misuse NOUN
misbehaviour
• *(Oth 4.2.108) Desdemona wonders what on earth she has done to allow Othello to 'stick / The smallest opinion on my least misuse'—misinterpret her tiniest misbehaviour.*

mo also spelled **moe** ADJECTIVE
more
• *(JC 2.1.72) Lucius tells Brutus that Cassius has arrived and 'there are mo with him'.*

mobbled also spelled **mobled** ADJECTIVE
with face muffled up
• *(Ham 2.2.490) The First Player asks who 'had seen the mobbled queen'.*

mock VERB
as well as meaning 'making fun of', you'll find: deceive
• *(Mac 1.7.81) Macbeth tells his wife that they must 'mock the time with fairest show'.*

modern ADJECTIVE
everyday
• *(Mac 4.3.172) Ross bemoans Scotland, 'where violent sorrow seems / A modern ecstasy'—a daily emotion.*

modesty NOUN
as well as meaning 'moderation' and 'without boasting', you'll find:
1 sense of propriety
• *(TN 5.1.323) Malvolio asks Olivia, 'in the modesty of honour', to explain her apparent favour to him—in a proper and honourable way.*
2 chastity
• *(Tem 3.1.53) Miranda swears companionship with Ferdinand 'by my modesty'.*

› **modestly** ADVERB
without exaggeration
• *(JC 1.2.69) Cassius tells Brutus that he 'Will modestly discover to yourself'—reveal things to him without exaggeration.*

Modo NOUN [pronounced **moh**-doh]
one of the fiends of hell
• *(KL 4.1.60) Poor Tom says five fiends have possessed him, including 'Modo, of murder'.*

moe see **mo**

moiety NOUN [pronounced **moy**-uh-tee]
portion
• *(MV 4.1.26) The Duke asks Shylock to 'Forgive a moiety of the principal'—a bit of the original sum lent.*

moist star
the moon (thought of as the 'wet planet', because of its influence on the tides)
• *(Ham 1.1.121) Horatio describes the moon as 'the moist star / Upon whose influence Neptune's empire stands'.*

molestation NOUN
disturbance
• *(Oth 2.1.16) The Second Gentleman says he 'never did like molestation view / On the enchafed flood'—has never seen the sea so rough.*

mollification NOUN
placating
• *(TN 1.5.190) Cesario, talking about Maria (presumably small of stature), asks Olivia for 'Some mollification for your giant'—calm down the great one protecting you.*

moment NOUN
importance
• *(Ham 3.1.86) Hamlet reflects on 'enterprises of great pitch and moment'—magnitude and importance.*

momentany ADJECTIVE
fleeting
• *(MND 1.1.143) Lysander talks of the factors that make love 'momentany as a sound'.*

monster NOUN
as well as meaning 'a large, frightening creature', you'll find:
1 monstrosity
• *(H5 2.2.82) Henry describes the traitors as 'English monsters'.*
2 victim of adultery
• *(Ham 3.1.139) Hamlet finds fault with wives: 'wise men know well enough what monsters you make of them'.*

monster VERB
make monstrous
• *(KL 1.1.219) France thinks that Cordelia's offence 'Must be of such unnatural degree / That monsters it'.*

MONEY

Before 1971, in Britain, there were
— 20 shillings in a pound
— 12 pence in a shilling
— 2 halfpence in a penny
— 2 farthings in a halfpenny

Here are some examples of the types of money mentioned in the plays, going from the smallest to the largest values.

halfpence
• *(H5 3.2.40) The Boy says that Bardolph stole a lute-case and sold it 'for three halfpence'—for next to nothing.*

groat
a coin worth four old pence
• *(H5 5.1.53) The Welsh Captain beats Pistol on the head and then gives him 'a groat to heal your pate'—some money to pay for a surgeon (but only a cheap one).*

sixpence
a silver coin worth six old pence
• *(MND 4.2.16) Flute thinks that Bottom would get 'sixpence a day during his life' for playing Pyramus at Theseus' wedding—extremely good pay.*

testril
a slang name for a sixpence; the word comes from Italian, referring to a silver coin with the head *(testa)* of a ruler on it
• *(TN 2.3.30) Sir Toby gives Feste sixpence to sing a song for him, and Sir Andrew follows suit: 'There's a testril of me too'—a generous tip.*

noble
a gold coin worth about a third of a pound
• *(H5 2.1.93) Nym wants Pistol to pay him the eight shillings he won at betting, and Pistol agrees: 'A noble shalt thou have'—a substantial sum, worth fighting over.*

angel
a gold coin worth about half a pound
• *(MV 2.7.56) Morocco describes how in England there is 'A coin that bears the figure of an angel / Stamped in gold'—of great value, therefore.*

crown (1)
in England, a silver or gold coin worth about 5 shillings
• *(H5 4.8.53) King Henry tells Exeter to 'fill this glove with crowns' and give it to Williams—a considerable amount of money for a soldier.*

crown (2)
in the countries of mainland Europe, a gold coin whose value varied from country to country
• *(Ham 2.2.73) The Norwegian king Fortinbras gives his son 'three thousand crowns in annual fee'—a huge amount of money, equal to about £750 then and over £75,000 today.*

› **monstrous** ADJECTIVE
unnatural
• *(JC 2.1.81) Brutus reflects on the 'monstrous visage' of conspiracy.*

› **monstrous** ADVERB
exceedingly
• *(MND 1.2.45) Bottom promises to speak 'in a monstrous little voice'.*

Montanto see **Mountanto**

monument NOUN
as well as meaning 'memorial structure', you'll find:
tomb
• *(RJ 5.1.18) Balthasar tells Romeo that Juliet's body 'sleeps in Capel's monument'—in the family tomb.*

mood NOUN
as well as meaning 'the way someone feels', you'll find:
1 anger
• *(MND 3.2.74) Demetrius tells Hermia: 'You spend your passion on a mispris'd mood'—your anger is mistaken.*
2 manner
• *(Ham 1.2.82) Hamlet says there are no 'forms, moods, shapes of grief, / That can denote me truly'—that can really express his feelings.*

› **moody** ADJECTIVE
angry
• *(Tem 1.2.244) Prospero gets annoyed with Ariel: 'How now? Moody?'*

mooncalf NOUN
monster
• *(Tem 2.2.130) Stephano greets Caliban: 'How now, mooncalf'.*

moonshine NOUN
as well as meaning 'moonlight', you'll find:
month
• *(KL 1.2.5) Edmund says he is 'some twelve or fourteen moonshines' younger than Edgar.*

Moor NOUN
dark-skinned person of North African descent
• *(Oth 1.1.40) Iago asks Roderigo, in view of the way Othello has treated him, whether he has any reason 'To love the Moor'.*

> **Moorship** NOUN
Moorish lordship—an insulting description
• *(Oth 1.1.33) Iago describes himself angrily as 'his Moorship's ancient'—merely an ensign (standard-bearer) to Othello.*
Expressions such as 'his lordship' have often been mocked in everyday use, by adding the '-ship' ending to a word that does not normally take it.

mop and mow
grimaces
• *(Tem 4.1.47) Ariel recites a verse saying that the spirits will arrive 'with mop and mow'—pulling funny faces.*

> **mopping and mowing**
grimacing
• *(KL 4.1.60) Poor Tom describes one of the devils as the prince 'of mopping and mowing'.*

mope VERB
⚠*Don't read the meaning of 'being sad' into these senses.*
wander about aimlessly
• *(H5 3.8.119) Orléans describes Henry as a man coming 'to mope with his fat-brained followers'.*

> **moping** ADJECTIVE
angry
• *(Tem 5.1.240) The Boatswain says he and his crew 'were brought moping hither'.*

moral NOUN
as well as meaning 'a lesson from a story about right behaviour', you'll find:
1 significance
• *(MA 3.4.71) Beatrice asks Margaret, who has just named a medicine as 'carduus benedictus', if there is 'some moral in this benedictus'.*
2 symbolic figure
• *(H5 3.7.36) The Welsh Captain describes Fortune as 'an excellent moral'.*

> **moral** ADJECTIVE
full of virtuous sentiments
• *(KL 4.2.58) Goneril calls Albany 'a moral fool'.*

> **moraller** also spelled **moraler** NOUN
self-critic
• *(Oth 2.3.279) Iago tells Cassio: 'You are too severe a moraler'.*

more and less
1 men of high and low rank
• *(Mac 5.4.12) Malcolm reports about Macbeth: 'Both more and less have given him the revolt'.*
2 great and small
• *(Ham 5.2.350) Hamlet asks Horatio to tell Fortinbras, who will beome king of Denmark, about all the events that have happened—'with th'occurrents, more and less / Which have solicited'.*

morris in the phrase **nine-men's morris** see **RECREATION, p.170**

morrow see **GOODBYE, p.121**

mortal ADJECTIVE
as well as meaning 'human', you'll find:
lethal
• *(RJ 5.1.66) The Apothecary tells Romeo he has 'mortal drugs'.*

mortified ADJECTIVE
⚠*Don't read the modern meaning of 'deeply embarrassed' into these senses.*
1 deadened
• *(JC 2.1.324) Ligarius says Brutus has 'conjur'd up / My mortified spirit'.*
2 put under control
• *(H5 1.1.26) Canterbury says Henry's 'wildness, mortified in him, / Seem'd to die too'.*

> **mortifying** ADJECTIVE
deadly
• *(MA 1.3.10) Don John criticizes Conrad for trying to apply 'a moral medicine to a mortifying mischief'—a medicine of philosophy to a deadly disease.*

mote NOUN
speck of dust
• *(H5 4.1.170) Henry says every soldier should 'wash every mote out of his conscience'.*

motion NOUN
as well as meaning 'movement' and 'formal proposal', you'll find:
1 inward prompting
• *(MV 5.1.86) Lorenzo describes a man without music: 'The motions of his spirit are dull as night'.*
2 emotion
• *(TN 2.4.96) Orsino tells Cesario that woman's love has 'No motion of the liver'.*
see **liver** ; see also **HUMOURS, p.137**
3 power to act normally
• *(Oth 1.2.75) Brabantio accuses Othello of abusing Desdemona's youth 'with drugs or minerals / That weakens motion'.*
4 attack (in fencing)
• *(Ham 4.7.157) Claudius advises Laertes what to do 'When in your motion you are hot and dry'.*

motive NOUN
⚠ *Don't read the modern meaning of 'reason to commit a criminal act' into these senses.*
1 cause
• *(Oth 4.2.42) Desdemona asks Othello: 'Am I the motive of these tears?'*
2 inspiration
• *(Mac 4.3.27) Malcolm describes Macduff's wife and child as 'Those precious motives'.*
3 impulse
• *(Ham 5.2.229) Laertes tells Hamlet that he is satisfied in 'nature, / Whose motive in this case should stir me most / To my revenge'.*

motley NOUN
the distinctive, patchwork, multi-coloured clothes of a fool
• *(TN 1.5.51) Feste tells Olivia: 'I wear not motley in my brain'.*

mould NOUN
1 clay
• *(H5 3.2.20) Pistol pleads with the Welsh Captain to be merciful 'to men of mould!'*
2 model
• *(Ham 3.1.153) Ophelia describes Hamlet as 'the mould of form'—the model of courteous behaviour.*

mount in the phrase **on mount**
for all to see
• *(Ham 4.7.28) Laertes describes Ophelia as 'challenger on mount of all the age / For her perfections'—her excellent qualities clearly surpass those of anyone alive.*

mountaineer NOUN
mountain-dweller
• *(Tem 3.3.44) Gonzalo recalls stories of 'mountaineers / Dewlapp'd like bulls'.*

mountain-squire NOUN
landlord of barren land
• *(H5 5.1.32) The Welsh Captain strikes Pistol for calling him a 'mountain-squire'.*

mountant ADJECTIVE
climbing to the peak of success
• *(H5 2.4.57) The French King describes the father of Edward the Black Prince as 'his mountant sire, on mountain standing'.*
The word appears as 'mountaine' in the First Folio, meaning 'pre-eminent'.

Mountanto also spelled **Montanto** NOUN
fencer (the name of an upward thrust in fencing)
• *(MA 1.1.28) Beatrice asks about Benedick: 'is Signor Montanto returned from the wars, or no?'*

mountebank NOUN
[pronounced **mount**-i-bank]
travelling drug-seller
• *(Oth 1.3.61) Brabantio says Desdemona is 'corrupted / By spells and medicines bought of mountebanks'.*

mouse-hunt NOUN
women-chaser
• *(RJ 4.4.11) Lady Capulet teases her husband: 'you have been a mouse-hunt in your time'.*

mouths in the phrase **make mouths**
make faces
• *(Ham 4.4.50) Hamlet says Fortinbras 'Makes mouths at the invisible event'—scorns the hidden future.*

move VERB
as well as meanings to do with 'movement' and 'affecting emotions', you'll find:
1 provoke
• *(RJ 1.1.5) Sampson says he strikes quickly with his sword, 'being moved'.*
2 encourage
• *(Ham 3.2.174) The Player Queen says thrift, not love, are 'The instances that second marriage move'.*
3 urge
• *(JC 1.2.167) Brutus tells Cassius he does not want to 'Be any further moved'.*
4 persuade
• *(RJ 3.4.2) Capulet tells Paris 'we have had no time to move our daughter'.*

› **moved** also spelled **mov'd** ADJECTIVE
1 upset
• *(Tem 4.1.146) Prospero says Ferdinand looks 'in a mov'd sort / As if you were dismay'd'.*
2 exasperated
• *(RJ 1.1.82) The Prince intervenes to stop the*

a b c d e f g h i j k l Mm n o p q r s t u v w x y z

fighting: 'hear the sentence of your moved prince'.

mow see **mop and now**

moy NOUN
a misunderstanding by Pistol of his French prisoner's use of 'moi' ('me'), thinking it is a type of coin
• *(H5 4.4.11) Pistol tells his prisoner: 'I will have forty moys'.*

muddy ADJECTIVE
made of clay
• *(MV 5.1.64) Lorenzo describes the human body as 'this muddy vesture of decay'.*

muddy-mettled ADJECTIVE
sluggish
• *(Ham 2.2.553) Hamlet describes himself as 'A dull and muddy-mettled rascal'.*

muffled ADJECTIVE
blindfolded (the usual representation of Cupid, the god of love)
• *(RJ 1.1.165) Romeo describes 'Love, whose view is muffled still'.*

multitudinous ADJECTIVE
innumerable
• *(Mac 2.2.65) Macbeth thinks the blood on his hand will 'The multitudinous seas incarnadine, / Making the green one red'.*

mum see **ATTENTION SIGNALS, p.23**

mural or **mure** NOUN
⚠ *Don't read in the meaning of a 'wall-painting'.*
wall
• *(MND 5.1.202) Theseus comments on the departure of Snout as Wall: 'Now is the mural down between the two neighbours'.*

murder also spelled **murther** NOUN
wound
• *(Mac 3.4.81) Macbeth imagines dead men rising again 'With twenty mortal murders on their crowns'.*

murdering-piece also spelled **murd'ring-** NOUN
a type of weapon that scatters lethal projectiles
• *(Ham 4.5.94) Claudius describes the rumours against him coming 'Like to a murd'ring-piece, in many places'.*

mure see **mural**

murrain NOUN [pronounced **muh**-run]
plague
• *(Tem 3.2.76) Trinculo curses Caliban: 'A murrain on your monster'.*

murrion ADJECTIVE
infected with plague
• *(MND 2.1.97) Titania tells Oberon: 'crows are fatted with the murrion flock'.*

murther see **murder**

muse VERB
as well as meaning 'think deeply', you'll find:
wonder at
• *(Tem 3.3.36) Alonso, after seeing the spirits, says he 'cannot too much muse / Such shapes'.*

Muses, the
in Greek mythology, the nine goddesses who were patrons of the arts and learning
• *(MND 5.1.52) Theseus reads the summary of a play about 'The thrice three Muses mourning for the death / Of learning'.*
The Chorus opens 'Henry V' by asking for a 'Muse of fire' to help the theatre company put on their play. Fire was thought of as the lightest of the four elements (earth, water, air, fire), and was especially associated with poetry and creativity.

mushrump NOUN
mushroom
• *(Tem 5.1.39) Prospero addresses the spirits 'whose pastime / Is to make midnight mushrumps'—mushrooms that appear overnight.*
This is the word that appears in the First Folio, as 'midnight-Mushrumps'. Some editions replace this with 'mushrooms'.

mute NOUN
1 silent spectator
• *(Ham 5.2.328) Hamlet addresses those 'That are but mutes or audience to this act'.*
2 dumb servant
• *(TN 1.2.62) The Captain promises Viola: 'Your mute I'll be'.*

mutine NOUN
mutineer
• *(Ham 5.2.6) Hamlet remembers lying in his bed and feeling 'Worse than the mutines in the bilboes'—in shackles.*

mutine VERB
rebel
• *(Ham 3.4.83) Hamlet wonders how shame can 'mutine in a matron's bones'—how a mature and dignified woman can lose her sense of shame.*

mutuality NOUN
exchanged intimacies
• *(Oth 2.1.251) Iago, talking about Desdemona's behaviour towards Cassio, suggests what happens when 'mutualities so marshal the way'—lead the way (to greater intimacy).*

Myrmidons NOUN [pronounced **mur**-mid-ons]
a band of warriors who went to the Trojan War with Achilles—here presumably the name of some upmarket tavern
• *(TN 2.3.26) Feste talks nonsense to Sir Andrew, concluding: 'the Myrmidons are no bottle-ale houses'.*

mystery NOUN
as well as meaning 'hidden or secret matter', you'll find:
occupation
• *(Oth 4.2.29) Othello tells Emilia to watch at the door: 'Your mystery, your mystery!'—this is what you do for a living.*

Night

Many of Shakespeare's plays were first performed outside at 2 pm in bright sunshine at the Globe. So, if a scene was set at night, actors would carry flaming torches, and rely on their audience to imagine the gloom. It possibly also involved some 'darkness' acting, with actors pretending they couldn't see each other.

naked ADJECTIVE
as well as meaning 'having no clothing on the body', you'll find:
1 defenceless
• *(Oth 5.2.256) Othello threatens Gratiano: 'naked as I am, I will assault thee'.*
2 stripped of all belongings
• *(Ham 4.7.43) Hamlet tells Claudius in a letter: 'I am set naked on your kingdom'.*

napkin NOUN
⚠ *Don't read in the meaning of 'a cloth used at mealtimes'.*
handkerchief
• *(JC 3.2.132) Antony says when people hear the content of Caesar's Will they'll 'dip their napkins in his sacred blood'.*

narrowly ADVERB
carefully
• *(MA 5.4.115) Claudio thinks Benedick will be unfaithful 'if my cousin do not look exceeding narrowly to thee'.*

natural ADJECTIVE
as well as meanings to do with 'formed by nature', you'll find:
1 feeling proper affection
• *(H5 2.Chorus.19) The Chorus addresses 'England', wishing that 'all thy children were kind and natural'—thinking of the traitors.*
2 inherent
• *(Ham 3.2.248) Lucianus describes his poisonous drug as having 'natural magic'.*

natural NOUN
half-wit
• *(Tem 3.2.31) Trinculo describes Caliban as 'such a natural!'*

natural ADVERB
like a half-wit
• *(TN 1.3.26) Maria describes Sir Andrew's gifts as 'most natural'—also making a pun on Sir Toby's comment that Andrew 'hath all the good gifts of nature' (meaning 'formed by nature').*

nature NOUN
as well as meanings to do with 'the world of nature' and 'human nature', you'll find cases where further shades of meaning are present:
1 normal feelings
• *(Ham 1.5.81) The Ghost asks Hamlet not to put up with his murder, 'If thou hast nature in thee'.*

a b c d e f g h i j k l m Nn o p q r s t u v w x y z

2 normal state of mind
- *(Mac 5.1.8) The Doctor describes Lady Macbeth's sleepwalking as 'A great perturbation in nature'.*

3 human life
- *(Ham 1.5.12) The Ghost regrets 'the foul crimes done in my days of nature'—when I was alive.*

4 ungoverned state
- *(KL 1.2.1) Edmund addresses Nature: 'Thou, Nature, art my goddess'—the law of the jungle.*

› **demi-natured** also spelled **-natur'd** ADJECTIVE
of a shared nature
- *(Ham 4.7.87) Claudius describes Lamord's horse-riding ability as if he had been 'demi-natur'd / With the brave beast'.*

› **disnatured** also spelled **disnatur'd** ADJECTIVE
unnatural
- *(KL 1.4.273) Lear asks Nature to make any child of Goneril a 'disnatur'd torment to her!'—an unnatural nightmare!*

› **unnatural** ADJECTIVE
1 against normal feelings of kinship
- *(Tem 5.1.79) Prospero addresses Antonio: 'Unnatural though thou art'.*

2 monstrous
- *(Mac 5.1.63) The Doctor reflects on Lady Macbeth's behaviour: 'unnatural deeds / Do breed unnatural troubles'.*

› **unnaturalness** NOUN
behaviour going against normal feelings of kinship
- *(KL 1.2.137) Edmund describes an author who writes about 'unnaturalness between the child and the parent'.*

naught also spelled **nought** ADJECTIVE
as well as meaning 'nothing', you'll find:
1 improper
- *(Ham 3.2.140) Ophelia tells Hamlet: 'You are naught'.*

2 wicked
- *(RJ 3.2.87) The Nurse attacks men: 'All forsworn, all naught, all dissemblers'.*

naught NOUN
wickedness
- *(MND 4.2.12) Flute says a paramour (a lover) is 'a thing of naught'.*

› **naughty** ADJECTIVE
⚠ *Don't read in the modern meaning of 'badly behaved' or 'slightly rude'.*
wicked
- *(MV 5.1.91) Portia, returning home at night, sees a light in her hallway and reflects: 'So shines a good deed in a naughty world'.*

Servants, tradesmen, and other people considered lower-class are often called 'naughty' by their superiors when they are angry—'naughty knave', 'naughty varlet', 'naughty gaoler'.

nave NOUN
1 navel
- *(Mac 1.2.22) The Captain reports how Macbeth killed Macdonald: 'he unseam'd him from the nave to th'chaps'—split him in two from navel to jaws.*

2 hub
- *(Ham 2.2.484) The First Player asks the gods to take away the power of Fortune, destroying the spokes of her wheel, and rolling 'the round nave down the hill of heaven'.*

nayword NOUN
proverb
- *(TN 2.3.121) Maria promises to trick Malvolio so much that his name will become proverbial for 'fool': 'gull him into a nayword'.*

Nazarite NOUN
someone from the city of Nazareth in present-day Israel—here referring specifically to Jesus Christ.
- *(MV 1.3.30) Shylock refuses to dine with Bassanio, 'to smell pork, to eat of the habitation which your prophet the Nazarite conjured the devil into'—referring to the biblical story of Jesus casting out demons from a man into a herd of pigs.*

neaf NOUN
fist
- *(MND 4.1.19) Bottom asks Mustardseed: 'Give me your neaf'—he wants to shake hands with him.*

Neapolitan NOUN
someone from the city of Naples in Italy
- *(Tem 1.2.161) Prospero describes Gonzalo as 'a noble Neapolitan'.*

near ADJECTIVE
close to the throne (in order of succession)
- *(Mac 1.4.36) Duncan addresses everyone: 'Sons, kinsmen, thanes, / And you whose places are the nearest'.*

near ADVERB
closely
- *(Oth 2.3.204) Iago tells Montano his remark has really got to him: 'Touch me not so near'—don't be so hurtful.*

› **nearest of life**
most vital part of the body
- *(Mac 3.1.120) Macbeth says that every minute Banquo remains alive 'thrusts / Against my*

near'st of life'—like a sword entering his vital organs.

› nearly ADVERB

⚠*Don't read in the meaning of 'not far away'.*

particularly

• *(MND 1.1.126) Theseus tells Demetrius and Egeus that he wants to talk to them 'Of something nearly that concerns yourselves'.*

neat ADJECTIVE

posh

• *(KL 2.2.38) Kent addresses Oswald: 'stand; you neat slave'.*

neat NOUN

ox

• *(JC 1.1.27) The Cobbler boasts that the best men 'as ever trod upon neat's leather' have used his shoes.*

neeze VERB

sneeze

• *(MND 2.1.56) Puck tells a story where all the people laugh 'and neeze, and swear'.*

neglected ADJECTIVE

underrated

• *(H5 2.4.13) The French King reminds his nobles of the harm caused by 'the fatal and neglected English'—the deaths caused by underestimating them.*

negligence NOUN

⚠*Don't read in the meaning of 'carelessness'.*

indifference

• *(Ham 4.5.133) Laertes tells Claudius that 'both the worlds I give to negligence'—he cares nothing about this world or the one he believes will come after death.*

Nemean lion [pronounced **nee**-mee-an]

a monstrous lion, from the region of Nemea, in Greece; it was said to be invulnerable, but Hercules managed to kill it.

• *(Ham 1.4.83) Hamlet, wrenching himself free from his companions to follow the Ghost, feels 'As hardy as the Nemean lion's nerve'.*

nephew NOUN

as well as meaning 'the son of a brother or sister', you'll find:

grandson

• *(Oth 1.1.112) Iago warns Brabantio that if he lets a horse (that is, Othello) take Desdemona, 'you'll have your nephews neigh to you'.*

Neptune NOUN

the Roman water god, chiefly associated with the sea (and often pictured as holding a trident)

• *(Mac 2.2.63) Macbeth asks himself: 'Will all great Neptune's ocean wash this blood / Clean from my hand?'*

Nero NOUN

1st-century Roman emperor, who slew his mother, Agrippina; considered a model of cruelty

• *(Ham 3.3.378) Hamlet, on going to meet his mother, hopes that cruelty won't possess him: 'Let not ever / The soul of Nero enter this firm bosom'.*

nerve NOUN

sinew

• *(Mac 3.4.102) Macbeth says that, seeing any apparition other than Banquo's, 'my firm nerves / Shall never tremble'—he won't shake with fear.*

› unnerved ADJECTIVE

drained of strength

• *(Ham 2.2.462) The First Player describes the death of Priam: 'Th'unnerved father falls'.*

Nervii NOUN [pronounced **ner**-vee-ee]

Belgian tribe, defeated by Caesar in 57 BC

• *(JC 3.2.171) Antony recalls the day Caesar first wore the cloak in which he was killed—'That day he overcame the Nervii'.*

Nestor NOUN

Greek leader in the siege of Troy, reputed for his age, wisdom, and seriousness

• *(MV 1.1.56) Solanio describes people who are so sour they never laugh at a joke, 'Though Nestor swear the jest be laughable'.*

nether ADJECTIVE

1 lower

• *(Oth 5.2.43) Desdemona asks Othello: 'why gnaw you so your nether lip?'*

2 earthly

• *(KL 4.2.79) Albany reflects on the way the gods can avenge 'our nether crimes'.*

nether-stock see **CLOTHING, p.158**

never-surfeited ADJECTIVE

never filled to excess

• *(Tem 3.3.55) Ariel tells Alonso, Sebastian, and Antonio that the 'never-surfeited' sea has belched them up—as if it had eaten too much by swallowing them.*

new-trothed see **troth**

nice ADJECTIVE

⚠*Don't read in the modern meaning of 'pleasant' or 'kind' into these senses.*

as well as meaning 'good', 'precise', or 'subtle',

you'll find:
1 fussy
• *(H5 5.2.257) Henry tells Kate that 'nice customs curtsy to great kings'.*
2 carefully accurate
• *(Mac 4.3.176) Macduff listens to Ross's account of the state of Scotland: 'O relation / Too nice and yet too true'.*
3 trivial
• *(RJ 5.2.18) The Friar says his letter to Romeo 'was not nice, but full of charge'.*
4 skilful
• *(MA 5.1.75) Leonato says he will fight Claudio, 'Despite his nice fence and his active practice'.*

› nicely ADVERB
1 fastidiously
• *(KL 2.2.100) Cornwall says Kent is far craftier than toadying courtiers 'That stretch their duties nicely'.*
2 subtly
• *(TN 3.1.13) Cesario chats with Feste about those 'that dally nicely with words'.*

nickname VERB
invent new names for
• *(Ham 3.1.145) Hamlet finds fault with women: 'You nickname God's creatures'.*

niësse see **nyas**

niggard ADJECTIVE
as well as meaning 'miserly', you'll find:
reluctant
• *(Ham 3.1.13) Rosencrantz reports that Hamlet is 'Niggard of question'—unwilling to be direct with them in conversation.*

niggard NOUN
miser
• *(Mac 4.3.182) Macduff tells Ross to say what he means: 'Be not a niggard of your speech'.*

niggard VERB
as well as meaning 'be miserly', you'll find:
put off
• *(JC 4.3.228) Brutus suggests to Cassius that, because it is so late at night, 'nature must obey necessity, / Which we will niggard with a little rest'.*

› niggardly ADJECTIVE
mean-minded
• *(TN 2.5.4) Sir Toby calls Malvolio a 'niggardly, rascally sheep-biter'.*

night-cap see **HATS, p.160**

nighted ADJECTIVE
1 blacked out
• *(KL 4.5.13) Regan says that Edmund has gone to deal with blinded Gloucester, 'to dispatch / His nighted life'.*
2 black
• *(Ham 1.2.68) Gertrude pleads with Hamlet: 'cast thy nighted colour off'.*

nightgown also spelled **night-gown** NOUN
dressing-gown
• *(Oth 1.1.159) Stage direction: 'Enter Brabantio in his nightgown'.*

nightly ADJECTIVE
⚠ *Don't read in the meaning of 'every night'.*
of the night
• *(MND 5.1.353) Theseus says they will celebrate 'In nightly revels and new jollity'.*

night-rule NOUN
night-time activity
• *(MND 3.2.5) Oberon asks Puck what's been going on: 'What night-rule now about this haunted grove?'*

nill he see **will he**

nimble ADJECTIVE
sudden
• *(KL 4.7.34) Cordelia imagines Lear on the heath 'In the most terrible and nimble stroke / Of quick, cross lightning'—forks of lightning.*

nimble-pinioned also spelled **-pinion'd** ADJECTIVE
swift-winged
• *(RJ 2.5.7) Juliet reflects on the speed of love: 'Therefore do nimble-pinion'd doves draw Love'—birds that pull the chariot that Venus, the goddess of love, rides in.*

nine-men's morris see **RECREATION, p.170**

Ninus NOUN [pronounced **nigh**-nus]
the founder of the Assyrian city of Nineveh
• *(MND 3.1.84) In the rustics' play, Pyramus has to meet Thisbe at 'Ninus' tomb'.*

Niobe NOUN [pronounced **ny**-uh-be]
in Greek mythology, a heroine who boasted about her many sons and daughters, causing the anger of the gods; her children were slain by Apollo and Diana, and she was turned into a rock—but her eyes continued to weep in the form of a spring
• *(Ham 1.2.149) Hamlet recalls Gertrude following his father's body 'Like Niobe, all tears'.*

nob see **hob, nob**

noble (money) see **MONEY, p.197**

noise NOUN
as well as meaning 'loud or unpleasant sound', you'll find:

1 news
• *(KL 3.6.109) Edgar thinks of how he needs to 'Mark the high noises'—the stories circulating in high government places.*
2 musical sound
• *(Tem 3.2.131) Caliban says: 'the isle is full of noises'.*

> **noiseless** ADJECTIVE
> peaceful
> • *(KL 4.2.56) Goneril reminds Albany that 'France spreads his banners in our noiseless land'—where war-drums haven't yet been heard.*

noisome ADJECTIVE
foul-smelling
• *(MA 5.2.49) Beatrice informs Benedick that 'foul breath is noisome'.*

nole NOUN
headpiece
• *(MND 3.2.17) Puck reports to Oberon what he did to Bottom: 'An ass's nole I fixed on his head'.*

nomination NOUN
mention
• *(Ham 5.2.124) Hamlet asks Osric about Laertes: 'What imports the nomination of this gentleman?'—why are we talking about him?*

nonce in the phrase **for the nonce**
for the occasion
• *(Ham 4.7.160) Claudius tells Laertes he will offer Hamlet 'A chalice for the nonce'—a ceremonial cup.*

non-come also spelled **non-com** NOUN
intended for the Latin expression *non compos mentis* ('not sound of mind')
• *(MA 3.5.59) Dogberry thinks the examination of the two prisoners 'shall drive some of them to a non-com'—the news will drive some people out of their minds.*
Some think Dogberry is trying to say 'nonplus' (meaning 'state of perplexity').

nonpareil NOUN [pronounced **non**-pa-**rail**]
person without equal
• *(Mac 3.4.19) Macbeth tells the First Murderer that if he killed Fleance as well as Banquo 'thou art the nonpareil'—the best!*

non-regardance see **regard**

non-suit see **suit**

nook-shotten ADJECTIVE
crookedly shaped
• *(H5 3.6.14) Bourbon describes Britain as 'that nook-shotten isle of Albion'.*

north NOUN
north wind
• *(Oth 5.2.218) Emilia says she 'will speak as liberal as the north'.*

Norweyan ADJECTIVE
Norwegian
• *(Mac 1.2.31) The Captain describes how 'the Norweyan lord' began a fresh attack.*
This is the name in the First Folio. Some editions replace this with 'Norwegian'.

notary NOUN
a clerk authorized to draw up contracts
• *(MV 1.3.140) Shylock tells Antonio: 'Go with me to a notary'.*

note VERB
as well as meaning 'notice' or 'observe', you'll find:
publicly discredit
• *(JC 4.3.2) Cassius quarrels with Brutus: 'You have condemn'd and noted Lucius Pella / For taking bribes'.*

note NOUN
list
• *(Mac 3.3.10) The Second Murderer says that, apart from Banquo, everyone is in the court 'That are within the note of expectation'—on the invitation list.*

> **by note**
> with a bill of dues
> • *(MV 3.2.140) Bassanio tells Portia that he comes 'by note to give, and to receive'—thinking of love as if it were a commercial transaction.*

nothing NOUN
as well as meaning 'not anything', you'll find:
nonsense
• *(Ham 4.5.7) A Gentleman describes Ophelia's behaviour: 'Her speech is nothing'.*

> **all the world to nothing**
> the odds are a million to one
> • *(RJ 3.5.213) The Nurse tells Juliet that 'Romeo is banish'd, and all the world to nothing / That he dares ne'er come back'—I'll bet the world!*

notion NOUN
understanding
• *(KL 1.4.217) Lear thinks, after hearing what Goneril has to say, that 'his notion weakens'.*

notorious ADJECTIVE
Don't read in the meaning of 'well known for doing something bad'.
evident, obvious
• *(Oth 5.2.237) Montano calls Iago 'a notorious villain'.*

warning note *usage note* *theatre note*

a b c d e f g h i j k l m **Nn** o p q r s t u v w x y z

noyance NOUN
harm
• *(Ham 3.3.13) Rosencrantz observes that every individual life finds it necessary 'To keep itself from noyance'.*

numbers NOUN
1 lines of verse
• *(Ham 2.2.119) Polonius reads Hamlet's verse-letter to Ophelia: 'I am ill at these numbers' —bad at writing poetry.*
2 metre
• *(TN 2.5.94) Malvolio reads Olivia's verse: 'The numbers altered!'—the rhythm of the writing has changed.*

nuncio NOUN
messenger
• *(TN 1.4.28) Orsino thinks Olivia will listen to young Cesario's message more 'Than in a nuncio's of more grave aspect'.*

nyas also spelled **niësse** NOUN
[pronounced **ny**-us]
young, untrained hawk
• *(RJ 2.2.167) Romeo calls Juliet 'My nyas'—she has left her nest (her bedroom) to talk to Romeo, whom she has just referred to as a 'tassel-gentle' (a male peregrine falcon).*

NUMBERS

People in Shakespeare's time usually counted with the units before the tens.

three and thirty
• *(JC 5.1.53) Octavius tells Brutus he will keep his sword drawn 'till Caesar's three and thirty wounds / Be well aveng'd'.*

five and thirty
• *(Tem 3.2.13) Stephano boasts he swam 'five and thirty leagues off and on' before he got to the shore—that would be 105 miles!*

two and forty
• *(RJ 4.1.105) Friar Lawrence tells Juliet that his potion will make her sleep for 'two and forty hours'.*

They also counted in twenties (scores) as well as in tens.

three score
• *(H5 4.3.3) Westmorland reports that the French have 'full threescore thousand' soldiers—60,000.*

four score
• *(MV 3.1.97) Tubal tells Shylock that Jessica spent in Genoa 'one night four score ducats'—a lot of money, as in Italy at the time 1 ducat = about a quarter of a pound, so 80 ducats = £20—like spending £2000 today!*

eight score
• *(Oth 3.4.169) Bianca computes how long Cassio has stayed away from her: 'Seven days and nights? / Eight score eight hours?'—8 x 20 + 8 = 168 hours.*

O plural **oes** NOUN
1 sphere
• *(MND 3.2.188) Lysander says Helena brightens the night more 'Than all yon fiery oes and eyes of light'—the stars.*
2 zero
• *(KL 1.4.182) The Fool tells Lear: 'now thou art an O without a figure'—a nothing (without a number before it to make it significant).*
3 sorrowful exclamation
• *(RJ 3.3.90) The Nurse asks Romeo: 'Why should you fall into so deep an O?'*

O INTERJECTION
As an exclamation, 'O' is used before directly addressing a person, a thing, or an abstract notion. It's also used, like modern 'Oh!', to express emotion. Ben thinks it is the most important word in all of Shakespeare. Here's a small sample of its uses:
• *(KL 3.7.88) Gloucester exclaims: 'O my follies! Then Edgar was abus'd'.*
• *(MND 5.1.167) Bottom exclaims: 'O grim-look'd night, O night with hue so black'.*
• *(Mac 3.2.36) Macbeth exclaims: 'O, full of scorpions is my mind, dear wife!'*
• *(Ham 1.5.92) Hamlet exclaims: 'O all you host of heaven! O earth!'*
• *(RJ 2.2.10) Romeo exclaims: 'It is my lady, O it is my love'.*
• *(JC 5.3.5) Titinius exclaims: 'O Cassius, Brutus gave the word too early'.*
• *(Tem 1.2.116) Miranda exclaims, 'O, the heavens!'*
• *(MA 1.1.70) Beatrice exclaims: 'O Lord, he will hang upon him like a disease'.*
• *(Oth 3.3.167) Iago exclaims: 'O beware, my lord, of jealousy'.*
• *(MV 2.8.15) Shylock exclaims: 'O my ducats! O my daughter!'*
• *(H5 Prologue.1) The Chorus exclaims: 'O for a muse of fire'.*
• *(TN 1.2.7) Viola exclaims: 'O my poor brother!'*
Editors vary in whether they place an exclamation mark after the sentence in which it appears. 'O' has traditionally been pronounced [oh], but it's rarely actually meant to be pronounced this way. No one pronunciation would capture all the emotional meanings expressed in these examples by that simple black circle, 'O'. Surprise? Anger? Frustration? Longing? The possibilities are endless.

Obidicut NOUN [pronounced o-**bid**-i-cut]
one of the fiends of hell
• *(KL 4.1.58) Poor Tom says five fiends have possessed him, including 'Obidicut, of lust'.*

object NOUN
spectacle
• *(JC 4.1.37) Antony describes Lepidus as a dull-minded person who 'feeds / On objects, arts, and imitations'—things that are showy, artificial, and unoriginal.*

obliged ADJECTIVE
bound by marriage
• *(MV 2.6.8) Salarino observes that the chariot of the goddess of love (Venus) flies faster for new love than it does 'To keep obliged faith unforfeited'—marriage vows unbroken.*

a b c d e f g h i j k l m n **Oo** p q r s t u v w x y z

obscenely ADVERB
intended for 'seemly' (decorously)
• *(MND 1.2.100) Bottom says the forest is a place where they 'may rehearse most obscenely'.*

obscured ADJECTIVE
disguised
• *(KL 2.2.163) Kent says that Cordelia has 'been inform'd / Of my obscured course'—of my course of action while in disguise.*

obsequy NOUN
funeral rite
• *(RJ 5.3.16) Paris speaks as if to Juliet in her tomb of 'The obsequies that I for thee will keep'.*

› **obsequious** ADJECTIVE
⚠ *Don't read in the meaning of 'being unduly attentive'.*
dutiful (after a death)
• *(Ham 1.2.92) Claudius tells Hamlet that a bereaved son has 'To do obsequious sorrow'.*

observation NOUN
1 ceremony
• *(MND 4.1.103) Theseus tells his attendants: 'now our observation is perform'd'—celebrating the rites of May-day.*
2 observance
• *(Tem 3.3.87) Prospero praises his spirits for performing their tasks 'with good life / And observation strange'—particularly careful attention.*

› **observancy** NOUN
proper attention
• *(Oth 3.4.144) Desdemona thinks that women should not look in men 'for such observancy / As fits the bridal'—the same kind of attention they give to their brides on their wedding day.*

› **observant** NOUN
ingratiating attendant
• *(KL 2.2.99) Cornwall thinks men like Kent are craftier 'Than twenty silly-ducking observants'—servants and subjects who bow too much.*

› **observe** VERB
indulge
• *(JC 4.3.45) Brutus asks Cassius: 'Must I observe you?'*

› **observed** NOUN
one deserving of honour
• *(Ham 3.1.154) Ophelia describes Hamlet as 'Th'observ'd of all observers'.*

› **observingly** ADVERB
perceptively
• *(H5 4.1.5) Henry thinks 'There is some soul of goodness in things evil / Would men observingly distil it out'.*

occasion NOUN
1 opportunity
• *(MV 3.5.48) Lorenzo tells off Lancelot for 'Yet more quarrelling with occasion!'—quibbling at every chance he gets.*
2 reason
• *(Oth 4.1.58) Iago addresses Cassio: 'I would on great occasion speak with you'.*
3 need
• *(TN 5.1.148) Olivia says she had intended to keep secret 'what occasion now / Reveals'—that which necessity is forcing her to reveal.*
4 course of events
• *(Mac 2.2.74) Lady Macbeth tells Macbeth to put on his dressing-gown 'lest occasion call us / And show us to be watchers'—lest what happens next shows us to be awake when we should be asleep.*

occulted ADJECTIVE
concealed
• *(Ham 3.2.78) Hamlet expects the play to reveal Claudius' 'occulted guilt'.*

odd-even ADJECTIVE
between 12 and 1 at night
• *(Oth 1.1.123) Roderigo tells Brabantio that his daughter is missing 'At this odd-even and dull watch o'the night'.*

Od's see **SWEARING, p.298**

oeillade also spelled **oeilliad** NOUN
[pronounced **ill**-yad]
amorous glance
• *(KL 4.5.25) Regan says Goneril 'gave strange oeilliads' to Edmund.*

o'erbear past form **o'erborne** also spelled **overbear** VERB
1 overwhelm
• *(MA 2.3.148) Leonato says Beatrice's emotion relating to Benedick 'hath so much overborne her'.*
2 overrule
• *(MND 4.1.178) Theseus tells Egeus: 'I will overbear your will'—go against your wishes.*

o'ercharged see **charge**

o'ercome also spelled **o'er-come, overcome** VERB
⚠ *Don't read in the meaning of 'defeat'.*
suddenly come over
• *(Mac 3.4.111) Macbeth asks if things like Banquo's ghost can 'overcome us like a summer's cloud'.*

o'ercrow also spelled **o'er-crow, overcrow** VERB
overpower
• *(Ham 5.2.346) Hamlet says: 'The potent poison quite o'ercrows my spirit'.*

o'erflourish also spelled **o'er-flourish, overflourish** VERB
richly decorated
• *(TN 3.4.344) Antonio describes beautiful people who are evil as 'empty trunks, o'er-flourish'd by the devil'.*

o'erfraught see **fraught**

o'erleaven also spelled **o'er-leaven, overleaven** VERB
pervade
• *(Ham 1.4.29) Hamlet describes men who have a 'habit, that too much o'er-leavens' their behaviour—that seeps through their whole character.*

o'erlook also spelled **o'er-look, overlook** VERB
⚠ *Don't read the meaning of 'fail to notice' or 'ignore' into these senses.*
as well as meaning 'look down on', you'll find:
1 read through
• *(KL 5.1.50) Albany tells Edgar: 'I will o'erlook thy paper'.*
2 bewitch
• *(MV 3.2.15) Portia says Bassanio's eyes 'have o'erlook'd me'.*

› **o'erlooking** also spelled **overlooking** NOUN
perusal
• *(KL 1.2.38) Edmund says to Gloucester that Edgar's letter is 'not fit for your o'erlooking'.*

o'ername also spelled **o'er-name, overname** VERB
read through the list of
• *(MV 1.2.34) Portia asks Nerissa to 'over-name' the suitors.*

o'eroffice also spelled **o'er-office, overoffice** VERB
lord it over
• *(Ham 5.1.74) Hamlet sees the First Gravedigger handling a skull which 'might be the pate of a politician which this ass now o'er-offices'.*
✒ *This is the word in the First Folio. Some editions follow the Second Quarto text, which has 'ore-reaches'—'get the better of'.*

o'erperch also spelled **o'er-perch, overperch** VERB
fly over
• *(RJ 2.2.66) Romeo tells Juliet how he entered the garden: 'With love's light wings did I o'erperch these walls'.*

o'erprize also spelled **o'er-prize, overprize** VERB
overvalue
• *(Tem 1.2.92) Prospero says his studies 'O'er-priz'd all popular rate'—were more valuable than people rated them.*

o'erreach past form **o'erraught** also spelled **o'er-reach, overreach** VERB
1 overtake
• *(Ham 3.1.17) Rosencrantz tells Gertrude of the players: 'We o'erraught on the way'.*
2 get the better of
• *(Ham 5.1.74) Hamlet sees the First Gravedigger handling a skull which 'might be the pate of a politician which this ass now o'erreaches'—treats in such a disrespectful way.*
✒ *This is the word in the Second Quarto text. Some editions follow the First Folio, which has 'o're Offices'—'lord it over'.*

o'erred also spelled **o'er-red, over-red** VERB
cover over with blood
• *(Mac 5.3.14) Macbeth tells the Servant: 'Go prick thy face and over-red thy fear'.*

o'erset also spelled **o'er-set, overset** VERB
overwhelm
• *(RJ 3.5.136) Capulet warns Juliet that her sighs 'Without a sudden calm, will overset / Thy tempest-tossed body'.*

o'ershoot also spelled **o'er-shoot, overshoot** VERB
go astray in aim
• *(JC 3.2.149) Antony says he should not have mentioned Caesar's Will to the people: 'I have o'ershot myself to tell you of it'.*

o'ersize also spelled **o'er-size, oversize** VERB
smear
• *(Ham 2.2.450) Hamlet quotes a line about Pyrrhus being 'o'ersized with coagulate gore'.*

o'erskip also spelled **o'er-skip, overskip** VERB
pass over without noticing
• *(KL 3.6.104) Edgar reflects on how 'the mind much sufferance doth o'erskip'—how your mind can ignore the pain you're going through when it becomes aware of the suffering of others.*

o'erstare see **stare**

o'ersway see **sway**

o'erswell also spelled **o'er-swell, overswell** VERB
overflow
• *(JC 4.3.161) Cassius tells Lucius to pour wine 'till the wine o'erswell the cup'.*

a b c d e f g h i j k l m n Oo p q r s t u v w x y z

o'ertake also spelled **o'er-take, overtake** VERB
as well as meaning 'catch up with', you'll find:
1 accomplish
• *(Mac 4.1.144) Macbeth reflects that 'The flighty purpose never is o'ertook / Unless the deed go with it'—one's intention is never achieved unless one acts as soon as the thought is formed, before the intention flies away.*
2 overpower by drink
• *(Ham 2.1.58) Polonius imagines Laertes being 'o'ertook in's rouse'—while carousing.*

o'erteemed see **teem**

o'ertrip also spelled **o'er-trip, overtrip** VERB
pass lightly over
• *(MV 5.1.7) Jessica imagines 'In such a night / Did Thisbe fearfully o'ertrip the dew'.*

offal NOUN
waste
• *(JC 1.3.109) Cassius condemns Rome: 'What trash is Rome, / What rubbish and what offal'.*

off-cap see **HATS, p.160**

offence NOUN
⚠ *Don't read the milder meaning of 'annoyance' into these senses.*
1 harm
• *(MND 2.2.23) The Fairy guarding Titania sings: 'Worm nor snail, do no offence'.*
2 annoying matter
• *(JC 2.1.268) Portia accuses Brutus: 'You have some sick offence within your mind'.*

› **offenceless** ADJECTIVE
harmless
• *(Oth 2.3.257) Iago says Othello has punished Cassio 'as one would beat his offenceless dog to affright an imperious lion'—punish a harmless creature to deter a dangerous one.*

› **offend** VERB
as well as meaning 'wrong', you'll find:
harm
• *(MV 4.1.140) Shylock tells Gratiano he is wasting his breath: 'Thou but offend'st thy lungs to speak so loud'.*

offer VERB
start
• *(RJ 3.4.11) Stage direction: 'Paris offers to go in'.*

offering also spelled **off'ring** NOUN
ritual
• *(Mac 2.1.52) Macbeth reflects on the night: 'Witchcraft celebrates / Pale Hecate's off'rings'.*

office NOUN
⚠ *Don't read the meaning of 'a room used for business' into these senses.*
1 task
• *(MA 4.1.264) Beatrice tells Benedick that the service she has in mind 'is a man's office'.*
2 role
• *(JC 5.5.29) Volumnius tells Brutus that helping him commit suicide is 'not an office for a friend'.*
3 red-tape bureaucracy
• *(Ham 3.1.73) Hamlet reflects on 'the insolence of office'.*
4 performance
• *(H5 5.2.343) Queen Isabel hopes that 'never may ill office' come between England and France.*

› **offices** NOUN
serving-rooms for food and drink
• *(Oth 2.2.8) A Herald makes an announcement: 'All offices are open'.*

› **officed** also spelled **offic'd** ADJECTIVE
functional
• *(Oth 1.3.267) Othello denies that love will ever blind his 'speculative and officed instruments' —his means of seeing and acting.*
➠ *'Offic'd instrument' is the reading in the First Folio. Some editions replace this with 'active instruments' from the First and Second Quarto texts; others choose a word from each.*

› **officers** NOUN
⚠ *Don't read in the meaning of 'senior member of the armed forces'.*
servants
• *(Ham 4.5.104) A Messenger reports that 'Laertes, in a riotous head, / O'erbears your officers'—with a rebellious uprising, has overcome your servants.*

old ADJECTIVE
as well as meaning 'having existed for a long time', you'll find:
1 bygone
• *(TN 2.4.47) Orsino describes a song that 'dallies with the innocence of love, / Like the old age'.*
2 normal
• *(KL 3.7.98) One of Gloucester's servants says that there is no justice if Regan 'in the end meet the old course of death'—if she dies naturally of old age.*
3 experienced
• *(RJ 3.3.94) Romeo asks the Nurse if Juliet doesn't 'think me an old murderer'.*
4 worn out
• *(TN 1.5.102) Olivia tells Feste that his 'fooling grows old'.*
5 abundant
• *(Tem 1.2.368) Prospero threatens Caliban: 'I'll rack thee with old cramps'.*

olive NOUN
olive-branch—a symbol of peace
• *(TN 1.5.195) Cesario tells Olivia: 'I hold the olive in my hand'.*

Olympus NOUN [pronounced o-**lim**-pus]
a mountain in northern Greece, the home of the gods
• *(JC 3.1.74) Caesar rejects Cinna's pleas as impossible: 'Wilt thou lift up Olympus?'*
see MAP, p.176

omit VERB
neglect
• *(Tem 1.2.183) Prospero tells Miranda of a star 'whose influence / If now I court not, but omit, my fortunes / Will ever after droop'—expressing the commonly held view that the positions of the stars influenced human life.*

once ADVERB
as well as meaning 'on one occasion only', you'll find:
1 in a word
• *(MA 1.1.292) Don Pedro sums up Claudio's situation: ''Tis once. Thou lovest'.*
2 ever
• *(Mac 5.5.15) Macbeth claims horror 'Cannot once start me'—can't alarm him.*
2 one day
• *(JC 4.3.191) Brutus has prepared himself for the thought that Portia 'must die once'.*

open ADJECTIVE
as well as meaning 'not closed', you'll find:
1 public
• *(H5 1.1.59) Canterbury recalls the way Henry frequented 'open haunts and popularity'—public and popular places (both considered unfit for a prince to visit).*
2 displayed
• *(KL 3.1.34) Kent says the French are ready 'To show their open banner'—unfurl their flag (a sign that they're ready for battle).*

open ADVERB
in public
• *(TN 3.3.37) Sebastian warns Antonio: 'Do not then walk too open'.*

open VERB
reveal
• *(Ham 2.2.18) Claudius asks Rosencrantz and Guildenstern to find out whether there is something unknown afflicting Hamlet 'That, open'd, lies within our remedy'.*

open-arse NOUN
the rude name for the medlar fruit (from its buttock-like shape)
• *(RJ 2.1.38) Mercutio wishes Romeo's mistress were 'An open-arse'.*

operant ADJECTIVE
active
• *(Ham 3.2.166) The Player King tells his Queen that his 'operant powers their functions leave to do'—his faculties are ceasing to function (a very poetic way of saying that he is dying).*

operation NOUN
power
• *(KL 1.1.110) Lear swears 'By all the operation of the orbs / From whom we do exist'—all the power of the stars, which gave us life.*

opinioned ADJECTIVE
intended to mean 'pinioned'
• *(MA 4.2.64) Dogberry commands his men to hold Conrad and Borachio. 'let them be opinioned'.*

opposeless ADJECTIVE
unable to be resisted
• *(KL 4.6.38) Gloucester prays to the gods, hoping not 'To quarrel with your great opposeless wills'.*

opposite ADJECTIVE
hostile
• *(TN 3.4.63) Olivia's letter tells Malvolio to 'be opposite with a kinsman'—be nasty to your relatives.*

opposite NOUN
1 adversity
• *(Ham 3.2.212) The Player Queen invites 'Each opposite that blanks the face of joy'—anything that ignores happiness—to come upon her if ever she marries again.*
2 opponent
• *(TN 3.4.245) Fabian tells Cesario that Sir Andrew is 'the most skilful, bloody, and fatal opposite'.*

oppressed also spelled **oppress'd** ADJECTIVE
distressed
• *(Ham 1.2.203) Horatio describes the Ghost walking past the 'oppress'd and fear-surprised eyes' of the observers.*

orb NOUN
1 planet or star
• *(MV 5.1.60) Lorenzo tells Jessica that even 'the smallest orb' sings like an angel when it moves.*
Lorenzo is thinking of the music of the spheres—the noise thought to be produced by the orbits of the planets moving past each other.
see THE COSMOS, p.174
2 orbit
• *(RJ 2.2.110) Juliet asks Romeo not to swear by the*

warning note *usage note* 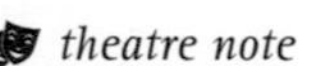 *theatre note*

moon, that makes 'monthly changes in her circl'd orb', and so is inconstant and cannot be trusted.
3 earth
• *(Ham 2.2.473) The First Player describes the calm before a storm: 'the orb below / As hush as death'.*
4 fairy ring
• *(MND 2.1.9) The Fairy says she serves Titania, 'To dew her orbs upon the green'—to moisten with dew the round grassy spaces where Titania dances.*

› **orbed** ADJECTIVE
spherical
• *(TN 5.1.262) Viola swears she will keep true to Orsino 'As doth that orbed continent the fire' —as the sun maintains its fire.*

orchard NOUN
garden
• *(JC 2.1.1) Stage direction: 'Enter Brutus in his orchard'.*

order NOUN
as well as meaning 'command' and 'request', you'll find:
1 arrangement
• *(H5 3.3.10) Gower says the Duke of Gloucester has been given 'the order of the siege'—put in charge of arranging how the attack will proceed.*
2 regular procedure
• *(KL 1.1.18) Gloucester says he has a son 'by order of law'—born within wedlock, and thus legitimate in the eyes of the law.*

order VERB
arrange
• *(Tem 1.2.29) Prospero tells Miranda that everything is 'So safely order'd' that nobody has been hurt in the wreck.*

› **take order**
make arrangements
• *(Oth 5.2.73) Othello says Cassio will be dealt with: 'Honest Iago hath tane order for't'.*

ordinance NOUN
⚠ *Don't confuse this with a different word, 'ordnance', meaning 'artillery'.*
as well as meaning 'command', you'll find:
1 appointed place in nature
• *(JC 1.3.66) Cassius, wondering about the unnatural events in Rome, asks 'Why all these things change from their ordinance'.*
2 normal practice
• *(H5 2.4.84) Exeter states the English claim to the honours belonging 'By custom and the ordinance of times / Unto the crown of France'.*

› **ordinant** ADJECTIVE
providential, giving luck
• *(Ham 5.2.48) Hamlet says that having his father's ring (used to seal letters) with him on the ship to England 'was heaven ordinant'.*

› **preordinance** also spelled **pre-ordinance** NOUN
previously established law
• *(JC 3.1.38) Caesar criticizes Metellus for trying to make him change his mind, saying it turns 'preordinance and first decree / Into the law of children'—decisions already made and agreed can't be changed at a whim, as if they were part of a children's game.*

ordure NOUN
dung
• *(H5 2.4.39) The Constable compares Henry to a plant once hidden, 'As gardeners do with ordure hide those roots / That shall first spring'.*

ore NOUN
precious metal
• *(Ham 4.1.25) Gertrude compares Hamlet's madness to 'some ore / Among a mineral of metals base'—a diamond in the rough.*

organ NOUN
⚠ *Don't read the meanings of 'a part of the body' or 'an instrument with many pipes' into these senses.*
1 agent
• *(Ham 4.7.70) Laertes hopes that he 'might be the organ' of revenge upon Hamlet.*
2 feature
• *(MA 4.1.225) The Friar says, once Hero is thought to have died, 'every lovely organ of her life' will appear more beautiful.*
3 musical instrument
• *(Ham 3.2.353) Hamlet says, of a recorder, that there is 'much music, excellent voice, in this little organ' (though he also means his own body).*

orient ADJECTIVE
lustrous
• *(MND 4.1.53) Oberon describes dew swelling on flower-buds 'like round and orient pearls'.*

original NOUN
source
• *(MND 2.1.117) Titania tells Oberon, of the evils arising from their quarrel: 'We are their parents and original'.*

orison NOUN [pronounced **o**-rizz-on]
prayer
• *(RJ 4.3.3) Juliet says she has 'need of many orisons'.*

ornaments NOUN
garments
• *(RJ 1.1.87) The Prince says the quarrel has made Verona's citizens throw aside 'their grave*

beseeming ornaments'—their smart, dignified clothes.

Orpheus NOUN [pronounced **aw**-fee-us]
in Greek mythology, a poet whose music could charm beasts and bring life to inanimate objects
• *(MV 5.1.80) Lorenzo recalls how 'Orpheus drew trees, stones, and floods'—charmed them with his music.*

orthography in the phrase **turn orthography**
become a user of elegant speech
• *(MA 2.3.19) Benedick regrets that Claudio, who used to speak plain, 'now is he turned orthography'—using phrases one expects to see only in writing.*

Ossa NOUN
a very high mountain in northern Greece, where in Greek mythology the giants fought the gods
• *(Ham 5.1.269) Hamlet says he would pile such a high burial mound above him and Laertes that it would 'Make Ossa like a wart'—seem as small as a wart.*
see MAP, p.176

ostent NOUN
⚠ *Don't read the meaning of 'a showy display to impress' into these senses.*
display
• *(MV 2.2.183) Gratiano promises to behave 'Like one well studied in a sad ostent'.*

› **ostentation** NOUN
1 display
• *(MA 4.1.204) The Friar tells Leonato to 'Maintain a mourning ostentation'.*
2 ceremony
• *(Ham 4.5.211) Laertes asks why Polonius was buried with 'No noble rite, nor formal ostentation'.*

othergates ADVERB
differently
• *(TN 5.1.186) Sir Andrew tells Cesario that if Sir Toby hadn't been drunk, 'he would have tickled you othergates than he did'—dealt with you differently.*

Ottomite NOUN
Turk (from the Ottoman Empire, one of the most powerful states in the world during Shakespeare's time)
• *(Oth 1.3.33) A Messenger reports how 'the Ottomites' are heading for Rhodes.*

› **Ottoman** ADJECTIVE
• *(Oth 1.3.49) The Duke tells Othello that he must be employed 'Against the general enemy Ottoman'—the enemies that all oppose (because they are not Christian).*

ounce see ANIMALS, p.162

ousel cock NOUN [pronounced **oo**-zul cock]
blackbird
• *(MND 3.1.109) Bottom sings about 'The ousel cock so black of hue'.*

out ADVERB
1 as well as meaning 'opposite of *in*', you'll find: angry
• *(JC 1.1.17) A Cobbler tells Flavius: 'be not out with me'—which he follows with a pun on being 'worn out': 'yet if you be out, sir, I can mend you'.*
2 unfriendly
• *(MV 3.5.28) Jessica tells Lorenzo that 'Lancelot and I are out'.*
3 up in arms
• *(Mac 4.3.185) Ross reports a rumour 'Of many worthy fellows that were out'.*
4 finished
• *(Tem 3.2.1) Stephano talks of when they run out of alcohol: 'When the butt is out, we will drink water'.*
5 fully
• *(Tem 1.2.41) Prospero tells Miranda of what happened when 'thou wast not / Out three years old'.*
6 out of pocket
• *(TN 2.3.167) Sir Andrew grumbles that, if he cannot obtain Olivia (and her wealth), 'I am a foul way out'—having spent (or rather, given) so much money to Sir Toby.*
7 out-of-date
• *(RJ 1.4.3) Benvolio says there is no need to make a formal excuse for their presence at the Capulets' party: 'The date is out of such prolixity'—such tedious explanation (prolixity) isn't the fashion any more.*
8 abroad
• *(KL 1.1.31) Gloucester says Edmund 'hath been out nine years'.*

› **out on**
enough of, shame on
• *(MA 4.1.55) Claudio reacts angrily to Hero's use of the word 'seem'd': 'Out on thy seeming!'*
✎ *The First Folio has 'thee' instead of 'thy', so some editions print the sentence as 'Out on thee, seeming!'*

outdwell VERB
stay beyond
• *(MV 2.6.4) Gratiano is surprised that Lorenzo 'outdwells his hour'—is late.*

outface see **face**

outnight VERB
outdo in making references to the night
• *(MV 5.1.23) Jessica ends a series of 'in such a*

night' speeches with 'I would outnight you, did nobody come'—if nobody interrupted us.

out of joint see **joint**

out-paramour see **paramour**

outrage NOUN
as well as meaning 'violent act' and 'anger', you'll find:
passionate expression
• *(RJ 5.3.216) The Prince tells everyone to 'Seal up the mouth of outrage for a while'.*

outrageous ADJECTIVE
⚠ *Don't read in the meaning of 'very shocking'.*
capricious
• *(Ham 3.1.58) Hamlet reflects on 'The slings and arrows of outrageous fortune'.*

outsport see **sport**

outstretched ADJECTIVE
puffed up, egotistical
• *(Ham 2.2.260) Hamlet talks of 'outstretched heroes' being like beggars.*

out-tongue VERB
speak more loudly than
• *(Oth 1.2.19) Othello says that his services to Venice 'Shall out-tongue' Brabantio's complaints.*

out-wall NOUN
external appearance
• *(KL 3.1.45) Kent tells a Gentleman: 'I am much more / Than my out-wall'.*

outward ADJECTIVE
external
• *(KL 4.4.10) Cordelia pleads for her father: 'He that helps him take all my outward worth'—all my worldly wealth.*

outwear see **wear**

over- (beginning a word) **see also words beginning with o'er-**

overlusty see **lusty**

overtopping NOUN
becoming too ambitious
• *(Tem 1.2.81) Prospero talks of making decisions about people at court: 'who t'advance, and who / To trash for overtopping'—who to keep in check for getting above themselves.*

overture NOUN
revelation
• *(KL 3.7.86) Regan tells Gloucester it was Edmund 'That made the overture of thy treasons to us'.*

overwatch, overwatched see **watch**

overweathered also spelled **overweather'd**
ADJECTIVE
weather-worn
• *(MV 2.6.19) Gratiano describes a returning ship 'With overweather'd ribs and ragged sails'.*

overweening ADJECTIVE
arrogant
• *(TN 2.5.27) Sir Toby calls Malvolio 'an overweening rogue'.*

overwhelming ADJECTIVE
⚠ *Don't read in the meaning of 'having a strong emotional effect'.*
overhanging
• *(RJ 5.1.39) Romeo remembers an apothecary 'with overwhelming brows'.*

owe VERB
⚠ *Don't read the meaning of 'have to pay money' into these senses.*
1 own
• *(MND 2.2.85) Puck anoints Lysander's eyes with 'All the power this charm doth owe'.*
2 give back
• *(MA 3.3.94) Conrad promises Borachio a response to his insult: 'I will owe thee an answer for that'—I'll remember what you've said and pay you back.*

owlet see **ANIMALS, p.162**

Plague

The Bubonic Plague, also known as the Black Death, hit London three times while Shakespeare was working there. People died in the thousands in London, more than halving the city's population. It was very infectious, so to avoid crowds the theatres had to close when there was an outbreak. It's thought that Shakespeare made money at these times by writing sonnets and poems for noblemen instead of plays.

pack NOUN
as well as meaning 'bundle', you'll find:
clique
• *(KL 5.3.18) Lear tells Cordelia that they will outlast 'packs and sects of great ones'—the cliques and political parties at court that come and go.*

pack VERB
be off
• *(MV 2.2.9) Lancelot describes the conflict with his conscience about leaving Shylock, where his conscience tells him to stay, but: 'the most courageous fiend bids me pack'.*

> **packed** ADJECTIVE
> in league
> • *(MA 5.1.292) Leonato says to the offenders that Margaret 'was pack'd in all this wrong'—part of the conspiracy.*

> **packing** NOUN
> plotting
> • *(KL 3.1.26) Kent tells a Gentleman of the 'snuffs and packings of the dukes'—their quarrels and plots.*

packthread NOUN
string used for tying up bundles
• *(RJ 5.1.47) Romeo describes the apothecary's shelves, containing 'Remnants of packthread'.*

paction NOUN
compact
• *(H5 5.2.345) Queen Isabel hopes that discord will not 'Thrust in between the paction of these kingdoms'.*

paddock see ANIMALS, p.162

pain NOUN
effort
• *(MND 5.1.80) Philostrate says the rustics' play has been 'conn'd with cruel pain'.*

> **painful** ADJECTIVE
> as well as meaning 'causing pain', you'll find:
> 1 laborious
> • *(Tem 3.1.1) Ferdinand reflects: 'There be some sports are painful'.*
> 2 arduous
> • *(H5 4.3.111) Henry describes the dirty appearance of his army due to 'rainy marching in the painful field'.*

painted ADJECTIVE
⚠ *Don't read the meaning of 'covered over with paint' into these senses.*
as well as a meaning in relation to art, you'll find:
1 disguised, feigned
• *(Ham 3.1.53) Claudius reflects on his 'most painted word'.*
2 depicted (as on a sign, to advertise a spectacle)
• *(Tem 2.2.28) Trinculo thinks of how much money he would make in England if he had Caliban 'painted'.*
3 motionless (as in a painting)
• *(Ham 2.2.468) The First Player describes Pyrrhus standing 'as a painted tyrant'.*

> **painting** NOUN
> cosmetics
> • *(Ham 3.1.142) Hamlet finds fault with women: 'I have heard of your paintings well enough'.*

> **paint out** VERB
> depict fully
> • *(MA 3.2.95) Don John says, of Hero, that the word 'disloyal' 'is too good to paint out her wickedness'.*

a b c d e f g h i j k l m n o Pp q r s t u v w x y z

pajock NOUN [pronounced **pa**-jock]
savage or peacock
• *(Ham 3.2.273) Hamlet improvises some lines about Claudius: 'now reigns here / A very, very—pajock'.*
A peacock has a reputation for vanity and foolishness, strutting around and showing off his feathers to attract females.

palabras NOUN [pronounced pa-**la**-brass]
Spanish for 'words', an abbreviation of the phrase *pocas palabras* 'few words', a popular expression of the time
• *(MA 3.5.15) Dogberry suggests that Verges is talking too much: "Palabras', neighbour Verges'.*

Palatine NOUN
a nobleman (with the title of Count) who has been given charge of a province within an empire
• *(MV 1.2.43) Nerissa lists among Portia's suitors 'the County Palatine'.*

pale NOUN
1 fence
• *(Ham 1.4.28) Hamlet describes some men who have a defect 'Oft breaking down the pales and forts of reason'—they become irrational.*
2 fenced land
• *(MND 2.1.4) A Fairy tells Puck where she wanders: 'Over park, over pale'.*

› **pale in** VERB
fence in
• *(H5 5.Prologue.10) The Chorus describes how 'the English beach / Pales in the flood with men'—seems to enclose the sea with a throng of people.*

pale ADJECTIVE
as well as referring to 'colour', you'll find:
cowardly
• *(H5 2.Chorus.14) The Chorus says the French try to divert the English purposes 'with pale policy'.*

pale VERB
dim
• *(Ham 1.5.90) The Ghost says the glow-worm begins 'to pale his uneffectual fire'.*

› **paly** ADJECTIVE
faint
• *(H5 4.Chorus.8) The Chorus describes how the two armies see each other through the 'paly flames' of their fires.*

palfrey NOUN
a horse for everyday riding, as used by the knights of old
• *(H5 3.8.26) Bourbon describes his horse as 'the prince of palfreys'.*

pall VERB
1 fail
• *(Ham 5.2.9) Hamlet reflects on how 'Our indiscretion sometime serves us well / When our deep plots do pall'—our sudden, unthinking actions sometimes benefit us more than a carefully thought out course of action.*
2 cover
• *(Mac 1.5.50) Lady Macbeth, thinking of her husband, asks night to 'pall thee in the dunnest smoke of hell'.*

palm NOUN
a palm leaf as a symbol of victory
• *(JC 1.2.131) Cassius is amazed that Caesar should 'bear the palm alone'.*

› **palmer** NOUN
pilgrim (who would carry a palm leaf after visiting Jerusalem)
• *(RJ 1.5.100) Romeo asks Juliet: 'Have not saints lips, and holy palmers too?'*

› **palmy** ADJECTIVE
triumphant
• *(Ham 1.1.116) Horatio recalls 'the most high and palmy state of Rome'.*

palpable-gross ADJECTIVE
plainly ignorant
• *(MND 5.1.350) Theseus remarks that 'This palpable-gross play' has helped them pass the time.*

palter VERB
deal evasively
• *(Mac 5.8.20) Macbeth rejects the evil spirits 'That palter with us in a double sense'.*

paly see **pale 2**

Pandarus NOUN [pronounced **pan**-da-rus]
a Trojan prince whose scheming enabled his niece Cressida and Troilus to be lovers
• *(TN 3.1.49) Feste, having had a coin from Cesario, tries to get another one by saying he 'would play Lord Pandarus of Phrygia, ... to bring a Cressida to this Troilus'.*

pander NOUN
pimp
• *(MA 5.2.29) Benedick describes Troilus as 'the first employer of panders'.*

pander VERB
gratify
• *(Ham 3.4.88) Hamlet describes what happens when 'reason panders will'—judgement acts as a go-between for lust.*

Paphos NOUN
a region of Cyprus, the favourite home of Venus, the goddess of love
• *(Tem 4.1.93) Iris says she saw Venus 'Cutting the clouds towards Paphos'—speeding through the clouds.*
see MAP, p.176

paragon VERB
surpass
• *(Oth 2.1.62) Cassio says Othello 'hath achiev'd a maid / That paragons description'.*

paramour VERB
1 lover
• *(RJ 5.3.105) Romeo, seeing Juliet's apparently dead body in the crypt, says death 'keeps / Thee here in dark to be his paramour'.*
2 intended to mean 'paragon' (a perfect model)
• *(MND 4.2.9) Quince says that Bottom 'is a very paramour for a sweet voice'.*

› **out-paramour** VERB
have more lovers than
• *(KL 3.4.87) Poor Tom tells Lear that in his former life he 'in woman out-paramour'd the Turk'—had more women than the Grand Sultan (who famously had a harem filled with wives).*

Parca NOUN
in Greek mythology, one of the three goddesses, or Fates, who decide human destiny by spinning and cutting the threads of life
• *(H5 5.1.18) Pistol asks the Welsh Captain if he thirsts 'to have me fold up Parca's fatal web'—cut off your life.*

parcel NOUN
⚠ *Don't read the meaning of 'something wrapped up to be carried or posted' into these senses.*
1 part
• *(Oth 1.3.153) Othello recalls how he gave a full account of his travels to Desdemona, 'Whereof by parcels she had something heard'.*
2 small group
• *(MV 1.2.100) Portia says she is glad that 'this parcel of wooers are so reasonable' (for deciding to return home).*

pard see ANIMALS, p.162

pardon NOUN
as well as meaning 'act of forgiving', you'll find:
permission
• *(Ham 1.2.56) Laertes asks Claudius for 'your gracious leave and pardon' to return to France.*

parish top
a large spinning-top kept as a pastime for people in a parish
• *(TN 1.3.38) Sir Toby says people should drink toasts to his niece until their brains spin round 'like a parish top'.*

park NOUN
⚠ *Don't read in the meanings of 'area of recreational land' or 'theme park'.*
hunting ground
• *(MND 2.1.4) A Fairy tells Puck where she wanders: 'Over park, over pale'.*

parle or **parley** NOUN
1 negotiation (between enemies under a truce)
• *(H5 3.4.2) Henry tells the citizens of Harfleur: 'This is the latest parle we will admit'—his final offer.*
2 discussion
• *(Mac 2.3.78) Lady Macbeth asks why the bell 'calls to parley / The sleepers of the house'.*

parle or **parley** VERB
have a conversation
• *(Ham 1.3.123) Polonius advises Ophelia not to respond immediately to 'a command to parley' from Hamlet.*

parlous ADJECTIVE
perilous
• *(MND 3.1.12) Snout thinks it 'a parlous fear!' that Pyramus should kill himself in front of the ladies at the court.*

parricide NOUN
1 murder of a father
• *(Mac 3.1.33) Macbeth says that Malcolm and Donaldbain have not confessed 'Their cruel parricide'.*
2 murderer of a father
• *(KL 2.1.45) Edmund says 'the revenging gods / 'Gainst parricides did all the thunder bend'.*

parrot NOUN
nonsense
• *(Oth 2.3.261) Cassio criticizes himself: 'Drunk! And speak parrot!'*

part NOUN
as well as meaning 'fragment' and 'side', you'll find:
1 quality
• *(RJ 3.5.181) Capulet says Paris is stuffed 'with honourable parts'.*
2 task
• *(MV 4.1.92) Shylock says the Venetians use their slaves 'in object and in slavish parts'.*

parti-coloured see COLOURS, p.164

particular NOUN
as well as meaning 'a detail', you'll find:
an individual person
• *(KL 2.4.289) Regan says, of her father, 'For his*

particular, I'll receive him gladly, / But not one follower'.

parti-eyed ADJECTIVE

with eyes of mixed colour—presumably, because of blood

• *(KL 4.1.10) Edgar sees Gloucester: 'My father, parti-eyed!'*

✒ *This word appears in the First Quarto text of the play. Some editions replace this with 'poorly led', derived from the First Folio.*

partisan see SWORDS AND DAGGERS, p.156

party NOUN

⚠ *Don't read the meaning of 'enjoyable social gathering' into these senses.*

1 faction

• *(KL 2.1.26) Edmund asks if Edgar has said anything about Cornwall—'Upon his party 'gainst the Duke of Albany'.*

2 fellow

• *(Tem 3.2.57) Stephano asks Caliban to lead him to Prospero: 'Canst thou bring me to the party?'*

pass NOUN

as well as meaning 'passage', you'll find:

1 swordthrust

• *(Ham 4.7.138) Claudius tells Laertes that 'a pass of practice' would deal with Hamlet—a treacherous thrust.*

2 bout

• *(TN 3.4.252) Sir Toby tells Sir Andrew he had a fencing round with Cesario: 'I had a pass with him'.*

3 quip

• *(Tem 4.1.240) Stephano praises what Trinculo has said as 'an excellent pass of pate'—a very clever piece of wit.*

pass VERB

as well as meanings to do with 'moving', you'll find:

1 go over (the points in an argument)

• *(Mac 3.1.81) Macbeth reminds the Murderers how he 'passed in probation'—how he demonstrated, or gave them proof (that Banquo had deceived them).*

2 show

• *(H5 2.1.110) Nym says that Henry 'passes some humours and careers'—strange moods and wild actions.*

3 ignore

• *(Oth 2.3.230) Iago says that Cassio must have received an insult 'Which patience could not pass'.*

4 pass sentence

• *(KL 3.7.23) Cornwall says, of Gloucester, 'well we may not pass upon his life / Without the form of justice'—we can't condemn him without a trial.*

5 die

• *(KL 4.6.47) Edgar says, after Gloucester's imagined fall, 'Thus might he pass indeed; yet he revives'.*

› pass upon VERB

jest at

• *(TN 3.1.40) Cesario reacts to what Feste has just said: 'an' thou pass upon me, I'll no more with thee'.*

passado see RECREATION, p.170

passage NOUN

⚠ *Don't read the meaning of 'passageway' into these senses.*

as well as meaning 'passing by', you'll find:

1 occurrence

• *(RJ Prologue.9) The Prologue introduces the lovers and 'The fearful passage of their death-mark'd love'.*

2 line of descent

• *(H5 1.1.86) Canterbury says he has yet to tell Henry of the 'unhidden passages / Of his true titles to some certain dukedoms'.*

3 departure from life

• *(Ham 3.3.86) Hamlet decides not to kill Claudius 'When he is fit and season'd for his passage'—when he is forgiven for his sins and ready to die (unlike Hamlet's father).*

4 passers-by

• *(Oth 5.1.37) Cassio calls out for help: 'No watch? No passage?'*

5 combat

• *(H5 3.7.85) The Welsh Captain tells Henry that 'there is gallant and most prave passages' at the bridge—some splendid ('brave') fighting is going on.*

passing ADVERB

extremely

• *(MA 2.1.72) Leonato tells Beatrice that she grasps things 'passing shrewdly'.*

passion NOUN

as well as meaning 'very strong emotion', you'll find:

1 general emotional state

• *(JC 1.2.48) Cassius admits to Brutus: 'I have much mistook your passion'.*

2 torment

• *(TN 2.4.4) Orsino asks for a song which he says 'did relieve my passion much'.*

3 fit of anger

• *(Mac 3.4.57) Lady Macbeth asks the nobles to*

a b c d e f g h i j k l m n o Pp q r s t u v w x y z

ignore Macbeth's behaviour, otherwise 'You shall offend him and extend his passion'.
4 emotional outburst
• *(MND 5.1.301) Theseus says of Thisbe, 'her passion ends the play'.*

passion VERB
experience deep feeling
• *(Tem 5.1.24) Prospero says he is capable of being moved in the same way as his enemies—'Passion as they'.*

passy-measures pavin
dance (a pavane) with a slow pace
• *(TN 5.1.193) Sir Toby calls the surgeon 'a rogue, and a passy-measures pavin', with a pun on 'past measure' (beyond all proportion)—his slowness is beyond belief.*

paste NOUN
pastry
• *(KL 2.4.119) The Fool tells Lear of the squeamish woman who put eels 'i'th' paste alive'—to avoid having to kill them first.*

pastry NOUN
pastry-making part of a kitchen
• *(RJ 4.4.2) The Nurse says they are calling 'for dates and quinces in the pastry'.*

pasture NOUN
upbringing
• *(H5 3.1.27) Henry asks his soldiers to 'show us here / The mettle of your pasture'—the quality of your breeding.*

pat ADVERB
1 opportunely
• *(Ham 3.3.73) Hamlet sees a chance to kill Claudius: 'Now might I do it pat'.*
2 very timely
• *(MND 3.1.2) Quince replies to Bottom's 'Are we all met?' with 'Pat, pat'.*
3 exactly
• *(MND 5.1.182) Bottom tells Theseus of the play's outcome: 'it will fall pat as I told you'.*

patch NOUN
fool
• *(MV 2.5.44) Shylock criticizes Lancelot: 'The patch is kind enough, but a huge feeder'—he's a pleasant enough fool, but he eats a lot.*

› **patched** ADJECTIVE
wearing a patchwork costume (like a jester)
• *(MND 4.1.207) Bottom reflects: 'man is but a patched fool'.*

paten NOUN
shining circle
• *(MV 5.1.59) Lorenzo describes the night sky as 'thick inlaid with patens of bright gold'.*

patent NOUN
1 right
• *(MND 1.1.80) Hermia says she would rather be a nun than 'yield my virgin patent up' to Demetrius.*
2 formal permission
• *(Oth 4.1.193) Iago suggests to Othello that he give Desdemona 'patent to offend'.*

path VERB
go on one's way
• *(JC 2.1.83) Brutus says if the conspiracy went on its way showing its real face—'if thou path, thy native semblance on'—nothing could prevent its discovery.*

patience NOUN
⚠ *Don't read the meaning of 'waiting calmly for a long time' into these senses.*
1 permission
• *(Ham 3.2.103) Rosencrantz tells Hamlet that the players 'stay upon your patience'—are waiting for your permission to enter.*
2 composure
• *(KL 4.3.16) A Gentleman describes how Cordelia received Kent's letters: 'Patience and sorrow strove / Who should express her goodliest'.*

› **patient** ADJECTIVE
serene
• *(KL 4.6.80) Edgar tells Gloucester to 'Bear free and patient thoughts'.*

› **patiently** ADVERB
with fortitude
• *(KL 4.6.36) Gloucester tells the gods that he will renounce the world and 'Shake patiently my great affliction off'—kill himself.*

Patrick, Saint
Irish saint of the 5th century, believed to be a guardian of purgatory (from where Hamlet's father's Ghost comes)
• *(Ham 1.5.142) Hamlet, having spoken to the Ghost, swears 'by Saint Patrick' that there has been an offence.*

patrimony NOUN
estate
• *(KL 5.3.76) Regan offers Edmund her 'soldiers, prisoners, patrimony'.*

pauser NOUN
delayer
• *(Mac 2.3.107) Macbeth says he killed the grooms because his 'violent love / Outran the pauser, reason'.*
✒ *There is a comma in the First Folio. Some editions omit the comma, turning 'pauser' into an adjective meaning 'prompting a pause'.*

pavin see **passy-measures pavin**

⚠ *warning note* ✒ *usage note* 🎭 *theatre note*

a b c d e f g h i j k l m n o Pp q r s t u v w x y z

pawn NOUN
pledge
• *(KL 1.1.154) Kent tells Lear that he held his life only as 'a pawn / To wage against thine enemies'—with a pun on the chess piece, often used as a sacrifice to save the king.*

pawn or **pawn down** VERB
pledge
• *(MV 3.5.73) Jessica says if the gods were to bet on two women, and Portia were one, 'there must be something else / Pawn'd with the other', for she has no equal.*

pax NOUN
a religious tablet, usually made of a precious metal, used during a Catholic Mass
• *(H5 3.7.38) Pistol reports that Bardolph 'hath stolen a pax'.*

pay VERB
as well as meaning 'give money', you'll find:
1 repay (something other than money)
• *(Tem 5.1.70) Prospero promises Gonzalo to 'pay thy graces home'—repay his favours in full.*
2 pay back (something other than money)
• *(TN 3.4.254) Sir Toby describes Sir Andrew's fencing riposte: 'he pays you as surely as your feet hits the ground'.*

peace see ATTENTION SIGNALS, p.23

peak VERB
1 mope about
• *(Ham 2.2.554) Hamlet reflects on how he can only 'peak / Like John-a-dreams'.*
2 waste away
• *(Mac 1.3.22) The First Witch says her charms will make a sailor 'dwindle, peak, and pine'.*

peascod NOUN
pea-plant
• *(TN 1.5.147) Malvolio compares Cesario's age to an unripe pea-pod 'before 'tis a peascod'.*

peck NOUN
heap
• *(MND 4.1.31) Bottom asks for 'a peck of provender'—a bundle of hay.*
A peck was a measure of quantity equivalent to about 9 litres today. Bottom is evidently quite hungry.

peculiar ADJECTIVE
⚠ *Don't read in the meaning of 'strange' or 'odd'.*
personal
• *(Oth 1.1.61) Iago says he follows (works for) Othello 'for my peculiar end'.*

pedant NOUN
⚠ *Don't read in the meaning of 'someone who insists on strictly keeping to rules'.*
schoolmaster
• *(TN 3.2.68) Maria describes Malvolio's cross-gartering as 'like a pedant that keeps a school i' th' church'.*

peer VERB
appear
• *(H5 4.7.79) Henry wonders why French horsemen still 'peer / And gallop o'er the field'.*

› **overpeer** VERB
1 look down on
• *(MV 1.1.12) A friend compliments Antonio on his large ships, which 'overpeer the petty traffickers / That curtsy to them'.*
2 rise above
• *(Ham 4.5.98) A Messenger compares the arrival of Laertes to 'The ocean, overpeering of his list'—rising above its limits.*

peevish ADJECTIVE
as well as meaning 'irritable', you'll find:
1 foolish
• *(JC 5.1.61) Cassius describes Octavius as 'A peevish schoolboy'.*
2 obstinate
• *(Ham 1.2.100) Claudius criticizes Hamlet's continued mourning for his father as 'peevish opposition' to the law of nature, where death is inevitable.*

peg NOUN
the pin on a stringed instrument to which the strings are fastened
• *(Oth 2.1.193) Othello has used musical terms to describe his love for Desdemona, and Iago continues the same theme: 'I'll set down the pegs that make this music'.*

Peg-a-Ramsey NOUN
the name of a spying wife in a contemporary ballad
• *(TN 2.3.67) Sir Toby calls Malvolio 'a Peg-a-Ramsey'.*

Pegasus NOUN [pronounced **peg**-a-sus]
in Greek mythology, the winged horse who brought thunder and lightning from Mount Olympus
• *(H5 3.8.14) Bourbon describes his horse as 'the Pegasus' with nostrils of fire.*

peise also spelled **peize** VERB [pronounced payz]
prolong
• *(MV 3.2.22) Portia apologizes to Bassanio for speaking too long, 'but 'tis to peize the time'*

that she can have with him before he makes his choice.

Pelion NOUN [pronounced **peel**-ee-on]
in Greek mythology, a high mountain in northern Greece, where the giants fought the gods
• *(Ham 5.1.237) Laertes asks for the burial mound above Ophelia's grave to be so high that it would 'o'ertop old Pelion'.*

pelting ADJECTIVE
paltry
• *(MND 2.1.91) Titania describes how 'every pelting river' has flooded, because of her quarrel with Oberon.*

pencil NOUN
⚠*Don't read in the meaning of a 'lead pencil'.*
a finely pointed paint-brush
• *(RJ 1.2.40) The Servant mixes up his professions, saying that a fisherman should meddle 'with his pencil and the painter with his nets'.*

pennon NOUN
banner
• *(H5 3.6.49) The French King describes Henry's progress in France 'With pennons painted in the blood of Harfleur'.*

pennyworth also spelled **penny-worth, penn'orth** NOUN
1 small amount
• *(MV 1.2.66) Portia says she has 'a poor penny-worth in the English'—a very small amount.*
2 bargain
• *(MA 2.3.42) Claudio says, of Benedick hiding himself, that they will 'fit the hid fox with a pennyworth'—pay him well (by mocking him) for being out of sight so craftily.*

pensioner NOUN
a gentleman of the royal bodyguard
• *(MND 2.1.10) A Fairy says, of Titania, 'The cowslips tall her pensioners be'.*

pensive ADJECTIVE
sorrowfully thoughtful
• *(RJ 4.1.39) The Friar calls Juliet a 'pensive daughter'.*

Pentecost NOUN
in the Christian calendar, the feast celebrating the descent of the Holy Spirit on the apostles—a time of festivals of renewal
• *(RJ 1.5.35) Capulet says it's been twenty-five years since he last wore a mask at a party, 'Come Pentecost as quickly as it will'—referring to the feast-day as we might say 'It'll be summer again before you know it'.*

Penthesilea NOUN
[pronounced penth-eh-si-**lay**-a]
in Greek mythology, an Amazonian queen who helped King Priam at Troy
• *(TN 2.3.160) Sir Toby calls Maria 'Penthesilea' for thinking up her plan to fool Malvolio.*

penthouse also spelled **pent-house** NOUN
⚠*Don't read the modern meaning of 'an apartment at the top of a building' into these senses.*
overhanging roof
• *(MA 3.3.96) Borachio tells Conrad to stand near him 'under this penthouse'.*

penthouse ADJECTIVE
like an overhanging roof
• *(Mac 1.3.19) The First Witch says her charms will affect a sailor so that sleep will not 'Hang upon his penthouse lid'—he won't be able to close his eyes.*

peradventure ADVERB
perhaps
• *(H5 4.1.153) Henry reflects on men dying in a battle: 'Some, peradventure, have on them the guilt of premeditated and contrived murder'.*

perchance ADVERB
1 perhaps
• *(TN 1.2.5) Viola asks the Captain about Sebastian: 'Perchance he is not drown'd'—and see sense 2.*
2 by good fortune
• *(TN 1.2.6) The Captain replies to Viola: 'It is perchance that you yourself were sav'd'.*

perdition NOUN
1 ruins
• *(Tem 3.3.77) Ariel threatens Alonso and the others with 'Ling'ring perdition'.*
2 loss
• *(Ham 5.2.110) Hamlet compliments Osric on the way he has described Laertes: 'his definement suffers no perdition in you'.*

perdu NOUN [pronounced per-**doo**]
sentry exposed to danger
• *(KL 4.7.35) Cordelia describes Lear on the heath as a 'poor perdu!'*

perdurable ADJECTIVE
[pronounced **per**-dyoo-rabble]
everlasting

• *(H5 4.5.8) Bourbon calls the French defeat a 'perdurable shame'.*

perdy see SWEARING, p.298

peremptory ADJECTIVE
⚠ *Don't read in the meaning of 'dictatorial' here—which would hardly be appropriate, especially as the French have been defeated.*
resolved
• *(H5 5.2.82) The French King promises to send Henry his 'peremptory answer'.*

perfect ADJECTIVE
as well as meaning 'complete' and 'flawless', you'll find:
1 innocent
• *(Oth 1.2.31) Othello says his 'perfect soul' will show him to be in the right.*
2 mature
• *(KL 1.2.68) Edmund reports Edgar's views on 'sons at perfect age, and fathers declin'd'.*
3 well aware
• *(Mac 4.2.63) A Messenger tells Lady Macduff: 'in your state of honour I am perfect'.*

perfect VERB
inform fully
• *(Tem 1.2.79) Prospero tells Miranda what happened when Antonio was 'once perfected how to grant suits'.*

perforce ADVERB
1 by force
• *(MND 2.1.26) Puck says that Titania 'perforce withholds the loved boy'—the changeling—from Oberon.*
2 of necessity
• *(KL 1.4.288) Lear regrets the 'hot tears, which break from me perforce'.*

perfumer NOUN
someone employed to make rooms smell sweetly
• *(MA 1.3.50) Borachio says he overheard a conversation when he was hired 'for a perfumer'.*

Perigenia NOUN [pronounced pe-ri-**jean**-ee-a]
in Greek mythology, one of the women abducted (and then deserted) by Theseus
• *(MND 2.1.78) Oberon reminds Titania of how she led Theseus away 'From Perigenia, whom he ravished'—raped.*

peril in the phrase **at peril**
at risk of death
• *(KL 3.7.50) Regan tells Gloucester that he had been 'charg'd at peril'.*

period NOUN
1 conclusion
• *(Oth 5.2.353) Lodovico reacts to Othello's suicide: 'O bloody period!'*
2 pause
• *(MND 5.1.96) Theseus recalls clerks who 'Make periods in the midst of sentences'.*
3 goal
• *(KL 4.7.95) Kent reflects that after the battle his 'point and period will be throughly wrought'—his purpose in life will be complete.*

periwig-pated ADJECTIVE
wearing a wig
• *(Ham 3.2.9) Hamlet says it offends him to hear 'a robustious periwig-pated fellow' shouting on stage.*

perpend VERB
consider
• *(H5 4.4.6) Pistol tells a French prisoner to 'Perpend my words'.*

Perseus NOUN [pronounced **per**-see-us]
in Greek mythology, the son of Zeus, whose killing of the Gorgon released the winged horse, Pegasus
• *(H5 3.8.19) Bourbon describes his horse as being 'a beast for Perseus'.*

person NOUN
physical appearance
• *(MND 4.2.9) Quince says Bottom has 'the best person' to play Pyramus.*

personage NOUN
appearance
• *(TN 1.5.145) Olivia asks about Cesario: 'Of what personage and years is he?'*

personate VERB
⚠ *Don't read in the meaning of 'impersonate'.*
describe
• *(TN 2.3.143) Maria says Malvolio 'shall find himself most feelingly personated' in the letter she will write.*

perspectively ADVERB
as if through an optical instrument
• *(H5 5.2.303) The French king describes how Henry sees the unentered walls of his cities: 'you see them perspectively, the cities turned into a maid'—with maiden walls that war has never entered.*

persuade VERB
1 urge
• *(Ham 4.5.166) Laertes says he is more moved by*

seeing Ophelia as she is than if she had her wits 'and didst persuade revenge'.
2 plead
• *(MV 3.2.279) Salarino says, of Shylock, that leading nobles 'have all persuaded with him'.*

› **persuasion** NOUN
conviction
• *(MND 1.1.156) Lysander accepts Hermia's argument for patience: 'A good persuasion'.*

pert ADJECTIVE
⚠ *Don't read meanings to do with 'being cheeky' or 'well-shaped' into these senses.*
lively
• *(MND 1.1.13) Theseus tells Philostrate to 'Awake the pert and nimble spirit of mirth'.*

› **pertly** ADVERB
quickly
• *(Tem 4.1.58) Prospero tells Ariel: 'Appear, and pertly!'*

pestered ADJECTIVE
⚠ *Don't read in a meaning to do with 'annoying'.*
afflicted
• *(Mac 5.2.23) Menteith describes the effect of Macbeth's 'pester'd senses'.*

petar also spelled **petard** NOUN
explosive
• *(Ham 3.4.209) Hamlet finds it amusing 'to have the enginer / Hoist with his own petard'—see the plotter's plots blow up in his face.*
✒ *This line is not in all editions of 'Hamlet', as it appears in the Second Quarto text of the play, but not the First Folio.*

Peter, Saint
in Christian tradition, the keeper of the gates of heaven
• *(MA 2.1.41) Beatrice says that after visiting hell she will 'away to Saint Peter fore the heavens'.*

Petrarch NOUN [pronounced **pet**-rark]
Italian poet of the 14th century, a major influence on later love poetry
• *(RJ 2.4.38) Mercutio mocks Romeo's romantic state: 'Now is he for the numbers that Petrarch flowed in'—the sonnets that Petrarch wrote so fluently.*

Phaëton NOUN [pronounced **fa**-ee-ton]
in Greek mythology, the son of the sun-god, who borrowed his father's chariot (but was unable to control it)
• *(RJ 3.2.3) Juliet, as if addressing the sun-god's horses, thinks a charioteer such as 'Phaëton would whip you to the west', making night come more quickly.*

phantasime see **fantastico**

phantasma NOUN [pronounced fan-**taz**-ma]
nightmare
• *(JC 2.1.65) Brutus describes the time between having a dreadful thought and acting it out as 'a phantasma or a hideous dream'.*

Pharamond NOUN [pronounced **fa**-ra-mond]
a legendary king of the Franks in the 5th century
• *(H5 1.2.37) Canterbury cites 'from Pharamond' the French objection to Henry's claim to France.*

Pharaoh NOUN [pronounced **fair**-oh]
a king in ancient Egypt—especially the biblical king whose soldiers fatally pursued the Israelites into the Red Sea
• *(MA 3.3.124) Borachio talks of fashions like those of 'Pharaoh's soldiers' that he has seen portrayed.*

Phibbus see **Phoebus**

Philemon NOUN [pronounced fie-**lee**-mon]
in Roman mythology, a peasant who entertained the gods when they visited the Earth to test people's hospitality
• *(MA 2.1.87) Masked Don Pedro describes himself to Hero: 'My visor is Philemon's roof'—inside the mask there is a god.*

Philippi NOUN [pronounced **fi**-li-pie]
a battle site in north-east Greece, where Antony defeated Brutus and Cassius in 42 BC
• *(JC 4.3.170) Brutus learns that his enemy's army is marching 'toward Philippi'.* see **MAP, p.176**

Phillida NOUN [pronounced **fi**-li-da]
in pastoral poetry, the traditional name given to the beloved of a love-sick shepherd
• *(MND 2.1.68) Titania reminds Oberon of when he assumed the shape of Corin 'versing love / To amorous Phillida'.*

Philomel NOUN [pronounced **fil**-o-mel]
in Greek mythology, a princess of Athens who was turned into a nightingale (the bird of the night with beautiful song) by the gods
• *(MND 2.2.13) A Fairy sings Titania to sleep: 'Philomel with melody'.*

philosopher NOUN
sage
• *(KL 3.4.165) Lear addresses Poor Tom as 'Noble philosopher'.*

› **philosophy** NOUN
science (known as 'natural philosophy')
• *(Ham 2.2.357) Hamlet puzzles over changes in popular attitude: 'there is something in this more than natural, if philosophy could find it out'.*

phlegm (a type of humour) see **HUMOURS, p.137**

Phoebe NOUN [pronounced **fee**-bee]
in Greek mythology, one of the names for the goddess of the Moon
• *(MND 1.1.209) Lysander tells Hermia they will leave Athens 'when Phoebe doth behold / Her silver visage in the watery glass'—when they see the Moon reflected in water.*

Phoebus NOUN [pronounced **fee**-bus]
in Greek mythology, the sun-god (Phoebus Apollo)
• *(H5 4.1.261) Henry reflects on the worker who 'Sweats in the eye of Phoebus'—in the heat of the sun.*
• *(MND 1.2.29) Bottom calls the sun-god's chariot 'Phibbus' car'—the spelling suggests a mispronunciation.*

Phrygia NOUN [pronounced **fri**-jee-a]
a region of Asia Minor where the city of Troy was situated
• *(TN 3.1.49) Feste imagines himself playing 'Lord Pandarus of Phrygia'.*
see **MAP, p.176**

physic NOUN
medicine
• *(TN 2.3.155) Maria assures Sir Toby about her plan for Malvolio: 'I know my physic will work with him'.*

physic VERB
cure
• *(Mac 2.3.47) Macbeth tells Macduff: 'The labour we delight in physics pain'—the work we enjoy cures us of any suffering we might feel while doing it.*

> **physical** ADJECTIVE
medicinal
• *(JC 2.1.261) Portia asks Brutus if it is 'physical / To walk unbraced'—with clothes not laced up.*

pia mater NOUN [pronounced **pee**-a **mah**-ter]
brain—the Latin name of the membrane that covers the brain
• *(TN 1.5.106) Feste says that Sir Toby 'has a most weak pia mater'.*

picked ADJECTIVE
1 over-refined
• *(Ham 5.1.128) Hamlet thinks 'the age is grown so picked'.*
2 specially chosen
• *(Tem 5.1.247) Prospero assures Alonso that he will tell his whole story 'At pick'd leisure'—in spare time set aside for the purpose.*

pickers and stealers
fingers and hands
• *(Ham 3.2.321) Hamlet swears 'by these pickers and stealers' that he is still friends with Rosencrantz.*
In the Catechism of the Book of Common Prayer, people pray to keep their hands 'from picking and stealing'.

piece NOUN
as well as meaning a 'part' of something, you'll find:
1 masterpiece
• *(Ham 2.2.299) Hamlet reflects: 'What piece of work is a man'.*
2 model
• *(Tem 1.2.56) Prospero tells Miranda that her mother 'was a piece of virtue'.*

piece VERB
add
• *(KL 1.1.198) Lear says Burgundy can have Cordelia 'with our displeasure piec'd, / And nothing more'.*

> **piece out** VERB
increase
• *(KL 3.6.2) Gloucester tells Kent, of a place to stay, that he will 'piece out the comfort with what addition I can'.*

pied see **COLOURS, p.164**

pierce VERB
as well as meaning 'make a hole', you'll find:
1 move
• *(MV 4.1.126) Gratiano asks Shylock: 'Can no prayers pierce thee?'*
2 see
• *(Tem 2.1.237) Antonio tells Sebastian, about becoming King of Naples, that 'Ambition cannot pierce a wink beyond'—can't glimpse anything greater.*

pight ADJECTIVE
determined
• *(KL 2.1.64) Edmund tells Gloucester that he was unable to dissuade Edgar from planning to commit murder, finding him 'pight to do it'.*

Pigmies NOUN
a legendary race of dwarfs thought to live in the Far East
• *(MA 2.1.250) Benedick asks Don Pedro to send him on 'any embassage to the pigmies' rather than talk to Beatrice.*

pignut also spelled **pig-nut** NOUN
a type of earth chestnut
• *(Tem 2.2.163) Caliban promises Stephano to 'dig thee pig-nuts'.*

Doublet and Hose

see CLOTHING, p158

a b c d e f g h i j k l m n o Pp q r s t u v w x y z

Pigrogromitus NOUN
[pronounced pig-roh-**grom**-i-tus]
an invented scholarly name (either made up by Feste or misremembered by Sir Andrew)
• *(TN 2.3.21) Sir Andrew recalls Feste's story 'of Pigrogromitus'.*

pike NOUN
1 spear: see **SWORDS AND DAGGERS, p.156**
2 central spike in a buckler (a small shield)
• *(MA 5.2.18) Benedick jests with Margaret about a shield: 'you must put in the pikes with a vice'—a screw.*

pilcher NOUN
pilchard
• *(TN 3.1.32) Feste observes that 'fools are as like husbands as pilchers are to herrings'.*
'Pilchers' is the word in the First Folio. Some editions replace this with 'pilchards'.

pilcher see **SWORDS AND DAGGERS, p.156**

pill VERB
peel (bark from a stick)
• *(MV 1.3.79) Shylock tells a biblical story in which 'The skilful shepherd pill'd me certain wands'—thin strips of wood.*

pillicock NOUN
a slang name for 'penis'
• *(KL 3.4.73) Poor Tom sings about 'Pillicock sat on Pillicock Hill'.*

pin NOUN
the peg at the centre of an archery target
• *(RJ 2.4.15) Mercutio says, of Romeo, that love has hit 'the very pin of his heart'.*

> **pin's fee**
> the value of a trifle
> • *(Ham 1.4.65) Hamlet tells Horatio and Marcellus: 'I do not set my life at a pin's fee'.*

See also **web and pin**

pinch NOUN
as well as meaning 'squeezing with a finger and thumb' and 'hardship', you'll find:
1 pang
• *(Tem 5.1.77) Prospero describes Sebastian's 'inward pinches' as very strong.*
2 tiny bite
• *(Tem 4.1.231) Caliban says Prospero 'will fill our skins with pinches'.*

pinch VERB
torment
• *(Tem 5.1.276) Caliban thinks he will be 'pinch'd to death!'*

> **pinch-spotted** ADJECTIVE
> discoloured with pinch-marks
> • *(Tem 4.1.258) Prospero tells Ariel to make Caliban and the others 'more pinch-spotted' than a leopard.*

pinfold NOUN
a pen for holding stray animals
• *(KL 2.2.8) Kent threatens to have Oswald 'in Lipsbury pinfold'—trapped between his teeth.*

pioned and twilled [pronounced **pee**-und]
channelled and woven
• *(Tem 4.1.64) Iris describes meadow banks 'with pioned and twilled brims'—with edges channelled and protected by a network of woven sticks.*
No other example of these words is known from the time, so the suggested meanings are tentative.

pioner also spelled **pioneer** NOUN
[pronounced pie-uh-**neer**]
⚠ *Don't read in the meaning of 'the first person to do something'.*
1 labouring foot-soldier
• *(Oth 3.3.347) Othello tells Iago: 'I had been happy if the general camp, / Pioners and all, had tasted her sweet body / So I had nothing known'—I wouldn't mind the whole camp, including the lowest soldiers, having sex with her, as long as I didn't know of it.*
2 miner
• *(Ham 1.5.171) Hamlet describes the Ghost, under the ground, as 'A worthy pioner!'*

pipe NOUN
voice
• *(TN 1.4.32) Orsino describes Cesario's 'small pipe'—his high-pitched voice—as like a woman's.*

pish see **EXCLAMATIONS, p.99**

pit NOUN
hole prepared to trap hunted animals
• *(JC 5.5.23) Brutus tells Volumnius: 'Our enemies have beat us to the pit'.*

pitch NOUN
1 height (to which a bird of prey soars before swooping)
• *(RJ 1.4.21) Romeo regrets he 'cannot bound a pitch above dull woe'.*
2 high aspiration
• *(Ham 3.1.86) Hamlet reflects about 'enterprises of great pitch and moment'.*
'Pitch' is a Second Quarto text reading from 'Hamlet'. In the First Folio, the word is 'pith', meaning 'importance'.

> **pitch and pay**
> pay as you go
> • *(H5 2.3.43) Pistol advises his wife how to look after things while he is away: 'the word is, pitch and pay'—give no credit.*

piteous ADJECTIVE
⚠ *Don't read in the meaning of 'deserving pity'.*
full of pity
• *(Tem 1.2.14) Prospero assures Miranda about the wreck: 'Tell your piteous heart / There's no harm done'.*

pitfall NOUN
a kind of bird-trap–a trapdoor that covers a hole in the ground
• *(Mac 4.2.35) Lady Macduff calls her son a bird who has never feared 'the net, nor lime, the pitfall, nor the gin'–different ways of catching birds.*

pith NOUN
1 strength
• *(Oth 1.3.83) Othello says his arms have been used with 'seven years' pith' in fighting.*
2 importance
see **pitch**

pitiful ADJECTIVE
⚠ *Don't read in the meaning of 'pathetic'.*
full of pity
• *(JC 3.1.169) Brutus tells Antony that the hearts of the conspirators 'are pitiful'.*

placket NOUN
opening in the front of a skirt or petticoat
• *(KL 3.4.93) Poor Tom advises: 'keep thy foot out of brothels, thy hand out of plackets'.*

plague NOUN
as well as meaning a disease, you'll find:
calamity
• *(KL 4.1.46) Gloucester reflects that it is 'the times' plague, when madmen lead the blind'.*

plain VERB
lament
• *(KL 3.1.39) Kent asks a Gentleman to report to Cordelia how 'The King hath cause to plain'.*

plainness NOUN
plain-speaking
• *(KL 1.1.147) Kent tells Lear: 'To plainness honour's bound, / When majesty falls to folly'–honour can rely on plain-speaking only, when the monarchy descends into madness.*

plainsong also spelled **plain-song** ADJECTIVE
lacking ornament
• *(MND 3.1.115) Bottom sings to himself: 'The plainsong cuckoo grey'.*

plainsong also spelled **plain-song** NOUN
plain truth
• *(H5 3.2.4) Nym says the fighting is too hot, 'that is the very plain-song of it'.*

Plantagenet NOUN
[pronounced plan-**taj**-a-net]
the family name of English kings between 1154 and 1485
• *(H5 5.2.230) Henry tells Katherine that 'Henry Plantagenet is thine'.*

plantain NOUN
a type of medicinal plant with a broad leaf
• *(RJ 1.2.51) Romeo says a 'plantain leaf is excellent' for a scratched shin.*

plate NOUN
⚠ *Don't read in the meaning of a single plate.*
special tableware
• *(RJ 1.5.6) One Servingman tells another: 'look to the plate'.*

platform NOUN
⚠ *Don't read in the meaning of 'a raised area in a hall or railway station'.*
gun position on a castle rampart
• *(Ham 1.2.252) Hamlet says he will visit Horatio and the sentinels 'Upon the platform 'twixt eleven and twelve'.*

plausive ADJECTIVE
pleasing
• *(Ham 1.4.30) Hamlet describes a fault in some men that excessively corrupts 'The form of plausive manners'–the pattern of approved behaviour.*

Plautus NOUN [pronounced **plaw**-tus]
Roman comic playwright of the 2nd century BC
• *(Ham 2.2.390) Polonius describes what the players can perform: the tragedian 'Seneca cannot be too heavy, nor Plautus too light'.*

play VERB
as well as meanings to do with 'games', 'music', and 'acting', you'll find:
1 show
• *(Tem 1.2.209) Ariel says that everyone on the sinking ship 'play'd / Some tricks of desperation'–showed signs of despair.*
2 play for
• *(H5 4.Chorus.19) The Chorus says the French 'Do the low-rated English play at dice'–make bets about their likely losses.*
3 fence
• *(Ham 4.7.105) Claudius tells Laertes how much Hamlet, when he heard Laertes was returning, wanted 'Your sudden coming o'er to play with you'.*

pleached ADJECTIVE
with hedges made of interlaced branches
• *(MA 3.1.7) Hero asks Margaret to tell Beatrice to hide in 'the pleached bower' to overhear their conversation.*

a b c d e f g h i j k l m n o Pp q r s t u v w x y z

pleasance NOUN
pleasure
• *(Oth 2.3.272) Cassio regrets the way men turn into beasts 'with joy, pleasance, revel, and applause'.*

pleasant ADJECTIVE
as well as meaning 'pleasing', you'll find:
facetious
• *(H5 1.2.259) Henry says he is 'glad the Dauphin is so pleasant with us'.*

pleasure NOUN
as well as meaning 'enjoyment', you'll find:
1 wish
• *(JC 4.3.249) Varrus tells Brutus 'we will stand and watch your pleasure'—be here staying awake in case you want something.*
2 intention
• *(KL 5.1.4) Edmund asks an officer to go to Albany and 'bring his constant pleasure'—his definite intention.*
3 pleasure ground
• *(JC 3.2.247) Antony tells the people that Caesar has left them 'common pleasures, / To walk abroad and recreate yourselves'.*

pledge NOUN
toast (in drinking)
• *(Ham 1.4.12) Hamlet explains to Horatio that drums and trumpets sound when Claudius celebrates 'The triumph of his pledge'.*

pleurisy NOUN
⚠ *Don't read in the meaning of 'a lung disease'.*
excess
• *(Ham 4.7.117) Claudius advises Laertes that 'goodness, growing to a pleurisy, / Dies in his own too-much'.*

pliant ADJECTIVE
suitable
• *(Oth 1.3.150) Othello says he 'Took once a pliant hour' to talk to Desdemona.*

plight NOUN
⚠ *Don't read in the meaning of 'an unfortunate situation'.*
marriage-vow
• *(KL 1.1.100) Cordelia tells Lear that the lord 'whose hand must take my plight shall carry / Half my love with him.'*

› **plighted** ADJECTIVE
hidden
• *(KL 1.1.279) Cordelia tells her sisters that 'Time shall unfold what plighted cunning hides'.*

pluck VERB
draw down
• *(JC 2.1.73) Lucius says that the people with Cassius have their hats 'pluck'd about their ears'.*

› **pluck up** VERB
take hold
• *(MA 5.1.198) Don Pedro reflects: 'Pluck up, my heart, and be sad'—let me be serious.*

› **pluck upon** VERB
bring to ruin
• *(KL 4.2.85) Goneril reflects about Edmund being with Regan: 'May all the building in my fancy pluck / Upon my hateful life'—her life will be hateful because she will have lost everything she has dreamed of.*

Pluto NOUN
in Greek mythology, one of the names of the god of the underworld
• *(JC 4.3.102) Cassius assures Brutus that his heart is 'Dearer than Pluto's mine'—more precious than anything in a mine of valuable metal.*
Cassius says 'Pluto', who would have charge of the mines beneath the ground; but he might have meant to say another god, 'Plutus', the god of riches.

ply one's music
go one's own way
• *(Ham 2.1.72) Polonius tells Reynaldo, of Laertes: 'let him ply his music'.*

pocky ADJECTIVE
infected with smallpox (or some other disease)
• *(Ham 5.1.152) The First Gravedigger tells Hamlet: 'we have many pocky corses nowadays'.*

point NOUN
1 sword-point
• *(Mac 1.2.56) Ross reports Macbeth's fight with the Norwegian king, 'Point against point'.*
2 summit
• *(MND 2.2.125) Lysander says he has reached 'the point of human skill' in preferring Helena to Hermia.*
3 punctuation
• *(MND 5.1.118) Theseus says that Quince 'doth not stand upon points'—he ignores punctuation (but punning on points meaning 'trivialities').*
4 purpose
• *(KL 4.7.95) Kent reflects that after the battle his 'point and period will be throughly wrought'—his purpose in life will be complete.*

› **points** NOUN
lace (for attaching hose to a doublet)
• *(TN 1.5.20) Feste says he is 'resolved on two*

points'—he means 'matters', but Maria in the next line interprets him to mean 'laces'.

› **at point** or **at a point**
prepared (for battle)
• *(Ham 1.2.200) Horatio tells Hamlet that the Ghost was 'Armed at point exactly'.*

› **to point**
⚠*Don't read in the meaning of 'direct (with your finger)'.*
exactly
• *(Tem 1.2.194) Prospero asks Ariel if he has 'Perform'd to point the tempest'.*

› **point-device** also spelled **-devise** ADJECTIVE
to the last detail
• *(TN 2.5.151) Malvolio promises to follow the description in Olivia's letter: 'I will be point-device the very man'.*

poise NOUN
importance
• *(Oth 3.3.82) Desdemona tells Othello that when she has a request that will really test his love, 'It shall be full of poise'.*

poise VERB
balance
• *(RJ 1.2.97) Benvolio says Romeo saw Rosaline with no other woman near, so that all he saw was 'Herself pois'd with herself in either eye'—his eyes were filled only with Rosaline.*

Polack NOUN
Pole
• *(Ham 1.1.66) Horatio describes the way King Hamlet 'smote the sledded Polacks on the ice' —Polish soldiers fighting on sledges.*
This word is derived from 'Pollax', found in the First Folio and the First and Second Quarto texts. Some editions emend it to 'poleaxe', so that the phrase would mean 'a battle-axe made like a sledge-hammer'.

› **Polack** ADJECTIVE
Polish
• *(Ham 5.2.369) Horatio addresses Fortinbras, who has arrived at Elsinore 'from the Polack wars'.*

poleaxe see **Polack**

pole-clipped also spelled **-clipp'd, -clipt** ADJECTIVE
hedged in by poles
• *(Tem 4.1.68) Iris describes the places where Ceres walks: 'thy pole-clipt vineyard'.*
Some editions think that 'pole' is a spelling of 'poll', in which case the word would mean 'pruned short'.

policy NOUN
1 diplomacy
• *(TN 3.2.26) Fabian advises Sir Andrew he needs to attract Olivia 'by some laudable attempt, either of valour or policy'.*
2 intrigue
• *(H5 2.Chorus.14) The Chorus describes how the French are using 'pale policy' to change the English course of action—cowardly cunning.*

› **politic** ADJECTIVE
as well as meaning 'prudent', you'll find:
wily
• *(Ham 4.3.20) Hamlet says Polonius is being eaten by 'A certain convocation of politic worms'.*

› **politician** NOUN
⚠*Don't read in the meaning of 'someone professionally involved in politics'.*
schemer
• *(TN 2.3.67) Sir Toby describes himself and his friends as 'politicians'.*

poll NOUN
head
• *(Ham 4.5.192) Ophelia sings of her father: 'All flaxen was his poll'.*

poll-clipped see **pole-clipped**

ponderous ADJECTIVE
⚠*Don't read in the meaning of 'heavy and awkward'.*
substantial
• *(KL 1.1.77) Cordelia reflects that her love is 'More ponderous than my tongue'—greater than she can ever say.*

poniard see **SWORDS AND DAGGERS, p.156**

Pontic Sea
Black Sea
• *(Oth 3.3.454) Othello says his bloody thoughts race on like the fast current that flows out of 'the Pontic Sea'.* see **MAP, p.176**

poor-John NOUN
dried, salted fish—cheaply available
• *(Tem 2.2.26) Trinculo describes Caliban as 'not-of-the-newest poor-John'—he smells like poor-quality old fish.*

poppering also spelled **poperin, pop'rin** ADJECTIVE
a variety of pear—from Poperinghe in Belgium
• *(RJ 2.1.38) Mercutio wishes that Romeo was 'a pop'rin pear' (the shape of the pear allows a sexual pun on 'penis', reinforced by the name of this particular variety, which sounds like 'pop 'er in').*

poppy NOUN
opium
• *(Oth 3.3.331) Iago reflects that neither 'poppy nor mandragora' will help Othello sleep from now on.*

a b c d e f g h i j k l m n o **Pp** q r s t u v w x y z

POLITENESS

Asking for something

Today we would say 'please' or 'may I'.

prithee or **I prithee**
short form of 'pray thee/you', said to someone you know very well
• *(Ham 5.1.179) Hamlet asks Horatio for his views: 'Prithee, Horatio, tell me one thing.'*

pray you or **I pray you**
a rather more formal request
• *(MND 1.2.58) Snug hopes his part in the play is written out: 'Pray you, if it be, give it me.'*

beseech you or **I beseech you**
stronger in force, expressing a much greater need
• *(Oth 1.3.114) Othello asks the senators to send for Desdemona to support what he has said: 'I do beseech you / Send for the lady.'*

Permitting

Today we would say 'with your permission' or 'if you don't mind'.

please you
• *(Tem 1.2.65) Miranda asks Prospero to carry on with his story: 'Please you, farther.'*

by your patience
• *(TN 2.1.3) Sebastian politely refuses Antonio's request to accompany him: 'By your patience, no.'*

by your pardon
• *(JC 3.1.235) Brutus disagrees with what Cassius has said: 'By your pardon, / I will myself into the pulpit first.'*

by your leave
• *(Mac 1.6.32) Duncan offers Lady Macbeth a kiss of welcome before entering her house: 'By your leave, hostess.'*

by your favour
• *(KL 4.6.206) Edgar apologises to a Gentleman for bothering him with another question: 'But, by your favour, / How near's the other army?'*

Apologizing

Today we would say 'I beg your pardon' or 'I'm sorry'.

cry you mercy
• *(MA 1.2.22) Leonato apologizes to Balthasar for ignoring him: 'I cry you mercy, friend. Go you with me and I will use your skill.'*

Apologizing for saying something that might offend

Today we would say 'pardon my language'.

God save the mark
a phrase originally thought to be used by midwives at the birth of a baby with a birthmark
• *(RJ 3.2.53) The Nurse is embarrassed about referring to the wound on Tybalt's bare chest: 'I saw it with mine eyes / (God save the mark!), here on his manly breast.'*

God bless the mark
• *(MV 2.2.21) Lancelot is superstitious about using the word 'devil': 'I should stay with the Jew my master who—God bless the mark!—is a kind of devil.'*

save your reverence
with all due respect to holiness
• *(MV 2.2.23) Lancelot is even more superstitious about mentioning the real devil: 'I should be ruled by the fiend who—saving your reverence—is the devil himself.'*

Thanking

Today we would say 'thank you (very much)' or '(many) thanks'.

God dild/'ild you
a way of writing 'God yield you', meaning 'God reward you'
• *(Ham 4.5.42) Claudius asks Ophelia how she is, and she replies: 'Well, God dild you.'*
'God' is in the First Folio; the Second Quarto text has 'good'.

God-a-mercy
a way of saying 'God have mercy'
• *(H5 4.1.34) Henry thanks Erpingham for wishing him heaven's blessing: 'God a mercy, old heart, thou speak'st cheerfully.'*

gramercy
from the Old French words *grant merci*, meaning 'great thanks'
• *(MV 2.2.112) Bassanio thanks old Gobbo for greeting him with the very respectful 'God bless your worship!': 'Gramercy; wouldst thou aught with me?'*

popular ADJECTIVE
of the common people
• *(H5 4.1.38) Pistol asks disguised King Henry: 'art thou officer, or art thou base, common, and popular?'—of low rank.*

› **popularity** NOUN
⚠ *Don't read the meaning of 'liked by people' into these senses.*
common people
• *(H5 1.1.59) Canterbury describes how Henry frequented 'open haunts and popularity'.*

poring ADJECTIVE
eye-straining
• *(H5 4.Chorus.2) The Chorus describes a time when 'the poring dark' is everywhere.*

porpentine NOUN
porcupine
• *(Ham 1.5.20) The Ghost says Hamlet's hair would stand on end 'Like quills upon the fretful porpentine'.*

porridge NOUN
meat and vegetable broth
• *(KL 3.4.54) Poor Tom says that the fiend has 'set ratsbane by his porridge'—rat poison, prompting him to kill himself.*

port NOUN
1 gateway or seaport
• *(KL 2.1.79) Gloucester says Edgar will not escape: 'All ports I'll bar'.*
2 bearing
• *(H5 Prologue.6) The Chorus describes Henry taking on 'the port of Mars'—the appearance of the god of war.*
3 rank
• *(MV 3.2.279) Salarino says that nobles 'Of greatest port' have argued with Shylock.*
4 style of living
• *(MV 1.1.124) Bassanio admits he has enjoyed 'a more swelling port' than he can afford.*

portable ADJECTIVE
⚠ *Don't read in the meaning of 'easy to carry around'.*
bearable
• *(KL 3.6.106) Edgar reflects 'How light and portable my pain seems now'.*

portage NOUN
openings
• *(H5 3.1.10) Henry tells his soldiers to look fierce in their attack, letting their eyes 'pry through the portage of the head, / Like the brass cannon'—look out fiercely like cannons through portholes.*

portance NOUN
behaviour
• *(Oth 1.3.138) Othello recounts the stories he told Desdemona 'And portance in my travels' history' -in all the events of my travelling life.*
✒ *This is the word in the First Folio. Some editions replace 'portance in' by 'with it all' from the First Quarto text.*

Portia NOUN [pronounced **paw**-sha]
the wife of Brutus, one of the assassins of Julius Caesar
• *(MV 1.1.166) Bassanio says his Portia is no less worthy than 'Cato's daughter, Brutus' Portia'.*

portion NOUN
as well as meaning 'a piece or part of something', you'll find:
dowry
• *(KL 1.1.241) Burgundy requests from Lear: 'that portion which yourself propos'd'.*

portly ADJECTIVE
⚠ *Don't read in the meaning of 'rather fat'.*
stately
• *(RJ 1.5.65) Capulet describes Romeo as 'a portly gentleman'.*

position NOUN
as well as meaning 'place' and 'arrangement', you'll find:
deliberate statement
• *(Oth 3.3.236) Iago, after talking about human nature in general, says he is not thinking of Desdemona specifically: 'I do not in position / Distinctly speak of her'.*

possess VERB
1 inform
• *(MV 4.1.35) Shylock tells the Duke: 'I have possess'd your grace of what I purpose'.*
2 fill
• *(RJ 5.1.10) Romeo reflects: 'how sweet is love itself possess'd'—love is filled with so much sweetness.*

› **possessed** ADJECTIVE
propertied
• *(MND 1.1.100) Lysander argues that he is 'As well possess'd' as Demetrius—just as wealthy.*

› **unpossessing** ADJECTIVE
unable to inherit property
• *(KL 2.1.66) Edmund recounts how Edgar called him 'Thou unpossessing bastard!'*

posset NOUN
a hot drink made of milk, liquor, and spices
• *(Mac 2.2.6) Lady Macbeth says, of the king's attendants, 'I have drugg'd their possets'.*
› **posset** VERB
make clots
• *(Ham 1.5.68) The Ghost says the poison made his blood 'posset / And curd'.*

post NOUN
⚠ *Don't read the modern meaning of 'mail' into these senses. The 'post' is the person who carries a message, not the message itself.*
courier
• *(MV 5.1.46) Lancelot tells Lorenzo: 'there's a post come from my master'.*

post VERB
hasten
• *(KL 4.5.8) Regan says that Edmund 'is posted hence on serious matter'.*
› **in post**
in haste
• *(RJ 5.3.273) Balthasar tells the Prince about Romeo: 'in post he came from Mantua'.*
› **posthaste** also spelled **post-haste** NOUN
speed of preparation
• *(Ham 1.1.110) Horatio describes the 'post-haste and rummage' taking place in Denmark—furious activity and turmoil.*
› **post-post-haste** also spelled **post post-haste** ADVERB
with all possible speed
• *(Oth 1.3.46) The Duke instructs that a letter be sent, 'Post-post-haste dispatch'.*
› **poster** NOUN
fast traveller
• *(Mac 1.3.31) The Witches describe themselves as 'posters of the sea and land'.*
› **posthorse** also spelled **post-horse** NOUN
fast horse
• *(RJ 5.1.26) Romeo tells his servant: 'hire post-horses'.*

post NOUN
door-post
• *(TN 1.5.139) Malvolio tells Olivia that Cesario intends to 'stand at your door like a sheriff's post'.*

posture NOUN
nature
• *(JC 5.1.33) Cassius tells Antony that 'The posture of your blows are yet unknown'.*

posy NOUN
a short piece of poetry often inscribed inside a ring
• *(Ham 3.2.144) Hamlet, after hearing the Player's short prologue, asks: 'Is this a prologue, or the posy of a ring?'*

potation NOUN
drinking-bout
• *(Oth 2.3.47) Iago reflects that Roderigo 'hath tonight carous'd / Potations pottle-deep'—draining large tankards full of (alcoholic) drink.*

potent ADJECTIVE
as well as meaning 'powerful', you'll find:
accomplished
• *(Oth 2.3.68) Iago says the English 'are most potent in potting'—great drinkers.*
› **potential** ADJECTIVE
⚠ *Don't read in the meaning of 'possible'.*
powerful
• *(KL 2.1.75) Edmund describes a scenario in which he would have 'potential spirits' to seek Edgar's death—powerful motives.*

pothecary see **apothecary**

potion ADJECTIVE
as well as meaning a liquid that does good, you'll find:
poison
• *(MND 3.2.264) Lysander calls Hermia a 'hated potion'.*

potting NOUN
tippling
• *(Oth 2.3.68) Iago says the English 'are most potent in potting'—great drinkers.*

pottle-deep ADJECTIVE
to the bottom of a drinking-vessel that can hold half a gallon (4 pints / 2.3 litres)
• *(Oth 2.3.47) Iago reflects that Roderigo 'hath tonight carous'd / Potations pottle-deep'—draining large tankards in a great alcoholic drinking-bout.*

powder NOUN
gunpowder
• *(RJ 2.6.10) The Friar compares Romeo's passionate outburst to 'fire and powder, / Which as they kiss consume'.*

powdering tub also spelled **-tub** NOUN
a sweating-tub for the treatment of venereal disease
• *(H5 2.1.65) Pistol tells Nym to go to the hospital, where Doll Tearsheet is being treated in 'the powdering tub of infamy'.*

power NOUN
as well as meaning 'strength', 'authority', 'control', and 'ability', you'll find:
1 armed force (often used in the plural)
• *(JC 4.2.30) Stage direction: 'Enter Cassius and his powers'.*
2 gods (usually in the plural)
• *(Ham 3.1.141) Ophelia prays for Hamlet: 'Heavenly powers, restore him'.*

pox see SWEARING, p.298

practice NOUN
⚠ *Don't read the meaning of 'repeated action to improve ability' into these senses.*
as well as meaning 'the activity of doing something', you'll find:
1 scheme
• *(KL 1.2.172) Edmund reflects that it is easy to dupe Edgar, 'on whose foolish honesty / My practices ride easy!'*
2 trickery
• *(TN 5.1.340) Olivia sympathizes with Malvolio: 'This practice hath most shrewdly pass'd upon thee'—been very wickedly imposed on you.*
3 treachery
• *(Ham 4.7.138) Claudius advises Laertes to use 'a pass of practice' when fencing with Hamlet.*
4 carrying out (of a plot)
• *(MA 5.1.241) Borachio reveals, regarding the plot against Hero, that Don John paid him well 'for the practice of it'.*
5 profession
• *(TN 3.1.62) Viola admires Feste's jesting: 'This is a practice / As full of labour as a wise man's art'.*

› **practise on** or **upon** VERB
1 plot against
• *(H5 2.2.96) Henry asks Scroop: 'Wouldst thou have practis'd on me for thy use?'—for your own purposes.*
2 work upon
• *(MA 2.1.353) Don Pedro plans to 'practise on Benedick' to make him fall in love with Beatrice.*

praise VERB
as well as meaning 'saying that someone or something is very good', you'll find:
evaluate
• *(TN 1.5.229) Olivia lists her features and asks Cesario: 'Were you sent hither to praise me?'*

prank NOUN
⚠ *Don't read in the meaning of a 'mischievous joke'.*
outrageous deed
• *(Ham 3.4.2) Polonius says, of Hamlet: 'his pranks have been too broad to bear with'.*

prank VERB
dress up
• *(TN 2.4.84) Orsino says he is attracted by Olivia's beauty 'That nature pranks her in'.*

prate VERB
chatter
• *(Mac 2.1.58) Macbeth feels that 'The very stones prate of my whereabout'.*

› **prater** NOUN
chatterer
• *(H5 5.2.155) Henry tells Katherine: 'A speaker is but a prater'.*

› **prating** ADJECTIVE
chattering
• *(RJ 2.4.183) The Nurse talks of Juliet when she was 'a little prating thing'.*

precedent ADJECTIVE
previous
• *(Ham 3.4.98) Hamlet tells Gertrude that Claudius is not worth a twentieth 'Of your precedent lord'.*

precedent NOUN
instance
• *(KL 2.3.13) Edgar thinks of what he will do: 'The country gives me proof and precedent / Of Bedlam beggars'—he can imitate the behaviour of mad beggars in the countryside.*

preceptial ADJECTIVE
full of wise instructions
• *(MA 5.1.24) Leonato reflects on the situation when good counsel can give 'preceptial medicine to rage'.*

preciously ADVERB
profitably
• *(Tem 1.2.241) Prospero tells Ariel that the next few hours 'must by us both be spent most preciously'.*

precurse NOUN
forerunner
• *(Ham 1.1.124) Horatio recalls unnatural events in ancient Rome, and 'the like precurse of fear'd events' in Denmark.*

predestinate ADJECTIVE
predictable
• *(MA 1.1.122) Benedick is relieved to hear that Beatrice will not marry, as 'some gentleman or other shall scape a predestinate scratched face'.*

predominance NOUN
greater influence
• *(Mac 2.4.8) Ross wonders whether the darkness in daytime is due to 'night's predominance, or the day's shame'.*

a b c d e f g h i j k l m n o **Pp** q r s t u v w x y z

a b c d e f g h i j k l m n o Pp q r s t u v w x y z

prefer VERB
1 recommend
• *(MND 4.2.31) Bottom reports: 'our play is preferred'.*
2 offer
• *(Ham 4.7.159) Claudius says, of Hamlet, 'I'll have preferr'd him / A chalice'.*
'Preferred' is the word in the Second Quarto text. Some editions use the First Folio word 'prepar'd'.

› **preferment** NOUN
advancement
• *(KL 4.5.38) Regan tells Oswald that 'Preferment falls on him' who kills Gloucester.*

pregnant ADJECTIVE
Don't read the meaning of 'having a baby' into these senses.
1 ready to act
• *(Ham 3.2.59) Hamlet describes flatterers who 'crook the pregnant hinges of the knee'.*
2 obvious
• *(Oth 2.1.228) Iago says his point is 'a most pregnant and unforced position'.*
3 meaningful (yet obscure)
• *(Ham 2.2.206) Polonius reflects on Hamlet's answers: 'How pregnant sometimes his replies are'.*
4 wily
• *(TN 2.2.27) Viola describes her disguise as 'a wickedness / Wherein the pregnant enemy does much'—a means used by Satan (the Devil, known to be a master of disguise).*

› **unpregnant of**
unresponsive to
• *(Ham 2.2.554) Hamlet describes himself as a dreamer, 'unpregnant of my cause'—not stirred to action by his cause.*

premise NOUN
condition
• *(Tem 1.2.123) We hear how the King of Naples agreed to help Antonio get rid of Prospero in return for 'premises / Of homage'—in return for special honours (we're not told what they are).*

prenominate ADJECTIVE
aforesaid
• *(Ham 2.1.44) Polonius refers to 'the prenominate crimes' that Laertes might have committed.*

pre-ordinance see **ordinance**

preparation NOUN
force ready for war
• *(Oth 1.3.14) A Sailor reports that 'The Turkish preparation makes for Rhodes'.*

preposterous ADJECTIVE
Don't read meanings to do with being 'completely ridiculous' into these senses.
unnatural
• *(Oth 1.3.325) Iago tells Roderigo that reason is the force which stops people leaping 'to most preposterous conclusions'.*

› **preposterously** also spelled **prepost'rously** ADVERB
unnaturally
• *(MND 3.2.121) Puck says he is happiest when events 'befall prepost'rously'.*

prerogatived also spelled **prerogativ'd** ADJECTIVE
privileged
• *(Oth 3.3.276) Othello reflects that it is 'the plague of great ones, / Prerogativ'd are they less than the base'.*

presage VERB
1 signify
• *(MV 3.2.173) Portia tells Bassanio that giving away her ring will 'presage the ruin of your love'.*
2 predict
• *(RJ 5.1.2) Romeo reflects: 'My dreams presage some joyful news at hand'.*

presage NOUN
sign
• *(TN 3.2.59) Fabian says that Cesario shows in his face 'no great presage of cruelty'.*

prescience NOUN [pronounced **press**-ee-uns]
foreknowledge
• *(Tem 1.2.180) Prospero says his 'prescience' tells him of the star that controls his fortune.*

prescribe VERB
limit
• *(KL 1.2.24) Gloucester is amazed that Lear has 'prescrib'd his power'.*

› **prescript** NOUN
instruction
• *(Ham 2.2.142) Polonius explains how he gave 'prescripts' to Ophelia about dealing with Hamlet.*

› **prescript** ADJECTIVE
appropriate
• *(H5 3.8.43) Bourbon says bearing well is 'the prescript praise and perfection' of a good mistress.*

presence NOUN
as well as meaning 'the state of being present' and a person's 'impressive bearing', you'll find:
1 royal assembly
• *(Ham 5.2.212) Hamlet tells Laertes how 'This*

presence knows' of his madness (though not that the madness was feigned).
2 royal reception chamber
• *(RJ 5.3.86) Romeo says that Juliet's beauty 'makes / This vault a feasting presence full of light'.*

present NOUN
1 immediate moment
• *(JC 1.1.165) Brutus tells Cassius that he would rather not be further urged 'For this present'—he doesn't want to talk about it right now.*
2 available means
• *(TN 3.4.319) Cesario says he will help Sebastian as much as he can: 'I'll make division of my present with you'—what I have with me right now.*
› **this present**
just now
• *(TN 1.5.215) Olivia removes her veil, telling Cesario: 'such a one I was this present'.*
› **presently** ADVERB
⚠ *Look carefully at the context of what is being said, to whom, and why, to decide whether this word means 'right now' or 'after a short time'.*
as well as meaning 'soon', you'll find:
immediately
• *(MV 4.1.385) Antonio asks that Shylock 'presently become a Christian'.*

present VERB
represent
• *(MA 3.3.69) Dogberry tells one of the watch that he is 'to present the prince's own person'.*

presentment NOUN
depiction
• *(Ham 3.4.54) Hamlet asks Gertrude to look at two pictures, 'The counterfeit presentment of two brothers'.*

press-money NOUN
money paid to a recruit when conscripted
• *(KL 4.6.87) Lear talks to an imaginary recruit: 'There's your press-money'.*

pressure NOUN
impression
• *(Ham 1.5.100) Hamlet reflects that he will wipe away 'all pressures past' so that he can remember the Ghost well.*

prest ADJECTIVE
engaged
• *(MV 1.1.160) Antonio asks Bassanio to say what he must do 'And I am prest unto it'—ready to do it.*

Prester John
a legendary Christian king of Africa or Asia
• *(MA 2.1.248) Benedick asks Don Pedro to send him on an errand to 'bring you the length of Prester John's foot'—rather than talk to Beatrice.*

pretence NOUN
⚠ *Don't read meanings to do with 'behaving as if something is true while knowing it is not' into these senses.*
intention
• *(Mac 2.3.127) Banquo affirms he will fight 'Against the undivulg'd pretence'—the unrevealed purpose (behind acts of treason).*
› **pretend** VERB
intend
• *(Mac 2.4.24) Ross asks, of Duncan's attendants: 'What good could they pretend?'—what did they think they would gain from killing Duncan?*

pretty ADJECTIVE
1 ingenious
• *(H5 1.2.177) Exeter says the English have 'pretty traps' to catch invading Scots.*
2 impressive
• *(H5 4.6.28) Exeter admits he cried to see 'The pretty and sweet manner' of York's death.*
3 fine-looking
• *(KL 1.4.91) Lear addresses his Fool as a 'pretty knave!'*
🎭 *'Pretty' could be used for men as well as for women.*
› **prettily** ADVERB
ingeniously
• *(MND 2.2.59) Hermia says that 'Lysander riddles very prettily'.*

prevailment NOUN
influence
• *(MND 1.1.35) Egeus claims that Lysander has won Hermia by sending her gifts—'messengers / Of strong prevailment in unharden'd youth'—that greatly influence impressionable youngsters.*

prevent VERB
as well as meaning 'stop from happening', you'll find:
1 anticipate
• *(TN 3.1.80) Cesario is about to enter the house with Sir Toby to see Olivia when she arrives, causing him to say: 'we are prevented'.*
2 confuse
• *(KL 3.4.152) Poor Tom tells Lear that his study is 'How to prevent the fiend'.*

prey in the phrase **in prey**
in pursuit of prey
• *(H5 1.2.169) Ely describes England as an eagle 'being in prey' and leaving her nest unguarded.*

Priam NOUN [pronounced **pry**-am]
the King of Troy, killed by Pyrrhus during the Greek attack on Troy
• *(Ham 2.2.435) Hamlet recalls a speech where the narrator 'speaks of Priam's slaughter'.*

prick NOUN
1 spike
• *(KL 2.3.16) Edgar describes beggars who pierce their arms with 'wooden pricks'.*
2 spine
• *(Tem 2.2.12) Caliban fears the hedgehogs which 'mount / Their pricks at my footfall'.*

prick VERB
as well as meaning 'urge on' (as if by pricking someone), you'll find:
torment
• *(RJ 1.4.28) Mercutio tells Romeo to be rough with love: 'Prick love for pricking, and you beat love down' (with a sexual pun).*

› **prick down** or **prick** VERB
put on a list
• *(JC 4.1.3) Octavius says the brother of Lepidus must be added to the list of those who are to be killed: 'Prick him down'.*

prick-song also spelled **pricksong** NOUN
vocal music written down
• *(RJ 2.4.20) Mercutio describes Tybalt as someone who 'fights as you sing prick-song, keeps time, distance, and proportion'—someone who fights 'by the book', and doesn't improvise.*

pride NOUN
as well as meaning 'high opinion of oneself', you'll find:
1 pomp
• *(KL 2.4.182) Lear describes Oswald's 'easy-borrow'd pride' as undeserved, coming solely from Goneril.*
2 sexual desire
• *(Oth 3.3.405) Iago imagines Desdemona and Cassio 'As salt as wolves in pride'—as lecherous as wolves on heat.*

› **pride of place**
the highest point reached by a bird of prey before it swoops down
• *(Mac 2.4.12) An Old Man reports 'A falcon tow'ring in her pride of place'.*

primal ADJECTIVE
original
• *(Ham 3.3.37) Claudius reflects on his crime, which 'hath the primal eldest curse upon't—/ A brother's murder'—in the Bible, the first and earliest recorded crime—Cain killing his brother Abel.*

prime ADJECTIVE
as well as meaning 'chief', you'll find:
lecherous
• *(Oth 3.3.404) Iago imagines Cassio and Desdemona being 'as prime as goats'.*

› **primy** ADJECTIVE
at its most active
• *(Ham 1.3.7) Laertes describes Hamlet's love for Ophelia as 'A violet in the youth of primy nature'.*

princox NOUN
impertinent fellow
• *(RJ 1.5.85) Capulet calls Tybalt 'a princox'.*

prithee see **POLITENESS, p.230**

private NOUN
⚠ *Don't read the meaning of an 'army rank' into these senses.*
1 intimate friend
• *(Ham 2.2.231) Rosencrantz and Guildenstern describe their relationship to Fortune: 'her privates we'—with a pun on 'private parts'.*
2 ordinary person
• *(H5 4.1.226) Henry reflects: 'what have kings that privates have not too, / Save ceremony'.*
3 privacy
• *(TN 3.4.83) Malvolio tells Fabian: 'Let me enjoy my private'—my private time.*

› **privily** ADVERB
secretly
• *(KL 3.3.13) Gloucester says he will look for Lear and 'privily relieve him'.*

prived ADJECTIVE
bereaved
• *(H5 2.4.108) Exeter warns the French King of the consequences of war, such as 'the prived maiden's groans'.*

probable ADJECTIVE
⚠ *Don't read in the meaning of 'likely to be true'.*
provable
• *(Tem 5.1.249) Prospero tells Alonso that his account of the events 'shall seem probable' to him.*

probal ADJECTIVE [pronounced **proh**-bal]
reasonable
• *(Oth 2.3.316) Iago reflects that the advice he is giving Cassio is 'Probal to thinking'.*

probation NOUN
1 demonstration
• *(Ham 1.1.161) Horatio says the Ghost 'made*

probation' of the belief that spirits return to their prison at dawn.
2 investigation
• *(TN 2.5.121) Malvolio is puzzled by the way Olivia's letter seems inconsistent 'under probation'.*

proclaim VERB
officially declare to be an outlaw
• *(KL 2.3.1) Edgar says: 'I heard myself proclaim'd'.*

procreant ADJECTIVE
for the purposes of producing offspring
• *(Mac 1.6.8) Banquo describes where the martlet bird has made a nest with its hanging bed—'his pendent bed and procreant cradle'.*

procreant NOUN
person engaged in the act of having sex
• *(Oth 4.2.27) Othello instructs Emilia: 'Leave procreants alone and shut the door'.*

Procrus NOUN [pronounced **proh**-crus]
Bottom (as Pyramus) mispronounces 'Procris'—in Greek mythology a princess whose love for Cephalus ends in tragedy
• *(MND 5.1.194) Pyramus finds a comparison for his love to Thisbe: 'Not Shafalus to Procrus was so true'.*

prodigal ADJECTIVE
foolishly extravagant
• *(MV 2.5.15) Shylock accepts an invitation to supper, 'to feed upon / The prodigal Christian'.*

prodigal ADVERB
extravagantly
• *(Ham 1.3.116) Polonius warns Ophelia: 'When the blood burns, how prodigal the soul / Lends the tongue vows'—it's amazing what you find yourself promising when you feel passionately.*

prodigal NOUN
waster
• *(TN 1.3.22) Maria calls Sir Andrew 'a very fool, and a prodigal'.*

prodigious ADJECTIVE
⚠ *Don't read in the meaning of 'extremely impressive'.*
ominous
• *(MND 5.1.395) Theseus promises that the children of the Athenians will not have a 'mark prodigious'—a birthmark (thought in Shakespeare's time to be the mark of the devil).*

› **prodigy** NOUN
⚠ *Don't read in the meaning of 'young person with exceptional ability'.*
omen
• *(JC 2.1.198) Cassius worries that the strange events—'these apparent prodigies'—may keep Caesar at home.*

professed ADJECTIVE
with openly declared affection
• *(KL 1.1.271) Cordelia says to her sisters, of her father: 'To your professed bosoms I commit him'.*

› **profession** NOUN
solemn vow
• *(KL 5.3.129) Edgar claims the right to fight Edmund because of 'mine honours, / My oath, and my profession'.*

profit NOUN
1 self-improvement
• *(MV 2.5.45) Shylock complains that Lancelot is 'Snail-slow in profit'.*
2 furtherance
• *(Ham 2.2.24) Gertrude asks Rosencrantz and Guildenstern to stay at Elsinore 'For the supply and profit of our hope'.*

profit VERB
⚠ *Don't read the meaning of 'making money' into these senses.*
benefit
• *(Tem 1.2.313) Prospero tells Miranda that Caliban 'serves in offices / That profit us'.*

projection NOUN
plan
• *(H5 2.4.46) The Dauphin warns the French King to avoid 'a weak and niggardly projection'—a serious underestimation—in calculating the size of the English forces.*

prolixity NOUN
long-windedness
• *(RJ 1.4.3) Benvolio says there is no need to make an excuse for attending the Capulets' party: 'The date is out of such prolixity'—such an apology is outdated.*

prolong VERB
⚠ *Don't read in the meaning of 'make something last for a longer time'.*
postpone
• *(MA 4.1.253) The Friar tells Hero that her wedding day 'Perhaps is but prolong'd'.*

Promethean ADJECTIVE
[pronounced pro-**meeth**-ee-an]
In Greek mythology, associated with Prometheus, a giant who stole fire from the gods that could make clay figures come alive
• *(Oth 5.2.12) Othello reflects that, if Desdemona's light is put out (by killing her), 'I know not where is that Promethean heat / That can thy light relume'.*

a b c d e f g h i j k l m n o **Pp** q r s t u v w x y z

a b c d e f g h i j k l m n o Pp q r s t u v w x y z

promise forth VERB
have an engagement elsewhere
• *(JC 1.2.287) Casca says he cannot dine with Cassius because he is 'promised forth'.*

pronounce VERB
⚠*Don't read in the meaning of 'say sounds in a particular way'.*
speak
• *(MV 1.2.10) Portia compliments Nerissa on her speech: 'Good sentences, and well pronounced'.*

proof NOUN
1 test
• *(KL 4.6.181) Lear says, of shoeing horses in felt, 'I'll put't in proof'—put it to the test.*
2 tested strength
• *(Mac 1.2.54) Ross describes a soldier as being 'lapp'd in proof'—clad in impenetrable armour.*
see **Bellona**
3 experience
• *(JC 2.1.21) Brutus reflects that it is 'a common proof / That lowliness is young ambition's ladder'.*
4 evidence
• *(KL 2.3.13) Edgar sees in the country 'proof and precedent / Of Bedlam beggars'.*

› **prove** VERB
as well as meaning 'show to be true', you'll find:
try out
• *(MA 1.3.64) Don John proposes: 'Shall we go prove what's to be done?'*

› **disprove** VERB
show to be wrong
• *(Oth 5.2.171) Emilia tells Iago to reveal Othello's wrong-doing: 'Disprove this villain'.*

proper ADJECTIVE
as well as meaning 'thorough', you'll find:
1 good-looking
• *(MA 2.3.177) Claudio says Benedick 'is a very proper man'.*
2 very own
• *(Ham 5.2.66) Hamlet tells Horatio how Claudius has 'Thrown out his angle for my proper life'—cast out his (fishing) line to catch my life.*
3 personal
• *(TN 5.1.307) Olivia proposes that the weddings will take place 'Here at my house, and at my proper cost'.*
4 characteristic
• *(KL 4.2.60) Albany tells Goneril that 'Proper deformity shows not in the fiend / So horrid as in woman'.*

› **unproper** ADJECTIVE
shared with another
• *(Oth 4.1.68) Iago talks of men who lie every night in 'unproper beds / Which they dare swear peculiar'—they thought belonged to them alone.*

properties NOUN
props (for a stage play)
• *(MND 1.2.91) Quince plans to 'draw a bill of properties'.*

property VERB
treat as an object
• *(TN 4.2.87) Malvolio complains about his captors: 'They have here propertied me'.*

propinquity NOUN
close kinship
• *(KL 1.1.113) Lear declares to Cordelia that he renounces all 'Propinquity and property of blood' with her.*

Propontic [pronounced proh-**pon**-tic]
the Sea of Marmara in north-west Turkey
• *(Oth 3.3.457) Othello says his bloody thoughts race on like the fast current that flows from the Black Sea 'To the Propontic and the Hellespont'.*
see MAP, p.176

proportions NOUN
as well as meaning 'proper relationship', you'll find:
forces and supplies needed for war
• *(H5 1.2.137) Henry says the English must 'lay down our proportions to defend / Against the Scot'.*

› **disproportioned** also spelled **disproportion'd** ADJECTIVE
inconsistent
• *(Oth 1.3.2) The First Senator agrees that the reports about the size of the Turkish fleet 'are disproportion'd'.*

› **unproportioned** also spelled **unproportion'd** ADJECTIVE
immoderate
• *(Ham 1.3.60) Polonius advises Laertes not to give 'any unproportion'd thought his act'—don't act out every reckless thought that comes into your head.*

propose VERB
⚠*Don't read in the meanings of 'suggest an idea' or 'ask to marry'.*
converse
• *(MA 3.1.3) Hero says Margaret will 'find my cousin Beatrice / Proposing with the prince and Claudio'.*

propriety NOUN
⚠ *Don't read the meaning of 'correct behaviour' into these senses.*
1 normal condition
• *(Oth 2.3.160) Othello says the alarm bell 'frights the isle / From her propriety'.*
2 real identity
• *(TN 5.1.145) Olivia tells Cesario that it is fear 'That makes thee strangle thy propriety' as a husband.*

prorogue VERB
postpone
• *(RJ 4.1.48) The Friar tells Juliet that 'nothing may prorogue' her marriage to Paris.*

proscription NOUN
condemnation
• *(JC 4.1.17) Octavius and Antony decide who is to die 'In our black sentence and proscription'.*

prosperous ADJECTIVE
⚠ *Don't read the meaning of 'rich' into these senses.*
as well as meaning 'successful', you'll find:
1 profitable
• *(Mac 3.1.22) Macbeth compliments Banquo on his 'good advice / Which still hath been both grave and prosperous'.*
2 sympathetic
• *(Oth 1.3.242) Desdemona asks the Duke to 'lend your prosperous ear' to her plea.*

protest VERB
⚠ *Don't read a meaning to do with 'disapproval' into these senses.*
1 avow
• *(KL 3.4.78) Benedick tells Beatrice: 'I protest I love thee'.*
2 declare
• *(RJ 2.4.156) Romeo is about to tell the Nurse something, but she interrupts him: 'I protest unto thee -'.*

> **protestation** NOUN
> solemn declaration
> • *(Ham 3.2.130) In the stage direction for the dumb show, the Queen kneels 'and makes show of protestation' before the King.*
>
> **protester** NOUN
> declarer of friendship
> • *(JC 1.2.74) Cassius tells Brutus he does not offer his love 'To every new protester'.*

proud ADJECTIVE
as well as meaning 'taking pride in' something, you'll find:
1 fine
• *(KL 3.4.78) Poor Tom advises his companions: 'set not thy sweet heart on proud array'—on fine clothing.*
2 high-spirited
• *(H5 Prologue.27) The Chorus describes horses 'Printing their proud hooves i'th' receiving earth'.*
3 swollen
• *(MND 2.1.91) Titania describes the way her quarrel with Oberon has 'every pelting river made so proud' that they have flooded.*

prove see **proof**

proverb VERB
provide with worldly wisdom
• *(RJ 1.4.37) Romeo says he is 'proverb'd with a grandsire phrase'—by an expression used by grandfathers.*

providence NOUN
1 foresight
• *(Ham 4.1.17) Claudius regrets his 'providence' did not keep Hamlet under control.*
2 destiny
• *(JC 5.1.106) Brutus says he is arming himself 'with patience / To stay the providence of some high powers'—await his fate from the gods.*

Provincial ADJECTIVE
from Provins or Provence in France
• *(Ham 3.2.265) Hamlet imagines 'two Provincial roses' decorating his shoes.*

provulgate VERB
make public
• *(Oth 1.2.21) Othello refers to his royal ancestry: 'when I know that boasting is an honour, / I shall provulgate'.*

publican NOUN
⚠ *Don't read in the meaning of 'a person in charge of a pub'.*
tax-collector
• *(MV 1.3.36) Shylock reflects on Antonio: 'How like a fawning publican he looks!'*

pudder NOUN
din
• *(KL 3.2.50) In the storm, Lear calls on the gods 'That keep this dreadful pudder o'er our heads'.*

pudding NOUN
large savoury dish
• *(H5 2.1.75) The Hostess says Falstaff will 'yield the crow a pudding one of these days'—die and be food for birds.*

a b c d e f g h i j k l m n o Pp q r s t u v w x y z

puissance NOUN [pronounced **pwee**-suns]
power
• *(H5 2.2.186) Henry rouses everyone to action: 'Let us deliver / Our puissance into the hand of God'.*
> **puissant** ADJECTIVE
powerful
• *(JC 3.1.33) Metellus addresses Caesar: 'Most high, most mighty, and most puissant Caesar'.*

puling ADJECTIVE
whimpering
• *(RJ 3.5.183) Capulet calls Juliet 'a wretched puling fool'.*

pulpit NOUN
⚠*Don't read in the meaning of 'preaching place in a church'.*
public speaking place
• *(JC 3.1.84) Casca tells Brutus: 'Go to the pulpit'.*

punto reverso see **RECREATION, p.170**

purblind ADJECTIVE
completely blind
• *(RJ 2.1.12) Mercutio describes Cupid as Venus' 'purblind son and heir'.*

purchase out VERB
buy off punishment for
• *(RJ 3.1.189) The Prince tells Montague: 'Nor tears nor prayer shall purchase out abuses'.*

purge VERB
⚠*Don't read the meaning of 'get rid of unwanted people or things' into these senses.*
1 cleanse
• *(Mac 5.3.52) Macbeth, thinking of Scotland, wishes the Doctor could 'find her disease, / And purge it'.*
2 expel
• *(RJ 1.5.106) Romeo, describing a kiss as a sin, tells Juliet: 'Thus from my lips, by thine, my sin is purg'd'.*
3 clear (of a charge)
• *(RJ 5.3.226) The Friar says he is ready 'both to impeach and purge'—to be both accused and cleared.*
4 discharge
• *(Ham 2.2.197) Hamlet describes old men as having 'eyes purging thick amber'.*
> **purge** NOUN
cleansing
• *(Mac 5.2.28) Caithness urges: 'pour we in our country's purge, / Each drop of us'—be ready to shed our blood to cleanse the country.*
> **purgation** NOUN
cleansing
• *(Ham 3.2.292) Hamlet suggests that it woudl be better for a doctor to treat Claudius' temper than for Hamlet to 'put him to his purgation'.*
> **purged** ADJECTIVE
purified
• *(H5 2.2.133) Henry describes the traitors as men who should have acted 'in purged judgement'.*
> **purger** NOUN
cleanser
• *(JC 2.1.180) Brutus affirms that the conspirators 'shall be called purgers, not murderers'.*
> **unpurged** ADJECTIVE
not cleansed
• *(JC 2.1.266) Portia warns Brutus against 'the rheumy and unpurged air' of night-time.*

Puritan NOUN
someone who behaves in a serious and moral way, or who belongs to the group of 16th-century Protestants demanding the reform of ritual in the Church
• *(TN 2.3.125) Maria describes Malvolio: 'sometimes he is a kind of Puritan'.*

purple ADJECTIVE
bright red
• *(RJ 1.1.79) The Prince condemns the fighters for trying to quell their rage 'With purple fountains issuing from your veins'—by bloodshed.*
> **purpled** ADJECTIVE
bloodstained
• *(JC 3.1.158) Antony describes Caesar's murderers as having 'purpled hands'.*
> **purple-in-grain** ADJECTIVE
dyed bright red
• *(MND 1.2.81) Bottom describes a possible beard for the play as 'your purple-in-grain beard'.*

purpose NOUN
as well as meaning 'plan' or 'aim', you'll find:
1 point at issue
• *(MA 2.3.18) Benedick recalls the time when Claudio spoke 'plain and to the purpose'.*
2 result
• *(H5 1.2.212) Canterbury describes how a thousand actions can 'End in one purpose'.*

purpose VERB
1 intend to do
• *(MV 4.1.35) Shylock tells the Duke: 'I have possess'd your grace of what I purpose'.*
2 decide
• *(JC 2.2.27) Caesar asks 'What can be avoided / Whose end is purpos'd by the mighty gods?'*
> **purposed** also spelled **purpos'd** ADJECTIVE
intended
• *(KL 2.2.137) Gloucester protests against the 'purpos'd low correction' of Kent in the stocks.*

pursy ADJECTIVE
flabby
• *(Ham 3.4.155) Hamlet comments on 'the fatness of these pursy times'—the poor moral state.*

purveyor NOUN [pronounced **pur**-vay-er]
steward sent ahead to make preparations for the arrival of someone important
• *(Mac 1.6.23) Duncan tells Lady Macbeth that he had hoped to reach her castle before Macbeth: 'To be his purveyor'.*

push NOUN
1 attack
• *(JC 5.2.5) Brutus thinks he can overthrow the enemy with a 'sudden push'.*
2 test
• *(Ham 5.1.281) Claudius tells Laertes he will 'put the matter to the present push'—act immediately.*

putter-out NOUN
investor
• *(Tem 3.3.48) Gonzalo thinks their unusual experiences on the island would satisfy 'Each putter-out of five for one'—guarantee a fivefold financial return for investing in a successful foreign journey.*

putting-on NOUN
prompting
• *(Oth 2.1.293) Iago hopes Roderigo will 'stand the putting on'—keep on doing what Iago wants.*

Pyramus NOUN [pronounced **pi**-ra-mus]
in Roman mythology, a hero whose love for Thisbe ended in tragedy
• *(MND 1.2.17) Peter Quince tells Bottom he is 'set down for Pyramus' in the play.*

Pyrrhus NOUN [pronounced **pi**-rus]
in Greek mythology, a general who entered Troy hidden in the wooden horse and killed King Priam
• *(Ham 2.2.439) Hamlet recalls a speech which 'begins with Pyrrhus'.*

Pythagoras NOUN
[pronounced pic-**thag**-o-ras]
Greek philosopher of the 6th century BC
• *(MV 4.1.131) Gratiano says Shylock's behaviour makes him want 'To hold opinion with Pythagoras' that the souls of animal can enter men—to agree with him.*

Quarto 1 and Quarto 2

There are two quarto editions of Hamlet. Quarto 1 is sometimes called the 'Bad Quarto', as there are so many mistakes in it.

'To be or not to be, I there's the point, To die, to sleepe, is that all? I all...'

It may have been compiled by a member of Shakespeare's company whose memory let him down — or it might have been produced by an actor from a rival company, trying to steal the play.

quail VERB
destroy
• *(MND 5.1.274) Bottom addresses the Fates: 'Quail, crush, conclude, and quell'.*

quaint ADJECTIVE
⚠ *Don't read the meanings to do with being 'attractively old-fashioned' into these senses.*
1 clever
• *(Tem 3.3.52) Stage direction: 'with a quaint device, the banquet vanishes'.*
🎭 *Sadly, few of the stage techniques of Shakespeare's theatre are known, so we can only guess how 'the banquet disappears with a clever trick'—but it's interesting to see that he set his company challenges!*
2 artful
• *(MV 3.4.69) Portia says, dressed as a man, she'll 'tell quaint lies' about love.*

3 elaborate
• *(MND 2.1.99) Titania regrets that 'the quaint mazes in the wanton green' can no longer be seen.*
4 pretty
• *(MND 2.2.7) Titania describes how the owl 'hoots and wonders / At our quaint spirits'.*

› **quaintly** ADVERB
1 subtly
• *(Ham 2.1.31) Polonius tells Reynaldo to mention Laertes' faults 'quaintly'.*
2 artistically
• *(MV 2.4.6) Solanio says that torchbearers need to be 'quaintly order'd'—arranged with style.*

qualification NOUN
normal condition (of being peaceful)
• *(Oth 2.1.266) Iago promises Roderigo that he will make the Cypriots quarrel, and their 'qualification shall come into no true taste again but by the displanting of Cassio'—the only way they will enjoy peace again will be by the removal of Cassio.*

› **qualify** VERB
1 explain
• *(MA 5.4.67) The Friar assures Don Pedro and Claudio that 'All this amazement can I qualify'.*
2 dilute
• *(Oth 2.3.33) Cassio says he has had only one drink, 'and that was craftily qualified too'.*

quality NOUN
as well as meaning 'character' and 'characteristic', you'll find:
1 rank
• *(H5 4.8.85) Henry reads out the list of the 'gentlemen of blood and quality' killed in the battle of Agincourt.*
2 profession
• *(Ham 2.2.339) Hamlet wonders if the child players 'will pursue the quality no longer than they can sing'—only as long as they can sing (after their voices break their falsetto singing voices will be gone).*
3 companions
• *(Tem 1.2.193) Ariel asks to do Prospero's bidding with 'all his quality'.*

qualm NOUN
⚠ *Don't read in the meaning of 'misgiving'.*
sudden sickness
• *(MA 3.4.69) Margaret insists that 'carduus benedictus' (the 'Benedick plant') 'is the only thing for a qualm'.*

quantity NOUN
as well as meaning 'amount', you'll find:
equal amount
• *(Ham 3.2.159) The Player Queen tells her King that 'women's fear and love hold quantity'—are equal in proportion to each other.*

› **disquantity** VERB
cut down
• *(KL 1.4.238) Goneril asks Lear 'A little to disquantity your train'—reduce the number of your followers a little.*

quarrel NOUN
cause of complaint
• *(JC 2.1.28) Brutus reflects, of Caesar, that 'the quarrel / Will bear no colour for the thing he is' —there are no grounds for complaining about him in his present state.*

quarrel VERB
quibble
• *(MV 3.5.48) Lorenzo loses patience with Lancelot: 'Yet more quarrelling with occasion!'—quibbling at every opportunity.*

quarry NOUN
heap of dead
• *(Ham 5.2.357) Fortinbras surveys the scene after Hamlet's death: 'This quarry cries on havoc'—all the dead people indicate total disorder in the state.*

quarter NOUN
1 conduct
• *(Oth 2.3.164) Iago says that Cassio and Montano were good friends 'In quarter and in terms'—in how they behaved with and spoke to each other before their quarrel.*
2 direction
• *(Mac 1.3.15) The First Witch describes winds blowing 'All the quarters that they know'—from all directions.*

quat NOUN
pimple
• *(Oth 5.1.11) Iago describes Roderigo as a 'young quat'.*

queasy ADJECTIVE
as well as meaning 'feeling sick' or 'easily upset', you'll find:
uncertain
• *(KL 2.1.17) Edmund reflects that he has 'a queasy question' to act out with Edgar—he'll have to draw his sword on him.*

quell NOUN
murder
• *(Mac 1.7.72) Lady Macbeth anticipates that*

Duncan's attendants 'shall bear the guilt / Of our great quell'.

quell VERB
kill
• *(MND 5.1.274) Bottom addresses the Fates: 'Quail, crush, conclude, and quell'.*

quern NOUN
hand-mill for grinding corn
• *(MND 2.1.36) A Fairy asks Puck if it is he who does 'sometimes labour in the quern'.*

quest NOUN
inquest
• *(Ham 5.1.20) The First Gravedigger affirms that the decision about Ophelia's burial (as a presumed suicide) is under the jurisdiction of 'crowner's quest law'.*

question NOUN
as well as meaning 'matter to be dealt with' and 'request for information', you'll find:
1 dispute
• *(MV 4.1.170) The Duke asks Balthazar if he understands 'the difference / That holds this present question in the court?'*
2 debate
• *(H5 3.3.60) The Scots Captain Jamy hopes to hear 'some question' between the other two Captains.*
3 interrogation
• *(MA 5.4.6) Leonato says it appears 'In the true course of the question' that Margaret acted against her will.*
4 conversation
• *(Oth 1.3.113) The First Senator asks Othello if Desdemona's affection arose 'by request and such fair question / As soul to soul affordeth'.*
5 cause
• *(JC 3.2.37) Brutus says, of Caesar, that 'The question of his death is enrolled in the Capitol'.*
6 fighting
• *(Oth 1.3.23) The First Senator believes that 'the Turk' (meaning the Turkish fleet) will head for Cyprus, 'So may he with more facile question bear it'—overcome Cyprus with an easy battle.*

question VERB
argue
• *(MV 4.1.70) Antonio reminds Bassanio that it is pointless to 'question with the Jew'.*

› call in question
discuss
• *(JC 4.3.165) Brutus says he and the others must sit down and 'call in question our necessities'—what needs to be done.*

› in contempt of question
without the shadow of a doubt
• *(TN 2.5.82) Malvolio is sure Olivia has written the letter: 'It is in contempt of question her hand'—her handwriting.*

› in question
under examination
• *(MA 3.3.166) Conrad comments on Borachio's description of the two of them as a commodity, now they've been arrested: 'A commodity in question, I warrant you'—to be interrogated.*

› questionable ADJECTIVE
inviting interrogation
• *(Ham 1.4.43) Hamlet addresses the Ghost (who looks so much like his dead father): 'Thou com'st in such a questionable shape / That I will speak to thee'.*

› questionless ADVERB
undoubtedly
• *(MV 1.1.176) Bassanio thinks, if he had the means to visit Portia, he 'should questionless be fortunate' in winning her affections.*

questrist NOUN
seeker
• *(KL 3.7.16) Oswald says that Lear's knights are 'Hot questrists after him'—they are looking for him as if on a quest.*

Queubus NOUN [pronounced kway-**oo**-bus]
an invented location on the equator (either made up by Feste or misremembered by Sir Andrew)
• *(TN 2.3.22) Sir Andrew recalls Feste's story of the Vapians 'passing the equinoctial of Queubus'.*

quick ADJECTIVE
as well as meaning 'in a short time', you'll find:
1 living
• *(H5 2.2.76) Henry tells the traitors that their words have killed 'The mercy that was quick in us but late'—the readiness to be merciful that was alive in him but recently.*
2 lively
• *(JC 1.2.294) Brutus says Casca 'was quick mettle when he went to school'.*
3 keen
• *(TN 1.1.9) Orsino describes love as 'quick and fresh'.*
4 flowing
• *(Tem 3.2.65) Caliban says he will not show Trinculo 'Where the quick freshes are'—the fresh-water streams.*

quick NOUN
1 living
• *(Ham 5.1.117) Hamlet tells the First Gravedigger his grave is 'for the dead, not for the quick'.*
2 tender flesh
• *(Ham 2.2.584) Hamlet decides about Claudius: 'I'll*

a b c d e f g h i j k l m n o p Qq r s t u v w x y z

tent him to the quick'—probe him to his most sensitive spot to find out if he's guilty.

› quicken VERB

1 revive

• *(Tem 3.1.6) Ferdinand says he is happy to work because 'The mistress which I serve quickens what's dead'—makes fresh the parts of me that are tired.*

2 receive life

• *(Oth 3.3.279) Othello reflects that having an unfaithful wife 'is fated to us / When we do quicken'—ordained by Fate as soon as we're conceived.*

quiddity NOUN
subtlety (coming from a lawyer, using sharp and subtle turns of phrase)

• *(Ham 5.1.92) Hamlet reflects on the skull of a lawyer: 'Where be his quiddities now?'*

see also **quillet**

quietus NOUN [pronounced kwie-**ay**-tus, kwee-**ay**-tus, kwie-**ee**-tus]
release

• *(Ham 3.1.75) Hamlet reflects that anyone 'might his quietus make / With a bare bodkin'—use a dagger on himself to leave life behind.*

The word is related to 'quiet', but its Latin appearance (the '-us' ending) has led to various pronunciations.

quill NOUN
voice

• *(MND 3.1.112) Bottom sings of a 'wren with little quill'.*

quillet or **quillity** NOUN
subtlety (coming from a lawyer, using sharp and subtle turns of phrase)

• *(Ham 5.1.92) Hamlet reflects on the skull of a lawyer, and asks where 'his quillets' are now.*

see also **quiddity**

'Quillets' is the word in the First Folio; the Second Quarto text has 'quillites', and this is emended to 'quillities' in some editions.

Quinapalus NOUN [pronounced kwi-**na**-pa-lus]
an invented name for a scholarly authority

• *(TN 1.5.31) Feste thinks up some support for his argument: 'For what says Quinapalus?'*

quintessence NOUN
purest form

• *(Ham 2.2.304) Hamlet reflects on man as a 'quintessence of dust'.*

quire see **choir**

quirk NOUN
as well as meaning 'peculiarity', you'll find:

1 quip

• *(MA 2.3.225) Benedick thinks he may have 'some odd quirks and remnants of wit broken on me' —that people might mock him, for changing his mind about marriage.*

2 verbal flourish

• *(Oth 2.1.63) Cassio describes Desdemona as 'One that excels the quirks of blazoning pens'—her character is too extraordinary to be written down, even by those who know how to write vivid descriptions.*

quit VERB

1 rid

• *(H5 3.6.47) The French King tells the nobles to 'quit you of great shames' by joining battle.*

2 release from

• *(MV 4.1.379) Antonio says, of Shylock, he is happy 'To quit the fine for one half of his goods'—he will let the matter be settled for a fine of half of Shylock's property.*

3 forgive

• *(H5 2.2.162) Henry tells the traitors: 'God quit you in His mercy'.*

4 release from service

• *(TN 5.1.309) Orsino tells Viola: 'Your master quits you'.*

5 reward

• *(RJ 2.4.175) Romeo tells the Nurse: 'be trusty, and I'll quit thy pains'.*

6 avenge

• *(KL 3.7.84) Blinded Gloucester asks Edmund 'To quit this horrid act'.*

7 draw level

• *(Ham 5.2.254) Claudius announces how he will celebrate if Hamlet 'quit in answer of the third exchange'—if Hamlet manages an equal score with Laertes in the third bout.*

8 do one's part

• *(KL 2.1.30) Edmund tells Edgar to appear to fight and with good skill: 'quit you well'.*

quittance NOUN
repayment

• *(H5 2.2.34) Henry says he would rather lose the use of his hand than fail to provide 'quittance of desert and merit'—not repay those who deserve, and have earned, such rewards.*

quondam ADJECTIVE
former

• *(MA 5.2.30) Benedick reflects on 'quondam carpet-mongers'—ladies' men from olden times.*

see **carpet-monger**

quote VERB
1 closely observe
• *(Ham 2.1.112) Polonius, reflecting on Hamlet, regrets that 'with better heed and judgement / I had not quoted him'.*
2 note
• *(Ham 3.2.45) Hamlet describes a type of clown for whom 'gentlemen quote his jests down in their tables'—in their notebooks.*
This line appears only in the First Quarto text of the play. It is sometimes omitted from modern editions.

quoth VERB
said
• *(Mac 1.3.4) The First Witch tells a story of how she asked a sailor's wife for some chestnuts: '"Give me", quoth I'.*

quotidian NOUN [pronounced kwoh-**tid**-ee-an]
type of fever with attacks every day
• *(H5 2.1.103) The Hostess reports that Falstaff is 'shaked of a burning quotidian tertian'.*
see also **tertian**

QUOTE IT!

Many famous lines that Shakespeare wrote are good to learn by heart. Here are twelve examples.

Famous lines

• *(Hamlet, Ham 3.1.56) To be, or not to be, that is the question.*
• *(Olivia reading, TN 2.5.132) Some are born great, some achieve greatness, and some have greatness thrust upon 'em.*
• *(Ariel, Tem 1.2.214) Hell is empty, / And all the devils are here.*
• *(Lysander, MND 1.1.134) The course of true love never did run smooth.*
• *(Juliet, RJ 2.2.184) Parting is such sweet sorrow.*
• *(Antony, JC 3.2.72) Friends, Romans, countrymen, lend me your ears! / I come to bury Caesar, not to praise him.*
• *(Macbeth, Mac 2.1.33) Is this a dagger which I see before me, / The handle toward my hand?*
• *(Lear, KL 1.1.89) Nothing will come of nothing.*
• *(Portia, as Balthazar, MV 4.1.182) The quality of mercy is not strain'd, / It droppeth as the gentle rain from heaven / Upon the place beneath.*
• *(Henry, H5 3.1.1) Once more unto the breach, dear friends, once more, / Or close the wall up with our English dead!*
• *(Othello, Oth 5.2.339) Then must you speak / Of one that lov'd not wisely, but too well.*
• *(Balthasar singing, MA 2.3.63) Men were deceivers ever.*

There are also a number of phrases that are so famous they are used every day.

Famous phrases

• *(Hamlet, Ham 3.4.180) I must be cruel only to be kind*
• *(Henry, H5 5.2.286) love is blind*
• *(Arragon, MV 2.9.53) a blinking idiot*
• *(Macbeth, Mac 1.7.5) the be-all and the end-all*
• *(Maria, TN 3.2.61) laugh yourselves into stitches*
• *(Stephano, Tem 3.2.33) keep a good tongue in your head*
• *(Othello, Oth 3.3.429) a foregone conclusion*
• *(Edmund, KL 5.3.173) The wheel is come full circle*
• *(Casca, JC 1.2.281) it was Greek to me*
• *(Oberon, MND 2.1.60) Ill met by moonlight*
• *(Nurse, RJ 2.4.151) in a fool's paradise*
• *(Benedick, MA 2.3.101) Sits the wind in that corner?*

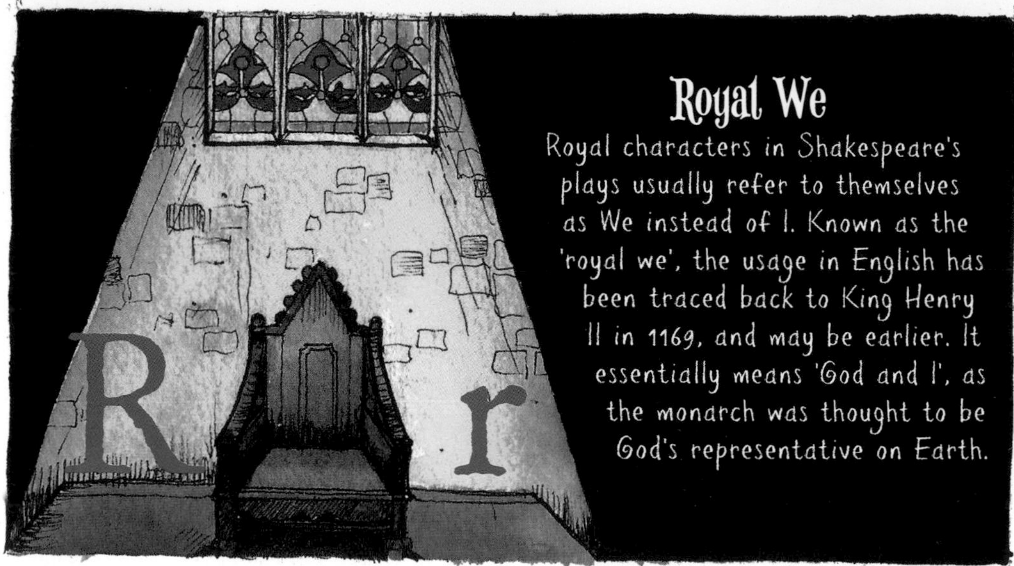

rabblement NOUN
mob
• *(JC 1.2.243) Casca reports that 'the rabblement hooted' when Caesar was offered the crown.*

rack NOUN
1 cloud formations
• *(Ham 2.2.472) The First Player observes that just before a storm 'the rack stand still'.*
2 shred of cloud
• *(Tem 4.1.156) Prospero describes the fading away of everything, leaving 'not a rack behind'.*

rack NOUN
machine of torture that stretches the limbs
• *(MV 3.2.25) Bassanio asks Portia to let him choose the casket, 'For as I am, I live upon the rack'—the tension is unbearable.*

rack VERB
1 stretch
• *(MV 1.1.181) Antonio says his credit 'shall be rack'd even to the uttermost'.*
2 increase
• *(MA 4.1.219) The Friar observes that, when a prized thing is lost, 'then we rack the value'.*

rage NOUN
⚠ *Don't read the meaning of 'great anger' into these senses.*
1 strong passion
• *(KL 4.3.16) A Gentleman reports that Kent's letters moved Cordelia, but to a gentle sorrow, 'Not to a rage'.*
2 madness
• *(RJ 4.3.53) Juliet fears that waking in the tomb will make her go mad, so that 'in this rage' she might kill herself.*
3 wild jest
• *(MV 2.1.35) Morocco fears someone less worthy than him might win Portia, just as Lichas (the servant to Hercules, also known as Alcides) beat his famous master at a game of dice: 'So is Alcides beaten by his rage'—strength losing out to cunning when it comes to luck.*
✒ *This is the word used in the First Folio and Quarto texts, but some editions replace it by 'page'.*

› **raging** ADJECTIVE
violent
• *(Oth 1.3.326) Iago says that 'we have reason to cool our raging motions'—control our intense desires.*

rail VERB
rant
• *(MA 2.3.226) Benedick reflects that he has 'railed so long against marriage'.*

› **railing** NOUN
abuse
• *(TN 1.5.87) Olivia says there is 'no railing in a known discreet man'.*

rake up VERB
bury
• *(KL 4.6.269) Edgar says he will 'rake up' dead Oswald in the sands.*

rank ADJECTIVE
1 growing in abundance
• *(Ham 1.2.136) Hamlet reflects on the world: 'Things rank and gross in nature / Possess it merely' —cover it completely.*

2 foul-smelling

• *(Ham 3.4.92) Hamlet condemns Gertrude for living 'In the rank sweat' of a slimy bed.*

3 festering

• *(RJ 1.2.50) Benvolio argues that a new infection in the eye kills off 'the rank poison' of an old one.*

4 outlandish

• *(KL 1.4.193) Goneril accuses Lear's retinue of 'breaking forth / In rank and not-to-be-endured riots'.*

5 grievous

• *(Tem 5.1.132) Prospero tells Antonio: 'I do forgive / Thy rankest fault'.*

6 lustful

• *(MV 1.3.75) Shylock recounts a story from the Bible in which 'the ewes being rank, / In end of autumn turned to the rams'.*

7 high

• *(Ham 4.4.22) The Captain thinks the land being fought over would not yield 'A ranker rate' than five ducats, should it be sold outright.*

> **rankly** ADVERB
> completely
> • *(Ham 1.5.38) The Ghost says those in Denmark who hear the false story of his death are 'Rankly abus'd'.*

rapier see p.283

rare ADJECTIVE

⚠ *Don't read the meaning of 'not often found' into these senses.*

1 splendid

• *(MA 1.1.126) Benedick calls Beatrice 'a rare parrot-teacher'—an excellent chatterer.*

2 striking

• *(Mac 5.8.25) Macduff compares Macbeth to one of 'our rarer monsters'—a really notable monstrosity.*

> **rarely** ADVERB
> splendidly
> • *(MND 1.2.24) Bottom boasts: 'I could play Ercles rarely'.*

> **rareness** NOUN
> exceptional character
> • *(Ham 5.2.115) Hamlet describes Laertes as someone of 'dearth and rareness'—of high value and great character.*

> **rarity** NOUN
> striking quality
> • *(Tem 2.1.57) Gonzalo observes that the (clean and dry) state of their clothes is 'the rarity of' their situation—its most noticeable feature.*

rash ADJECTIVE

⚠ *Don't read a meaning of 'not thinking of the consequences of an action' into these senses.*

1 quickly acting

• *(JC 4.3.120) Cassius apologizes to Brutus for 'that rash humour which my mother gave me'—his choleric temperament.*

2 hasty

• *(Tem 1.2.468) Miranda begs Prospero not to make 'too rash a trial' of Ferdinand.*

rash ADVERB

impulsively

• *(Oth 3.4.79) Desdemona asks Othello why he speaks 'so startingly and rash'.*

rash VERB

slash with

• *(KL 3.7.56) Gloucester imagines Goneril attacking her father like a wild animal: 'in his anointed flesh / Rash boarish fangs'.*

rate NOUN

1 opinion

• *(Tem 2.1.105) Alonso sorrows for his lost son, 'and, in my rate', for his lost daughter too (as she is newly married).*

2 style of living

• *(MV 1.1.127) Bassanio says he is not complaining about being 'abridg'd / From such a noble rate' —forced to cut down on his spending.*

3 worth

• *(MND 3.1.136) Titania describes herself as 'a spirit of no common rate'.*

rate VERB

as well as meaning 'put a value on', you'll find: scold

• *(RJ .5.169) The Nurse criticizes Capulet for shouting at Juliet: 'to rate her so'.*

ratsbane NOUN

rat poison

• *(KL 3.4.54) Poor Tom says that the Devil has 'set ratsbane by his porridge'—trying to trick him into killing himself.*

raught see **reach**

ravelled ADJECTIVE

tangled

• *(Mac 2.2.40) Macbeth reflects on 'Sleep that knits up the ravell'd sleeve of care'—that patches up the damage caused in the mind by daily worry.*

> **ravel out** VERB
> unravel
> • *(Ham 3.4.188) Hamlet warns Gertrude against letting Claudius 'Make you to ravel all this matter out'—so that Claudius won't find out that Hamlet's madness is not genuine.*

a b c d e f g h i j k l m n o p q **Rr** s t u v w x y z

ravin up also spelled **raven** VERB
feed ravenously on
• *(Mac 2.4.28) Ross reflects on 'ambition that will ravin up / Thine own life's means'—devour everything needed for life.*

› **ravined** also spelled **ravin'd, ravened** ADJECTIVE
stuffed with prey
• *(Mac 4.1.24) The Third Witch adds to the cauldron the guts 'Of the ravin'd salt-sea shark'.*

ravish VERB
as well as meaning 'fill with joy', you'll find:
snatch
• *(KL 3.7.37) Gloucester tells Regan that 'These hairs, which thou dost ravish from my chin', will come to life and accuse her.*

raw ADJECTIVE
unrefined
• *(Ham 5.2.120) Hamlet ironically asks Osric why they are talking about Laertes 'in our more rawer breath'—in such an unrefined way.*

› **rawly** ADVERB
so young
• *(H5 4.1.134) Williams talks of those who die in battle crying for 'their children rawly left'.*

› **rawness** NOUN
unprotected state
• *(Mac 4.3.26) Malcolm asks Macduff why 'in that rawness left you wife and child'.*

raze VERB
alter
• *(KL 1.4.4) Kent talks about why 'I raz'd my likeness'—altered his appearance.*

› **raze out** VERB
wipe out
• *(Mac 5.3.43) Macbeth asks the Doctor if he can 'Raze out the written troubles of the brain'—the cares imprinted there.*

› **razed** ADJECTIVE
cut in a decorative way
• *(Ham 3.2.266) Hamlet imagines decorative roses on his 'razed shoes'.*

reach past form **raught** VERB
hold out
• *(H5 4.6.21) Exeter says dying York 'raught me his hand'.*

reach NOUN
mental capability
• *(Ham 2.1.64) Polonius explains how people 'of wisdom and of reach' find things out.*

rearward also spelled **rear-ward** NOUN
rearguard
• *(RJ 3.2.121) Juliet complains to the Nurse of the way she mentioned Romeo's banishment 'with a rear-ward following Tybalt's death'—as an additional thought.*

reason NOUN
as well as meaning 'explanation', you'll find:
1 ability to make judgements
• *(Oth 1.3.18) The First Senator insists that 'By no assay of reason' is the Turkish fleet making for Rhodes—by no test of common-sense (they can't understand why the Turkish fleet looks as if it is preparing to attack Rhodes).*
2 sensible judgement
• *(MA 5.1.41) Leonato tells Antonio: 'thou speak'st reason'—that's good advice.*
3 reasonable treatment
• *(Tem 3.2.116) Stephano responds to Caliban's request to sing, saying 'I will do reason, any reason'—anything within reason.*

reason VERB
1 speak
• *(MV 2.8.28) Salarino says he 'reason'd with a Frenchman yesterday'.*
2 debate the pros and cons of
• *(KL 2.4.261) Lear reacts to Regan's suggestion that he needs no followers: 'O, reason not the need!'*
3 discuss
• *(RJ 3.1.49) Benvolio tells Mercutio and Tybalt to 'reason coldly of your grievances'.*

› **reasonable** ADJECTIVE
endowed with the ability to make judgements
• *(Tem 5.1.81) Prospero describes his spellbound enemies' growing awareness as a tide that 'Will shortly fill the reasonable shore'.*

› **unreasonable** ADJECTIVE
lacking the ability to make judgements
• *(RJ 3.3.111) The Friar says Romeo's 'wild acts denote / The unreasonable fury of a beast'.*

reave past form **reft** VERB
deprive
• *(MA 4.1.195) Leonato declares that, if Hero has been wronged, he will avenge her, for his life has not 'reft me so much of friends' who would help.*

rebato see CLOTHING, p.158

rebel ADJECTIVE
uncontrollable
• *(JC 3.1.40) Caesar says he does not bear 'such rebel blood' that would allow him to be influenced by fine words.*

rebuke VERB
put down
• *(H5 3.7.114) Montjoy tells Henry that the French 'could have rebuked him at Harfleur'.*

receiving NOUN
perception
• *(TN 3.1.116) Olivia reveals her feelings to Cesario: 'To one of your receiving / Enough is shown'.*

recheat NOUN
a horn call for bringing hounds together
• *(MA 1.1.219) Benedick says he will not 'have a recheat winded in my forehead'—sounded to show he has horns (the sign of a man whose wife has cheated on him).*
see also **cuckold**

reck VERB
regard
• *(Ham 1.3.51) Ophelia hopes Laertes will not be one who 'recks not his own rede'—doesn't follow his own advice.*

reclaim VERB
make obedient
• *(RJ 4.2.47) Capulet is happy to find that Juliet, 'this same wayward girl is so reclaim'd'.*
› **unreclaimed** ADJECTIVE
untamed
• *(Ham 2.1.34) Polonius suggests Reynaldo describes Laertes' faults as 'A savageness in unreclaimed blood'—wildness typical of untamed youth.*

recognizance NOUN
[pronounced ri-**cog**-ni-zans]
1 token
• *(Oth 5.2.213) Othello describes his handkerchief as a 'recognizance and pledge of love'.*
2 bond recognizing a debt
• *(Ham 5.1.97) Hamlet imagines the owner of a skull to be 'a great buyer of land, with his statutes, his recognizances'.*

recoil VERB
give way
• *(Mac 4.3.19) Malcolm wonders if Macduff has stayed honourable in the face of Macbeth's tyrannical reign: 'A good and virtuous nature may recoil / In an imperial charge'—yield to a royal command (from the tyrant Macbeth).*

recollected ADJECTIVE
artificial
• *(TN 2.4.5) Orsino says he prefers an old song to modern 'light airs and recollected terms'—artificial phrases.*

recommend VERB
1 commit
• *(TN 5.1.86) Antonio complains that Cesario 'denied me mine own purse, / Which I had recommended to his use'.*
2 inform
• *(Oth 1.3.41) News of the Turkish fleet is received from Montano, who 'With his free duty recommends you thus'—informs you with the greatest respect.*

recover VERB
⚠ *Don't read in the meaning of 'regain'.*
1 revive
• *(Tem 2.2.89) Stephano believes wine will 'recover' Caliban.*
2 obtain
• *(TN 2.3.167) Sir Andrew tells Sir Toby: 'If I cannot recover your niece, I am a foul way out'—I shall have lost a huge amount of time and money.*
3 reach
• *(Tem 3.2.13) Stephano says how far he swam before he 'could recover the shore'.*
› **recovery** NOUN
1 attainment [*first use below*]
2 legal procedure for transferring property into full ownership [*second use below*]
• *(Ham 5.1.99) Hamlet wonders, of a great buyer of land, if a skull full of dirt is 'the recovery of his recoveries'.*

recreant NOUN [pronounced **reck**-ree-ant]
1 coward
• *(MND 3.2.409) Puck calls Demetrius: 'Come, recreant'.*
2 heretic
• *(KL 1.1.165) Lear addresses Kent: 'Hear me, recreant!'*

recreation NOUN
figure of fun
• *(TN 2.3.122) Maria promises to make Malvolio 'a common recreation'.*

rede NOUN
advice
• *(Ham 1.3.51) Ophelia hopes Laertes will not be one who 'recks not his own rede'—doesn't follow his own advice.*

redeliver see **deliver**

redoubted see **doubt**

reduce VERB
restore
• *(H5 5.2.63) Burgundy hopes the meeting between the kings will enable France to 'reduce into our former favour'—to appear as once it was.*

a b c d e f g h i j k l m n o p q Rr s t u v w x y z

reechy ADJECTIVE
1 dirty
• *(Ham 3.4.186) Hamlet imagines Claudius giving Gertrude 'a pair of reechy kisses'.*
2 begrimed by smoke
• *(MA 3.3.125) Borachio talks of fashions like those of 'Pharaoh's soldiers in the reechy painting'—thinking of some painting he has seen in a tavern.*

reed ADJECTIVE
reedy (nasal)
• *(MV 3.4.67) Portia says she will adopt 'a reed voice' when dressed as a man.*

reek VERB
steam
• *(JC 3.1.158) Antony says that the bloodstained hands of Caesar's assassins 'do reek and smoke'.*

› **reeking** ADJECTIVE
sweaty
• *(KL 2.4.29) Kent reports the arrival of 'a reeking post'—a sweating messenger bringing a message.*

› **reeky** ADJECTIVE
foul-smelling
• *(RJ 4.1.83) Juliet imagines being in a charnel-house 'with dead men's rattling bones, / With reeky shanks'.*

reeling-ripe see **ripe**

reels NOUN
revels
• *(Ham 1.4.9) Hamlet describes how Claudius celebrates with 'swagg'ring upspring reels'.*

reflection NOUN
return (at the spring equinox)
• *(Mac 1.2.25) The Captain compares the reversal of fortunes in the battle to when 'the sun 'gins his reflection'—returns to the beginning of its journey again at springtime (when storms are common).*

reflex NOUN
reflection
• *(RJ 3.5.20) Romeo describes the morning light as 'the pale reflex of Cynthia's brow'—a reflection of the light cast by the Moon.*

reform VERB
intended to mean 'inform'
• *(MA 5.1.247) Dogberry says the sexton 'hath reformed Signor Leonato of the matter'.*

reft see **reave**

refuse VERB
disown
• *(RJ 2.2.34) Juliet wishes Romeo to 'Deny thy father and refuse thy name'.*

REGRETTING

Several words could be used to express unhappy emotions such as grief, anxiety, pity, or regret, with varying amounts of intensity.

alack
• *(MND 2.2.159) Hermia panics when she sees Lysander is not with her: 'Alack, where are you?'—a strong expression.*

alas
• *(Ham 4.7.183) Laertes hears the news of Ophelia's death: 'Alas, then she is drown'd'—a very strong expression.*

ay me
• *(JC 2.4.39) Portia reflects sadly: 'Ay me, how weak a thing / The heart of woman is!'—a mild expression.*

well-a-day or **weraday**
• *(TN 4.2.104) Malvolio says he is as well in his wits as any man in Illyria, but Feste doubts it: 'Well-a-day that you were, sir!'—a strong expression, typically used by comic characters.*

woe
• *(RJ 5.3.13) Paris visits Juliet's grave: 'O woe, thy canopy is dust and stones!'—the strongest expression.*

People can repeat these words, or join them together, if they want to express a really strong emotion.
• *(Mac 2.3.83) Lady Macbeth reacts to the news of Duncan's death: 'Woe, alas, / What, in our house?'*
And if you wanted to relate a sad event to a particular day, you would add 'the day' to one of these words.
• *(TN 2.1.21) Antonio replies to Sebastian's belief that Viola was drowned in the shipwreck: 'Alas the day!'*
• *(RJ 4.5.23) The Nurse finds Juliet apparently dead: 'she's dead, alack the day!'*
• *(Tem 1.2.15) Miranda is distraught at seeing the shipwreck: 'O, woe the day!'*

regard NOUN
as well as meaning 'consideration' or 'gaze', you'll find:
1 respect
• *(H5 2.4.118) Exeter tells the Dauphin of Henry's 'slight regard, contempt'.*
2 view
• *(Oth 2.1.39) Montano tells everyone to look out for Othello's ship as far as where the sea and sky are 'An indistinct regard'—as far as the horizon.*

regard VERB
as well as meaning 'gaze upon', you'll find:
respect
• *(JC 5.3.88) Titinius reflects on 'how I regarded Caius Cassius'—how highly he esteemed him.*

› **non-regardance** NOUN
failure to respect
• *(TN 5.1.116) Orsino expresses his anger to Olivia—'Since you to non-regardance cast my faith'.*

region NOUN
sky
• *(RJ 2.2.21) Romeo thinks Juliet's eyes in heaven 'Would through the airy region stream so bright'.*

region ADJECTIVE
in the sky
• *(Ham 2.2.566) Hamlet reflects on feeding Claudius to 'all the region kites'.*

regreet NOUN
fresh greeting
• *(MV 2.9.88) Portia is told that Bassanio's messenger 'bringeth sensible regreets'—return of greetings, along with something tangible ('sensible'—gifts).*

rehearse VERB
⚠ *Don't read in the meaning of 'practise'.*
utter
• *(MND 5.1.380) Titania tells the Fairies: 'rehearse your song by rote'.*

relapse NOUN
return
• *(H5 4.3.107) Henry predicts that any English dead bodies would cause a plague in France, 'Killing in relapse of mortality'—with a deadly second effect.*

relative ADJECTIVE
relevant
• *(Ham 2.2.591) Hamlet reflects he'll 'have grounds more relative' than what the Ghost has told him, to determine Claudius' guilt.*

relic NOUN
souvenir
• *(JC 2.2.89) Decius interprets Calpurnia's dream as great men rushing to get from Caesar's blood 'tinctures, stains, relics'—any kind of memorial.*

relieve VERB
aid
• *(KL 3.3.13) Gloucester says he will look for Lear and 'privily relieve him'—give him secret help.*

religious ADJECTIVE
1 conscientious
• *(TN 3.4.363) Fabian says Cesario is 'a most devout coward, religious in it!'—making a religion out of cowardice.*
2 solemn
• *(Ham 3.3.8) Guildenstern affirms that keeping the king's dependents safe is a 'Most holy and religious fear'—a sacred duty.*

reliques NOUN [pronounced **rel**-iks]
antiquities
• *(TN 3.3.19) Sebastian asks Antonio whether they might 'go see the reliques of this town'.*

relish NOUN
as well as meanings to do with 'liking', you'll find:
1 trace
• *(Mac 4.3.95) Malcolm claims he has 'no relish' of good qualities in his character.*
2 kind
• *(H5 4.1.106) Henry tells Bates that the king has fears 'of the same relish as ours are'.*

relish VERB
feel
• *(Tem 5.1.23) Prospero says he is someone who can 'relish all as sharply / Passion as they'—he has feelings as his enemies do.*

› **disrelish** VERB
cause distaste in
• *(Oth 2.1.225) Iago predicts that Desdemona's tenderness will 'disrelish and abhor the Moor'.*

relume VERB [pronounced **re-lyoom**]
relight
• *(Oth 5.2.13) Othello reflects that, once Desdemona's light (life) has been extinguished, there is nothing 'That can thy light relume'.*

remain VERB
dwell
• *(Tem 1.2.424) Ferdinand asks Miranda 'if you remain upon this island'.*

› **here-remain** NOUN
stay
• *(Mac 4.3.150) Malcolm talks of what he has seen during 'my here-remain in England'.*

a b c d e f g h i j k l m n o p q Rr s t u v w x y z

remediate ADJECTIVE
healing
• *(KL 4.4.17) Cordelia asks the herbs of the earth to be 'aidant and remediate' in helping her father.*

remember VERB
1 remind
• *(H5 5.Chorus.43) The Chorus tells the audience that his role has been to play 'The interim, by remembering you 'tis past'—that time has gone by.*
2 call to mind
• *(Tem 1.2.406) Ferdinand thinks the singing 'does remember my drown'd father'.*
3 acknowledge
• *(MA 1.1.11) A Messenger reports that Claudio's feats have been 'remembered by Don Pedro'.*

› **remembrance** NOUN
1 memory
• *(TN 3.4.207) Cesario insists that his 'remembrance is very free and clear from any image of offence done to any man'.*
2 notice
• *(Ham 2.2.26) Claudius says he will thank Rosencrantz and Guildenstern 'As fits a king's remembrance'—they will get appropriate reward.*
3 keepsake
• *(Oth 3.3.293) Emilia recalls that Desdemona's handkerchief 'was her first remembrance from the Moor'.*

› **remembrancer** NOUN
official reminder
• *(Mac 3.4.37) Macbeth thanks his wife for reminding him to welcome everyone: 'Sweet remembrancer!'*

remorse NOUN
as well as meaning 'deep regret', you'll find:
1 pity
• *(MV 4.1.20) The Duke hopes Shylock will show 'mercy and remorse'.*
2 thoughtfulness for others
• *(TN 2.3.81) Malvolio condemns Sir Toby and the others for singing 'without any mitigation or remorse of voice'—considerately keeping their voices down.*

remotion NOUN
removal
• *(KL 2.4.110) Lear senses that the visit by Cornwall and Regan to Gloucester is a plot: 'this remotion of the duke and her / Is practice only'.*

removed ADJECTIVE
1 further away
• *(Ham 1.4.61) Marcellus describes how the Ghost is gesturing Hamlet to go 'to a more removed ground'.*
2 estranged
• *(TN 5.1.84) Antonio complains that Cesario 'grew a twenty years' removed thing / While one would wink'—in the blink of an eye treated him as if they hadn't met for twenty years.*

render VERB
1 give up
• *(Mac 5.7.25) Siward reports that Macbeth's castle is 'gently render'd'.*
2 give an account of
• *(H5 1.2.238) The French Ambassadors ask Henry if they may deliver their message frankly: 'Freely to render what we have in charge'.*

rendezvous NOUN
⚠ *Don't read the meaning of 'meeting-place' into these senses.*
1 refuge
• *(H5 5.1.76) Pistol reflects on the death of Doll Tearsheet: 'there my rendezvous is quite cut off'.*
2 last resort
• *(H5 2.1.15) Nym summarizes his view: 'that is the rendezvous of it'—that's the end of it.*

renegado NOUN [pronounced re-ni-**gah**-doh]
turncoat
• *(TN 3.2.63) Maria reports that Malvolio has 'turned heathen, a very renegado'—turned away from all forms of belief.*

renege VERB
deny
• *(KL 2.2.74) Kent attacks people like Oswald who 'Renege, affirm'—say whatever their master wants.*

repair VERB
as well as meaning 'mend', you'll find:
make one's way
• *(JC 1.3.147) Cassius tells Cinna: 'Repair to Pompey's Porch'.*

repair NOUN
arrival
• *(Ham 5.2.203) Horatio offers to prevent everyone coming to see Hamlet fence with Laertes—'forestall their repair hither'.*

repeal VERB
recall (from exile)
• *(KL 3.6.111) Edgar, giving himself courage, reflects on the day when proof of his innocence 'repeals and reconciles thee'.*

› **repeal, repealing** NOUN
recall (from exile)
• *(JC 3.1.54) Brutus asks Caesar that Publius Cimber 'may / Have an immediate freedom of repeal'.*

replication NOUN
1 reply
• *(Ham 4.2.12) Hamlet asks Rosencrantz 'what replication' he should make to him.*
2 echo
• *(JC 1.1.48) Murellus describes how the shouts of the people made the river Tiber tremble 'To hear the replication of your sounds'.*

reportingly ADVERB
by hearsay
• *(MA 3.1.116) Beatrice reflects that Benedick is a worthy man, which she believes 'better than reportingly'—not just because other people say he is.*

reposal NOUN
placing
• *(KL 2.1.67) According to Edmund, Edgar once claimed that, despite 'the reposal of any trust' in what Edmund (an illegitimate son) might say, he would never be believed.*

reproach NOUN
1 disgrace
• *(Oth 4.1.47) Iago reflects on how schemes can make innocent women 'meet reproach'.*
2 intended to mean 'approach'
• *(MV 2.5.20) Lancelot tells Shylock: 'My young master doth expect your reproach'—but Shylock takes him to mean 'criticism'.*

reprobance or **reprobation** NOUN
damnation
• *(Oth 5.2.208) Gratiano reflects that if Desdemona's father were alive to see her dead body, he would curse so much that he would 'fall to reprobance'.*
'Reprobance' is the word in the First Folio. The First and Second Quarto texts have 'reprobation', with the same meaning.

reprove VERB
deny
• *(MA 2.3.221) Benedick admits that Beatrice is virtuous: 'I cannot reprove it'.*

repugnant ADJECTIVE
Don't read in the meaning of 'very unpleasant'.
opposing
• *(Ham 2.2.459) The First Player describes Priam's sword as being 'repugnant to command'—not doing as it was told.*

requite past form **requit** VERB
pay back
• *(TN 4.2.113) Malvolio pleads with Feste to help him, saying he will 'requite it in the highest degree'.*

reremouse plural **reremice** NOUN
[pronounced **rear**-mouse]
bat
• *(MND 2.2.4) Titania instructs some of her faries to 'war with reremice for their leathern wings'.*

reserve VERB
retain
• *(KL 3.4.63) The Fool tells Lear that Poor Tom 'reserv'd a blanket' to cover his nakedness.*

residence NOUN
as well as meaning 'house where one lives', you'll find:
normal place of performance (in the city)
• *(Ham 2.2.323) Hamlet wonders why the Players are travelling about, as 'Their residence, both in reputation and profit, was better both ways'—they were thought of in higher regard, and made more money, when they had a permanent base.*

resolute NOUN
desperado
• *(Ham 1.1.101) Horatio describes Fortinbras gathering together 'a list of lawless resolutes'.*

resolve VERB
1 satisfy
• *(H5 1.2.4) Henry says there are certain important matters about which 'We would be resolved'.*
2 inform
• *(Tem 5.1.248) Prospero tells Alonso: 'I'll resolve you' of all that has happened.*
3 decide
• *(Mac 3.1.140) Macbeth tells the Murderers: 'Resolve yourselves apart'—go away to make up your minds.*
4 dissolve
• *(Ham 1.2.130) Hamlet wishes his flesh 'would melt, / Thaw, and resolve itself into a dew'.*

respect NOUN
as well as meaning 'consideration' and 'admiration', you'll find:
1 circumstance
• *(MV 5.1.99) Portia finds music at night sweeter than during the day: 'Nothing is good, I see, without respect'—everything depends on circumstances.*
2 attention
• *(MV 1.1.74) Gratiano says Antonio has 'too much respect upon the world'—he worries about worldly things too much.*
3 status
• *(KL 1.1.247) Cordelia says she will not marry Burgundy, 'Since that respect and fortunes are his love'.*

a b c d e f g h i j k l m n o p q Rr s t u v w x y z

respective ADJECTIVE
careful
• *(MV 5.1.156) Nerissa tells Gratiano that he 'should have been respective and have kept' her ring.*

responsive ADJECTIVE
suited
• *(Ham 5.2.144) Osric describes straps for carrying a sword as being 'very responsive to the hilts'.*

rest NOUN
as well as meaning 'period of repose', you'll find:
final stake (as a bet in a card-game)
• *(H5 2.1.15) Nym concludes his remarks: 'That is my rest'.*

rest VERB
remain
• *(Ham 3.3.64) Claudius wonders what else he can do: 'What rests?'*

restem see **stem**

retention NOUN
as well as meaning 'retaining', you'll find:
1 power to retain emotion (a medical term)
• *(TN 2.4.94) Orsino tells Cesario that a woman's heart does 'lack retention'.*
2 place of confinement
• *(KL 5.3.48) Edmund says he has sent Lear 'To some retention'.*

› **retentive** ADJECTIVE
confining
• *(JC 1.3.95) Cassius affirms that nothing 'Can be retentive to the strength of spirit'.*

retire VERB
⚠ *Don't read a meaning to do with 'giving up a job' into these senses.*
withdraw
• *(RJ 5.3.11) Stage direction: Page 'Retires'.*

retire NOUN
retreat
• *(H5 4.3.86) Montjoy asks Henry for permission for the French to make 'a sweet retire / From off these fields'.*

› **retired** also spelled **retir'd** ADJECTIVE
secluded
• *(Tem 1.2.91) Prospero recalls a time in Milan when he lived in a way that was 'so retir'd'.*

› **retirement** NOUN
withdrawal
• *(Ham 3.2.288) Guildenstern tells Hamlet that Claudius is 'in his retirement marvellous distempered'—very upset after seeing the 'play within a play'.*

retort VERB
return
• *(RJ 3.1.160) Benvolio describes how Tybalt 'Retorts' a sword-thrust from Mercutio.*

retrograde ADJECTIVE
contrary
• *(Ham 1.2.114) Claudius tells Hamlet that going back to Wittenberg 'is most retrograde to our desire'.*

reverence NOUN
⚠ *Don't read a religious meaning into these senses.*
respected state
• *(MA 5.1.64) Angry Leonato tells Claudio: 'I am forc'd to lay my reverence by'.*
See also POLITENESS, p.230

› **do reverence**
show respect (to someone)
• *(JC 3.2.119) Antony talks about the dead Caesar: 'And none so poor to do him reverence'—not even the lowest person will now pay him homage.*

› **reverend** ADJECTIVE
respected
• *(MV 4.1.161) Bellario says Balthazar's youth should not stop him being given 'a reverend estimation'.*

revolt NOUN
as well as meaning 'rebellion against a government', you'll find:
1 act of disobedience
• *(Oth 1.1.134) Roderigo tells Brabantio that his daughter 'hath made a gross revolt'.*
2 betrayal
• *(RJ 4.1.58) Juliet says she will kill herself before her 'true heart with treacherous revolt / Turn to another'.*

› **revolution** NOUN
reversal (of fortune)
• *(Ham 5.1.84) Hamlet reflects on the skulls being dug up: 'Here's fine revolution'.*

revolve VERB
⚠ *Don't read in the meaning of 'physically turn around'.*
consider
• *(TN 2.5.131) Malvolio reads his letter: 'If this fall into thy hand, revolve'.*

rhapsody NOUN
muddled collection
• *(Ham 3.4.48) Hamlet describes Claudius' act as so monstrous that it turns religion into 'A rhapsody of words'.*

Rhenish NOUN
white wine from the Rhineland
• *(MV 3.1.36) Salarino says there is more difference between Jessica and Shylock than there is 'between red wine and Rhenish'.*

rheum NOUN [pronounced **room**]
1 tears
• *(MA 5.2.76) Benedick describes mourning after the death of a husband: 'an hour in clamour and a quarter in rheum'—mostly in shouting and only partly in tears.*
2 head-cold
• *(Oth 3.4.47) Othello asks Desdemona for the handkerchief he gave her, to deal with his 'salt and sorry rheum'.*
3 spit
• *(MV 1.3.112) Shylock reminds Antonio of how he was treated: 'You, that did void your rheum upon my beard'.*

› **rheumy** ADJECTIVE
damp
• *(JC 2.1.266) Portia warns Brutus of the dangers of going out into 'the rheumy and unpurged air'.*

rheumatic ADJECTIVE
⚠ *Don't read the modern meaning of 'disease causing pain in the joints and muscles' into these senses.*
1 with watery discharge
• *(MND 2.1.105) Titania describes the effects of the quarrel with Oberon: 'rheumatic diseases do abound'—lots of colds and coughs.*
2 a mistake for 'choleric' or 'lunatic'
• *(H5 2.3.34) The Hostess describes Falstaff as 'rheumatic'.*

Rialto NOUN [pronounced ree-**al**-toe]
the name of the only bridge spanning the Grand Canal in Venice, Italy, in Shakespeare's time; also used as the commercial exchange centre
• *(MV 1.3.17) Shylock says he has heard about Antonio's ventures 'upon the Rialto'.*

rib VERB
enclose
• *(MV 2.7.51) Morocco thinks lead would be too inferior for Portia's coffin—'To rib her cerecloth in the obscure grave'—to enclose her shroud.*

riband NOUN
ribbon
• *(RJ 3.1.28) Mercutio describes a man who tied 'his new shoes with old riband'.*

right in the phrase **do one right**
give one satisfaction
• *(MA 5.1.144) Benedick challenges Claudio to a duel: 'Do me right, or I will protest thy cowardice'.*

right on
straight out
• *(JC 3.2.220) Antony tells the crowd: 'I only speak right on'—without any art.*

right out
ordinary
• *(Tem 4.1.101) Iris says Cupid has decided to break his arrows and 'be a boy right out'—simply be a boy.*

rim NOUN
midriff (the rim of the belly)
• *(H5 4.4.12) Pistol threatens a French prisoner: 'I will fetch thy rim out at thy throat'—reach down your throat and pull out your insides.*

ring NOUN
as well as meaning 'a piece of jewellery for the finger', you'll find:
a circle surrounding the sovereign's head on a coin
• *(Ham 2.2.416) Hamlet compares a young player's voice to a gold coin, hoping it is 'not cracked within the ring'—not broken (and thus, losing its value).*
🎭 *High-pitched male voices that hadn't yet broken were more useful to an acting company, as these children could play the female roles.*

› **ringlet** NOUN
fairy dance in a ring
• *(Tem 5.1.37) Prospero describes spirits who 'By moonshine do the green, sour ringlets make'—dance rings in the grass under the light of the moon.*

ripe ADJECTIVE
as well as meaning 'ready' and 'mature', you'll find:
1 red and full (like ripe fruit)
• *(KL 4.3.20) A Gentleman describes Cordelia's little smiles 'That play'd on her ripe lip'.*
2 drunk
• *(Tem 5.1.279) Alonso describes Trinculo as 'reeling-ripe!'*

› **riping** NOUN
coming to readiness
• *(MV 2.8.41) Antonio advises Bassanio to 'stay the very riping of the time' in visiting Portia—wait until the time is right.*

a b c d e f g h i j k l m n o p q **Rr** s t u v w x y z

rivage NOUN [pronounced **ri**-vidge]
shore
• *(H5 3.Chorus.14) The Chorus asks the audience to 'stand upon the rivage, and behold / A city'.*

rival NOUN
⚠*Don't read in the meaning of 'competitor'.*
partner
• *(Ham 1.1.14) Barnardo, a sentinel, describes Horatio and Marcellus as 'The rivals of my watch'.*

rive VERB
1 split
• *(JC 4.3.85) Cassius tells Brutus that he 'hath riv'd my heart'.*
2 burst out of
• *(KL 3.2.58) Lear imagines telling a criminal that his hidden crimes will 'Rive your concealing continents'—your hiding places.*

road NOUN
as well as meaning 'route', you'll find:
1 harbour
• *(MV 5.1.288) Antonio says all his ships 'Are safely come to road'.*
2 raid
• *(H5 1.2.138) Henry anticipates the Scots 'will make road upon us'.*

robustious ADJECTIVE
boisterous
• *(Ham 3.2.9) Hamlet says it offends him to hear 'a robustious periwig-pated fellow' shouting on stage.*

rogue NOUN
as well as meaning 'wicked person', you'll find:
vagrant
• *(KL 4.7.39) Cordelia imagines her father living on the heath 'with swine and rogues forlorn'.*

› **roguish** ADJECTIVE
wild (like a vagabond)
• *(KL 3.7.101) A Servant describes Poor Tom as displaying a 'roguish madness'.*

romage also spelled **rummage** NOUN
turmoil
• *(Ham 1.1.110) Horatio describes the 'post-haste and rummage' taking place in Denmark.*

ronyon also spelled **runnion** NOUN
mangy creature
• *(Mac 1.3.5) The First Witch describes an old woman as a 'rump-fed runnion'.*

rood see **SWEARING, p.298**

ropery NOUN
rascal ways
• *(RJ 2.4.133) The Nurse asks Romeo who was the person that 'was so full of his ropery'.*

roping ADJECTIVE
forming rope-like threads
• *(H5 3.6.23) The Constable rouses his companions not to 'hang like roping icicles / Upon our houses' thatch'.*

› **down-rope** VERB
trickle down
• *(H5 4.2.48) The French describe the English horses, with 'gum down-roping from their pale-dead eyes'.*

Roscius NOUN [pronounced **ro**-see-us]
the most famous actor of ancient Rome, in the 2nd century BC
• *(Ham 2.2.380) Hamlet pretends to tell Polonius a story: 'When Roscius was an actor in Rome...'.*

round ADJECTIVE
blunt
• *(TN 2.3.84) Malvolio tells Sir Toby: 'I must be round with you'.*

round ADVERB
thoroughly
• *(Ham 2.2.139) Polonius tells Claudius and Gertrude that he 'went round to work' in talking to Ophelia—he acted straight away.*

round NOUN
1 circle dance
• *(MND 3.1.93) Puck says he will lead the rustics 'about a round'.*
2 crown
• *(Mac 1.5.27) Lady Macbeth imagines her husband wearing 'the golden round'.*
3 rung
• *(JC 2.1.24) Brutus reflects on the way an ambitious young man 'attains the upmost round' and then scorns the means that got him there.*

› **roundel** NOUN
circle dance
• *(MND 2.2.1) Titania asks the fairies for 'a roundel and a fairy song'.*

round hose see **CLOTHING, p.158**

rouse NOUN
full draught of wine
• *(Ham 1.4.8) Hamlet explains that 'The King doth wake tonight and takes his rouse'.*

rout NOUN
1 rabble
• *(JC 1.2.78) Cassius cannot imagine himself dining and befriending 'all the rout'.*

2 brawl

• *(Oth 2.3.194) Othello asks, of the fight between Cassio and Montano, 'How this foul rout began'.*

row NOUN

verse

• *(Ham 2.2.407) Hamlet breaks off his quotation, telling Polonius to look in the Bible: 'The first row of the pious chanson will show you more'.*

royal ADJECTIVE

as well as meaning 'kingly', you'll find:

generous

• *(JC 3.2.241) The Third Plebeian, after hearing the terms of Caesar's will, exclaims 'O royal Caesar!'*

› **royal merchant**

prince among merchants

• *(MV 3.2.237) Gratiano describes Antonio as 'that royal merchant'.*

rub NOUN

1 obstacle (as when something hinders the run of a ball in bowling)

• *(Ham 3.1.65) Hamlet reflects on a difficulty: 'there's the rub'.*

2 impediment

• *(Mac 3.1.136) Macbeth tells the Murderers 'To leave no rubs nor botches in the work' of killing Banquo.*

rub VERB

hinder

• *(KL 2.2.149) Gloucester says Cornwall's intentions 'Will not be rubb'd or stopp'd'.*

rubious see **COLOURS, p.164**

rude ADJECTIVE

⚠ *Don't read the modern meaning of 'indecent' into these senses.*

1 violent

• *(RJ 3.1.185) The Prince condemns Montague's 'rude brawls'.*

2 stormy

• *(MND 2.1.152) Oberon remembers a mermaid singing so beautifully 'That the rude sea grew civil at her song'.*

3 uncultivated

• *(JC 3.2.30) Brutus asks the crowd: 'Who is here so rude that would not be a Roman?'*

4 ignorant

• *(H5 1.1.55) Canterbury describes Henry's former companions as 'unletter'd, rude, and shallow'.*

5 inexpert

• *(Oth 1.3.81) Othello acknowledges a limitation: 'Rude am I in my speech'.*

6 raucous

• *(MV 2.2.168) Bassanio says Gratiano is 'too wild, too rude, and bold of voice'.*

7 uncontrolled

• *(RJ 2.3.28) The Friar reflects on the two chief characteristics in men—'grace and rude will'.*

› **rudeness** NOUN

rough manner

• *(JC 1.2.298) Cassius describes Casca's behaviour: 'This rudeness is a sauce to his good wit'—his rough manner makes people enjoy his sharp mind all the more.*

rudesby NOUN

ruffian

• *(TN 4.1.45) Olivia rebukes Sir Toby for fighting: 'Rudesby, be gone!'*

ruffian VERB

rage

• *(Oth 2.1.7) Montano describes the wind which 'hath ruffian'd so upon the sea'.*

rugged ADJECTIVE

1 hairy

• *(Ham 2.2.438) Hamlet remembers lines from a play about 'The rugged Pyrrhus'.*

2 frowning

• *(Mac 3.2.28) Lady Macbeth tells her husband to 'sleek o'er your rugged looks'—smooth over your frowning face (as with a smile).*

rummage see **romage**

rumour NOUN

as well as meaning 'information that may not be true', you'll find:

tumult

• *(JC 2.4.18) Portia says she 'heard a bustling rumour, like a fray'—like the noise of a fight.*

runagate NOUN

runaway

• *(RJ 3.5.89) Lady Capulet says, of Romeo, she will send a message to Mantua, 'Where that same banish'd runagate doth live'.*

runnion see **ronyon**

russet see **COLOURS, p.164**

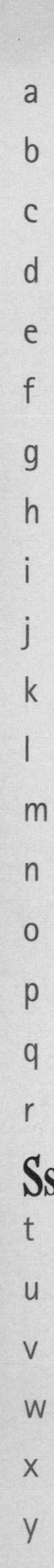

Ss

Soliloquy

A soliloquy is a speech in which a character is alone on stage and speaks thoughts aloud. Since the 18th century it has been considered an inner monologue that the audience must listen to silently. But in Shakespeare's time, it was an opportunity to 'ask the audience', who might shout out and respond as the character explored an idea.

sa' VERB
Shakespeare's way of showing an Irish pronunciation of 'save'
• *(H5 3.3.53) Macmorris wants action: 'So God sa' me, 'tis shame to stand still'.*

sable NOUN
rich dark-coloured fur
• *(Ham 3.2.125) Hamlet says 'I'll have a suit of sables'—a very expensive set of clothes (to wear while mourning).*
See also COLOURS, p.164

sack NOUN
a type of white wine
• *(Tem 3.2.11) Stephano says Caliban 'hath drowned his tongue in sack'.*

sad ADJECTIVE
as well as meaning 'sorrowful', you'll find:
1 serious
• *(MA 2.1.318) Leonato says Beatrice 'is never sad but when she sleeps'.*
2 morose
• *(MND 3.2.439) Puck sees Hermia: 'Here she comes, curst and sad'—in a very bad temper.*

› **sadly** ADVERB
seriously
• *(Ham 2.2.168) Gertrude sees Hamlet approaching: 'But look where sadly the poor wretch comes reading'.*

› **in sadness**
seriously
• *(RJ 1.1.193) Benvolio asks Romeo who he loves: 'Tell me in sadness, who is that you love?'*

› **sad-eyed** ADJECTIVE
serious-looking
• *(H5 1.2.202) Canterbury compares to a bee 'the sad-ey'd justice with his surly hum'—the serious-looking magistrate who keeps saying 'hmm', sounding like a bee.*

safe ADJECTIVE
1 certain
• *(Mac 3.4.25) Macbeth asks the First Murderer: 'But Banquo's safe?'—definitely dead.*
2 sane
• *(KL 4.6.81) Edgar reacts to Lear dressed in wild flowers: 'The safer sense will ne'er accommodate / His master thus'—someone in his right mind would never appear like this.*
3 out of the way
• *(Tem 3.1.21) Miranda tells Ferdinand to rest, as Prospero is 'safe for these three hours'.*

› **safely** ADVERB
trustworthily
• *(Mac 1.4.27) Macbeth affirms to Duncan that his duty is 'doing everything / Safe toward your love and honour'.*

saffron see **COLOURS, p.164**

said in the phrase **well said** see **say**

Saint Colm's Inch
Inchcolm, a small island in the Firth of Forth, eastern Scotland
• *(Mac 1.2.61) Ross reports how the Norwegian king was made to pay a ransom 'at Saint Colm's Inch'.*

sake in the phrase **for your sake**
because of you
• *(Oth 1.3.193) Brabantio tells Desdemona that 'For your sake' he is glad he has no other children.*

salary NOUN
reward
• *(Ham 3.3.79) Hamlet reflects about killing Claudius while he is praying: 'this is hire and salary, not*

revenge'—payment or reward for a deed, rather than revenge for a crime.

Salic also spelled **Salique** ADJECTIVE
[pronounced **sa**-lik]
the name of a law stating that the French crown could be passed on only through male descendants
• *(H5 1.2.11) Henry asks Canterbury to say if 'the law Salic that they have in France' bars him from the French throne.*

sallet NOUN
1 salad
• *(KL 3.4.125) Poor Tom says he 'eats cow-dung for sallets'.*
2 tasty bit
• *(Ham 2.2.429) Hamlet tells one of the Players of a play where 'there were no sallets in the lines to make the matter savoury'—no vulgarity*

sallied, sally see **sully**

salt ADJECTIVE
1 bitter
• *(Oth 3.4.47) Othello asks Desdemona for a handkerchief for his 'salt and sorry rheum'—his heavy cold.*
2 lecherous
• *(Oth 2.1.232) Iago describes Cassio as having a 'salt and most hidden loose affection'.*

salt NOUN
salt tears
• *(KL 4.6.191) Lear comments that his situation 'would make a man a man of salt'—move a man to tears.*

salvage NOUN
savage
• *(Tem 2.2.57) Stephano asks Caliban: 'Do you put tricks upon's with salvages and men of Ind?'—are you playing tricks on us with savages and men from the Indies.*
This is the spelling in the First Folio. Several editions replace it with 'savages'.

salve VERB
make more acceptable
• *(MA 1.1.289) Claudio assures Don Pedro that, though his admission of love for Hero was brief, he 'would have salv'd it with a longer treatise'.*

sampire also spelled **samphire** NOUN
a type of marine plant, used in pickling
• *(KL 4.6.15) Edgar describes a person climbing on the cliffs at Dover: 'halfway down / Hangs one that gathers sampire'.*

sanctified ADJECTIVE
as well as meaning 'having a saintly character', you'll find:
appearing to be holy
• *(Ham 1.3.130) Polonius describes Hamlet's vows to Ophelia as 'Breathing like sanctified and pious bawds'—with pretended sincerity.*
› **unsanctified** ADJECTIVE
wicked
• *(Mac 4.2.78) Macduff's wife tells a Murderer that she hopes her husband is 'in no place so unsanctified / Where such as thou mayst find him'.*

sanctimonious ADJECTIVE
Don't read in the meaning of 'appearing or pretending to be holy'.
holy
• *(Tem 4.1.16) Prospero warns Ferdinand not to have sex with Miranda 'before / All sanctimonious ceremonies' have taken place.*

sanctimony NOUN
sacred bond
• *(Oth 1.3.349) Iago thinks he will be able to arrange matters so that the 'sanctimony and a frail vow' between Desdemona and Othello will not prevent Roderigo from having her.*

sanctuarize VERB
shelter
• *(Ham 4.7.127) Claudius agrees with Laertes that 'No place indeed should murder sanctuarize'—not even a church should give sanctuary to a murder.*

sand-blind ADJECTIVE
half-blind
• *(MV 2.2.69) Gobbo tells Lancelot: 'Alack, sir, I am sand-blind'.*
The word has nothing to do with grains of sand; the first part is a popular version of an Old English prefix 'sam-', meaning 'half'.

sanded ADJECTIVE
sandy-coloured
• *(MND 4.1.119) Theseus describes his hounds as being of Spartan origin, 'so sanded'.*

sans PREPOSITION [pronounced **sanz**]
without
• *(Tem 1.2.97) Prospero recalls his state of mind in Milan: 'A confidence sans bound'.*

sapient ADJECTIVE
wise
• *(KL 3.6.22) Lear asks one of his companions (either Poor Tom or the Fool) to sit down: 'Thou, sapient sir, sit here'.*

a b c d e f g h i j k l m n o p q r Ss t u v w x y z

Sardis NOUN [pronounced **sah**-diss]
the capital of Lydia (present-day Turkey) in Asia Minor
• *(JC 4.2.28) Lucilius reports that the army of Cassius 'mean this night in Sardis to be quarter'd'.*
see MAP, p.176

Sarum NOUN [pronounced **sair**-um]
the old name for Salisbury, in present-day Wiltshire—Salisbury Plain being a possible location for King Arthur's legendary kingdom
• *(KL 2.2.80) Kent, calling Oswald a goose (a whore), says that if he had him 'upon Sarum plain, / I'd drive ye cackling home to Camelot'.*

satiety NOUN
tedious satisfaction
• *(Oth 2.1.222) Iago assures Roderigo there will come a point when the relationship between Desdemona and Othello will 'give satiety a fresh appetite'—want something new (they'll get bored with each other).*

satisfaction NOUN
as well as meaning 'removal of doubt', you'll find:
compensation
• *(Ham 4.5.205) Claudius promises that if he is found guilty of Polonius' death he will transfer the kingdom to Laertes 'in satisfaction'.*

› **satisfy** VERB
convince
• *(JC 3.2.1) The Plebeians shout at Brutus: 'We will be satisfied!'*

› **unsatisfied** ADJECTIVE
(people) unaware of all the facts
• *(Ham 5.2.333) Hamlet asks Horatio to 'Report me and my cause aright / To the unsatisfied'.*

Saturn see COSMOS, p.174

save your reverence see **reverence, sir-reverence**

saw NOUN
old saying
• *(TN 3.4.352) Sir Toby tells his companions they will talk of 'most sage saws'—the wisest reflections about life.*

say VERB
as well as meaning 'speak', you'll find:
speak the truth
• *(TN 3.1.10) Feste responds to Cesario's remarks: 'You have said, sir'.*

› **well said**
well done
• *(Oth 2.1.163) Iago sees Cassio taking Desdemona's hand: 'Ay, well said'.*

'sblood see SWEARING, p.298

scaffold NOUN
stage
• *(H5 Prologue.10) The Chorus apologizes for performing 'On this unworthy scaffold'.*

scald also spelled **scall, scaul, scauld** ADJECTIVE
vile
• *(H5 5.1.29) The Welsh Captain calls Pistol a 'scald knave'.*

scambling ADJECTIVE
quarrelsome
• *(MA 5.1.94) Antonio calls Claudio and Don Pedro 'Scambling, outfacing, fashion-monging boys'.*

scambling NOUN
struggling
• *(H5 5.2.197) Henry tells Kate he will 'get thee with scambling'—he will have to work hard to win her affections.*

scamel NOUN
a type of edible bird or shellfish
• *(Tem 2.2.167) Caliban promises to get Stephano 'Young scamels from the rock'.*
No other instance of the word is known, so a more precise meaning cannot be given. That's something we have to expect sometimes, when we're reading old texts.

scan VERB
examine
• *(Oth 3.3.247) Iago suggests to Othello that he 'scan this thing no farther'—the possible affair between Cassio and Desdemona.*

scandal VERB
pour scorn on
• *(JC 1.2.76) Cassius denies he is someone who would fawn on people 'And after scandal them'.*

› **scandalled** also spelled **scandall'd** ADJECTIVE
shameful
• *(Tem 4.1.90) Ceres says she has given up Venus and Cupid's 'scandall'd company'.*

scant VERB
1 neglect
• *(KL 1.1.277) Goneril criticizes Cordelia: 'you have obedience scanted'.*
2 restrict
• *(MV 2.1.17) Portia reflects on what might have happened 'If my father had not scanted me'—in choosing a husband.*
3 cut short
• *(MV 5.1.141) Portia welcomes Antonio briefly: 'I scant this breathing courtesy'.*

scant ADJECTIVE
sparing
• *(Ham 1.3.121) Polonius advises Ophelia to be 'something scanter of your maiden presence' —limit the amount of time she spends with Hamlet.*

scant ADVERB
scarcely
• *(RJ 1.2.101) Benvolio assures Romeo that Rosaline 'shall scant show well that now seems best'—she (who now appears best to you) is not going to appear as well as she does now when you see other beautiful women.*

› **scanted** ADJECTIVE
withheld
• *(KL 3.2.67) Kent tells Lear he will return to Regan's castle and 'force / Their scanted courtesy' to gain them entrance.*

scape also spelled **'scape** VERB
a short form of 'escape'
• *(Mac 3.4.20) The First Murderer tells Macbeth: 'Fleance is scap'd'—he's got away.*

scape NOUN
a short form of 'escape'
• *(Oth 1.3.135) Othello recalls how he spoke 'Of hair-breadth scapes' from danger.*

scarf NOUN
⚠ *Don't read in the meaning of something worn around the neck or head.*
military sash
• *(MA 2.1.178) Benedick asks Claudio how he will wear the sign of a forsaken lover—'under your arm, like a lieutenant's scarf?'*

scarf VERB
wrap round (like a sash)
• *(Ham 5.2.13) Hamlet describes how he had a 'sea-gown scarf'd about me'.*

› **scarf up** VERB
blindfold
• *(Mac 3.2.47) Macbeth talks as if to the night, asking it to 'Scarf up the tender eye of pitiful day'.*

› **scarfed** ADJECTIVE
fully decked out
• *(MV 2.6.16) Gratiano describes how 'The scarfed bark puts from her native bay'—the ship sets sail in all its glory from her harbour.*

scathe also spelled **scath** VERB
harm
• *(RJ 1.5.83) Capulet tells off Tybalt for his attitude: 'This trick may chance to scathe you'.*

› **scatheful** also spelled **scathful** ADJECTIVE
harmful
• *(TN 5.1.51) Orsino describes how Antonio made 'such scathful grapple' with the best ships in his fleet—a destructive battle.*

scattered also spelled **scatter'd** ADJECTIVE
divided
• *(KL 3.1.31) Kent reports how an army is coming 'Into this scatter'd kingdom'.*

› **scattering** ADJECTIVE
haphazard
• *(Oth 3.3.152) Iago tells Othello not to be concerned about 'his scattering and unsure observance' of Cassio and Desdemona.*

scaul see **scald**

schedule NOUN
⚠ *Don't read the meaning of 'timetable' into these senses.*
1 inventory
• *(TN 1.5.225) Olivia says she will 'give out divers schedules of my beauty'.*
2 document
• *(JC 3.1.3) Artemidorus asks Caesar to 'Read this schedule'.*

scholar NOUN
learned man (who knows Latin, the language of religion, and of exorcism)
• *(MA 2.1.238) Benedick wishes that 'some scholar would conjure' Beatrice—cast the devil out of her.*

school NOUN
university
• *(Ham 1.2.113) Claudius denies Hamlet the chance of 'going back to school in Wittenberg'.*

school VERB
control
• *(Mac 4.2.15) Ross asks Macduff's wife to 'school yourself'—calm down.*

› **schooling** NOUN
counsel
• *(MND 1.1.116) Theseus says he has 'some private schooling' for Egeus and Demetrius.*

scimitar see **SWORDS AND DAGGERS, p.156**

scion NOUN [pronounced **sigh**-on]
shoot taken from a plant (to grow a new plant), used here to mean 'offspring'
• *(H5 3.6.7) The Dauphin asks if the English—whom he calls 'Our scions'—will grow bigger than the French.*
🎭 *The English are in part descended from the Normans, who were also ancestors of the French.*

sconce NOUN
1 head
• *(Ham 5.1.94) Hamlet asks why a dead lawyer would allow the First Gravedigger to treat his*

skull so carelessly—'knock him about the sconce with a dirty shovel'.

This is a jocular usage, much as people often say 'bonce', 'melon', 'loaf', or 'noggin' today.

2 fort

• *(H5 3.7.67) Gower describes those who talk of military actions 'at such and such a sconce'.*

scorch VERB

Don't read in the meaning of 'burn the surface' of something.

slash

• *(Mac 3.2.13) Macbeth tells his wife: 'We have scorch'd the snake, not kill'd it'.*

score NOUN

1 account

• *(Mac 5.9.19) Siward says his son 'parted well, and paid his score'—did his duty, giving up his life as a soldier should.*

2 tavern-bill

• *(RJ 2.4.125) Mercutio sings: 'a hare that is hoar / Is too much for a score'—a hare that is old and white should not be put on the bill (because it is mouldy).*

See also **NUMBERS, p.206**

score VERB

make a mark on or wound

• *(Oth 4.1.126) Othello asks, unheard by Cassio: 'Have you scored me?'*

scout VERB

as well as meaning 'look out for', you'll find:

mock

• *(Tem 3.2.118) Stephano sings: 'Flout 'em and scout 'em'.*

The word in the First Folio and some modern editions is 'cout', but 'scout' also appears in the next line, so some editions use it here too. The meaning of 'cout', used in some editions, is unclear, though from the context it probably has a similar meaning to 'scout'.

screw VERB

Don't read in modern meanings to do with 'insert by twisting'.

wrench

• *(TN 5.1.118) Orsino tells Olivia he knows what it is 'That screws me from my true place in your favour'.*

scrimer NOUN

swordsman

• *(Ham 4.7.100) Claudius talks of those among the French who have praised Laertes' fencing skills—'the scrimers of their nation'.*

scrip NOUN

script

• *(MND 1.2.3) Bottom tells Quince to call the company together 'according to the scrip'.*

scrubbed ADJECTIVE

undersized

• *(MV 5.1.162) Gratiano says he gave Nerissa's ring to 'a little scrubbed boy'.*

scruple NOUN

as well as meaning 'doubt', you'll find:

tiny amount

• *(MA 5.1.93) Antonio says he knows how much Claudio and Don Pedro weigh, 'even to the utmost scruple'.*

In talking of their weight, he doesn't actually know how heavy they are. Today we might say he knows them even down to their shoe-size—from top to bottom.

scullion NOUN

domestic servant

• *(Ham 2.2.574) Hamlet criticizes himself for cursing like 'A scullion!'*

This is the word used in the First Folio. The Second Quarto text has 'stallyon', which has led some editions to use 'stallion', a slang word for a prostitute.

scurvy ADJECTIVE

contemptible

• *(Tem 2.2.150) Trinculo describes Caliban as 'A most scurvy monster!'*

scuse also spelled **'scuse** NOUN

a short form of 'excuse'

• *(Oth 4.1.79) Iago tells Othello that he got Cassio to leave, laying 'good scuse upon your ecstasy' —giving as a reason Othello's fit.*

Scylla NOUN [pronounced **sil**-a]

in Greek mythology, a dangerous rock (or sea-monster) in the narrow strait between Sicily and the Italian mainland

• *(MV 3.5.14) Lancelot says each of Jessica's parents invite damnation: 'when I shun Scylla your father, I fall into Charybdis your mother'.*

Scylla was opposite the whirlpool of Charybdis, so ships that avoided the one were in danger of being wrecked by the other. The dilemma is also expressed by the idiom 'between the devil and the deep blue sea'.

see also **Charybdis**

see **MAP, p.176**

Scythian NOUN [pronounced **si**-thee-an]

someone from Scythia, an ancient region of eastern Europe, where the people were known for

their savagery
• *(KL 1.1.115) Lear affirms that he would favour 'The barbarous Scythian' rather than Cordelia.*

sea-cap see HATS, p.160

sea-gown see CLOTHING, p.158

seal NOUN
1 confirming action
• *(Ham 3.2.383) Hamlet affirms that, though he may use harsh words to his mother, he will never 'give them seals'—turn them into deeds.*
2 promise
• *(MND 3.2.144) Demetrius describes Helena as 'this seal of bliss!'*

seal VERB
1 confirm
• *(Ham 4.7.1) Claudius tells Laertes: 'Now must your conscience my acquittance seal'—you must accept that I am not guilty.*
2 agree
• *(MV 1.3.148) Antonio agrees Shylock's terms: 'I'll seal to such a bond'.*
3 mark (as if by a wax seal, identifying the owner or sender of a letter by the imprint made in the wax)
• *(Ham 3.2.63) Hamlet tells Horatio that his soul had 'sealed thee for herself'—made a bond of friendship.*

› **seal under** VERB
become security for
• *(MV 1.2.75) Portia says the English suitor has boxed the ear of the Scottish suitor, who has promised to repay him for the blow, and the French suitor has 'sealed under for another'—agreed to do the same.*

› **sealed** also spelled **seal'd** ADJECTIVE
certified (by being marked with a wax seal)
• *(Ham 1.1.89) Horatio describes a 'seal'd compact' between the Danes and the Norwegians.*

› **sealing day** also spelled **-day** NOUN
wedding-day
• *(MND 1.1.84) Theseus says the arrival of the new moon will be 'The sealing-day betwixt my love and me'.*

sea-maid NOUN
mermaid
• *(MND 2.1.154) Oberon describes 'the sea-maid's music'.*

sea-marge NOUN
coast
• *(Tem 4.1.69) Iris lists the places where Ceres walks: 'thy sea-marge, sterile and rocky-hard'.*

sea-mark NOUN
landmark
• *(Oth 5.2.266) Othello says he has reached the 'very sea-mark of my utmost sail'—of his last voyage (the end of his life).*

sear also spelled **sere** NOUN [pronounced **seer**]
trigger-catch (of a gun)
• *(Ham 2.2.318) Hamlet predicts that 'the clown shall make those laugh whose lungs are tickle a th' sear'—ready to go off like a gun.*

search VERB
as well as meaning 'look for', you'll find:
probe
• *(JC 5.3.42) Cassius asks Pindarus to use his sword to 'search this bosom'—to kill him.*

search NOUN
search-party
• *(Oth 1.1.158) Iago tells Roderigo to 'lead to the Sagittary the raised search'—to find Othello (the Sagittary is probably the name of the inn where Othello is staying).*
Sagittarius is the name today of a sign of the zodiac—a centaur who is an archer.

› **searcher** NOUN
an official appointed to view corpses and report on the cause of death
• *(RJ 5.2.8) Friar John recounts how 'the searchers of the town' locked the doors.*

seasick ADJECTIVE
⚠ *Don't read in the meaning of 'feeling ill'.*
tired of voyaging
• *(RJ 5.3.119) Romeo, about to commit suicide, sees himself as a ship about to be wrecked: 'run on / The dashing rocks thy seasick weary bark!'*

season NOUN
1 time
• *(Ham 1.4.5) Horatio says midnight 'draws near the season / Wherein the spirit held his wont to walk'.*
2 opportunity
• *(Ham 3.2.245) Lucianus finds it a 'Confederate season' to commit murder—the right time.*
3 preservative
• *(Mac 3.4.141) Lady Macbeth tells her husband that he lacks 'the season of all natures, sleep'.*

season VERB
1 ripen
• *(Ham 1.3.81) Polonius comments on the advice he has just given Laertes: 'My blessing season this in thee'.*
2 preserve
• *(TN 1.1.30) Valentine describes Olivia's actions and

a b c d e f g h i j k l m n o p q r **Ss** t u v w x y z

tears 'to season / A brother's dead love'—her grief in mourning the loss of her brother.
3 moderate
• *(Ham 1.2.192) Horatio tells Hamlet of the Ghost: 'Season your admiration for a while'—control your wonder.*
4 turn into
• *(Ham 3.2.201) The Player King tells his Queen that anyone who tests an insincere friend 'Directly seasons him his enemy'.*
5 delight
• *(MV 4.1.97) Shylock asks if masters would let the palates of their slaves 'Be season'd with such viands'—eat the same food as them.*
6 prepare
• *(Ham 3.3.86) Hamlet decides not to kill Claudius while 'he is fit and season'd for his passage'.*

› **out of season**
at an inconvenient time
• *(KL 2.1.118) Regan explains why she and Cornwall have visited Gloucester 'Thus out of season'.*

seat NOUN
1 throne
• *(H5 1.1.88) Canterbury explains Henry's claim to 'the crown and seat of France'.*
2 estate
• *(MV 1.1.171) Bassanio talks of where Portia lives: 'her seat of Belmont'.*
3 location
• *(Mac 1.6.1) Duncan says Macbeth's 'castle hath a pleasant seat'.*

seat VERB
establish
• *(H5 1.2.62) Canterbury explains how Charles the Great 'did seat the French / Beyond the River Sala'.*

› **seated** ADJECTIVE
firmly placed
• *(Mac 1.3.135) Macbeth finds his thoughts 'make my seated heart knock at my ribs'.*

› **disseat** also spelled **dis-seat** VERB
remove from the throne
• *(Mac 5.3.21) Macbeth reflects that the battle 'Will cheer me ever or disseat me now'.*

second NOUN
1 supporter
• *(KL 4.6.190) Lear asks: 'No seconds? All myself?'—no-one to back me up? All by myself?*
2 supporting action
• *(Ham 4.7.153) Claudius wants his plan to 'have a back or second'.*

second VERB
assist
• *(MA 5.1.2) Antonio tells Leonato it is not wise 'to second grief against yourself'—to make his grief worse.*

secret ADJECTIVE
as well as meaning 'not to be told', you'll find:
magical
• *(Tem 1.2.77) Prospero describes himself 'rapt in secret studies'.*

sect NOUN
1 faction
• *(KL 5.3.18) Lear promises Cordelia that they will wear out 'packs and sects of great ones'—survive the cliques and political factions that come and go in the world of the court.*
2 cutting
• *(Oth 1.3.327) Iago says that lust is 'a sect or scion' of love—an offshoot or graft.*

sectary astronomical
devotee of astrology
• *(KL 1.2.143) Edgar asks his brother: 'How long have you been a sectary astronomical?'*
The fields of astronomy and astrology overlapped until well into the 18th century.

secure ADJECTIVE
as well as meaning 'safe', you'll find:
carefree
• *(Ham 1.5.61) The Ghost describes how Claudius came 'Upon my secure hour'—in an unguarded time, as he slept in his orchard.*

› **secure** VERB
1 protect
• *(Tem 2.1.305) Sebastian tells Alonso that 'we stood here securing your repose'.*
2 make over-confident
• *(KL 4.1.20) Gloucester reflects that 'Our means secure us'—the things we own keep us from suspecting we will suffer any harm.*
3 take comfort
• *(Oth 1.3.10) The Duke says the contradictory reports about the Turkish fleet do not make him feel any safer: 'I do not so secure me in the error'.*

› **security** NOUN
over-confidence
• *(JC 2.3.7) Artemidorus warns Caesar that 'security gives way to conspiracy'.*

sedge NOUN
a grassy plant that grows near water
• *(MA 2.1.189) Benedick describes Claudio as a hurt fowl who will 'creep into sedges' to hide himself.*

› **sedged** also spelled **sedg'd** ADJECTIVE
made from sedges
• *(Tem 4.1.129) Iris calls to the nymphs 'With your sedg'd crowns'.*

seel VERB
close up
• *(Oth 3.3.212) Iago describes Desdemona as someone who could 'seel her father's eyes up close as oak'—hide from her father any bad behaviour (as if enclosed within an oak tree).*
The word is from falconry, when a bird's eyelids are sewed up ('seeled') as part of taming.

› **seeling** ADJECTIVE
concealing
• *(Mac 3.2.46) Macbeth asks 'seeling night' to come quickly to hide his actions.*

seeming NOUN
1 appearance
• *(Oth 1.3.109) The Duke asks for more substantial arguments against Othello than ones 'Of modern seeming'—that are used every day.*
2 deceiver
• *(MA 4.1.55) Claudio attacks Hero: 'Out on thee, seeming!'*
'Out on thee seeming' is in the First Folio. Some editions keep this punctuation and change 'thee' to 'thy', in which case the word would mean 'deception'.
3 demeanour
• *(Ham 3.2.85) Hamlet plans with Horatio to observe Claudius 'In censure of his seeming'—to judge his behaviour.*

seeming ADJECTIVE
apparent
• *(RJ 3.3.112) The Friar criticizes Romeo for being an 'Unseemly woman in a seeming man!'*

› **well-seeming** ADJECTIVE
attractive-looking
• *(RJ 1.1.173) Romeo reflects on love as a 'Misshapen chaos of well-seeming forms'.*

segregation NOUN
Don't read in a meaning to do with 'separating racial groups'.
scattering
• *(KL 2.1.10) A Gentleman describes the 'segregation of the Turkish fleet'.*

seize upon NOUN
take possession of
• *(Oth 5.2.362) Lodovico says Gratiano may 'seize upon the fortunes of the Moor'.*

› **seised** also spelled **seized, seiz'd** VERB
possessed
• *(Ham 1.1.92) Horatio talks of the lands that old Fortinbras 'stood seiz'd of'.*

self ADJECTIVE
same
• *(KL 1.1.68) Regan says she is 'made of that self mettle as my sister'.*
Some editions have 'made of that self same mettle as my sister'.

› **one self**
one and the same
• *(TN 1.1.39) Orsino says all of Olivia's feelings are governed by 'one self king'—one and the same ruler.*

self-abuse see **abuser**

self-bounty NOUN
inner virtue
• *(Oth 3.3.202) Iago tells Othello that he 'would not have your free and noble nature, / Out of self-bounty, be abus'd'—would not have you exploited because of your natural generosity of spirit.*

self-covered see **cover**

self-endeared also spelled **-endear'd** ADJECTIVE
in love with oneself
• *(MA 3.1.56) Hero says that Beatrice 'is so self-endear'd'.*

self-subdued see **subdued**

semblable NOUN
likeness
• *(Ham 5.2.116) Hamlet says Laertes' 'semblable is his mirror'—he is matched in fighting only by his own reflection.*

› **semblative** ADJECTIVE
resembling
• *(TN 1.4.34) Orsino says Cesario's qualities are all 'semblative a woman's part'.*

semblance NOUN
1 appearance
• *(RJ 1.5.73) Capulet tells Tybalt that frowns are 'An ill-beseeming semblance for a feast'.*
2 likeness
• *(MA 5.1.245) Claudio, having learned the truth, thinks of Hero 'In the rare semblance that I lov'd it first'.*

Seneca NOUN [pronounced **sen**-e-ka]
Roman tragic playwright of the 1st-century AD
• *(Ham 2.2.389) Polonius describes what the players can present: 'Seneca cannot be too heavy'—Seneca's tragedies aren't too tough for them to perform.*

senna see note at **cynne**

sennet NOUN
a trumpet-call signalling a procession
• *(JC 1.2.214) Stage direction: 'Sennet. Exeunt Caesar and his train.'*

sennight see **seven-night**

sense NOUN
as well as meaning 'organ of sense' and 'ability to perceive or feel', you'll find:
1 power of reason
• *(Ham 5.1.232) Laertes curses Hamlet for depriving Ophelia of her 'most ingenious sense'—her ability to think clearly.*
2 opinion
• *(Oth 5.2.287) Othello feels, after all that has happened, 'in my sense 'tis happiness to die'.*
3 intuition
• *(Ham 3.4.194) Hamlet asks Gertrude not to ignore 'sense and secrecy' and reveal his true nature to Claudius.*

> **to the sense**
to the quick (the most sensitive parts of the body)
• *(Oth 5.1.11) Iago reflects on the way he has rubbed Roderigo 'almost to the sense'.*

> **senseless** ADJECTIVE
incapable of feeling
• *(JC 1.1.37) Murellus calls the people 'you blocks, you stones, you worse than senseless things'.*

> **sensible** ADJECTIVE
as well as meaning 'endowed with good sense', you'll find:
1 capable of feeling
• *(MND 5.1.179) Theseus thinks that the character of Wall, 'being sensible, should curse again'.*
2 perceptible by the senses
• *(Mac 2.1.36) Macbeth addresses a dagger in the air: 'Art thou not, fatal vision, sensible / To feeling as to sight?'*

> **sensibly** ADVERB
⚠*Don't read in the meaning of 'wisely'.*
acutely
• *(Ham 4.5.149) Claudius tells Laertes he is 'most sensibly in grief' for Polonius' death.*

sentence NOUN
⚠*Don't read meanings to do with 'grammar' or 'punishment' into these senses.*
1 maxim—a short statement expressing a general truth
• *(RJ 2.3.79) The Friar instructs Romeo: 'Pronounce this sentence then: / Women may fall, when there's no strength in men'.*
2 authoritative decision
• *(KL 1.1.169) Lear harangues Kent for coming 'betwixt our sentence and our power'—between his decision and its implementation.*

sententious NOUN
intended to mean 'sentences'
• *(RJ 2.4.194) The Nurse says Juliet 'hath the prettiest sententious of it'—she speaks beautfully.*

se offendendo see **LATIN, p.352**

sepulchre VERB
serve as a burial-place for
• *(KL 2.4.128) Lear says that if Regan were not pleased to see him, she would be the daughter of someone else, so that her mother's tomb would be 'Sepulchring an adult'ress'—serving as a place for a woman that was unfaithful to him.*

sequent ADJECTIVE
1 following
• *(Ham 5.2.54) Hamlet finishes telling Horatio his story: 'what to this was sequent / Thou knowest already'.*
2 successive
• *(Oth 1.2.41) Cassio tells Othello that 'a dozen sequent messengers' have arrived at the court.*

sequester NOUN
withdrawal
• *(Oth 3.4.36) Othello tells Desdemona that her hand 'requires / A sequester from liberty'—she must not be free to do as she likes.*

sequestration NOUN
1 removal
• *(H5 1.1.58) Canterbury recalls how Henry never had 'Any retirement, any sequestration, / From open haunts'—he never kept away from public places.*
2 separation
• *(Oth 1.3.341) Iago says the love between Othello and Desdemona had a violent start and will have 'an answerable sequestration'—a corresponding end.*

sere also spelled **sear** ADJECTIVE
withered
• *(Mac 5.3.23) Macbeth reflects how his 'way of life / Is fall'n into the sere, the yellow leaf'.*
✒ *'Sere' isn't a noun here, but an adjective describing 'leaf'. The use of an extra 'the' allows the metre in the line to be regular.*

sere NOUN see **sear**

sergeant NOUN
1 army officer
• *(Mac 1.2.3) Malcolm introduces 'the sergeant' (who is actually a captain by rank) who saved him from captivity.*
2 sheriff's officer
• *(Ham 5.2.329) Hamlet's dying words: 'this fell sergeant, Death, / Is strict in his arrest'.*

serve VERB
as well as meaning 'be useful', you'll find:
1 be favourable
• *(JC 4.3.223) Brutus tells Cassius they 'must take the current when it serves'—go with the tide, act when it's easiest.*
2 work as a servant
• *(MV 1.3.86) Antonio comments on the venture 'that Jacob serv'd for'—in the Bible, a plan Jacob devised to gain a flock of sheep (he worked hard to get it—unlike usurers, who simply sit back and wait for the money to roll in).*

service NOUN
as well as meaning 'work activity' and 'military service', you'll find:
1 situation (of employment)
• *(TN 2.5.146) Malvolio reads in the letter from Olivia: 'She that would alter services with thee'—change social positions, by making Malvolio master of the house, and she, his servant.*
2 respect
• *(KL 1.1.28) Edmund is introduced to Kent and says: 'My services to your lordship'.*
3 course (in a meal)
• *(Ham 4.3.23) Hamlet tells Claudius: 'Your fat king and your lean beggar is but variable service'—different courses in the same meal for worms.*
4 table preparations (for a meal)
• *(Mac 1.7.1) Stage direction: Enter 'Servants with dishes and service'.*

serviceable ADJECTIVE
ready to do any job (no matter how wicked)
• *(KL 4.6.247) Edgar describes Oswald as 'a serviceable villain'.*

> **› super-serviceable** ADJECTIVE
> offering service beyond what is needed
> • *(KL 2.2.16) Kent describes Oswald as a 'super-serviceable, finical rogue'—officious and fussy.*

servile ADJECTIVE
slavish
• *(KL 3.2.21) Lear calls the elements of the storm 'servile ministers'—agents serving his daughters' unpleasant ways.*

servitor NOUN
servant
• *(Oth 1.3.40) A Messenger brings the Duke a report from Montano, 'Your trusty and most valiant servitor'.*

sessa also spelled **sesey, sese** INTERJECTION
off you go (a cry of encouragement used to a horse)
• *(KL 3.4.96) Poor Tom imagines himself talking to a horse: 'sessa! let him trot by'.*

session see **direct session**

set ADJECTIVE
1 with jests carefully composed (pre-written comedy, not spontaneous or improvised)
• *(TN 1.5.80) Malvolio is contemptuous of people who laugh at 'these set kind of fools' such as Feste.*
2 rigidly staring
• *(Tem 3.2.8) Stephano tells drunken Caliban: 'Thy eyes are almost set in thy head'.*

set NOUN
cycle
• *(Oth 2.3.116) Iago says that Cassio will stay awake to drink while the clock goes round 'a double set'.*

set VERB
as well as meanings to do with 'putting' and 'placing', you'll find:
1 rate
• *(TN 5.1.184) Sir Andrew complains of Cesario: 'I think you set nothing by a bloody coxcomb'—you think nothing of an injured head.*
2 stake
• *(KL 1.4.116) The Fool rhymes: 'Set less than thou throwest'—don't stake all your winnings on a single throw of the dice.*
A popular Elizabethan pastime was to bet on the outcome of a roll of the dice.
see **RECREATION, p.170**
3 direct
• *(Ham 3.4.16) Gertrude tells Hamlet she will 'set those to you that can speak' -send people to talk to you that you will have to listen to.*

> **› set down** VERB
> 1 decide
> • *(Ham 3.1.169) Claudius says he has 'set it down'—decided what to do with Hamlet.*
> 2 make a note
> • *(Ham 1.5.107) Hamlet thinks it right 'to set it down / That one may smile, and smile, and be a villain'.*
> 3 loosen
> • *(Oth 2.1.193) Iago continues with Othello's use of musical terms to describe his love for Desdemona: 'I'll set down the pegs that make this music'—I'll loosen the pins that the strings

of an instrument are fastened to (I'll destroy this love).

› set forth VERB

1 praise

• *(MV 3.5.81) Jessica tells Lorenzo: 'I'll set you forth'.*

2 display

• *(Mac 1.4.6) Malcolm says Cawdor 'set forth / A deep repentance' for his treachery.*

› set up one's rest

stake all (in a card-game)

• *(MV 2.2.96) Lancelot tells Gobbo: 'I have set up my rest to run away'.*

set cock-a-hoop see **cock-a-hoop**

sevennight also spelled **seven-night, sennight, se'nnight** NOUN

week

• *(MA 2.1.332) Leonato tells Claudio he cannot have his wedding until 'a just sevennight'—exactly a week away.*

several ADJECTIVE

⚠ *Don't read the meaning of 'more than two but not many' into these senses.*

1 different

• *(TN 2.2.1) Stage direction: 'enter Viola and Malvolio, at several doors'.*

2 various

• *(KL 1.1.43) Lear announces that he will 'publish / Our daughters' several dowers'—announce their inheritances.*

› severally ADVERB

separately

• *(JC 3.2.10) The Second Plebeian says they can compare the arguments of Brutus and Cassius 'When severally we hear them rendered'.*

› severals NOUN

details

• *(H5 1.1.86) Canterbury says he has yet to tell Henry of 'the severals and unhidden passages / Of his true titles'.*

severed ADJECTIVE

⚠ *Don't read in the meaning of 'cut apart'.*

opened

• *(MV 3.2.118) Bassanio finds Portia's portrait in the casket he has chosen: 'Here are sever'd lips / Parted with sugar breath'—sweet-smelling breath.*

sewer NOUN [pronounced **syoo**-er]

⚠ *Don't read in the meaning of 'underground drain'.*

master of ceremonies (who presides over a formal meal)

• *(Mac 1.7.1) Stage direction: 'Enter a Sewer and divers Servants'.*

shadow NOUN

1 image

• *(MV 3.2.127) Bassanio says his praise of Portia's portrait 'doth wrong this shadow / In underprizing it'—isn't enough to do justice to the real woman.*

2 reflection

• *(JC 1.2.58) Cassius tells Brutus that he needs mirrors to 'see your shadow' of worthiness.*

3 illusion

• *(Ham 2.2.256) Hamlet observes that 'A dream itself is but a shadow'.*

4 spirit

• *(MND 3.2.347) Puck calls Oberon 'King of Shadows'—Oberon can make himself invisible, and move as fast as a shadow.*

5 shade

• *(Tem 4.1.67) Iris describes Ceres' 'broom groves, / Whose shadow the dismissed bachelor loves'—the yellow-flowered shrubs under which love-sick men sit to mope (yellow being the colour of cowardice).*

shadow VERB

conceal

• *(Mac 5.4.5) Malcolm points to the advantage of using branches as camouflage: 'thereby shall we shadow / The numbers of our host'.*

› shadowed also spelled **shadow'd** ADJECTIVE

darkened

• *(MV 2.1.2) Morocco describes his complexion as 'The shadow'd livery of the burnish'd sun'—the dark clothes of the polished sun.*

› shadowing ADJECTIVE

darkening

• *(Oth 4.1.40) The trembling Othello says there must be a good reason for his nature to give way to 'such shadowing passion'.*

› shadowy ADJECTIVE

shady

• *(KL 1.1.63) Lear gives Goneril land 'With shadowy forests'.*

Shafalus NOUN [pronounced **sha**-fa-lus]

a mispronunciation of 'Cephalus', in Greek mythology a man who (in one version of the story), despite being abducted by Aurora (the Roman goddess of the dawn), remained faithful to his wife Procris

• *(MND 5.1.194) Pyramus finds a comparison for his love to Thisbe: 'Not Shafalus to Procrus was so true'.*

shale NOUN

shell

• *(H5 4.2.18) The Constable says the French will suck*

away the souls of the English, 'Leaving them but the shales and husks of men'.
✒ *This is the spelling in the First Folio. Several editions replace it with 'shells'.*

shambles NOUN
slaughter-house
• *(Oth 4.2.65) Othello says Desdemona is as chaste 'as summer flies are in the shambles'—feeding on everything (in other words, not chaste at all).*

shape NOUN
as well as meaning 'visible form', you'll find:
1 posture
• *(Ham 4.7.89) Claudius recalls the 'shapes and tricks' performed by Lamord on his horse.*
2 role
• *(Ham 4.7.150) Claudius discusses with Laertes what else needs to be done to 'fit us to our shape'—to help us achieve what we want.*
> **shaping** ADJECTIVE
> imaginative
> • *(MND 5.1.5) Theseus talks about the 'shaping fantasies' of lovers and madmen.*

shard NOUN
fragment of a broken pot
• *(Ham 5.1.215) The Priest explains how Ophelia might have been buried with 'Shards, flints, and pebbles' thrown on her (because she is thought to have committed suicide, she should not receive any formal burial rites or prayers).*

shard-born or **-borne** ADJECTIVE
born in dung or carried [with the spelling *borne*] on scaly wings
• *(Mac 3.2.42) Macbeth talks of 'The shard-born beetle, with his drowsy hum'.*

shark up VERB
hastily gather together
• *(Ham 1.1.101) Horatio describes how Fortinbras has 'Shark'd up a list of lawless resolutes'.*

sharp NOUN
shrill sound
• *(RJ 3.5.28) Juliet describes the lark singing with 'harsh discords and unpleasing sharps'.*

shealed also spelled **sheal'd** ADJECTIVE
shelled
• *(KL 1.4.189) 'The Fool describes Lear as 'a sheal'd peascod'—the pod of a pea, with nothing left inside.*
✒ *'Sheal'd' is the spelling in the First Folio. Several editions replace it with 'shelled'.*

sheep-biter NOUN
shifty fellow
• *(TN 2.5.5) Sir Toby calls Malvolio a 'rascally sheep-biter'.*

sheepcote also spelled **sheep-cote** NOUN
building where sheep shelter
• *(KL 2.3.18) Edgar recalls beggars who travel around 'Poor pelting villages, sheep-cotes, and mills'.*

shent VERB
rebuked, told off
• *(TN 4.2.100) Feste tells the imprisoned Malvolio: 'I am shent for speaking to you'.*

sheriff see OCCUPATIONS, p.166

shift NOUN
arrangement
• *(MV 1.2.83) Portia hopes she 'will make shift to go without' her German suitor.*
> **for a shift**
> for lack of a better alternative
> • *(MA 2.3.80) Don Pedro tells Balthasar: 'thou sing'st well enough for a shift'.*

shift VERB
as well as meaning 'move', you'll find:
1 look out
• *(Tem 5.1.256) Stephano tells Trinculo and Caliban: 'Every man shift for all the rest'.*
2 change
• *(KL 5.3.185) Edgar explains how he had 'to shift / Into a madman's rags'.*

shiver VERB
⚠ *Don't read in the meaning of 'tremble'.*
smash to pieces
• *(KL 4.6.51) Edgar tells Gloucester what would happen to anyone falling from a cliff-top who wasn't light as air: 'Thoud'st shiver'd like an egg'.*
> **shivering** ADJECTIVE
> shattering
> • *(MND 1.2.26) Bottom declaims: 'The raging rocks / And shivering shocks'.*

shog or **shog off** VERB
be gone
• *(H5 2.3.39) Nym says it's time to leave: 'Shall we shog?'*

shoon NOUN
an old-fashioned word in Shakespeare's time for 'shoes'
• *(Ham 4.5.26) Ophelia sings of the 'sandal shoon' of a true love.*

shoot VERB
⚠ *Don't read in the meaning of 'fire a gun'.*
let fly
• *(KL 2.4.224) Lear tells Goneril he will not 'bid the thunder-bearer shoot'—call on Jove (the god*

of thunder) to send down a thunder-bolt as vengeance.

Kings were believed to have the power to bid the gods perform their wishes.

short ADJECTIVE
controlled
• *(Ham 4.1.18) Claudius reflects with regret that he 'Should have kept short' Hamlet's behaviour.*

› **shorten** VERB
1 undermine
• *(KL 4.7.9) Disguised Kent explains to Cordelia that 'to be known shortens my made intent'—he must stay disguised if he wants to stick to his plan of serving the king.*
2 leave out
• *(MA 3.2.89) Don John informs on Hero: 'circumstances shortened ... the lady is disloyal'—to cut a long story short.*

shough see ANIMALS, p.162

show NOUN
as well as meaning 'display' and 'sight', you'll find:
1 pretence
• *(Mac 1.7.81) Macbeth tells his wife they must 'mock the time with fairest show'—they must pass the time by showing they are enjoying themselves.*
2 dumbshow
• *(Ham 3.2.133) Ophelia asks Hamlet: 'Belike this show imports the argument of the play'—perhaps the dumbshow explains the plot.*

shrew also spelled **shrow** NOUN
vexatious person (literally, a small, mouse-like animal that scuttles and skitters around)
• *(TN 1.3.43) Sir Andrew calls Maria a 'fair shrew'.*

Anyone might be called a shrew, but the label was usually applied to women.

› **shrewishly** ADVERB
in a shrill voice (like a woman)
• *(TN 1.5.150) Malvolio describes Cesario as speaking 'very shrewishly'.*

shrewd also spelled **shrowd** ADJECTIVE
⚠ *Don't read meanings to do with 'having good judgement' into these senses.*
1 harsh
• *(MA 2.1.17) Leonato says Beatrice will never get a husband 'if thou be so shrewd of thy tongue'.*
2 bad-tempered
• *(MND 3.2.323) Helena describes Hermia as 'keen and shrewd'—sharp and short-tempered when she's angry.*
3 cunning
• *(JC 2.1.158) Cassius describes Antony as 'A shrewd contriver'—a cunning conspirator.*
4 ominous or bitter
• *(MV 3.2.241) Portia thinks 'There are some shrewd contents' in Bassanio's letter.*

› **shrewdly** also spelled **shrowdly** ADVERB
1 very much
• *(H5 3.8.136) Orléans says that the English 'are shrewdly out of beef'.*

He's mocking the belief that the English are always eating roast beef.
2 sharply
• *(Ham 1.4.1) Hamlet comments on the temperature: 'The air bites shrewdly'.*
3 mischievously
• *(TN 5.1.340) Olivia sympathizes with Malvolio: 'This practice hath most shrewdly pass'd upon thee'— been very wickedly imposed on you.*

shrift NOUN
1 confession of sins (to a priest)
• *(RJ 2.4.164) Romeo asks the Nurse to arrange for Juliet 'to come to shrift this afternoon'.*
2 forgiveness of sins (from a priest)
• *(RJ 2.3.56) The Friar tells Romeo: 'Riddling confession finds but riddling shrift'—an ambiguous confession will receive ambiguous forgiveness.*
3 place for hearing confession
• *(Oth 3.3.24) Desdemona assures Cassio that she will make his case to Othello so that 'His bed shall seem a school, his board a shrift'.*

Marriage was thought of as a bond of 'bed and board'. She will school (teach) Othello while he sleeps, and counsel him like a priest while he eats.

› **shrive** VERB
hear confession
• *(MV 1.2.119) Portia says she would rather Morocco 'should shrive me than wive me'.*

› **shriving-time** NOUN
time to make a confession
• *(Ham 5.2.47) Hamlet tells how his letter asked the English King to put Rosencrantz and Guildenstern to death, 'Not shriving-time allow'd'.*

Even the worst criminals were normally given time to pray for their sins before death. The rewritten letter denies his friends this chance. It was considered a terrible way to die.

shrill-gorged also spelled **-gorg'd** ADJECTIVE
shrill-sounding
• *(KL 4.6.58) Edgar tells Gloucester that 'the shrill-*

gorg'd lark' is so high above them it cannot be heard.

shrive VERB see **shrift**

shroud VERB
shelter
• *(Tem 2.2.39) Trinculo, seeing Caliban's cloak, says he 'will here shroud till the dregs of the storm be past'.*

shrow see **shrew**

shrowd see **shrewd**

shuffling NOUN
trickery
• *(Ham 3.3.61) Claudius reflects that 'There is no shuffling' in heaven.*

Sibylla NOUN [pronounced si-**bill**-a]
in Greek mythology, a prophetic priestess to whom Apollo granted as many years of life as she could hold grains of sand in her hand
• *(MV 1.2.98) Portia says she will not disregard her father's will even 'If I live to be as old as Sibylla'.*

› **sibyl** NOUN
wise woman (the modern equivalent might be a 'good or white witch')
• *(Oth 3.4.66) Othello tells Desdemona that 'A sibyl' sewed her handkerchief.*

sick ADJECTIVE
as well as meaning 'ill', you'll find:
1 full of loathing
• *(MND 2.1.212) Demetrius tells Helena: 'I am sick when I do look on thee'.*
2 pale
• *(RJ 2.2.8) Romeo describes the moon as being 'sick and green'—pale and envious (green was the colour of jealousy).*
3 harmful
• *(JC 2.1.268) Portia says Brutus has 'some sick offence' in his mind.*

› **sickly** ADJECTIVE
weak
• *(JC 5.1.86) Cassius sees birds looking down on his army as if 'we were sickly prey'.*

› **sickly over** or **o'er** VERB
cover with a pale hue
• *(Ham 3.1.85) Hamlet reflects how 'the native hue of resolution / Is sicklied o'er with the pale cast of thought'—the natural colour of a decision to do something is made pale by over-thinking.*

sickle-man also spelled **sickleman** NOUN
a harvester who uses a sickle to cut corn
• *(Tem 4.1.134) Iris calls the reapers 'sunburn'd sickle-men'.*

side-piercing ADJECTIVE
heart-breaking
• *(KL 4.6.85) Edgar calls Lear a 'side-piercing sight!'*

siege NOUN
as well as its military meaning, you'll find:
1 onslaught
• *(RJ 5.3.237) The Friar describes what Capulet did 'to remove that siege of grief' from Juliet.*
2 status
• *(Oth 1.2.22) Othello says he gets 'his life and being / From men of royal siege'.*
3 excrement
• *(Tem 2.2.102) Stephano asks Trinculo how he seemed to be 'the siege of this mooncalf'—emerging from under Caliban's cloak.*

sightless ADJECTIVE
as well as meaning 'blind', you'll find:
invisible
• *(Mac 1.5.48) Lady Macbeth calls on agents of evil in their 'sightless substances'.*

sign NOUN
as well as meaning 'indication' or 'appearance', you'll find:
1 banner
• *(H5 2.2.188) Henry urges on his troops: 'The signs of war advance'.*
2 outward appearance
• *(Oth 1.1.157) Iago says he must give Othello 'a flag and sign [sense 1] of love, / Which is indeed but sign'—his demonstrations of love to Othello are really just a show.*

signal NOUN
token (of victory)
• *(H5 5.Chorus.21) The Chorus describes how Henry gives 'full trophy, signal, and ostent / Quite from himself to God'—all signs of honour to God.*

signify VERB
make known
• *(MV 5.1.118) Lorenzo says that a messenger has arrived ahead of Bassanio and Gratiano 'To signify their coming'.*

signiory also spelled **signory** NOUN
state (in Italy)
• *(Oth 1.2.18) Othello recalls the services 'which I have done the signiory'.*

signor see **TERMS OF ADDRESS, p.306**

silly ADJECTIVE
as well as meaning 'foolish', you'll find:
simple
• *(TN 2.4.45) Orsino describes a song as 'silly sooth'—simple truth.*

a b c d e f g h i j k l m n o p q r **Ss** t u v w x y z

silly-ducking ADJECTIVE
foolishly and excessively bowing in respect
• *(KL 2.2.99) Cornwall thinks men like Kent are craftier 'Than twenty silly-ducking observants'.*

simple ADJECTIVE
⚠ *Don't read the meaning of 'easy, uncomplicated' into these senses.*
1 ordinary
• *(MV 2.2.149) Lancelot sees in the lines in his hand 'a simple line of life'.*
2 foolish
• *(RJ 2.5.38) The Nurse tells Juliet that she has 'made a simple choice' in Romeo.*
3 uninformed
• *(Ham 1.2.97) Claudius says Hamlet's grieving behaviour shows 'An understanding simple and unschool'd'.*
4 sincere
• *(OTH 1.1.108) Roderigo tells Brabantio that he comes to him 'In simple and pure soul'.*
5 small
• *(MV 3.2.81) Bassanio reflects that 'There is no vice so simple' that has no outward mark of virtue—even the smallest vice will hide behind an outward appearance of goodness (bad always hides behind good).*

› **simple** NOUN
medicinal herb
• *(RJ 5.1.40) Romeo recalls an apothecary 'culling of simples'—gathering herbs.*

› **simpleness** NOUN
1 sincerity
• *(MND 5.1.83) Theseus says, of the rustics' play, that 'never anything can be amiss / When simpleness and duty tender it'.*
2 honour
• *(Oth 1.3.244) Desdemona asks the Duke for his support, 'T'assist my simpleness'.*
3 stupidity
• *(RJ 3.3.77) The Friar criticizes Romeo for not hiding: 'What simpleness is this?'*

› **simplicity** NOUN
1 sincerity
• *(MND 5.1.104) Theseus says that love and 'tongue-tied simplicity / In least speak most' —are most effective when accompanied by few words.*
2 innocence
• *(MND 1.1.171) Hermia swears to meet Lysander 'By the simplicity of Venus' doves'.*
She isn't arranging a place to meet. People would swear (make promises) by a heavenly body, a virtue, or (as here) something associated with a god or goddess.
3 foolishness
• *(MV 1.3.38) Shylock criticizes Antonio for his 'low simplicity' in lending money without charging interest.*

› **simple-answered** also spelled **-answer'd** ADJECTIVE
straight in reply
• *(KL 3.7.42) Regan tells Gloucester: 'Be simple-answer'd, for we know the truth'.*

simular NOUN
pretender
• *(KL 3.2.54) Lear calls down the gods on anyone who is a 'simular of virtue'—a hypocrite about chastity.*

simulation NOUN
disguised meaning
• *(TN 2.5.128) Malvolio puzzles over the letter from Olivia: 'This simulation is not as the former'—not like the earlier one.*

sinew NOUN
⚠ *Don't read the meaning of 'tissue that connects muscle to bone' into these senses.*
1 muscle (as distinct from connecting tissue)
• *(Tem 3.1.26) Ferdinand tells Miranda he would rather 'crack my sinews' than have her carry logs—rupture his muscles.*
2 nerve
• *(H5 3.1.7) Henry urges his troops to 'Stiffen the sinews'.*
3 main strength
• *(TN 2.5.70) Fabian advises his companions to have 'patience, or we break the sinews of our plot'.*

› **unsinewed** also spelled **unsinew'd** ADJECTIVE
weak
• *(Ham 4.7.10) Claudius gives Laertes his reasons for not punishing Hamlet, 'Which may to you perhaps seem much unsinew'd / But yet to me th'are strong'.*

sinfully ADVERB
without repenting of sins
• *(H5 4.1.141) Henry talks of a man who does 'sinfully miscarry upon the sea'—dies in a state of sin.*

single ADJECTIVE
1 individual
• *(MV 1.3.141) Shylock asks Antonio to go with him to a notary to seal 'Your single bond'.*
2 solitary
• *(Tem 1.2.433) Ferdinand describes himself as 'A single thing' (or sense 3).*

3 feeble

• *(Mac 1.6.17) Lady Macbeth, speaking on behalf of her husband, describes service to Duncan as 'poor and single business' compared with the honours he has bestowed on them.*

4 unaided

• *(KL 5.3.103) Albany says (presumably to the disguised Edgar): 'Trust to thy single virtue'—trust your single-handed courage.*

› **singleness** NOUN

feebleness

• *(RJ 2.4.63) Romeo calls Mercutio's wordplay a thin joke, like a poorly-soled shoe: 'O single-soled jest, solely singular for the singleness!' —notable only for it being so feeble.*

single-soled, singular see **singleness**

singularity NOUN

eccentric behaviour

• *(TN 2.5.140) Malvolio reads an invitation in Olivia's letter: 'Put thyself into the trick of singularity'—make eccentricity your most noticeable feature.*

sinister ADJECTIVE

⚠ *Don't read the meaning of 'looking evil' into these senses.*

1 left (the Latin source of the word meant 'left-hand')

• *(MND 5.1.161) Snout describes the cranny in the wall as 'right and sinister'—horizontal from right to left.*

2 illegitimate

• *(H5 2.4.86) Exeter tells the French king that Henry has made 'no sinister nor no awkward claim' to France.*

3 impolite

• *(TN 1.5.163) Cesario tells Olivia he is very sensitive, 'even to the least sinister usage'—even the smallest unkindness upsets him.*

sink NOUN

waste pit

• *(H5 3.6.59) The French believe that Henry will 'drop his heart into the sink of fear'.*

sirrah see **TERMS OF ADDRESS, p.306**

sir-reverence NOUN

an apologetic expression: begging your pardon

• *(RJ 1.4.42) Mercutio says he will save Romeo from 'this sir-reverence love'—this (excuse the word) love!*

The First Folio has 'save your reverence', and this is used in several editions.

see **POLITENESS, p.230**

sisters three

in Greek mythology, the three goddesses (the Fates) who control human destiny, and end a life by cutting its string

• *(MND 5.1.321) Thisbe asks the Fates to come to her: 'O sisters three'.*

sith that CONJUNCTION

since

• *(KL 2.4.236) Regan asks Lear why he needs so many knights, 'sith that both charge and danger / Speak 'gainst so great a number'—because they cost so much to maintain and Lear is in no danger in her castle (so she says...).*

size NOUN

allowance

• *(KL 2.4.172) Lear says Regan is not the kind of person who would 'scant my sizes'—cut down my allowances.*

size VERB

measure

• *(Ham 3.2.162) The Player Queen tells her husband: 'as my love is siz'd, my fear is so'—measure the size of my fear by the size of my love for you.*

skains-mate NOUN

cut-throat companion

• *(RJ 2.4.140) The Nurse is contemptuous of Mercutio: 'I am none of his skains-mates'.*

skill VERB

matter

• *(TN 5.1.278) Feste says 'it skills not much' when the letters of a madman are delivered.*

skillet NOUN

saucepan

• *(Oth 1.3.269) Othello says, if love interferes with his official duties, 'Let housewives make a skillet of my helm'.*

skipping ADJECTIVE

1 frivolous

• *(MV 2.2.174) Bassanio tells Gratiano to make an effort to quell 'Thy skipping spirit'.*

2 fleeing

• *(Mac 1.2.30) The Captain tells how the 'skipping kerns'—the hired mercenaries—left the battlefield.*

skirr VERB

1 scour

• *(Mac 5.3.36) Macbeth tells Seyton to 'skirr the country round' to find people to fight his cause.*

a b c d e f g h i j k l m n o p q r Ss t u v w x y z

2 scurry

• *(H5 4.7.55) Henry says he will make the French army 'skirr away as swift as stones' sent from slings.*

skirts NOUN

as well as meaning an item of clothing, you'll find:

borders

• *(Ham 1.1.100) Horatio describes how Fortinbras has gathered men 'in the skirts of Norway'.*

› **wide-skirted** ADJECTIVE

with wide borders

• *(KL 1.1.64) Lear gives Goneril land 'With plenteous rivers and wide-skirted meads'.*

skittish ADJECTIVE

⚠ *Don't read in the meaning of 'frisky'.*

changeable

• *(TN 2.4.17) Orsino says lovers are unsettled and 'skittish in all motions' other than in relation to the person they love.*

skyish ADJECTIVE

reaching to the sky

• *(Ham 5.1.237) Laertes imagines making a mountain of Ophelia's grave that is higher than 'the skyish head / Of blue Olympus' (an unimaginably high mountain).*

slab ADJECTIVE

congealed

• *(Mac 4.1.32) The Third Witch wants to 'Make the gruel thick and slab'.*

slack ADJECTIVE

lax

• *(KL 1.3.10) Goneril tells Oswald to 'come slack of former services' in attending on Lear—treat him badly.*

slander VERB

as well as meaning 'defame', you'll find:

disgrace

• *(MA 2.3.45) Balthasar asks Don Pedro not to make him sing again: 'tax not so bad a voice / To slander music any more than once'.*

slander NOUN

disgraceful rogue

• *(H5 3.7.74) Gower describes Pistol as one of the 'slanders of the age'.*

slave NOUN

as well as meaning 'someone owned by another', you'll find:

villain

• *(Oth 5.2.289) Lodovico calls Iago 'a damned slave'.*

slave VERB

bring into subjection

• *(KL 4.1.67) Gloucester calls the heavens down on any man 'That slaves your ordinance'—treats your commands as if they were his.*

sleave NOUN

strands of silk

• *(Mac 2.2.40) Macbeth reflects on the way sleep 'knits up the ravell'd sleave of care'—sleep can repair the unravelled cover of health (the mind).*

☛ *The First Folio has 'sleeve', and this is used in some editions.*

sledded ADJECTIVE

on sledges

• *(Ham 1.1.66) Horatio describes the way King Hamlet 'smote the sledded Polacks on the ice' —Polish soldiers fighting on sledges.*

sleight NOUN

trickery

• *(Mac 3.5.26) Hecate describes a powerful liquid 'distilled by magic sleights'.*

'slid, 'slight see **SWEARING, p.298**

slight ADJECTIVE

⚠ *Don't read in the meaning of being physically very small.*

worthless

• *(JC 4.1.12) Antony describes Lepidus as 'a slight unmeritable man'.*

› **slightly** ADVERB

easily

• *(MV 5.1.167) Portia tells Gratiano he is to blame 'To part so slightly with your wife's first gift'.*

› **slight off** VERB

dismiss with contempt

• *(JC 4.3.5) Cassius complains to Brutus that his letters had been 'slighted off'.*

slip NOUN

as well as meaning 'lapse', you'll find:

1 sprig

• *(Mac 4.1.27) The Third Witch adds 'slips of yew' to the cauldron.*

2 leash

• *(H5 3.1.31) Henry sees his men standing 'like*

greyhounds in the slips'- ready and eager to be loosed.

3 counterfeit coin

• *(RJ 2.4.48) Mercutio chides Romeo for giving them 'the slip'—paying with a false coin (tricking them).*

› **slipper** ADJECTIVE

evasive

• *(Oth 2.1.233) Iago describes Cassio as 'a slipper and subtle knave'.*

› **slip** VERB

fail to keep

• *(Mac 2.3.43) Macduff says he has 'almost slipp'd the hour' to wake Duncan—he was almost late.*

› **let slip**

unleash

• *(JC 3.1.273) Antony imagines Caesar's spirit shouting: 'Cry havoc and let slip the dogs of war'.*

slipshod also spelled **slip-shod** ADJECTIVE

⚠ *Don't read in the modern meaning of 'careless'.*

wearing slippers

• *(KL 1.5.10) The Fool jokes with Lear about his brains being in his feet and getting blisters, but says: 'Thy wit shall not go slip-shod'—your way of thinking will never be comforted.*

sliver VERB

split off

• *(KL 4.2.34) Albany tells Goneril that a person who will 'sliver and disbranch / From her material sap' will wither (grow sick and die)'.*

slobbery ADJECTIVE

slimy

• *(H5 3.6.13) Bourbon says, if the English remain unfought, he will sell his dukedom and 'buy a slobbery and a dirty farm' in England.*

slop or **slops** see **CLOTHING, p.158**

slough NOUN [pronounced sluff]

outer skin

• *(TN 2.5.137) Malvolio reads Olivia's letter: 'cast thy humble slough, and appear fresh'—throw off your old look.*

slovenry NOUN

negligence

• *(H5 4.3.114) Henry tells Montjoy that 'time hath worn us into slovenry'—they have fought and marched so hard, they haven't had time to smarten their appearances.*

slubber VERB

1 smear

• *(Oth 1.3.224) The Duke tells Othello he needs to 'slubber the gloss of your new fortunes' with a tougher expedition.*

2 be careless with

• *(MV 2.8.40) Antonio tells Bassanio not to rush back home: 'Slubber not business for my sake'.*

slug-a-bed also spelled **-abed** NOUN

lazy-bones

• *(RJ 4.5.2) The Nurse tries to wake Juliet: 'fie, you slug-a-bed!'*

smack VERB

have a taste

• *(MV 2.2.15) Lancelot reflects that his 'father did something smack'—have a bit of a taste for women.*

small ADJECTIVE

as well as meanings to do with size, you'll find:

high-pitched

• *(MND 1.2.43) Quince tells Flute: 'you may speak as small as you will'.*

small beer

trivialities

• *(Oth 2.1.157) Iago cynically tells Desdemona that one of the things 'a deserving woman'—a woman of merit—can do is 'suckle fools and chronicle small beer'—breast-feed idiots and talk about matters of little consequence.*

🎭 *'Small beer', literally, was beer of a very poor quality.*

smatch NOUN

taste

• *(JC 5.5.46) Brutus tells Strato: 'Thy life hath had some smatch of honour in it'.*

smatter VERB

prattle

• *(RJ 3.5.171) Capulet tells the Nurse to go and 'smatter with your gossips'—go and talk with your gossiping friends.*

smilet NOUN

little smile

• *(KL 4.3.19) A Gentleman describes Cordelia's 'happy smilets' in receiving Kent's news of her father.*

smirched ADJECTIVE

stained

• *(MA 3.3.127) Borachio describes a picture of Hercules in a 'smirched, worm-eaten tapestry'.*

› **unsmirched** ADJECTIVE

unstained

• *(Ham 4.5.118) Laertes rejects calmness as originating in a source other than 'the chaste unsmirched brow' of his mother.*

a b c d e f g h i j k l m n o p q r Ss t u v w x y z

smite past form **smote** VERB
strike (usually with great force)
• *(Tem 4.1.172) Ariel describes how Stephano and his companions 'smote the air / For breathing in their faces'—they were so hot they fanned themselves vigorously with their hands, trying to cool down.*

smock NOUN
⚠ *Don't read in the modern meaning of 'overall' or 'loose dress'.*
woman's undergarment
• *(Oth 5.3.271) Othello describes dead Desdemona as being 'Pale as thy smock!'*

smoke VERB
as well as meaning 'smoke from a fire', you'll find:
1 give off steam (of blood)
• *(Mac 1.2.18) The Captain describes Macbeth's sword, 'Which smok'd with bloody execution'.*
2 perfume
• *(MA 1.3.50) Borachio says he 'was smoking a musty room'—making a damp-smelling room smell nicer.*

smooth also spelled **smoothe** VERB
1 indulge
• *(KL 2.2.71) Kent describes Oswald as one of those who 'smooth every passion' of their masters.*
2 speak well of
• *(RJ 3.2.98) Juliet, thinking of Romeo, asks 'what tongue shall smooth thy name' after she has mangled it (crushed it with her harsh words).*

smote see **smite**

smug ADJECTIVE
⚠ *Don't read in the meaning of 'self-satisfied'.*
smartly dressed
• *(MV 3.1.41) Shylock recalls Antonio as 'a beggar that was used to come so smug upon the mart'—when he was a young merchant, working his way up.*

Smulkin NOUN
the name of a devil
• *(KL 3.4.133) Poor Tom tells one of the fiends possessing him to be quiet: 'Peace, Smulkin!'*

snatcher NOUN
thief
• *(H5 1.2.143) Henry describes the Scots as 'coursing snatchers'—thieves who make quick raids into England.*

sneck up VERB
go hang yourself!
• *(TN 2.3.83) Sir Toby tells Malvolio: 'Sneck up!'*

snipe NOUN
dupe
• *(Oth 1.3.376) Iago describes Roderigo as 'a snipe'.*
🎭 *A 'snipe' is a type of long-billed wading bird; the sound of the name ('sn-', which is often used in words to convey unpleasantness, such as 'snout' and 'snivel') gave it an appeal as a contemptuous label for a fool.*

snuff NOUN
1 smouldering candle-end
• *(KL 4.6.39) Gloucester tells the gods that, if he lived longer, his 'snuff and loathed part of nature should / Burn itself out'—the last (and hated) bit of his life would come to a natural end.*
2 resentment
• *(KL 3.1.26) Kent tells a Gentleman of the 'snuffs and packings of the dukes'—Albany and Cornwall's quarrels and plots.*

› **in snuff**
in need of snuffing out; also, in a rage
• *(MND 5.1.239) Demetrius says that the candle in Starveling's lantern 'is already in snuff'.*

sober ADJECTIVE
⚠ *Don't read the meaning of 'not drunk' into these senses.*
1 sedate
• *(JC 4.2.40) Cassius tells Brutus he has a 'sober form'—a grave manner.*
2 serious
• *(MA 1.1.155) Claudio asks Benedick to 'speak in sober judgement' about Hero.*

› **sober-suited** ADJECTIVE
sedately dressed
• *(RJ 3.2.11) Juliet describes night as a 'sober-suited matron all in black'.*

sociable ADJECTIVE
responsive
• *(Tem 5.1.63) Prospero, looking at the spell-bound Gonzalo, says his own eyes are 'sociable to the show of thine'—as both men are weeping.*

society NOUN
as well as meaning 'companionship' and 'groups of people', you'll find:
social graces
• *(Ham 5.2.106) Osric describes Laertes as 'of very soft society'—pleasing manners.*

sodden ADJECTIVE
boiled
• *(H5 3.6.18) The Constable describes English beer as 'sodden water'.*

soft ADJECTIVE
as well as meaning 'not hard' and 'quiet', you'll find:
1 pleasing
• *(Oth 3.3.266) Othello reflects that he does not have 'soft parts of conversation'—he's no good at small-talk.*
2 tender
• *(H5 3.4.48) The Governor of Harfleur tells Henry he yields 'our town and lives to thy soft mercy'.*
3 weak
• *(MV 3.3.14) Shylock tells Antonio he will 'not be made a soft and dull-eyed fool'.*

› **softly** ADVERB
slowly
• *(TN 2.5.113) Malvolio tries to work out the meaning of the initials in the letter he has found, and slowly speaks them out: 'Softly! "M.O.A.I."'*

› **soft and fair**
not so fast
• *(MA 5.4.72) Benedick stops the Friar from going to the chapel: 'Soft and fair, friar'.*

See also ATTENTION SIGNALS, p.23

soil NOUN
as well as meaning 'earth', you'll find:
blemish
• *(JC 1.2.42) Brutus admits to having had ideas that 'give some soil' to his behaviour.*

soiled ADJECTIVE
lively (because filled with fresh fodder)
• *(KL 4.6.120) Lear remarks, speaking of a prostitute's sexual behaviour, that neither the pole-cat 'nor the soiled horse goes to't / With a more riotous appetite'.*

sojourn VERB
[pronounced **sodge**-urn or **soh**-jurn]
stay for a while
• *(RJ 3.3.169) The Friar advises Romeo: 'Sojourn in Mantua'.*

sojourn NOUN
visit
• *(KL 1.1.46) Lear says France and Burgundy 'Long in our court have made their amorous sojourn'.*

sold ADJECTIVE
made commercial
• *(Mac 3.4.33) Lady Macbeth tells her husband that 'the feast is sold / That is not often vouch'd'—it needs personal pledges (toasts to be made) to make the meal different from the kind of event one would pay to attend.*

solemn NOUN
⚠ *Don't read meanings to do with 'not being cheerful' into these senses.*
formal
• *(Mac 3.1.14) Macbeth tells Banquo: 'Tonight we hold a solemn supper'.*

› **solemnity** NOUN
celebration
• *(MND 4.1.184) Theseus promises to 'hold a feast in great solemnity'.*

› **solemnly** ADVERB
ceremoniously
• *(H5 5.Chorus.14) The Chorus tells the audience how they will see Henry land from France and 'solemnly see him set on to London'.*

solicit VERB
⚠ *Don't read a 'sexual' meaning into these senses ('solicitation' is the formal charge given to prostitutes when arrested).*
1 urge, persuade
• *(Mac 4.3.151) Malcolm wonders how the English king 'solicits heaven' to enable him to cure people.*
2 beg pardon
• *(Oth 5.2.28) Othello advises Desdemona that if any sin of hers is still unforgiven by God, she should 'Solicit for it straight'.*

› **soliciting** NOUN
urging
• *(Mac 1.3.129) Macbeth reflects on 'This supernatural soliciting' from the witches.*

› **still-soliciting** ADJECTIVE
always begging
• *(KL 1.1.230) Cordelia says she is glad she has no 'still-soliciting eye'.*

› **solicitor** NOUN
⚠ *Don't read in the meaning of 'lawyer'.*
presenter: (on behalf of someone else)
• *(Oth 3.3.27) Desdemona tells Cassio what she will do for him: 'Thy solicitor shall rather die / Than give thy cause away'—she will never abandon his case.*

solidity NOUN
solid body
• *(Ham 3.4.49) Hamlet says the face of heaven is sad 'O'er this solidity and compound mass'—over the world.*

solus **see LATIN, p.352**

Solyman NOUN [pronounced **sol**-i-man]
a Turkish sultan (also spelled Suleiman) who fought in many parts of Europe and North Africa in the 16th century
• *(MV 2.1.26) The Prince of Morocco boasts of his sword 'That won three fields of Sultan Solyman'.*

a b c d e f g h i j k l m n o p q r Ss t u v w x y z

something ADVERB
somewhat
• *(Ham 1.3.121) Polonius advises Ophelia to be 'something scanter of your maiden presence' —don't give Hamlet opportunity to spend time with you.*

sometime ADVERB
1 formerly
• *(Tem 5.1.86) Prospero says he will clothe himself 'As I was sometime Milan'—dress in the clothes he wore as the Duke of Milan.*
2 sometimes
• *(MND 3.2.362) Oberon tells Puck to 'sometime rail thou like Demetrius'.*

sometime ADJECTIVE
former
• *(KL 1.1.119) Lear disowns Cordelia and calls her 'my sometime daughter'.*

son see FAMILY, p.103

sonance NOUN
sound
• *(H5 4.2.35) The Constable commands a trumpet call: 'The tucket sonance and the note to mount'.*

sonnet NOUN
as well as meaning a type of poem, you'll find:
song
• *(TN 3.4.22) Malvolio quotes a line from a popular song, a 'very true sonnet'.*

sonties see SWEARING, p.298

soon-speeding ADJECTIVE
quickly acting
• *(RJ 5.1.60) Romeo asks an Apothecary for a 'soon-speeding' poison.*

sooth NOUN
truth
• *(TN 2.4.45) Orsino describes a song as 'silly sooth'—simple truth.*

sooth ADJECTIVE
true
• *(Mac 5.5.39) Macbeth asks a Messenger 'if thy speech be sooth'.*
See also SWEARING, p.298

soothe VERB
indulge
• *(KL 3.4.170) Kent advises Gloucester to let Lear take Poor Tom with him: 'soothe him'—humour him.*

soothsayer NOUN
foreteller of events
• *(JC 1.2.19) Brutus tells Caesar: 'A soothsayer bids you beware the ides of March'.*

sop NOUN
piece of bread or cake steeped in liquid
• *(KL 2.2.29) Kent tells Oswald he will 'make a sop o'th' moonshine of you'—beat you into a soggy mess and leave you lying to soak up the moonshine.*

sophisticated ADJECTIVE
⚠ *Don't read in the meaning of 'socially refined' or 'complicated'.*
not in a natural state
• *(KL 3.4.101) Lear tells Poor Tom and the Fool that the three of them 'are sophisticated'—wearing clothes, because the 'natural' human state is to be naked.*

Sophy NOUN [pronounced **soh**-fee]
a title of the Shah of Persia, a member of the monarchy of what is now Iran
• *(TN 2.5.168) Fabian says he would not have missed seeing Malvolio 'for a pension of thousands to be paid from the Sophy'—Persia was considered a land of riches.*

sore ADJECTIVE
1 severe
• *(Ham 5.1.157) The First Gravedigger says water is 'a sore decayer' of a dead body.*
2 serious
• *(MV 5.1.307) Gratiano says he can think of nothing 'So sore as keeping safe Nerissa's ring'.*
3 violent
• *(Mac 2.4.3) An Old Man cannot recall ever seeing such a 'sore night'.*

sore ADVERB
seriously
• *(RJ 1.4.19) Romeo says he cannot be merry as he is 'too sore enpierced' with Cupid's arrow.*

› **sorely** ADVERB
1 severely
• *(KL 2.4.299) Gloucester worries that 'the bleak winds / Do sorely ruffle'—are very strong.*
2 heavily
• *(Mac 5.1.46) The Doctor describes Lady Macbeth's heart as 'sorely charged'.*

sorry ADJECTIVE
1 sad
• *(Mac 3.2.9) Lady Macbeth asks her husband why he remains alone, 'Of sorriest fancies your companions making'—making sad imaginings your closest friends.*
2 wretched
• *(Oth 3.4.47) Othello says he has a 'salt and sorry rheum'—a heavy cold.*

sort NOUN
as well as meaning 'kind' or 'manner', you'll find:
1 social rank
• *(H5 4.8.70) Henry asks 'What prisoners of good sort are taken'.*
2 crowd
• *(MND 3.2.21) Puck describes how jackdaws fly away at the sound of a gun, 'many in sort'—a great flock.*
3 assigned portion
• *(JC 2.1.283) Portia asks Brutus if he won't confide in her because he sees her as his wife only 'in sort or limitation'—in particular ways.*

sort VERB
as well as meaning 'arrange', you'll find:
1 suit
• *(MND 5.1.55) Theseus rejects a proposed play as 'Not sorting with a nuptial ceremony'.*
2 classify
• *(Ham 2.2.263) Hamlet tells Rosencrantz and Guildenstern: 'I will not sort you with the rest of my servants'.*
3 turn out
• *(MA 5.4.7) Antonio says he is 'glad that all things sorts so well'.*

sot NOUN
idiot
• *(KL 4.2.8) Oswald complains that Albany 'call'd me sot'.*

soul NOUN
as well as meaning the 'inner being' of a person, you'll find:
essence
• *(Ham 2.2.90) Polonius observes that 'brevity is the soul of wit'.*

› **half a soul**
halfwit
• *(Mac 3.1.84) Macbeth tells the Murderers that the evil of Banquo's actions would be obvious even 'to half a soul and to a notion crazed'—to a fool or a madman.*

sound VERB
as well as meaning 'pronounce', you'll find:
1 question
• *(Ham 3.1.7) Guildenstern says Hamlet is not 'forward to be sounded'—not receptive to being questioned.*
2 cry out
• *(JC 1.2.143) Cassius asks Brutus why the name of Caesar should 'be sounded more than yours'.*
See also **swoon**

sound ADJECTIVE
not yet broken
• *(TN 1.4.33) Orsino describes Cesario's voice as 'shrill and sound'.*

› **sounding** NOUN
1 making music
• *(RJ 4.5.133) Peter tells the musicians that they 'have no gold for sounding'—with a pun on the jingling of coins.*
2 gauging depth (as in testing the depth of water)
• *(RJ 1.1.144) Montague wonders why Romeo is 'so far from sounding or discovery'—won't have his thoughts and feelings probed.*

sovereign ADJECTIVE
overpowering
• *(KL 4.3.42) Kent says Lear is overcome by 'A sovereign shame'.*

› **sovereignty** NOUN
power of control
• *(Ham 1.4.73) Horatio warns Hamlet that the Ghost 'might deprive your sovereignty of reason'.*

'Your sovereignty' was also a respectful way of referring to someone royal, similar to 'your grace' or 'your majesty'.

Sowter NOUN
a name for a stupid hound
• *(TN 2.5.115) Fabian says Malvolio will find a meaning in what he reads despite being so stupid: 'Sowter will cry upon't'—when even a dumb dog would bark at it.*

space NOUN
freedom or possession of property
• *(KL 1.1.55) Goneril says she loves Lear 'Dearer than eye-sight, space, and liberty'.*

spare ADJECTIVE
1 frugal
• *(H5 2.2.128) Henry talks about men who are 'spare in diet'—who don't eat much.*
2 gaunt
• *(JC 1.2.201) Caesar thinks he should avoid 'that spare Cassius'.*

› **spare** VERB
as well as meaning 'avoid', you'll find:
stop
• *(Tem 2.1.25) Alonso stops Gonzalo from talking: 'I prithee, spare'.*

› **sparing** NOUN
economy
• *(RJ 1.1.212) Romeo talks critically of Rosaline*

for wanting to live chastely: 'in that sparing makes huge waste'.

› sparingly ADVERB
with restraint
• *(H5 1.2.239) The French Ambassador asks Henry if he can speak freely, rather than 'sparingly show you far off / The Dauphin's meaning' —rather than speaking vaguely and formally.*

Spartan ADJECTIVE
from Sparta, a city of southern Greece, famous for its hunting hounds
• *(MND 4.1.118) Theseus says his hounds 'are bred out of the Spartan kind'.*
see MAP, p.176

speak VERB
as well as meaning 'talk' and 'report', you'll find:
1 call upon
• *(Tem 2.1.202) Antonio tells Sebastian: 'Th'occasion speaks thee'—this is your opportunity.*
2 reveal
• *(Mac 4.3.161) Malcolm says the English king has 'blessings hang about his throne / That speak him full of grace'.*
3 be announced
• *(Ham 5.2.187) Hamlet replies to a message from Claudius about fighting Laertes: 'If his fitness speaks, mine is ready'—I am ready if Laertes is.*
4 rebuke
• *(KL 1.3.26) Goneril says she will make opportunities 'That I may speak'—find occasions to tell Lear off.*

› speak for VERB
demand
• *(KL 1.4.236) Goneril says Lear's men's behaviour 'doth speak / For instant remedy'- they're behaving so badly she wants something done immediately.*

› speak within door
don't speak so loudly
• *(Oth 4.2.143) Iago tells Emilia: 'Speak within door'.*

› unspeak VERB
renounce
• *(Mac 4.3.123) Malcolm says he will 'Unspeak mine own detraction'—take back the bad things he said about himself.*

speculation NOUN
1 power of sight
• *(Mac 3.4.95) Macbeth tells Banquo's ghost that it has 'no speculation in those eyes / Which thou dost glare with'.*
2 looking on
• *(H5 4.2.31) The Constable boasts that French peasants would defeat the English while the nobles 'Took stand for idle speculation'.*
3 observer
• *(KL 3.1.24) Kent says servants of Albany and Cornwall 'are to France the spies and speculations / Intelligent of our state'—providing the French with information.*

› speculative ADJECTIVE
observing
• *(Oth 1.3.267) Othello denies that love will ever blind his 'speculative and officed instruments' —his means of seeing and acting.*

speed NOUN
as well as meaning 'swiftness', you'll find:
1 good luck
• *(Oth 2.1.67) Cassio says Iago has 'had most favourable and happy speed'.*
2 aid
• *(RJ 5.3.121) The Friar prays: 'Saint Francis be my speed!' (St Francis was the founder of the religious order to which the Friar belongs).*

speed VERB
1 prosper
• *(KL 1.2.19) Edmund reflects: 'if this letter speed / And my invention thrive' he will come out on top of Edgar.*
2 bring to an end
• *(MV 2.9.71) Arragon reads the words in the casket: 'So be gone, you are sped'.*

spell backward
misrepresent
• *(MA 3.1.61) Hero says that Beatrice never yet saw a man 'But she would spell him backward'—she mocks whichever man she sees.*

spell-stopped also spelled **-stopp'd**
ADJECTIVE
spellbound
• *(Tem 5.1.61) Prospero tells his enemies: 'There stand, / For you are spell-stopp'd'.*

spend VERB
as well as meaning 'expend' and 'use money', you'll find:
use up
• *(RJ 3.2.130) Juliet says her tears 'shall be spent' for Romeo's banishment.*

› spend one's mouth
bark
• *(H5 2.5.71) The Dauphin compares the English to cowardly dogs that 'Most spend their mouths when what they seem to threaten / Runs far before them'.*

sphere NOUN
as well as meaning 'Earth' or 'heavenly body', you'll find:
1 orbit
• *(MND 2.1.7) A Fairy says she wanders everywhere, 'Swifter than the moon's sphere'.*
2 socket
• *(Ham 1.5.17) The Ghost says his tale would make Hamlet's eyes 'like stars start from their spheres'.*

› **spherical** ADJECTIVE
of heavenly bodies
• *(KL 1.2.117) Edmund dismisses the notion that people could be 'knaves, thieves, and treachers by spherical predominance'.*
Edmund is talking about the popular idea in Shakespeare's time that the position of the stars at your birth would dictate aspects of your personality.

› **sphery** ADJECTIVE
of heavenly bodies
• *(MND 2.2.105) Helena compares herself to 'Hermia's sphery eyne'—eyes that shine like stars.*

spill VERB
destroy
• *(Ham 4.5.20) Gertrude reflects that guilt 'spills itself in fearing to be spilt'—guilty people are found out because they show their fear of being found out.*

spinster NOUN
Don't read in the meaning of 'unmarried woman'.
woman who stays at home spinning
• *(TN 2.4.43) Orsino describes a song sung by 'The spinsters and the knitters in the sun'.*

spirituality NOUN
ecclesiastical estate
• *(H5 1.2.132) Canterbury promises that 'we of the spirituality' will raise money for Henry's war.*

spirt up VERB
shoot up (as a plant does)
• *(H5 3.6.8) The Dauphin asks whether a few offshoots of the French ancestry (the English) can 'Spirt up so suddenly into the clouds'—rise so high (and become royal).*
The word is spelled 'spirt' in the First Folio, but some editions change this to 'spurt'.

spital NOUN
hospital
• *(H5 2.1.65) Pistol tells Nym to go 'to the Spital'.*

spite NOUN
1 vexation
• *(MND 3.2.194) Helena believes that the others have joined together 'To fashion this false sport in spite of me'—to make up these jokes in order to irritate me.*
2 hatred
• *(RJ 1.5.61) Tybalt believes that Romeo has come to the Capulets' party 'in spite, / To scorn at our solemnity'.*

spite VERB
vex
• *(Mac 3.1.113) The Second Murderer says he is reckless and does what he does 'To spite the world'.*

spleen NOUN
1 passion
• *(Oth 4.1.88) Iago bids Othello be patient, 'Or I shall say you're all in all in spleen / And nothing of a man'.*
2 malice
• *(KL 1.4.272) Lear asks Nature, if Goneril ever gives birth, to 'Create her child of spleen'.*
3 delight
• *(TN 3.2.61) Maria asks Sir Toby and Fabian to go with her, 'If you desire the spleen, and will laugh yourselves into stitches'.*
4 impulse or temper
• *(MND 1.1.146) Lysander talks of lightning 'That in a spleen unfolds both heaven and earth'.*
All emotions, dark or bright, were thought to come from the spleen—an abdominal organ that controls changes in the blood. It was the source of one of the four humours, responsible for melancholy, sleeplessness, and irritability.
see **HUMOURS, p.137**

› **spleenitive** also spelled **splenative, splenitive** ADJECTIVE
hot-headed
• *(Ham 5.1.245) Hamlet tells Laertes he is 'not splenative and rash'.*

splinter VERB
Don't read in the meaning of 'split into pieces'.
put in a splint
• *(Oth 2.3.303) Iago advises Cassio to ask Desdemona to mend the break with Othello: 'This broken joint between you and her husband entreat her to splinter'.*

a b c d e f g h i j k l m n o p q r Ss t u v w x y z

spoil VERB
1 destroy
• *(H5 4.5.18) The Constable appeals: 'Disorder, that hath spoil'd us, friend us now'.*
2 ravage
• *(KL 5.3.277) Lear says his troubles make him unable to fight: 'these same crosses spoil me'.*
3 badly injure
• *(Oth 5.1.54) Cassio tells Iago 'I am spoil'd, undone by villains!'*

spoil NOUN
1 plundering
• *(MV 5.1.85) Lorenzo says a man without music 'Is fit for treasons, stratagems, and spoils'.*
2 destruction
• *(JC 5.3.7) Titinius says Brutus' soldiers 'fell to spoil'.*

spongy ADJECTIVE
1 rainy
• *(Tem 4.1.65) Iris describes Ceres' banks, 'Which spongy April at thy hest betrims'—beautifies at your command.*
2 soaked with drink
• *(Mac 1.7.71) Lady Macbeth plots against Duncan's 'spongy officers'.*

sport NOUN
as well as meaning 'athletic activity', you'll find:
1 recreation
• *(MND 2.1.87) Titania is angry with Oberon: 'with thy brawls thou hast disturb'd our sport'.*
2 amorous dalliance
• *(KL 1.1.22) Gloucester says, of Edmund, 'there was good sport at his making'—the sex was good.*

sport VERB
make merry
• *(Tem 4.1.74) Iris invites Ceres to 'come and sport'.*

› **sportful** ADJECTIVE
playful
• *(TN 5.1.353) Fabian says the plot against Malvolio was carried out 'with a sportful malice'.*

› **outsport** also spelled **out-sport** VERB
make merry beyond the bounds of
• *(Oth 2.3.3) Othello advises Cassio 'Not to out-sport discretion'—celebrate too much.*

spotted ADJECTIVE
1 blemished
• *(MND 1.1.110) Lysander calls Demetrius a 'spotted and inconstant man'.*
2 embroidered
• *(Oth 3.3.436) Iago describes Desdemona's handkerchief, 'Spotted with strawberries'.*

› **unspotted** ADJECTIVE
unblemished
• *(H5 4.1.153) Henry asserts that there is no such thing as an army of 'all unspotted soldiers'.*

spousal NOUN
married union
• *(H5 5.2.342) Queen Isabel hopes for 'a spousal' between France and England.*

spray NOUN
offshoot
• *(H5 3.6.5) The Dauphin asks if 'a few sprays' of French ancestry can overpower them (King Henry has distant French relations in his family tree).*

sprighting see **spriting**

spring NOUN
as well as meaning the season, you'll find:
first moment
• *(MND 2.1.82) Titania says Oberon's arguing has disturbed her 'since the middle summer's spring'.*

springe NOUN
snare
• *(Ham 5.2.300) Laertes says he has been killed by his own treachery—'as a woodcock to mine own springe'—the woodcock being thought of as a stupid bird, easy to catch.*

sprite also spelled **spright** NOUN
1 spirit
• *(Tem 2.2.112) Caliban admires Stephano and Trinculo, 'if they be not sprites'.*
2 feeling
• *(Mac 4.1.126) The First Witch invites her fellows to brighten Macbeth: 'cheer we up his sprites'.*

› **spriting** also spelled **sprighting** NOUN
activities as a spirit
• *(Tem 1.2.298) Ariel promises Prospero to 'do my spriting gently'.*
➨ *Some editions have 'spiriting'.*

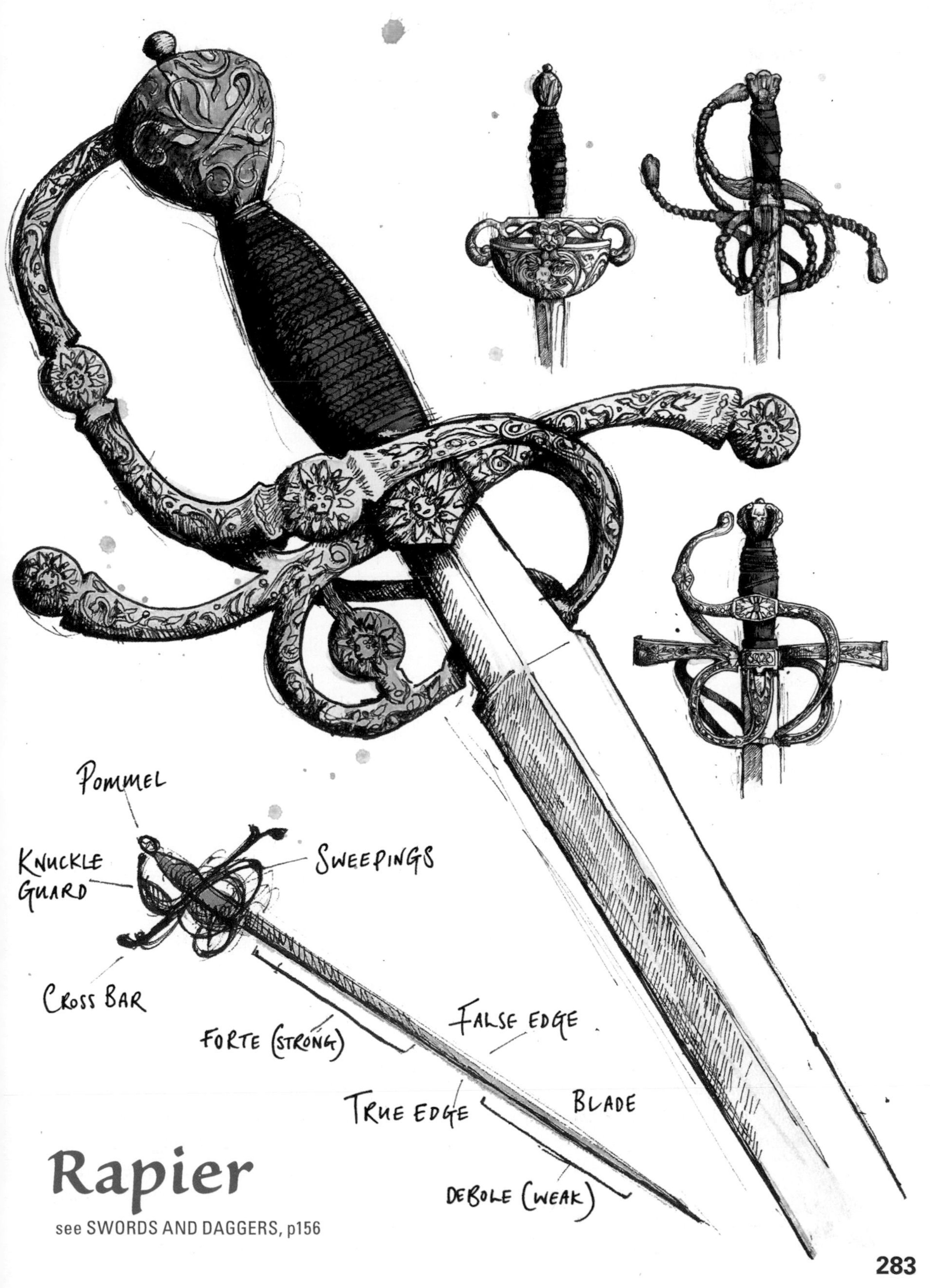

Rapier

see SWORDS AND DAGGERS, p156

a b c d e f g h i j k l m n o p q r Ss t u v w x y z

spur NOUN
as well as meaning 'a device to make a horse go faster', you'll find:
tree-root
• *(Tem 5.1.47) Prospero reflects on how he plucked up pines and cedars 'by the spurs'.*
› forespurrer also spelled **fore-spurrer** NOUN
one who has ridden ahead
• *(MV 2.9.94) The arrival of Bassanio's messenger is announced: 'this forespurrer comes before his lord'.*
› on the spur
at a gallop
• *(JC 5.3.29) Pindarus reports that Titinius is surrounded by horsemen 'that make to him on the spur'.*

spurn VERB
1 scorn
• *(KL 5.3.144) Edmund says he will 'disdain and spurn' any delay in fighting disguised Edgar.*
2 kick
• *(MV 1.3.113) Shylock says Antonio did 'foot me as you spurn a stranger cur / Over your threshold' —as you would kick an unwelcome dog out of your house.*
› spurn at VERB
kick out at
• *(Ham 4.5.6) A gentleman reports that Ophelia 'Spurns enviously at straws'—takes offence at the smallest thing.*

spurn NOUN
contemptuous treatment
• *(Ham 3.1.73) Hamlet reflects on bearing 'the spurns / That patient merit of th'unworthy takes'—the treatment that patient people receive from others who themselves don't deserve to be treated with patience.*

square NOUN
1 normal condition
• *(KL 1.1.73) Regan says she will reject 'all other joys / Which the most precious square of sense possesses'.*
2 formation (of troops)
• *(H5 4.2.28) The Constable describes the French peasants who swarm 'About our squares of battle'.*
› square VERB
quarrel (as in the modern fighting term 'square up')
• *(MND 2.1.30) Puck says Titania and Oberon never meet 'But they do square'.*
› squarer NOUN
quarrelsome person
• *(MA 1.1.72) Beatrice asks, of Benedick, if there is 'no young squarer now that will make a voyage with him to the devil'—no new young companion who behaves in the same quarrelsome way.*

squash NOUN
unripe pea-pod
• *(TN 1.5.147) Malvolio compares Cesario's age to what 'a squash is before 'tis a peascod'—before it is a fully grown pea-plant.*

squeny also spelled **squiny** VERB
squint
• *(KL 4.6.134) Lear asks Gloucester: 'Dost thou squiny at me?'*

squire NOUN
as well as meaning an 'attendant on a knight', you'll find:
1 young lover
• *(MA 1.3.46) Don John describes Claudio as 'A proper squire'.*
2 lad
• *(MND 2.1.131) Titania recalls the way her 'young squire'—the changeling—was born.*
3 fellow (used contemptuously)
• *(Oth 4.2.144) Emilia is sure Othello has been abused by a villain—'Some such squire'.*
› squire-like ADJECTIVE
like an attendant
• *(KL 2.4.211) Lear says he would rather kneel before the King of France and 'squire-like, pension beg' than return to Goneril.*

staff plural **staves** NOUN
as well as meaning 'stick', you'll find:
spear
• *(Mac 5.7.19) Macduff refuses to fight with ordinary soldiers 'whose arms / Are hir'd to bear their staves'—the mercenary troops (kerns) that Macbeth has paid to fight for him.*
See also **stave**

stage NOUN
raised surface
• *(Ham 5.2.389) Fortinbras commands: 'Bear Hamlet like a soldier to the stage'—a platform of some kind where people can view and pay respects to his body.*

stain NOUN
as well as meaning 'dirty mark', you'll find:
object stained with blood (as a relic)
• *(JC 2.2.89) Decius imagines people coming to a blood-spouting statue of Caesar 'for tinctures, stains, relics'.*

stairs see **keep below stairs**

STAGE DIRECTIONS

Quite often a speech is preceded by words telling you where on the stage a character is entering or speaking.

A CHARACTER IS ON THE GALLERY ABOVE THE STAGE

above

• *(Oth 1.1.83) Iago and Roderigo wake Brabantio up with their shouting: 'Brabantio appears above, at a window.'*

aloft

• *(RJ 3.5.1) A new scene: 'Enter Romeo and Juliet aloft as at the window.'*

on the top

• *(Tem 3.3.18) Prospero looks down at the banquet being prepared for his enemies: 'Solemn and strange music, and Prospero on the top, invisible.'*

A CHARACTER IS ON ONE SIDE OF THE STAGE, AWAY FROM THE OTHERS

apart

• *(JC 4.2.13) Brutus wants a private word with Lucilius: 'Brutus and Lucilius draw apart.'*

A CHARACTER IS ON THE PART OF THE STAGE BENEATH THE GALLERY

below

• *(MV 2.6.58) Jessica has spoken to Lorenzo from the balcony of her house, and now comes downstairs to meet him: 'Enter Jessica below.'*

Some editions omit the word 'below'.

A CHARACTER IS BEHIND THE BACK OF THE STAGE OR UNDER THE STAGE

within

• *(TN 4.2.20) Feste calls out to the imprisoned Malvolio, who replies: '(Within) Who calls there?'*

A CHARACTER SAYS SOMETHING TO THE AUDIENCE
—THAT NO-ONE ELSE ON STAGE CAN HEAR
—THAT ONLY CERTAIN CHARACTERS ON STAGE CAN HEAR

aside

• *(Mac 1.3.115) Macbeth has just heard the news that he has been made Thane of Cawdor, and says: '(Aside) Glamis, and Thane of Cawdor: / The greatest is behind.'*

• *(MA 3.3.99) The members of the Watch overhear Borachio talking to Conrad, and one tells his companions: '(Aside) Some treason, masters.'*

A CHARACTER LEAVES THE STAGE

exit

• *(MND 1.1.15) Philostrate responds to Theseus' command to go and organize some revels: 'Exit Philostrate.'*

MORE THAN ONE CHARACTER LEAVES THE STAGE

exeunt

a Latin word meaning 'they go out' (the plural of 'exit')

• *(KL 3.2.78) 'Exeunt Lear and Kent', leaving the Fool alone.*

stake in the phrase **at the stake**
at risk (as in gambling) or under attack (as in bear-baiting)

• *(TN 3.1.114) Olivia asks Cesario: 'Have you not set mine honour at the stake'.*

stale NOUN

1 decoy

• *(Tem 4.1.187) Prospero uses showy garments to attract Stephano and his companions—'For stale to catch these thieves'.*

2 prostitute

• *(MA 2.2.24) Borachio describes Hero as 'a contaminated stale'.*

stale VERB
wear out

• *(JC 1.2.73) Cassius says he would never 'stale with ordinary oaths my love / To every new protester' —smother a new friend with declarations of love and make the word meaningless.*

stalk on VERB
move stealthily in hiding

• *(MA 2.3.95) Claudio talks to himself, thinking of Benedick: 'stalk on, stalk on; the fowl sits'.*

When hunting game, the hunters would often hide behind a screen—such as an artificial 'stalking horse'—so that the target would not see them. Claudio and the Prince are stalking Benedick by hiding in a similar way.

warning note *usage note* *theatre note*

a b c d e f g h i j k l m n o p q r Ss t u v w x y z

stallion see **scullion, staniel**

stamp NOUN
Don't read in the modern meaning of 'postage stamp' into these senses.
as well as meaning 'imprint', you'll find:
coin (with the impression of the monarch's head on it)
• *(Mac 4.3.155) Malcolm describes how the English king treats the sick—'Hanging a golden stamp about their necks'.*
King James, who was king at the time Shakespeare was writing Macbeth, would give coins like this to people he had 'touched' in this way.

stamp VERB
1 press (as in forging coins)
• *(Oth 2.1.235) Iago says Cassio has 'an eye that can stamp and counterfeit advantages'.*
2 validate
• *(MA 1.2.6) Antonio says his news may be good 'As the event stamps them'—as time will tell.*

stanchless also spelled **staunchless** ADJECTIVE
insatiable
• *(Mac 4.3.78) Malcolm claims he has 'A stanchless avarice'.*

stand VERB
as well as meaning 'be upright', 'continue', and 'tolerate', you'll find:
1 stop
• *(Ham 1.1.144) Horatio tells Marcellus to strike at the Ghost 'if it will not stand'.*
2 delay
• *(JC 5.3.43) Cassius asks Pindarus to kill him: 'Stand not to answer'.*
3 impersonate
• *(KL 1.4.135) The Fool describes a lord, and asks Lear: 'Do thou for him stand'.*
4 depend
• *(Ham 1.1.122) Horatio describes the moon 'Upon whose influence Neptune's empire stands'.*
Neptune was the God of the sea, and the moon controls the tides.
5 fight
• *(KL 2.2.38) Kent tells Oswald to fight him: 'stand, rogue, stand'.*

› **stand by** VERB
1 stand aside
• *(MA 4.1.22) Claudio tells the Friar: 'Stand thee by'.*
2 maintain
• *(TN 3.1.8) Cesario continues Feste's punning by suggesting that 'the Church stands by thy tabor, if thy tabor stand by the church'—the Church (financially) supports his drum-playing if his drum is being played next to the church building.*

› **stand on** VERB
insist on
• *(RJ 2.3.93) Romeo tells the Friar: 'I stand on sudden haste'.*

› **stand to** VERB
1 perform
• *(RJ 2.4.135) Romeo says Mercutio 'will speak more in a minute than he will stand to in a month'—with a sexual pun (have an erection, have sex).*
2 come forward
• *(Tem 3.3.49) Alonso, after seeing food arrive, says he will 'stand to, and feed'.*

› **stand to it**
get down to business
• *(Mac 3.3.17) The First Murderer urges the attack on Banquo: 'Stand to't!'*

› **stand upon** VERB
1 bother about
• *(MND 5.1.118) Theseus reacts to Quince's opening speech: 'This fellow does not stand upon points'—pay attention to punctuation marks.*
2 be the duty of
• *(Ham 5.2.63) Hamlet asks Horatio if it does not 'stand me now upon' to kill Claudius.*

standard NOUN
flag-bearer (also, the flag that is carried)
• *(Tem 3.2.15) Stephano says Caliban can be his lieutenant—his deputy or 'standard'.*

staniel NOUN
kestrel (known to be useless in falconry)
• *(TN 2.5.107) Sir Toby says, of Malvolio: 'with what wing the staniel checks at it'—pounces on the bait in Olivia's letter.*
The word appears as 'stallion' (an uncastrated male horse) in the First Folio, but some editions emend to 'staniel'.

star NOUN
as well as meaning 'heavenly body' (including planets), you'll find:
1 pole-star (as an aid to navigation)
• *(MA 3.4.53) Margaret jests with Beatrice that 'there's no more sailing by the star'—from now on, she will be guided by a lover (rather than by the stars).*
The main way of navigating your way

around the world was by checking your position in relation to the stars in the sky.

2 fortune (as determined by the stars)

• *(KL 3.1.22) Kent refers to Albany and Cornwall's 'great stars / Thron'd and set high'.*

3 sphere

• *(Ham 2.2.141) Polonius says he told Ophelia that Hamlet was 'a prince, out of thy star'—with a position beyond your social sphere.*

› **star-blasting** NOUN

bad influence of the stars (following the commonly held belief that the position of the stars affected the destiny of humans)

• *(KL 3.4.58) Poor Tom addresses Lear: 'Bless thee from whirlwinds, star-blasting'.*

› **star-crossed** also spelled **-cross'd** ADJECTIVE

thwarted by a malicious star (see *star-blasting*)

• *(RJ Prologue.6) The Chorus describes how 'A pair of star-cross'd lovers take their life'.*

stare VERB

as well as meaning 'look intensely', you'll find: stand on end

• *(JC 4.3.280) Brutus says the sight of Caesar's ghost makes his 'hair to stare'.*

› **o'erstare** also spelled **o'er-stare, overstare** ADVERB

outstare

• *(MV 2.1.27) Morocco says to win Portia he 'would o'er-stare the sternest eyes that look'.*

stark VERB

rigid

• *(RJ 4.1.103) The Friar says the potion will make Juliet's body 'stiff and stark and cold'.*

start VERB

as well as meaning 'jump' or 'jump away', you'll find:

1 disturb

• *(Mac 5.5.15) Macbeth reflects that terror 'Cannot once start me'—can never alarm him.*

2 rush

• *(MA 4.1.159) The Friar notes the way Hero's blushes 'start into her face'.*

3 raise up

• *(JC 1.2.147) Cassius says the name of Brutus 'will start a spirit' as much as the name of Caesar.*

start NOUN

as well as meaning 'sudden movement', you'll find:

1 advantage

• *(MV 2.2.5) Lancelot gives himself advice: 'use your legs, take the start, run away'.*

2 outburst

• *(KL 1.1.297) Regan complains about Lear's 'unconstant starts'.*

› **starting** NOUN

startled reaction

• *(Mac 5.1.40) Lady Macbeth, as she sleepwalks, talks as if to her husband: 'You mar all with this starting'.*

› **by starts**

in fits and starts

• *(H5 5.3.4) The Chorus apologizes for the characters in the play 'Mangling by starts the full course of their glory'.*

› **startingly** ADVERB

in fits and starts

• *(Oth 3.4.75) Desdemona asks Othello why he speaks 'so startingly and rash'.*

start-up NOUN

upstart, one who has risen suddenly in rank

• *(MA 1.3.57) Don John describes Claudio as a 'young start-up'.*

state NOUN

as well as meaning 'condition' and 'government', you'll find:

1 rank

• *(Oth 1.3.233) Othello addresses the Duke, humbly 'bending to your state'.*

2 persons of rank

• *(Ham 5.2.209) Stage direction: 'Enter King, Queen, Laertes, Osric, and all the State'.*

3 splendour

• *(RJ 1.4.70) Mercutio says, after describing Queen Mab: 'in this state she gallops night by night'.*

4 ceremony

• *(RJ 4.3.8) Juliet says she has gathered together what is needed 'for our state tomorrow'.*

5 throne

• *(Mac 3.4.5) Macbeth greets his guests, saying 'Our hostess keeps her state'—remains sitting.*

6 property

• *(MV 3.2.257) Bassanio reminds Portia that his 'state was nothing'—he has no assets.*

7 stately phrasing

• *(TN 2.3.132) Maria describes Malvolio as 'an affectioned ass that cons state without book'—*

a b c d e f g h i j k l m n o p q r Ss t u v w x y z

learns courtly etiquette by heart, even though (as a steward) he'll never get to put it into practice.

› unstate VERB
give up everything
• *(KL 1.2.94) Gloucester tells Edmund: 'I would unstate myself to be in a due resolution'—to get the issue of Edgar resolved.*

station NOUN
stance
• *(Ham 3.4.58) Hamlet describes his father's appearance: 'A station like the herald Mercury'.*
Mercury was the gods' winged messenger—the implication being that Hamlet's father stood ready to spring into action (he was ready for anything).

statist NOUN [pronounced **stay**-tist]
statesman
• *(Ham 5.2.33) Hamlet recalls once believing, 'as our statists do', that good handwriting was for social inferiors.*

statute NOUN
as well as meaning 'law', you'll find:
legal security (when buying land)
• *(Ham 5.1.97) Hamlet describes a lawyer—'a great buyer of land, with his statutes'.*

stave NOUN
staff
• *(TN 5.1.275) Feste says Malvolio 'holds Beelzebub at the stave's end'—keeps the devil at bay.*
See also **staff**

stay VERB
as well as meaning 'remain', you'll find:
1 wait
• *(MND 2.1.235) Demetrius tells Helena: 'I will not stay thy questions'—I won't wait to hear what you have to say.*
2 detain
• *(MA 4.1.281) Beatrice tells Benedick: 'You have stayed me in a happy hour'—at a favourable time.*
3 stop
• *(RJ 5.2.12) Friar John says his journey to Mantua 'was stay'd'.*
4 endure
• *(MV 4.1.344) Shylock says he will 'stay no longer question'.*

stead VERB
help
• *(MV 1.3.6) Bassanio asks Shylock for a loan: 'May you stead me?'*

steal VERB
as well as meaning 'take dishonestly', you'll find:
hide furtively
• *(Ham 3.2.86) Horatio says he will watch to see if Claudius 'steal aught the whilst this play is playing'—tries to hide his reactions.*

› stealing ADJECTIVE
stealthily moving
• *(Ham 5.1.67) The First Gravedigger sings of growing old: 'age with his stealing steps'.*

› stealth NOUN
1 furtive journey
• *(MND 3.2.310) Helena tells Hermia she had informed Demetrius 'of your stealth unto this wood'—leaving Athens secretly with a plan to elope with Lysander.*
2 theft
• *(KL 3.4.89) Poor Tom says he is a 'fox in stealth'—he steals with great cunning.*

› stolen also spelled **stol'n** ADJECTIVE
secret
• *(RJ 5.3.233) The Friar explains what happened on Romeo and Juliet's 'stol'n marriage day'.*

stealers see **pickers and stealers**

steeled ADJECTIVE
hardened (like steel)
• *(H5 2.2.36) Scroop says that service to the King 'shall with steeled sinews toil'.*

steep-down ADJECTIVE
precipitous
• *(Oth 5.2.278) Othello calls on devils to wash him 'in steep-down gulfs of liquid fire!'*

stelled ADJECTIVE
[pronounced in this line as two syllables: **stel**-id]
starry
• *(KL 3.7.58) Gloucester compares the storm to a sea that would have risen up 'and quench'd the stelled fires'—the waves crashing so high they would extinguish the stars.*

stem VERB
make headway against
• *(JC 1.2.109) Cassius recalls how he and Caesar swam against the current in the river, 'stemming it with hearts of controversy'—crossing the river with bold competitive spirit.*

› re-stem also spelled **restem** VERB
retrace
• *(Oth 1.3.37) A Messenger reports that the Ottomites (the Turkish fleet) 'do restem / Their backward course'—steer back to their original course, away from their offensive position.*

step NOUN
distance
• *(MND 2.1.69) Titania says Oberon has come 'from the farthest step of India'.*
Some editions have 'steppe'—a large area of flat, unforested grassland.

stepdame see FAMILY, p.103

sterling NOUN
genuine (said of money)
• *(Ham 1.3.107) Polonius says Hamlet's advances to Ophelia are 'not sterling'.*

sternage NOUN
sterns (of a fleet of ships)
• *(H5 3.Chorus.18) The Chorus asks the audience to follow the English navy in their imaginations: 'Grapple your minds to sternage of this navy'.*

steward NOUN
Don't read in the meaning of 'someone who looks after people on a ship or at a public event'.
controller of a household's domestic affairs—the top of the servant hierarchy
• *(KL 1.3.1) Stage direction: 'Enter Goneril, and Oswald, her Steward'.*

stick VERB
as well as meaning 'fix' and 'pierce', you'll find:
hesitate
• *(Ham 4.5.92) Claudius thinks people will spread rumours that 'Will nothing stick our person to arraign'—won't think twice about accusing us.*

› **stick off** NOUN
shine out
• *(Ham 5.2.242) Hamlet says Laertes' skill will, like a star, 'Stick fiery off indeed'.*

sticking-place VERB
place where something is held tight (such as on a stringed instrument or crossbow)
• *(Mac 1.7.60) Lady Macbeth tells her husband to screw his courage 'to the sticking place'.*

stiffly ADVERB
strongly
• *(Ham 1.5.95) Hamlet asks his muscles to 'bear me stiffly up'—so he can stand up again.*

still ADVERB
1 always
• *(TN 2.5.164) Malvolio reads in Olivia's letter: 'in my presence still smile'.*
2 now (as it was before)
• *(KL 3.2.1) Stage direction: 'Storm still'.*

still-soliciting see **solicit**

still-vexed see **vex**

stint VERB
stop
• *(RJ 1.3.49) The Nurse describes how baby Juliet stopped crying: 'pretty fool, it stinted'.*

stithy NOUN
forge
• *(Ham 3.2.82) Hamlet says, if the Ghost was lying, then his 'imaginations are as foul / As Vulcan's stithy'.*
Vulcan was the gods' blacksmith, who forged thunderbolts for Zeus (the supreme god of the ancient Greeks).

stoccado, stoccata see RECREATION, p.170

stock NOUN
ancestry
• *(RJ 1.5.57) Tybalt swears 'by the stock and honour of my kin'.*
See also CLOTHING, p.158

stockfish NOUN
dried cod
• *(Tem 3.2.68) Stephano tells Trinculo that he will 'make a stockfish of thee'—beat you as if tenderising a piece of fish before cooking.*

stockish NOUN
wooden
• *(MV 5.1.81) Lorenzo says that music can change the nature even of someone who is 'stockish, hard, and full of rage'.*

stock-punished also spelled **-punish'd**
ADJECTIVE
punished by being put in the stocks
• *(KL 3.4.127) Poor Tom says how he was whipped and 'stock-punish'd'.*

stocks NOUN
a wooden structure used for punishment, in which people sat with their ankles locked in holes between two planks of wood, so that they were forced to stay in an uncomfortable position
• *(KL 2.2.121) Cornwall decides to punish Kent for his bad behaviour: 'Fetch forth the stocks'.*

stolen see **steal**

stomach NOUN
as well as meaning a part of the body, you'll find:
1 appetite
• *(MV 3.5.42) Lancelot says the people in the house are ready for dinner: 'they have all stomachs'.*
2 desire
• *(H5 4.3.35) Henry tells any soldier to leave if he 'hath no stomach to this fight'.*
3 courage
• *(Tem 1.2.157) Prospero says Miranda's smile 'rais'd in me / An undergoing stomach'—the will to carry on.*
4 anger
• *(KL 5.3.75) Regan tells Goneril she is not well,*

otherwise she would answer 'From a full-flowing stomach'—with a great deal of anger.

stone NOUN
1 highly polished stone used as a mirror
• *(KL 5.3.261) Lear hopes Cordelia's breath 'will mist or stain the stone'.*
2 thunderbolt
• *(Oth 5.2.232) Othello asks: 'Are there no stones in heaven / But what serves for the thunder?'—to hurl at Iago.*
3 testicle
• *(RJ 1.3.54) The Nurse describes a bump on baby Juliet's brow 'as big as a young cock'rel's stone'.*

stone VERB
turn to stone
• *(Oth 5.2.63) Othello tells Desdemona: 'Thou dost stone my heart'.*

stone-bow NOUN
type of crossbow that shoots stones
• *(TN 2.5.43) Sir Toby, listening to Malvolio, wishes for 'a stone-bow to hit him in the eye!'*

stoop VERB
swoop down (as a falcon)
• *(H5 4.1.103) Henry says that the king's feelings 'stoop with the like wing'—he can feel down-hearted (just like anyone else) as quickly as a falcon swoops down.*

stople VERB [pronounced **stop**-ul]
stop up
• *(KL 5.3.154) Albany tells Goneril to shut her mouth, 'Or with this paper shall I stople it'.*

store NOUN
as well as meaning 'supply', you'll find:
1 resources
• *(TN 3.3.45) Antonio tells Sebastian that 'your store' is not enough to make trifling purchases —even to buy small things.*
2 group
• *(RJ 1.2.22) Capulet invites Paris to his feast: 'you among the store' will be most welcome—you'll be guest of honour.*

store VERB
populate
• *(Oth 4.3.83) Emilia talks of the number of unfaithful women who 'would store the world they played for'—fill with children the world they gambled for.*

stoup NOUN
jug
• *(Ham 5.1.57) The First Gravedigger tells his assistant: 'fetch me a stoup of liquor'—get me a (alcoholic) drink.*

stout ADJECTIVE
proud
• *(TN 2.5.158) Malvolio says he will be 'strange, stout, in yellow stockings'.*

stover NOUN [pronounced **stoh**-ver]
fodder grass
• *(Tem 4.1.63) Iris describes Ceres' 'flat meads thatch'd with stover'—open fields covered with grass.*

Strachy NOUN [pronounced **stray**-chee]
an unknown meaning—presumably the name of a local family, house, or institution
• *(TN 2.5.36) Malvolio reflects that 'The Lady of the Strachy married the yeoman of the wardrobe'.*
Malvolio is taking hope from the fact that there has been another noble lady who married her servant. It was extremely unusual for servants and nobles, being of distinctly different social classes, to marry.

straight ADVERB
immediately
• *(RJ 5.1.33) Romeo tells Balthasar to hire horses: 'I'll be with thee straight'.*

strain VERB
1 constrain
• *(MV 4.1.182) Balthazar explains that 'The quality of mercy is not strain'd'—cannot be forced in anyone.*
2 encourage
• *(Oth 3.3.252) Iago, referring to Cassio, tells Othello to 'Note if your lady strain his entertainment'.*
› **strained** also spelled **strain'd** ADJECTIVE
excessive
• *(KL 1.1.168) Lear condemns Kent for talking to him 'with strain'd pride'.*

strait ADJECTIVE
close-fitting
• *(H5 3.8.51) Bourbon jests with the Constable about his riding like an Irish peasant soldier 'in your strait strossers'—tight trousers.*

strand also spelled **strond** NOUN
shore
• *(MV 1.1.171) Bassanio says Portia's hair reminds him of the mythological story of Jason's golden fleece, which makes 'her seat of Belmont Colchos' strand'—her house reminiscent of Colchis, the grand palace where Jason came in search of the fleece.*

strange ADJECTIVE
as well as meaning 'unusual' and 'not experienced before', you'll find:

1 unnatural
• *(KL 2.1.76) Gloucester describes Edgar as a 'strange and fast'ned villain!'—abnormal and steadfast in his villainy.*
2 special
• *(Tem 3.3.87) Prospero says his spirits have carried out their tasks with 'observation strange'—paying attention to detail.*
3 aloof
• *(RJ 2.2.102) Juliet tells Romeo that she 'should have been more strange' towards him—she feels she should have played harder to get.*
4 diffident
• *(MA 2.3.47) Don Pedro tells the singer it is a sign of excellence 'To put a strange face on his own perfection'—to appear humble rather than proud of one's talents.*

› **strangely** ADVERB
1 unaccountably
• *(Tem 3.3.40) Francisco says the spirits 'vanish'd strangely'.*
2 admirably
• *(Tem 4.1.7) Prospero tells Ferdinand he has 'strangely stood the test'.*
2 extremely
• *(Mac 4.3.152) Malcolm describes how the English king cures 'strangely visited people'—greatly afflicted.*

› **strangeness** NOUN
aloofness
• *(TN 4.1.13) Feste asks Sebastian to 'ungird thy strangeness'—remove your distant manner.*

› **stranger** VERB
disown
• *(KL 1.1.203) Lear tells Burgundy that Cordelia has been 'stranger'd with our oath'—he has vowed to disown her.*

strange-disposed see **dispose**

straw NOUN
trivial matter
• *(Ham 4.5.6) A gentleman reports that Ophelia 'Spurns enviously at straws'—treats little matters with contempt, and takes offence easily.*

strength NOUN
as well as meanings to do with 'power' and 'ability', you'll find:
resources
• *(KL 2.1.111) Cornwall tells Gloucester: 'Make your own purpose / How in my strength you please' —draw on my resources for your purpose, in any way you wish.*

strewments NOUN
scattered flowers [on a grave]
• *(Ham 5.1.217) The Priest says that Ophelia's grave is allowed 'Her maiden strewments'—a sign of chastity.*

stride VERB
bestride
• *(Mac 1.7.22) Macbeth imagines pity 'like a naked newborn babe / Striding the blast'—the storm of indignation that will follow news of Duncan's murder.*

strife NOUN
⚠ *Don't read in the meaning of 'fighting'.*
striving, great effort
• *(RJ 2.2.152) Juliet asks Romeo 'To cease thy strife and leave me to my grief'.*

strike past form **struck** VERB
as well as meaning 'hit' and 'beat', you'll find:
1 fight
• *(H5 2.4.54) The French king recalls when the Battle of Crécy 'was struck'.*
2 have an evil influence
• *(Ham 1.1.167) Marcellus says, alluding to the belief that the movements of planets affect human behaviour, that on Christmas night 'no planets strike'.*

› **strike off** VERB
cancel
• *(Oth 3.4.173) Cassio, not having seen Bianca for some time, promises he will 'Strike off this score of absence'—pay off his debt.*

stripe NOUN
stroke of a whip, and the mark it leaves on the skin
• *(Tem 1.2.345) Prospero harangues Caliban, 'Whom stripes may move, not kindness'.*

stroke NOUN
⚠ *Don't read meanings to do with 'gentle movement' into these senses.*
1 blow
• *(Mac 5.4.20) Siward says for there to be a certain outcome, sword 'strokes must arbitrate'—there has to be a battle.*
2 affliction
• *(KL 4.1.64) Gloucester describes Poor Tom as someone 'whom the heav'ns' plagues / Have humbled to all strokes'.*

strossers NOUN
trousers
• *(H5 3.8.51) Bourbon jests with the Constable about his riding like an Irish peasant soldier 'in your strait strossers'.*

strumpet NOUN
prostitute
• *(Oth 4.2.80) Othello calls Desdemona an 'Impudent strumpet!'*

stubborn ADJECTIVE
as well as meaning 'obstinate', you'll find:
1 hostile
• *(MV 4.1.32) The Duke says Antonio's woes are enough to get sympathy even 'From stubborn Turks'—a people believed to be tough in their business dealings.*
2 challenging
• *(Oth 1.3.225) The Duke describes Othello's mission to Cyprus as 'stubborn and boisterous'—difficult and violent.*

stuck or **stuck-in** NOUN
thrust (in fencing)
• *(Ham 4.7.161) Claudius plans with Laertes what to do if Hamlet 'escape your venom'd stuck'—thrust from a poisoned sword.*

study VERB
1 learn by heart
• *(Ham 2.2.525) Hamlet asks the First Player to 'study a speech'.*
2 reflect
• *(Tem 2.1.78) Adrian ponders Gonzalo's reference to Dido: 'You make me study of that'—I'll have to think about that.*

study NOUN
as well as meaning 'learning', you'll find:
1 aim
• *(KL 1.1.276) Goneril advises Cordelia: 'Let your study / Be to content your lord'.*
2 reflection (in thought)
• *(MA 4.1.224) The Friar predicts how Claudio will think about Hero: 'Th'idea of her life shall sweetly creep / Into his study of imagination'.*

› **studied** ADJECTIVE
1 experienced
• *(MV 2.2.183) Gratiano assures Bassanio he will behave 'Like one well studied in a sad ostent'—someone thoroughly accustomed to looking serious.*
2 learned by heart (as when preparing a part in a play)
• *(Mac 1.4.9) Malcolm says that Cawdor died 'As one that had been studied in his death'—prepared and ready for it.*

stuff NOUN
as well as meaning 'substance', you'll find:
1 nonsense
• *(Mac 3.4.60) Lady Macbeth dismisses her husband's fears: 'O proper stuff!'*
2 equipment
• *(Tem 1.2.164) Prospero remembers the help Gonzalo gave him: 'Rich garments, linens, stuffs'.*

› **stuffed** ADJECTIVE
as well as meaning 'filled up', you'll find:
clogged
• *(Mac 5.3.45) Macbeth describes his wife as having a 'stuff'd bosom'—an oppressed heart.*

› **unstuffed** ADJECTIVE
unclogged (by troubles)
• *(RJ 2.3.37) The Friar says sleep readily comes to a 'youth with unstuff'd brain'.*

sty VERB
confine (as in an animal's sty)
• *(Tem 1.2.342) Caliban complains to Prospero: 'here you sty me / In this hard rock'.*

sub-contracted see **contraction**

subdued ADJECTIVE
subjugated
• *(Tem 1.2.490) Ferdinand describes Prospero as someone 'To whom I am subdued'.*

› **self-subdued** also spelled **-subdu'd** ADJECTIVE
unresisting
• *(KL 2.2.118) Oswald complains of the way Kent attacked someone who 'was self-subdu'd'—unwilling to fight.*

subject NOUN
1 subjects [in a state]
• *(Ham 1.1.75) Marcellus asks why 'nightly toils the subject of the land'—why people are working night and day.*
2 subordinate
• *(KL 5.3.61) Albany tells Edmund he holds him 'but a subject of this war, / Not as a brother'—not as an equal (with a possible pun, as Edmund might one day be his brother-in-law).*

› **subjection** NOUN
obedience
• *(H5 4.1.139) Williams says to disobey the king would be 'against all proportion of subjection'—against all proper relation of subject to ruler.*

a b c d e f g h i j k l m n o p q r Ss t u v w x y z

suborn VERB
bribe
• *(Mac 2.4.24) Macduff believes Duncan's attendants 'were suborn'd' by Malcolm and Donaldbain.*

subscribe VERB
1 sign
• *(Ham 5.2.52) Hamlet says he folded his version of the letter to the English king and 'Subscrib'd it'.*
2 proclaim to be
• *(MA 5.2.54) Benedick promises Beatrice, if he does not hear a response from Claudio to his challenge, 'I will subscribe him a coward'.*
3 consent
• *(KL 3.7.62) Gloucester imagines wolves howling at the gate of Regan's castle, and her telling the porter to open the door, 'All cruels else subscribe'—every other cruel thing would do so.*
See the usage note at cruels
› **subscribe for** VERB
answer on behalf of
• *(MA 1.1.37) Beatrice describes how her uncle's fool 'subscribed for Cupid', responding to a challenge from Benedick.*
› **subscription** NOUN
obedience
• *(KL 3.2.18) Lear tells the storm: 'You owe me no subscription'.*

substantial ADJECTIVE
real
• *(RJ 2.2.141) Romeo thinks his meeting with Juliet is a dream, 'Too flattering-sweet to be substantial'.*
› **unsubstantial** ADJECTIVE
intangible
• *(KL 4.1.7) Edgar embraces his life outside in the 'unsubstantial air'.*

substitute NOUN
deputy
• *(Oth 1.3.221) The Duke refers to his 'substitute' in Cyprus.*

substractor NOUN
detractor
• *(TN 1.3.31) Sir Toby says those who criticize Sir Andrew are 'scoundrels and substractors'.*

subtle ADJECTIVE
1 crafty
• *(TN 1.5.277) Olivia reflects on how Cesario's perfections have affected her 'With an invisible and subtle stealth'.*
2 refined
• *(Tem 2.1.42) Adrian describes the island as being of 'subtle, tender, and delicate temperance'.*
› **super-subtle** ADJECTIVE
specially refined
• *(Oth 1.3.350) Iago describes Desdemona as 'a super-subtle Venetian'.*
› **subtlety** ADJECTIVE
ingenious contrivance
• *(Tem 5.1.124) Prospero tells his visitors that they 'do yet taste / Some subtleties o'th' isle'.*
› **subtly** ADVERB
deceitfully
• *(RJ 4.3.25) Juliet worries that the potion might be 'a poison which the Friar / Subtly hath minister'd to have me dead'.*

suburbs NOUN
part of a city lying outside the walls, and so outside the city's laws (an area known for its brothels and theatres)
• *(JC 2.1.285) Portia asks Brutus: 'Dwell I but in the suburbs / Of your good pleasure?'*

success NOUN
as well as meaning 'successful outcome', you'll find:
1 outcome (whether good or bad)
• *(Oth 3.3.224) Iago hopes his speech would not 'fall into such vile success / As my thoughts aim'd not at'.*
2 process of time
• *(MA 4.1.233) The Friar assures Leonato that 'success / Will fashion the event in better shape' —the situation will improve in due course.*
› **succession** NOUN
1 system of legal inheritance
• *(Tem 2.1.147) Gonzalo says in his imaginary commonwealth there would be no 'succession'.*
2 future
• *(Ham 2.2.344) Hamlet says the child players 'exclaim against their own succession'—insult the profession that they will one day belong to as adults.*

sudden ADJECTIVE
1 swift to act
• *(JC 3.1.19) Cassius tells Casca to 'be sudden, for we fear prevention'.*
2 early
• *(RJ 3.5.109) Lady Capulet tells Juliet that her husband has 'sorted out a sudden day of joy' for her.*
3 unpredictable
• *(Oth 2.1.262) Iago says Cassio is 'rash and very*

sudden in choler'—when he's angry, no-one knows what he will do next.

> **on a sudden**
suddenly
• *(RJ 2.3.50) Romeo tells the Friar that 'on a sudden one hath wounded me / That's by me wounded'.*

> **suddenly** ADVERB
at once
• *(Ham 2.2.210) Polonius says he will 'suddenly contrive the means of meeting'—arrange an immediate meeting between Ophelia and Hamlet.*

sue VERB
⚠*Don't read in the meaning of 'start a lawsuit'.*
beg
• *(KL 1.1.29) Kent, on being introduced to Edmund: 'I must love you, and sue to know you better'.*

suffer VERB
as well as meaning 'feel pain', you'll find:
1 allow
• *(MV 5.1.213) Bassanio says he did not wish to give his ring to Balthazar, but 'suffer'd him to go displeas'd away'.*
2 put up with
• *(KL 1.2.49) Gloucester reads in Edgar's letter that old age rules, not because it has power, but 'as it is suffer'd'—young people have to put up with it.*
3 endure
• *(Tem 1.2.401) Ariel sings about a drowned Alonso who 'doth suffer a sea-change'.*
4 hold up
• *(TN 2.5.121) Malvolio, reading Olivia's letter, finds no consistency in the sequence of letters 'that suffers under probation'—no meaning in the order that makes sense under examination.*
5 perish
• *(Mac 3.2.16) Macbeth says he will let 'both the worlds suffer, / Ere we will eat our meal in fear'—this world and the next will fall before he will feel fear.*

> **sufferance** also spelled **suff'rance** NOUN
1 suffering
• *(JC 2.1.115) Brutus affirms that his motives for action include 'The sufferance of our souls'.*
2 patience
• *(MV 1.3.105) Shylock tells Antonio: 'suff'rance is the badge of all our tribe'—all Jews have to be patient (to put up with the way they are treated).*
3 reprieve
• *(H5 2.2.46) Scroop says an offender needs to be punished 'lest example / Breed by his sufferance more of such a kind'.*

> **suffered** also spelled **suffer'd** ADJECTIVE
undergone
• *(Tem 1.2.231) Ariel says he has left the mariners sleeping, through 'a charm join'd to their suffer'd labour'—the trouble they have endured is helping to make them rest.*

> **suffering** ADJECTIVE
patient
• *(JC 2.1.130) Brutus says the kind of people who swear an oath include 'such suffering souls / That welcome wrongs'.*

sufficiency NOUN
competence
• *(Oth 1.3.222) The Duke says he has a deputy in Cyprus 'of most allowed sufficiency'—of well-recognized ability.*

> **sufficient** ADJECTIVE
capable
• *(MV 1.3.14) Shylock wants to be reassured that Antonio 'is sufficient'—is capable of acting as a guarantor for Bassanio.*

suffigance NOUN [pronounced suh-**fidge**-ans]
intended to mean 'sufficient'
• *(MA 3.5.49) Dogberry assures Leonato that he can examine the prisoners: 'It shall be suffigance'.*

suggest VERB
⚠*Don't read the meaning of 'propose' or 'proposal' into these senses.*
tempt
• *(H5 2.2.111) Henry compares Scroop to 'other devils that suggest by treasons'—tempt people to commit acts of treason.*

> **suggestion** NOUN
temptation
• *(Mac 1.3.133) Macbeth asks himself: 'why do I yield to that suggestion, / Whose horrid image doth unfix my hair'.*

suit NOUN
as well as meaning 'lawsuit', you'll find:
1 petition
• *(Ham 1.2.43) Claudius asks Laertes: 'You told us of some suit'.*
2 wooing
• *(MV 2.7.73) Morocco reads from a scroll: 'your suit is cold'.*
3 clothing (in general)
⚠*Don't read in the modern meaning of 'matching jacket and skirt/trousers'.*
• *(TN 5.1.226) Cesario, seeing Sebastian, wonders 'If spirits can assume both form and suit'.*

> **suited** ADJECTIVE
dressed up
• *(MV 3.5.56) Lorenzo comments on Lancelot's*

a b c d e f g h i j k l m n o p q r Ss t u v w x y z

speech: 'how his words are suited!'—he speaks in a fancy way.

› **three-suited** ADJECTIVE
allowed only three suits of clothes a year (the usual allocation to servants)
• *(KL 2.2.14) Kent calls Oswald 'three-suited' —servile.*

suit VERB
1 clothe
• *(KL 4.7.6) Cordelia suggests to Kent, still disguised, that he 'Be better suited'.*
2 compare
• *(MA 5.1.7) Leonato says he can be comforted only by 'such a one whose wrongs do suit with mine'.*

› **non-suit** VERB
refuse
• *(Oth 1.1.16) Iago complains that Othello 'Non-suits my mediators'—rejects petitions made on his behalf.*

› **suitor** ADJECTIVE
petitioner
• *(JC 2.4.15) Portia asks Lucius to watch Caesar carefully and see 'what suitors press to him'.*

sully also spelled **sally** NOUN
blemish
• *(Ham 2.1.40) Polonius instructs Reynaldo about laying 'slight sullies on my son'.*

› **sullied** ADJECTIVE
blemished
• *(Ham 1.2.129) Hamlet wishes his 'too too sullied flesh would melt'.*
This is the word used in several editions. Some editions have 'solid', from the First Folio, or 'sallied' ('assailed'), from the First and Second Quarto texts of the play.

sumless ADJECTIVE
incalculable
• *(H5 1.2.165) Canterbury talks of the 'sunken wreck and sumless treasuries' at the bottom of the sea.*

summer-seeming ADJECTIVE
befitting the summer-time of life (early manhood)
• *(Mac 4.3.86) Macduff says that avarice grows more 'Than summer-seeming lust'.*

summoner NOUN
court-officer who ensures attendance
• *(KL 3.2.59) Lear in the noisy storm imagines crimes emerging from their hiding-places to 'cry / These dreadul summoners grace'—ask for mercy.*

sumpter NOUN
pack-horse
• *(KL 2.4.213) Lear says, of Oswald, he would rather 'be slave and sumpter / To this detested groom' than return to Goneril.*

sunburnt ADJECTIVE
of dark complexion
• *(MA 2.1.296) Beatrice says getting married is the way of the world 'and I am sunburnt'—out of fashion because not fair-skinned.*
Elizabethans rated fair skin as more attractive than dark—whether naturally so, or through the action of the sun. Dark skin meant 'foreigner' or (if tanned) 'low-born' (because you worked in the sun).

sup VERB
have supper
• *(Mac 1.7.29) Lady Macbeth says Duncan 'has almost supp'd'—he's almost finished supper.*

superfluity NOUN
immoderate living
• *(MV 1.2.8) Nerissa observes that 'superfluity comes sooner by white hairs'—it ages a person who lives a life of excess.*

› **superfluous** ADJECTIVE
1 immoderate
• *(Ham 4.5.95) Claudius says that Laertes' arrival 'Gives me superfluous death'—kills me over and over.*
2 over-supplied
• *(KL 4.1.66) Gloucester hopes the heavens will deal with 'the superfluous and lust-dieted man'—the man who has lots of possessions and gets whatever he wants.*

superflux NOUN
surplus possessions
• *(KL 3.4.35) Lear wants himself 'to feel what wretches feel, / That thou mayst shake the superflux to them'—so he may give all he doesn't need to them.*

super-serviceable see **serviceable**

super-subtle see **subtle**

supervise NOUN
perusal
• *(Ham 5.2.23) Hamlet says his letter to the English king asked for the death of Rosencrantz and Guildenstern 'on the supervise'—as soon as the letter had been read.*

› **supervisor** NOUN
Don't read in the meaning of 'someone in charge'.
onlooker
• *(Oth 3.3.396) Iago asks Othello if he would be a 'supervisor' of Desdemona having sex with another man.*

supplant VERB
root out
• *(Tem 3.2.47) Stephano threatens Trinculo: 'I will*

a b c d e f g h i j k l m n o p q r **Ss** t u v w x y z

warning note *usage note* *theatre note*

supplant some of your teeth'—I'll knock your teeth out.

suppliance NOUN
pastime
• *(Ham 1.3.9) Laertes says that Hamlet's love is 'The perfume and suppliance of a minute'—momentary, like a wave of perfume.*

supply VERB
as well as meaning 'provide', you'll find:
1 satisfy (sexually)
• *(Oth 4.1.28) Iago describes knaves who either overpowered a woman or found her willing to be 'supplied'.*
2 reinforce
• *(Mac 1.2.13) The Captain describes how Macdonald 'Of kerns and galloglasses is supplied'—the traitor has hired mercenaries from other countries to fight for him (because he couldn't get enough support from his own countrymen).*

supportance NOUN
support
• *(TN 3.4.274) Sir Toby tells Cesario to 'draw for the supportance of his vow'—draw your sword so that Sir Andrew can keep his vow to fight.*

supposal NOUN
opinion
• *(Ham 1.2.18) Claudius says that young Fortinbras holds 'a weak supposal of our worth'—a poor opinion.*

> **supposed** ADJECTIVE
> false
> • *(KL 5.3.111) The Herald announces Edmund as the 'supposed Earl of Gloucester'.*

> **supposition** NOUN
> 1 belief
> • *(MA 4.1.237) The Friar explains what people will think of Hero if there is 'supposition of the lady's death'.*
> 2 doubt
> • *(MV 1.3.15) Shylock says that Antonio's financial 'means are in supposition'.*

surcease NOUN
completion
• *(Mac 1.7.4) Macbeth wonders if assassinating Duncan would 'catch / With his surcease, success'—whether, with the completion of Duncan's life, Macbeth might find success with his own life.*

surcease VERB
stop
• *(RJ 4.1.97) The Friar describes what happens when Juliet drinks his potion: 'no pulse / Shall keep his native progress, but surcease'—its natural movement will cease.*

sure ADJECTIVE
as well as meaning 'certain', you'll find:
loyal
• *(MA 1.3.59) Don John asks Borachio and Conrad: 'You are both sure, and will assist me?'*

sure ADVERB
as well as meaning 'certainly', you'll find:
securely
• *(JC 1.2.319) Cassius reflects: 'let Caesar seat him sure, / For we will shake him, or worse days endure'—Caesar had better hold on tight, because we're going to rock his world.*

surety NOUN [pronounced **sure**-uh-tee]
1 guarantee
• *(H5 5.2.352) Henry tells the French lords he will take their oath 'for surety of our leagues'—to ratify the alliance.*
2 guarantor
• *(Tem 1.2.476) Miranda tells her father that she will take responsibility for Ferdinand: 'I'll be his surety'.*
3 certainty
• *(Oth 1.3.381) Iago decides to take as 'surety' the rumour that Othello has slept with Emilia.*

surfeit VERB [pronounced **sir**-fit]
1 overindulge
• *(TN 1.1.2) Orsino wants an excess of music (which he sees as the food of love), so that 'surfeiting, / The appetite may sicken, and so die'—by taking so much of it, the desire for music (and so, he hopes, his love-sickness for Olivia) will wane.*
2 become sick through excess
• *(MV 3.2.114) Portia, as if talking to Love, asks it to moderate its effect on her: 'make it less, / For fear I surfeit'.*

> **surfeited** ADJECTIVE
> overfilled (with drink)
> • *(Mac 2.2.5) Lady Macbeth knows that 'the surfeited grooms / Do mock their charge with snores'.*

surgeon NOUN
doctor (who also treats wounds—unlike today, where a surgeon is the specialist who performs operations)
• *(RJ 3.1.90) Mercutio tells his servant to 'fetch a surgeon'.*

surly ADJECTIVE
⚠ *Don't read in the meaning of 'bad-tempered'.*
haughty
• *(TN 2.5.138) Olivia's letter tells Malvolio to be 'surly with servants'.*

surmise NOUN
imagining
• *(Mac 1.3.140) Macbeth says his thoughts have so taken him over that 'function / Is smother'd in surmise'—imaginings have taken away his power to act.*

surmise VERB
suppose
• *(Ham 2.2.108) Polonius tells Claudius and Gertrude to read Hamlet's letter, then 'gather, and surmise'—work out for yourselves what is happening.*

surprise VERB
⚠ *Don't read in the meaning of 'do something unexpected'.*
take prisoner
• *(TN 1.4.25) Orsino tells Cesario to visit Olivia and 'Surprise her with discourse of my dear faith' —capture her (heart) by telling her how loyal he is.*

sur-reined ADJECTIVE [pronounced **sir**-raind]
worn out (because ridden too hard)
• *(H5 3.6.19) The Constable describes English ale as 'A drench for sur-reined jades'—a drink only for over-worked nags.*

suspiration NOUN
deep sighing
• *(Ham 1.2.79) Hamlet says his feelings of grief can't be judged simply by the way he sighs: 'windy suspiration of forc'd breath'.*

sustain VERB
1 have a place
• *(Oth 5.2.258) Othello says, of his sword, that a better weapon 'never did itself sustain / Upon a soldier's thigh'.*
2 provide for
• *(KL 3.3.5) Gloucester says he has been told not to speak of Lear, 'entreat for him, or any way sustain him'.*

› **sustaining** ADJECTIVE
life-supporting
• *(KL 4.4.6) Cordelia says Lear is crowned with 'all the idle weeds that grow / In our sustaining corn'.*

sutler see **OCCUPATIONS, p.166**

swabber NOUN
deckhand
• *(TN 1.5.189) Cesario, told to 'hoist sail' (to leave) by Maria, replies: 'No, good swabber'.*

swag-bellied ADJECTIVE
with a sagging paunch
• *(Oth 2.3.69) Iago describes a Dutchman as a 'swag-bellied Hollander'.*

swagger VERB
⚠ *Don't read meanings to do with 'strutting' into these senses.*
1 talk blusteringly
• *(Oth 2.3.262) Cassio is appalled at his own behaviour: 'Swagger! Swear!'*
2 quarrel
• *(H5 4.7.117) Williams tells the king of 'a rascal that swaggered with me last night'.*

› **swaggering** ADJECTIVE
quarrelling
• *(TN 5.1.386) Feste sings: 'By swaggering could I never thrive'.*

swain NOUN
yokel
• *(MND 4.1.64) Oberon tells Puck to take the ass's scalp 'From off the head of this Athenian swain'.*

swarth NOUN
chunk
• *(TN 2.3.133) Maria says Malvolio is one who learns etiquette off by heart 'and utters it by great swarths'.*

swasher NOUN
braggart
• *(H5 3.2.25) The Boy reflects on Pistol, Nym, and Bardolph: 'I have observed these three swashers'.*

swathing clouts NOUN
swaddling clothes (the kind of tight, restrictive clothes that you dress a young baby in)
• *(Ham 2.2.373) Hamlet describes Polonius as a baby 'not yet out of his swathing clouts'.*
This is the word used in the First Folio. Some editions follow the First and Second Quarto texts and use 'swaddling-clouts'.

sway NOUN
1 rule
• *(RJ 4.1.10) Capulet thinks it dangerous that Juliet 'do give her sorrow so much sway'.*
2 direction
• *(KL 4.7.20) Cordelia asks the Doctor to proceed 'I'th' sway of your own will'—do what he thinks best.*
3 position of authority
• *(KL 1.1.135) Lear gives Cornwall and Albany 'the sway'.*

sway VERB
⚠ *Don't read the meaning of 'move gently from side to side' into these senses.*
1 direct
• *(MA 4.1.200) The Friar asks Leonato: 'let my counsel sway you in this case'.*

⚠ *warning note* *usage note* *theatre note*

SWEARING

Characters swear when they want to say something in an especially emotional or powerful way, or for emphasis. As in modern English, the swear-words are often just emotional noises that have lost their original meaning. Some are quite mild in their force; some are very strong.

SWEARING ON YOUR HONOUR OR FAITH

forsooth

in truth; *sooth* was an Old English word meaning 'truth'

• *(RJ 4.2.12) Capulet asks the Nurse if Juliet has gone to see Friar Lawrence, and she replies: 'Ay forsooth'.*

sooth, good sooth, in sooth, in good sooth

• *(JC 2.4.20) Portia nervously asks Lucius a second time if he heard a noise: 'Sooth, madam, I hear nothing'.*

by my troth, good troth

• *(TN 1.3.3) Maria tells Sir Toby off for coming in late: 'By my troth, Sir Toby, you must come in earlier o'nights'.*

i'faith, in faith, in good faith, by my faith, by my fay

• *(RJ 2.5.53) Juliet sympathizes with the Nurse: 'I'faith, I am sorry that thou art not well'.*

SWEARING ON YOUR BODY OR A DISEASE

by my hand, by this hand

• *(Ham 5.2.243) Hamlet insists he is not mocking Laertes: 'No, by this hand'—which is raised in oath-taking and which carries a sword.*

pox, a pox

the disease of smallpox, a really nasty outcome

• *(Oth 1.3.352) Iago tells Roderigo to forget any thought of killing himself: 'A pox of drowning thyself!'*

SWEARING BY THE ANCIENT GODS

by Apollo

• *(KL 1.1.159) King Lear swears 'by Apollo', the Greek sun-god, and therefore an indication of strong feeling.*

by Jupiter

• *(KL 2.4.20) King Lear also swears 'By Jupiter'—the Roman supreme god, and therefore expressing the strongest emotion.*

by Juno

• *(KL 2.4.21) in reply, Kent matches him with 'By Juno'—the Roman supreme goddess, the wife of Jupiter, and, as queen of the gods, expressing just as strong an emotion.*

by Jove

• *(H5 4.3.24) King Henry swears 'By Jove'—another name for Jupiter, but, coming from the mouth of a Christian king, largely empty of meaning (as in the usage of older people today).*

by Janus

• *(Oth 1.2.33) Iago swears 'By Janus'—the Roman god who guards gates and doors, shown with two faces, one at the back of his head, so that he can see comings and goings (an appropriate swear-word for a two-faced character).*

Swearing by the Christian God

In a period when virtually everyone believed in God, to swear by his name was taken very seriously, though some characters would use it lightly (as today when people say 'Oh my God').

God in full

'fore God
short for 'before God'
• *(Oth 2.3.66) Cassio loves Iago's song: ' 'Fore God, an excellent song.'*

perdy also spelled **perdie**
from the French words for 'by God' (par Dieu)
• *(Ham 3.2.282) Hamlet is delighted that Claudius did not like the play: 'he likes it not, perdie.'*

Things to do with God

• *(Ham 2.2.516) Hamlet swears by **God's bodkin** ('God's dear body').*
• *(RJ 3.5.176) Capulet swears by **God's bread**.*
• *(MV 2.2.41) Gobbo swears by **God's sonties**—an old way of saying 'saints'.*

God totally hidden

This is an example of 'having your cake and eating it'—the swearer expresses a strong emotion without actually saying the original swear-word (and thus avoiding a charge of blasphemy).

sblood also spelled **'sblood**
short for 'God's blood'
• *(Ham 3.2.354) Hamlet gets angry with Guildenstern: ' 'Sblood, do you think I am easier to be played on than a pipe?'*

swounds also spelled **'swounds, zounds**
short for 'God's wounds'
• *(Oth 5.2.217) Iago angrily tells Emilia to keep quiet: 'Zounds, hold your peace!'*

Sir Andrew uses the rather dainty **'slid,** 'God's eyelid' *(TN 3.4.364)* and **'slight** 'God's light' *(TN 2.5.30)*. God also appears in **by Cock**—a euphemistic softening of the name—which allows people to swear and make a rude joke at the same time.
• *(Ham 4.5.61) Ophelia sings in her madness of young men: 'By Cock, they are to blame.'*

God partly hidden

Another way of avoiding the force of the full form of the word.
• *(TN 5.1.177) Sir Andrew swears by 'Od's lifelings ('God's dear life').*
• *(Oth 4.3.73) Emilia swears by 'Ud's pity ('God's pity').*

Swearing by other Christian beliefs

Jesu
the Latin form of Jesus (the full form is hardly ever used as a swear-word in Shakespeare, unlike today)
• *(RJ 2.5.29) The Nurse doesn't want Juliet to rush her: 'Jesu, what haste!'*
Jesus is also softed to **Gis** by Ophelia *(Ham 4.5.58)* and given a Welsh accent by the Welsh Captain: **By Cheshu** *(H5 3.3.15)*.

Christ
The full form is never used alone as a swear-word in Shakespeare (unlike today).
• *(H5 4.1.64) The Welsh Captain advises Gower to keep his voice down: 'In the name of Jesu Christ, speak fewer.'*
• *(H5 3.3.31) Macmorris gives the name an Irish accent: 'By Chrish.'*

by the rood
rood is an Old English word for the 'cross' on which Christ was crucified, and thus a very strong oath
• *(Ham 3.4.13) Gertrude asks Hamlet if he has forgotten her, and he replies angrily: 'No, by the rood, not so.'*

mass or **by the mass**
the main Christian celebration, and originally a strong oath, but often used in a very weak way
• *(Ham 3.2.362) Polonius agrees with Hamlet that a cloud looks like a camel: 'By th' mass, and 'tis.'*

marry
from *Mary*, the mother of Jesus; usually said at the beginning of a reply to emphasize it; used by everyone with a very weak force
• *(Ham 1.4.13) Horatio asks if Elsinore's noisy celebration is a custom, and Hamlet replies: 'Ay marry is't.'*

by'r lady
short for *Our Lady*, another name for the mother of Jesus, a mild oath
• *(MA 3.3.77) Verges firmly agrees with Dogberry: 'By'r Lady, I think it be so.'*

The Nurse also swears **by my holidam**— 'holy dame' *(RJ 1.3.44)*. And other characters swear by the saints: Hamlet swears **by St Patrick** *(Ham 1.5.142)* and Friar Lawrence by **Saint Francis** *(RJ 2.3.65)*
see the alphabetical entries at **Francis** and **Patrick**.

2 be directed

• *(Mac 5.3.9) Macbeth asserts that 'the mind I sway by and the heart I bear / Shall never sag with doubt'.*

3 move

• *(TN 2.4.30) Orsino says, of a younger wife: 'So sways she level in her husband's heart'—she will always follow his heart's desire rather than her own.*

> **o'ersway** VERB
> persuade
> • *(JC 2.1.203) Decius says, if Caesar is resolved to stay at home, 'I can o'ersway him'—make him change his mind.*

swear VERB

⚠*Don't read in the meaning of 'use curse words'.*

promise

• *(Mac 4.2.47) Lady Macduff tells her son that a traitor is 'one that swears and lies'—takes an oath and then breaks it.*

> **unswear** VERB
> retract
> • *(Oth 4.1.31) Iago tells Othello that what Cassio has said is 'No more than he'll unswear'—no more than he'll take back.*

sweet ADJECTIVE

sweet-scented

• *(MND 2.1.252) Oberon describes a bank covered with 'sweet musk-roses'.*

sweet NOUN

1 sweet-scented flower

• *(Ham 5.1.227) Gertrude strews flowers on Ophelia's grave: 'Sweets to the sweet'—sweet-smelling flowers for the sweetheart.*

2 sweetness

• *(RJ 1.1.188) Romeo describes love as 'A choking gall, and a preserving sweet'—something that drags you down yet at the same time gives you life.*

> **sweeting** NOUN
> 1 sweetheart
> • *(Oth 2.3.236) Othello tells Desdemona, after the fight: 'All's well now, sweeting'.*
> 2 sweet-flavoured type of apple (used as a sauce for roast goose)
> • *(RJ 2.4.74) Mercutio tells Romeo: 'Thy wit is very bitter sweeting'.*

swelling ADJECTIVE

1 magnificent

• *(H5 Prologue.4) The Chorus imagines on the stage 'monarchs to behold the swelling scene'.*

2 arrogant

• *(Oth 2.3.48) Iago describes three men of Cyprus as 'noble swelling spirits'.*

sweltered also spelled **swelter'd** ADJECTIVE

oozing

• *(Mac 4.1.8) The First Witch puts 'Swelter'd venom' into the cauldron.*

swim VERB

as well as meaning 'move one's body through water', you'll find:

sail

• *(JC 5.1.67) Cassius says he is ready for battle: 'blow wind, swell billow, and swim bark!'—let the waves swell and the ship sail!*

swits and spurs

use a whip and spurs (to make a horse go faster)

• *(RJ 2.4.65) Romeo tells Mercutio: 'Swits and spurs, swits and spurs, or I'll cry a match'—keep going or I'll claim victory.*

Switzer NOUN

Swiss guard

• *(Ham 4.5.96) Claudius calls: 'Where is my Switzers?'*

The Swiss were often used as hired troops to form a royal guard. (Claudius is not being ungrammatical when he says 'is'—at that period in English, a plural subject was often accompanied by a singular verb.)

swoon, swound or **sound** VERB

faint

• *(Ham 5.2.302) Claudius says Gertrude 'swoons to see them bleed'.*

The First Folio prints the word as 'sounds'. 'Swounds' is found in the Third Folio. 'Swoons' is in the First Quarto text.

swoopstake ADVERB

indiscriminately (as if taking all stakes at once)

• *(Ham 4.5.141) Claudius asks Laertes if, 'swoopstake, you will draw both friend and foe' —if he is ready to kill both friend and enemy in obtaining his revenge.*

sword NOUN

as well as meaning the weapon, you'll find:

soldier (who wields a sword)

• *(KL 5.3.33) Edmund tells a Captain: 'to be tender-minded / Does not become a sword'.*

sworn brother see **brother**

swound see **swoon**

'swounds see SWEARING, p.298

sympathy NOUN
⚠ *Don't read the meaning of 'pity' into these senses.*
agreement
• *(RJ 3.3.85) The Nurse describes Romeo and Juliet's situation as a 'woeful sympathy'—shared misery.*

› sympathize with VERB
resemble
• *(H5 3.8.131) The Constable says the English 'do sympathize with the mastiffs'—they resemble large dogs in their rough and noisy attacks.*

synod NOUN [pronounced **sin**-od]
assembly
• *(Ham 2.2.482) The First Player addresses 'All you gods / In general synod'.*

Tt

Theatre

Theatre in the time of Queen Elizabeth I became virtually illegal unless performed by licensed actors who had a nobleman as a patron. Laws had been passed to control wandering beggars – but these laws also applied to touring actors. To avoid being arrested, they had to be perform outside the city walls, near the brothels and often in the same venue as the vicious sport of bear-baiting.

table or **table-book** NOUN
notebook
• *(Ham 1.5.98) Hamlet says he will wipe all trivial recollections 'from the table of my memory'.*

tabor see MUSIC, p.172

taborer NOUN
player of a tabor (a small drum)
• *(Tem 3.2.147) Stephano wonders: 'I would I could see this taborer' (as Ariel invisibly creates music).*

tackled also spelled **tackl'd** ADJECTIVE
made of rope
• *(RJ 2.4.172) Romeo says his man will bring cords 'made like a tackl'd stair'—a rope-ladder.*

ta'en see **take**

tag-rag ADJECTIVE
raggedly dressed
• *(JC 1.2.257) Casca reports the way 'the tag-rag people' applauded Caesar—the rabble.*

take past form **taken, ta'en, tane** VERB
as well as meanings to do with 'possessing' and 'carrying', you'll find:
1 hit
• *(H5 4.1.204) Williams tells Henry 'I will take thee a box on the ear'.*
2 appreciate
• *(MND 5.1.90) Theseus says, of the rustics' play: 'Our sport shall be to take what they mistake'—to be entertained when they get it wrong.*
3 captivate
• *(Tem 5.1.313) Alonso says that Prospero's story will 'Take the ear strangely'.*
4 bewitch
• *(Ham 1.1.168) Marcellus says that on Christmas night 'No fairy takes'—has the power to cast spells.*
5 pretend
• *(Ham 2.1.13) Polonius tells Reynaldo: 'Take you as 'twere some distant knowledge' of Laertes.*

a b c d e f g h i j k l m n o p q r s **Tt** u v w x y z

6 put up with
• *(KL 2.2.96) Cornwall describes Kent as one who 'must speak truth: / And they will take it'.*
7 believe
• *(KL 4.6.138) Edgar says, seeing Lear's behaviour, that he 'would not take this from report'—if somebody had told him about it.*
8 find
• *(H5 4.1.207) Henry says he will accept Williams' challenge, even 'though I take thee in the king's company'.*

› take down VERB
cut down to size
• *(RJ 2.4.137) The Nurse threatens that, if Mercutio says anything against her, 'I'll take him down'—put him in his place.*

› take me with you
I don't understand you
• *(RJ 3.5.141) Capulet hears the news from Lady Capulet that Juliet doesn't want to marry Paris: 'take me with you, wife'.*

› take on VERB
pretend
• *(MND 3.2.258) Demetrius says Lysander will 'take on as you would follow'—pretend that he would follow him to a place to fight.*

› take out VERB
copy
• *(Oth 3.3.298) Emilia looks at Desdemona's handkerchief: 'I'll have the work tane out'.*

› take up VERB
1 settle
• *(TN 3.4.267) Sir Toby says Sir Andrew has promised to give him his horse 'to take up the quarrel'—to stop the fight before it starts.*
2 arrest
• *(MA 3.3.165) Borachio tells Conrad they will 'prove a goodly commodity, being taken up of these men's bills'—we will be sold like prize fish, being caught by these men's spears.*

take the wall see **wall**

taking NOUN
infection
• *(KL 3.4.58) Poor Tom addresses Lear: 'Bless thee from whirlwinds, star-blasting, and taking!'*

taking ADJECTIVE
infectious
• *(KL 2.4.160) Lear curses Goneril: 'Strike her young bones, / You taking airs, with lameness!'*

› taking off also spelled **-off** NOUN
killing
• *(KL 5.1.65) Edmund thinks how to get rid of Albany: 'Let her who would be rid of him devise / His speedy taking off'—if Albany's wife, Goneril, wants to marry Edmund, she can get rid of her husband.*

tale NOUN
as well as meaning 'story', you'll find:
false rumour
• *(MND 3.2.133) Helena says that Lysander's vows are 'as light as tales'—unbelievable.*

› in a tale
in agreement
• *(MA 4.2.30) Dogberry says that Conrad and Borachio 'are both in a tale'.*

tall ADJECTIVE
as well as meaning 'high of stature', you'll find:
1 brave
• *(TN 1.3.18) Sir Toby says Sir Andrew is 'as tall a man as any's in Illyria'.*
2 fine
• *(MV 3.1.5) Salarino describes the dangerous stretch of sea known as the Goodwins, 'where the carcasses of many a tall ship lie buried'.*

tallow-face NOUN
face as pale as wax
• *(RJ 3.5.157) Capulet calls Juliet 'You tallow-face!'*

tame also spelled **'tame** VERB
break into (a short form of *attame*—break into)
• *(H5 1.2.173) Ely describes Scotland as a weasel sucking the eggs of eagle England, 'To 'tame and havoc more than she can eat'.*

tane see **take**

tang VERB
ring out
• *(TN 2.5.138) Malvolio is asked in the letter: 'Let thy tongue tang arguments of state'—speak openly about politics (one of the most demanding subjects to talk about in public).*

tang NOUN
sting
• *(Tem 2.2.49) Stephano sings of a girl called Kate who 'had a tongue with a tang'—she could speak sharply and wittily.*

tar see **tarre**

tardy ADJECTIVE
⚠ *Don't read the meaning of 'being late' into these senses.*
reluctant
• *(JC 1.2.297) Cassius explains why Casca 'puts on this tardy form'.*

tardy ADVERB
inadequately
• *(Ham 3.2.24) Hamlet criticizes a play that is 'overdone, or come tardy off'—carried out badly.*

› tardy-gaited ADJECTIVE
slow-moving
• *(H5 4.Chorus.20) The Chorus describes how the French nobles 'chide the tardy-gaited night'.*

› tardiness NOUN
reserve
• *(KL 1.1.234) France describes Cordelia's behaviour as 'a tardiness in nature'—a natural reluctance.*

target see **ARMOUR, p.154**

Tarquin NOUN
Tarquinius Superbus, king of Rome in the 6th-c BC, here remembered for his terrible rape of Lucrece
• *(Mac 2.1.55) Macbeth reflects on how the murderer moves stealthily towards his victim —'With Tarquin's ravishing strides'.*

tarre also spelled **tar** VERB
arouse
• *(Ham 2.2.346) Rosencrantz talks of the two sides in a theatre dispute, and how people are ready to 'tar them to controversy'—get them arguing.*

tarry VERB
stay a while longer
• *(MV 3.2.1) Portia begs Bassanio: 'I pray you tarry'.*

Tartar NOUN
someone from Tartary, in central Asia, known for their dark, yellowish-brown (tawny) complexion
• *(MND 3.2.263) Lysander calls Hermia a 'tawny Tartar'.*

Tartar NOUN
in Greek mythology, Tartarus, the underworld place of confinement for those who incurred the wrath of the gods
• *(TN 2.5.191) Sir Toby says he will follow Maria 'To the gates of Tartar'—to the gates of hell.*

tassel-gentle NOUN
male peregrine falcon
• *(RJ 2.2.159) Juliet wishes she was a falconer to bring Romeo back—'To lure this tassel-gentle back again!'*

taste VERB
try out
• *(TN 3.1.75) Sir Toby tells Cesario to 'Taste your legs, sir; put them to motion'—move!*

taste NOUN
1 testing
• *(KL 1.2.44) Edmund says he hopes Edgar's letter (and the disturbing message it contained) was only 'an essay or taste of my virtue'.*
2 degree
• *(JC 4.1.34) Antony compares Lepidus to a horse 'in some taste'—to some extent.*

Taurus see **COSMOS, p.174**

tax VERB
as well as meaning 'take a percentage of your income for the government', you'll find:
1 censure
• *(Ham 1.4.18) Hamlet says Claudius' revelling makes Denmark 'tax'd of other nations'—criticized by other states.*
2 order
• *(MA 2.3.44) Balthasar asks Don Pedro: 'tax not so bad a voice' to sing again.*

› taxation NOUN
demand for money
• *(TN 1.5.195) Viola tells Olivia she comes in peace, bringing 'no taxation of homage'—no claim arising out of an obligation.*

Te Deum see **LATIN, p.352**

tedious ADJECTIVE
⚠ *Don't read in the meaning of 'boringly slow'.*
laborious
• *(Mac 3.4.138) Macbeth, thinking of the river of blood he has created, says he is so far in that 'Returning were as tedious as go o'er'—he has gone so far, trying to turn back would be just as hard as to carry on and finish the job.*

teem VERB
1 bring forth
• *(Mac 4.3.178) Ross thinks of the sorrows in Scotland: 'Each minute teems a new one'.*
2 be made pregnant
• *(Oth 4.1.242) Othello says if the earth 'could teem with woman's tears, / Each drop she falls would prove a crocodile'—the tears would be feigned.*
3 give birth
• *(KL 1.4.271) Lear asks Nature to curse Goneril's children 'If she must teem'.*

› o'erteemed also spelled **o'er-teemed** ADJECTIVE [pronounced oar-**tee**-med]
excessively productive
• *(Ham 2.2.496) The First Player describes Hecuba's 'lank and all o'erteemed loins' —exhausted by child-bearing (Hecuba had 18 children).*

a b c d e f g h i j k l m n o p q r s Tt u v w x y z

The word would normally have two syllables, but in this line the metre requires a pronunciation with three.

teen NOUN
Don't read in the modern meaning of 'teenager'.
trouble
• *(Tem 1.2.64) Miranda says to her father: 'To think o'th' teen that I have turn'd you to'.*

teeth in the phrase
to the teeth and forehead of
in the very face of
• *(Ham 3.3.63) Claudius reflects that in the sight of heaven people have to face up to their wrongs —'Even to the teeth and forehead of our faults'.*

tell VERB
as well as meaning 'say' and 'reveal', you'll find:
1 count
• *(KL 3.2.89) The Fool prophesies what will happen to England 'When usurers tell their gold i'th'field'—count their money for anyone to see.*
2 tell the time on
• *(Tem 2.1.284) Antonio says to Sebastian that the other lords will 'tell the clock to any business that / We say befits the hour'—they'll agree to anything we say.*

Tellus NOUN
in Roman mythology, the goddess of the Earth
• *(Ham 3.2.148) The Player King describes the orb-shaped Earth as 'Tellus' orbed ground'.*

temper NOUN
Don't read the meaning of an 'angry mood' into these senses.
1 frame of mind
• *(H5 5.2.144) Henry, outlining his character, asks Katherine if she can 'love a fellow of this temper'.*
2 stable mind
• *(KL 1.5.42) Lear hopes he will not go mad, and asks the heavens: 'keep me in temper'.*

temper VERB
as well as meaning 'soften' or 'moderate', you'll find:
1 balance
• *(RJ 3.3.115) The Friar criticizes Romeo: 'I thought thy disposition better temper'd'.*
2 mould
• *(H5 2.2.115) Henry tells Scroop about the devil 'that temper'd thee'.*

› **ill-tempered** also spelled **-temper'd** ADJECTIVE
with unbalanced elements
• *(JC 4.3.115) Cassius finds Brutus vexed by 'grief and blood ill-temper'd'.*

see HUMOURS, p.137

› **mistempered** also spelled **mistemper'd** ADJECTIVE
made with evil intent
• *(RJ 1.1.81) The Prince commands the fighters to 'Throw your mistemper'd weapons to the ground'.*

› **untempering** ADJECTIVE
unsoftening
• *(H5 5.2.215) Henry hopes Katherine loves him, 'notwithstanding the poor and untempering effect of my visage'—his off-putting appearance (he doesn't think himself handsome).*

temperance NOUN
as well as meanings to do with 'moderation', you'll find:
climate
• *(Tem 2.1.42) Adrian describes the island as of 'subtle, tender, and delicate temperance'.*

› **temperate** ADJECTIVE
gentle-natured
• *(Tem 4.1.132) Iris calls to her 'temperate nymphs'.*

temple NOUN
1 church
• *(MA 3.3.149) Borachio says Claudio and Hero will meet 'next morning at the temple'.*
2 human body (thought of, in Christian belief, as the temple of the Holy Ghost)
• *(Ham 1.3.12) Laertes explains that the mind changes 'as this temple waxes'—as the body grows.*

temporal ADJECTIVE
worldly
• *(Tem 1.2.110) Prospero says Alonso thought him incapable 'Of temporal royalties'—unable to carry out the civil duties of a ruler.*

temporize VERB
become amenable
• *(MA 1.1.250) Don Pedro predicts that Benedick 'will temporize with the hours'—be more disposed to falling in love as time goes by.*

tempt VERB
as well as meaning 'persuade to do something wrong', you'll find:
make trial of
• *(JC 4.3.36) Cassius tells Brutus: 'tempt me no farther!'*

tenable ADJECTIVE
kept secret
• *(Ham 1.2.248) Hamlet asks his companions not to talk about the Ghost: 'Let it be tenable in your silence still'.*

tend VERB
as well as meaning 'serve', you'll find:
1 await
• *(Ham 1.3.83) Polonius tells Laertes: 'your servants tend'.*
2 pay attention
• *(Tem 1.1.6) The Boatswain orders the Mariners to 'Tend to th' master's whistle!'*
3 relate
• *(JC 3.2.57) Brutus tells the crowd to honour Antony's speech 'Tending to Caesar's glories'.*

tender NOUN
1 offer
• *(Ham 1.3.99) Ophelia tells her father that Hamlet has 'made many tenders / Of his affection to me'.*
2 offer of betrothal
• *(RJ 3.4.12) Capulet tells Paris he will 'make a desperate tender / Of my child's love'—a bold offer.*
3 concern
• *(KL 1.4.200) Goneril tells her father her intentions are 'in the tender of a wholesome weal'—concerned about having a healthy country.*

tender VERB
1 offer
• *(Tem 4.1.5) Prospero gives Ferdinand his daughter: 'I tender to thy hand'.*
2 care for
• *(Ham 4.3.39) Claudius assures Hamlet that he is concerned about his safety, 'Which we do tender'.*
3 regard
• *(RJ 3.1.68) Romeo calls Tybalt a Capulet, 'which name I tender / As dearly as mine own'.*

> **tender-hefted** ADJECTIVE
> gently fashioned
> • *(KL 2.4.168) Lear hopes that Regan's 'tender-hefted nature shall not give / Thee o'er to harshness'—he believes her character is set in a delicate, womanly frame.*

> **untender** ADJECTIVE
> unkind
> • *(KL 1.1.105) Lear asks Cordelia: 'So young, and so untender?'*

tenor also spelled **tenour** NOUN
1 general meaning
• *(H5 5.2.72) Henry tells the French that they have the 'tenors and particular effects' of his demands—the general aims and the details.*
2 exact meaning
• *(MV 4.1.233) Shylock says he will tear up his bond 'When it is paid, according to the tenour'.*

tent VERB
probe
• *(Ham 2.2.584) Hamlet decides about Claudius: 'I'll tent him to the quick'—reach his most sensitive psychological spot.*

> **untented** ADJECTIVE
> too deep to be cleansed with lint (a type of fabric used for dressing wounds)
> • *(KL 1.4.290) Lear berates Goneril: 'Th'untented woundings of a father's curse / Pierce every sense about thee!'*

tents NOUN
camp
• *(JC 5.3.10) Pindarus reports to Cassius that 'Mark Antony is in your tents'.*

tenure NOUN
condition for holding property
• *(Ham 5.1.93) Hamlet reflects on the skull of a lawyer, and asks where are 'his tenures' now.*

term NOUN
as well as meaning 'word' or 'expression', you'll find:
circumstance
• *(TN 5.1.66) Orsino asks Antonio why he has appeared among the people he made enemies of 'in terms so bloody and so dear'—in such warlike and grievous circumstances.*

Termagant NOUN [pronounced **term**-a-gant]
a noisy and overbearing character in 16th-century mystery plays
• *(Ham 3.2.13) Hamlet condemns noisy actors 'for o'erdoing Termagant'.*

termination NOUN
sentence ending
• *(MA 2.1.230) Benedick says there would be no living near Beatrice 'If her breath were as terrible as her terminations'.*

tertian NOUN
type of fever which attacks every third day
• *(H5 2.1.103) The Hostess reports that Falstaff is 'shaked of a burning quotidian tertian'.*
A quotidian fever occurs every day. Is Falstaff suffering from both kinds of fever, or (rather more likely) is the Hostess simply upset and getting confused?

TERMS OF ADDRESS

When characters address each other, the names they use show their attitude, such as courteous, friendly, sarcastic, or insulting.

bawcock
'fine fellow', from French words for a 'fine cockerel' (*beau coq*)
• *(H5 3.2.22) Pistol tries to calm the Welsh Captain down: 'Good bawcock, bate thy rage'.*

biddy
a childish word for a chicken
• *(TN 3.4.106) Sir Toby is being highly insulting when he addresses Malvolio in this way: 'Ay, biddy, come with me'.*

bully
⚠ *Don't read in the modern meaning of 'someone who tries to hurt or frighten people who are weaker'.*
'good friend'
• *(MND 3.1.7) Peter Quince is full of warmth when he asks Bottom what he wants: 'What sayest thou, bully Bottom?'*

dame
'woman, lady', a word that could be used politely or rudely
• *(Mac 4.2.62) A Messenger is being very respectful when he addresses Lady Macduff: 'Bless you, fair dame'.*
• *(KL 5.3.153) Albany is being very rude when he tells Goneril: 'Shut your mouth, dame'.*

gallants
'fine gentlemen'
• *(MA 3.2.13) Benedick addresses his friends: 'Gallants, I am not as I have been'.*

gentles
'ladies and gentlemen'
• *(MND 5.1.126) Peter Quince respectfully addresses the audience of lords and ladies: 'Gentles, perchance you wonder at this show'.*

goodman
'mister, master', usually very polite, but could be used sarcastically
• *(MA 3.5.9) Dogberry describes his companion as 'Goodman Verges'.*
• *(KL 2.2.42) Kent picks a fight with Oswald and calls him 'goodman boy'.*

hearts
'dear friends'
• *(TN 2.3.14) Feste greets Sir Toby and Sir Andrew: 'How now, my hearts?'*

lady or **my lady**
'madam', a very formal address
• *(TN 1.2.2) The Captain tells Viola where she is: 'This is Illyria, lady'.*

my liege
a formal way of addressing a king
• *(H5 1.2.3) Westmorland asks King Henry: 'Shall we call in th'ambassador, my liege?'*

masters
'sirs, gentlemen', a polite way of addressing a group of men
• *(Ham 2.2.409) Hamlet greets the players: 'You are welcome, masters'.*

signor also spelled **signior**
an Italian word, but used outside of Italy as a friendly way of saying 'sir'
• *(MND 4.1.17) Bottom addresses Cobweb: 'I would be loath to have you overflown with a honey-bag, signior'.*

sirrah
'sir', usually used by a high-ranking person to someone lower, but often used in a playful or familiar way
• *(Ham 5.1.109) Hamlet talks to the Gravedigger: 'Whose grave's this, sirrah?'*
• *(JC 4.3.134) Brutus is angry at the Poet: 'Get you hence, sirrah'.*
• *(KL 1.4.108) the Fool playfully addresses King Lear: 'Sirrah, I'll teach thee a speech'.*

wench
'lass', usually showing an affectionate relationship
• *(Tem 1.2.139) Prospero responds to his daughter's question: 'Well demanded, wench'.*

tester or **testril** see MONEY, p.197

tetter NOUN
irritation of the skin, similar to serious eczema
• *(Ham 1.5.71) The Ghost tells Hamlet how, after he was poisoned, 'a most instant tetter' spread all over his body.*

text NOUN
subject
• *(TN 1.5.213) Olivia tells Cesario, who has asked to see her face: 'You are now out of your text' —departing from what he had planned to say.*

text VERB
⚠ *Don't read in a meaning to do with 'text-messaging'.*
inscribe
• *(MA 5.1.177) Don Pedro asks when horns will be set on Benedick's head, 'and text underneath: "Here dwells Benedick, the married man".'*
🎭 *Horns were an image associated with men who were victims of adultery.*

Thasos also spelled **Thassos** NOUN
an island in the Aegean Sea near Philippi, northern Greece
• *(JC 5.3.104) Brutus commands that the body of Titinius be sent 'to Thasos'—a nearby city (presumably to avoid a funeral upsetting the battling soldiers).*
see MAP, p.176

Theban NOUN [pronounced **thee**-ban]
someone from Thebes, a city in south-east Greece, associated with wisdom and learning
• *(KL 3.4.150) Lear calls Poor Tom a 'learned Theban'—perhaps because Tom's rags resemble the poor clothing of a philosopher, or because, in his madness, Lear interprets Tom's ramblings as being incredibly profound.*
see MAP, p.176

theoric NOUN
theory
• *(Oth 1.1.24) Iago calls Cassio's military knowledge 'bookish theoric'—not based on experience in battle.*

Thessalian ADJECTIVE
[pronounced theh-**sail**-ee-an]
from Thessaly, an ancient region of northern Greece
• *(MND 4.1.121) Theseus compares the look of his hounds to 'Thessalian bulls'.*
see MAP, p.176

thews NOUN
bodily strength (sinews)
• *(JC 1.3.81) Cassius says that 'Romans now / Have thews and limbs like to their ancestors'.'*

thick ADJECTIVE
as well as a physical meaning of breadth, you'll find:
1 poor
• *(JC 5.3.21) Cassius tells Pindarus he needs his help to see what is happening on the battlefield: 'My sight was ever thick'.*
2 confused
• *(Ham 4.5.81) Claudius worries that the Danes are 'muddied, / Thick and unwholesome in their thoughts'.*

thick-coming ADJECTIVE
coming in crowds
• *(Mac 5.3.39) The Doctor says that Lady Macbeth is 'troubled with thick-coming fancies'—crowds of wildly inventive thoughts.*

thick-pleached ADJECTIVE
with hedges made of closely interlaced branches
• *(MA 1.2.8) Antonio tells Leonato what he overheard while 'walking in a thick-pleached alley in mine orchard'.*

thickskin also spelled **thick-skin** NOUN
blockhead
• *(MND 3.2.13) Puck describes Bottom as 'the shallowest thick-skin' among the rustics—the stupidest of them all.*

thief NOUN
villain
• *(MA 3.3.121) Borachio describes fashion as a 'deformed thief'—it makes people often change what they wear (like a maddening rogue who keeps stealing their outfits).*

› **thievish** ADJECTIVE
frequented by thieves
• *(RJ 4.1.79) Juliet says she would rather 'walk in thievish ways' than marry Paris.*

think on VERB
be remembered
• *(Ham 3.2.128) Hamlet says any great man needs to build churches, 'or else shall 'a suffer not thinking on'—or else he will be forgotten.*

Thisbe NOUN [pronounced **thiz**-be]
in Roman mythology, a heroine whose love for Pyramus ends in tragedy
• *(RJ 2.4.42) Mercutio mocks Romeo's romantic view of his lady Rosaline as someone who allows 'Thisbe a grey eye or so'—Thisbe's eyes are pretty enough, but that's the best one can say about her.*

thorough PREPOSITION
through
• *(MND 2.1.5) A Fairy says she travels 'Thorough flood, thorough fire'.*

a b c d e f g h i j k l m n o p q r s Tt u v w x y z

thought in the phrase **upon a thought**
in a moment
• *(Mac 3.4.55) Lady Macbeth assures everyone about her husband: 'upon a thought / He will again be well'.*

thought-executing ADJECTIVE
acting as fast as thought
• *(KL 3.2.4) Lear addresses the storm: 'You sulph'rous and thought-executing fires'.*

thought is free
think what you like
• *(TN 1.3.63) Maria responds to Sir Andrew's question with 'Now, sir, thought is free'.*

thought-sick ADJECTIVE
filled with dread
• *(Ham 3.4.51) Hamlet says heaven is 'thought-sick at the act'—the murder of his father.*

thrall NOUN
slave
• *(Mac 3.6.13) Lennox says Duncan's attendants were the 'thralls of sleep'.*

thralled also spelled **thrall'd** ADJECTIVE
enslaved
• *(Ham 3.4.74) Hamlet tells his mother that, in her relationship with Claudius, 'sense to ecstasy was ne'er so thrall'd'—reasonable thinking had never been so enslaved by passion.*

thread VERB
trace a path through
• *(KL 2.1.118) Regan explains why they have arrived late at Gloucester's castle, 'threading dark-ey'd night'.*

threaden ADJECTIVE
made of linen thread
• *(H5 3.Chorus.10) The Chorus asks the audience to imagine 'the threaden sails' of the English fleet.*

three-suited see **suit**

thrice-driven ADJECTIVE
three-times winnowed (having had air blown through to remove the less desirable parts)
• *(Oth 1.3.229) Othello says he is used to the steel couch of war being his 'thrice-driven bed of down'—a very comfortable bed (because it contains the lightest feathers, having been winnowed—to get rid of the chaff—three times).*

thrift NOUN
as well as meaning 'careful spending', you'll find:
profit
• *(Ham 3.2.60) Hamlet is dismissive of flatterers, for whom 'thrift may follow fawning'—they thrive because of their flattery.*

› **thriftless** ADJECTIVE
useless
• *(TN 2.2.38) Viola reflects on Olivia falling in love with her: 'What thriftless sighs shall poor Olivia breathe?'*

› **unthrift** ADJECTIVE
spendthrift
• *(MV 5.1.16) Lorenzo teases Jessica as someone who 'with an unthrift love did run from Venice'.*

› **unthrifty** ADJECTIVE
1 wasteful
• *(MV 1.3.172) Shylock describes Lancelot as 'an unthrifty knave'.*
2 harmful
• *(RJ 5.3.136) The Friar worries about what Romeo may have done: 'O much I fear some ill unthrifty thing'.*

thrill VERB
⚠ *Don't read the meaning of 'being excited' into these senses.*
tremble
• *(RJ 4.3.15) Juliet reflects on taking the Friar's drug: 'I have a faint cold fear thrills through my veins'.*

› **thrilled** ADJECTIVE
pierced
• *(KL 4.2.73) A Messenger reports how Cornwall was killed by 'A servant that he bred, thrill'd with remorse'—the servant was so upset at the torture of Gloucester that he attacked Cornwall.*

throe VERB
give pain (as in childbirth)
• *(Tem 2.1.226) Sebastian senses that Antonio has a thought 'Which throes thee much to yield'.*

throstle NOUN
thrush
• *(MND 3.1.111) Bottom sings about 'The throstle with his note so true'.*

throughfare NOUN
thoroughfare
• *(MV 2.7.42) Morocco describes deserts and wildernesses as 'throughfares now / For princes to come view fair Portia'.*

throughly ADVERB
thoroughly
• *(Ham 4.5.135) Laertes assures Claudius that he will 'be reveng'd / Most throughly for my father'.*

thrum NOUN
the unwoven end of the lengthwise threads on a weaving loom
• *(MND 5.1.273) Pyramus, seeing dead Thisbe, asks*

the Fates to 'Cut thread and thrum'—cut the thread of life completely, the good part as well as the bad.

Bottom the weaver, playing the part of Pyramus, would be very familiar with such materials, and perhaps slips off-script into his own language here.

thrusting on NOUN
imposition
• *(KL 1.2.120) Edmund reflects on the stupidity of those who believe that evil acts come from 'a divine thrusting on'—the result of supernatural control.*

thunderstone also spelled **thunder-stone** NOUN
thunderbolt
• *(JC 1.3.49) Cassius says he has presented his chest to the lightning: 'bar'd my bosom to the thunderstone'.*

thwart ADJECTIVE
obstinate
• *(KL 1.4.273) Lear asks Nature to make any child of Goneril's 'a thwart disnatur'd torment to her!'*

Tiber NOUN [pronounced **tie-ber**]
the river that flows through Rome
• *(JC 1.1.60) Flavius calls for all the poor men to come 'to Tiber banks'.*

tickle VERB
as well as meaning 'move the fingers against the skin to cause a reaction', you'll find:
1 move easily
• *(Ham 2.2.318) Hamlet predicts that 'the clown shall make those laugh whose lungs are tickle a th' sear'—they are quick to start laughing (ready to go off like a gun's trigger).*
2 beat
• *(TN 5.1.186) Sir Andrew tells Cesario that, if Sir Toby hadn't been drunk, 'he would have tickled you othergates than he did'—dealt with you differently.*

tide NOUN
season
• *(RJ 3.5.176) Capulet says how often he has tried to get Juliet a husband—'Day, night, hour, tide, time, work, play'.*
'Tide' appears in the Second Quarto text, but not in other sources, and is sometimes omitted.

tide VERB
come (from *betide*)
• *(MND 5.1.199) Thisbe assures Pyramus: 'Tide life, tide death, I come without delay'—whether life or death happens, she will meet him.*

tie over VERB
restrict
• *(H5 5.2.296) Henry reacts to Burgundy's comparison of maids and flies during summer-time: 'This moral ties me over to time, and a hot summer'—this kind of argument restricts the time he has to woo Kate properly.*

tight ADJECTIVE
water-tight
• *(Tem 5.1.224) The Boatswain reports that his ship 'Is tight and yare'—ready for sea.*

tike NOUN
mongrel
• *(KL 3.6.68) Poor Tom says he shouts at all dogs, including a 'bobtail tike'—a mixed breed dog with a docked tail.*

tilly-vally see **EXCLAMATIONS, p.99**

tilt VERB
thrust
• *(Oth 2.3.167) Iago describes how Cassio and Montano were 'tilting one at other's breasts'.*

tilth NOUN
tilled land
• *(Tem 2.1.148) Gonzalo says he would have no 'bound of land, tilth, vineyard' no boundaries in his imaginary commonwealth.*

time in the phrase **in good time**
just at the right moment!
• *(RJ 1.2.44) A Servant is relieved to see Benvolio and Romeo arriving: 'In good time!'*

time in the phrase **keep time** see **keep**

time in the phrase **when time was**
once upon a time
• *(Tem 2.2.134) Stephano tells Caliban he 'was the man i' th' moon when time was'.*

timeless ADJECTIVE
untimely
• *(RJ 5.3.162) Juliet wakes to find Romeo: 'Poison I see hath been his timeless end'.*

time-pleaser NOUN
follower of fashion
• *(TN 2.3.132) Maria describes Malvolio as 'a time-pleaser'.*

timorous ADJECTIVE
Don't read in the meaning of 'nervous'.
terrifying
• *(Oth 1.1.76) Iago advises Roderigo to call Brabantio with a 'timorous accent'—a scary voice.*

tinct NOUN
colour
• *(Ham 3.4.91) Gertrude says she sees in her soul 'such black and grained spots / As will not leave their tinct'—the colour will never disappear.*

tincture NOUN
as well as meaning 'colour, dye', you'll find:
keepsake infused with blood (as of a martyr)
• *(JC 2.2.89) Decius imagines people coming to a blood-spouting statue of Caesar 'for tinctures, stains, relics'.*

tire see **HATS, p.160**

tiring-house NOUN
dressing room
• *(MND 3.1.4) Quince tells his companions that 'This green plot shall be our stage, this hawthorn brake our tiring-house'—they will get ready for their play's rehearsal behind a bush.*

Titan NOUN [pronounced **tie**-tan]
one of the titles of the Roman sun-god (also called Hyperion), whose chariot pulled the sun
• *(RJ 2.3.4) Friar Lawrence sees night moving away 'From forth day's path and Titan's fiery wheels'.*

tithe NOUN
tenth part—originally, a pledge of a tenth of one's goods to support the church
• *(Ham 3.4.97) Hamlet says Claudius is worth 'not twentieth part the tithe' of his father—a twentieth of a tenth (less than 1 percent).*

> **tithing** NOUN
> parish—originally, a hamlet (small village) of ten households
> • *(KL 3.4.127) Poor Tom describes himself as a man 'whipp'd from tithing to tithing'.*

> **tithe-pig** NOUN
> pig given as part of a tithe
> • *(RJ 1.4.79) Mercutio says Queen Mab sometimes tickles a parson's nose 'with a tithe-pig's tail'.*

title NOUN
as well as meaning a 'legal right', you'll find:
possession
• *(Mac 4.2.7) Lady Macduff wonders why her husband left 'his babes, / His mansion, and his titles'.*

> **untitled** also spelled **untitl'd** ADJECTIVE
> with no right to rule
> • *(Mac 4.3.104) Macduff describes Macbeth as 'an untitl'd tyrant'.*

toged ADJECTIVE [pronounced **toe**-guhd]
toga-wearing
• *(Oth 1.1.25) Iago dismisses Cassio as someone who knows as little of war as 'toged consuls'—officials in their gowns.*

toil NOUN
trap
• *(Ham 3.2.332) Hamlet asks Rosencrantz and Guildenstern why they 'would drive me into a toil?'*

to it or **to't**
to death
• *(Ham 5.2.56) Horatio reflects: 'So Guildenstern and Rosencrantz go to't'.*

token NOUN
as well as meaning a 'sign' or 'signal', you'll find:
1 omen
• *(JC 1.3.55) Casca says men should tremble when 'the most mighty gods by tokens send / Such dreadful heralds to astonish us'.*
2 keepsake
• *(Ham 2.2.144) Polonius says he advised Ophelia to 'receive no tokens' from Hamlet.*

Tom o'Bedlam see **Bedlam**

tongs and bones see **MUSIC, p.172**

tonight NOUN
as well as meaning 'the night to come', you'll find:
last night
• *(RJ 1.4.50) Romeo tells Mercutio: 'I dreamt a dream tonight'.*
This would normally be said in the morning, to avoid confusion with 'the night to come'.

tool NOUN
sword
• *(RJ 1.1.29) Gregory tells Sampson: 'Draw thy tool'—with a sexual pun (just as it would have today).*

tooth NOUN
as well as its usual meaning of a part of the body, you'll find:
fangs
• *(Mac 3.2.15) Macbeth, thinking of his rivals as a snake, tells his wife that they are still 'in danger of her former tooth'.*

top NOUN
as well as meaning 'highest part', you'll find:
head
• *(MA 1.2.14) Antonio says Don Pedro intends 'to take the present time by the top'—seize the opportunity.*
See also **STAGE DIRECTIONS, p.285**

top VERB
1 exceed
• *(Mac 4.3.57) Macduff says there is no devil in hell that could 'top Macbeth' in his evil.*
2 have sex with
• *(Oth 5.2.137) Othello tells Emilia of Desdemona: 'Cassio did top her'.*

top-gallant, topmast, topsail
see SHIPS, p.168

tosspot also spelled **toss-pot** NOUN
drunkard
• *(TN 5.1.390) Feste sings of how, when he got older, 'With toss-pots still had drunken heads'—he was always drunk, or had a hangover.*

touch VERB
as well as meaning 'place one thing against another' and 'affect someone', you'll find:
1 test the quality of
• *(Oth 3.3.81) Desdemona tells Othello that when she has a request that will 'touch your love indeed', it will be full of weight.*
2 endanger
• *(JC 2.1.154) Decius asks: 'Shall no man else be touch'd but only Caesar?'*
3 wound
• *(Oth 2.3.204) Iago is offended at Montano's suggestion that he would not tell the truth: 'Touch me not so near'.*
4 play on
• *(JC 4.3.257) Brutus asks Lucius to play for him—'touch thy instrument a strain or two'.*
5 fire off
• *(H5 3.Chorus.33) The Chorus describes how the gunner with a match 'the devilish cannon touches'.*

touch NOUN
as well as meaning 'small amount' and 'quality', you'll find:
1 action
• *(MND 3.2.70) Hermia accuses Demetrius of killing Lysander: 'O, brave touch!'*
2 skill in playing
• *(Ham 3.2.341) Guildenstern protests that he can't play the recorder: 'I know no touch of it'.*

toward ADVERB
in preparation
• *(MND 3.1.67) Puck sees the rustics in the wood and exclaims: 'What, a play toward?'*

› **towards** ADVERB
at hand
• *(RJ 1.5.121) Capulet says he has 'a trifling foolish banquet towards'—taking place soon.*

town crier see OCCUPATIONS, p.166

toy NOUN
⚠ *Don't read the meaning of 'a child's plaything' into these senses.*
1 trifling matter
• *(Ham 4.5.18) Gertrude reflects that 'each toy seems prologue to some great amiss'—every slight mishap seems to be part of some bigger misfortune to come.*
2 fancy
• *(Oth 3.4.150) Emilia tells Desdemona she hopes that Othello's mood is 'no jealous toy / Concerning you'.*
3 trinket
• *(TN 3.3.44) Antonio gives Sebastian some money in case his eye should 'light upon some toy / You have desire to purchase'.*
4 old wives' tale
• *(MND 5.1.3) Theseus says he doesn't believe 'these fairy toys'—foolish tales of fairies.*

trace VERB
1 imitate
• *(Ham 5.2.117) Hamlet says, of Laertes, anyone who 'would trace him' would end up being his shadow, nothing more.*
2 follow on from
• *(Mac 4.1.152) Macbeth says, of Macduff, he will kill everyone who 'trace him in his line'—all his family and descendants.*
3 pass through
• *(MA 3.1.16) Hero tells Ursula that they will 'trace this alley up and down'.*

traduce VERB
defame
• *(Ham 1.4.18) Hamlet says that the Danish revelling 'Makes us traduc'd and tax'd of other nations'—mocked by all the other countries.*

traffic NOUN
⚠ *Don't read modern meanings to do with 'vehicles' into these senses.*
1 trading
• *(Tem 2.1.144) Gonzalo says he would have 'no kind of traffic' in his imaginary commonwealth.*
2 dealings
• *(RJ Prologue.12) The Prologue estimates the story will take up 'two hours' traffic of our stage'.*

› **trafficker** NOUN
merchant vessel
• *(MV 1.1.12) Salarino says Antonio's great ships 'Do overpeer the petty traffickers'.*

tragedian NOUN
actor (not only of tragedy)
• *(Ham 2.2.322) Rosencrantz tells Hamlet of the arrival of 'the tragedians of the city'.*

a b c d e f g h i j k l m n o p q r s Tt u v w x y z

a b c d e f g h i j k l m n o p q r s Tt u v w x y z

train NOUN
retinue
• *(H5 3.4.1) Stage direction: 'Enter the King, Exeter, and all his train'.*

train NOUN
stratagem
• *(Mac 4.3.118) Malcolm says that Macbeth 'By many of these trains hath sought to win me / Into his power'.*

traject NOUN
ferry boat
• *(MV 3.4.53) Portia asks Balthazar to bring her disguise 'Unto the traject' that regularly travels to Venice.*

trammel up VERB
catch up (as in a fishing net)
• *(Mac 1.7.3) Macbeth wonders if assassinating Duncan would 'trammel up the consequence'—have no further repercussions preventing his path to the crown.*

translate VERB
⚠*Don't read the meaning of 'turn into another language' into these senses.*
1 transform
• *(MND 3.1.104) Quince sees Bottom with an ass's head and exclaims: 'Thou art translated!'*
2 explain
• *(Ham 4.1.2) Claudius tells Gertrude that 'These profound heaves / Thou must translate'.*

transpose VERB
alter
• *(Mac 4.3.21) Malcolm tells Macduff: 'That which you are, my thoughts cannot transpose'.*

trans-shape VERB
transform
• *(MA 5.1.165) Don Pedro tells Benedick how Beatrice did 'trans-shape thy particular virtues'.*

trapically see **tropically**

trash NOUN
as well as meaning 'rubbish', you'll find:
dirty money
• *(JC 4.3.26) Brutus asks Cassius if they will sell their honours 'For so much trash'*

trash VERB
keep in check (as with a dog while hunting)
• *(Tem 1.2.81) Prospero talks of people at court: 'who t'advance, and who / To trash for overtopping'.*

travail NOUN [pronounced **tra**-vale]
1 exertion or journeying
• *(Tem 3.3.15) Antonio tells Sebastian that the others 'are oppress'd with travail'.*
✒*Some editions replace this with 'travel', which is very similar in sound and meaning to 'travail'.*
2 distress or labour (as in childbirth)
• *(MA 4.1.212) The Friar advises Leonato of his plan for Hero: 'on this travail look for greater birth'—more trouble will come.*

traverse VERB
about turn (as in a military command)
• *(Oth 1.3.363) Iago tells Roderigo: 'Traverse!'*

tray-trip see **RECREATION, p.170**

treacher NOUN
traitor
• *(KL 1.2.117) Edmund reflects on whether the stars form the character of 'knaves, thieves, and treachers'.*

treatise NOUN
narrative
• *(MA 1.1.289) Claudio assures Don Pedro that, though he only briefly mentioned his love for Hero, he would like to have made it 'a longer treatise'.*

trenched ADJECTIVE
[pronounced in this line as two syllables: **trench**-id]
deep
• *(Mac 3.4.27) The First Murderer tells Macbeth that Banquo is dead 'With twenty trenched gashes on his head'.*

trencher NOUN
plate
• *(RJ 1.5.2) The First Servingman asks why Potpan isn't helping to clear the table: 'He shift a trencher?'*

> **trenchering** NOUN
> plates
> • *(Tem 2.2.178) Caliban sings about how he will no longer have to 'scrape trenchering'—do the washing-up.*
>
> **trencherman** also spelled **trencher-man** NOUN
> hearty eater
> • *(MA 1.1.45) Beatrice describes Benedick as 'a very valiant trencherman'.*

tributary NOUN
defeated ruler who pays tribute to the victor
• *(JC 1.1.35) Murellus asks the commoners about Caesar: 'What tributaries follow him to Rome?'*

tributary ADJECTIVE
paying a tribute
• *(RJ 3.2.103) Juliet talks to her tears, as she cries over her cousin Tybalt's death and Romeo's banishment: 'Your tributary drops belong to woe'.*

trice NOUN
brief period
• *(KL 1.1.216) France wonders what monstrous thing Cordelia must have done to change Lear's attitude so much 'in this trice of time'.*

trick NOUN
⚠ *Don't read the meaning of 'practical joke' into these senses.*
1 natural behaviour
• *(Ham 4.7.187) Laertes weeps, despite himself: 'It is our trick'.*
2 knack
• *(Ham 5.1.84) Hamlet reflects on the First Gravedigger's treatment of skulls: 'Here's fine revolution and we had the trick to see't'—a fine change of fortune, if we had the ability to see it (that the skulls of noble people are now being battered about by a common gravedigger).*
3 distinguishing trait
• *(TN 2.5.139) Malvolio reads Olivia's letter: 'Put thyself into the trick of singularity'—make yourself look as unique as possible.*
4 feat
• *(Ham 4.7.89) Claudius cannot imagine anyone ever surpassing Lamord's 'shapes and tricks' on his horse.*
5 trifle
• *(Ham 4.4.61) Hamlet reflects on soldiers who are prepared to die for 'a fantasy and trick of fame' —the smallest amount.*
6 delusion
• *(Oth 4.2.128) Iago asks Desdemona about Othello's strange behaviour: 'How comes this trick upon him?'*

› **trick up** VERB
decorate
• *(H5 3.7.70) Gower describes men who behave like Pistol, who boast about the wars in language 'which they trick up with new-tuned oaths'—they exaggerate their stories of heroism.*

› **tricked** also spelled **trick'd** ADJECTIVE
spotted (like a pattern on a coat of arms)
• *(Ham 2.2.445) Hamlet recites lines about Pyrrhus being 'horridly trick'd / With blood'.*

› **tricksy** ADJECTIVE
cleverly playful
• *(Tem 5.1.226) Prospero calls Ariel his 'tricksy spirit'.*

trifle VERB
1 waste
• *(MV 4.1.296) Shylock tells Balthazar: 'We trifle time'.*
2 make insignificant
• *(Mac 2.4.4) An Old Man tells Ross that 'this sore night / Hath trifled former knowings'—he has never seen anything like it before.*

trifle NOUN
illusion
• *(Tem 5.1.112) Alonso wonders if Prospero is 'some enchanted trifle'—he can't believe his eyes.*

trim ADJECTIVE
1 fine
• *(MND 3.2.157) Helena ironically compliments Lysander and Demetrius on their behaviour: 'A trim exploit'.*
2 insincere
• *(MA 4.1.317) Beatrice condemns manhood: 'men are only turned into tongue, and trim ones, too' —men can only talk, and talk glibly too.*

trim NOUN
readiness
• *(Tem 5.1.236) The Boatswain reports how the mariners woke up 'in all our trim'—either referring to their boat or their clothes (or both).*

trim ADVERB
well
• *(RJ 2.1.13) Mercutio describes Cupid as 'he that shot so trim'.*
🎭 *Cupid, the god of love, shoots arrows of love. Those the arrows hit (and he has a very good aim) immediately fall in love with the next person they see.*

› **trim up** VERB
dress (in fine array)
• *(RJ 4.4.25) Capulet tells the Nurse to get Juliet ready to meet Paris: 'Go and trim her up'.*

› **in the trim**
in fine condition
• *(H5 4.3.115) Henry tells Montjoy that their English 'hearts are in the trim'.*

trip NOUN
(in wrestling) a foot movement that causes an opponent to fall
• *(TN 5.1.162) Orsino warns Cesario that 'thine own trip shall be thine overthrow'—if Cesario continues to be so deceitful, sooner or later he'll trip himself up (get caught).*

› **tripping** ADJECTIVE
light-footed
• *(TN 5.1.35) Feste describes 'a good tripping measure'—a nimble dance.*

a b c d e f g h i j k l m n o p q r s Tt u v w x y z

triplex NOUN
(in music) triple time
• *(TN 5.1.34) Feste, hoping for a third coin from Orsino, tells him that 'the triplex, sir, is a good tripping measure'—the rhythm of the music is easy to dance to.*

tristful ADJECTIVE
sorrowful
• *(Ham 3.4.50) Hamlet describes the whole world having a 'tristful visage' at the sight of what Claudius has done.*

Troilus NOUN [pronounced **troy**-lus]
in the Trojan Wars, a Trojan prince who loved Cressida, but who lost her love after she was traded to the Greeks
• *(MV 5.1.4) Lorenzo imagines a night when 'Troilus methinks mounted the Troyan walls' to secretly see Cressida.*

Trojan see **Troyan**

troll VERB
⚠ *Don't read in the modern meaning to do with internet activity.*
sing out
• *(Tem 3.2.114) Caliban asks Stephano to 'troll the catch / You taught me'.*

troop with
accompany
• *(RJ 1.5.47) Romeo sees Juliet for the first time—'So shows a snowy dove trooping with crows'—and sees her as a beautiful white dove (a symbol of peace and love) surrounded by crows (black birds thought to be symbols of death or bad luck).*

trophy NOUN
as well as meaning 'souvenir of success', you'll find:
memorial
• *(Ham 4.5.210) Laertes asks Claudius why there was 'No trophy, sword, nor hatchment' (coat-of-arms) hung over Polonius' grave—a noticeable lack of ceremony for a noble lord.*

tropically ADVERB
figuratively (like a trope—a figure of speech)
• *(Ham 3.2.228) Hamlet explains the name of the play 'The Mousetrap': 'Marry, how tropically!'—with a possible pun 'trap-ically', depending on how it's pronounced.*

troth NOUN
good faith
• *(MND 2.2.42) Lysander tells Hermia 'to speak troth'.*
'Troth' is the form in the First Folio. Some editions replace this with 'truth'.
See also SWEARING, p.298

> **troth-plight** ADJECTIVE
> engaged
> • *(H5 2.1.17) Bardolph recalls that Nym was 'troth-plight' to the Hostess before Pistol married her.*

> **new-trothed** ADJECTIVE
> recently engaged
> • *(MA 3.1.38) Hero reports remarks by 'the Prince and my new-trothed lord'.*

trow VERB
1 know
• *(MA 3.4.54) Beatrice asks Hero what Margaret is talking about: 'What means the fool, trow?' —d'y'know? (an informal way of talking).*
2 accept as true
• *(KL 1.4.115) The Fool advises Lear: 'Learn more than thou trowest'.*

Troyan also spelled **Trojan** NOUN
fellow (after the people of Troy, a city famed for its invasion and capture)
• *(H5 5.1.17) Pistol calls the Welsh Captain a 'base Troyan'.*
The word came to be used in both positive and negative ways. Someone might be described as a 'true Trojan', meaning 'good fellow', but here Pistol is being insulting, calling the Captain a low character.

truant NOUN
⚠ *Don't read in the meaning of 'someone who misses school without permission'.*
rogue
• *(MA 3.2.16) Don Pedro mocks Benedick: 'Hang him, truant!'*

truce in the phrase **take truce**
come to terms
• *(RJ 3.1.153) Benvolio describes how Romeo 'Could not take truce with the unruly spleen / Of Tybalt'—he could not make peace or agree to stop fighting with Tybalt.*

truckle-bed NOUN
low-lying bed on castors
• *(RJ 2.1.39) Mercutio says he is going 'to my truckle-bed'.*

trudge VERB
go away
• *(RJ 1.3.35) The Nurse, telling a story to Lady*

Capulet, says the shaking of the dove-house during a huge earthquake was no reason 'To bid me trudge'—she didn't need an earthquake as a hint to leave.

true ADJECTIVE
as well as meaning 'faithful' and 'genuine', you'll find:
1 honest
• *(MA 3.3.49) Dogberry says (quite rightly) that a thief is 'no true man'.*
2 proper
• *(JC 3.1.241) Brutus says he will tell the people that 'Caesar shall / Have all true rites and lawful ceremonies'.*

› **true-fixed** also spelled **-fix'd** ADJECTIVE
immovable
• *(JC 3.1.61) Caesar describes the north star as having a 'true-fix'd and resting quality'.*
The north star was—and is—for travellers in the northern hemisphere a central part of navigation by sea or land to find the direction of north, as it appears to stay in the same place, over the north pole.

› **truly falsely** also spelled **truly-falsely** ADVERB
with faithful heart but incorrect grammar
• *(H5 5.2.185) Henry tells Katherine that his tongue speaks 'most truly falsely'.*

truepenny NOUN
honest fellow
• *(Ham 1.5.158) Hamlet calls to the unseen Ghost: 'Art thou there, truepenny?'*

trump see MUSIC, p.172

trumpery NOUN
fancy garments
• *(Tem 4.1.186) Prospero asks Ariel to fetch 'The trumpery in my house'.*

trumpet NOUN
as well as meaning the instrument, you'll find:
1 trumpeter
• *(H5 4.7.50) King Henry tells his herald: 'Take a trumpet'—he isn't expecting the herald to make the trumpet-call (heralds made announcements).*
2 trumpet-call
• *(Oth 2.1.173) Iago says he hears Othello's arrival: 'I know his trumpet'.*
see also **tucket**

truncheon NOUN
Don't read in the modern meaning of a policeman's stick.
military staff or baton—a symbol of authority
• *(Ham 1.2.204) Horatio says the Ghost passed by them 'Within his truncheon's length'—as near as the length of the Ghost's baton (very near).*

trundle-tail NOUN
dog with a tail that trails on the ground
• *(KL 3.6.69) Poor Tom says he shouts at all dogs, including a 'trundle-tail'.*

try VERB
as well as meaning 'attempt', you'll find:
1 prove
• *(RJ 4.3.29) Juliet thinks the Friar has always 'been tried a holy man'.*
2 put to the test
• *(JC 4.3.214) Brutus points out to Cassius: 'we have tried the utmost of our friends'—found as many supporters as we can.*
3 fight out
• *(Mac 5.8.32) Macbeth tells Macduff he will 'try the last'—fight to the end.*
4 refine
• *(MV 2.9.62) Arragon reads the script inside the silver casket: 'The fire seven times tried this'.*
Shakespeare is using a passage from the Bible: 'the words of the Lord are flawless, like silver tried in a furnace of earth, purified seven times'. Those that don't work their judgement over and over will never reach perfection.
5 adjust the sails of a ship so that the bow comes into the wind
• *(Tem 1.1.33) The Boatswain shouts: 'Bring her to try with main-course'.*

try conclusions
see what happens
• *(Ham 3.4.197) Hamlet reminds Gertrude of the fable about an ape that crept into a basket 'To try conclusions'.*
The original and fantastical story isn't known any more, but it must have been about an ape that saw a cage of birds at the top of a house, released them from the basket, and then assumed that if he entered the basket himself he would be able to fly—with disastrous results. Essentially, Hamlet is telling his mother that, if she reveals his secret, she will come to grief herself.

tuck see SWORDS AND DAGGERS, p.156

tucket NOUN
personal trumpet call
• *(H5 4.2.35) The Constable commands 'The tucket sonance'—make a trumpet call.*
Nobles would have their own distinctive trumpet call, which would be sounded to signal their impending arrival.

tuition NOUN
Don't read in the meaning of 'teaching'.
safe-keeping
• *(MA 1.1.257) Claudio mocks the way Benedick ends*

a letter, committing his addressee 'To the tuition of God'.

It was normal in Shakespeare's time to write letters with great formality, especially wishing for the health of the addressee, or that they would be in good grace with God.

tumble VERB
have sex with
• *(Ham 4.5.62) Ophelia sings of a woman thinking of her lover: 'Before you tumbled me'.*

tun NOUN
box
• *(H5 1.2.255) The French Ambassador presents Henry with a 'tun of treasure'.*

tune NOUN
as well as having a musical sense, you'll find:
1 state of mind
• *(MA 3.4.38) Hero asks Beatrice: 'Do you speak in the sick tune?'—in a sad mood.*
2 fashionable (and artificial) speech
• *(Ham 5.2.177) Hamlet describes Osric as speaking in 'the tune of the time'.*

> **untuned** ADJECTIVE
> disordered
> • *(KL 4.7.16) Cordelia calls on the gods to cure Lear's 'untuned and jarring sense'.*

Tunis NOUN
a former state in North Africa (in present-day Tunisia)
• *(Tem 2.1.68) Gonzalo remembers the clothes he was wearing at the wedding of Alonso's 'daughter Claribel to the King of Tunis'.*
see MAP, p.176

tup VERB
have sex with
• *(Oth 1.1.90) Iago tells Brabantio that 'an old black ram / Is tupping your white ewe'—he says Othello is having sex with Desdmona.*

Turk NOUN
heathen (the Turkish people were considered so, believing in a non-Christian God)
• *(Oth 2.1.113) Iago says his remarks are true, 'or else I am a Turk'.*

> **turn Turk**
> change completely (as from Christian to heathen—a hugely dramatic shift for the Christian culture in England at the time)
> • *(Ham 3.2.265) Hamlet (after seeing Claudius' reaction to the play) thinks he would succeed as a theatre man even 'if the rest of my fortunes turn Turk with me'.*

Turlygod NOUN
a nonsense name (used by Edgar as a possible name for himself when disguised as a beggar)
• *(KL 2.3.20) Edgar calls out: 'Poor Turlygod!'*

turn NOUN
as well as meaning the 'action of turning something', you'll find:
1 need
• *(Ham 5.2.173) Hamlet comments on Osric commending himself: 'There are no tongues else for's turn'—nobody else will do it for him.*
2 act
• *(Oth 5.2.206) Gratiano says the sight of dead Desdemona would make her father 'do a desperate turn'.*

tush see **EXCLAMATIONS, p.99**

twae see **tway**

twain NOUN
two
• *(Ham 3.4.158) Gertrude tells Hamlet: 'thou hast cleft my heart in twain'.*

twain ADJECTIVE
separated
• *(RJ 3.5.240) Juliet decides to no longer confide in her Nurse: 'Thou and my bosom henceforth shall be twain'.*

tway also spelled **twae** NOUN
two (in a Scottish accent)
• *(H5 3.3.60) Jamy tells the Welsh and Irish captains that he would like to 'hear some question 'tween you twae'.*

twenty in the phrase **and twenty**
and many more
• *(TN 2.3.46) Feste sings: 'Then come kiss me, sweet and twenty'—someone who is twenty times sweet; or, come and kiss me sweet(heart), twenty times over.*

twiggen bottle also spelled **twiggen-bottle** NOUN
bottle cased in wickerwork
• *(Oth 2.3.134) Cassio says, of Roderigo, 'I'll beat the knave into a twiggen bottle'.*

twilled see **pioned and twilled**

twink NOUN
twinkling (of an eye)
• *(Tem 4.1.43) Prospero tells Ariel to do something immediately: 'with a twink'—as fast as an eye twinkles.*

tyrant NOUN
as well as meaning 'ruthless dictator', you'll find: pitiless ruffian
• *(MA 1.1.153) Benedick describes himself, in relation to women, as 'a professed tyrant to their sex'.*

› **tyrannically** ADVERB
outrageously
• *(Ham 2.2.333) Rosencrantz says the child players 'are most tyrannically clapped'—heavily applauded for what they do.*

› **tyrannous** ADJECTIVE
pitiless
• *(KL 3.4.144) Gloucester describes the forthcoming storm: 'this tyrannous night'.*

› **tyranny** NOUN
cruelty
• *(MV 4.1.13) Antonio says he is ready to suffer 'The very tyranny and rage' of Shylock.*

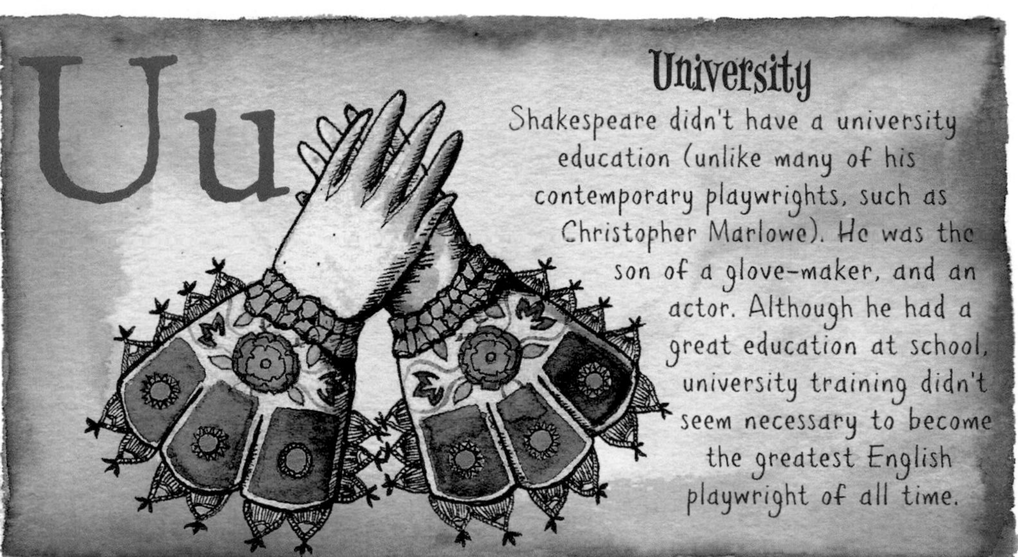

Ud's see **SWEARING, p.298**

umbrage NOUN
shadow
• *(Ham 5.2.117) Hamlet says anyone who tries to imitate the skill of Laertes is 'his umbrage, nothing more'—will, like his shadow, never catch up with him.*

› **umbered** also spelled **umber'd** ADJECTIVE
shadowed
• *(H5 4.Chorus.9) The Chorus describes how each army 'sees the other's umber'd face'.*

umpire NOUN
mediator
• *(RJ 4.1.63) Juliet threatens to use a knife to 'play the umpire' between herself and the desperate situation she finds herself in.*

unction NOUN
1 ointment
• *(Ham 4.7.141) Laertes says he 'bought an unction of a mountebank'—a poison from a medicine-seller.*
2 balm
• *(Ham 3.4.147) Hamlet urges Gertrude not to use his supposed madness as an excuse to distract herself from what he has told her: 'Lay not that flattering unction to your soul'.*

underborne ADJECTIVE
trimmed at the bottom
• *(MA 3.4.20) Margaret describes the Duchess of Milan's gown as having 'skirts round underborne with a bluish tinsel'.*

undergo VERB
1 carry out
• *(JC 1.3.123) Cassius says he has asked various Romans to 'undergo with me an enterprise / Of honourable dangerous consequence'.*
2 support
• *(Ham 1.4.34) Hamlet describes men condemned for their one fault, even though they may have virtues 'As infinite as man may undergo'.*
3 face up to
• *(MA 5.2.53) Benedick tells Beatrice: 'Claudio undergoes my challenge'.*

a b c d e f g h i j k l m n o p q r s t Uu v w x y z

un-

One of the most important ways in which Shakespeare made up words was to add the *un-* prefix to a word that already existed. This way of making words had been used in English since Anglo-Saxon times, to express an opposite (as in *happy—unhappy*) or to reverse a meaning (as in *do—undo*).
In this panel we bring together all the examples of *un-* words where the word is no longer used or where there is a meaning different from that found today. If an *un-* word is not explained here, you will find it in the dictionary along with its related word: for example, you will find *unaccommodated* under the entry for *accommodate*.

unaneled also spelled **unanel'd** ADJECTIVE
[pronounced un-an-**eeld**]
without being anointed by a priest (especially as part of the last rites before death)
• *(Ham 1.5.77) The Ghost tells Hamlet that he was unprepared for death—'unaneled'.*

unauspicious ADJECTIVE
discouraging
• *(TN 5.1.108) Orsino describes himself as making offerings to Olivia's 'ingrate and unauspicious altars'—thinking of her as holy and himself as a worshipper.*

unbacked also spelled **unback'd** ADJECTIVE
unrestrained
• *(Tem 4.1.176) Ariel describes Stephano and his companions as acting like 'unback'd colts'—like wild horses.*

unbitted ADJECTIVE
unbridled
• *(Oth 1.3.326) Iago tells Roderigo that people are able to control their 'unbitted lusts'.*

unbonneted **see HATS, p.160**

unburthen also spelled **unburden** VERB
reveal or unload
• *(MV 1.1.133) Bassanio tells Antonio that he is going to 'unburden all my plots and purposes' to him.*

unchary ADVERB
carelessly
• *(TN 3.4.182) Olivia says she has 'laid mine honour too unchary out' by saying so much—risked her reputation by speaking so openly to Cesario.*

uncoined also spelled **uncoin'd** ADJECTIVE
genuine or not yet in circulation
• *(H5 5.2.150) Henry asks Katherine to 'take a fellow of plain and uncoined constancy'—he seems to be telling her he's still a virgin.*

unconfirmed also spelled **unconfirm'd** ADJECTIVE
ignorant (of the ways of the world)
• *(MA 3.3.108) Borachio tells Conrad: 'thou art unconfirmed'.*

uncouple VERB
release pairs of hunting dogs for the chase
• *(MND 4.1.106) Theseus tells his attendants: 'Uncouple in the western valley'.*

uncovered see **cover**

uncurrent ADJECTIVE
worthless
• *(TN 3.3.16) Sebastian apologizes for being unable to repay Antonio other than by thanking him: 'and oft good turns / Are shuffled off with such uncurrent pay'.*

undeeded ADJECTIVE
without any deeds performed
• *(Mac 5.7.21) Macduff vows to fight with Macbeth himself or else his sword he will 'sheathe again undeeded'—or he won't fight at all (strong words from a man so loyal to his country).*

undo past form **undone** VERB
1 ruin
• *(MA 2.2.27) Borachio tells Don John he has enough proof 'to undo Hero'.*
2 eliminate
• *(KL 4.1.69) Gloucester reflects on how 'distribution should undo excess'—sharing would balance out some people having too much.*

› **undone** ADJECTIVE
brought down
• *(Oth 5.1.54) Cassio says he has been 'undone by villains!'*

unfold VERB
reveal
• *(MND 1.1.146) Lysander compares love to lightning that suddenly 'unfolds both heaven and earth'—it strikes so hard and fast it lights up everything.*

› **unfolding** NOUN
proposal
• *(Oth 1.3.242) Desdemona asks the Duke: 'To my unfolding lend your prosperous ear'.*

unforfeited ADJECTIVE
unbroken
• *(MV 2.6.8) Salarino says the pigeons of the goddess of love (Venus) fly faster to form new bonds of love than 'To keep obliged faith unforfeited'—than to maintain the faithfulness of those bound by marriage.*

ungored also spelled **ungor'd** ADJECTIVE
unharmed
• *(Ham 5.2.234) Laertes says he needs proof of Hamlet's innocence 'To keep my name ungor'd'—to preserve his reputation.*

ungotten ADJECTIVE
not yet conceived
• *(H5 1.2.287) Henry says 'some are yet ungotten and unborn' who will come to regret what the Dauphin has done.*

unhallowed also spelled **unhallow'd** ADJECTIVE
unholy
• *(RJ 5.3.54) Paris tells Romeo, who is opening Juliet's tomb: 'Stop thy unhallow'd toil'.*

unhatched also spelled **unhatch'd** ADJECTIVE
1 still evolving
• *(Oth 3.4.135) Desdemona thinks Othello is being affected by 'some unhatch'd practice' in Cyprus—a developing conspiracy being plotted against him.*
2 unmarked
• *(TN 3.4.214) Sir Toby mockingly describes Sir Andrew as a 'knight dubbed with unhatched rapier'—a sword never used on the battlefield.*
Andrew was knighted (where one kneels, and is touched lightly on each shoulder) with the blade of a sword never used on the battlefield, so the phrase carries an implication of weakness.

unheedy ADJECTIVE
reckless
• *(MND 1.1.237) Helena reflects on Cupid, the blind god of love: 'Wings, and no eyes, figure unheedy haste'—if love has wings but no eyes, no wonder it makes people rush into things without thought.*

unhoused ADJECTIVE
independent
• *(Oth 1.2.26) Othello says it is only his love for Desdemona that lets his 'unhoused free condition'—his life as a travelling bachelor—be confined.*

unhouseled also spelled **unhousel'd** ADJECTIVE
without receiving holy communion
• *(Ham 1.5.77) The Ghost tells Hamlet that his father was 'unhousel'd'—unprepared for death when he was killed.*
In Catholic theology, those who could not be forgiven of their sins and receive the last rites and holy communion from a priest risked going to hell.

unkennel VERB
be revealed
• *(Ham 3.2.79) Hamlet anticipates that Claudius' guilt will 'unkennel in one speech' while he is watching the play.*

unlimited ADJECTIVE
⚠ *Don't read in the general meaning of 'not limited'.*
allowing changes in the location of the action or on any subject
• *(Ham 2.2.389) Polonius describes what the players can perform, including 'poem unlimited'.*

unmanned also spelled **unmann'd** ADJECTIVE
not yet broken in (as an untrained falcon)
• *(RJ 3.2.14) Juliet asks night to 'Hood my unmann'd blood, bating in my cheeks'—to cover her rising blushes (also making a pun on 'being unknown to a man'—being a virgin).*

unmastered also spelled **unmaster'd** ADJECTIVE
uncontrolled
• *(Ham 1.3.32) Laertes warns Ophelia not to let herself be seduced by Hamlet's 'unmaster'd importunity'—his unrestrained soliciting.*

unmitigable ADJECTIVE
implacable, unstoppable
• *(Tem 1.2.276) Prospero reminds Ariel of Sycorax's 'most unmitigable rage'.*

unordinate also spelled **inordinate** ADJECTIVE
excessive
• *(Oth 2.3.287) Cassio says a drink too many is a curse: 'Every unordinate cup is unblessed'—every drink after the first isn't toasted, and so is not blessed (and thus is the work of the devil).*

unprevailing ADJECTIVE
ineffective
• *(Ham 1.2.107) Claudius tries to persuade Hamlet to 'throw to earth / This unprevailing woe'—his grief won't change anything.*

unprizable ADJECTIVE
worthless
• *(TN 5.1.50) Orsino describes Antonio's vessel as 'unprizable'.*

unprized also spelled **unpriz'd** ADJECTIVE
unvalued
• *(KL 1.1.258) France describes Cordelia as an 'unpriz'd precious maid'.*
The word could also mean 'priceless' —invaluable.

unprovide VERB
make unready
• *(Oth 4.1.201) Othello says he will not argue with Desdemona, 'lest her body and beauty unprovide*

my mind again'—sway his mind away from the decision he's prepared himself to act out.

› unprovided ADJECTIVE
unprepared
• *(KL 2.1.51) Edmund tells Gloucester how Edgar attacked his 'unprovided body'—Edmund says he was unarmed (or, if he was armed, he hadn't time to draw his weapon) when Edgar attacked.*

unpublished also spelled **unpublish'd** ADJECTIVE
concealed
• *(KL 4.4.16) Cordelia asks all the 'unpublish'd virtues of the earth' to help her father—all the unknown restorative herbs that the earth grows.*

unraised ADJECTIVE [pronounced un-**ray**-zid]
ordinary
• *(H5 Prologue.9) The Chorus apologizes for the 'flat unraised spirits' that have dared to put on a play about the Battle of Agincourt—the dull, unimaginative actors.*
Normally 'unraised' would be pronounced with two syllables, but in this line the metre requires three.
see **INTRODUCTION, pp.4–5**

unrighteous ADJECTIVE
insincere
• *(Ham 1.2.154) Hamlet describes his mother's grief after his father's death as 'most unrighteous tears'.*

unrough ADJECTIVE
beardless
• *(Mac 5.2.10) Lennox says there are 'many unrough youths' in the English army.*

unseam VERB
split in two
• *(Mac 1.2.22) The Captain reports how Macbeth killed Macdonald: 'he unseam'd him from the nave to th'chaps'—from the navel to the jaws.*

unsex VERB
remove all qualities and infirmities associated with being a woman (or a man)
• *(Mac 1.5.40) Lady Macbeth asks the spirits to 'unsex me here'.*

unsifted ADJECTIVE
inexperienced
• *(Ham 1.3.102) Polonius says Ophelia talks like a girl 'Unsifted in such perilous circumstance'.*

unskilful NOUN
undiscerning
• *(Ham 3.2.25) Hamlet says actors who overact only 'make the unskilful laugh'.*

unstaid ADJECTIVE
unsettled
• *(TN 2.4.17) Orsino says lovers are 'Unstaid and skittish in all motions'—manic in all aspects of their life, other than in relation to the one they love.*

unstanched ADJECTIVE
with uncontrollable bleeding
• *(Tem 1.1.44) Gonzalo imagines the ship 'as leaky as an unstanched wench'—a graphic image of a woman who can't stop bleeding (though fitting, as ships are always referred to with the feminine pronoun).*

untowardly ADVERB
wretchedly
• *(MA 3.2.117) Don Pedro reflects on Don John's news: 'O day untowardly turned!'*

untread VERB
retrace
• *(MV 2.6.11) Gratiano says no horse 'doth untread' his steps with the same energy as when it first set out on a journey.*

› untrod ADJECTIVE
unprecedented
• *(JC 3.1.136) Antony says he will follow Brutus through 'the hazards of this untrod state'—the unusual situation that has arisen after Caesar's assassination.*

You will find these words and their definitions in this dictionary at entries without un-: unaccommodated, unattainted, unbated, unbolted, unbookish, unbreathed, uncharge, unchecked, uncomfortable, unfellowed, unfurnished, ungalled, ungently, ungoverned, ungracious, unhandsome, unhappily, unhappy, unimproved, unkind, unkindly, unkindness, unknown, unlineal, unluckily, unlucky, unmannerly, unmeet, unmeritable, unproper, unproportioned, unnatural, unnaturalness, unnerved, unpossessing, unpregnant of, unpurged, unreasonable, unreclaimed, unsanctified, unsatisfied, unsinewed, unsmirched, unspeak, unspotted, unstate, unstuffed, unsubstantial, unswear, untempering, untender, untented, unthrift, unthrifty, untitled, untuned, unvalued, unwholesome, unwit, unwonted, unwrung, unyoke

› undergoing ADJECTIVE
sustaining
• *(Tem 1.2.157) Prospero says young Miranda's smile 'rais'd in me / An undergoing stomach' —gave him courage to endure.*

understanding NOUN
knowledge
• *(KL 4.5.28) Regan tells Oswald she knows he is Goneril's confidante: 'I speak in understanding'.*

undertake VERB
as well as meaning 'take on a task', you'll find: make overtures to (begin the process of a wooing with an aim to marry—with a sexual pun)
• *(TN 1.3.53) Sir Andrew tells Sir Toby, of Maria, he 'would not undertake her in this company'—in front of all these people (the theatre audience).*

› undertaker NOUN
⚠ *Don't read in the modern meaning of 'someone who arranges a funeral'.*
person who takes on a task
• *(Oth 4.1.205) Iago tells Othello that he will handle Cassio: 'let me be his undertaker'—let me deal with him.*

union NOUN
large pearl
• *(Ham 5.2.257) Claudius says, if Hamlet succeeds at fencing, he will throw 'in the cup an union'.*
🎭 *An ostentatious act: pearls would dissolve in red wine.*

up and down
in every respect
• *(MA 2.1.108) Masked Ursula says she can tell her masked partner is Antonio: 'Here's his dry hand up and down'.*

uphoard VERB
amass
• *(Ham 1.1.139) Horatio asks the Ghost 'if thou hast uphoarded in thy life / Extorted treasure'—kept treasure that wasn't rightfully yours while you were alive (as this might explain the Ghost's appearance).*

upshot NOUN
1 final shot that determines the result (in archery)
• *(TN 4.2.67) Sir Toby realizes he 'cannot pursue with any safety this sport to the upshot'.*
2 outcome
• *(Ham 5.2.377) Horatio outlines the events that have taken place, and 'in this upshot, purposes mistook'—the way things have ended make people's true intentions misunderstood.*

upspring ADJECTIVE
trendy or lively
• *(Ham 1.4.9) Hamlet describes how Claudius celebrates with 'swagg'ring upspring reels'.*

up-staring ADJECTIVE
standing on end (out of fear)
• *(Tem 1.2.213) Ariel describes Ferdinand 'With hair up-staring'.*

urchin NOUN
⚠ *Don't read in the meaning of 'a poorly dressed boy'.*
spirit in the form of a hedgehog
• *(Tem 1.2.326) Prospero threatens Caliban: 'Urchins / Shall, for that vast of night that they may work, / All exercise on thee'.*

› urchin-show NOUN
spirit apparition in the form of a hedgehog
• *(Tem 2.2.5) Caliban says only Prospero can 'Fright me with urchin-shows'.*

Ursa Major see **COSMOS, p.174**

usance NOUN [pronounced **yooz**-uns]
interest on a loan
• *(MV 1.3.40) Shylock says Antonio 'brings down / The rate of usance'—because Antonio lends money without charging interest on the loan.*
see also **usurer**

use NOUN
as well as meaning 'the action of using something', you'll find:
1 usual practice
• *(JC 2.2.25) Calpurnia says the night's events 'are beyond all use'.*
2 outcome
• *(KL 4.2.36) Albany tells Goneril she 'must wither / And come to deadly use'—have a horrible death.*
3 trust (temporary possession)
• *(MV 4.1.381) Antonio asks the Duke to let him have half of Shylock's property 'in use'—so that he can later give it to Lorenzo, the fiancé of Shylock's daughter.*
4 interest
• *(MA 2.1.259) Beatrice says Benedick lent her his heart for a while 'and I gave him use for it, a double heart for his single one'.*

a b c d e f g h i j k l m n o p q r s t **Uu** v w x y z

⚠ *warning note* ✒ *usage note* 🎭 *theatre note*

use VERB
as well as meaning 'perform an action', you'll find:
1 make a habit
• *(RJ 3.5.189) Capulet tells Juliet: 'I do not use to jest'.*
2 treat
• *(KL 2.2.132) Kent, who is to be kept in the stocks all night, tells Regan 'You should not use me so!'*
3 keep company with
• *(Mac 3.2.10) Lady Macbeth asks her husband why he is still 'Using those thoughts which should indeed have died' when Duncan was killed.*

usurer NOUN
money-lender who charges excessive interest
• *(KL 4.6.159) Lear imagines a money-lender condemning a cozener (a fraudster) to death, even though the lender himself cheats and lies: 'The usurer hangs the cozener'.*
Fraud and usury (lending someone money, but charging them interest on how much they borrow) were both illegal in Shakespeare's time.

usurped also spelled **usurp'd** ADJECTIVE
disguising
• *(TN 5.1.241) Viola tells Sebastian of her 'masculine usurp'd attire'—the way she disguised herself as a young man.*

utensil NOUN
1 distinctive feature
• *(TN 1.5.226) Olivia tells Cesario she will list 'every particle and utensil' of her beauty.*
2 pieces of equipment (household or magical)
• *(Tem 3.2.93) Caliban tells Stephano that Prospero 'has brave utensils'.*

utmost NOUN
largest number
• *(JC 4.3.214) Brutus tells Cassius that they have asked for help from 'the utmost of our friends'—all the supporters they have.*

utter VERB
as well as meaning 'speak', you'll find:
1 exhale
• *(MND 4.2.35) Bottom tells his companions to 'eat no onions nor garlic; for we are to utter sweet breath'.*
2 offer for sale
• *(RJ 5.1.67) The Apothecary tells Romeo about his drugs: 'Mantua's law / Is death to any he that utters them'.*
3 commemorate
• *(MA 5.3.20) Balthasar sings: 'Graves yawn, and yield your dead / Till death be uttered'—a Biblical reference: graves open and give up the dead on the Day of Judgement.*

utterance in the phrase **to the utterance**
to the bitter end
• *(Mac 3.1.73) Macbeth invites Fate to 'champion me to th'utterance'—to fight for him until the last word of his life.*

uttermost NOUN
very latest time
• *(JC 2.1.213) Brutus asks his companions when they should bring Caesar to the Capitol: 'By the eighth hour, is that the uttermost?'*

Vv

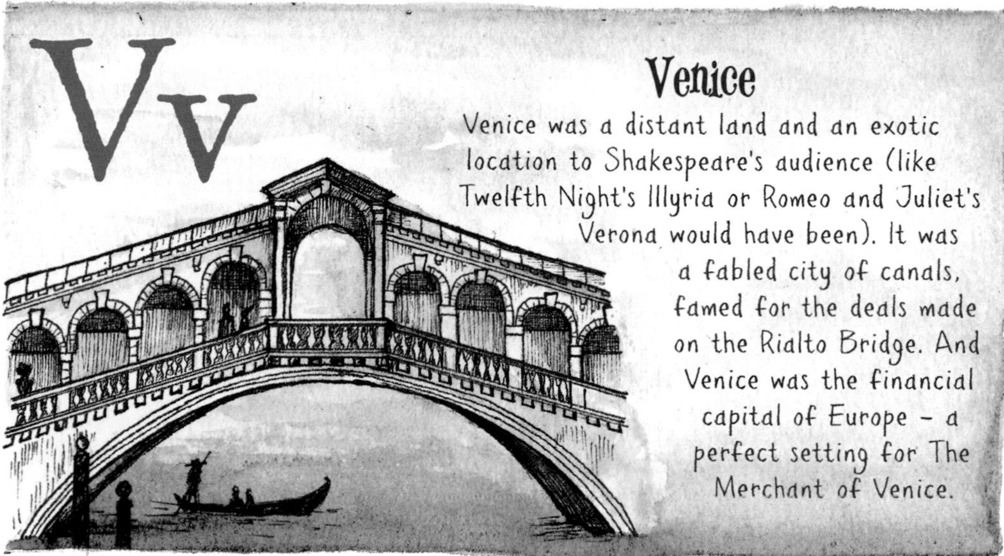

vacancy NOUN
empty space
• *(Ham 3.4.117) Gertrude tells Hamlet, who is looking at the Ghost: 'you do bend your eye on vacancy'—you're looking at nothing.*

vagrom ADJECTIVE
intended to mean 'vagrant'
• *(MA 3.3.24) Dogberry tells his men: 'you shall comprehend all vagrom men' -apprehend (arrest) all vagrants.*

vail VERB
cast down
• *(MV 1.1.28) Salarino imagines his ship wrecked, 'Vailing her high top lower than her ribs'—the top of the highest sail would be closer to the ground than the curving beams (ribs) that make up the bottom of the ship.* see **SHIPS, p.168**

› **vailed** ADJECTIVE
lowered
• *(Ham 1.2.70) Gertrude pleads with Hamlet not to go around 'with thy vailed lids'—with downcast eyes.*

vain ADJECTIVE
⚠ *Don't read in the meaning of 'conceited' here (unlike in vainness below).*
silly
• *(KL 4.2.61) Goneril calls Albany a 'vain fool!'*

› **vainly** ADVERB
uselessly
• *(RJ 5.3.125) The Friar, approaching the crypt, asks what torch 'vainly lends his light / To grubs and eyeless skulls?'—to things that can't see anything.*

› **vainness** NOUN
vanity
• *(H5 5.Chorus.20) The Chorus says Henry is 'free from vainness and self-glorious pride'.*

valanced also spelled **valanc'd** ADJECTIVE
fringed (with a beard)
• *(Ham 2.2.411) Hamlet tells one of the players: 'thy face is valanced since I saw thee last'.*

Valentine, Saint
the patron saint of lovers—a 3rd century Roman saint whose feast day (14 February) is the day when, according to tradition, the first person you meet will be your true love
• *(Ham 4.5.48) Ophelia sings: 'Tomorrow is Saint Valentine's day, / All in the morning betime'—in the early morning.*

validity NOUN
1 value
• *(KL 1.1.80) Lear gives Regan land 'No less in space, validity, and pleasure / Than that conferr'd on Goneril'.*
2 robustness
• *(Ham 3.2.181) The Player King says that often we intend to do something, but our memory can let us down, similar to someone 'Of violent birth but poor validity'—born in a violent birth, but growing up physically weak.*

valued also spelled **valu'd** ADJECTIVE
discriminating, showing value
• *(Mac 3.1.97) Macbeth describes the usefulness of a catalogue that lists different kinds of dogs: 'The*

valu'd file / Distinguishes the swift, the slow, the subtle'.

› unvalued also spelled **unvalu'd** ADJECTIVE
unimportant
• *(Ham 1.3.19) Laertes tells Ophelia that Hamlet 'may not, as unvalu'd persons do, / Carve for himself'—choose the person he wants to marry.*

vanity NOUN
⚠ *Don't read the meaning of 'being vain' into these senses.*
1 unprofitable way of life
• *(RJ 1.1.172) Romeo describes the fight between the Capulets and the Montagues as a conflict between hate and love, using a series of contradictions: 'heavy lightness, serious vanity'.*
2 trifling display
• *(Tem 4.1.41) Prospero says he must show Ferdinand and Miranda 'Some vanity of mine art'.*

vantage NOUN
1 right moment
• *(Mac 1.2.31) The Captain reports that the Norwegian commander, 'surveying vantage', began a fresh assault.*
2 advantageous position
• *(Ham 5.2.383) Fortinbras says he has some rights in Denmark, which he intends to claim because 'my vantage doth invite me'.*
3 benefit
• *(Mac 1.3.112) Angus is uncertain whether the Thane of Cawdor gave the King of Norway 'hidden help / And vantage'.*

› of vantage or **to the vantage**
in addition
• *(Ham 3.3.33) Polonius thinks, of Hamlet's intended conversation with his mother, it would be fitting to have someone 'o'erhear / The speech of vantage'—in addition to Gertrude.*
➨ *The choice between 'vantage' and 'advantage' is often based on which word will fit the metre of a line.*

Vapians NOUN [pronounced **vay**-pee-anz]
an invented racial name (either made up by Feste or misremembered by Sir Andrew)
• *(TN 2.3.21) Sir Andrew recalls Feste's story 'of the Vapians passing the equinoctial'—a race of people crossing the Equator.*

varlet NOUN
rogue
• *(KL 2.4.184) Lear tells Oswald: 'Out, varlet, from my sight!'*

vary VERB
express in fresh words
• *(H5 3.8.30) Bourbon says a man has no wit if he cannot, all day long, 'vary deserved praise' on his horse—think of new ways of praising it.*

› vary NOUN
variation
• *(KL 2.2.75) Kent describes Oswald as one of those men who follow 'every gale and vary of their masters'—every whim.*

vassal NOUN
servant
• *(Tem 1.2.373) Caliban thinks Prospero's magic is so strong it would 'make a vassal' of his god Setebos.*
🎭 *Setebos was a deity worshipped by religious followers in Patagonia.*

vassal ADJECTIVE
subordinate
• *(H5 3.6.51) The French King urges his nobles to fall upon the English like snow rushing from Alpine mountains into the 'low vassal seat' of the valleys.*

vast NOUN
long deserted space of time
• *(Tem 1.2.327) Prospero talks of spirits working in the 'vast of night'.*

› vasty ADJECTIVE
vast
• *(MV 2.7.42) Morocco talks of the 'vasty wilds / Of wide Arabia' as one of the many routes now only used to gain access to Portia.*

vault NOUN
⚠ *Don't read the meaning of 'underground room' into these senses.*
1 roof
• *(KL 5.3.258) Lear asks why others are not using their voices so loudly that 'heaven's vault should crack'.*
2 sky
• *(Tem 5.1.43) Prospero reflects on the magic he has worked between 'the green sea and the azur'd vault'—the blue skies.*

› vaulty ADJECTIVE
arched
• *(RJ 3.5.22) Romeo tells Juliet it isn't the lark they hear in 'The vaulty heaven so high above our heads'.*

› vaultage NOUN
cavern
• *(H5 2.4.125) Exeter warns the French Dauphin that even the 'caves and womby vaultages of France' will rebuke him for his mockery of Henry.*

vaunt-currier also spelled **-courier** NOUN
herald
• *(KL 3.2.5) Lear describes the storm's lightning flashes as 'Vaunt-curriers of oak-cleaving*

thunderbolts'—anticipating tree-splitting thunder (normally lightning would split a tree, but perhaps here Lear is calling on thunder loud enough to do so).

vaunting ADJECTIVE
boastful
• *(H5 2.3.4) Pistol encourages Nym: 'rouse thy vaunting veins'.*

vaunting NOUN
boasting
• *(JC 4.3.52) Brutus dares Cassius to 'make your vaunting true' over who is the better soldier.*

vaward NOUN
1 vanguard—the foremost division of an army
• *(H5 4.3.131) York asks Henry for 'The leading of the vaward'—he wants to lead the charge against the French.*
'Vaward' is the word in the First Folio. Some editions replace this with 'vanguard'.
2 foremost part
• *(MND 4.1.104) Theseus tells his hunting companions that 'we have the vaward of the day'—it is still early.*

vendible ADJECTIVE
marriageable
• *(MV 1.1.112) Gratiano thinks that one of the places where silence is desirable is in 'a maid not vendible'.*

venge VERB
a short form of 'avenge' or 'revenge'
• *(RJ 3.5.86) Juliet wishes that 'none but I might venge my cousin's death!'*

vent VERB
1 utter
• *(TN 4.1.8) Sebastian tells Feste: 'vent thy folly somewhere else'.*
2 excrete
• *(Tem 2.2.103) Stephano wonders how it is that Trinculo emerges from under Caliban's cloak: 'Can he vent Trinculos?'*

ventage NOUN
finger-hole of a musical instrument
• *(Ham 3.2.342) Hamlet gives Guildenstern a recorder and tells him to 'Govern these ventages with your fingers and thumb'.*

venture NOUN
as well as meaning 'risky enterprise', you'll find:
1 business deal
• *(MV 1.3.18) Shylock reflects on Antonio's 'ventures he hath squandered abroad'.*
2 cargo
• *(MV 1.1.42) Antonio tells Salarino: 'My ventures are not in one bottom trusted'—not in only one ship.*

Venus NOUN
in classical mythology, the goddess of love
• *(MA 4.1.59) Claudio accuses Hero of being 'more intemperate in your blood / Than Venus'—unable to control her passions.*

verdure NOUN
vitality
• *(Tem 1.2.87) Prospero compares himself to a tree-trunk and Antonio to ivy that 'suck'd my verdure out'—as the ivy plant wraps itself around and often strangles other plants and trees.*

verily ADJECTIVE
true
• *(Tem 2.1.316) Gonzalo tells Alonso: 'There was a noise, / That's verily'.*

verity NOUN
truth
• *(Mac 3.1.8) Banquo reflects on the way the witches' prophecies have come true for Macbeth—'the verities on thee made good'.*

versal ADJECTIVE
intended to mean 'universal'
• *(RJ 2.4.188) The Nurse describes Juliet as looking 'as pale as any clout in the versal world'—as white as any sheet in the whole wide world.*

vestal NOUN
woman vowed to chastity
• *(MND 2.1.158) Oberon describes how Cupid aimed his love arrow 'At a fair vestal'.*

vestal ADJECTIVE
virgin
• *(RJ 2.2.8) Romeo describes the moon as dressed in a 'vestal livery'—all in pure white (the colour virgins wore to show their purity).*

vesture NOUN
clothing
• *(JC 3.2.194) Antony tells the people, weeping at the sight of 'Our Caesar's vesture wounded', they will weep more when they see his body.*

vex VERB
Don't read meanings to do with 'mild annoyance' into these senses.
torment
• *(MA 2.2.26) Borachio has a plan 'to vex Claudio'.*
> **still-vexed** also spelled **-vex'd** ADJECTIVE
> always troubled
> • *(Tem 1.2.229) Ariel recalls Prospero sending him*

a b c d e f g h i j k l m n o p q r s t u **Vv** w x y z

'to fetch dew / From the still-vex'd Bermudas' —always beset by storms.

› vexation NOUN
disturbance
• *(MND 4.1.68) Oberon says the lovers will think of what has happened only 'as the fierce vexation of a dream'.*

› vexed also spelled **vex'd, vext** ADJECTIVE
1 disturbed
• *(Tem 4.1.158) Prospero apologizes to Ferdinand: 'Sir, I am vex'd'.*
2 stormy
• *(KL 4.4.2) Cordelia says her father is 'As mad as the vex'd sea'.*

via also spelled **fia** VERB
go on
• *(MV 2.2.9) Lancelot imagines a fiend advising him to leave Shylock: '"Fia!" says the fiend'—get on with it!*

viands NOUN [pronounced **vie**-andz]
items of food
• *(Tem 3.3.41) Sebastian says, of the spirits that appeared to them: 'They have left their viands behind'.*

Vice NOUN
stage jester
• *(TN 4.2.117) Feste sings 'I'll be with you again, / In a trice, like to the old Vice'—I'll be back straight away, in the manner of the old stage jester.*
The Vice was a stock character of medieval morality plays in the 15th and 16th centuries, and the forerunner of the clown or fool. Feste goes on to sing about how the Vice would hit the Devil with a wooden sword and drive him off the stage.

vice NOUN
screw
• *(MA 5.2.19) Benedick tells Margaret that pikes have to be put into a shield 'with a vice'—probably intending a sexual pun.*

viceroy NOUN
deputy monarch
• *(Tem 3.2.105) Stephano, imagining himself king of the island, tells Trinculo and Caliban that they 'shall be viceroys'.*

vicious ADJECTIVE
⚠ *Don't read the modern meaning of 'nastily aggressive' into these senses.*
1 defective
• *(Oth 3.3.146) Iago tells Othello he could be 'vicious in my guess'—he might be wrong.*
2 caused by vice
• *(KL 1.1.226) Cordelia begs Lear to make it known that her situation is due to 'no vicious blot, murther or foulness'.*

victual NOUN [pronounced **vit**-uhl]
food and drink
• *(MA 1.1.44) Beatrice says that Benedick's service in the war was that he helped to eat 'musty victual'—he helped to eat all the leftovers.*

vile also spelled **vild** ADJECTIVE
as well as meaning 'disgusting', you'll find:
1 degrading
• *(MV 2.4.6) Solanio thinks that arranging torchbearers is 'vile unless it may be quaintly order'd'—done artistically.*
2 shameful
• *(H5 4.Chorus.50) The Chorus apologizes for the actors' 'four or five most vile and ragged foils'—the fake swords they will use to show the battle.*
3 of humble birth
• *(H5 4.3.62) Henry says, of the men about to fight: 'be he ne'er so vile, / This day shall gentle his condition'—however low-born he may be, today he will be seen as a nobleman.*

› vilely also spelled **vildly** ADVERB
terribly
• *(JC 4.3.133) Cassius says of the Poet: 'how vildly doth this cynic rhyme!'*

villain NOUN
as well as meaning 'rogue', you'll find:
servant
• *(Tem 1.2.309) Miranda tells her father that Caliban is 'a villain, sir, / I do not love to look on'.*

› villainous ADVERB
detestably
• *(Tem 4.1.247) Caliban worries that Prospero might turn them all into apes 'With foreheads villainous low'.*

› villainy NOUN
rudeness
• *(MA 2.1.129) Beatrice says that Benedick's best quality or 'commendation is not in his wit but in his villainy'.*

viol-de-gamboys see MUSIC, p.172

virtue NOUN
as well as meaning 'a good quality in someone's character', you'll find:

1 essence
• *(MND 4.1.168) Demetrius says that Helena is 'the virtue of my heart'.*
2 courage
• *(KL 5.3.103) Albany tells Edmund to 'Trust to thy single virtue'—your unaided valour.*
3 power
• *(RJ 2.3.13) The Friar says that plants have 'many virtues excellent'.*
4 chastity
• *(KL 3.2.54) Lear calls down the gods on anyone who is a 'simular of virtue'—anyone who pretends to be sexually pure.*

> **virtuous** ADJECTIVE
> powerful
> • *(Oth 3.4.105) Cassio asks Desdemona to use her 'virtuous means' to regain Othello's favour.*

visage NOUN [pronounced **viz**-idge]
as well as meaning 'face', you'll find:
general outward appearance
• *(Oth 1.1.50) Iago talks of bad servants 'trimm'd in forms and visages of duty'—who take on the manners and appearance of dutiful servants.*

visit VERB
as well as meaning 'go to see a person or place', you'll find:
punish
• *(H5 4.1.167) Henry talks about the sins of soldiers 'for which they are now visited' through death on the battlefield.*

visitor NOUN
parish visitor (of the sick)—an official position
• *(Tem 2.1.12) Antonio compares Gonzalo (who is attempting to comfort Alonso) to a church worker who will not stop trying to help: 'The visitor will not give him o'er so'.*

visor NOUN
mask
• *(RJ 1.5.23) Capulet tells his guests: 'I have seen the day / That I have worn a visor'—he used to wear a mask at parties when he was younger.*

vizard NOUN [pronounced **viz**-uhd]
mask
• *(Mac 3.2.34) Macbeth tells his wife that they must 'make our faces vizards to our hearts, / Disguising what they are'.*

voice NOUN
as well as meaning 'sound coming from the mouth', you'll find:
1 support
• *(Oth 1.3.257) Othello asks the Duke to agree to Desdemona's request: 'Let her have your voice'.*
2 authoritative opinion
• *(Ham 5.2.233) Laertes says he needs those who are expert in matters of honour to give him 'a voice and precedent of peace / To keep my name ungored'—to assure him that fighting a duel will keep his honour unharmed.*
3 talk
• *(TN 1.5.240) Olivia admits that Orsino's good qualities are recognized 'In voices well divulg'd'—many people speak well of him.*

void VERB
1 empty
• *(MV 1.3.112) Shylock reminds Antonio: 'You that did void your rheum upon my beard'—discharge your spit.*
2 leave
• *(H5 4.7.53) Henry says the French horsemen up on a nearby hill must 'come down, / Or void the field'.*

void ADJECTIVE
uncrowded
• *(JC 2.4.37) The Soothsayer says he will go 'to a place more void' to speak to Caesar.*

voluble ADJECTIVE
glib, insincere
• *(Oth 2.1.230) Iago describes Cassio as 'a knave very voluble'.*

voluntary ADJECTIVE
⚠ *Don't read in the meaning of 'doing work without pay'.*
enthusiastic
• *(Oth 4.1.27) Iago describes men who boast of their sexual prowess, having had 'voluntary dotage of some mistress'—a woman enthusiastically making love to him.*

vor VERB
a dialect form of 'warn'
• *(KL 4.6.235) Edgar tells Oswald to keep away from Gloucester, 'che vor' ye'—I warn you.*

votaress also spelled **votress, vot'ress** NOUN
devotee
• *(MND 2.1.123) Titania says her changeling's mother 'was a votress of my order'—a follower of Titania's (religious) order.*

> **votarist** NOUN
> religious vow-taker
> • *(Oth 4.2.186) Roderigo says he has had no acknowledgement of the jewels he has given to Desdemona, though they 'would half have*

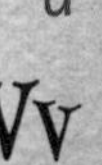
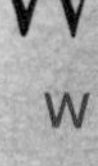

corrupted a votarist'—the jewels would even have persuaded a nun to marry him.

vouch VERB
as well as meaning 'guarantee', you'll find: pledge, make a toast
• *(Mac 3.4.34) Lady Macbeth tells her husband that 'The feast is sold / That is not often vouch'd'—a feast is no different from a meal you have to pay for if it doesn't begin with toasts from the host.*

vouch NOUN
approval
• *(Oth 2.1.144) Desdemona talks of a woman who was so well-thought of that she 'did justly put on the vouch of very malice itself'—even spitefulness would approve of her.*

› **vouched** ADJECTIVE
attested
• *(Tem 2.1.59) Gonzalo is explaining that unusual or rare events can be beyond belief, when Sebastian interrupts: 'As many vouched rarities are'.*

› **voucher** NOUN
legal warrant of a right to property
• *(Ham 5.1.100) Hamlet wonders if one of the skulls in the graveyard might have belonged to a great buyer of land who would have all sorts of legal documents, including 'vouchers'.*

› **fore-vouched** also spelled **-vouch'd** ADJECTIVE
previously declared
• *(KL 1.1.219) The King of France tells Lear he believes Cordelia's offence has to be great, otherwise 'your fore-vouch'd affection / Fall into taint'—becomes discredited.*

vouchsafe VERB
1 permit
• *(Ham 3.2.284) Guildenstern asks Hamlet: 'vouchsafe me a word with you'.*
2 graciously receive
• *(JC 2.1.313) Ligarius greets Brutus: 'Vouchsafe good morrow from a feeble tongue'.*

› **vouchsafed** also spelled **vouchsaf'd** ADJECTIVE
kindly granted
• *(TN 3.1.85) Cesario tells Olivia that his message is only for her own 'most pregnant and vouchsafed ear'—an ear that is ready and willing to receive it.*

vox NOUN
proper voice
• *(TN 5.1.285) Feste tells Olivia that if he is to read the letter of a madman (Malvolio's letter) then 'you must allow vox'—let him read it in a madman's voice.*

Vulcan NOUN
the Roman god of fire, and the gods' blacksmith
• *(TN 5.1.48) Orsino says the last time he saw Antonio's face 'it was besmear'd / As black as Vulcan'—Antonio's face was blackened by the fire and smoke of battle (as black as if it had been in a blacksmith's forge).*

vulgar ADJECTIVE
1 generally known
• *(KL 4.6.205) A Gentleman says the impending battle is 'Most sure and vulgar'—it's definitely happening, and everyone knows of it.*
2 common to all
• *(Ham 1.3.61) Polonius advises Laertes to be 'familiar, but by no means vulgar' on his travels—don't socialize with absolutely everybody.*

vulgar NOUN
common people
• *(JC 1.1.72) Flavius says he will go and 'drive away the vulgar from the streets'.*

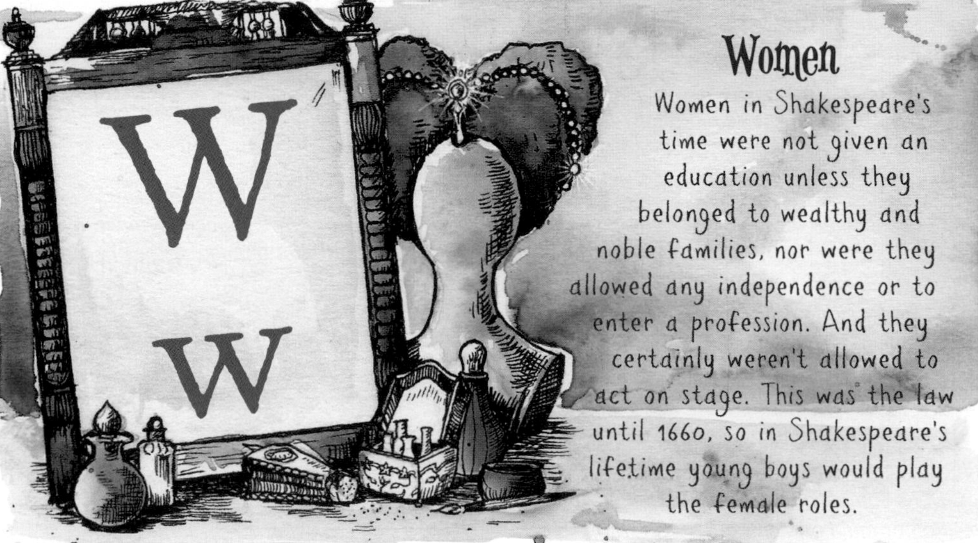

wafer-cake NOUN
type of thin, lightweight cake
• *(H5 2.3.44) Pistol tells the Hostess to trust nobody, for 'men's faiths are wafer-cakes'—extremely fragile.*

waft VERB
beckon
• *(MV 5.1.11) Lorenzo imagines Dido (the queen and founder of the city of Carthage) standing on the shore to 'waft her love / To come again to Carthage'.*

› **wafture** NOUN
waving
• *(JC 2.1.246) Portia reminds Brutus of how he told her to leave him 'with an angry wafture of your hand'.*

wag VERB
as well as meaning 'move to and fro like a dog's tail', you'll find:
go away
• *(MA 5.1.16) Leonato imagines someone who is able to 'Bid sorrow wag'.*

wage VERB
1 risk
• *(Oth 1.3.30) The First Senator thinks it unlikely that the Turks would 'wake and wage a danger profitless'—take on a risky venture.*
2 stake
• *(KL 1.1.155) Kent tells Lear he held his life 'but as a pawn / To wage against thine enemies'.*
3 do battle
• *(KL 2.4.206) Lear says he chooses 'To wage against the enmity o'th' air'—to head out into the wildness of the countryside, rather than return to Goneril's castle.*

waggoner also spelled **wagoner** NOUN
charioteer
• *(RJ 3.2.2) Juliet wants 'such a waggoner / As Phaëton' to pull the sun away—in Greek mythology, the son of the sun-god Phoebus (who pulls the sun around the Earth).*

wain-rope also spelled **wainrope** NOUN
waggon-rope
• *(TN 3.2.54) Sir Toby thinks 'oxen and wainropes' wouldn't be able to bring Sir Andrew and Cesario close enough together to fight.*

waist see **SHIPS, p.168**

wait on or **upon** VERB
1 accompany
• *(Mac 3.4.38) Macbeth greets his dinner-guests: 'Now good digestion wait on appetite'.*
2 obey
• *(Ham 3.4.70) Hamlet tells Gertrude that at her age sexual passion 'waits upon the judgement'—her desire should be subordinate to her powers of reason.*

wake VERB
1 disturb
• *(MA 5.1.102) Don Pedro tells Antonio and Leonato: 'we will not wake your patience'—we won't disturb you further.*
2 urge on
• *(Mac 3.6.31) A Lord says Macduff has gone 'To wake Northumberland'.*
3 stay up
• *(Ham 1.4.8) Hamlet explains the noisy revels: 'The King doth wake tonight and takes his rouse'.*

a b c d e f g h i j k l m n o p q r s t u v Ww x y z

wake NOUN
fete
- *(KL 3.6.72) Poor Tom calls on imaginary companions to 'march to wakes and fairs'.*

walk VERB
as well as meaning 'move about on foot', you'll find:
walk aside (to fight a duel)
- *(RJ 3.1.72) Mercutio calls to Tybalt: 'you rat-catcher, will you walk?'*

walk a bout see **bout**

wall in the phrase **take the wall**
keep to the cleaner side of a path
- *(RJ 1.1.10) Sampson says: 'I will take the wall of any man or maid of Montague's'—show myself to be better (the roadside is made dirtier by passing traffic, so it's better to stay close to the wall).*

wallet NOUN
⚠ *Don't read in the modern meaning of 'a container for money and credit cards'.*
bulging growth
- *(Tem 3.3.46) Gonzalo talks of mountain-dwellers 'whose throats had hanging at 'em / Wallets of flesh'.*

wall-newt NOUN
type of lizard that frequents walls
- *(KL 3.4.123) Poor Tom says he eats 'the wall-newt, and the water'—two types of lizard.*

wan VERB
turn pale
- *(Ham 2.2.539) Hamlet describes the First Player as having 'all his visage wann'd'.*

  › **wanny** ADJECTIVE
  pale
  - *(RJ 4.1.100) The Friar says his potion will make Juliet's rosy cheeks 'fade / To wanny ashes'.*

wand NOUN
a straight, slender stick
- *(MV 1.3.79) Shylock tells a biblical story in which 'The skilful shepherd pill'd me certain wands'—stripped the bark from some thin sticks.*

wandering ADJECTIVE
⚠ *Don't read in the meaning of 'moving in no particular direction' here.*
having its own motion
- *(MND 4.1.97) Oberon says he and Titania can travel around the globe 'Swifter than the wandering moon'.*

wanton ADJECTIVE
1 unrestrained
- *(MV 5.1.71) Lorenzo describes the behaviour of 'a wild and wanton herd' of colts.*

2 out of control
- *(TN 3.1.14) Cesario tells Feste that those who play with words 'may quickly make them wanton'—make them so full of ambiguity they become meaningless.*

3 lewd
- *(Tem 4.1.95) Iris tells of Venus and Cupid wanting to do 'Some wanton charm' upon Ferdinand and Miranda—to make them lustful.*

4 sexually passionate
- *(Oth 2.3.16) Iago says Othello 'hath not yet made wanton the night' with Desdemona.*

5 badly behaved
- *(KL 4.1.36) Gloucester reflects: 'As flies to wanton boys, are we to th'gods; / They kill us for their sport'.*

6 luxuriant
- *(MND 2.1.99) Titania bemoans what has happened to the countryside, and to 'the quaint mazes in the wanton green'.*

7 gentle
- *(RJ 2.6.19) The Friar describes the webs floating 'in the wanton summer air'.*

wanton ADVERB
lustfully
- *(Ham 3.4.185) Hamlet tells Gertrude not to let Claudius 'Pinch wanton on your cheek'.*

wanton NOUN
1 seducer
- *(RJ 1.4.35) Romeo says that dancing at a party is for 'wantons light of heart'.*

2 lover
- *(Oth 4.1.71) Iago reflects on those who 'lip a wanton in a secure couch'.*

3 prostitute
- *(MA 4.1.43) Claudio says he will not 'knit my soul to an approved wanton'.*

4 wilful creature
- *(MND 2.1.63) Oberon calls to Titania: 'Tarry, rash wanton!'*

5 young rascal
- *(RJ 2.2.177) Juliet wants Romeo to move away from her 'no farther than a wanton's bird, / That lets it hop a little from his hand'.*

6 spoilt child
- *(Ham 5.2.291) Hamlet taunts Laertes' fencing skills: 'I am afeard you make a wanton of me' —you're just playing with me.*

  › **wantonness** NOUN
  foolish behaviour
  - *(Ham 3.1.145) Hamlet accuses women of making 'your wantonness your ignorance'—that they*

behave foolishly and pretend they're unaware they're doing so.

want-wit ADJECTIVE
stupid
• *(MV 1.1.6) Antonio describes himself as having 'a want-wit sadness'—idiotic seriousness.*

ward NOUN
1 defensive posture
⚠ *Don't read in the meaning of a 'hospital ward'.*
• *(Tem 1.2.472) Prospero tells Ferdinand to put up his sword: 'Come from thy ward'.*
2 prison cell
• *(Ham 2.2.242) Hamlet describes the world as a place where 'there are many confines, wards, and dungeons'.*
3 minor (a young person legally under an elder's protection)
• *(KL 1.2.69) Edgar is supposed to have written: 'the father should be as ward to the son'.*

Ware in the phrase **Bed of Ware**
a bed, famous for its great size, in the town of Ware, Hertfordshire
• *(TN 3.2.42) Sir Toby advises Sir Andrew to fill his sheet of paper (his letter to Cesario) with insults, even though 'the sheet were big enough for the bed of Ware in England'.*

ware ADJECTIVE
aware
• *(RJ 1.1.118) Benvolio says he saw Romeo out walking and tried to talk to him, 'but he was ware of me' and hid himself.*

warn VERB
as well as meaning 'advise of danger', you'll find:
confront
• *(JC 5.1.5) Octavius tells Antony of the enemy's intentions: 'They mean to warn us at Philippi here'.*

war-proof NOUN
valour tested in war
• *(H5 3.1.18) Henry describes his soldiers as descended 'from fathers of war-proof'.*

warrant VERB
1 give an assurance about
• *(Tem 1.1.43) Gonzalo, certain the Boatswain is to be hanged one day, says 'I'll warrant him for drowning'—he's equally certain the man won't drown.*
2 promise
• *(TN 2.3.155) Maria says tricking Malvolio will be 'Sport royal, I warrant you'.*
3 authorize
• *(MA 4.1.178) Hero denies she knows any man more than 'maiden modesty doth warrant'.*
4 protect
• *(MND 5.1.305) Demetrius wonders whether Pyramus or Thisbe is the better actor: 'he for a man, God warrant us; she for a woman, God bless us'—they're both good in their own way (the oaths help point the joke, much as comedians today use a swear-word to make a joke sound funnier).*

warrant NOUN
⚠ *Don't read the modern meaning to do with 'being arrested' into these senses.*
1 assurance
• *(Oth 3.3.20) Desdemona promises Cassio: 'I give thee warrant of thy place'—I guarantee your military standing won't change.*
2 authorization
• *(Mac 2.3.141) Malcolm and Donaldbain plan to leave (steal away from) Macbeth's castle: 'There's warrant in that theft / Which steals itself when there's no mercy left'.*
3 evidence
• *(MA 3.2.98) Don John tells Claudio not to be shocked by the charge against Hero until he provides 'further warrant'.*

› **of warrant**
allowed
• *(Ham 2.1.39) Polonius assures Reynaldo that attributing faults to Laertes 'is a fetch of warrant'—a justifiable stratagem.*

› **out of warrant**
unlawful
• *(Oth 1.2.79) Brabantio accuses Othello of being 'a practiser / Of arts inhibited, and out of warrant'—of black magic.*

› **warranted** ADJECTIVE
justified
• *(Mac 4.3.137) Malcolm tells Macduff he hopes 'the chance of goodness / Be like our warranted quarrel!'—their success will reflect the rightfulness of their cause.*

› **warranty** NOUN
⚠ *Don't read in the modern meaning to do with a manufacturer's guarantee.*
authorization
• *(MV 1.1.132) Bassanio says Antonio's love gives him 'a warranty / To unburden all my plots and purposes'.*

warren NOUN

⚠*Don't read in the meaning of a 'rabbit warren'.*

hunting park

• *(MA 2.1.199) Benedick says Claudio is 'as melancholy as a lodge in a warren'—a lonely place to live.*

washing ADJECTIVE

slashing

• *(RJ 1.1.56) Sampson tells Gregory to prepare for the fight: 'remember thy washing blow'.*

wassail NOUN

drinking-party

• *(Ham 1.4.9) Hamlet, explaining the revels at Elsinore, says the king 'Keeps wassail'.*

waste VERB

⚠*Don't read meanings to do with 'wastefulness' in these senses.*

1 pass

• *(MV 3.4.12) Portia talks of companions 'That do converse and waste the time together'.*

2 use up

• *(JC 2.1.59) Lucius tells Brutus that 'March is wasted fifteen days'.*

› **wasted** ADJECTIVE

used up

• *(MND 5.1.358) Puck reflects on fires dying down: 'Now the wasted brands do glow'—the burned logs are giving off a red-orange glow.*

› **wasteful** ADJECTIVE

destructive

• *(H5 3.1.14) Henry describes a rock 'Swill'd with the wild and wasteful ocean'.*

watch NOUN

1 watchmen (an early sort of police force, who patrolled the streets at night to safeguard life and property)

• *(RJ 5.3.71) The Page, seeing Romeo fighting with Paris, says he will 'go call the Watch'.*

2 sleepless state

• *(Ham 2.2.148) Polonius thinks Hamlet fell 'into a fast, / Thence to a watch'—stopped eating, then sat staring into space and not sleeping.*

3 period of time

• *(Oth 1.1.123) Roderigo asks Brabantio what his daughter is up to 'At this odd-even and dull watch o'the night'—at this very late hour.*

4 signal

• *(Mac 2.1.54) Macbeth describes the wolf, 'Whose howl's his watch'—whose howl is the sign of his presence.*

watch VERB

1 stay awake

• *(KL 2.2.150) Kent tells Gloucester he has 'watch'd and travell'd hard'.*

2 keep the watch

• *(Oth 2.3.47) Iago says the drunken Roderigo is 'to watch' tonight—keep guard.*

3 look out for

• *(JC 4.3.249) Brutus' servants tell him they will 'stand and watch your pleasure'—be there in case you want anything.*

› **watcher** NOUN

one who stays awake

• *(Mac 2.2.74) Lady Macbeth tells her husband to put on his dressing-gown in case they are called and proven 'to be watchers'—awake while the murder took place.*

› **watchful** ADJECTIVE

sleepless

• *(JC 2.1.98) Brutus asks his visitors 'What watchful cares do interpose themselves / Betwixt your eyes and night?'*

› **watching** NOUN

wakefulness

• *(RJ 4.4.8) The Nurse tells Capulet he will 'be sick tomorrow / For this night's watching'.*

› **watch him tame**

keep him awake (a technique used when taming a hawk)

• *(Oth 3.3.23) Desdemona promises Cassio she will make his case to Othello at all times: 'I'll watch him tame'.*

› **all-watched** ADJECTIVE

maintaining a watch (guard) throughout

• *(H5 4.Chorus.38) The Chorus describes Henry in 'the weary and all-watched night'.*

› **overwatch** VERB

stay up late

• *(MND 5.1.349) Theseus fears 'we shall outsleep the coming morn / As much as we this night have overwatch'd'.*

› **o'erwatched** also spelled **o'erwatch'd** ADJECTIVE

exhausted from lack of sleep

• *(KL 2.2.165) Kent says he is 'All weary and o'erwatch'd'.*

water NOUN

1 tears

• *(Oth 4.2.103) Desdemona says she has no answers to questions about Othello 'But what should go by water'.*

2 lustre

• *(TN 4.2.60) Feste responds to the compliment of being called Sir Topas (also the name of a precious stone) by saying 'I am for all waters'—he can turn his hand to anything.*

🎭*The transparency and quality of pearls and diamonds were described in terms of 'waters'. The three highest grades were known as the 'first water', 'second water', and 'third water'.*

3 urine

• *(TN 3.4.95) Fabian tells Maria, of Malvolio, that she should 'Carry his water to th' wise woman'—a fortune-teller who might be able to say what is wrong with him by studying his urine.*

see also **cast the water**

4 water-newt

• *(KL 3.4.123) Poor Tom says he eats 'the wall-newt, and the water'—two types of lizard.*

> **› watery** also spelled **wat'ry** ADJECTIVE
> made of water-drops
> • *(Tem 4.1.71) Iris, goddess of the rainbow, describes herself as Ceres' 'watery arch and messenger'—her chief messenger made of water-drops, only seen through sunlight (the rainbow).*

water-rug see **ANIMALS, p.162**

wawl VERB

howl

• *(KL 4.6.176) Lear tells Gloucester: 'the first time that we smell the air / We wawl and cry'.*

wax NOUN see **man of wax**

wax or **waxen** VERB

grow

• *(H5 5.1.76) Pistol reflects: 'Old I do wax'.*

🎭*The phrase is used to describe the moon, which is said to 'wax' when it approaches its full visible extent, and 'wane' when it appears smaller.*

waxen ADJECTIVE

written on wax (and thus perishable)

• *(H5 1.2.233) Henry says, if France cannot be won, his grave will not be worth commemorating, not even with 'a waxen epitaph'.*

ways in the phrase **come thy/your ways** or **go thy/your ways**

come along or get along

• *(TN 2.5.1) Sir Toby invites Fabian to accompany him: 'Come thy ways, Signior Fabian'.*

waywardness NOUN

wrong-headedness

• *(KL 1.1.295) Goneril anticipates in Lear 'unruly waywardness that infirm and choleric years bring with them'.*

🎭*In Shakespeare's time, old age was thought to bring a tendency of physical instability (infirmity) as well as the humour choler, making the elderly irrationally angry. see HUMOURS, p.137*

weal NOUN

1 state

• *(Mac 5.2.27) Caithness and his companions go to meet 'the med'cine of the sickly weal'—Malcolm is seen as the doctor who will heal Scotland.*

2 well-being

• *(RJ 3.2.51) Juliet asks the Nurse to simply say yes or no: 'Brief sounds determine my weal or woe'.*

wealth NOUN

as well as meaning 'prosperity', you'll find:

well-being

• *(MV 5.1.249) Antonio, defending Bassanio, tells Portia: 'I once did lend my body for his wealth' —through his bond with Shylock.*

wear VERB

as well as meanings to do with clothes, you'll find:

1 adapt

• *(TN 2.4.29) Orsino tells Cesario that a woman should have an older man as a husband: 'so wears she to him'—adapts herself to his ways.*

2 possess

• *(MA 5.1.82) Antonio says of Claudio: 'Win me and wear me'—if he defeats me, he can do what he likes with me.*

> **› wear out** VERB
> outlive
> • *(KL 5.3.17) Lear tells Cordelia: 'we'll wear out, / In a wall'd prison, packs and sects of great ones'—all political cliques at court.*
>
> **› outwear** VERB
> use up
> • *(H5 4.2.63) The Constable urges the nobles to the field: 'The sun is high, and we outwear the day'.*

weasand also spelled **wezand** NOUN

windpipe

• *(Tem 3.2.88) Caliban tells Stephano a way to kill Prospero—'cut his weasand with thy knife'—slit his throat.*

weather-fend VERB

shelter

• *(Tem 5.1.10) Ariel says he has left Prospero's enemies 'In the line-grove which weather-fends your cell'—in the grove of lime-trees that shelters the place where you live.*

web and pin

cataract in the eye, causing blindness

• *(KL 3.4.110) Poor Tom imagines Gloucester as a devil: 'He gives the web and the pin'.*

a b c d e f g h i j k l m n o p q r s t u v **Ww** x y z

weeds NOUN
garments
• *(MND 2.2.77) Puck sees Lysander: 'Weeds of Athens he doth wear'.*
'Weed' (in the sense of 'garment') is usually found as a plural, but occasionally it is a singular:
• *(MND 2.1.256) Oberon describes a shedded snakeskin as 'Weed wide enough to wrap a fairy in'.*

welked also spelled **whelked, whelk'd** ADJECTIVE
twisted
• *(KL 4.6.71) Edgar describes the imagined fiend to Gloucester: 'Horns whelk'd and wav'd like the enridged sea'.*

welkin NOUN
sky
• *(Tem 1.2.4) Miranda describes the sea 'mounting to th' welkin's cheek'—to the edges of the clouds.*

› **out of my welkin**
none of my business
• *(TN 3.1.55) Feste tells Cesario: 'who you are and what you would are out of my welkin'.*

well-a-day see **REGRETTING, p.250**

well-apparelled see **apparel**

well-appointed see **appoint**

well-compact see **compact**

well-favoured see **favour**

well-hallowed also spelled **-hallow'd** ADJECTIVE
well-blessed
• *(H5 1.2.293) Henry tells the French ambassadors he is coming to put forth his 'rightful hand in a well-hallow'd cause'—to conquer France, as God intends.*

well-possessed see **possess**

well-seeming see **seeming**

well to live ADJECTIVE
intended to mean 'well-to-do'
• *(MV 2.2.49) Gobbo describes himself as a poor man and 'well to live'—he probably means 'alive and well', but uses the wrong idiom.*

wench see **TERMS OF ADDRESS, p.306**

weraday see **REGRETTING, p.250**

wether NOUN
castrated ram
• *(MV 4.1.114) Antonio describes himself as 'a tainted wether of the flock'—a sick sheep fit only for death.*

wharf NOUN
river bank
• *(Ham 1.5.33) The Ghost tells Hamlet that if he does not act he will be duller than the oblivion-causing weed 'That roots itself in ease on Lethe wharf'.*
In Greek mythology, Lethe was the river in the underworld (Hades). When the souls of the dead drank its water they would forget their life on earth.

what the good year see **goodyear**

wheel NOUN
refrain
• *(Ham 4.5.169) Ophelia tells her listeners to sing, but with two different rhythms: 'O, how the wheel becomes it!'—how the unrhythmical tune suits her maddened mood.*

› **wheeling** ADJECTIVE
roving
• *(Oth 1.1.136) Roderigo describes Othello as 'an extravagant and wheeling stranger'—a wandering or travelling foreigner.*
Travelling in Shakespeare's time was a very dangerous affair, considered suitable only for solitary men if they were able to defend themselves, or (as Roderigo is implying) those wanting to attack the defenceless.

whelk NOUN
pimple
• *(H5 3.7.95) The Welsh Captain describes Bardolph's face as full of 'whelks, and knobs'.*

whelked see **welked**

whey-face NOUN
pale-face (the colour of milk)
• *(Mac 5.3.17) Macbeth asks his frightened servant: 'What soldiers, whey-face?'*

whiffler see **OCCUPATIONS, p.166**

while in the phrase **the while**
1 in the meantime
• *(Tem 3.1.24) Miranda offers to help Ferdinand: 'I'll bear your logs the while'.*
2 the times
• *(JC 1.3.82) Cassius laments about the times: 'woe the while'.*

while-ere also spelled **whilere** ADVERB
a short time ago
• *(Tem 3.2.115) Caliban asks Stephano if he will sing the song 'You taught me but whilere?'*

whipster NOUN
wretch
• *(Oth 5.2.242) Othello says 'every puny whipster gets my sword'—any weak wretch can defeat me.*

whipstock NOUN
handle of a whip
• *(TN 2.3.25) Feste says 'Malvolio's nose is no whipstock'—he can't grab hold of his nose to ask for money.*

whirligig see **RECREATION, p.170**

whist ADJECTIVE
quiet
• *(Tem 1.2.377) Ariel sings of spirits kissing 'The wild waves whist'—kissing them into silence.*

whit in the phrase **no whit**
not at all
• *(JC 2.1.148) Metellus thinks that, if Cicero is involved in the conspiracy, 'Our youths and wildness shall no whit appear'.*

white ADJECTIVE
1 almost fully ripened
• *(KL 3.4.112) Poor Tom imagines a devil who 'mildews the white wheat'—who makes the wheat wet (and thereby useless).*
2 unsmoked
• *(KL 3.6.31) Poor Tom says a devil cries in his belly 'for two white herring'.*

white and black
black-and-white
• *(MA 5.1.298) Dogberry complains that he was called an ass, though it is 'not under white and black'—not written down.*

white-livered ADJECTIVE
cowardly (lily-livered)
• *(H5 3.2.29) The Boy describes Bardolph as 'white-livered and red-faced'—from the idea that a deficiency of bile caused a pale liver, and thereby a lack of vigour or courage.*

Whitsun NOUN
in the Christian calendar, the feast-day celebrating the descent of the Holy Spirit on the apostles (in Shakespeare's England, celebrated with dancing)
• *(H5 2.4.25) The Dauphin dismisses England as a country 'busied with a Whitsun morris dance'.*

wholesome ADJECTIVE
1 beneficial
• *(Oth 1.1.145) Iago tells Roderigo it would not be 'wholesome to my place'—not good for my military standing—if he were called as a witness against Othello.*
2 sensible
• *(Ham 3.2.301) Guildenstern asks Hamlet for a sensible response: 'make me a wholesome answer'.*
3 free from disease
• *(Mac 4.3.105) Macduff wonders when Scotland will ever see its 'wholesome days again' (the disease being the tyrannical reign of Macbeth).*
4 health-giving
• *(Ham 1.1.167) Marcellus says that during the Christmas season 'The nights are wholesome'—because they are fresh and brisk.*

› **unwholesome** ADJECTIVE
1 harmful
• *(H5 2.3.49) The Boy says horse-blood is 'unwholesome food'.*
2 corrupted
• *(Ham 4.5.81) Claudius worries that the Danes are 'unwholesome in their thoughts'.*
3 impaired
• *(Oth 4.1.120) Cassio asks Iago not to think his judgement (about marrying Bianca) 'so unwholesome'.*

whoremaster ADJECTIVE
lecherous
• *(KL 1.2.120) Edmund finds it 'An admirable evasion of whoremaster man' to blame astrology for everything—it's easy to blame the movement of the stars and planets to let yourself behave however you like.*

Whore of Babylon
an evil female figure named in the Bible's Book of Revelation
• *(H5 2.3.34) The Hostess remembers Falstaff talking 'of the Whore of Babylon'.*

whoreson NOUN
literally, the son of a prostitute (and so probably fatherless)—bastard
• *(KL 1.1.22) Gloucester says, of Edmund, 'The whoreson must be acknowledged'.*

› **whoreson** ADJECTIVE
bastard
• *(KL 1.4.77) Lear calls Oswald a 'whoreson dog!'*
• *(Ham 5.1.161) The First Gravedigger calls Yorick 'A whoreson mad fellow'.*

The word is usually used in an abusive way, to add force to the meaning, but it can be either serious (as in the 'King Lear' quotation) or jocular (as in the 'Hamlet').

wide ADJECTIVE
as well as its meaning of extent in space, you'll find:

confused
• *(KL 4.7.50) Cordelia describes her father as 'still, far wide!'*

wide ADVERB
1 in error
• *(MA 4.1.61) Hero asks Claudio if he is (psychologically, emotionally) well, 'that he doth speak so wide?'*
2 enlarged
• *(Ham 1.3.14) Laertes explains that, as the body grows, the mind 'Grows wide withal'—has more to think about.*

wide-skirted see **skirts**

wide-stretched ADJECTIVE
extensive
• *(H5 2.4.83) Exeter presents Henry's claim to the French throne and 'all wide-stretched honours' belonging to it.*

wife NOUN
as well as its usual meaning of 'spouse', you'll find:
woman
• *(H5 5.Chorus.10) The Chorus describes the English beach full 'with men, with wives, and boys' greeting the return of Henry.*

wight NOUN
person
• *(Oth 2.3.82) Iago sings of King Stephen: 'He was a wight of high renown'.*

wild NOUN
wilderness
• *(MV 3.2.182) Bassanio talks of how a multitude of noises, 'being blent together / Turns to a wild of nothing'.*

will NOUN
as well as meaning 'power to decide', you'll find:
1 desire
• *(RJ 3.5.23) Romeo tells Juliet he has 'more care to stay than will to go'.*
2 lust
• *(Ham 3.4.88) Hamlet is appalled to find that in Gertrude 'reason panders will'—that she is in the service of lust.*

will he, nill he
willy-nilly—like it or not
• *(Ham 5.1.15) The First Gravedigger argues: 'If the man go to this water and drown himself, it is, will he nill he, he goes'.*

win VERB
get the better of
• *(MA 5.1.82) Antonio says of Claudio: 'Win me and wear me'—if he defeats me, he can do what he likes with me.*

wind in the phrase **recover the wind**
(in hunting) go to the windward side, allowing the quarry to scent the hunter
• *(Ham 3.2.331) Hamlet asks Rosencrantz: 'why do you go about to recover the wind of me'.*

› **windy** ADJECTIVE
windward (in hunting, so that the scent of the hunter will travel away from the animal)
• *(TN 3.4.148) Fabian tells Sir Andrew that he keeps 'o' th' windy side of the law'—on the safe side.*

wind VERB
as well as meaning 'turn something in twists', you'll find:
1 manoeuvre into a favourable position
• *(KL 1.2.92) Gloucester asks Edmund, of Edgar, 'Wind me into him'—get yourself into his confidence for me.*
2 make [something] wheel about in a circle
• *(JC 4.1.32) Antony says he teaches his horse 'to fight, / To wind, to stop'.*

wind VERB [also pronounced to rhyme with 'find']
sound
• *(MA 1.1.219) Benedick says he will not have the call of a hunting-horn 'winded in my forehead'—to show he has horns (has an adulterous wife).*
see **cuckold**

› **wind up** VERB
1 occupy
• *(H5 4.1.267) Henry talks of a wretched slave 'Winding up days with toil'.*
2 ready for action
• *(Mac 1.3.35) The Witches conclude: 'the charm's wound up'.*
3 put in order
• *(KL 4.7.16) Cordelia asks the gods to help Lear: 'Th'untuned and jarring sense, O, wind up'.*

windlass NOUN
(in hunting) a circuit made to intercept game
• *(Ham 2.1.65) Polonius advises Reynaldo to deal with Laertes 'With windlasses and assays of bias'—in roundabout or indirect ways, and unfair comments.*

window NOUN
as well as its meaning of 'opening in a wall', you'll find:
shutter (for a window)

- *(JC 3.2.256) A Plebeian calls on others to 'Pluck down forms, windows, anything!'*

› eye's windows
eyelids
- *(RJ 4.1.100) The Friar explains about the effects of his potion: 'the eyes' windows fall'.*

› windowed also spelled **window'd** ADJECTIVE
full of holes
- *(KL 3.4.31) Lear thinks of wretches everywhere, with holes in their clothes: 'You loop'd and window'd raggedness'.*

windring ADJECTIVE
winding
- *(Tem 4.1.128) Iris talks to the nymphs 'of the windring brooks'.*

wink NOUN
as well as meaning 'quick closing and opening of the eye as a signal', you'll find:
1 shutting
- *(Tem 2.1.280) Antonio thinks of killing Gonzalo, putting him 'To the perpetual wink for aye' —closing Gonzalo's eyes for ever.*

2 smallest amount
- *(Tem 2.1.237) Antonio describes the height of Sebastian's hopes: 'even / Ambition cannot pierce a wink beyond'—even a personification of ambition could not see so high.*

wink VERB
1 shut one's eyes
- *(RJ 5.3.294) The Prince addresses Capulet and Montague, regretting that he has been 'winking at your discords'.*

2 fail to look
- *(Mac 1.4.52) Macbeth wants 'The eye wink at the hand'—to not see what his hand might do.*

3 blink
- *(TN 5.1.85) Antonio remarks on the sudden change in Cesario 'While one would wink'—he changed in the blink of an eye.*

4 doze
- *(Tem 2.1.211) Antonio tells Sebastian that he is ignoring an opportunity to seize his fortune: thou 'wink'st / Whiles thou art waking'.*

› wink at VERB
ignore
- *(H5 2.2.54) Henry wonders how one can be merciful towards major crimes if little faults 'Shall not be wink'd at'.*

› wink on VERB
give someone a significant glance
- *(H5 5.2.291) Burgundy tells Henry, regarding Katherine, 'I will wink on her to consent'.*

› winking NOUN
shutting the eyes
- *(Ham 2.2.137) Polonius tells Claudius how he would not have 'given my heart a winking mute and dumb'—shut the eyes of his heart (closed off his feelings) to the meetings between Hamlet and Ophelia.*

wise woman
fortune-teller
- *(TN 3.4.95) Fabian tells Maria that she should take a sample of Malvolio's urine 'to th' wise woman', to find out what is wrong with him.*

When sick or mentally ill, doctors or healers would study a person's urine for indications of how they might be healed.

wit NOUN
Don't read the meaning of 'clever humour' into these senses.

1 good sense
- *(Ham 2.2.90) Polonius observes that 'brevity is the soul of wit'.*

2 mental sharpness
- *(MA 1.1.55) Leonato says Beatrice and Benedick 'never meet but there's a skirmish of wit between them'—they banter with each other.*

3 reasoning
- *(Tem 2.1.13) Sebastian sees Gonzalo 'winding up the watch of his wit'.*

4 cunning plan
- *(TN 1.2.61) Viola asks the Captain to keep knowledge of her plans to himself: 'shape thou thy silence to my wit'.*

5 mind
- *(Ham 1.5.43) The Ghost says that Claudius acted 'With witchcraft of his wit'—with an almost magical ability of his mind.*

6 lively person
- *(H5 3.7.73) Gower predicts how Pistol will boast of the wars among 'foaming bottles and ale-washed wits'.*

› wits or **five wits**
faculties of the mind or body
- *(KL 3.2.67) Lear tells the Fool: 'My wits begin to turn'.*
- *(TN 4.2.82) Feste asks Malvolio: 'how fell you beside your five wits?'*

In Shakespeare's time, the five mental wits were thought to be common sense, imagination, fantasy, estimation, and

a b c d e f g h i j k l m n o p q r s t u v Ww x y z

a b c d e f g h i j k l m n o p q r s t u v **Ww** x y z

memory; the five senses (as today) were sound, vision, touch, smell, taste.

› witty ADJECTIVE
1 intelligent
• *(Oth 2.1.130) Desdemona asks Iago what he thinks of a woman who is 'black and witty'.*
2 cunning
• *(MA 4.2.25) Dogberry describes Conrad as 'A marvellous witty fellow'.*

› unwit VERB
make crazy
• *(Oth 2.3.166) Iago describes the quarrel between Cassio and Montano 'As if some planet had unwitted men'—referring to the astrological belief that the position of planets changed people's moods.*

› witsnapper also spelled **wit-snapper** NOUN
wisecracker
• *(MV 3.5.43) Lorenzo responds to Lancelot: 'what a witsnapper are you!'*

witching ADJECTIVE
witchcraft-practising
• *(Ham 3.2.372) Hamlet reflects on 'the very witching time of night'.*
Witches were said to meet, dance, and make spells at night-time under the moon.

withal ADVERB
1 in addition
• *(JC 2.1.292) Portia says she is a woman, 'but withal / A woman that Lord Brutus took to wife'.*
2 nevertheless
• *(MA 1.2.19) Leonato says he can hardly believe the news that Don Pedro loves Hero, 'But I will acquaint my daughter withal'.*
3 with this
• *(H5 1.2.216) Canterbury tells Henry he needs to take to France (Gallia) only a quarter of his power 'and you withal shall make all Gallia shake'.*

withal PREPOSITION
with
• *(RJ 1.5.114) The Nurse tells Romeo that she nursed the girl (Juliet) 'that you talk'd withal'.*

wither out VERB
make less
• *(MND 1.1.6) Theseus talks of a stepmother 'Long withering out a young man's revenue'—by living for a long time, she spends all his inheritance.*

withers NOUN
ridge between the shoulder-blades of a horse
• *(Ham 3.2.233) Hamlet tells Claudius that a horse with ill-fitting tack (harness, reins, saddle) might be in pain, but 'our withers are unwrung'—our shoulders are unchafed because we're innocent of wrong-doing—aren't we?*

within see STAGE DIRECTIONS, p.285

Withold, Saint also spelled **Swithold**
a saint sometimes mentioned in Elizabethan literature as a defender against harms
• *(KL 3.4.113) Poor Tom recites: 'Swithold footed thrice the wold'—the saint walked around the English Downs three times.*

without PREPOSITION
as well as meaning 'not having', you'll find:
outside (of)
• *(RJ 3.3.17) Romeo bemoans his banishment: 'There is no world without Verona walls'.*

witness NOUN
evidence
• *(Mac 2.2.50) Lady Macbeth tells her husband to 'wash this filthy witness from your hand' —Duncan's blood.*

witness VERB
provide evidence
• *(MND 5.1.25) Hippolyta says the lovers' agreement about the night's events 'More witnesseth than fancy's images'—provides so much evidence that what happened must be more than just a dream.*

woe see REGRETTING, p.250

wold also appears as **'old** NOUN
rolling hills
• *(KL 3.4.113) Poor Tom recites: 'Swithold footed thrice the wold'—St Withold walked around the downs three times.*

wolvish-ravening ADJECTIVE
devouring like a wolf
• *(RJ 3.2.76) Juliet describes Romeo as a 'wolvish-ravening lamb!'—a lamb who devours like a wolf.*

womby ADJECTIVE
cavernous
• *(H5 2.4.125) Exeter warns the French Dauphin that even the 'caves and womby vaultages of France' will rebuke him for his mockery of Henry.*

wonder NOUN
as well as meanings to do with 'marvelling', you'll find:
1 astonishment, shock
• *(MA 4.1.238) The Friar says the news of Hero's death 'Will quench the wonder of her infamy'.*
2 special power
• *(Oth 3.4.95) Desdemona believes there must be*

'some wonder in this handkerchief' to make Othello behave in the way he does.

3 calamity, event that causes distress

• *(Ham 5.2.356) Horatio tells Fortinbras he need look no further if he wants to see 'woe and wonder'.*

4 astonishing course of events

• *(Ham 4.5.88) Claudius says Laertes 'Feeds on this wonder'.*

The Second Quarto text has 'this wonder'. The First Folio has 'his wonder' (which would mean 'his grief').

wonder VERB

1 be astonished

• *(MA 3.3.107) Conrad is amazed that villainy can be so profitable: 'I wonder at it'.*

2 stare in curiosity

• *(TN 1.5.184) Olivia tells Cesario that 'I ... allowed your approach rather to wonder at you than to hear you'—more to stare at you than to listen to you.*

› **wondered** also spelled **wonder'd** ADJECTIVE
performing amazing feats (wonders)

• *(Tem 4.1.123) Ferdinand calls Prospero: 'So rare a wonder'd father'.*

› **wonderful** ADJECTIVE
astonishing (full of wonder)

• *(JC 1.3.14) Cicero asks Casca about the storm: 'saw you anything more wonderful?'*

› **wonder-wounded** ADJECTIVE
awestruck

• *(Ham 5.1.241) Hamlet says Laertes' grief is so huge it makes the stars 'stand / Like wonder-wounded hearers'—makes them appear to stop moving, in awe.*

wont VERB [pronounced wohnt]

accustomed

• *(MND 4.1.70) Oberon takes the spell away from Titania: 'Be as thou wast wont to be'.*

wont NOUN [pronounced wohnt]

habit

• *(Ham 1.4.6) Horatio says it is near the time 'Wherein the spirit held his wont to walk'.*

› **wonted** ADJECTIVE
usual

• *(Ham 3.1.41) Gertrude hopes Ophelia will bring Hamlet 'to his wonted way again'.*

› **unwonted** ADJECTIVE
unusual

• *(Tem 1.2.498) Miranda apologizes to Ferdinand for Prospero's attitude: 'This is unwonted / Which now came from him'.*

wood ADJECTIVE

furious

• *(MND 2.1.192) Demetrius, in the forest, says he is 'wood within this wood / Because I cannot meet my Hermia'.*

woodbine NOUN

1 honeysuckle

• *(MA 3.1.30) Ursula says Beatrice 'Is couched in the woodbine coverture'—hiding in the honeysuckle-covered shelter.*

2 bindweed

• *(MND 4.1.41) Titania winds Bottom in her arms: 'So doth the woodbine the sweet honeysuckle / Gently entwist'.*

woodcock NOUN

type of game bird, thought to be easily snared in a gin (trap)

• *(TN 2.5.77) Fabian says Malvolio (calling him a woodcock) has seen the letter they've left out for him: 'Now is the woodcock near the gin'.*

wooingly ADVERB

enticingly

• *(Mac 1.6.6) Banquo says, of Macbeth's castle, that 'the heaven's breath / Smells wooingly here'.*

woollen in the phrase **lie in the woollen**

sleep in rough blankets

• *(MA 2.1.26) Beatrice says she would 'rather lie in the woollen' than have a husband with a beard.*

word NOUN

as well as meaning a 'meaningful unit of speech or writing', you'll find:

saying

• *(Ham 4.5.104) A Messenger says antiquity and custom are 'The ratifiers and props of every word'.*

› **words** NOUN
talk

• *(Mac 3.6.21) Lennox says he has heard 'from broad words' that Macduff lives in disgrace —from talk everywhere.*

› **at a word**

1 once and for all

• *(MA 2.1.104) Masked Antonio denies he is really Antonio: 'At a word, I am not'.*

2 without any fuss

• *(JC 1.2.266) Casca reflects on the chance he had to kill Caesar 'at a word'.*

work past form **wrought** VERB

as well as meanings to do with 'effortful activity', you'll find:

1 bring about

• *(RJ 5.3.245) The Friar reports the effect of the*

potion on Juliet: 'it wrought on her / The form of death'.
2 affect
• *(Tem 4.1.144) Ferdinand observes Prospero in 'some passion / That works him strongly'.*
3 act upon
• *(H5 Prologue 18) The Chorus asks the audience to let the players 'On your imaginary forces work' —get your imaginations working.*
4 behave
• *(Ham 4.7.20) Claudius describes the common people who 'Work like the spring that turneth wood to stone'.*
The spring refers to sources of limestone water that covers wood with a hard layer of lime. Because the people love Hamlet (says Claudius), they don't see the harm he does, but protect him, covering up his faults and turning them into virtues.
5 persuade
• *(JC 1.2.163) Brutus can guess what Cassius 'would work me to'.*
6 plot
• *(Mac 3.1.83) Macbeth reminds the Murderers of how they were abused by Banquo—'the instruments, / Who wrought with them'—the methods he used to afflict them, and who plotted to use them.*
7 manipulate
• *(JC 1.2.307) Cassius reflects on how Brutus' 'honourable mettle may be wrought / From that it is dispos'd'—his loyal nature may be twisted out of its natural inclination.*

work NOUN
needlework
• *(Oth 3.4.174) Cassio asks Bianca to copy the embroidery on a handkerchief: 'Take me this work out'.*

> **works** NOUN
> fortifications
> • *(Oth 3.2.3) Othello says he will be 'walking on the works'.*

> **in the working**
> while being made
> • *(Ham 2.1.41) Polonius says Reynaldo can mention Laertes' faults as 'a thing a little soil'd i'th' working'—the result of worldly contact (as hardly-noticed faults appear in manufacturing).*

world in the phrase **go to the world**
a proverbial expression for getting married
• *(MA 2.1.295) Beatrice, after hearing that Hero and Claudio are to be married, says 'Thus goes every one to the world but I'—getting married is the way of the world for everybody except me.*

world in the phrase **it is a world**
it's a great thing
• *(MA 3.5.34) Dogberry comments on Verges' remarks: 'it is a world to see'.*

worm NOUN
as well as meaning the 'soil-living animal', you'll find:
1 large snake (as opposed to an adder, a smaller snake)
• *(MND 3.2.71) Hermia accuses Demetrius of killing Lysander: 'Could not a worm, an adder do so much?'*
2 bug
• *(TN 2.4.109) Cesario tells Orsino of a woman whose concealment of her love ate away her beauty, 'like a worm i' th' bud'—like an insect that eats a flower.*

wormwood NOUN
1 absinthe plant (known for its bitter taste)
• *(RJ 1.3.27) The Nurse describes weaning Juliet: 'I had then laid wormwood to my dug'—put it on my nipple to stop the baby wanting milk.*
2 bitterness
• *(Ham 3.2.173) Hamlet says, of the Player Queen's remarks, 'That's wormwood'.*

worried ADJECTIVE
savaged
• *(H5 1.2.219) Canterbury says, of the Scots (the dog), that if the English 'Cannot defend our own doors from the dog, / Let us be worried'.*

worser ADJECTIVE
evil
• *(KL 4.6.213) Gloucester asks the gods: 'Let not my worser spirit tempt me again' to commit suicide (considered to be a grave sin).*

worsted ADJECTIVE
made of a cheap woollen fabric
• *(KL 2.2.15) Kent calls Oswald a 'filthy worsted-stocking knave'—not a gentleman (who would wear silk stockings).*

worthy VERB
give honour to
• *(KL 2.2.117) Oswald says when Kent tripped him up in front of the King, he put on a show of bravery 'That worthied him'—that gave him honour.*

wot VERB
know
• *(RJ 3.2.139) The Nurse tells Juliet, of Romeo: 'I wot well where he is'.*

woundless ADJECTIVE
invulnerable
• *(Ham 4.1.44) Claudius takes the idea of arrows*

being shot at him, and hopes that any slanders directed at him will miss him 'And hit the woundless air'.

wrack NOUN

1 wreck

• *(Tem 1.2.26) Prospero comforts Miranda about 'The direful spectacle of the wrack'—the terrible image of the shipwreck she saw.*

2 destruction

• *(Mac 1.3.113) Angus says that the traitor Cawdor 'labour'd / In his country's wrack'—worked to betray and destroy his own country.*

wrack VERB

1 wreck

• *(MV 3.1.3) Salarino reports that Antonio has a ship filled with riches 'wracked on the Narrow Seas'.*

2 destroy (psychologically, emotionally)

• *(Ham 2.1.113) Polonius explains to Ophelia that he feared Hamlet 'did but trifle / And meant to wrack thee'.*

Some editions replace 'wrack' with 'wreck' in all these uses.

wrest VERB

distort

• *(H5 1.2.14) Henry hopes Canterbury will not 'fashion, wrest, or bow' his interpretation of the claim to the French throne.*

wring VERB

1 struggle

• *(MA 5.1.28) Leonato knows that it is wise to advise patience 'To those that wring under the load of sorrow'.*

2 force tears from

• *(Tem 1.2.135) Miranda says Prospero's account of her crying as a child makes her cry again—'a hint / That wrings mine eyes to't'.*

› **wringing** NOUN

aches and pains

• *(H5 4.1.223) Henry reflects on being 'Subject to the breath of every fool, whose sense / No more can feel but his own wringing'—people who can observe or complain only about their own troubles.*

› **unwrung** ADJECTIVE

not rubbed sore

• *(Ham 3.2.233) Hamlet tells Claudius that a horse with ill-fitting tack (saddle, rein, harness) might be in pain, but 'our withers are unwrung'—the moral of the play they're watching doesn't hurt their shoulders (withers) because they are all innocent.*

writ NOUN

1 document

• *(Ham 5.2.51) Hamlet recounts how he replaced Claudius' letter to England, folding it in the form (the same way) as the first: 'Folded the writ up in the form of th'other'.*

2 written authority

• *(KL 5.3.244) Edmund says: 'my writ / Is on the life of Lear and on Cordelia'—a warrant for their execution.*

3 the Bible

• *(Oth 3.3.325) Iago reflects on how jealousy can make unimportant things seem like 'proofs of holy writ'.*

4 writing that follows traditional rules of drama

• *(Ham 2.2.391) Polonius describes the players as the best men 'For the law of writ'.*

› **written** ADJECTIVE

as well as meaning 'inscribed (as on paper)', you'll find:

engraved

• *(Mac 5.3.43) Macbeth asks the Doctor if he can get rid of 'the written troubles of the brain'—troubles that are deeply and permanently ingrained.*

wrong NOUN

as well as meaning 'injustice', you'll find:

1 dishonour

• *(Tem 1.2.444) Prospero says to Ferdinand: 'I fear you have done yourself some wrong'—in claiming to be King of Naples.*

2 insult

• *(MND 3.2.361) Oberon tells Puck to 'stir Demetrius up with bitter wrong'.*

3 wrongful gain

• *(H5 1.2.27) Henry recognizes the sin of a war caused by anyone 'whose wrongs give edge unto the swords'—starting a war for the wrong reasons (and so giving a sharp edge to unused swords in a time of peace).*

wroth NOUN

misfortune, grief

• *(MV 2.9.77) Arragon says he will keep his oath, 'Patiently to bear my wroth'—he will bear his grief without complaint.*

wrought see **work**

wry-necked also spelled **-neck'd** ADJECTIVE

having a crooked neck (from playing a musical instrument)

• *(MV 2.5.29) Shylock tells Jessica not to look out at 'the vile squealing of the wry-neck'd fife'—not to listen to someone playing the flute to serenade her.*

Yorick

Yorick was old King Hamlet's jester who used to entertain the young Prince Hamlet. In the play, Hamlet discovers his old play-fellow's skull in a grave, holds it in his hands, and contemplates life – an image that has become one of the most famous in English theatre.

a b c d e f g h i j k l m n o p q r s t u v w x **Yy** z

yard NOUN
measuring-rod (a long piece of wood, like a metre-stick, used by a tailor)
• *(RJ 1.2.39) A Servant reflects that 'the shoemaker should meddle with his yard'—he's mixing up the crafts of a cobbler and a tailor (and probably making a sexual pun).*

yard NOUN
see SHIPS, p.168

yare ADVERB [pronounced yair]
quickly
• *(Tem 1.1.5) The Boatswain shouts at his Mariners: 'Yare, yare!'*

yare ADJECTIVE
1 ready for sea
• *(Tem 5.1.224) The Boatswain says his ship 'Is tight and yare'.*
2 quick
• *(TN 3.4.203) Sir Toby advises Cesario: 'be yare in thy preparation'.*

› **yarely** ADVERB
quickly
• *(Tem 1.1.3) The Master calls to the Boatswain: 'Fall to't, yarely, or we run ourselves aground'.*

yaw VERB
move unsteadily
• *(Ham 5.2.112) Hamlet says, of Laertes, that people would 'yaw neither, in respect of his quick sail' —would falter in trying to keep up with him.*

yawn VERB
open wide
• *(JC 2.2.18) Calpurnia tells Caesar that 'graves have yawn'd and yielded up their dead'.*

yearn VERB
⚠ *Don't read in the meaning of 'long for' something.*
grieve
• *(H5 4.3.26) Henry says he is not concerned with outward things: 'It yearns me not if men my garments wear'.*

yeasty also spelled **yesty** ADJECTIVE
1 superficial
• *(Ham 5.2.178) Hamlet describes Osric as one who carries on 'a kind of yeasty collection'—a frothy conversation.*
2 foaming
• *(Mac 4.1.52) Macbeth conjures the Witches to answer his question, 'though the yeasty waves / Confound and swallow navigation up'.*

yeoman **see OCCUPATIONS, p.166**

yeoman's service
good and faithful service
• *(Ham 5.2.36) Hamlet says his good handwriting 'did me yeoman's service', as he could copy the writing style of Claudius' letter accurately.*

yerk VERB
thrust (with a weapon)
• *(Oth 1.2.5) Iago says, of Roderigo, 'Nine or ten times / I had thought to have yerk'd him here, under the ribs'—thrust at him with my sword.*

yesternight NOUN
last night
• *(MA 4.1.82) Claudio asks Hero: 'What man was he talk'd with you yesternight?'*

yielder NOUN
someone who gives up
• *(MND 3.2.30) Puck describes the way the bushes pull at the frightened rustics' clothes while they are running away: 'from yielders all things catch'—everything catches at the timid.*

› **yielding** NOUN
consent
• *(RJ 2.2.105) Juliet asks Romeo to 'not impute this yielding to light love'.*

yoke NOUN
servitude (literally, a piece of wood that harnesses

an animal to make it work)

• *(JC 1.3.84) Cassius tells Casca: 'Our yoke and sufferance show us womanish'.*

› **yoked** ADJECTIVE
wedded

• *(Oth 4.1.66) Iago assures Othello: 'Think every bearded fellow that's but yoked / May draw with you'—all married men share your situation and think as you do.*

› **yoke-devil** NOUN
associate in evil

• *(H5 2.2.103) Henry says treason and murder are 'two yoke-devils sworn to either's purpose'—both crimes vow to support each other.*

› **yoke-fellow** NOUN
comrade

• *(H5 2.3.46) Pistol encourages his companions: 'Yoke-fellows in arms, / let us to France'.*

› **unyoke** VERB
cease labouring

• *(Ham 5.1.49) The First Gravedigger asks his companion to answer his riddle: 'tell me that and unyoke'—tell me and stop digging.*

yond ADVERB
over there

• *(Tem 1.2.410) Prospero asks Miranda: 'say what thou seest yond'.*

young days in the phrase **of so young days**
from such an early age

• *(Ham 2.2.11) Claudius explains to Rosencrantz and Guildenstern why they are visiting Hamlet, 'being of so young days brought up with him'.*

younger NOUN
younger son

• *(MV 2.6.15) Gratiano describes a ship leaving her home port with all flags flying, 'like a younger or a prodigal' embarking on a journey.*

Zany

A zany was a Fool or a jester's assistant, a bit like a clown. A Fool was paid to entertain the nobility. Over the course of his writing career, Shakespeare's 'silly-Clownish' characters (like Dogberry in Much Ado About Nothing) became much more 'wise-Foolish' (like Feste in Twelfth Night).

zany NOUN
comic assistant

• *(TN 1.5.81) Malvolio describes fools like Feste as being 'no better than the fools' zanies'.*

zenith NOUN
highest point (in someone's fortune)

• *(Tem 1.2.181) Prospero knows his 'zenith doth depend upon / A most auspicious star'- good luck depends on the position of a favourable star (a belief from astrology).*

zir NOUN
a dialect form of 'sir'

• *(KL 4.6.230) Edgar tells Oswald he will not let go of Gloucester's arm: 'Chill not let go, zir'.*

zo ADVERB
a dialect form of 'so'

• *(KL 4.6.234) Edgar tells Oswald he would never have lived so long if he had been scared of him: 'twould not ha' bin zo long'.*

zone in the phrase **burning zone** see COSMOS, p.174

zounds see SWEARING, p.298

zwaggered also spelled **zwagger'd** VERB
a dialect form of 'swaggered'—using bullying or blustering language

• *(KL 4.6.233) Edgar tells Oswald he is not scared of his bullying manner: 'And 'chud ha' bin zwagger'd out of my life'—if I was, I would've been bullied out of my life long ago.*

SHAKESPEAREAN GRAMMAR

Most of the time, English grammar in the period when Shakespeare was writing was exactly the same as it is now, but you'll notice some differences compared to the Standard English of today. (Some of these usages can still be heard in regional dialects and in non-standard English.) We've chosen the examples below to show the kind of thing to look out for.

Verb endings

After *he*, *she* and *it*, you sometimes find the old *-eth* ending, rather than *-s*. Shakespeare uses this especially when he wants an extra syllable to make a verb fit into the rhythm of a line.

- *(KL 3.2.77) Though the rain it raineth every day.*
- *(MND 1.1.199) The more I love, the more he hateth me.*

After *thou*, you will find the *-est* ending, often shortened to *'st*:

- *(RJ 2.2.85) Thou knowest the mask of night is on my face.*
- *(Mac 2.1.42) Thou marshall'st me the way that I was going.*

Verb forms

Several common verbs have a different form:

SHAKESPEARE'S USE	TODAY WE WOULD SAY
thou art, beest, wast, wert	you are, were
thou hast, hadst; he hath	you have, had; he has
thou dost, didst, didest; he doth	you do, did; he does
thou canst	you can
thou mayst	you may
thou shalt, thou's	you shall
thou shouldst	you should
thou wilt	you will
thou wouldst	you would
woo't	would you

Past tenses

Some verbs have a different form when referring to past time:

SHAKESPEARE'S USE	TODAY WE WOULD SAY
bended *(Ham 2.1.100)*	bent
bidden *(MA 3.3.30)*	bid
create *(MND 5.1.388)*	created
digged *(Ham 5.1.34)*	dug
durst *(MND 2.2.82)*	dared
fretten *(MV 4.1.77)*	fretted
holp *(Mac 1.6.24)*	helped
mistook *(TN 5.1.250)*	mistaken
shore *(Oth 5.2.205)*	sheared
spake *(Ham 3.1.163)*	spoke
stricken *(JC 2.1.192)*	struck
well-foughten *(H5 4.6.18)*	well-fought

Singulars and plurals

Some nouns are used as plurals which are now singular:

SHAKESPEARE'S USE	TODAY WE WOULD SAY
behaviours *(JC 1.2.42)*	behaviour
companies *(Ham 2.2:14)*	company
funerals *(JC 5.3.105)*	funeral
moneys *(MV 1.3.103)*	money
revenges *(Mac 5.2.3)*	revenge

Some nouns are used as singular which are now plural:

SHAKESPEARE'S USE	TODAY WE WOULD SAY
our nuptial *(MND 1.1.125)*	our nuptials
musty victual *(MA 1.1.44)*	musty victuals

Comparisons

SHAKESPEARE'S USE	TODAY WE WOULD SAY
more nearer	nearer
most unkindest	unkindest or most unkind
oftener	more often
perfectest	most perfect

'An' for 'a'

SHAKESPEARE'S USE	TODAY WE WOULD SAY
an usurer	a usurer
an universal shout	a universal shout
an hair	a hair
an habit	a habit

Two negative words together

SHAKESPEARE'S USE	TODAY WE WOULD SAY
nothing neither	nothing either *or* anything neither
never none	never shall anyone *or* none shall ever

Using 'me' to mean 'for me'

SHAKESPEARE'S USE	TODAY WE WOULD SAY
(Ham 2.1.7) Polonius asks Reynaldo: 'Inquire me first what Danskers are in Paris'	inquire for me
(MND 4.1.11) Bottom asks Cobweb: 'kill me a red-hipped humble-bee'	kill for me

Word order

Among the everyday constructions that have a different word-order, you'll find:

SHAKESPEARE'S USE	TODAY WE WOULD SAY
I like not	I do not like
Good my lord	My good lord

Word-order often changes to suit the rhythm of a line:

SHAKESPEARE'S USE	TODAY WE WOULD SAY
(RJ 1.4.73) Then dreams he of another benefice	Then he dreams

THOU AND YOU

Thou-forms are *thou, thee, thy, thine, thyself.*
You-forms are *you, your, yours, yourself, yourselves.*

People of the 'upper class' normally would use *you*-forms to each other; those from the 'lower class' used *thou*-forms to each other.

- *(MV 1.1.73) Gratiano addresses Antonio: 'You look not well'.*
- *(Mac 3.1.1) One Murderer greets another: 'But who did bid thee join with us?'*

You-forms would also be used by people considered low down on the social scale to people who were considered higher up—such as servants to masters and children to parents; *thou*-forms would be used in return.

- *(Tem 1.2.54) Prospero explains to Miranda: 'Thy father was the Duke of Milan'.*
- *(Tem 1.2.55) Miranda replies: 'Sir, are you not my father?'*

You-forms would be used by all when talking to more than one person:

- *(H5 3.1.17) Henry addresses his soldiers: 'On, on, you noble English'.*
- *(MND 1.2.14) Bottom tells his players: 'Masters, spread yourselves'.*

People of the 'lower class' would also use *you*-forms when on official business

- *(MND 1.2.13) Bottom tells Quince: 'call forth your actors by the scroll'.*

or when *you* means 'one':

- *(MND 3.1.56) Snout says to everyone: 'You can never bring in a wall'.*

But people of the 'upper class' would use *thou*-forms when talking to a supernatural being,

- *(JC 4.3.279) Brutus sees a vision: 'Art thou some god, some angel, or some devil'.*

when addressing a country,

- *(Mac 4.3.105) Macduff cries to Scotland: 'When shalt thou see thy wholesome days again'.*

at times of special friendship or intimacy,

- *(RJ 2.2.60) Juliet asks: 'Art thou not Romeo, and a Montague?'*

at times of high emotion,

- *(Oth 4.2.37) Othello addresses Desdemona: 'Swear thou art honest'.*

and when thinking of someone who is absent:

- *(MA 3.1.111) Beatrice, alone: 'Benedick, love on. I will requite thee' (this speech is the only time in the play she talks to him using* thou-*forms).*

Sometimes the *thou*-form is friendly and loving:

- *(MND 3.1.131) Titania to Bottom: 'Thou art as wise as thou art beautiful'.*

Sometimes the *thou*-form is insulting and angry:

- *(TN 3.2.39) Sir Toby tells Sir Andrew how to write to Cesario: 'If thou thou'st him some thrice, it shall not be amiss'.*

»

Changing the pronoun always signals a change in attitude or a difference in relationship from *thou*-form to *you*-form

- *(MA 4.1.321) Benedick opens his heart to Beatrice: 'By this hand, I love thee'.*
- *(MA 4.1.326) Benedick becomes business-like: 'I will kiss your hand, and so I leave you'.*

- *(Ham 1.1.7) Barnardo is being friendly: 'Get thee to bed, Francisco'.*
- *(Ham 1.1.10) Barnardo is being a soldier: 'Have you had quiet guard?'*

from *you*-form to *thou*-form

- *(KL 1.1.84) Lear asks Cordelia politely: 'what can you say'.*
- *(KL 1.1.107) Lear gets angry with Cordelia: 'thy truth then be thy dower'.*

- *(MV 2.2.81) Gobbo isn't sure Lancelot is his son: 'I cannot think you are my son'.*
- *(MV 2.2.86) Gobbo then realises he is: 'thou art mine own flesh and blood'.*

SHAKESPEAREAN PRONUNCIATION

When you read a Shakespeare play, you see many words appearing with apostrophes. This can look odd on the page, so remember that they are simply ways of showing the speed and rhythm of everyday speech. On this page we show some of the most commonly used shortened word forms.

SHORT FORM	FULL FORM	EXAMPLE
'a, a	he	*(RJ 1.3.41)* 'A was a merry man
e'en	even	*(Ham 5.1.184)* E'en so
'em	them	*(Tem 5.1.49)* let 'em forth
gi'	give	*(RJ 1.2.57)* God gi' good-e'en
ha'	have	*(Ham 5.1.21)* will you ha' the truth on't
i'	in	*(KL 2.4.195)* How came my man i'th'stocks?
ne'er	never	*(RJ 1.5.52)* I ne'er saw true beauty
o'	of	*(H5 2.3.12)* the turning o'the tide
o'	on	*(TN 1.3.38)* turn o' th' toe
o'er	over	*(MND 3.2.130)* Will you give her o'er?'
'r	our	*(MA 3.3.77)* By'r Lady, I think it be so
's	us	*(Mac 1.3.124)* to betray's
's	his	*(TN 3.4.13)* the man is tainted in's wits
-'st	-est	*(MV 3.2.249)* a few of the unpleasant'st words
-'st	-est	*(JC 2.1.48)* Brutus, thou sleep'st
't	it (after a word)	*(Ham 1.5.112)* I have sworn't
't	it (before a word)	*(MND 5.1.347)* 'tis almost fairy time
t'	to	*(Mac 4.3.17)* T'appease an angry god
ta'en	taken	*(TN 3.3.28)* were I ta'en here
th'	thou	*(Mac 1.3.11)* Th'art kind
th'	the	*(H5 1.2.3)* call in th'ambassador
whoe'er	whoever	*(Oth 1.3.65)* Whoe'er he be
wi'	with	*(Tem 1.1.60)* Let's all sink wi'th' king
y'	you	*(TN 3.1.96)* Y'are servant to the Count Orsino

Original pronunciation

Pronunciation has changed in several ways over the past 400 years. You notice it especially when pairs of lines don't rhyme properly. Here are some examples where you have to use the old pronunciation if you want the lines to rhyme:

MND 3.2.407	Thou coward, art thou bragging to the stars, Telling the bushes that thou look'st for wars	*wars* was pronounced like *stars*
Mac 4.1.6	Toad, that under cold stone Days and nights has thirty-one	*one* was pronounced like *stone*
Ham 3.2.174	The instances that second marriage move Are base respects of thrift, but none of love	*move* was pronounced like *love*
MA 5.3.3	Done to death by slanderous tongues, ... Death, in guerdon of her wrongs	*tongues* was pronounced like *wrongs*
TN 2.4.59	On my black coffin let there be strewn... My poor corpse, where my bones shall be thrown	*strewn* was pronounced like *thrown*
RJ 1.2.20	This night I hold an old accustom'd feast, Whereto I have invited many a guest	*feast* was pronounced like *guest*

Word stress

Sometimes the stress pattern of a word is different from today. You can tell this from the way the word needs to be pronounced within the rhythm of a line. Knowing that Shakespeare's poetic lines tended to use iambic pentameter (see Introduction) will help you see the pronunciation of words like these:

	SHAKESPEARE'S STRESS	TODAY WE SAY
Ham 1.4.47	Why thy canonized bones, hearsed in death	canonized
Tem 3.2.93	He has brave utensils, for so he calls them	utensils
RJ 3.3.98	My conceal'd lady to our cancell'd love	concealed
MND 5.1.8	Are of imagination all compact	compact
H5 5.2.82	Pass our accept and peremptory answer	peremptory

SHAKESPEARE'S FRENCH

Here are some of the French words and phrases used by Shakespeare in his plays. The meanings are given in English to help you.

Twelfth Night

LINE	FRENCH	ENGLISH
1.3.82	Pourquoi	Why
3.1.68	Dieu vous garde, monsieur	God keep you, sir
3.1.69	Et vous aussi, votre serviteur	And you too, at your service

Romeo and Juliet

LINE	FRENCH	ENGLISH
2.4.43	bon jour	good day

Henry V

All of Act 3 Scene 5 in *Henry V* in written in French. All the lines of that scene are given below with English translations to help you.

LINE	FRENCH	ENGLISH
3.5.1	Alice, tu as été en Angleterre, et tu bien parles le langage.	Alice, you have been in England, and you speak the language well.
3.5.2	Un peu, madame.	A little, ma'am.
3.5.3	Je te prie, m'enseignez.	I beg you, teach me.
3.5.3	Il faut que j'apprenne à parler.	I need to learn to speak it.
3.5.4	Comment appelez-vous la main en anglais?	What do you call the hand in English?
3.5.5	La main. Elle est appelée de hand	The hand. It is called 'the hand'.
3.5.6	De hand. Et les doigts?	'The hand'. And the fingers?
3.5.7	Les doigts, ma foi, j'ai oublié les doigts, mais je me souviendrai les doigts.	The fingers, gosh, I've forgotten the fingers, but I'll remember the fingers.
3.5.8	Je pense qu'ils sont appelés de fingres. Oui, de fingres.	I think they are called 'the fingers'. Yes, 'the fingers'.
3.5.10	Je pense que je suis le bon écolier.	I think I am a good student.
3.5.11	J'ai gagné deux mots d'anglais vitement.	I've learned two words of English quickly.
3.5.12	Comment appelez-vous les ongles?	What do you call the nails?
3.5.13	Les ongles, nous les appelons de nails.	The nails, we call them 'the nails'.
3.5.14	Écoutez! Dites-moi si je parle bien: de hand, de fingres, et de nails.	Listen! Tell me if `I speak correctly: 'the hand', 'the fingers', and 'the nails'.
3.5.16	C'est bien dit, madame.	That's well spoken, ma'am.
3.5.16	Il est fort bon anglais.	It is very good English.
3.5.17	Dites-moi l'anglais pour le bras.	Tell me the English for the arm.
3.5.19	Et le coude.	And the elbow.
3.5.21	Je m'en fais la répétition de tous les mots que vous m'avez appris dès à présent.	I'm going to repeat all the words that you have taught me up to now.
3.5.23	Il est trop difficile, madame, comme je pense.	It is too difficult, ma'am, as I think,
3.5.24	Excusez-moi, Alice. Écoutez.	Not at all, Alice. Listen.
3.5.27	O Seigneur Dieu, j m'en oublié d'elbow.	O Lord God, I've forgotten 'the elbow'.
3.5.27	Comment appelez-vous le col?	What do you call the neck?
3.5.30	Et le menton?	And the chin?
3.5.33	Oui. Sauf votre honneur, en vérité vous prononcez les mots aussi droits que les natifs d'Angleterre.	Yes. if it please your honour, you really pronounce the words as well as the natives of England.
3.5.35	Je ne doute point d'apprendre, par la grâce de Dieu, et en peu de temps.	I've no doubt at all that I'll learn, with God's help, and very quickly.
3.5.36	N'avez-vous pas déjà oublié ce que je vous ai enseigné?	Haven't you already forgotten what I've taught you?
3.5.37	Non, et je réciterai à vous promptment.	No, and I'll recite to you right now.
3.5.42	Sauf votre honneur, de elbow.	If it please your honour, 'the elbow'
3.5.43	Ainsi dis-je.	That's what I said.
3.5.43	Comment appelez-vous les pieds et la robe?	What do you call the feet and the gown?
3.5.45	De foot, madame, et de count.	The words in Alice's pronunciation remind her of the two rudest words in French, foutre and con.

LINE	FRENCH	ENGLISH
3.5.46	O Seigneur Dieu, ils sont les mots de son mauvais, corruptible, gros, et impudique, et non pour les dames d'honneur d'user!	O Lord God, they are words with a wicked, corrupting, obscene, and rude sound, and not for ladies of honour to use!
3.5.48	Je ne voudrais prononcer ces mots devant les seigneurs de France pour tout le monde! Foh!	I wouldn't like to speak these words in front of the gentlemen of France for all the world! Ugh!
3.5.50	Néanmoins, je réciterai une autre fois ma leçon ensemble.	Nevertheless, I will recite my lesson once again all together.
3.5.55	C'est assez pour une fois.	That's enough for one time.
3.5.55	Allon-nous à dîner.	Let's go to dinner.
3.6.5	O Dieu vivant!	O living God!
3.6.11	Mort de ma vie	Death of my life
3.6.15	Dieu de batailles	God of battles
3.8.12	Ça, ha! or Ch'ha!	That one, ha! or a horse's neigh
3.8.14	le cheval volant ... qui a les narines de feu	the flying horse ... which has nostrils of fire
3.8.60	Le chien est retourné à son propre vomissement, et la truie lavée au bourbier.	The dog has returned to its own vomit, and the washed sow to its wallowing. [a biblical quotation]
4.1.35	Qui vous là? [he means Qui va là?]	Who you there? [Who goes there?]
4.1.48	Harry le roi.	Harry the king.
4.2.2	Montez à cheval!	Get on your horse!
4.2.4	Via les eaux et terres!	Go across water and land!
4.2.5	Rien puis l'air et feu?	Not air and fire, then?
4.2.6	Cieux	Heavens
4.4.2	Je pense que vous êtes le gentilhomme de bon qualité.	I think you are a gentleman of high rank.
4.4.5	O Seigneur Dieu!	O Lord God!
4.4.10	Oh, prenez miséricorde!	Oh, be merciful!
4.4.10	Ayez pitié de moi!	Take pity on me!
4.4.14	Est-il impossible d'échapper la force de ton bras?	Is it impossible to escape the power of your arm?
4.4.17	Oh, pardonnez-moi!	Oh, pardon me!
4.4.20	Écoutez. Comment êtes-vous appelé?	Listen. What's your name?
4.4.21	Monsieur le Fer.	Mr Fer. [fer = iron]
4.4.27	Que dit-il, monsieur?	What does he say, sir?
4.4.28	Il me commande à vous dire que vous faites-vous prêt, car ce soldat ici est disposé tout à cette heure de couper votre gorge.	He orders me to tell you that you should make yourself ready to die, because this here soldier is inclined to cut your throat right now.
4.4.31	Oui, coupe la gorge, par ma foi.	Yes, cut the throat, by my faith.
4.4.34	Je vous supplie, pour l'amour de Dieu, me pardonner!	I beg you, for the love of God, pardon me!
4.4.35	Je suis le gentilhomme de bonne maison.	I am a gentleman from a good family.
4.4.36	Gardez ma vie, et je vous donnerai deux cents écus.	Save my life, and I will give you two hundred crowns.
4.4.42	Petit monsieur, que dit-il?	Little gentleman, what does he say?

LINE	FRENCH	ENGLISH
4.4.43	Encore qu'il est contre son jurement de pardonner aucun prisonnier, néanmoins, pour les écus que vous l'ayez promis, il est content à vous donner la liberté, le franchisement.	Although it is against his oath to have mercy on any prisoner, nevertheless, for the crowns that you've promised him, he is happy to give you liberty, freedom.
4.4.47	Sur mes genoux je vous donne mille remerciements, et je m'estime heureux que je suis tombé entre les mains d'un chevalier – je pense le plus brave, vaillant, et tres distingué seigneur d'Angleterre.	On my knees I give you a thousand thanks, and I count myself fortunate that I have fallen into the hands of a gentleman – I think the bravest, most valiant, and very distinguished lord of England.
4.4.57	Suivez-vous le grand capitaine.	Follow the great captain.
4.5.1	O diable!	Oh the devil!
4.5.2	O Seigneur! Le jour est perdu, tout est perdu!	O Lord! The day is lost, all is lost.
4.5.3	Mort de ma vie	Death of my life
4.5.6	O méchante fortune!	O evil chance!
5.2.107	Pardonnez-moi	Excuse me
5.2.110	Que dit-il - que je suis semblable à les anges?	What does he say – that I am like the angels?
5.2.111	Oui, vraiment, sauf votre grâce, ainsi dit-il.	Yes, indeed, begging your grace's pardon, that is what he says.
5.2.114	O bon Dieu, les langues des hommes sont pleines de tromperies!	O good God, the tongues of men are full of deceits!
5.2.129	Sauf votre honneur	Saving your grace
5.2.165	ennemi	enemy
5.2.176	Je quand sur le possession de France, et quand vous avez le possession de moi	I when upon possession of France, and when you have possession of me
5.2.178	Donc vôtre est France, et vous êtes mienne.	Then yours is France, and you are mine
5.2.182	Sauf votre honneur, le français que vous parlez, il est meilleur que l'anglais lequel je parle.	Saving your grace, the French that you speak is better than the English I speak.
5.2.207	la plus belle Katherine du monde, mon très cher et divin déesse [the grammar should be 'ma chère et divine', hence Katherine's next remark about his fausse 'incorrect' (as well as 'deceitful') French]	the most beautiful Katherine in the world, and my very dear and divine goddess
5.2.210	sage demoiselle ... en France	wise maiden ... in France
5.2.237	roi mon pere	king my father
5.2.242	Laissez, mon seigneur, laissez, laissez!	Let go, my lord, let go, let go!
5.2.242	Ma foi, je ne veux point que vous abaissiez votre grandeur, en baisant la main d'une de votre seigneurie indigne serviteur.	By my faith, I would not at all want you to lower your dignity by kissing the hand of one of your majesty's unworthy servants.
5.2.244	Excusez-moi, je vous supplie, mon très puissant seigneur.	Pardon me, I beg you, my most mighty lord.
5.2.247	Les dames et demoiselles, pour être baisées devant leurs noces, il n'est pas la coutume de France.	It isn't the custom in France for women and maidens to be kissed before their marriage.
5.2.250	façon pour les	fashion for the
5.2.253	entends bettre que moi	understands better than me
5.2.256	Oui, vraiment.	Yes, indeed.
5.2.320	Notre très cher fils Henri, roi d'Angleterre, héritier de France.	Our most renowned son Henry, king of England, heir of France.

SHAKESPEARE'S LATIN

benedicite [pronounced be-ne-**die**-si-tee]
God bless you
• *(RJ 2.3.31) Friar Lawrence greets Romeo: 'Benedicite!'*

bonos dies [pronounced **boh**-nos | **dee**-ayz]
good day (mock Latin—it should be *bonus dies*)
• *(TN 4.2.12) Feste, disguised as Sir Topas, utters a greeting: 'Bonos dies, Sir Toby'.*

diluculo surgere
[pronounced di-**loo**-ku-loh | **soor**-ge-ray]
to rise at dawn—part of a popular proverb saying it is healthy to rise early
• *(TN 2.3.2) Sir Toby suggests that being up after midnight has the same effect as getting up early: diluculo surgere, thou knowest'.*

ergo ADVERB [pronounced **air**-go]
therefore
• *(MV 2.2.53) Lancelot addresses Gobbo: 'I pray you, ergo old man, ergo I beseech you'.*

et tu, Brute [pronounced et | **too** | **broo**-tay]
and you, O Brutus
• *(JC 3.1.77) Julius Ceasar's last words as Brutus stabs him: 'Et tu, Brute?—Then fall Caesar!'*

exeunt see STAGE DIRECTIONS, p.285

hic et ubique
[pronounced **hik** | et | oo-**bee**-kway]
here and everywhere
• *(Ham 1.5.164) Hamlet reacts to the Ghost's voice from beneath the ground: 'Hic et ubique? Then we'll shift our ground'.*

hysterica passio
[pronounced hiss-**te**-ri-ka | **pass**-ee-oh]
hysterical passion—hysteria
• *(KL 2.4.55) Lear tells himself : 'Hysterica passio! down, thou climbing sorrow!'*

In terram Salicam mulieres ne succedant
[pronounced in | **te**-ram | **sa**-li-cam | moo-lee-**air**-ez | nay | suk-**say**-dant]
(literally) in land Salic women not will-succeed
• *(H5 1.2.38) Canterbury translates as 'No woman shall succeed in Salic land'.*

Non nobis [pronounced **non noh**-biss]
the opening words of Psalm 115 in the Bible (113 in the Vulgate version), meaning 'not unto us'—in full, 'Not unto us, O Lord, not unto us, but to thy Name, give the praise'
• *(H5 4.8.118) Henry commands 'Let there be sung Non nobis'.*

Praeclarissimus filius noster Henricus, rex Angliae et heres Franciae
[pronounced pray-kla-**riss**-i-mus | **feel**-i-us | **noss**-tair | hen-**ree**-kus, | reks | **ang**-lee-ie | et | **hay**-rez | **frank**-ee-ie]
our most renowned son Henry, King of England and heir of France
• *(H5 5.2.321) Exeter requests the French king for a Latin title to be used for Henry.*

primo, secundo, tertio
[pronounced **pree**-moh | se-**kun**-doh | **tairt**-see-oh]
first, second, third
• *(TN 5.1.33) Feste hopes for a third gift from Orsino: 'Primo, secondo, tertio, is a good play'—thinking of 'third time lucky'.*

se offendendo
[pronounced **say** | off-en-**den**-doh]
a mistake for 'se defendendo'—in self-defence
• *(Ham 5.1.8) The First Clown says Ophelia's death 'must be se offendendo'.*

solus ADVERB [pronounced **soh**-lus]
alone
• *(H5 2.1.41) Nym tells Pistol: 'I would have you solus'—with no-one else around.*

Te Deum [pronounced **tay** | **day**-um]
the opening Latin words of a canticle from the Book of Common Prayer, short for *Te Deum laudamus*—'we praise thee, O God'.
• *(H5 4.8.118) Henry commands the singing of 'Te Deum'.*

videlicet [pronounced vi-**day**-li-set]
namely
• *(Ham 2.1.61) Polonius imagines Laertes entering 'a house of sale—/ Videlicet a brothel'.*